Third Edition

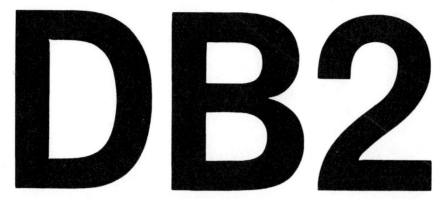

DB2
Design & Development Guide

Gabrielle Wiorkowski
David Kull

ADDISON-WESLEY PUBLISHING COMPANY, INC.
Reading, Massachusetts • Menlo Park, California • New York
Don Mills, Ontario • Wokingham, England • Amsterdam • Bonn
Sydney • Singapore • Tokyo • Madrid • San Juan • Milan • Paris

Library of Congress Cataloging-in-Publication Data

Wiorkowski, Gabrielle.
   DB2 : design and development guide / Gabrielle Wiorkowski, David
Kull.—3rd ed.
     p. cm.
   Includes index.
   ISBN 0-201-58049-7
   1. Data base management. 2. IBM Database 2. I. Kull, David.
II. Title. III. Title: DB two.
QA76.9.D3W58   1992
005.75'65—dc20   91-26771
                                                    CIP

4 5 6 7 8 9 10 –MA–9594

Preface

The first edition of this book was written in 1984 during the early support program and before DB2 was generally available as a database management product. It was the first practical guide to design and development of application systems published in book form. The book is based on over 1400 pages of seminar material developed and presented by Gabrielle Wiorkowski to over 5000 students in 23 countries on 6 continents. The material is constantly updated for each release/version (plus current PTFs) of DB2. Experience, gained through application design and development, of new features and the input of over 5000 seminar attendees have been incorporated into the book. The professionals attending the seminars have requested repeatedly that the book contain more indepth coverage as do the seminars. This current third edition of the book is an attempt to satisfy those requests within the bounds of a single volume.

A DB2 professional stated in a presentation at Guide that DB2 is easy to use but easier to abuse. This edition of the book continues to cover the ease of use but has expanded coverage on performance issues in each chapter to avoid the abuses. This indepth coverage of DB2 is for the experienced DB2 designers and developers as well as for the reader new to DB2. Because the features of DB2 are tightly interwoven, it is not possible to discuss a feature thoroughly without referring to related features that are discussed in other chapters. Therefore there are frequent references to the related features. Some chapters can be skipped by experienced DB2 professionals but are essential for the understanding of subsequent chapters for those new to DB2. For example, the chapters on concepts and components, normalization, and SQL data manipulation can be skipped by the experienced

DB2 professional but are necessary for the new DB2 reader before reading the chapters on programming for performance, optimization, and explaining the access path chosen by the optimizer.

Numerous hints, tips, and guidelines on the design and development of high performing application systems are given throughout the book based on the authors' experience and the input of professional seminar attendees. In order to apply the proven techniques, it is necessary to understand DB2 processing to maximize performance so that the guidelines can be applied to your specific application system. There are several techniques that can be used to accomplish an objective depending on the characteristics of the data and how the data will be processed. These techniques are discussed along with their advantages and disadvantages to allow the reader to choose or tailor a technique to satisfy their specific requirements.

ACKNOWLEDGMENTS

We have been very fortunate to have leading DB2 experts as reviewers of the book. Marilyn Bohl, a leading authority on DB2 and relational database management systems, and Barbara von Halle, the co-author of the widely read *Handbook of Relational Database Design,* have taken the time from their busy schedules to review all three editions of the book. William Favero, Dale Hoyt, Sheryl Larsen, Chris Loosley, and Colin White have applied their indepth understanding of DB2 to the review process. Their many comments and suggestions have contributed significantly to the content of the book. We are very grateful for their valuable assistance and hours of work in assuring the accuracy and readability of the book. Thanks also to John Wiorkowski, who was particularly helpful in reviewing and helping to shape some of the book's more mathematically intense portions. We are also indebted to Chris Date for sharing his Suppliers, Parts, and Jobs tables, which are used in most of this book's examples, and for his advice and support during the project. Without Dr. E.F. Codd and Sharon Weinberg, this book—and for that matter DB2—would not exist. Dr. Codd is a grand person and has provided the theoretical foundation on which all relational database management systems are built. And finally, many thanks to the fine editorial and support staff at Addison-Wesley for their assistance in preparing this significantly revised and expanded third edition.

Gabrielle Wiorkowski
David Kull

Contents

1

Concepts and Components

1.1 INTRODUCTION

A database management system (DBMS) physically stores information in electromagnetic form and makes it available for sharing by users or programs. The DBMS must provide ways for developers to define the data to the system and for users or programs to retrieve or change them. A DBMS must also provide facilities for security, recovery, and other tasks dictated by practical necessity. And it should relieve users of the work of maintaining the information's consistency throughout the database as parts of it are changed. But the data definition, physical storage, access capabilities, and data integrity are the essential business of a DBMS.

The database's physical structure, constrained by requirements of storage devices and input/output processes, must be relatively fixed and usually very different from the structure of the information as database users, including programmers, think of it. The DBMS translates a data request—ideally made in the user's terms—into a search through the physical structure to fulfill the request. To be as useful as possible, the DBMS should make it easy for users to formulate their requests, requiring them to know little or nothing about the database's physical structure. The relational model, invented by E.F. Codd at IBM in 1969, frees users from having to know the database structure or refer to it in their database requests. This is a valuable advance over the design of earlier DBMSs, which require users to include details of the physical database structure in their requests for data.

DB2 and the Relational Model

The relational database model is the foundation upon which DB2 has been built and in fact provides its reason for being. Because of its advantages, the relational model has become the technology of choice for DBMSs. In 1981, IBM announced SQL/DS, a DBMS based on the relational model for computers running under the DOS/VSE and later the VM/CMS operating systems. Many other companies have also based their DBMS products on the model. But IBM's announcement in 1983 of DB2 for computers running under MVS, its most advanced operating system for large computers, gave the movement toward the relational model perhaps its greatest impetus.

The model provides an uncomplicated, intuitive way for developers and users to think about and work with the information the DBMS manages. The model's basic elements are tables in which columns represent things and the attributes that describe them and rows represent specific instances of the things described. In Fig. 1.1, for example, the columns show that the table contains information about employees—their names, ages, project assignments, and salaries. Each row provides that information for a given employee.

The model also provides for operators for generating new tables from old, which is the way users manipulate the database and retrieve information from it. The language providing these operators for DB2 is SQL (structured query language), which has been standardized by ANSI (American

EMPLOYEE TABLE

EMPL_NUMBER	NAME	AGE	SALARY	ASSIGNMENT
29145	SMITH, J	55	45000	BOOSTER
36201	THOMAS, H	29	32000	BOOSTER
12596	GEORGE, R	46	94000	ACCOUNTING
42578	SMITH, T	32	50000	DESIGN
23820	JONES, L	34	25000	REENTRY
26899	RALPH, T	50	36000	ACCOUNTING
41020	PETERS, J	41	26000	DESIGN

Fig. 1.1 A relational table

National Standards Institute) and ISO (International Standards Organization) and has become the standard for all relational DBMSs. SQL also provides for the definition and control of DB2 databases.

The tables and operators are the basic elements of the relational model. The model includes many more elements, of course, many relating to the need for the DBMS to maintain various kinds of logical consistency as the data are manipulated. No current DBMS, including DB2, fully implements the model as Codd defined it, although IBM and other vendors have said they are working toward it.

We will cover SQL's data-manipulation capabilities in detail in two chapters and provide two brief introductory examples in this chapter. We will also review normalization, the database design method that is closely related to the relational model. And although a detailed examination of the relational model is beyond this book's scope, we will visit a number of its elements in the discussion of a variety of DB2 features.

Although this book provides a grounding in the relational model, its primary purpose is to describe how to employ effectively DB2's implementation of the relational model, including SQL. Our examinations will cover facilities and techniques for creating and controlling the use of databases, loading and backing up data, programming DB2 applications, and monitoring and tuning for performance.

1.2   DB2'S KEY COMPONENTS

DB2 cooperates with—*attaches to* is the technical term—any of three MVS subsystem environments: IMS, CICS, and TSO. These subsystems cooperate with DB2 facilities to provide such services as data communications and control of transactions, which are groups of database operations that must be coordinated to avoid the introduction of errors. CICS is a teleprocessing monitor, a program for controlling online transactions—those that execute as they are entered from a terminal—allowing users to interact with the computer. IMS/DB/DC is a well-established nonrelational DBMS, which includes a teleprocessing monitor. DB2 can use CICS only for online applications, but DB2 transactions running under CICS and IMS may access DB2 and IMS databases simultaneously (Fig. 1.2). A fourth attach, the call attach facility, allows an application to interact with DB2 without the help of the three subsystems, leaving many transaction management activities to the developer. TSO also contains a teleprocessing monitor that can be used by DB2. DB2 applications running under TSO may be online or batch, and they may not access IMS databases.

The two primary online facilities used with DB2 are QMF (query management facility) under CAF (call attach facility) or CICS and DB2 Interact-

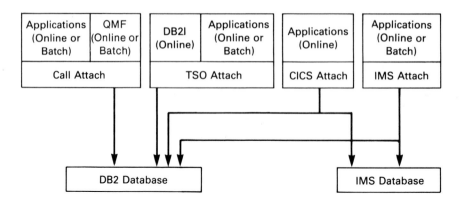

Fig. 1.2 Subsystem attaches

ive (DB2I) under TSO. QMF, an optional product, is designed primarily to help novices or occasional users formulate database requests and format reports. It has also proved useful for testing during application development. DB2I comes with DB2 and is directed primarily at allowing data processing professionals to enter SQL statements interactively through a component called SPUFI and at helping them prepare programs and utilities for execution.

Detailed knowledge of the subsystem environments is not required, however, to understand DB2 and develop databases and applications for it. Nor is it necessary for developers to have a detailed understanding of DB2's internal components. Subsequent chapters will present the necessary details during discussions of how to develop applications using DB2. The following overview of components provides a groundwork for those discussions.

Bind

DB2 translates database requests into code for fulfilling them through a process called *bind*, illustrated in Fig. 1.3. Bind reads and analyzes an SQL statement, determines an access path through the database's physical structure to the data in question, and generates machine code calls for locating and acting on the data, called an *application plan or package*. The access path depends on a number of characteristics of the data's structure—the sizes of tables, the number of distinct values in particular columns, and so on.

Chapter 10 will discuss in detail the distinction between an application plan and a package. Packages are particularly useful where a number of application programs constitutes a transaction or a program consists of a

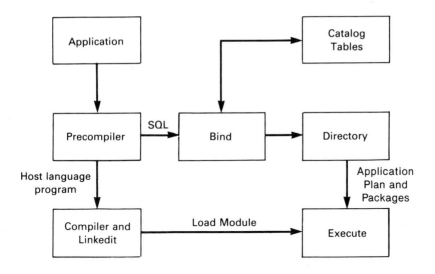

Fig. 1.3 The bind process

number of subprograms. Program maintenance is eased by managing each program and subprogram independently. A package can optionally be created for the SQL in each application program or subprogram and all of the packages for a transaction referenced in an application plan through a bind plan command.

Bind automatically creates an application plan for each interactive query or update entered from a terminal. For application programs, the application plans or packages cover all of the program's SQL statements. The plans and packages are saved in a component called a *directory*, to be used when needed as a program runs. Initially the developer invokes bind while preparing a program for execution. On subsequent executions of the program, if the data's structure has been changed in a way that makes the previous application plan or package unusable, DB2 automatically rebinds the plan or package to create a new one.

If the developer believes that the database structure has been changed to provide a more efficient access path, he or she can choose to rebind the plan or package to take advantage of it. Because SQL statements are separated from the rest of a program's code in a precompile process, an entire program need not be recompiled when an application plan or package is changed. The plan or package is simply rebound.

SQL statements can be embedded in a number of host-language programs including COBOL, PL/1, FORTRAN, C/370, and assembler. When the statements are embedded in one of these languages, the SQL is referred to as static SQL. Once the SQL is tested, it will not change unless a business requirement changes and new information is required. Thus the origin of the term static SQL. Static SQL is typically bound once and executed many times. SQL that is entered interactively using QMF, SPUFI, or any of a number of interactive tools is referred to as dynamic SQL. Dynamic SQL is used primarily for ad hoc processing where the request for information changes often. A bind occurs each time a dynamic SQL statement is executed and the application plan is not saved.

Catalog Tables, Statistics, and the Optimizer

The bind process eases the maintenance burden on programmers by allowing the database to be changed without requiring the programs that use it to be changed. It also saves programmers the trouble of determining access paths for their requests. Bind's intelligence for carrying out these tasks comes from a component called the *optimizer*, which estimates the most efficient access path for each request. It does this by applying rules for weighing database access options to statistics describing the particular database being accessed.

When tables and other elements of a DB2 database, called *objects*, are created or altered, DB2 stores information about them in a component called the *catalog tables*, which it uses to maintain a variety of operational information. A utility called RUNSTATS also collects statistics describing a table's data. These catalog tables provide the knowledge to which the optimizer applies its intelligence. They also provide monitoring information for developers and system administrators.

1.3   AN INTRODUCTION TO SQL

When a large subject is taught, the order in which information is presented is crucial. Background material needed to understand a particular aspect of the subject must be presented first. A problem arises, however, when the prerequisite information and primary subject are inextricably linked and the two parts of the problem are too big to be tackled together. We faced this problem in deciding how to order information about creating and using databases. Decisions made during development depend on anticipated use; use depends on an understanding of what is being used.

In subsequent chapters, we present the in-depth information on creating objects first, partly because the necessary prerequisite information about use—in this case use of SQL's data-manipulation capabilities—is relatively simple and largely intuitive. Therefore some example SQL statements appear in the early chapters on creating objects before SQL itself is fully taught. This brief introduction to SQL, however, should provide enough background to make those examples meaningful for newcomers to the language. SQL is presented in depth in Chapters 7 and 9.

Selecting from Tables

Under the relational model, data are logically stored and retrieved as tables. The SQL operator for retrieving data is the SELECT statement, which specifies the columns that are to return data and the rows to be included. The columns and rows may come from a single table or multiple tables. The SELECT's results are in the form of a result table with the specified columns and rows.

A SELECT from a single table identifies the desired columns, the table, and the condition or conditions that determine which rows should be returned. The following statement, which refers to the Employee table in Fig. 1.1, returns the names and salaries of employees older than 45 who earn more than $40,000:

```
SELECT NAME, SALARY
FROM    EMPLOYEE
WHERE   AGE > 45
AND     SALARY > 40000
```

The statement is straightforward. The SELECT clause identifies the desired columns; the FROM clause the table that contains them; and the WHERE clause the conditions that limit the returned rows. (Each condition in the WHERE clause is called a predicate.) The statement returns:

```
NAME      SALARY
----      ------
SMITH, J  45000
GEORGE, R 94000
```

Joining Tables

One way to combine information from multiple tables is with an operation called a *join*. To join two tables, the SELECT statement's FROM clause identifies them, and the WHERE clause includes a condition that relates values from a column in one table with corresponding values from a column in the other table. Usually this relationship is an equality, which produces what is called a *natural join*. (Chapters 2, 7, and 9 discuss natural and other kinds of joins in depth.)

The Projects table in Fig 1.4, for example, includes information on various projects, including their locations. Since the Assignment names in

PROJECTS TABLE

ASSIGNMENT	LOCATION	DEADLINE
BOOSTER	HOUSTON	MAY
REENTRY	NEW YORK	JUNE
ACCOUNTING	NEW YORK	SEPT
DESIGN	LOS ANGELES	JUNE

EMPLOYEE TABLE

EMPL_NUMBER	NAME	AGE	SALARY	ASSIGNMENT
29145	SMITH, J	55	45000	BOOSTER
36201	THOMAS, H	29	32000	BOOSTER
12596	GEORGE, R	46	94000	ACCOUNTING
42578	SMITH, T	32	50000	DESIGN
23820	JONES, L	34	25000	REENTRY
26899	RALPH, T	50	36000	ACCOUNTING
41020	PETERS, J	41	26000	DESIGN

Fig. 1.4 A join

the Projects table correspond to those in the Employee table, they can be used to join information from the two tables. To find Peters's job location, for example, look in the Employee table for his Assignment: Design. Then look up Design in the Projects table to find its location: Los Angeles. That, essentially, is a join.

A statement to find the job locations as well as salaries of employees over 45 requires such a join. Notice in the join's statement below that the names of the two ASSIGNMENT columns are prefixed by their table names:

```
SELECT NAME, SALARY, LOCATION
FROM   EMPLOYEE, PROJECT
WHERE  AGE > 45
AND    EMPLOYEE.ASSIGNMENT = PROJECT.ASSIGNMENT
```

Whenever the Assignment value from the row of an over-45 worker in the Employee table matches an Assignment value in the Job Table, the matched rows join and return the requested columns as part of the SELECT's answer. The shaded rows in Fig. 1.4 indicate those matches. The SELECT returns:

```
NAME     SALARY  LOCATION
____     _____  _____
SMITH, J   45000  HOUSTON
GEORGE, R  94000  NEW YORK
RALPH, T   36000  NEW YORK
```

In most cases, tables in a join are associated through columns exhibiting certain properties. These columns are called *primary* and *foreign keys*. Every value in a primary key column is unique, providing a way to identify each row. (Sometimes two or more columns must be combined to create unique key values, a subject discussed in Chapter 2.) In the example tables, EMPL_NUMBER provides the primary key for the Employee table. In the Projects table, the ASSIGNMENTS column provides the primary key. Each ASSIGNMENT value in the Employee table corresponds to a value in the Projects table's primary key. EMPLOYEE.ASSIGNMENT therefore provides a foreign key to the Projects table.

SQL provides many more operators and facilities for data manipulation. Chapter 7 tells how to use them, while Chapter 11 shows how to use them most efficiently with this release of DB2. Understanding the simple SELECT and JOIN presented here is sufficient to begin.

Status of an SQL Statement Execution

DB2 returns a code called an SQLCODE after each execution of an SQL statement indicating its status. Most frequently SQLCODE will contain a value of 0 or +100, indicating successful execution of the statement or that no rows qualified or no more rows qualify respectively. Any other positive three-digit value indicates that the statement did execute but that the result may not be what was expected. A negative three-digit value indicates that an error condition was encountered. The meaning of these codes will be discussed in Chapter 9.

Another code, SQLSTATE, is an alternative to the SQLCODE that allows a program to be insensitive to which DBMS is being accessed. It will indicate the same or similar condition for all system application architecture (SAA) DBMSs and provides compatibility with ANSI SQL2 used by many DBMSs available from software companies. It is a five-digit character standard code. The first two digits indicate the error class, and the last three digits indicate the specific error with a range of '00000' to '65535'.

A Unit of Work

A unit of work (UOW) begins when the first SQL statement is executed in a program. A number of SQL statements can be in a UOW. A UOW ends when the program issues a commit work statement or the program terminates normally at which point updates are written to the log dataset. If a failure occurs before the changes are actually written to the table, DB2 will apply the outstanding updates in the log to the table when DB2 is restarted. A UOW also ends when a rollback statement is issued or the program terminates as the result of an error. If any updates have been applied to the table, they will be removed. This processing is discussed in Chapter 8.

1.4 INTRODUCTION TO REFERENTIAL INTEGRITY

Referential integrity refers to a particular kind of consistency that must be maintained between primary and foreign keys. Simply stated the relational model requires that every foreign key value have a corresponding primary key value. The reason for this should be clear from the previous join example. If a row in the Employee table includes a value in the ASSIGNMENT column (the foreign key) that has no matching value in the Project table's ASSIGNMENT column (the primary key), there would be no way for the database management system or users to associate that row with the Project table's information. If the Employee table had employee George assigned to FINANCE, for example, how could the database management system determine his location?

Referential integrity is another topic whose position in the order of teaching presents difficulties. To fully understand referential integrity and how DB2 provides for it, an understanding of SQL is helpful. If the reader is not familiar with SQL, Chapter 7 can be read before reading the chapter on referential integrity.

1.5 TABLE NAMING

DB2 requires that each table, view (a virtual table created by an SQL data manipulation statement), alias (an alternative name of a table or view), and index have a two-part name. The first part of the name is a qualifier indicating the table, view, alias, or index's *owner*, usually an eight character string identifying the functional application system or subject area to which it belongs. The qualifier must be included in references to the table or view in SQL statements unless measures are taken to avoid that requirement. Unfortunately the qualifier can be the source of considerable confusion.

The qualifier is generally the authorization identification (AUTHID) of the individual who creates the table, view, alias, or index. DB2 automatically appends the qualifier if none is specified in the statement creating the table, view, alias, or index. For example, if Jenny creates the Employee table and her AUTHID is JENNY, the table's name would actually be

JENNY.EMPLOYEE. While Jenny could leave the qualifier off when referencing the table, any other user would have to include the qualifier to gain access to the table—again unless those special steps are taken. (It is best for Jenny to specify a qualifier like EMPSYS when creating the object rather than using her personal ID). For simplicity most examples in this book do not include the qualifiers. Chapter 4 discusses the use of qualifiers when a table is created; Chapter 10 discusses how to specify the qualifier when executing bind; and Chapter 15 on security provides a detailed discussion of qualifiers and how to avoid the need to use them.

Optionally, a three-part name can be used to identify objects. The third part can be a name describing the location. If Jenny's table is located in Dallas, the fully qualified name might be DALLAS.JENNY.EMPLOYEE. It is best not to give a specific city name since an office of the company might move to another city. Rather it is better to use a name that describes the office to avoid confusion and complexities if a move does occurs. Location will be discussed in Chapter 17.

1.6 A WORD ON PERFORMANCE

In their earliest days, relational DBMSs suffered from a reputation for using computer resources inefficiently compared with established, nonrelational systems. Their relatively poor performance, however, stemmed from their immaturity rather than a deficiency in the model. Nothing inherent in the relational model would inhibit performance.

Indeed a relational DBMS's ability to retrieve a set of rows with one access to the database rather than retrieving only one record at a time, as nonrelational systems must do, provides a performance advantage. And as query optimizers are improved, they should do better than programmers in developing access paths. An optimizer can know more about a database structure and keep up with changes to it better than a programmer. Nevertheless, the performance of any DBMS depends on the database design and how the DBMS is used, and performance is a critical issue for any user organization. The discussions in this book therefore will emphasize the most efficient use of DB2.

The question of performance covers a number of interrelated issues. The key points are the amount of processing required by a transaction or query and the number of times the computer must communicate with an external direct access storage device (DASD) to access data. These two factors combine to determine the length of time required to respond to a database request. A general understanding of these two factors will be helpful for later discussions of specific performance-related questions.

Processing needs are important because they determine the size of the computer needed for an application or, looked at from the other direction, the size and number of applications that can run on a given computer. Processing is actually the computer's execution of the program instructions that carry out a given task. This execution is performed by the computer's central processing unit (CPU), which executes instructions in cycles. Processing requirements are generally expressed therefore in terms of CPU cycles.

Communications between the computer and DASD, called *input/output* or *I/O operations*, are a key performance element because they require CPU cycles and can contribute a high proportion of the time it takes to fulfill database requests. Time needed for I/O includes the time it takes to find and transfer data between DASD and the computer. Because the number of communications channels between the storage device and computer is limited, however, an I/O operation can spend time just waiting for other I/O to complete and free a communications channel. And I/O to DASD can also slow down communications between the computer and other I/O devices, including terminals.

In general for DBMSs, I/O operations will have the greatest impact on response times and the rate at which transactions can be processed. But processing and I/O requirements are interrelated. As we will discuss in detail in subsequent chapters, the use of more CPU cycles can sometimes be traded for fewer I/O operations, or more I/O can save on processing. *Response time*, the time between when a request is entered and the results are provided, is a function of both processing and I/O requirements. Developers' decisions will usually depend on whether their installations can better afford CPU cycles or I/O operations and on how quickly users need results. In any event, developers will have many opportunities to affect processing requirements, I/O needs, and response times through their design and development decisions. Much of this book is devoted to describing the factors they should consider in making those decisions.

1.7 THE DB2 SYSTEM ARCHITECTURE

DB2 consists of three major components, each in its own address space, with an optional fourth address space for distributed processing. The systems services address space (SSAS) is the first component encountered when using DB2. It is responsible for establishing a thread that describes a program's connection existence, traces its progress, and provides the ability to perform processing in DB2. The thread consists of task control blocks (TCBs) that are allocated when the first SQL statement is executed in a plan, and the thread is deallocated at the end of execution.

SSAS also provides facilities for tracing the progress of the processing associated with a thread. In fact, the instrumentation facility within SSAS collects and records statistics on the work done by all of DB2's address spaces. The instrumentation facility records statistics on the work done by SSAS whenever DB2 is started and stopped, at user-specified intervals, when traces are started, and each time a new active log is used as record type 100. The records can be directed to system management facility (SMF) or general trace facility (GTF) datasets. The instrumentation facility will record information on the number of I/O issued and the CPU time used, starting when a thread is allocated. The record type of 101 is written to a SMF or GTF dataset when the thread is deallocated or the AUTHID is changed. This information is useful for billing users for the resources they use. The third record type, 102, is used to trace performance related events and to record audited SQL. The performance trace is useful for identifying tuning requirements for the DB2 system itself and application programs. The trace can be turned on for all plans or just one plan, AUTHID, or resource manager ID (RMID).

The last major responsibility of SSAS is to log before and after images of all changed data. The changed data is first written to a log buffer in main memory. The log buffer is written to an active log dataset usually on DASD to insure that the update will not be lost in case of a power failure when a commit work statement is issued. When the active log dataset becomes full to a specified percent, it is automatically written to an archive log. SSAS switches to using another active log dataset during the archiving process to avoid delaying any commits issued during the archive process. The boot strap dataset (BSDS) is used to maintain an inventory of all active and archived logs. SSAS is also responsible for starting and stopping the DB2 subsystem.

The second address space shown in Fig. 1.5, the database services address space (DSAS), is the address space that does most of the processing of application data. It manages all application tables and indexes as well as the catalog tables, directory, and work tables that are used for sorts, joins, and storing intermediate results.

Two important components of DSAS, the data manager (DM) and the relational data system (RDS) process the data requested by SQL statements in two stages. DM is the first component in DB2 to operate on the data. It applies conditions called *stage 1 predicates* that were specified by the programmer in the WHERE clauses of an SQL statement. It then passes all qualifying columns to the RDS, which applies all remaining conditions called *stage 2 predicates*. A stage 1 predicate means that it will be applied by DM and a stage 2 predicates means that it will be applied by RDS. Chapter 11 and 12 cover the distinction between stage 1 and 2 predicates in detail.

DM requests from another DSAS component, the buffer manager, the data and index pages that are required. The buffer manager attempts to

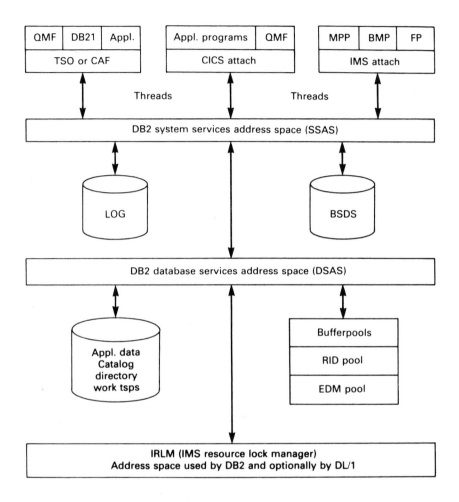

Fig. 1.5 DB2 System architecture

keep frequently read and updated pages in the bufferpools to minimize physical I/O to DASD. The buffer pages are reused on a least recently used (LRU) basis. That is, if a page is not marked in use, the space is available to another user. Those pages not referenced recently are the first to be re-used. The row identifier (RID, which gives the location of a row) pool is used to sort and eliminate duplicate RIDs obtained from the index pages before performing I/O to the data pages. This is done to minimize I/O to the data pages and makes the necessary I/O more efficient.

The buffer manager is responsible for opening and closing all datasets

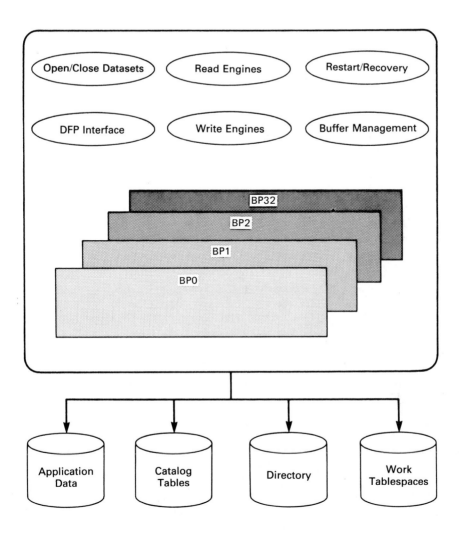

Fig. 1.6 Buffer pools and management

used for application data and work areas as indicated in Fig. 1.6. Indeed it is the first open that causes DB2 to create a buffer pool using a GETMAIN instruction, and when the last dataset using the buffer pool is closed, DB2 frees the buffer space in main memory. The buffer manager passes all read requests to data facility product (DFP) if the required pages are not in the buffer. It is the DFP media manger that actually issues the physical I/O.

Read and write engines are used to provide for processing 32 pages with a single I/O assuming a default bufferpool size of 4 MB (megabytes). The read engines manage asynchronous sequential prefetch and list prefetch that read ahead of the data currently being processed so that a program does not have to wait for the I/O to complete. Rather an attempt is made to have the required pages in the bufferpool before they are actually referenced. Thresholds are used to avoid any one user taking an excessive amount of space in the bufferpool as will be discussed in Chapter 3.

The write engines do write behind processing using asynchronous deferred writing of up to 10 percent of the buffer to a single dataset in 32 page chunks. Writes of updated pages are triggered by buffer manager thresholds, the number of updated pages for a given dataset, stopping a database, stopping DB2, and execution of the QUIESCE utility. Pages are written in sequence as they appear on DASD to minimize arm movement. Pages can be updated and read by many users without a physical write. A locking mechanism is used to avoid one user writing over updates of another user as will be discussed in Chapter 8.

RDS interfaces with the environmental descriptor manager (EDM), which manages application plans and packages. The EDM pool contains sections of the plan and packages that are currently being executed. When the first SQL statement in a plan or package is executed, the EDM checks to see if the plan is present or in the bufferpool; if it is not, buffer manager issues read requests for the plan or package from the directory and passes it to the EDM manager. At this point, the plan is called a SKCT (skeleton cursor table), a package is called a SKPT (skelton package table), and a copy is made called the CT (cursor table) and PT (package table). It is the CT or PT that is used in executing the SQL.

The EDM manager will attempt to maintain a copy of the SKCT and SKPT as long as space is available in the EDM pool so that subsequent executions require only that a copy of the SKCT or SKPT be made for the new person executing the plan or package. The space is reused on a least recently used basis. Each person executing a plan or package has one or more CT or PT sections. Each SKCT can have an authorization cache of from 256 to 4096 bytes that is used to store the AUTHID of the last 124 people (assuming a 1024-byte block) who executed the plan. This avoids having to read the catalog authorization tables each time the plan is executed by the same AUTHID. A single copy of the database descriptor (DBD) for all users processing data in a database is also maintained in the EDM pool. It contains a concise description of all the objects in a database and is used to identify the objects to be manipulated.

The IMS resource lock manager (IRLM) is the third address space required by DB2. It manages all locks taken when programs and users read and update data to insure data integrity as will be discussed in Chapter 8.

The fourth address space is distributed data facility (DDF) and is optional. It is required only if SQL is to be sent to a remote DBMS or if DB2 is to receive requests from a remote DBMS. A remote UOW and a distributed UOW are supported. Both provide for selecting and updating data at a remote DBMS using the TSO and CAF attaches but only select processing using the CICS and IMS attaches. A remote UOW allows the creation of objects and the granting of privileges at the remote site. It provides for support of multiple heterogenous relational DBMS unlike a distributed UOW that allows for only data manipulation between multiple DB2 subsystems. Distributed database facilities are discussed in Chapter 17.

1.8 SUMMARY

DB2 is based on the relational model for database management systems. It is relatively easy, therefore, for developers to create databases under DB2 and for programmers and business professionals to use them. This book provides grounding in the relational model and describes DB2's facilities for developing and using databases. The emphasis throughout is on obtaining optimum performance from the system.

EXERCISES

1.1 Name the MVS subsystems to which DB2 attaches. What are their primary services provided to DB2 applications?

1.2 Can an IMS database be accessed through a program developed under DB2I?

1.3 An index that provides an application efficient access to a table has been dropped. How will DB2 react to the application's next execution? How does it know what action to take?

1.4 Write a SELECT statement to determine from the Employee table (Fig. 1.4) those employees assigned to accounting who earn less than $50,000. Give the results.

1.5 Write a SELECT statement to find in the tables in Fig. 1.4 employee Peters's job location. Give the results.

1.6 Which is more important for system performance: processing or I/O requirements?

2

Review of Normalization

2.1 INTRODUCTION

Databases do not exist in a vacuum, acting according to arbitrary or artificial rules. A database contains information that is central to an enterprise; therefore its design must reflect the characteristics of the real-world situations the data describe. Normalization, a design procedure originally defined by E.F. Codd and elucidated by C.J. Date, provides a method for representing data and their relationships precisely in a tabular format that makes the database easy to understand and operationally efficient. The normalization process helps developers refine their understanding of the data, but it also requires from the start a firm grasp of the information's meaning.

Ideally normalization begins after an analysis of the organization's strategic information systems needs. Several methodologies provide frameworks for such analyses. One of the most widely known is IBM's Business Systems Planning (BSP). Whatever methodology is used, its purpose is to place in perspective the application system the database will serve: Where does the application fit within the organization's business processes? What data resources does the application generate or use? How does it relate to other planned or existing applications? What data repeat across applications, and how can the redundancy be reduced? If a strategic data model answering such questions is not available, the developer must begin with as complete an analysis as possible of the particular system's business role. It is not enough to know that the system will receive and store data, produce reports, and respond to queries.

The depth of understanding required by the designer for normalization will become clear as we explore the process in detail. To begin, normalization requires the identification and definition of the entities, attributes, and relationships that describe an application system. An *entity* is something fundamental to an enterprise about which data can be kept—a person, place, item, event, and so on. (*Entity type* is sometimes used to describe all instances of a particular entity—all employees, for example; *entity occurrence* refers to a specific case—an employee.) An *attribute* is a quantitative or descriptive characteristic of an entity—a name, identification number, price. A *relationship* is any association of one or more entity types with one or more other entity types that is inherent in and relevant to the enterprise. Employees and departments form a relationship, for example, if employees work in departments and that fact is relevant to the system.

Although Codd created normalization theory with the relational database model in mind, developers have used it widely in designing nonrelational hierarchical and network databases as well. While this takes advantage of many of normalization's benefits, manually translating the design from logical tables to hierarchies and networks requires considerable effort. With a relational DBMS such as DB2, logical and physical designs are frequently very similar to each other.

Normalization carries a number of benefits. One of the most important is that its rules reduce data redundancy, in the process ensuring the data's consistency by allowing for efficient, accurate updates and deletions. A normalized design also lends itself to change. Business processes rarely remain constant after the logical design is complete. If the data were well understood and represented initially, the addition or deletion of entities, attributes, or relationships is unlikely to require the total restructuring of normalized databases. Adding or dropping an entity is a simple matter of adding or dropping a table. Similarly adding an attribute requires only the altering of a table to add a column. Adding a relationship also usually requires only the addition of a foreign key column, the values of which relate its table to another. As Chapter 4 describes, DB2 makes adding or altering tables relatively easy. In addition, in most cases, applications accessing the database require little or no change when normalized tables are added, dropped, or altered.

Normalization and Performance

Normalization also offers several performance advantages. The process frequently results in separation of one table into two or more tables, resulting

Box 2.1   Advantages of normalization

- An excellent logical design methodology
- Direct translation from logical to physical design in relational DBMSs
- Reduced data redundancy
- Protection against update and delete anomalies
- The ability to add or delete entities, attributes, and relations without wholesale restructuring of tables
- Smaller tables and fewer total bytes
- Tables with fewer columns and therefore shorter rows, which allows more rows per data page, resulting in more rows of data being passed per I/O operation

in fewer columns per table. This logical change has implications for physical data storage. The page is DB2's basic unit of physical storage and therefore of input and output. The number of rows that can occupy a page depends on row length, and length depends partly on the number of columns in a row. Normalized tables therefore will fit more rows on a page than will unnormalized tables, and more rows will be processed in each I/O operation. This advantage depends on the way in which the data are used. An unnormalized table might have 30 columns totaling 400 bytes in length, for example. Since a page provides about 4,000 bytes, each I/O operation would process about 10 rows. If most transactions need only some of the columns, however, normalization will allow for more rows per I/O by placing in separate tables those columns that can be accessed independently. Normalization may split the 30-column table into three 10-column tables, each about 150 bytes long. Each I/O would then process about 26 rows. If, on the other hand, columns from separate tables are used together, DB2 must perform a join operation to unite them, which requires considerable processing. If normalized tables require frequent joins over a large number of rows, the developer might consider denormalization, explored in detail in Section 2.8.

Other performance gains are possible through normalization. The elimination of redundant data reduces the database's total size and processing requirements. Global updates are frequently eliminated since data are not stored redundantly.

2.2   THE FIRST NORMAL FORM

All of the advantages of normalization will become clear as we examine the procedure's rules. Normalization provides five design levels, called *normal*

```
Employee

Employee Number
Employee Name
Department Code
Department Name
Department Location
Dependent Name
Dependent Date of Birth
Skill Code
Skill Name
Skill Where Attained
Skill Level
```

Fig. 2.1 Unnormalized data items

forms. Each form's rules place additional conditions on the database design. By satisfying the first set of rules, the data are said to be in the first normal form. Moving on to satisfy the second set results in the second normal form, and so on up to the fifth normal form. Beginning analysts will usually work through the normal forms in order, refining their designs to satisfy each succeeding set of rules. With experience, most will move directly to the third normal form, with their original designs satisfying the rules for the first three normal forms. The fourth and fifth normal forms are needed only rarely.

Normalization results in one table, or relation, for each entity, with attributes shown as column headings and each occurrence shown as a row. To begin, though, a simple list beneath an entity's name of the attributes that describe it provides a convenient starting point for the normalization process. Consider, for example, the list of attributes for a hypothetical employee entity shown in Fig. 2.1. In actuality, such an entity is likely to encompass more attributes, but these few suffice to illustrate the concepts. By studying the list, the designer can begin to make judgments about the nature of the data.

In the example, each employee will have one employee number that is different from all other employee numbers. Each employee also works for only one department, described by a code, a name, and a location. Each employee might have no dependents or any number and one skill or several. The department, skill, and dependent attributes are themselves entities with attributes of their own, as will become evident during the normalization process.

If each employee row—or *record* in nonrelational terminology—contained all of the listed attributes, it would pose several problems for the database, problems that the normalization process solves. First, relational operations—the mathematically based data manipulations that underlie

Box 2.2   Conditions addressed by each normal form

1NF: Repeating groups

2NF: A column's dependency on only part of a composite key

3NF: A nonkey column's representing a fact about another nonkey column

4NF: Two or more independent, multivalued facts occurring for an entity

5NF: Interdependent columns (symmetric constraint)

data management in a relational system—do not allow for data items that could be repeated within a given record. Such items are called *repeating groups*, and the first normal form prohibits relations that include them. (COBOL programmers will recognize that this prohibition bars use of the Occurs clause, which defines repeating groups.) In the example, both dependent and skill attributes may repeat in a record. An employee might have more than one of each. Therefore those attributes must be removed from the employee relation and listed in their own tables for the design to satisfy the first normal form (Fig. 2.2).

```
                 Employee

Primary key-Employee Number
             Employee Name
             Department ID
             Department Name
             Department Location


                 Skill

Primary key┬Employee Number
           └Skill ID
             Skill Name
             Skill Where Attained
             Skill Level


                 Dependent

Primary key┬Employee Number
           └Dependent Name
             Dependent Date of Birth
```

Fig. 2.2 First normal form

2.3   THE KEY ISSUE

The higher-level normal forms all deal in one way or another with *keys*—
the attributes that uniquely identify rows and are often used to show the
relationships between tables. Every relation must have one attribute or
combination of attributes that will provide a unique identifier value for
each row occurrence. This attribute, or combination of attributes, is called
the *primary key*. (DB2 does not require identification of primary keys. They
are essential to normalization, however.) If the unique identifier is, in fact,
a combination of attributes, it is called a *composite key*. A relation may
also have one or more attributes whose values have matching values in a
primary key in another relation. These attributes, called *foreign keys*, establish the relationships between tables.

In Fig. 2.2, the employee number attribute provides a primary key for
the employee relation: Employees might have the same name, but each will
always have a unique number. In the skill relation, however, the employee
number will be repeated for each skill that particular employee holds. A
skill will also be repeated whenever more than one employee holds the skill.
But a combination of the employee number and skill code attributes will
provide a unique identifier for each occurrence of a row in the skill relation—a composite primary key. Similarly a combination of employee number and dependent name provides the primary key for the dependent relation.

The employee number attributes in the skill and dependent relations
match the primary key in the Employee table, providing foreign keys for
relating the three tables. Under the relational model, a DBMS makes connections between tables by cross-matching any two columns, a process
called *join*. (DB2 allows the joining of any columns irrespective of whether
the columns are keys, leaving it to users to ensure that the columns used in
this way exhibit the properties of primary and foreign keys.) The join's
crossmatch operation can require considerable processing. Think of a system search for all employees in Department A who can type. A Join operation to find this information might be done by searching the employee relation for those who work in Department A, and then searching the skills
relation to crossmatch those employees with employees who type. This
method requires much more processing than would a single search of one
table that included both pieces of information. There may be times, therefore, when selectively storing redundant data, a practice called *denormalization*, provides performance advantages. Before exploring that issue, however, we should look at the additional problems of unnormalized data and
how they may be avoided.

2.4   THE SECOND NORMAL FORM

The ways in which a relation's attributes may be associated with the primary key hold the potential for inefficiency in both the use of processing resources and the maintenance of the data's integrity. One problem occurs whenever an attribute depends for its definition on only one part of a composite primary key. Remember that in the example's skill relation, shown in Fig. 2.2, the employee number and skill code attributes combined to form the primary key. Attributes providing the skill's name, classification level, and location where the employee obtained it complete the relation. Only the attribute for where the skill was obtained will have values that vary in the table, depending on where each employee was trained. Notice, on the other hand, that the skill's name and classification level depend on, or are directly associated with, only its code. In other words, no matter which employee holds the particular skill, its name and level remain the same. With the design as it stands, however, the database repeats a skill's name and classification level in every listing for an employee who holds it, a waste of space. Moreover it requires unnecessary processing whenever those attributes are changed, and it opens the door for errors whenever changes are made.

If the organization decides to reclassify a skill, for example, the change has to be made wherever the skill is listed—that is, for every employee who holds it. A DBMS could miss some instances. For example, a programmer or occasional user, unaware that the skill level repeats throughout the database, may change it for only some employee rows. If the system misses some instances during an update, for whatever reason, the skill will have one classification level for some employees and another for the rest. This is called an *update anomaly*. Another problem with this design in the first normal form occurs if the last employee holding a particular skill leaves the company and his or her records are removed from the database. In that case, a *delete anomaly*, the skill will not be stored anywhere in the database.

Creating a separate relation for the attributes that depend only on the skill, not the employee who holds it, avoids these update and delete anomalies. In general, the second normal form mandates creation of a separate relation for any attributes that depend on only part of a composite key. Notice in Fig. 2.3 that the skill relation is split into two tables satisfying the second normal form. There, changes to the attributes depending on a skill alone need be made only in one place in the database.

2.5   THE THIRD NORMAL FORM

Yet another possibility for update and delete anomalies and unnecessary processing occurs when a nonkey attribute is a fact about another nonkey

This relation violates the second normal form:

```
              Skill

Primary key ┬─Employee Number
            │ ╱Skill Code ◄─┐ ◄──────────┐
            │  Skill Name ──┘             │
            └─Skill Where Attained        │
              Skill Level ────────────────┘
```

These provide second normal form:

```
       Employee Skill                        Skill

Primary key ┬─Employee Number      Primary key─Skill Code
            └─Skill Code    ─                  Skill Name
              Skill Where Attained             Skill Level
```

Skill name and skill level attributes need a separate relation because in the original design, they depend on only part of the primary key—that is, they remain the same no matter which employees hold the skill. Skill where attained, on the other hand, depends on the particular skill and on the employee. Arrows in the original skill relation indicate these dependencies.

Fig. 2.3 Second normal form

attribute in the relation. The employee relation from the example's first normal form, shown in Fig. 2.4, satisfies both first and second normal forms: It contains no repeating groups and no composite key. Still it poses a problem. The employee name and department code relate directly to the employee number—the employee name because it belongs to the employee and the department code because it tells where the particular employee works. The department name and department location attributes, on the other hand, depend on only the department code. They remain the same no matter which employees work in the department.

The problems this causes are the same as those that occur when an attribute depends on only part of a composite key. Although department name and location have nothing to do with individual employees, they are repeated in the database for every occurrence of an employee who works in the particular department. The redundancy requires unnecessary data storage and unnecessary processing for changes to the attributes. The solution is also the same as for the second normal form: Create another table, this one for the attributes that are not dependent on the original relation's key. Fig. 2.4 shows this solution.

A designer need not work through the first and second normal forms to get to the third. The rules leading to and including the third normal form can be summed up in a single statement: Each attribute must be a fact about the key, the whole key, and nothing but the key. Designers can use this

This relation violates the third normal form:

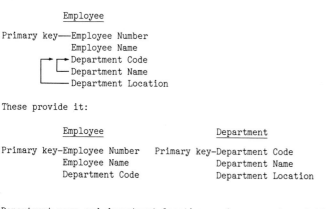

These provide it:

```
        Employee                          Department

Primary key–Employee Number      Primary key–Department Code
           Employee Name                    Department Name
           Department Code                  Department Location
```

Department name and department location need a separate relation because as the arrows in the original indicate, they depend only on department code, not a primary key.

Fig. 2.4 Third normal form

statement to test whether their designs are in the third normal form. The designer should ask if each attribute in a relation is a fact about the key, the whole key, and nothing but the key. If the answer is yes for each question about each attribute, the table is in the third normal form.

2.6 THE FOURTH NORMAL FORM

For the majority of databases, the third normal form is the extent of normalization needed or desired. Two additional normalization levels can improve the design in certain situations, however. The fourth and fifth normal forms apply only when the database includes one-to-many and many-to-many relationships, and then only in some special situations.

The example database illustrates the one-to-many and many-to-many concepts (Fig. 2.5). The relationship between employees and their departments is one-to-many, for example: Many employees can be assigned to each department, but each employee can work in only one department. The relationship between employees and skills is many-to-many: An employee can hold any number of skills, and each skill can be shared by any number of employees.

Many-to-many and one-to-many relationships can pose problems when a designer tries to include more than one of them in a single relation. The

```
One:One-For each occurrence of an entity, the other entity can occur only
        once.

            Department    : Location

            Accounting    : New York

One:Many-For each occurrence of an entity, the other entity can occur many
         times.

            Department    : Employee

            Accounting    : Mary Jefferson
                          : Peter Reynolds

Many:Many-For each occurrence of either entity, the other can occur many
          times.

            Employee          : Skill

            Mary Peterson     : Accountant
                              : Programmer

            Peter Reynolds    : Accountant
                              : Engineer
```

Fig. 2.5 Relationship types

problems can best be explained with an example. Consider adding a second attribute, language ability, to the employee-skill relation. Employees and skills share a many-to-many relationship. So do employees and languages; an employee might speak any number of languages, and each language may be spoken by any number of employees. Notice, however, that language and skill are not directly related. They might be indirectly related in that they can be shared by the same employee, but that indirect relationship may not be meaningful. In other words, an employee may have mastered the skill of programming and may be able to speak French. That does not mean that the employee can program in French. That being the case, representing the skill and language attributes in the same relation creates confusion.

Consider Employee Smith, who holds programmer and analyst skills and speaks French, German, and Greek. If there is no direct relationship between the skills and languages, they can be listed within the same relation in several, essentially arbitrary, ways (Fig. 2.6). Each method holds some drawbacks. In some cases, information is repeated, causing the familiar problems of redundancy—wasteful storage, unnecessary processing for updates, and the possibility of update and delete anomalies. In other cases, database maintenance policies must account for each design's quirks. Inserting a skill in the designs in Figs. 2.6(c) or 2.6(d), for example, might require looking for a row where the skill is blank and adding it there, or a

(a) A disjoint format in which a record contains either a skill or language but not both

EMPLOYEE	SKILL	LANGUAGE
SMITH	PROGRAMMER	
SMITH	ANALYST	
SMITH		FRENCH
SMITH		GERMAN
SMITH		GREEK

(b) Minimal number of records with repetitions

EMPLOYEE	SKILL	LANGUAGE
SMITH	PROGRAMMER	FRENCH
SMITH	ANALYST	GERMAN
SMITH	ANALYST	GREEK

(c) Minimal number of records with blanks

EMPLOYEE	SKILL	LANGUAGE
SMITH	PROGRAMMER	FRENCH
SMITH	ANALYST	GERMAN
SMITH		GREEK

(d) Unrestricted

EMPLOYEE	SKILL	LANGUAGE
SMITH	PROGRAMMER	FRENCH
SMITH	ANALYST	
SMITH		GERMAN
SMITH	ANALYST	GREEK

(e) Every possible pairing of skills and languages

EMPLOYEE	SKILL	LANGUAGE
SMITH	PROGRAMMER	FRENCH
SMITH	PROGRAMMER	GERMAN
SMITH	PROGRAMMER	GREEK
SMITH	ANALYST	FRENCH
SMITH	ANALYST	GERMAN
SMITH	ANALYST	GREEK

Fig. 2.6 Alternatives for representing two independent, multivalued facts

STORE	MANUFACTURER	PRODUCT
NY	ACME	REFRIGERATORS
NY	AJAX	RANGES
LA	ACME	RANGES

Fig. 2.7 Store, manufacturer, product table

new row might be added for the employee's new skill, leaving the language blank. In Fig. 2.6(e), adding a new skill would require inserting multiple rows, each with a different pairing of the skill and possible languages. Each of these alternatives causes confusion and wastes computer resources. The fourth normal form avoids these problems by providing for separate relations for each of the unrelated, one-to-many or many-to-many relationships. The rule here is that no relation may include two or more many-to-one or many-to-many relationships that are not directly related.

2.7 THE FIFTH NORMAL FORM

If some logical relationship between two one-to-many or many-to-many relations exists, however, it makes sense to keep them within the same table. If each employees exercises his or her skills only in certain languages, for example, each actual combination would represent a unique instance of the relation. In some cases, though, logical constraints that are inherent in the information's meaning allow for its even more efficient representation in the database. The fifth normal form encourages designers to take advantage of these situations. A simple example will clarify the concept.

Suppose a retailer's stores sell appliances from several manufacturers, each of which makes some combinations of refrigerators, ranges, microwave ovens, or dishwashers. If any outlet can sell any product, a relation describing which store sells which products requires three columns: one each for the store, manufacturer, and product. This relation includes two many-to-many relationships: stores to manufacturers and stores to products. But since the relationship between manufacturer and product is direct and meaningful for the system, the design does not violate the fourth normal form. Each actual combination of store, manufacturer, and product requires a separate row in the table. Fig. 2.7, for example, shows that the New York store sells Acme refrigerators and Ajax ranges. Although Acme may make ranges and Ajax may make refrigerators and the New York store sells both types of appliances, we know from the relation that that outlet does not carry Acme ranges or Ajax refrigerators; the database does not list those combinations.

Now suppose that each manufacturer instituted a rule stating that any outlet selling any of a particular type of appliance had to sell that company's brand of that appliance or lose all of its business. In other words, if the New York store sold any brand of refrigerator and wanted to sell any Ajax appliances, it would have to sell Ajax refrigerators. This logical constraint on the information allows the designer to represent it in three smaller tables rather than one larger table. Using the logical rule, each actual combination of store, manufacturer, and product can be reconstructed from three smaller relations: store-product, store-manufacturer, and manufacturer-product (Fig. 2.8[a]).

One can determine from the Store-Product table, for example, that the New York store sells refrigerators and from the Store-Manufacturer table that it sells Ajax products. Since the manufacturer-product relation shows that Ajax makes refrigerators, because of the special rule, we know that the New York store sells Ajax refrigerators. Any combination that can be expressed in the larger, unnormalized relation can be determined from the smaller ones.

The performance benefit of the fifth normal form can be seen when rows are added or deleted. Suppose the retailer adds an outlet that handles microwaves, ranges, and washers from three manufacturers. With the single, unnormalized relation, this would require the addition of nine new listings, one for each combination (Fig. 2.8[b]). The fifth normal form relations need only six additions: three in the Store-Product table and three in the Store-Manufacturer table (Fig. 2.8[a]). In such situations, new rows increase additively in the normalized design and multiplicatively in the unnormalized version. An organization that adds tens of thousands of entity occurrences to a fifth normal form database—or deletes them—can save hundreds of database insert or delete operations over a design that does not take advantage of the logical constraint.

2.8 MINIMIZING JOINS

We have concentrated on the advantages of normalization. There are situations, however, in which denormalization provides such performance benefits that risking loss of the advantages is a good bet—if the designer recognizes and minimizes the risks. Usually, the most processing-intensive relational operation is the join over a large number of rows, the cross-match process that reunites related data items that have been separated into different tables for normalization. Denormalization, reuniting these items within a single table during design, eliminates the need for joins. (Denormalization

a:

STORE	PRODUCT
NY	Ranges
NY	Refrigerators
LA	Washers
LA	Ranges
CHI	Microwaves
CHI	Washers
CHI	Ranges

MANUFACTURER	PRODUCT
Acme	Refrigerators
Acme	Ranges
Acme	Washers
Acme	Microwaves
Ajax	Refrigerators
Ajax	Ranges
Ajax	Microwaves
Ajax	Washers
Tops	Ranges
Tops	Microwaves
Tops	Washers

STORE	MANUFACTURER
NY	Acme
NY	Ajax
LA	Tops
LA	Ajax
CHI	Ajax
CHI	Acme
CHI	Tops

b:

To add a Chicago outlet representing all three manufacturers and selling ranges, microwaves, and washers requires only six new listings, shown above in red. With the unnormalized store/manufacturer/product table, nine new listings would be needed:

STORE	MANUFACTURER	PRODUCT
CHI	Ajax	Microwaves
CHI	Ajax	Washers
CHI	Ajax	Ranges
CHI	Acme	Microwaves
CHI	Acme	Washers
CHI	Acme	Ranges
CHI	Tops	Microwaves
CHI	Tops	Washers
CHI	Tops	Ranges

Fig. 2.8 Fifth normal form

also reduces the database's number of foreign keys, the attributes by which separate tables are related. And since foreign keys are often indexed, it reduces the number of indexes. Both reductions offer performance benefits—less storage, fewer items to be searched or updated—that should be weighed in any denormalization decision.)

Denormalization also reintroduces the need for redundancy and its attendant risks: update and delete anomalies, unnecessary processing for updates, and so on. Knowing when the redundancy-for-joins trade-off is worthwhile requires an understanding of how the data in question will be used. If users or programs will use two related data items in large tables together most of the time—say 80 percent of the time as a rule of thumb— and if the required join would cover hundreds of thousands of rows in each table, it is probably best to keep the items in the same table even if it violates the principles of normalization. If, for example, almost every database request for employees' names will also ask for their skills—a combination that would require a join in our normalized database example (Fig. 2.3)— recombining the employee and department relations makes sense. For large tables, the processing time saved by avoiding the join will outweigh the extra processing required to maintain the redundant records in the denormalized design. In summary, tables should be combined only if they are related via primary and foreign keys, are acted on by the same application function, and are used together for inquiry. The meaning of the data determines the logical design. The processing of the data influences the physical design.

The analyst can get a rough estimate from a system's prospective users about how often related items will be accessed together. Once the database is in use, DB2's EXPLAIN command will provide information for monitoring and tuning the database designs, allowing more informed decisions on the performance gains to be had from denormalization. Caution should be exercised in a shared data environment. Denormalization may benefit one application at a significant cost to another application.

Denormalization and Data Integrity

Denormalization reintroduces the possibility of update and delete anomalies, but the risks are fewer if the database is used carefully. Users and programmers must understand the potential problems so they can avoid them. For example, after denormalization of Employee and Skill tables, the Skill attributes will be repeated for every employee. SQL then offers two ways to select and update the skill information. First, to change a skill's name, the user might identify all employees known to hold the skill, have the system locate their rows, and change the skill name attribute in each one. This way is dangerous: If managers forget to change one or more employee records, they will have introduced inconsistencies.

Second, since SQL allows updates to sets of data, the user might specify that the skill name change be made in every row with the specific skill code. The command for this would be UPDATE EMPLOYEE SET SKILL_ NAME = 'NEW NAME' WHERE SKILL CODE = 702. DB2 would then be responsible for locating all instances of the code and making all the changes. DB2 is set up to carry out this responsibility without error. If a system failure occurs during the update, DB2 automatically rescinds, rolls back, the changes that have been made, ensuring that the skill name remains the same in all rows. It also issues an error code, alerting the user that no rows have been updated.

DB2, then, offers some safety from update anomalies but only if the user knows enough about the database's design to employ it properly. When deciding whether the potential improvement in performance through denormalization is worth the risk of data inconsistencies, the designer should consider the types of users who will have access to the data. If only a few programmers will be allowed to update it, the risks are relatively small. Programmers understand the general concept of update and delete anomalies and can be easily alerted to specific instances in the database where they are possible. If, on the other hand, a large number of casual users will be changing the data, teaching them to avoid the anomalies would be difficult, if not impossible. It would certainly be expensive—perhaps so expensive that the organization may rather pay the performance price for the joins that would let them avoid the issue.

2.9 STORING MONTHLY DATA

Organizations frequently need to store data by months—sales, expenses, and so on. There are two basic approaches for doing this, each appropriate

Account	Month	Amount	...
1000	01	5000	
1000	03	7000	
1000	06	3000	
1000	07	2000	
2000	02	9000	
2000	04	6000	
2000	06	4000	
Etc...			

Fig. 2.9 Months stored vertically

Account	Jan.	Feb.	Mar.	Apr	May	June	July	...
1000	5000		7000			3000	2000	
2000		9000		6000		4000		
3000	4000	1000	3000	9000	8000	6000	5000	
Etc..								

Fig. 2.10 Months stored horizontally

for different data and usage characteristics. In the vertical approach, the months are indicated by name or a code in a MONTH column with each monthly amount stored in another column in the particular month's row. In the horizontal approach, each month has its own column with each monthly amount stored as a value in the appropriate month column.

Consider the two tables shown in Fig. 2.9 and Fig. 2.10, either of which might be used to store monthly sales data by account.

The MONTHS_VERTICAL table is good when most months do not have a sales amount since it limits the number of rows. The MONTHS_HORIZONTAL table is good when most accounts have amounts. The approach chosen also depends on how the data is to be used. The two methods present differing levels of complexity in the SQL formulations needed for different types of requests.

A few example SELECT statements illustrate how each approach works. Consider requests for the January, February, and March amounts for ACCOUNT 1000. Using MONTHS_VERTICAL, the statement would read:

```
SELECT ACCOUNT, MONTH, AMOUNT
FROM   MONTHS_VERTICAL
WHERE  ACCOUNT = 1000
AND    (MONTH = 1
OR      MONTH = 2
OR      MONTH = 3)
```

Using MONTHS_HORIZONTAL, the same search would read:

```
SELECT ACCOUNT, JAN, FEB, MAR
FROM   MONTHS_HORIZONTAL
WHERE  ACCOUNT = 1000
```

To determine the maximum purchased by any account in any month the two statements would be:

```
SELECT ACCOUNT, MAX(AMOUNT)
FROM MONTHS_VERTICAL
```

and,

```
SELECT ACCOUNT, MAX(JAN),
MAX(FEB),MAX(MAR),MAX(APR),
MAX(MAY),MAX(JUNE),MAX(JULY),
MAX(AUG),MAX(SEPT),MAX(OCT),
MAX(NOV),MAX(DEC)
FROM MONTHS_HORIZONTAL
```

In addition, the **MONTHS_VERTICAL** table design would require host-language code to determine the maximum between the 12 months.

To determine the total amount for the year for all accounts:

```
SELECT ACCOUNT,SUM(AMOUNT)
FROM    MONTHS_VERTICAL
GROUP  BY ACCOUNT
```

and,

```
SELECT ACCOUNT, JAN + FEB
+ MAR + APR + MAY + JUNE
+ JULY + AUG + SEPT + OCT
+ NOV + DEC
FROM MONTHS_HORIZONTAL
```

To determine the accounts with an amount greater than 2000 in any month:

```
SELECT ACCOUNT
FROM    MONTHS_VERTICAL
WHERE  AMOUNT > 2000
```

and,

```
SELECT ACCOUNT
FROM    MONTHS_HORIZONTAL
WHERE  JAN > 2000
OR      FEB > 2000
OR      MAR > 2000
Etc.
OR      DEC > 2000
```

In most cases, storing the months vertically simplifies the SQL that is required to satisfy a request. If the months are stored horizontally, it may be necessary to create an index on each month to be able to locate the rows efficiently. This would be the case if searches are frequently specified on one or a few months when the months are stored horizontally. Having to maintain 12 indexes can be quite costly as will be seen in Chapter 6 in addition to the DASD (direct access storage device) space required for the indexes.

The DASD space required to store the data varies significantly between whether the months are stored vertically or horizontally. If months are stored vertically, it avoids having to store zero amounts for months that have not yet occurred early in the year. In fact, not all 12 months will have amounts until December. Consider the amount of DASD space that would be required to store 100,000 rows depending upon the time of year assuming a 38-byte row with a 30-byte primary key and an 8-byte amount.

```
 3,800,000 bytes (   950 pages) end of January
11,400,000 bytes ( 2,850 pages) end of March (1st qtr.)
22,810,000 bytes ( 5,700 pages) end of June  (2nd qtr.)
34,200,000 bytes ( 8,550 pages) end of Sept. (3rd qtr.)
45,600,000 bytes (11,400 pages) end of Dec.  (4th qtr.)
```

It would appear that a great deal of space is saved by not storing zeros for months that have not occurred. But before making a definite decision, consider the amount of space required for storing the monthly amounts horizontally. The row length would be 126 bytes with 30 bytes for the primary key and the 8-byte amount repeated 12 times. It would require about 12,600,000 bytes (3150 pages) for a table throughout the year beginning in January. Surprisingly, storing the months horizontally costs less starting in the beginning of the second quarter, and by the end of the second quarter, storing the months vertically requires almost twice the amount of space and the space requirements increase for the remainder of the year. If several years of history are retained with the monthly amounts stored horizontally, savings are more dramatic since all months of a year will have values.

This example is taken from a project where it was decided to store the months horizontally due to significant space savings in terms of dozens of disk devices. Indeed the calculated values were even more dramatic than was indicated in the example since the primary key was 81 bytes in length and several million rows were to be retained online for several years. It is suggested that for large tables, particularly historical tables, calculations be done to determine the cost tradeoffs even though storing the data vertically is more appealing particularly for simplifying SQL statements, which may be very costly. In any case, neither approach violates normalization requirements. The months are not a repeating group as was seen with skills and dependents because each has a separate business meaning.

2.10 SUMMARY

Normalization provides a design method that helps developers understand the data in the databases they design and, in fact, requires that they do so. Adhering to the rules of normalization produces designs that offer efficient performance and minimize the chances for inconsistencies in the data. In some cases, however, performance advantages may be obtained by violating normalization, a technique called denormalization, which should be practiced only with great care.

EXERCISE

Develop a logical design in third normal form for the following entities and attributes. The database manages information on professors, their departments and the courses they teach, and on students, the courses they take, and the grades they receive. Indicate each relation's primary key:

Student's name

Professor's name

Department name

Department ID

Student's grade in each course

Professor's department

Professor's age

Textbook ID for each course's text

Student's ID

Student's address

Professor's ID

Course ID

Professor's education

Professor's date of employment

Each student's courses

Each professor's courses

Department location

Student's major department

Student's minor department

Course name

What are the foreign keys within the tables you designed?

What characteristics of data use will require join operations on the tables you designed?

3

Creating Physical Objects

3.1 INTRODUCTION

DB2 manages data through a system of logical and physical entities called *objects*. Tables and indexes are objects, for example. A database, which is a collection of related tables, is also an object. Objects that describe a database in the way that users and developers think about it are called *logical objects*. Those that refer to the way data are actually stored in the system are called *physical objects*. The line between logical and physical objects is not sharp, however. In creating the physical database, the developer will work with several levels of objects ranging from the database's logical concept down to the *virtual sequential access method* (VSAM) datasets that physically store the information. Design decisions made at each level affect performance. Although DB2 can make database creation very easy by making many of the design decisions itself, its choices may or may not be the most efficient. Developers therefore should understand the design alternatives DB2 will use in order to intelligently override them.

Moving progressively toward the physical level, a database consists of tables and indexes that are stored in tablespaces and indexspaces that are made up of pages—blocks of physical storage that are the I/O units when the data is moved between the computer and storage devices. (Fig. 3.1 shows DB2's objects.) The tablespaces and indexspaces may be assigned to

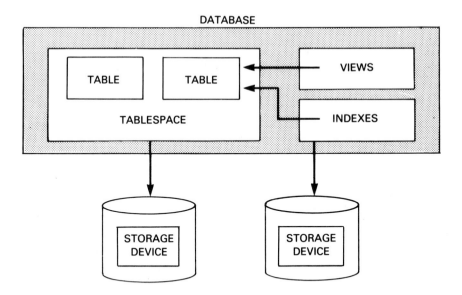

DATABASE

TABLE   TABLE   VIEWS

TABLESPACE   INDEXES

STORAGE DEVICE   STORAGE DEVICE

Fig 3.1 DB2 objects

storage groups, each of which is a collection of DASD (direct access storage devices) volumes.

This chapter examines the creation of the more physical of the objects—databases, tablespaces, and indexes. Chapter 4 covers the more logical of the objects—tables and views. There is some overlap between physical and logical design decisions, however. The amount of storage space allocated to a tablespace, for example, depends on the design of the table or tables it will hold.

3.2 DATABASES

One DB2 system can manage up to 65,279 separate databases. Although several application systems can operate on each database and each program can access many databases transparently, there are a number of advantages to defining a separate database for each subject area or functional group of objects. From an administrative standpoint, a database can be easily controlled, and therefore the application it serves can be easily controlled. For example, DB2 gives administrators the ability through AUTHIDs to authorize only certain employees to start, stop, or display the status of a database; to create or drop objects in it; or to load, reorganize, or copy objects in the database. Administrators will usually grant such authority on an application-by-application basis. In that case if functional application systems shared a database, an employee given authority to work within the database would have to be cleared to work with objects pertaining to all of its applications—an administrative strain if not an impossibility depending on how security is to be administered.

The DBD

Operational considerations also argue in favor of having one functional application system per database. One reason is that a DB2 component called the database descriptor (DBD) limits access to the database whenever objects are being created, altered, or dropped. Database developers, query management facility (QMF) users, and application programs all create objects. Each time they do, DB2 writes descriptive and control information about the object in the DBD. Each database has a DBD that is created when a database is created and maintained by DB2 as objects are created and altered in the database. The maximum size of a DBD is 2 gigabytes, allowing a virtually unlimited number of objects to be created in a database with a current limit of 10,000 objects in a database. However, the space occupied by a DBD should not exceed 5 to 10 percent of that allocated to the environmental description manager (EDM) pool of memory. Otherwise there is a good change that there will be contention for space between multiple DBD and application plans and packages, which also use the EDM pool that also use the EDM. Indeed DB2 limits the DBD size to 25 percent of the EDM pool. If there is insufficient space in the EDM pool at execution time, an error of SQLCODE = -904 will be received when an attempt is made to execute static SQL.

To maintain the integrity of the information about the objects, DB2 locks the DBD during object creation. Only one object at a time may be created therefore. If several objects being created require the DBD at the same time, each must wait its turn, a situation called *lock contention* may result. Placing more than one application system in a single database increases the likelihood of lock contention on the DBD.

The DBD enters into several other physical design decisions with performance implications. Lock contention on the DBD can also be troublesome when end users have access to the database through QMF. QMF users create a relatively large number of objects, often without realizing it. When a user saves data, for example, DB2 creates a table for it, locking the DBD and temporarily barring creation of any other objects in the database. A QMF user faced with a delay when saving data may well be waiting for other users who are also saving data. In addition whenever SQL statements are bound, DB2 locks the DBD. QMF users executing statements interactively can cause lock contention on the DBD for others attempting to create objects. Many early DB2 users erred in trying to isolate QMF users in one or two databases, which resulted in poor or unacceptable performance. As a rule of thumb, more than 20 or 25 active QMF users on a database will cause lock contention on the DBD. Generally it is most efficient to group QMF users by functional area with only a few assigned to each database.

Programs that frequently create temporary tables may also cause lock contention on the DBD. DB2 allows programmers to create such tables within COBOL and other host-language programs, a useful device for storing intermediate values during multistep processing. If a frequently executed program generates many temporary tables, however, lock contention on the DBD may result. The developer can minimize this problem by defining a separate database for the application's temporary tables so that they do not interfere with the production database.

Creating Objects

Developers create objects using SQL's CREATE statements, usually while working within a DB2 facility called SPUFI (SQL processor using file input), which allows interactive statement execution. The same statement format can be used to create many objects: the word CREATE, followed by the object type, followed by the object's name, which is usually dictated by an installation's naming conventions. The developer may add various descriptive information after the name, drawing on a set of keywords to identify the parameters that further define the object. With this information, the developer implements design decisions. Developers can also change objects easily with ALTER statements, which are similar in format to CREATE statements.

The initial statement for defining a database is, logically, the CREATE DATABASE statement, which takes this form:

```
CREATE DATABASE DASPJDB
    STOGROUP DASPJSTG
    BUFFERPOOL BP0
    ROSHARE NONE;
```

In this case, the database name, DASPJDB comprises codes specifying its location (DA), the application it serves (SPJ), and its object type (DB). For a database, storage group, and tablespace the object's name may be 8 characters; other objects' names may be 18 characters. An installation's naming conventions generally dictate how the characters may be used. The STOGROUP and BUFFERPOOL parameters specify the storage group and bufferpool to which objects created within the database will be assigned unless otherwise specified when objects are created in the database. The bufferpool is main or expanded memory set aside to hold data temporarily that DB2 expects to need for processing. The STOGROUP and BUFFER-POOL parameters have default assignments, however, which developers can override when they create a tablespace or indexspace within a database.

Shared Read-only Database

A database can be created in such a manner that data can be read from multiple DB2 subsystems. The data exists *only* in an owning database on a single DB2 subsystem. Programs using other DB2 subsystems can read the data but not update it. The DB2 subsystems can be on the same or different processors. If they are on different processors, these must be channel-to-channel-connected, and the data must be on shared data DASD that is channel-connected to DB2 subsystems that read the data. The MVS GRS (global resource serialization) and VSAM sharing options are used to enforce data integrity with a single ICF (integrated catalog facility) designated as shared. The owner of the data must create the database with the ROSHARE OWNER parameter like:

```
CREATE DATABASE DAREADB
STOGROUP DASPJSTG
BUFFERPOOL BP0
ROSHARE OWNER;
```

A CREATE DATABASE statement must be executed on each DB2 subsystem that will be allowed to read the data with the ROSHARE READ parameter like:

```
CREATE DATABASE DAREADB
STOGROUP DASPJSTG
BUFFERPOOL BP0
ROSHARE READ;
```

There are significant operational restrictions on the use of a shared read-only database. The type of processing dictates whether owner and reader database must be started or stopped with a specific access type. A change of access type requires stopping *all* owner and reader databases in most cases. The example of stopping the DAREADB database and starting it with read/write (RW) access will stop all tablespaces and indexes in the database. Optionally individual tablespace and indexes can be stopped.

```
-STOP  DATABASE (DAREADB) SPACENAM (*)
-START DATABASE (DAREADB) SPACENAM (*) ACCESS (RW)
```

Box 3.1 summaries the state of a shared read-only database for specific processing. The only time both the owner and all reader databases can be started at the same time is for read-only (RO) access. Almost all processing

Box 3.1   State of database for specific processing

Processing	Owner Database	Reader Databases
Create/drop/alter owner objects Create/drop/alter reader objects Update data Read data Utilities	Start RW Stopped Start RW Start RO	Stopped Start RW Stopped Start RO
RW = Read/write access RO = Read-only access UT = Utility-only access	Start UT	Stopped

requires that only the owner database be started and that all reader databases must be stopped. An exception is when objects are created in the reader databases in which case the reader database must be started and the owner database stopped. In addition, the order of operations is significant. Usually an operation is performed on the owner database before the reader databases.

The stopping and starting of databases results in significant complexities in the administration and operations of shared read-only data. Indeed to change the status of a reader database, it is necessary to drop the database and recreate it with the ROSHARE READ parameter. The owner-shared database, however, need not be dropped to change from nonshared to shared. No update activity is allowed by the owner or any readers while sharing data. The reader object definitions must be almost identical to the owner's object definitions as will be discussed in Chapter 4. All plans and packages must be bound on each DB2 subsystem where they will be executed, and any time a change is required the changed plans and packages must be bound on each owner's and reader's DB2 subsystem.

Despite these administration and operation complexities, there are advantages of shared RO data if the data needs to be available on multiple DB2 subsystems. Shared RO databases have performance advantages over distributed processing since it is not necessary to format messages to transmit them over communication links. There is a reduction in the amount of DASD space required since the data is stored in only one place, and there is no possibility of inconsistent copies of the data. The processing load can be spread load across multiple DB2s and processors. For example, ad hoc users can access the data from a separate processor to avoid impacting operational transactions on their processors. Select and update transactions can be processed during the day on the owning DB2 with RO batch jobs run in parallel on multiple DB2s and processors to accommodate a narrow batch

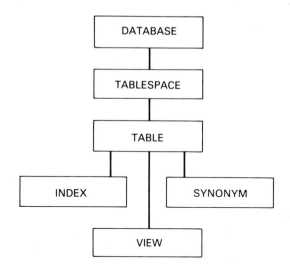

Before a dependent object can be created, the object upon which it depends must be created. A table cannot be created until the tablespace that will hold it has been, for example. Whenever an object is dropped, all objects that depend on it are also dropped.

Fig. 3.2 Hierarchy of object dependencies

window. Maintenance of the data including the execution of utilities is required on only the single copy of the data. (An exception is RUNSTATS, which should be executed on each shared database objects.)

Dropping Objects

DB2 organizes objects according to a hierarchy in which higher level objects must be created before lower level, dependent objects. For example, the database must be created before any of the objects its contains. A table cannot be created before the tablespace that will hold it. (Fig. 3.2 shows the hierarchy of dependencies.)

Objects can be dropped with simple DROP statements—the word DROP followed by the name of the object type followed by the object name. Developers may wish to drop objects when they no longer wish to allow access to them and when they wish to restructure an object and its dependents. They must drop objects carefully, however. In most cases, whenever an object is dropped, all its dependent objects will be dropped. For example, if a tablespace is dropped, all of its tables, indexes, and views will also be dropped.

Often developers will want to recreate dropped objects—as part of a restructuring, for example. This may not be a trivial task particularly if several professionals have been creating objects in the same space. If a single developer has responsibility for creating a tablespace's objects, the individual will usually create a SPUFI file containing all the CREATE statements associated with the space. The developer can use this file to recreate the object and its dependent objects. Frequently several professionals will create tables, views, and synonyms in a tablespace. These would be lost if someone unaware of them dropped the tablespaces. DBMAUI (Data Base Migration Aid Utility Interface) from IBM as well as a number of non-IBM product offerings can alleviate this problem. Before a table or database is dropped, DBMAUI will generate statements for them and their dependent objects from information in the catalog tables. Designed to aid in migration from a test to production environment, DBMAUI reads the catalog statements and generates the CREATE statements in a SPUFI file that can be used to recreate the objects. Alternatively developers can query the catalog tables to identify dependent objects and recreate their CREATE statements.

Box 3.2   Three types of tablespaces

A tablespace resides in a page set consisting of one or more VSAM data sets. Pages are 4K or 32K depending on the bufferpool choice. The data page format is the same for all types of tablespaces.

1) Segmented tablespace
    Can house one or more tables (no limit)

    Tablespace is divided into segments of 4 to 64 pages in increments of 4 pages Each segment is dedicated to a table A table can occupy multiple segments

2) Simple tablespace
    Can house one or more tables (no limit)

    Rows from multiple tables can be interleaved on a page under the developers control and maintenance

3) Partitioned tablespace
    Can house one table

    Tablespace is divided into parts

    Each part is housed in a separate VSAM data set

3.3 TABLESPACE AND INDEXSPACE

Tablespaces and indexspaces are of pivotal importance in DB2 designs because the system uses these objects to control the data's physical storage. There are three types of tablespaces: simple, segmented, and partitioned. (Partitioned tablespaces are discussed in Section 3.9.) Both simple and segmented types can provide storage space for one or more tables, but segmented tablespaces are better for managing multiple tables. Simple tablespaces should almost never be used for multiple tables. A nonsegmented tablespace may also be partitioned—or split—among VSAM data sets in which case it can contain only one table. An indexspace cannot hold more than one index. Therefore there is no need to create both indexes and indexspaces. DB2 creates the indexspace in carrying out the CREATE INDEX statement.

Using the parameters available with the CREATE TABLESPACE and CREATE INDEX statements, the developer instructs DB2 about how to employ the storage management options at its disposal. (Fig. 3.3 provides examples of CREATE TABLESPACE statements.) With these statement parameters, for example, the developer implements decisions about the size of the VSAM datasets that will hold the tables and indexes; the amount and distribution of space left free in the datasets when the data are loaded or reorganized; the amount of data covered by concurrency control locks, which prevent introduction of inconsistencies through simultaneous updating of the same data, and the placement of datasets in specific storage volumes. All of these decisions and others made during tablespace and indexspace creation hold performance implications. We will explore these considerations, along with the descriptions of the statements for implementing decisions about them.

If the developer does not specify choices for any of these parameters, DB2 will use default values. Indeed developers need not even create a tablespace in order to create a table. DB2 will automatically create a default tablespace for any table without an assigned tablespace with 12K bytes of primary and 12K of secondary space. This is a useful feature for casual users; however, because the parameters available for creating tablespaces hold performance implications, developers will usually want to specify their choices in CREATE statements for each application system.

STOGROUP versus VCAT (Volume Catalog)

DB2 offers two methods for creating tablespaces and indexspaces. Under the first method, in the CREATE TABLESPACE statement, the developer assigns the tablespace to a storage group (STOGROUP) that has been pre-

```
Using STOGROUP:

CREATE TABLESPACE PTSP
  IN DASPJDB
  USING STOGROUP DASPJSTG
   PRIQTY 7200
   SECQTY 720
  ERASE NO
  PCTFREE 10
  FREEPAGE 63
  LOCKSIZE PAGE
  CLOSE NO
  BUFFERPOOL BP0
  SEGSIZE 64
  DSETPASS SESAME;

Using VCAT:

    CREATE TABLESPACE PTSP
      IN DASPJDB
      USING VCAT AAXX2
      PCTFREE 10
      FREEPAGE 63
      LOCKSIZE PAGE
      CLOSE NO
      BUFFERPOOL BP0
      SEGSIZE 64
      DSETPASS SESAME;

Changing tablespace parameters:

    ALTER TABLESPACE DASPJDB.PTSP
      USING STOGROUP DATOMSTG
       PRIQTY 14400
       SECQTY 720
      ERASE YES
      PCTFREE 15
      FREEPAGE 7
      LOCKSIZE ANY
      CLOSE YES
      BUFFERPOOL BP1
      DSETPASS NEWPASS;
```

Fig. 3.3 CREATE and ALTER TABLESPACE statements

defined with a **CREATE STOGROUP** statement, which is discussed below. DB2 then automatically creates the VSAM linear datasets (LDS) needed for the tablespace within the specified storage group. Under the second method, the developer creates LDS or entry sequence datasets (ESDS) with the IDCAM utility. Then, when creating the tablespace or indexspace, the developer specifies a volume catalog (VCAT) name, indicating the VSAM

ICF catalog alias or name typically created by the MVS or DASD management group. ESDS and LDS datasets can be processed by VSAM AMS (assess method services) in CI (control internal) mode, including IMPORT and EXPORT. LDS can be processed by PRINT and REPRO utilities as well. Each method has advantages and disadvantages. We will examine the use of storage groups first.

It is usually the systems administrator that establishes the storage group with a CREATE statement including parameters identifying the volumes that will make up the storage group, their VCAT identifier, and password if the ICF catalog is password protected. The statement would look like this:

```
CREATE STOGROUP DASPJSTG
  VOLUMES (VOL1, VOL4)
  VCAT VCATID
  PASSWORD SESAME;
```

A storage group may contain a maximum of 133 DASD volumes. A volume assigned to a storage group is not dedicated to it.

The developer or other users can allocate sequential files, VSAM datasets, DL/1 files, or even other DB2 storage groups to the same volume. To control table placement by volume when using the storage group to create tablespaces, however, the developer can assign only one volume to each storage group. When DB2 uses the storage group to create a tablespace, it creates the necessary VSAM datasets in the storage group's first volume until it is full, and then automatically moves to the next volume. It is not possible to control the placement of a dataset on specific volumes of a multivolume storage group. If the data facility product SMS (system managed storage) is used with the parameter VOLUMES (*) when creating a storage group, however, SMS will place the datasets on the appropriate volumes to spread I/O evenly across volumes and channels.

Although the use of storage groups to create tablespaces and indexspaces surrenders some control and flexibility if SMS is not used, it still does have advantages. Primarily it relieves the developer of the chore of creating the VSAM datasets. A DB2 developer need not be conversant with VSAM. Even for expert VSAM programmers, creating the necessary datasets can be burdensome. Doing the work manually, the developer would have to create 20 VSAM datasets to accommodate 10 tables with one index per table, for example. If developers want to partition tables or indexes, they must create a separate VSAM dataset for each partition. And for extremely large tables, the developer would have to create a separate dataset for up to 64 partitions of data and 64 partitions of its index. Using a storage

Fig. 3.4 Place small datasets close together

group, DB2 does all this work automatically. When STOGROUP is used, DB2 also records space allocations in the catalog tables for use in monitoring, described in Chapter 14. When VCAT is used, space allocations are not recorded in the DB2 catalog tables. This is important for proper space management.

Cylinder or track allocation improves performance for inserts, load, reorganization, and recovery since space is preformatted in the allocated unit and the high used RBA is recorded in ICF catalog VVR for each space allocation. If the required space approaches the cylinder size of the DASD device used (720 KB for a 3390), the PRIQTY and SECQTY should be specified in multiples of the cylinder size. Otherwise multiples of the track size are a good choice (48 KB for a 3390). It is necessary to specify SECQTY in multiples of the cylinder or track size or zero to achieve preformatting of space in cylinders or tracks.

Volumes can be added to, or removed from, a storage group. There is no loss of data when removing a volume. It simply means that no more objects will be placed on the volume. Execution of the reorganization, load replace, or recover utilities will result in objects being placed in another volume in the storage group. If all volumes are removed from a storage group, the object can be altered to place it in another storage group. A sample ALTER statement looks like:

```
ALTER STOGROUP DASPJSTG
   ADD VOLUMES (VOL6)
   REMOVE VOLUMES (VOL4)
   PASSWORD NEWPASS;
```

A sometimes perceived advantage of using VCAT to create tablespaces and indexspaces is that it gives developers control over placement, allowing them, for example, to place small- and medium-sized (few cylinders) datasets close together if they are frequently used together as indicated in Fig. 3.4. This placement of tablespaces and indexes on contiguous DASD space will reduce seek time. Large tablespaces and indexes should be spread

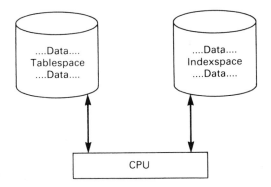

Fig. 3.5 Separate large datasets for parallelism

across volumes and channels as indicated in Fig. 3.5 in order to spread
I/O activity and to provide for parallel I/O across the channels. Placement
of datasets can be controlled using STOGROUP by assigning one volume
to a storage group.

A disadvantage of using VCAT is that the space allocated and used for
datasets are not recorded in the catalog tables. Chapter 14 has several SE-
LECT statements for space management to determine if too much or not
enough space has been allocated. It will not be possible to use these statements when using VCAT. Also a number of software products on the market make use of the space figures if they are available to determine if various utilities should be executed and automatically generate and submit the
appropriate utility. Chapter 14 discusses a technique for getting the space
figures in the catalog tables if using VCAT is a requirement.

Using VCAT lets the developer employ some, but not all, of the VSAM
AMS parameters that DB2 would not use automatically with a storage
group. DB2 uses VSAM's AMS to create a dataset, but it formats the dataset and manages the data itself. By specifying certain parameters during
creation of the dataset, however, the developer can take advantage of some
VSAM services. For example, the developer can specify the STAGE and
NONDESTAGE parameters necessary for DB2 to store the datasets on a
3850 Mass Storage System. That storage device, considerably slower than
3390 or 3380 DASD, might be used for less frequently accessed data, freeing
up space on the faster devices. To make this and similar choices about data
placement that require special VSAM parameters, the developer must use
VCAT to create the tablespace's datasets. The developer must use VSAM
parameters with care, however. DB2 will not accept some parameters. The

manual, *IBM Database 2 Administration Guide* (SC26–4374), provides detailed information on creating VSAM datasets for DB2.

VCAT Naming Conventions

The VCAT identification in the CREATE TABLESPACE statement's USING clause must match the first node of the VSAM datasets created for the space. That node names the VSAM ICF catalog to which the datasets have been assigned. One way installations can take advantage of the VCAT method's flexibility of data placement is to reassign tablespaces among VSAM catalogs and move them among direct access storage devices. As with changing between STOGROUP and VCAT space management, the tablespace must be stopped while the catalog change is made. After the tablespace has been stopped, it can be moved between ICF catalogs by using the VSAM rename utility to change the first node of the datasets' name. If the tablespace is to be moved to a new volume, any of four copy utilities external to DB2 may be used. These are DSN1COPY, DFDSS (data facility data system services), AMS REPRO, and AMS EXPORT/IMPORT. After the datasets have been renamed and moved, the first node of the tablespace is renamed with an ALTER statement that changes the USING parameter. For example, the tablespace PTSP defined with VCAT in Figure 3.2, can be reassigned from volume AAXX2 to volume NEWCAT with the statement:

```
ALTER TABLESPACE DASPJDB.PTSP
   USING VCAT NEWCAT;
```

After the changes have been made, the tablespace is restarted,which causes the updated DBD as a result of the ALTER to be used. The tablespace must be stopped before the alter and started after the alter as indicated in the example on changing space allocation. This is necessary to cause the updated DBD to be used.

Changing from VCAT to STOGROUP

An installation may want to switch from using one type of storage management to another. During the change,the tablespace must be stopped, shut off for access, and after the change, it must be started again. The STOP and START statements begin with those key words followed by the name of the database that holds the tablespace and the tablespace name. For example:

```
-STOP DATABASE (DASPJDB) SPACENAM (PTSP)
```

Although the statement must identify the database, it stops only the tablespace. The developer then simply includes in the ALTER statement the new parameters redefining the space through STOGROUP and starts the table-space and database.

```
ALTER TABLESPACE DASPJDB.PTSP
  USING STOGROUP DASPJSTG
  PRIQTY 14400
  SECQTY 720
  ERASE NO;
```

```
-START DATABASE (DASPJDB) SPACENAM (PTSP) ACCESS (RW).
```

The ACCESS(RW) part of the statement gives users read and write access to the database.

Storage Quantities

When a developer uses a storage group to define a tablespace, he or she must specify the size of the VSAM datasets DB2 will create for it. DB2 assigns the space to a primary area and a secondary area, which it uses if the primary area is full. The key to selecting the most efficient primary and secondary quantity sizes is determining a primary amount that is certain to hold the tablespace but not so large that it wastes storage. Contiguous space will probably not be assigned to the secondary areas after the primary area is filled. Indeed secondary storage may be placed on separate DASD devices. A tablespace scan therefore will expend excessive seek time if it must move from the primary to secondary areas to complete a search. On the other hand, setting the primary quantity too high wastes storage. Appendix A provides formulas for estimating the amount of space tables require. Those formulas provide the value for the primary quantity (PRIQTY) parameter. The maximum size of a tablespace is 64 gigabytes. This maximum size is determined by the first three bytes of the RID (row identifier also known as the record identifier) that is used to identify a page. Three bytes have 24 bits so 224 = 16 megabytes times 4K page gives the limit of 64 gigabytes. This is a great deal of space. It would require about 128 volumes of 3380D DASD devices.

If necessary, however, DB2 can allocate the secondary quantity 123 times—in 123 *extents* in storage terminology. While it is inefficient to store a tablespace across multiple extents, this characteristic of secondary storage provides a safety margin. It allows a tablespace whose data fill the primary storage and one or more extents of secondary storage to continue operating until a developer allocates additional space. The catalog tables contain information on space use (Chapter 14 describes how to use the catalog to monitor use.) If the primary allocation proves to be too small, it can be

Box 3.3 Allocating storage space

DB2 gives developers two methods for allocating storage to tablespaces and indexspaces in their CREATE statements: by instructing DB2 to create VSAM datasets in a predefined storage group (STOGROUP) or by assigning the object to predefined datasets identified by a volume catalog (VCAT) name. Each method has pros and cons:

STOGROUP

- Relieves developers of the need to know VSAM
- Saves developers the effort of creating VSAM datasets
- Saves developers from having to delete the dataset in addition to dropping the tablespace
- Makes placement of data on target storage devices difficult when a storage group contains more than one volume
- Allows altering of space allocation

VCAT

- Requires developers to create VSAM datasets
- Provides control over placement of data on storage devices
- Permits use of some VSAM access service parameters
- Does not allow altering of space allocation with the DB2 ALTER statement

---

expanded with an ALTER statement. The new allocation takes effect when the tablespace or index is reorganized or recovered.

The Erase Option

DB2 provides two methods for deleting the data when the tablespace is dropped. First it will merely drop the tablespace from the system, leaving the data on DASD until it is written over, a routine data management practice. In this case, while the data are not available through the system, they may still be recovered from DASD. This is a time-consuming, highly technical process in which DB2 and VSAM control information must be decoded but it is a possibility nevertheless. The second delete option negates the possibility. It actually "erases" the dropped tablespace's information by filling the tablespace with zeros. Since this requires many I/O operations and considerable CPU time—in effect, it means writing over the entire tablespace—the erase method should be used only when security consider- ations dictate, that is, only when the information is so sensitive that it should not be left on DASD after the table has been dropped. A value of YES for the ERASE parameter activates use of zeros to fill a dropped tablespace. A value of NO avoids it.

3.4 FREE SPACE

Developers can use two parameters to indicate the amount and distribution of free space DB2 leaves in a tablespace or indexspace's datasets when it loads or reorganizes data. Recovery of an index also returns free space to its indexspace. Free space provides room for insertion of new rows within a sequence or for the expansion of variable-length rows. The page is the basic unit of physical storage. The PCTFREE parameter allows developers to specify the percentage of each page to be left free. The FREEPAGE parameter lets them indicate the number of pages to be loaded with data between each free page. Either or both parameters may be used for an entire tablespace or indexspace or for a partition. Choices made about either pa- rameter affect I/O operations, CPU utilization, and the frequency with which the data must be reorganized. Developers must make tradeoffs among these factors.

Insertions within Sequence

We will explore the role of free space in row insertion first. In most cases, free space for row insertion should be provided on each page with the PCT- FREE parameter. Developers should specify that a table have a clustering index that causes DB2 to maintain the physical sequence of stored rows in close correspondence to their collating sequence. (This arrangement saves search time and I/O operations for many requests. Chapter 6 discusses clus- tering's benefits in detail.) With clustering, rows are stored in the sequence of the column designated as the clustering index. As programs or users in- sert rows and index values, DB2 places them in free space in their proper order within the clustering sequence. If there is no free space within the sequence, DB2 finds space for the new rows someplace else on a *near page* within the same segment or on a *far page*—in the last segment of a seg- mented tablespace. When using a nonsegmented tablespace, free space is located by reading forward and backward 16 pages, and if space is found, it is considered a near page. If space is not found, a far page is located by scanning the space map pages from the beginning of the tablespace. (Space map pages are discussed in section 3.8.) As this happens with more and

Box 3.4   Specifying free space

Developers can instruct DB2 to leave free space in a tablespace or index-space during data loads and reorganizations with two parameters in the CREATE statement: PCTFREE and FREEPAGE. PCTFREE specifies the percentage of space to be left free on each page. FREEPAGE indicates the number of pages to be loaded between each page left free. Both may be used in the same statement. The parameter values PCTFREE (20) FREE-PAGE (2) would produce a data load that looks like this:

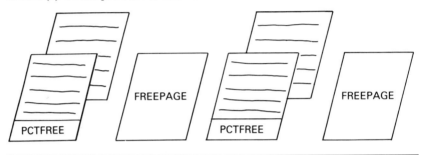

more insertions, the table becomes unclustered, losing the benefits of sequential storage. Then the tablespace and indexspace must be reorganized to reorder the rows and add more free space for subsequent insertions. The amount and type of free space the developer decides to leave in the tablespace to maintain clustering depends therefore on the nature of the data, the anticipated rate of insertions, the distribution of inserts throughout the tablespace and the acceptable frequency of reorganization. Examples will show how these points interact.

If new rows are added uniformly throughout the clustering sequence each week that expand the total number of rows by 10 percent and the developer has called for 10 percent free space, weekly reorganization will be necessary. To change to an every-other-week reorganization schedule, the developer would double the free space to 20 percent. The free space should be a multiple of the row length since a row must fit within the free space. If a table will be updated slowly—as with an employee table when new hires arrive infrequently—its tablespace and indexspace will require very little free space, perhaps less than the default value of 5 percent for a tablespace and 10 percent for an indexspace. And since DB2 will allocate free space by partition, partitions experiencing the most update activity should be given the most free space. This is often the case when some partitions hold historical information requiring few or no insertions, while other partitions accumulate new information with many insertions. If many rows will be deleted from the tablespace's table in about the same places in the clustering sequence as inserts, relatively little free space will be needed because DB2 immediately frees space that had been occupied by a deleted row for use by inserted rows. Read-only tables, which are not updated at all, require no free space.

A skewed distribution of update activity can result in free space in some pages rarely being used. This is a difficult situation with which to deal. A possible technique is to use a low percent of free space and load sections with low update activity. Then increase percent free with the ALTER statement and load sections with high update activity using the "resume" option of the load utility described in Chapter 16. This is cumbersome and results in index page splitting as is discussed in Chapter 6.

When rows are added sequentially to a table at the end of a clustering sequence—if sales are entered by consecutive invoice number, for example—the table's tablespace requires no free space. There will be no insertions within the sequence. Note, however, that the nonclustering indexes still need free space to maintain the B-tree indexes. A B-tree index has a tree like structure in which each branch contains a range of index values. (Chapter 6 describes the B-tree in detail.) To maintain balanced—or equal-length—access paths down the B-tree's branches when a page becomes full, DB2 splits it and redistributes the values, a process that requires significant CPU time and I/O operations. Free space within the indexspace pages minimizes this splitting. In general, free space for an index should be about twice that for its tablespace. The index will require frequent reorganization when inserting consecutive values.

Free pages are useful for providing near pages. A free page value of 63 will provide for a near page within a 64-page segment. A free page of 15 will provide for a near page for a search within plus or minus 16 pages for a nonsegmented tablespace.

Relocation of Rows

Free space also comes into play when a table is designed to have variable-length rows—those including a variable-length data type called VARCHAR or those whose data are compressed. (VARCHAR and data compression are discussed in the next chapter.) Free space is also needed when a column is added to a table, lengthening its rows as the column is filled. Whenever an update lengthens a row, DB2 tries first to expand it onto free space on the page that contains it. If no free space is there, it moves the entire row to a near or far page that can hold it and leaves a pointer on the original page pointing to the new location.

This pointer arrangement avoids the need to update indexes—perhaps many of them—with a row's new location. But displacing expanded rows costs processing time during the update and whenever the relocated row is accessed. The update requires a search for space. The access requires two I/O operations rather than one; the first finds the pointer, and the second finds the row. Assignment of free space to pages with the PCTFREE parameter helps avoid the need for such row relocation. The FREEPAGE parameter can help somewhat in this situation by providing free space on a nearby page for a relocated row. This at least reduces seek time when the disk access arm follows the pointer to the new location. If the row is moved a second time, a chain of pointers is not created. Rather the first pointer is updated to point to the third location of the row.

Estimating Free Space Needs

The matrix in Fig. 3.6 provides suggested PCTFREE values for various applications. To accommodate insertions without wasting space, the PCTFREE parameter should leave space in multiples of row length. For example, 5 percent free space equals about 200 bytes on each 4K page. If rows are longer than 200 bytes, that space will never be used, or if the row is 110 bytes in length, only one row will fit in the free space.

If a table's rows are 100 bytes long, each 4K-byte data page will hold about 40 rows. If the developer wants to add a 10-byte column, however, and hopes to keep the rows on their original pages, he or she must leave 400 bytes free. Since the PCTFREE parameter value is expressed as a percentage of the page to be left free, the value here would be 10–400 bytes free/4000 bytes total. This is only a rough estimate. When DB2 loads or reorganizes the tablespace, space is left in each row for the newly added column. If the column was added with NOT NULL WITH DEFAULT, the default value will be placed in the rows added column as discussed in the next chapter.

Similarly the amount by which a VARCHAR column will expand can be estimated only roughly. A VARCHAR column usually contains names or descriptions of various lengths. The possible amount of expansion of each row, therefore, is the difference between the minimum and maximum description or name length contained in the VARCHAR column. The probable amount of expansion depends on a number of factors related to update patterns—the percentage of rows changed and the average size of the changes, for example. An extreme example makes the point.

Suppose 10 percent of a VARCHAR column's values are unknown when the table is loaded. Their places are left empty and later updated with descriptions averaging 20 characters. The developer can expect that 10 percent of each page's rows will expand by 20 bytes. A page with 100 rows

Usage of Data	Percentage Free			
	0	Low (5-15)	Medium (10-30)	High (30-50)
Read-only tablespace and indexspace	Y			
10 percent of rows randomly inserted on a clustering index; weekly reorganization		Y		
10 percent of rows randomly inserted on a clustering index; biweekly reorganization			Y	
Large percentage of rows randomly inserted on a clustering index; infrequent reorganization				Y
Most rows (80 percent) inserted at end of clustering index TABLESPACE INDEX	Y	Y		
Variable-length rows frequently updated and expanded TABLESPACE INDEX (if not updated)	Y	Y		
Column added with ALTER TABLE statement values added gradually INDEX on new column		Y Y	Y	

Fig. 3.6 Percentage free guidelines

therefore would need 200 bytes, or 5 percent free space. The amount of row expansion possible when data are compressed is even more difficult to estimate, depending usually on the number of trailing blanks, leading zeros, and repeating characters in the data being compressed.

Frequently VARCHAR is used to avoid storing trailing blanks, and the column is seldom increased in length in which case little free space is required for expansion of the column value. If the use of VARCHAR does not result in saving enough space typically to store an additional row, there is no advantage to using VARCHAR since all I/O and space allocation is at the page level.

Free Space Adjustments

Fortunately estimates of free space requirements need not be exact. The developer can monitor the number and frequency of relocated rows in a table and the loss of clustering and adjust free space before reorganization to achieve the desired reorganization schedule. Developers would add free space if reorganizations have been needed more frequently than desired. They will also want to subtract unnecessary free space. Because free space reduces the number of rows that can fit on a page and the page is the basic I/O unit, the more free space that is used, the fewer rows can be processed for each I/O. Unnecessary free space means unnecessary I/Os.

For small production tables or tables used for testing, a developer may want to use free space to spread the rows over more pages than they would normally need. Reference, or *look-up*, tables in particular usually contain relatively few rows, which are often accessed concurrently by many programs. If the table occupies only a few pages, users are likely to encounter lock contention. A high percentage of free space on each table spreads the rows across more pages, reducing contention. "Padding" rows with unused columns is another way to spread rows over more pages in small tables and avoids having inserted rows use up the space.

Adding Columns

Timing the addition of free space is important when the space is needed to accommodate a new column. If free space had not been allocated for the column when the tablespace was created, the free space may be added by specifying it with the PCTFREE parameter in an ALTER TABLESPACE statement and then reorganizing the tablespace. If this is done before the column's values are entered, DB2 will not have to relocate rows as they are updated. An alternative method would be updating the table before adding free space, accepting the processing cost of row relocation, and reorganizing the table afterward. The proper alternative depends on the table's size and the expected rate of updates to add the new column's values. For large tables that can be updated in mass—when all of the column's values are known—it is best to reorganize the tablespace so that space will be left for the newly added column. The cost of relocating a large percentage of the updated rows can be excessive.

3.5   LOCKSIZE

When creating a tablespace, the developer specifies the size of locks that will be available to applications executing against it. (Programmers can influence locks in a variety of ways when they develop an application. Chapter 8 discusses these options in depth. This section provides only enough detail to allow informed decisions during tablespace creation.) The tablespace developer can instruct DB2 to impose locks in either of three sizes: by page, by table, or by tablespace. (The locksize of TABLE is available only in segmented tablespaces.) Or by specifying ANY, the developer can let DB2 make the choice for each program that executes against the tablespace. (ANY is also the default should the developer not specify a value for this parameter.) When DB2 makes the choice, it usually locks by page. The performance implications of locksizes are clearcut. A page locksize provides the best response times for most update transactions. Because locks are taken on individual pages, those not locked are free for access by concurrent users. A table or tablespace locksize, on the other hand, reduces CPU time and the need for virtual storage. The CPU must execute instructions each time it imposes a lock and use 200-250 bytes of virtual storage to record the fact that the lock exists. When a second transaction executes against the tablespace, the CPU spends time searching through the page locks to determine whether to permit the transaction. If a tablespace lock were in place, the CPU would have to check only one location to determine whether to allow the transaction. But since the entire tablespace is inaccessible for the duration of a tablespace lock, response times may be slow as transactions wait their turn at the tablespace.

When SQL statements are bound—prepared for execution—DB2 chooses the locksize, type, and duration of each lock depending on the locksize specified in the CREATE TABLESPACE statement, the type of SQL statement being executed, and the parameters specified when a user has DB2 bind SQL into an application plan or package. In other words, DB2 determines how to employ its locks from information implicit in each transaction. Programmers can also explicitly specify in code that a table or tablespace lock be used for particular transactions. The basic lock types are exclusive locks that bar all access to the locked data and that DB2 imposes for all updates, update locks that are taken while locating data to be updated before an exclusive lock is taken, and share locks that allow multiple users to read but not alter the data.

If the developer is creating a tablespace that will hold read-only tables, a tablespace locksize is the best choice. Since there will be no need for exclusive locks on the tablespace, this selection does not affect response times. It does, of course, provide the CPU and virtual storage savings of the larger locksize. In addition, no locks are taken on index pages. CPU savings would be about 5 to 15 percent.

If the tablespace must handle multiple update transactions executed concurrently, the page locksize provides the best response times by allowing the most concurrency. Pages not locked for one transaction will be available for other transactions. When too many page locks are taken, however, main memory and CPU time are wasted. To avoid these problems, when a lock size of ANY has been specified if more than a predetermined limit of page locks specified by the system administrator are actually taken in a tablespace, DB2 automatically escalates the locksize to table for a segmented tablespace and to tablespace for a nonsegmented tablespace. This escalation lasts until the transaction completes or a COMMIT WORK statement completes a unit of work for the transaction, depending upon the parameter specified in the BIND command.

Some tablespaces will experience a moderate rate of updates most of the time, with occasional extensive updates from a batch program. In these cases, developers can specify the page locksize in the CREATE TABLESPACE statement to ensure the best response time during normal use of the tablespace. A program that updates a large percentage of the table's rows at one time should issue an explicit tablespace lock that remains in force until a COMMIT WORK is issued. This avoids having numerous page locks during the mass update burden main memory and the CPU or prompt DB2 to escalate the locksize to table or tablespace after page locks have already been taken.

Developers can change a tablespace's locksize easily using the ALTER command. As the database is used, system monitoring will reveal locking patterns, allowing the developer to alter locksizes to fit usage.

Row Level Locking

It is anticipated that row-level locking will be made available in Version 3. The row level locking may require specific models of IBM computers that provide a hardware assist in microcode to achieve the required performance. Such locking may also be accompanied by the ability to avoid taking locks on index pages when reading data. Box 3.5 summarizes situations that can benefit from row-level locking and its associated costs. It remains to be seen what the performance tradeoffs will be for row level locking.

Row-level locking can cost as much as 40 times that of page-level locking with current technology assuming 40 rows with a length of 100 bytes on a 4K page and that most of the rows on a page need to be processed. In

Box 3.5 Row-level locking

Situations that can benefit from row-level locking:

High transaction rate required with high update activity

Programs process only a few rows

Very small tables frequently updated

Rows usually inserted at end of table or updates concentrated in specific areas of the table

The cost of row-level locking:

Lock contention is most often on index pages which will encourage a minimal number of indexes (1 or 2) that need to be updated. In addition, there is a need for value level locking in the indexes.

A page lock is necessary if a variable length row is increased in length or a page is dynamically reorganized to gather free space.

It can be 40 times as costly in CPU and virtual storage as data page locking assuming 40 rows on a page (row length of 100). Lock

Lock hardware assist will probably be necessary to achieve the required performance.

---

addition, indexed values must also be locked, and each index page can contain references to 400 rows assuming that the indexed value plus overhead is 10 bytes in length. Indeed if lock contention is a problem, chances are it is a result of locking index pages rather than data pages as will be seen later in Section 3.9 and in Chapter 8.

3.6 THE CLOSE OPTION

The developer uses the CLOSE parameter to instruct DB2 about how to handle the opening and closing of the tablespace's VSAM datasets. Opening and closing datasets can be costly. It requires CPU time, I/O operations, and additional space in log datasets. Each time a checkpoint is taken, log records are written from the log buffer to a log dataset, information must be written about all open datasets. More datasets must be closed when a database or DB2 is stopped and keeping a dataset open requires virtual storage for maintaining control information about it. For a frequently used tablespace or indexspace there, opening and closing datasets each time a plan or package is executed degrades performance. To avoid this, the developer can specify that a dataset be opened when a transaction or query first accesses it and that it be left open until the tablespace is stopped or DB2 is terminated. The parameter value for this option is NO. Unfortunately the default value is YES, which results in the opening and closing of each dataset at the start and end of each transaction or QMF user access as well as each time a COMMIT WORK is issued, depending on a threshold to be discussed in a moment. Close of NO is a good choice for tablespaces and indexes used frequently for daily processing.

The maximum number of open datasets is 10,000. This is an MVS limit that applies to each address space, and DB2 manages datasets in its database services address space (DBAS). While it is a generous limit, it can be a problem for companies with a large number of tablespaces and indexes. DB2 only logically closes datasets when they are not in use. That is, the RBA (relative byte address) is written to SYSLGRNG in the directory for recovery purposes. Updated pages in the bufferpool are not written to DASD at this time so that they need not be reread the next time they are referenced in most cases. The dataset is placed in a drain queue with a length of 1000 by default when the dataset no longer has users (a count of current users is decreased by one when a cursor is closed). If 99 percent of DSMAX (default value of 1000) is reached, a physical close of 3 percent of the drain queue datasets is done on a FIFO (first in, first out) basis. Both close of yes and no datasets are not closed until the threshold is reached. If physical closes are occurring too frequently, the developer may need to check with the system administrator to determine if the limit can be increased. (The 1000 default limit can be changed by the systems administrator using the parameter DSMAX in DSN6SPRM of DSNZPARM but should not exceed the MVS limit.)

Keeping the datasets open costs saves working storage in DBAS, however—about 1.8K plus 0.3K below the 16M line or 0.9K bytes above the 16M line per dataset. If virtual storage is in short supply, the developer might have to trade increased CPU time and I/O operations for decreased storage requirements by having the tablespace's datasets closed after each use. This would be appropriate for tablespaces that are used infrequently.

3.7 BUFFERPOOL OPTIONS

By analyzing usage patterns, DB2 can determine which data to keep in the bufferpool for likely processing later rather than sending them to disk and having to retrieve them repeatedly. The return to disk and retrieval require I/O operations, so bufferpools can save considerable I/O time. Main memory is finite and costly, however. Expanded memory, available as an option on larger IBM computers, is almost as fast as, and about one-third the cost of, main memory. Expanded storage is significantly faster than DASD I/O. An I/O from expanded storage is about 20 microseconds compared with an I/O from a 3390 at 16 milliseconds. Still the cost of whatever memory bufferpools use mandates that they be used with care.

DB2 can provide up to four bufferpools: BP0, BP1, BP2, and BP32. For the most part, it manages each bufferpool independently. The more memory allocated to a bufferpool, the more data it can hold and therefore the greater the likelihood that an application program or interactive user request will find the data it needs there. Generally a system administrator decides how much memory to allocate to each bufferpool. This decision sets the installation's bufferpool strategy, which developers follow when creating tablespaces and indexspaces.

The system administrator must allocate memory to BP0 because DB2 uses it for catalog tables and for work space for joins, utilities, and sorts. The administrator must also create BP32 if the database will include any table with rows longer than about 4K bytes or result tables from joins of more than 4K bytes. Since DB2 will not split rows across pages, any row longer than 4K bytes must reside on a 32K-byte page. Developers should avoid the need for the larger pages. The transfer time for each I/O operation for a 32K-byte page is eight times as long as that for a 4K-byte page. Indeed an I/O operation for a 32K-byte page can require eight physical I/Os depending upon the availability of bufferpool space. Sometimes a text column will run longer than 4K bytes. In those cases it is usually better to use BP32 rather than to artificially split the column into separate rows just to take advantage of the smaller pages.

Beyond the mandates concerning BP0 and BP32, administrators can allocate memory to the bufferpools as they see fit. Usually they will follow one of three scenarios. One approach places all tablespaces in one bufferpool and all indexspaces in another. A second strategy provides one bufferpool for use by most tablespaces and indexspaces and reserves another for tablespaces used by applications for which short response times are critical. The third method allocates all available bufferpool space to BP0 and uses the one large bufferpool for all tablespaces and indexspaces. Let us look at each scenario.

The idea behind the strategy of assigning tablespaces and indexspaces to separate bufferpools is that when an application accesses a table, it is also very likely to access an associated index. Keeping data from both tables and indexes in a bufferpool is likely to reduce the need for I/O operations. Assigning the tablespaces and indexspaces to separate bufferpools ensures that the table and index data will not have to contend for the same bufferpool space.

Separate bufferpools for data and indexes can be of value for very large tablespaces, say those of over 10 million rows. It is unlikely that the bufferpool can be made large enough so that the data pages will be reused. It is likely that the database and program design will result in frequent index use to locate data pages. The assignment of the indexes to a large bufferpool increases the possibility that the frequently used index pages will remain in the bufferpool, thus avoiding having to reread down through the various levels of a B-tree index as discussed in Chapter 6.

Providing a separate bufferpool for tables accessed by priority applications ensures that other applications do not steal bufferpool space. The less space that is left available for data from the performance-critical applications, the more likely it is they will be forced to use more I/O. This approach holds several drawbacks. First, bufferpool space will be largely wasted whenever the critical applications experience low usage. Second, the priority bufferpool is likely to fill up over time with tablespaces and indexspaces for more and more applications the developers consider critical. Third, as business circumstances change, each application's performance needs change. Although a developer can easily reassign a tablespace or indexspace from one bufferpool to another, keeping track of which belong in the priority pool and which do not requires careful attention. If the DB2 professionals do not have the time to manage multiple bufferpools carefully, it is best to leave it to DB2.

By assigning all tablespaces and indexspaces to one large bufferpool, the system administrator turns bufferpool management over to DB2. Its algorithms then determine how to use all the bufferspace strictly according to actual application system usage rather than according to what the administrator expects usage to be. DB2 may well allocate bufferpool space among tablespaces and their associated indexspaces more efficiently when it can consider the bufferspace needs of both object types together rather than being limited by the administrator's estimates about how much space should be provided for each. Similarly with DB2 managing the bufferpool, priority applications will probably enjoy the same performance levels as they would with a smaller amount of space in a separate bufferpool. Overall system performance will frequently be better with a single bufferpool because space not claimed by priority applications during low usage periods will be available for other applications.

In general, large bufferpools can significantly improve performance. The default BP0 bufferpool size of 4M bytes is insufficient once an organization has gotten beyond a few small application systems and should be increased to achieve good performance. As a bufferpool fills up, DB2 shuts off one sophisticated feature after another. If the stealable space falls below 10 percent, sequential and list prefetch of up to 32 pages with a single I/O will be discontinued. (Stealable space means that the page is not currently marked in use by the buffer manager.) If the stealable space falls below 50 percent, the buffer manager will discontinue accumulating up to 10 percent of the bufferspace with updated pages per dataset and writing chunks of 32 pages with a single I/O. If 95 percent of the pages are marked in use, an I/O will occur for each row read and written to DASD. And the worse case is when 97.5 percent of the pages are marked in use so the updates are logged and written to the tablespace synchronously (one after another).

Because DB2's algorithms for managing the bufferpool have proved to be efficient, many administrators are choosing to leave the job to DB2 by assigning all available bufferpool space to BP0.

In any event, administrators can gauge bufferpool efficiency by monitoring DB2's system monitoring facility (SMF) record type 100, which indicates the number of times data requests are satisfied by the bufferpool compared to the number of I/O operations. Then they can adjust bufferpool strategies accordingly.

Bufferpools in Hiperspace

It is anticipated that DB2 will have a new set of bufferpools that can be placed in hiperspace, which is analogous to holding the data in expanded or main storage. It is possible that the first access of a tablespace or index will cause all pages to be brought into hiperspace to avoid rereading the pages from DASD. This holds significant advantages for small reference tables that are frequently read, index pages, or any data frequently accessed that justifies the additional cost of expanded or main memory over the cost of DASD and the I/O and CPU time needed to move the data from DASD to main memory for processing.

3.8 SEGMENTED TABLESPACES

Segmented tablespaces provide for efficient performance when multiple small- or medium-sized tables occupy a single tablespace. Grouping tables within a tablespace helps in the administration of related tables. The approach is particularly useful for managing the recovery of referential structures, which can be troublesome when the various objects occupy separate tablespaces. On the other hand, there are disadvantages to storing multiple unrelated tables in a single tablespace, even if it is segmented. And it is rarely a good idea to store multiple tables in a nonsegmented tablespace. We will describe segmented tablespace first, then explore the choices they present to database designers. A segment size of 64 or 32 pages maximizes the benefits of prefetch and avoids reading pages for another table with innermixed segments. Prefetch is triggered one segment ahead.

Using the SEGSIZE keyword in the CREATE TABLESPACE statement, developers can define segment sizes in multiples of 4-pages ranging from 4 to 64 pages. For example, the 10,000K-byte tablespace will occupy 2500 4K-byte pages, which are segmented into 39 64-page segments. If segments do not divide equally into available pages, leftover pages take an additional segment. DB2 dedicates each segment to rows from only one of the tables assigned to the tablespace. That is, rows from multiple tables will not be included together—or interleaved—within the same segment. Tables larger than the specified segment size will be spread over multiple segments. A segment size of 64 or 32 pages maximizes the benefits of prefetch and avoids reading pages for another table with intermixed segments. Prefetch is triggered one segment ahead.

To avoid wasting storage space for tables smaller than 64 pages, table and segment sizes should be approximately the same. For example, if reference tables to be stored in the tablespace will each require about 1 page, segments set at 64 pages will waste 63 pages per table. Notice, too, that all segments will be the same size even if the assigned tables are not.

Because DB2 treats each segment separately when allocating free pages, FREEPAGE values should be set with segment sizes in mind. For example, if the CREATE TABLESPACE statement called for a free page every 24 pages and segments of only 20 pages and if DB2 did not account for the discrepancy, there would be no free pages left at all. DB2 does avoid this problem, however, by automatically adjusting FREEPAGE to SEGSIZE-1 whenever a statement's FREEPAGE parameter is greater than SEGSIZE. That adjustment assures one free page per segment. Segmented tablespaces provide their benefits largely because of the design of their space map pages, special pages within a tablespace that provide information about how the storage space has been used. This information helps DB2 find the most appropriate free space in which to store new data. All tablespaces include space map pages, but those within segmented tablespaces provide more information than others, allowing more efficient location of free space and tablespace scans.

Space map pages occur more frequently in segmented than they can in nonsegmented tablespaces. The interval between space map pages varies according to the size of the segments. For 4-page segments, they occur every 1712 pages when 4K data pages are used and every 13,784 pages when 32K data pages are used. For 64 page segments, they fall every 5504 pages when 4K pages are used and every 44,544 pages when 32K pages are used. In nonsegmented tablespaces, the corresponding intervals are 10,760 pages and 87,216 pages. The smaller intervals in the segmented tablespaces mini-

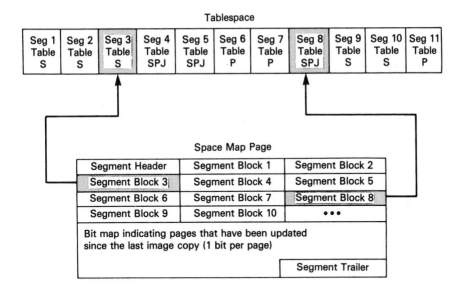

Fig. 3.7 Space Map Page

mize seek times when the disk reader moves from the space map page to the data page it indicates. The data page format is the same for segmented and simple tablespaces.

More important, however, is the detailed way the space map pages can describe available free space. A space map page is divided into segment blocks with each block containing information applying to a specific segment (Fig. 3.7). Typically a table occupies more than one segment; each segment block includes a pointer to the next segment block that applies to the same table. Each segment block includes a four-bit code describing the free space in each of the segment's data pages. The four bits can be set in 16 combinations, each representing a different free space condition, although four of the settings are not yet being used. The codes provide such information as whether there is space available on the appropriate data page for a row being inserted in sequence or for expansion of a variable-length row. If the code indicates there is not sufficient space, DB2 saves having to read the data page in a vain attempt to find it. Instead it can keep checking the space map code for the next best data page location for the update.

Space maps for pages in nonsegmented tablespaces, on the other hand, have only two bits per page to describe free space, giving DB2 much less information to go on in its search for free space. The two bits indicate whether there is available space on the page for the largest, average, or

Box 3.6   Meaning of four bit values for free space

---

0 – Page is empty and unformatted

1 – Page is emptied with mass delete

2 – Page is empty and formatted

3 – Page has space for longest row

4–10 Values indicates the difference between the minimum and maximum row size in 12.5 percent increments for placing variable length rows (minimizes the possibility of accessing a page with insufficient space)

11–14 Values reserved for future use

15 – Page has less than the minimum row space available or is full

---

smallest row or whether the page is full. A capability provided by the segmented tablespace's space maps is the mass delete algorithm.

This facility provides an efficient way to delete all the rows in a table and make the space they occupied available for storing new data without actually processing data pages. The algorithm is invoked with a DELETE statement without a predicate—DELETE FROM SPJ, for example. In addition, the mass delete cannot use a cursor or be performed on a table for which a primary key has been declared. With a nonsegmented tablespace, DB2 would respond by reading every data page that included rows from that table. With a segmented tablespace instead of processing data pages, DB2 notes in the table's space map segment blocks that the page is empty due to a mass delete and that the space can be reused. One minor drawback to a mass delete is that DB2 will not track how many rows it has deleted. With a conventional delete, that information is available to programs as they execute or is provided when the delete is executed interactively. Significantly less data must be logged when the mass delete algorithm is used. No data pages need to be accessed or logged; only the space map pages need to be processed.

The space maps in segmented tablespaces also provide performance advantages during database operations. In a tablespace scan, for example, the maps allow DB2 to skip pages that do not hold rows for the table being searched. On the other hand, a tablespace scan reads pages for all the tables in a multitable, nonsegmented tablespace even when only one of the tables needs to be searched. This is necessary since a given page can have rows from multiple tables in a simple tablespace.

The maps also allow space from dropped tables to be immediately reusable. This is a particularly useful feature for interactive users, who frequently create and drop tables without even being aware of it. And in a segmented tablespace, concurrency control locks can be managed at the table level rather than at the tablespace level as would be necessary in a nonsegmented tablespace. As we will discuss in Chapter 8, managing locks by table rather than by tablespace provides several performance advantages.

An advantage of placing multiple tables in a segmented tablespace is that most utilities including those for copying and recovering data operate on tablespaces, not on individual tables. Related tables, such as those that make up a referential integrity structure stored in a single tablespace, can be copied or recovered with a single execution of the utility rather than by coding and submitting multiple utilities as would be needed if each table were in a separate tablespace. This is significant for maintaining data integrity across related tables. If there is a failure of one tablespace and it is successfully recovered, there may be data inconsistencies between related tables in separate tablespaces. Indeed DB2 will set the check pending status on and not allow any selects or updates until the pending status has been removed. (The check pending status will be discussed at length in Chapters 5 and 16.)

There are disadvantages of placing more than one table in a tablespace regardless of whether it is a segmented or simple tablespace. The disadvantages have to do with the fact that tablespace parameters apply at the tablespace level (as the name indicates) and that most utilities operate at the tablespace level, not on specific tables in the tablespace. Free space is allocated at the tablespace level, but a different amount of free space may be needed for different tables in the tablespace. For example, companies typically do business with specific suppliers and do not change suppliers often. Little free space is needed to maintain clustering and variable length rows. Frequent shipments of parts are received from suppliers, however, requiring free space in the SPJ table. This also means that image copies and reorganizations would be required more frequently for the SPJ table than for the Supplier table but their schedule cannot be varied if they are in the same tablespace. More space might be required for the SPJ table and might be added with the ALTER statement, but the entire tablespace would require reorganization to obtain the free space. All tables in a tablespace have limited availability since utilities lock at the tablespace level and pending states apply at the tablespace level. The bottom line is that frequently updated tables and infrequently updated tables should not be mixed in a tablespace.

In some cases, multiple tables in a tablespace make sense. For example, most application systems have many reference tables used for validation of data or to translate a code to a name. A table of state codes and names might be used to translate CA stored in a row to California when a report is to be printed. A small table of this type may occupy only a page. It seems a waste of resources to have a separate VSAM dataset that must be managed with the utilities. In addition, a one page table would require a header page and a space map page, which triples the amount of space required for each of many small reference tables.

Placing multiple tables in a tablespace saves virtual storage. When data are accessed, DB2 opens the underlying VSAM dataset in which they reside, which requires 2.1 or 2.7K of storage. If multiple tables reside in a tablespace, they can all be accessed by opening a single tablespace. With all of the benefits segmented tablespaces provide, they should be used in most cases even for one table per tablespace.

3.9 CREATE INDEX

An index lists values from one or more of a table's columns. Along with each value, the index lists a pointer—the RID—to the data page containing the value's row. In many cases DB2 will find data more efficiently by scanning the index and following the pointer than by scanning the entire tablespace. (Chapter 6 discusses the use of indexes in detail.)

A nonunique index can reference duplicate values; a unique index will not. Unique indexes are required for the primary key columns, which by definition must be unique. Either nonunique or unique indexes may cluster rows, maintaining the physical placement of rows in sequential order. But each table may have only one clustering index. The keyword CLUSTER identifies the index as clustering.

Since DB2 allows only one index per indexspace, a CREATE INDEX statement actually creates the indexspace, a LDS VSAM dataset. The process of creating an index, therefore, is similar to that of creating a tablespace. As with the tablespace, the developer can create the VSAM dataset and assign the indexspace to it using the VCAT or have DB2 create the dataset in a specified storage group. In deciding which method to use, developers should weigh the same factors they consider when making the similar choice for a tablespace. Section 3.3 describes these considerations.

Most of the parameters available for creating indexes are the same as those used in creating tablespaces: USING, PCTFREE, FREEPAGE, BUFFERPOOL, CLOSE, and DSETPASS, for example. These parameters have the same performance impact on both kinds of objects. The UNIQUE, CLUSTER, and SUBPAGE parameters are specific to indexes and cannot be altered. It is necessary to drop and recreate an index to change these parameters. Fig. 3.8 shows typical statements for creating an index—one using a storage group and the other using VCAT. The first line in the exam-

```
Using STOGROUP:
CREATE UNIQUE INDEX PNX
  ON P_T (PN ASC)
  USING STOGROUP DASPJSTG
    PRIQTY 7200
    SECQTY 720
    ERASE NO
  PCTFREE 20
  FREEPAGE 10
  CLUSTER
  SUBPAGES 4
  BUFFERPOOL BPO
  CLOSE NO
  DSETPASS SESAME;
Using VCAT:
CREATE UNIQUE INDEX SNX
  ON SPJ_T (SN,PN,JN DESC)
  USING VCAT AAXX2
  PCTFREE 20
  FREEPAGE 10
  CLUSTER
  SUBPAGES 4
  BUFFERPOOL BPO
  CLOSE NO
  DSETPASS SESAME;

Changing index parameters:
ALTER INDEX PNX
  USING STOGROUP DATOMSTG
    PRIQTY 14400
    SECQTY 720
    ERASE NO
  PCTFREE 25
  FREEPAGE 5
  BUFFERPOOL BP1
  CLOSE YES
  DSETPASS NEWPASS;
```

Fig. 3.8 CREATE INDEX statements

ple identifies the index as being unique. If UNIQUE had not been specified, the index would allow duplicate values. If the developer uses VCAT to specify the indexspace's dataset, the index name determines part of the dataset's name. The index name must be the fourth node of the dataset name.

The developer stipulates the column or columns to be indexed using the keyword ON followed by the table name and in parentheses the column name. If the index is to be composite—that is, if it is to include more than one column—a comma separates adjacent column names. If CLUSTER is specified, DB2 will cluster according to the values in the columns listed. The developer can also specify within the parentheses whether the index should follow an ascending or descending order. (The code ASC indicates ascending and DESC descending. If neither is declared, DB2 uses ascending order by default.)

Subpage Locks

An index page, unlike a data page, always consists of 4K bytes. DB2 can lock the index page by subpage increments, however, including 1, 1/2, 1/4, 1/8, or 1/16 subpage sizes. The developer indicates the selected subpage size in the CREATE INDEX statement by using the denominator of the chosen fraction as the value for the SUBPAGE parameter. A SUBPAGE value of 1 indicates the entire page will be locked. If no value is specified, DB2 uses a SUBPAGE value of 4 by default and locks 1/4 of an index leaf page at a time.

A page locksize is the smallest locking increment for data pages. Indexes need the smaller locksizes because index pages hold many more index values than tablespace pages hold rows. A page lock for a table with 100-byte rows, for example, will lock only about 40 rows at a time (4000 byte/100 bytes per row). (The 4000 byte figure is used to simplify the example. Precise calculations are in Appendixes A and B.) A page lock for an index on a 6-byte column (plus its 4-byte RID), on the other hand, will lock more than 400 entries (4000 bytes/10 bytes per column). If there are three indexes on a table, about 1200 (3 * 400) rows are effectively locked when a row is inserted or deleted. (Because overhead space is needed to manage the subpages, these figures are approximate. Appendix B presents a formula for determining the number of index values per subpage more precisely. But rough estimates suffice to guide decisions on the SUBPAGE parameter value.)

Choosing the correct SUBPAGE size when creating an index is similar to choosing the correct locksize when creating a tablespace. When a transaction requires an index lock, the fewer values the lock covers, the more values it leaves available for access by concurrent transactions. A high SUBPAGE parameter value—and therefore a small SUBPAGE locksize—allows the most concurrency. The length of the column indexed also determines the number of values contained within a lockable unit. A 1K-byte subpage (SUBPAGE 4) will contain about as many entries for a 10-byte index column as a 2K-byte subpage (SUBPAGE 2) will contain for a 20-byte index column. Given the same transaction rates, indexes on these columns would require the two different subpage parameter values to provide the same concurrency levels. The subpage size must be large enough to contain at least one complete index value and their RID plus free space. In a unique index, for example, 13 pairs of 60-byte values and their 4-byte RIDs would use 832 bytes (13 * (60 + 4)). Since a subpage of 4 provides 890 bytes, 58 would be wasted per subpage, 232 per leaf page.

If response time for a tablespace degrades, the problem may be that concurrent users are contending for access to locked index values rather than for access to the table itself. This lock contention on an index can be eased by increasing the SUBPAGE parameter value. Unlike LOCKSIZE on a tablespace, the SUBPAGE parameter value cannot be changed with an ALTER statement because the value determines the physical layout of the index. Instead the index must be dropped and re-created with the new subpage parameter value.

DB2 must use CPU time and virtual storage to manage locks. If a high concurrency level is not needed or if the indexed column is relatively long— meaning that fewer entries fit within a lockable unit—a smaller SUBPAGE parameter value will minimize CPU and virtual storage needs. Insert activity, however, can require index page splitting to keep the index balanced, a subject discussed in Chapter 6.3. During splitting, the index cannot be used beneath the page split resulting in even more rows being effectively locked. For example, if a leaf page references 200 rows, the next higher index page would reference 40,000 rows and during the page split these rows are effectively locked. A larger subpage will reduce splitting and the need to reallocate free space dynamically spread across subpages. Therefore heavy insert requirements when they are concentrated on a few index pages suggest the need for larger subpages.

Free space as specified with the PCTFREE parameter is evenly distributed throughout the index page. If 16 percent free is specified with a subpage of 4, each subpage has 4 percent free space. If an inserted value will not fit within the 4 percent free space, the page is dynamically reorganized to gather all the free space together, which increases CPU time. The page is split if there is insufficient space on the page. Consideration should be given to whether a value will fit within the specified free space in a subpage.

When to Build an Index

When creating an index, issuing the CREATE INDEX statement before loading the data provides significant performance advantages. With this approach as the load utility reads in the records from the sequential file to be loaded into the table, it can extract indexed columns' values and write them on a work file. DB2 can then sort the index values, which allows it to build a compact index, leaving only the specified amount of free space.

DB2 will build an index after the data have been loaded. It must read the tablespace once for each index created this way, however. Therefore if a table is to have more than one index, it is probably best to create them all before loading the data. Even if there is only one index, this approach saves having to pass the data twice—once to build the table and once to build the index. There are also advantages to building unique indexes during the load rather than after. When building a unique index after the data are loaded, if DB2 encounters a duplicate value, it will not complete the index. The developer is responsible for locating and removing the duplicate before reissuing the CREATE INDEX statement. On the other hand, when building a unique index during a load, DB2 saves any duplicates in a discard dataset and completes the index without them.

3.10   PARTITIONING AND PERFORMANCE

A partitioned tablespace allows the developer to divide a table by rows into partitions that the system can manage separately, a method that provides for use of DB2's utilities on just part of the tablespace and placement of rows on differing direct access storage devices. A partitioned tablespace must have a clustering index that is considered the partitioning index and is used to determine which partition to use to process a row.

DB2 allows up to 64 1-gigabyte partitions, each in its own VSAM dataset. Partitions can be larger—up to 4 gigabytes each—but the total tablespace cannot exceed 64 gigabytes. Developers might consider partitioning a table with 1 million rows or more. For smaller tables, the advantages are probably not worth the effort needed to manage the partitions.

Partitioning lets the developer place frequently accessed and updated parts of a table on fast direct access storage devices and less frequently needed parts on slower devices. When tables collect and maintain information over time, for example, users typically access and update the recent data more often than they do the historical data. With partitioning, the system administrator might move partitions to a slower device as their information ages and alter the space and free space allocations. The older partitions will have little update activity and need little or no free space.

A primary reason for partitioning is to allow for the maintenance of a large table in parts. There may not be sufficient time available in the evening or on weekends to execute a utility or batch update program to process a very large number of rows. It is necessary to break the table into parts so that they can be processed separately and in some cases in parallel. Multiple partitions can be processed by multiple batch update jobs and image copied in parallel on multiple processors. Multiple partitioning and nonpartitioning indexes can be recovered in parallel with parallel tablespace scans. More resources are required, but damaged data can be recovered in less elapsed time, minimizing the time that the data is unavailable.

To avoid the introduction of inconsistencies, DB2's utilities lock data during data loading, reorganization, coping, and recovery. Indeed most utilities lock at the tablespace level as has been mentioned. Generally utilities work at the tablespace level; they can also operate on partitions, however. Since less time is needed to perform those tasks on partitions than on the entire tablespace, the utilities' locks are in force for shorter periods although they still cover the entire tablespace.

The benefits of partitioning decrease as the number of indexes on the table increases. The required partitioning index needs little additional processing to maintain. The clustering index, like the data, is split into partitions. The first 40 bytes of a partitioning index identifies the partition number. All other indexes cover the entire tablespace.

Reorganization of a partition requires reorganization of all of these large indexes and may cost almost as much in processing as does reorganizing the entire tablespace. The utility must delete each index value while it is unloading the data and reinsert the values during the reloading of the data. Indeed, it is the nonpartitioning indexes that cause the utilities to lock at the tablespace level resulting in the data being unavailable while work is being done on only one partition.

Creating Partitioned Tablespaces

The statement for creating a partitioned tablespace is similar to that for a simple tablespace, requiring only one additional parameter—NUMPARTS—to establish the partitions. If the developer wishes to allocate a different amount of space or percent free to various partitions or assign the partitions to different storage groups or volume catalogs, however, they must also be specified in the statement. A partitioned tablespace also requires a clustering index, created with its own CREATE statement. We will look first at the statement needed to create a partitioned tablespace and then at the statement for a clustering index.

A skeleton statement to create a partitioned tablespace (Fig. 3.9) for a zip code table looks like this:

```
CREATE TABLESPACE ZIPTBS
   IN DAZIPDB
   USING STOGROUP DAZPOSTG
     PRIQTY 7200
     SECQTY 0
     ERASE NO
   NUMPARTS 22
   (PART 1 USING STOGROUP DAZP1STG
          PRIQTY 14400
          SECQTY 720
          ERASE NO
          PCTFREE 20
```

Tablespace ZIPTBS

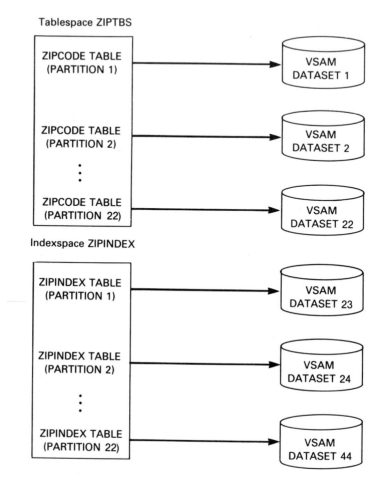

The 22-million-row zip code table is divided into 22 1,000,000-row partitions, each with its own dataset. An index on the table, divided into corresponding partitions, manages placement of rows in their proper partitions.

Fig. 3.9 Partitioned tablespace and indexspace

```
        FREEPAGE 7,
PART 2 USING STOGROUP DAZP2STG
       PRIQTY 14400
       SECQTY 720
       ERASE NO
      PCTFREE 15
      FREEPAGE 7)
```

```
PCTFREE 0
FREEPAGE 0
LOCKSIZE PAGE
BUFFERPOOL BP0
CLOSE NO;
```

After naming the tablespace (ZIPTBS in the example) and indicating its database (DAZIPDB), the developer might specify a default STO-GROUP or VCAT. This STOGROUP or VCAT assignment governs the placement of any partition not specifically assigned elsewhere by the statement. The developer indicates the assignment of specific partitions within parentheses immediately after the NUMPARTS parameter and its value, which determines the number of partitions. In this example, the statement calls for 22 partitions. Partitions 3 to 22, which are not assigned specifically, will reside on the default STOGROUP (DAZP0STG) and have the same amount of allocated space and the same free space. Partitions 1 and 2 will reside in STOGROUP DAZP1STG and DAZP2STG and are separately assigned space and free space.

Frequently, different partitions have different update activity. In the example, it is assumed that partition 1 is going to have heavy update activity and is given 20 percent free space. Partition 2 is to have moderate update activity and is given 15 percent free space. Partitions 3 through 22 are primarily for historical purposes and will have very little update activity so zero percent free is specified.

The statement for creating the clustering index assigns portions of the table to each tablespace partition. The statement indicates the table's column that will provide the index values and the ranges of values for the rows to be included in each partition. The index itself is partitioned into the same number of parts as the tablespace, with the CREATE statement assigning each index partition to a VSAM dataset in a STOGROUP or VCAT. When the tablespace is loaded, the rows containing the values of each partition are placed in each corresponding tablespace partition. The tablespace partitions were assigned to STOGROUPs or VCATs when the tablespace was created. A skeleton statement for creating a clustering index looks like this:

```
CREATE INDEX ZIPINDEX
  ON ZIPTB (ZIPCODE)
  CLUSTER
    (PART 1 VALUES(1000000)
      USING STOGROUP DAZ01STG
        PRIQTY 7200
          SECQTY 720
        PCTFREE 20,
      PART 2 VALUES(2000000)
        USING STOGROUP DAZ02STG
          PRIQTY 7200
```

```
        SECQTY 720
        PCTFREE 15,

           .
           .
           .
    PART 22 VALUES(22000000)
        USING STOGROUP DAZ22STG
          PRIQTY 14400
          SECQTY 720
        PCTFREE 0)
    PCTFREE  5
    FREEPAGE 0
    SUBPAGES 4
    BUFFERPOOL BP0
    CLOSE NO;
```

After naming the index (ZIPINDEX) and indicating the table to which it applies (ZIPTB), the developer indicates within parentheses the column that provides the index and partitioning values. The table for this example contains demographic and sales data broken down geographically by zip code. The zip codes themselves make a logical choice for the index. (Chapter 6 discusses index design in detail.) There are 22 million zip codes. Assuming for simplicity that entries will be distributed uniformly across the range of codes, we set aside a table partition for every 1,000,000 rows. The index therefore must have 22 partitions, one for each tablespace partition. The CLUSTER parameter identifies the index as a clustering index. The following information within parentheses assigns the zip code values to each index partition and therefore the table's rows with those values to the corresponding tablespace partition.

The statement format allows single numbers to specify index value ranges. In the example, the values in parentheses indicate ascending values. The developer might stipulate that the values be partitioned in descending order by inserting the word DESC after the word specifying the index column within the parentheses with a space separating the words. With the example's ascending order, the first value—1000000—indicates that the first partition is to include any zip codes $\leq$ 1,000,000. The next value sets partition 2's values at $>$ 1,000,000 and $\leq$ 2,000,000 and so on. If descending order were used, the value indicated for Partition 1 represents the highest index value. Subsequent values represent the low points for the following ranges.

The developer should be sure that the last partition leaves room for all the data to be loaded. In the example, the zip code index carries an upper limit of 22,000,000. When the data are loaded and the index is built, DB2 will place values exceeding that number in the final partition. If there are, in fact, more than 22 million zip codes, there will be too many to fit in the final partition. If DB2 fills the partition and there are more rows to be loaded, the load fails.

The potential for another difficult-to-detect error related to index range values arises when the indexed column contains decimal values. In this case, all index range values must end with a decimal point. If they do not, the load fails. Finally, values in a column used as a partitioning index cannot be updated. If such a value must be changed, its row must be deleted and a row with the new value inserted. This manipulation is problematic when referential integrity constraints cascade the deletion to multiple tables.

3.11 SUMMARY

DB2's more physical objects—databases, storage groups, and tablespaces—underlie the more logical objects—particularly tables and views—on which applications are built. The physical objects must be created first. Choices made during their creation play an important role in performance in and of themselves. In some ways, though, the desired characteristics of the more physical objects depend on choices made about tables. The next chapter discusses those decisions.

EXERCISES

3.1. Write a CREATE statement for a database named for yourself (with the designation DB following your name to indicate the object type). Use the default storage group SYSDEFLT and bufferpool BP0.

3.2. Write a CREATE statement for a tablespace that will hold an Employee table, EMP. Place the tablespace in the database created in Exercise 1, and use its storage group to define the space. Name the space after the table it will hold, followed by TSP to indicate the object type. Allocate 20,000K bytes for the primary quantity and the smallest possible value for the secondary quantity. Use the smallest possible locksize. The row length is a little less than 100 bytes. Choose a percent free so that two rows can be inserted on a page. Use a free page parameter consistent with a good segment size. Select the most efficient option for opening and closing the tablespace's datasets considering that the tablespace will be accessed frequently.

3.3. Write an ALTER statement for the tablespace created in Exercise 2 to double the default amount of free space and to change the bufferpool to which it is assigned to BP1. Determine the probable cause or causes and a solution for each performance problem presented in Exercises 4 through 9.

3.4. Whenever a program updates Table A, access to Table B is barred.

3.5. Table A experiences heavy update activity. The tablespace that contains Table A—and only Table A—carries a locksize of page. Response times are surprisingly long.

3.6. A negative SQL code is issued for the SQL statement, UPDATE P SET PN = 100 WHERE PN = 10.

3.7. DB2 fails to load a table's final partition, issuing an error message stating there is insufficient space. All partitions have the same space allocations. Rows are entered in numerical order.

3.8. Table A is very small, fewer than five pages, but access to it requires an excessive number of I/O operations and unusually long response times.

3.9. Analysis of statistics indicate that each row accessed requires a physical I/O to read the page from DASD. Pages are rarely found in the bufferpool to minimize I/O.

4

Creating Tables and Views

4.1 INTRODUCTION

The table is DB2's basic unit for data definition. Often a table is referred to as a base table to distinguish it from a view, which is a virtual table derived from one or more base tables. In a base table, each column holds values for an entity attribute, identified in the column headings. Each row contains a value for each column, with a few exceptions that will be explained later, with all the values in a given column being of the same data type.

4.2 CREATING TABLES

Fig. 4.1 shows a typical statement for creating a table—in this case for storing part information. The table's name (P_T) reflects a naming convention that provides for differentiation between base tables and views, virtual tables discussed later in this chapter. Under the convention, which some DB2 developers find helpful, a "T" at the end of a table name identifies it as a base table. The view of the same table would have the same name but without the "T," a distinction that helps administrators keep the objects straight. (To simplify the table names, we are leaving off the AUTHID qual-

```
CREATE TABLE P_T
  (PN      CHAR(6)         NOT NULL,
   PNAME   CHAR(20)        NOT NULL WITH DEFAULT,
   COLOR   CHAR(6)         NOT NULL WITH DEFAULT,
   WEIGHT  SMALLINT,
   CITY    CHAR(15)        NOT NULL WITH DEFAULT,
   DATE_RECORDED DATE NOT NULL WITH DEFAULT,
   PRIMARY KEY (PN))
IN DASPJDB.PTSP
AUDIT NONE
VALIDPROC CHECKP;

ALTER TABLE P_T
  ADD PRICE DECIMAL(15,2)
  FIELDPROC FPRICE
  VALIDPROC VALPART
  AUDIT ALL;
```

Fig. 4.1 CREATE TABLE and ALTER TABLE statements

ifier that is a part of each table name. See Chapters 1 and 15 for a discussion of this issue.)

The IN clause designates the database and tablespace to house the table. If the IN clause is not specified, the default database DSNDB04 is used and DB2 automatically creates the tablespace using the default storage group SYSDEFLT. In this case, very little space is allocated to the tablespace—12K of primary and 12K of secondary space. The default tablespace name is the same as the table name if the table name is $< = 8$ alphanumeric characters, first position is not a number, and name is not currently used for another table or index space. Otherwise the first 4 characters of table name are used followed by a digit and 3 characters for uniqueness. And if it is left to DB2 to create the tablespace, it will create a simple tablespace. It was seen in Chapter 3 that there are significant advantages to a segmented tablespace even for one table per tablespace. These factors suggest that the developers will, in most cases, want to create their own tablespace and database in which to house the table.

The developer lists within parentheses the table's column names, each followed by the data type the column will contain, the length of each data item for character items, and whether null values are allowed in the column. (A null indicates that an actual value is either unknown or inapplicable. Nulls hold practical and performance implications to be discussed in a moment.) The maximum number of columns in a table or view is 750 except for a dependent table, which has a maximum of 749.

Column order holds performance implications. When an update changes data, DB2 records the change in a log, which is used to recreate the change if the tablespace must be recovered after a failure. Because DB2 logs only that portion of a row from the first to the last changed byte, placing frequently updated columns next to each other will minimize logging, saving on both processing and storage. And, as we shall see, listing variable-length columns last provides the best performance. First, let us look at data types.

Data Types

Processors can operate on only one type of data—the zeros and ones of the binary system. Information systems, however, need to operate on many different kinds of data—text, decimal numbers, whole numbers, and so on. Programming-language compilers and DBMSs must provide for the representation of these types of data and for their translation into the zeros and ones the computer acts upon. DB2 offers a variety of data types, which can be used in conjunction with the data types available in the programming languages it supports (Fig. 4.2)—that is, data represented as a certain type in a DB2 database may be used by a program as the corresponding type in its language. DB2 offers all the standard data types: integers, decimals, and characters. It also offers special types, including graphic data types used for expressing the Japanese Kanji and Katakana ideograms and date and time data types, used to record data entries in standard date and time formats and to process dates, to subtract the current date from the date of an entry, for example.

Data type synonyms are available for compatibility with the ANSI (American National Standards Institute) and ISO (International Standards Organization). The synonym for DECIMAL is NUMERIC. The synonym for floating point numbers is FLOAT.

DB2's data types offer developers a number of performance choices. An INTEGER, for example, requires 4 bytes, which can represent a value of up to 2,147,483,648. The developer who knows that the item's value will never exceed 32,767 may use SMALLINT, which can represent values up to that amount but needs only 2 bytes. The shorter representation can save storage and speed processing and I/O operations.

Character Sets

Most string data types including CHAR, VARCHAR, and LONG VARCHAR use a single-byte character set (SBCS)—that is, each character requires one byte to represent it. Graphic data types use a double-byte character set (DBCS). Two bytes are used to represent a Kanji or extended Katakana character. Mixed data strings allow for a mixture of SBCS and DBCS with shift codes used to delimit DBCS characters. Data subtypes of SBCS,

Data Types	N B*	COBOL Declaration	PL/1 Declaration	C Declaration
SMALLINT	2	01 V PIC S9(4) COMP.	DCL V BIN FIXED(15);	SHORT INT ID;
INTEGER	4	01 V PIC S9(9) COMP.	DCL V BIN FIXED(31);	LONG INT ID;
DECIMAL NUMERIC	< =16	01 V PIC S9(N) V9(M) COMP-3.	DCL V DEC FIXED (S,P);	No exact equal
REAL	4	01 V COMP-1.	DCL V BIN FLOAT(21);	FLOAT ID;
FLOAT (n) n < 22				
FLOAT(n) n < 53	8	01 V COMP-2.	DCL V BIN FLOAT(53);	DOUBLE ID;
DOUBLE PRECISION				
CHAR	254	01 V PIC X(N).	DCL V CHAR(N);	CHAR ID [m];
VARCHAR	4046	01 V. 49 VL PIC S9(4) COMP. 49 VN PIC X (N).	DCL V CHAR(N) VAR;	STRUCT CHAR ID;
LONG VARCHAR 32714				
GRAPHIC	254	01 V PIC G(N). DISPLAY-1.	DCL V GRAPHIC (N);	
VARGRAPHIC	4046	01 V. 49 VL PIC S9(4) COMP. 49 VN PIC G(N). DISPLAY-1.	DCL V GRAPHIC (N) VAR:	
LONG VARGRAPHIC 32714				
DATE	4	01 V PIC X(10).	DCL V CHAR(10);	CHAR ID [> =11];
TIME	3	01 V PIC X(8).	DCL V CHAR(8);	CHAR ID [> =9];
TIMESTAMP	10	01 V PIC X(26).	DCL V CHAR(26);	CHAR ID [> =27];

*Number of Bytes
Add 1 byte if nulls are allowed

Fig. 4.2 Data types and lengths

MIXED, and FOR BIT DATA can be specified for string data types. FOR BIT DATA indicates that the bits need not conform to EBCDIC. This clause has a performance advantage in a distributed environment where it is necessary to convert from, say, the U.S. character set to an Italian character set that supports accent marks or to convert EBCDIC to ASCII character representation. FOR BIT DATA informs DB2 that character conversion is not required for a specified column when converting from one coded character set identifier (CCSID) to another. It is necessary for the system administrator to directly update the SYSIBM.SYSSTRINGS catalog table to indicate the character conversion required, and appropriate parameters must be specified at installation time.

VARCHAR with Care

The VARCHAR data type offers significant space savings, but developers must use it carefully. The type allocates storage according to the actual length of each data item, not including trailing blanks, up to the maximum specified in the CREATE TABLE statement. The CHAR data type, on the other hand, allocates the same amount of space—that specified in the statement—regardless of each item's length. If the value is, in fact, shorter than the allocated amount, the remaining space is filled with blanks.

It may seem at first that VARCHAR would always use space more efficiently than CHAR. This is not so, however, because each VARCHAR entry must carry a 2-byte prefix indicating its length. If the values' lengths do not vary significantly, this 2-byte cost on each item can outweigh the gains of space savings on the shorter items. Consider a 100,000 row table in which 80 percent of the rows are about 20 characters long and the rest average 15 characters. The variable allocations from VARCHAR gain 100,000 bytes— 5 bytes each on the 20,000 shorter rows. The variable lengths cost 200,000 bytes, though—2 bytes for each row. As a rule of thumb, VARCHAR provides its gains when a column's values vary in length and the average length is about half that of the maximum length. This is most often the case when a column contains a description. In any case, the savings should result in one or more additional rows fitting on a page. Otherwise there is no real saving in DASD space and I/O since storage and I/O is at the page level.

The use of VARCHAR also costs storage space when a VARCHAR column is indexed. The storage space used for each index value does not vary. Instead DB2 inserts blanks to pad each value to the item's maximum length. In any case, long columns make poor candidates for indexes because they place a burden on DB2's B-tree index scheme (detailed in Chapter 6), perhaps adding levels to the B-tree, which requires excessive I/O operations for an index search to work its way down to the data. In addition, index only processing is not possible since the data page has the length of the column that must be returned to the host-language program.

VARCHARs hold the potential for another processing inefficiency. A row can change length whenever a VARCHAR item is updated with a differing value. If a page has little or no free space, an update that expands a VARCHAR item will force the row onto another page. DB2 replaces the relocated row with a pointer to its new page. Accessing that row then requires two I/O operations—one finds the pointer, the second finds the row. Proper use of free space avoids this problem. (See Section 3.4.)

The table designer should usually place VARCHAR columns at the end of a row. When DB2 retrieves a row, it must know where each column begins and ends. If a VARCHAR column sits at the front of the row, DB2 must determine its length and then calculate each subsequent column's position in the variable-length row. If the VARCHAR column comes at the end of the row on the other hand, DB2 can simply lay out each fixed-length column and perform only one calculation to set the variable-length column's end point, a considerable savings in CPU time for the processing. Also a variable-length row frequently requires that more data be logged with an update. For example, if the row length is changed, the entire row is logged since the row length is in the 6-byte prefix of the row. If the row is fixed in length with no VARCHAR columns, however, only the first through last byte updated is logged. For example, if the third and fifth column is updated, then only columns three, four, and five are logged as indicated in Fig. 4.3. This suggests that placing frequently updated columns next to each other will reduce the total number of bytes that must be logged.

In many cases, though, users will want to see a VARCHAR column toward the beginning of a row because it logically belongs there according to the way they think about or use the information. A variable-length part description, for example, might logically follow the part ID at the beginning of a row. In this case, it is still best to place the VARCHAR column at the end of the row. Then the developer can create a logical view of the table with the columns in any desired order. This provides the performance advantage of placing the VARCHAR column at the row's end while allowing users the format they find most convenient.

COBOL does not calculate the number of characters before the trailing blanks. Consequently the programmer must define the variable, its type, and maximum length in this form:

```
01 VARIABLE.
   49 VARIABLE-LENGTH PICTURE S9(4) COMP.
   49 VARIABLE-VALUE PICTURE X(100).
```

The host variable value—shown in parentheses after ''X''—must match the maximum length designated in the CREATE TABLE statement. The vari-

Rows with a VARCHAR column

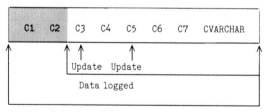

Data logged if row length changed

Fixed length rows

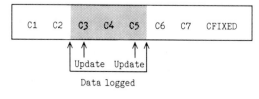

Fig. 4.3 Logged data with a variable and fixed-length row

able length must be calculated by the COBOL program and placed in VARI-ABLE-LENGTH. A couple of techniques for doing this are discussed in Chapter 9.

There are restrictions on the operations that can be performed on a column declared as VARCHAR with a length greater than 254 bytes since it is considered a long string like LONG VARCHAR. It is not possible to place an index on the column, it cannot be used with a predicate other than LIKE, a function other than SUBSTR, a subselect, a UNION without ALL, ORDER BY, GROUP BY, or DISTINCT. (These functions are discussed in Chapter 7.)

Numerals as Numeric Types

Developers sometimes are tempted to declare variables consisting of numeric identifiers—such as employee identifications or part numbers—as character types. These numbers will not be used in calculations so the developer feels safe in treating them as character variables. The perceived advantage is that the approach avoids the data exceptions that occur after data entry mistakes—the keying in of a character rather than a numeral for a numeric type. Ideally a validation procedure would catch such an error, but the lack of thorough validation does occur. Consequently data exceptions may occur, requiring costly program reruns. If a character type had been declared originally, however, the system would accept the mistake and keep running.

This shortcut can be expensive, however. Putting aside the question of tolerating misinformation, using a character type for numeric data holds tangible disadvantages. One is that it uses unnecessary storage space. SMALLINT, which can handle numbers up to 32,767, requires only 2 bytes. The five characters needed to represent values with five digits require 1 byte each—a 3-byte cost per data value. If the column is indexed, the space cost of this approach more than doubles.

Another reason to use the appropriate type is that occasional users find it confusing to have to enclose some numerals in quotation marks—those that have been declared as characters—in their database requests.

Finally when DB2 eventually supports enforcement of domains, existing violations will cause difficulties. The domain of a column with all numeric data is misrepresented when the column is declared as a character data type. Clearly all of these potential problems argue strongly in favor of declaring numeric identifiers as numeric types.

Domains

C.J. Date defines a domain as a pool of values from which one or more columns draw their actual values. E.F. Codd would like to see data types used to enforce domains. A date data type is a good example of enforcement of a domain through a DB2 data type. A column defined as a date data type must contain a year value between 1 and 9999, a month value between 1 and 12, and a day value between 1 and 31. Research is currently being done on defining domains to DB2 by specifying the conditions that a column value must meet and in terms of SELECT statements.

The ANSI SQL2 standard calls for a CREATE DOMAIN statement where domains are given a name, data type, default value, integrity rule, and constraint name. All but the domain and data type are optional. An example will demonstrate the definition of a domain.

```
CREATE DOMAIN COLORS AS CHAR(6) DEFAULT 'GREEN'
    CHECK (VALUE IN ('RED', 'YELLOW', 'BLUE,' 'GREEN'))
    CONSTRAINT INVALID_COLORS
```

The domain name is COLORS, and the column will contain six characters. The color green will be inserted into the column if a color is not specified when a row is inserted. The IN list is used to define the valid domain values in the example. Almost any predicate, however, can be used to define the valid values. All inserts and updates must specify a value of red, yellow, blue, or green for the color. If an attempt is made to place another color in the column, the constraint name of INVALID_COLORS will be returned to the program. The constraint name allows the program to determine which of perhaps many domain definitions have been violated.

Frequently the list of valid values is quite long, and it may change over time. A table can be created containing the valid values and a domain defined in terms of the values listed in the table. The following example is very similar to the previous example except that the valid colors are in the ALL_COLORS table.

```
CREATE DOMAIN COLORS AS CHAR(6) DEFAULT 'GREEN'
   CHECK (VALUE IN SELECT COLOR FROM ALL_COLORS'))
   CONSTRAINT INVALID_COLORS;
```

The domain name is specified in place of data type when a table is created.

```
CREATE TABLE P_T
  (PN      CHAR(6)     NOT NULL,
   PNAME   CHAR(6)     NOT NULL WITH DEFAULT,
   COLOR   COLORS, ...
```

Date and Time

Three data types allow for the manipulation of dates and times and for the automatic recording of when rows are inserted. This capability is useful for keeping track of when orders were entered, for example. The types are DATE, TIME, and TIMESTAMP. DATE represents the month, day, and year in a number of formats—MM/DD/YYYY, for example—that are discussed in Section 7.5. TIME represents the hour, minute, and second of insertion or the hour, minute, and whether AM or PM. TIMESTAMP, which represents both date and time plus six digits of microseconds, is used when a large number of sources are entering data into the same table at the same second and the organization wants to differentiate the entries by time. It is almost a million times less likely that two sources would enter data at the same microsecond than at the same second though it can happen, particularly in a multiprocessor system or across international time zones.

The time and date columns are declared in the CREATE TABLE statement by stating the column name followed by the type name: DATE_ RECORDED DATE, for example. As with numeric types, the lengths need not be declared. In fact, DATE requires 4 bytes, TIME 3 bytes, and TIMESTAMP 10 bytes. The internal representation is like a packed decimal without the four sign bits. Because the time and date types are very specialized, they do not correspond directly to types provided by host languages. Host-language variables that receive values from time and date columns must be declared as character types: 10 bytes long for DATE corresponding to the 10 characters in the standard date formats, 8 bytes for TIME, and 26 bytes for TIMESTAMP. When the DATE and TIME variables are used in calculations, a process discussed in Chapter 7, the host-language variable that receives the results must be declared as a decimal type: DECIMAL(8,0) for DATE, DECIMAL(6,0) for TIME, and DECIMAL(14,n) for TIMESTAMP, with n = 0 through 6, depending on the format required.

To Null or Not Null

Null values can be used when actual values are unknown or inapplicable. Their use is required for the most accurate data representation, but they are difficult to deal with in application development.

It is perhaps easiest to understand the concept of nulls by considering the problem that arises when they are unavailable. What value should be placed in the cost column of a product information table for an item whose cost has not been set? A value of 0 is inaccurate because the product surely has a cost. A null value solves the problem by showing that the item carries a cost but that it is not known.

The ability to make this distinction takes resources. The use of nulls requires 1 byte of storage for every value in a column that allows nulls and another byte for every value in an index created from a column with nulls. The extra byte provides a prefix for each value that indicates whether it is in fact null. The null prefix is HEX '00' if the value is present and HEX 'FF' if it is not. These extra bytes can add up. A 100,000-row table with 10 columns allowing nulls requires 1 million bytes for the capability. If five of those columns provide indexes, another one-half million bytes are needed. Application programmers that select data from a column with nulls must know that nulls are allowed in columns and remember to code a null indicator and that there is the processing time for testing the null indicators.

Null can also present difficulties for occasional database users and programmers. Null values do not compare as equals in joins, for example. Suppose a database includes one table describing projects and another describing employees who might work on them. A user may request a report requiring a join of columns from each table—perhaps a list of the salaries being paid to workers assigned to each project. If some projects have no workers assigned to them, that fact might be indicated with nulls in the project table assignment column because an employee identification would not be applicable as an entry. Those projects with null values for the assignment column will not show up in the report, however, because the join ignores them. This may be fine if the report's purpose is to show salaries being paid for active projects. If the report was meant to show how much was being paid in salaries, by project, however, it would be misleading since it would not show the projects for which no salaries were being paid.

The developer can avoid this and similar problems by using a nonmeaningful value in place of null as a code that, in this case, would relate to an "unassigned" row in the employee table. For example, an employee ID of zero in the employee table would carry "unassigned" in the name column, and inactive projects would list zeros for employee IDs in the open slots.

An advantage of using nulls is that they allow for accurate averages in columns that include them. The nulls do not enter into the sum of values or contribute to their count. Consider a column of salaries that must use zeros for employees whose salaries are unknown. If the salaries for 10 listed employees totaled $300,000, the average is $30,000. If information on a new hire whose salary was unknown were added to the table and the salary was listed as zero, the salary column would still total $300,000, but the count of employees would now be 11. The column average would be $27,272.72. If null was used, the average would not change. One way around this problem if the developer does not wish to use nulls is to specify NOT NULL for the salary column, use zero in place of nulls, and compute the average for values where the salary is not equal to zero. This scheme does not work if the column includes volunteers, and the average should reflect that fact. To avoid this additional problem, the developer might use an impossible salary—perhaps −1—as the null replacement and take the average of salaries not equal to −1.

When DB2 uses a null in a mathematical procedure, the result will be null unless the SQL statement specifies special handling for nulls. For example, if a statement requests the subtraction of employees' insurance payments from their salaries and the insurance payment value is null, the result is null. The same principle applies to addition and multiplication. Division by null is like division by zero and results in a negative SQLCODE. Chapter 7 discusses the use of the VALUE clause to substitute values for nulls in SQL calculations.

Not Null with Default

In some cases, DB2 itself will choose zero as a null replacement or at least as a default for values unknown to it. DB2 requires that some value be assigned to every row in every column for which NOT NULL is in effect. In other words, these places may not be left empty when the table is loaded or a row is inserted. If the developer specifies NOT NULL WITH DEFAULT for a column in the CREATE TABLE statement, DB2 automatically places zeros in empty numeric columns; blanks in empty character columns; and the current date, time, or timestamp in columns with the corresponding date data type. This avoids troublesome errors during data input into NOT NULL columns, but users and programmers must be aware that these default values may be present in the column.

NOT NULL WITH DEFAULT on a date or time column results in recording date or time when a row is inserted. DATE and TIME columns declared NOT NULL WITH DEFAULT receive the current date and time when a row is inserted if no other values are specified. If a table includes columns for ORDER_DATE and RECEIVED_DATE, current time would be appropriate for the first but not the second when a row is first inserted. An alternative for RECEIVED_DATE would be '0001-01-01' or '9999-12-31' (all zeros is not a valid date). The date of '0001-01-01' is used by the reorganization utility after a date column is added to a table with the ALTER statement.

Programmers must also be aware of which columns allow nulls. Whenever they write a program that selects data from a column with nulls, they must declare a null indicator variable and reference it in each SELECT statement for the column. This coding is not difficult, but if it is not done—if the programmer does not know or forgets that nulls apply—a negative SQLCODE will result. Chapter 9 discusses programming for nulls.

No-Choice Nulls

For certain kinds of columns, the developer will almost never allow nulls. A primary key, by definition, must uniquely identify each row. Therefore a unique value should always be inserted into the primary key column. A foreign key column usually should not contain nulls. An exception would be the project assignment table when an employee ID might be designated null if no employee is assigned to a particular project. The primary key column therefore and usually the foreign key column should be declared NOT NULL. DB2, but not the relational model, allows the primary key to be defined as NOT NULL WITH DEFAULT. This should be avoided, except perhaps to allow automatic insertion of a timestamp recording when the row is inserted. Any column can be declared unique by creating a unique index on it, meaning that DB2 will not allow duplicate values to be inserted in it. In fact, all primary key columns must be declared unique to guarantee that no values are repeated. Any unique column should be declared NOT NULL since it would allow only one null value in any case.

On the other hand, NOT NULL may not be specified for columns added to a table with the ALTER TABLE statement. A newly added column will obviously contain nulls until its values are inserted. If the developer wants to specify NOT NULL for a new column, he or she must drop the table and re-create it. A column specified NOT NULL WITH DEFAULT may be added to a table with an ALTER statement. The newly added column will contain the default values after a reorganization.

Developers frequently declare most columns as NOT NULL WITH DEFAULT except for the primary key and in some cases the foreign key. Even if no columns allow for nulls, it may be necessary to use a null indicator. For example, if the average salary of employees in Department X is computed and there are no employees in the department, the result is null and a null indicator must be coded on the SQL statement to avoid a negative SQLCODE.

Auditing a Table

DB2 will audit a table's use—keep a record of SQL statements that access it—if the table's creator requests such an audit in the table's CREATE statement and the system administrator specifies that the audit is to occur. With the clause AUDIT CHANGE, the developer requests that records be kept for each insert, update, or delete statement. An AUDIT ALL clause requests records for selects as well. An AUDIT NONE asks that no auditing be done. Since this is the default if no audit parameter is indicated, AUDIT NONE is used primarily for documentation. The system administrator can specify that the audit cover all access to the table or access by specific application plans or authorization IDs. An audit record consists of the SQL statement, the primary authorization ID of the individual issuing the statement, and a timestamp indicating when the statement was issued.

Before and after images of the data are not part of the audit record. The company's auditor may or may not find this acceptable. An image of the INSERT statement which includes the column values inserted will be recorded. The condition under which a row is deleted and updated as expressed in the predicates will be written as part of the statement image, and the values used in the set clause of the update statement will be logged. If this is not acceptable to the company's auditor, the IFI (instrumentation facility interface) exit can be used with application program code to write the audit.

The audit record is made when the statement first attempts to access the table, and the record will be kept even if the statement abends or the statement's work is rolled back as part of the recovery process after a fault. If a table is altered with respect to its audit status, application plans and packages that access the table are invalidated, and the plans and packages are automatically rebound prior to their next execution. This allows DB2 to add or remove codes needed for the audit. Audit applies to both static and dynamic SQL.

Auditing adds about 5 percent to the CPU costs plus the I/O to write an image of the SQL statement to the audit trace. It will be less costly than having an application program write an image of updated rows and can be used to perform occasional studies of how a table is being used. In any case, systems administrators control audits, turning them on when DB2 is installed or starting and stopping them dynamically as it runs.

An audit is only one of several traces DB2 provides. The administrator uses a START TRACE statement to begin an audit, specifying in the statement the type, or class, of audit to be performed. Any combination of eight audit classes may be specified, including those that track the granting and revocation of security authorizations, the creation, alteration, or dropping of objects, and instances of security violations—attempts by unauthorized users to access data. Of course, there are also classes for tracking the kinds of statements indicated by CREATE TABLE statements—those that update and those that only select from a table. The START TRACE statement also indicates where the audit records are to be stored. They may be directed to GTF (general trace facility) or SMF (systems management facility) datasets and will have a record type of 102. Here is a typical START TRACE statement for an audit:

```
-START TRACE (AUDIT) CLASS(4,6) DEST(GTF)
```

The first parameter indicates that the trace is for an audit. The class parameters 4 and 6 indicate respectively that the audit is to track SQL statements that update tables for which audits have been designated and to track binds of all SQL statements issued on audited tables. No reporting tools are provided with DB2 for audit traces. The records must be accessed with a user-written program, DB2PM from IBM, or with a product from another software company.

EDITPROC, FIELDPROC, and VALIDPROC

DB2 provides for the compression or encoding and validation of data when they are entered—and decompression and decoding when they are selected—through assembler programs invoked each time a row is inserted, updated, or retrieved. The developer specifies the names of these procedures in the CREATE TABLE statement using the EDITPROC, FIELD-PROC, or VALIDPROC parameters. The programs can be custom written for the table on which they operate. The program name follows the key word for the type of procedure to be used. Once the procedure has been developed and defined, its use is transparent to anyone issuing an SQL statement.

EDITPROC and FIELDPROC provide for the compression and en-

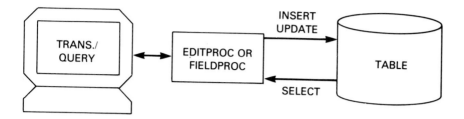

EDITPROC and FIELDPROC capture a row or field to compress or encode data before the row is updated or inserted in a table. Before a row is returned in response to a request, they decompress or decode its data. EDITPROC acts on an entire row and FIELDPROC on individual columns.

Fig. 4.4 EDITPROC and FIELDPROC

coding—EDITPROC for entire rows, FIELDPROC for individual columns (Fig. 4.4). Because EDITPROC and FIELDPROC routines affect the way DB2 stores the data, they cannot be added to or dropped from a table after it has been created, nor can a column be added to a table that includes an EDITPROC routine. A FIELDPROC routine, however, can be added to a table with a column that is added with an ALTER TABLE statement.

Use of EDITPROC or FIELDPROC requires CPU time for the assembler programs to compress or encrypt the data. But because more compressed rows can fit on each page, more rows can be processed in each I/O operation. And the compressed data take up less DASD space. These savings may outweigh the cost of the assembler program processing, depending on the amount of space that can be compressed. Keep in mind that compression of rows cause them to be variable in length. Recall that a variable-length row that is increased in length may have to be moved to another page if there is no free space available, and more bytes must be logged when columns are updated in most cases. In addition, decompression is done on all columns even though only a few columns are selected, which increases CPU usage. On the positive side, savings can be realized when using the reorganization, copy, and recover utilities since fewer pages need to be processed. Several software companies offer products for compressing data with the use of EDITPROC. IBM provides a sample procedure: DSN8HUFF in the sample library DSNSAMP.

Besides compressing data, EDITPROC and FIELDPROC routines can provide a means for representing a table's data in other than EBCDIC, which is standard on IBM computers. Developers can use this ability to encrypt data or change the usual EBCDIC collating sequence. Sorts done on data represented in EBCDIC result in strict alphabetical order, for example, while an organization may want to use exceptions to that order. In an employee list, for example, it may want MacDonald and McDonald next to each other rather than having MacGraw in between. An assembler program invoked using FIELDPROC could account for the special order. Similarly, sorts of EBCDIC represented data will not account for accent marks, sorting words that contain them out of alphabetical order. A FIELDPROC routine can solve the problem of handling accent marks, common in languages other than English. FIELDPROC can also be useful for translating a code to a name or description when data is selected. State code is frequently stored in a row rather than the longer state name. The state code of, say, 1 or 'AL' can be translated to Alabama automatically for reporting purposes when a row is processed through a FIELDPROC.

A VALIDPROC routine can check table data as they are entered to ensure the values are within permitted ranges. If the routine detects a mistake, it issues an error message and does not permit the update, insertion, or deletion. The assembler program spends some CPU time performing its checks when data are entered. It is not invoked when data are retrieved. A VALIDPROC routine can save overall CPU time—as well as development effort—for data validation by eliminating the need for each application updating a table to handle its own validation. Accounting for validation with VALIDPROC during table creation rather than through application programs makes it safer for occasional users to enter data interactively.

Since VALIDPROC does not affect how the data are stored, an ALTER TABLE statement may add or drop a VALIDPROC routine. A column may also be added to a table that employs a VALIDPROC routine. The routine, unless revised, will not, however, operate on the new column.

Row Length Considerations

To fit as many rows as possible on each page and avoid wasted space, developers should consider several factors related to row length. DB2 permits a maximum of 127 rows per 4K data page regardless of their length. (This limitation is due to a page's directory, which can list only that many rows. Seven bits of the last byte in the RID (row or record identifier) are used to locate a slot in the page directory. Thus, $2^7 - 1 = 127$, which is the maximum number of rows on a page.) Consequently a row length of 32 bytes including overhead will just fill the available space (32 bytes/row * 127 rows = 4064 bytes). A shorter row length will waste space on the page.

The developer should avoid row lengths of slightly more than 2037 bytes including overhead. Rows cannot be split across pages. Only one 2038-byte row will fit on a page, leaving almost half the page empty. This will require twice as many I/O operations to access the same number of rows as would be needed if the length were slightly less than 2037 bytes and two rows could fit on each page.

Similarly a row of more than 4074 bytes including overhead will not fit on a 4K page but will need a 32K page. Developers should avoid using 32K pages whenever possible because they require 32K of contiguous virtual storage to process and may result in fragmented space. The large pages also require use of bufferpool 32, which requires eight times the I/O transfer time as 4K bufferpools. If textual data are being stored, however, it is best to use a 32K page rather than artificially splitting the row across multiple 4K pages.

Creating Objects in a Read-only Database

The creation of a shared read-only database is discussed in Chapter 3. The creation of objects in the reader databases must be very similar to the owner-database objects. Most table parameter values must be the same including the IN clause, column data types, order of columns, and EDIT-PROC. (The AUDIT CHANGES and VALIDPROC do not apply to reader tables since the data resides only in the owner's database.) Some parameters can differ, for example, the table name, column names, and FIELDPROC. If the names are the same, however, a copy of plans and packages on the owner DB2 subsystem can be used. The OBID (object identifier) is recorded in the DBDs, plans, and packages and used at execution time. Therefore it is necessary to have the OBID match on the owner and reader databases. The owner's OBID can be determined from SYSTABLES like:

```
SELECT OBID
FROM   SYSIBM.SYSTABLES
WHERE  CREATOR = 'AUTHID'
AND    NAME = 'P_T'
```

The OBID can be specified when the table is created on the reader's database. In the following example, it is the last parameter on the CREATE TABLE statement.

```
CREATE TABLE P_T
   (PN     CHAR(6)   NOT NULL,
    PNAME  CHAR (20) NOT NULL WITH DEFAULT,
    COLOR  CHAR(6)   NOT NULL WITH DEFAULT,
    WEIGHT SMALLINT,
    CITY   CHAR (15) NOT NULL WITH DEFAULT,
    DATE_RECORDED DATE NOT NULL WITH DEFAULT,
    PRIMARY KEY (PN))
IN DAREADB.PTSP
OBID 1414;
```

The owner and reader indexes must be the same except that the BUFFERPOOL and CLOSE parameter values can differ. The owner and reader tablespaces must have mostly the same parameter values including the tablespace name, USING, PCTFREE, FREEPAGE, SEGSIZE, NUMPARTS, and DASETPASS parameters. The owner and reader tablespace need not use the same BUFFERPOOL as long as the same page size is used. The tablespace LOCKSIZE parameters need not agree. The locksize of tablespace is always used with a shared read-only database except when the owner data is updated in which case the specified locksize is used. The CLOSE parameter value for reader's objects need not be the same as the owner's objects. There is no data on the reader's DB2 subsystem. Although some parameters can differ between the owner and reader object definitions, administration is eased by having everything the same. The owner's CREATE statements can be copied to the reader DB2 subsystem and only a few changes are required like the ROSHARE parameter on the CREATE DATABASE statement and the OBID on the CREATE TABLE statement before they are executed.

Creating LIKE Tables

Frequently developers will want to create tables exactly like existing ones. For example, they may want to create a test table just like an existing production table. Management of referential integrity structures with the CHECK DATA utility discussed in Chapter 16 needs a duplicate table to receive foreign key rows that do not have a matching primary key.

Developers can create duplicate tables without having to retype entire CREATE TABLE statements or having to retrieve the statements from a file by using a CREATE TABLE . . . LIKE . . . statement. In this statement, the developer simply names the new table and indicates the existing table on which it is to be based. For example:

```
CREATE TABLE TEST.SPJ LIKE PROD.SPJ IN DATSTDB.DATESTSP;
```

This statement creates a test table, TEST.SPJ, with the same attributes as the production table, PROD.SPJ, and places it in the DATESTSP tablespace and DATSTDB database.

The new table can be placed in any tablespace. It will use the same FIELDPROC procedures as those specified for the original. However, EDITPROC and VALIDPROC procedures and referential constraints will not carry forward to the LIKE table. Primary and foreign keys can be added with an ALTER statement.

Synonyms and Aliases

Synonyms and aliases are useful for creating a more meaningful name for a person using a table or view. They are sometimes used by developers to manage the leading qualifier of a table or view. For example, a developer needs to select and update from the TEST.SPJ table in a program that is being developed in a test environment. It is known that when the program is migrated to the production environment, the table will have a different qualifier, say PROD.SPJ. The developer does not want to reference TEST.SPJ in all FROM clauses since it would be necessary to change the program to reference PROD.SPJ when the program is moved to production.

The developer can create a synonym like:

```
CREATE SYNONYM SPJ FOR TEST.SPJ;
```

This allows the developer to simply reference SPJ in all FROM clauses. Then after the move of the program to production, a synonym is created to point to the production table.

```
CREATE SYNONYM SPJ FOR PROD.SPJ;
```

This seems like a straightforward procedure, but there are some complicating factors that revolve around the fact that a synonym is specific to the AUTHID that created it. The consequences are that when a table or view is dropped directly or indirectly by dropping a tablespace or database, the synonym is also dropped. It is not uncommon in a development environment to drop and recreate objects. After this has occurred, a program that was working fine will no longer execute until the referenced synonym is recreated. Typically a number of developers are writing programs that reference a table and must recreate their synonyms to continue their work. This has proved quite cumbersome at a number of companies.

An alternative is to use an alias. Aliases were designed for a distributed environment to avoid having to reference the location qualifier of a table or view. They can be used in a local environment as well with or without specifying the location like:

```
CREATE ALIAS SPJ FOR DALLAS.TEST.SPJ;
```

The advantage is that the alias is not dropped when the table is dropped, and in fact the table does not need to exist when the alias is created.

Another alternative is the use of the secondary AUTHID discussed in Chapter 15. Each person can be assigned up to 245 secondary AUTHIDs, and each person on a project team can be assigned the same secondary AUTHID. For example, each person working on the TEST.SPJ table can be assigned the secondary AUTHID of TEST. This allows the developer to set their IDs to TEST and issue any SQL statement interactively without having to specify the qualifier of TEST. Also when the developer binds that SQL statement into a plan or package, the qualifier parameter can be specified as QUALIFIER (TEST), which will cause all unqualified table names to be qualified with TEST. Then the migration to production requires only that the bind statement specify QUALIFIER (PROD). Indeed the value specified as the qualifier does not have to be a secondary AUTHID. Secondary AUTHID do provide for avoiding qualifying interactive SQL, however, and allows for granting of privileges to a single ID shared by a number of developers as discussed in Chapter 15.

COMMENT ON Statements

Developers can use an SQL statement called a COMMENT ON statement to enter in the catalog tables, SYSIBM.SYSTABLES and SYSIBM.SYS-COLUMNS, textual descriptions of the tables and columns they have created. These descriptions are part of the documentation for the application system. In effect, the COMMENT ON statement inserts the developer's description in the catalog table REMARKS column in the row describing the table or column the statement specifies. Since the REMARKS column is a 254-character VARCHAR column, the description in the COMMENT ON statement cannot exceed 254 characters. In addition, COMMENT ON can be used on an alias. (Aliases will be discussed in Chapter 17.)

The COMMENT ON statement for a table identifies the table and, following the keyword IS, gives the description itself within single quotation marks—for example:

```
COMMENT ON TABLE AUTHID.SPJ IS
  'SPJ SHOWS THE RELATIONSHIP BETWEEN
   SN, PN, JN AND HAS THE PN QUANTITY';
```

The COMMENT ON statement for a single column also names the column:

```
COMMENT ON COLUMN AUTHID.SPJ.SN IS
  'SN IS THE SUPPLIER ID';
```

Developers can, however, use a single statement to enter descriptions of several of a table's columns. To do that, they name the table in the COMMENT ON statement and, within parentheses, specify the column names and their associated descriptions—for example:

```
COMMENT ON AUTHID.SPJ
  (SN IS 'SN IS THE SUPPLIER ID',
```

```
PN IS 'PN IS THE PART ID',
JN IS 'JN IS THE JOB ID');
```

LABEL ON Statements

The LABEL ON statement's purpose is to create labels that substitute for table or column names when interactive reports are generated. For example, a LABEL ON statement may create a label "SUPPLIER ID" for the SN column in the example SPJ table. Whenever an interactive request generates a report using the column, it is returned with the label rather than column name as a heading. Labels may be up to 30 characters.

The LABEL ON syntax is similar to that of the COMMENT ON statement. Columns can be labeled individually, or several from the same table can be labeled with a single statement—for example:

```
LABEL ON COLUMN AUTHID.SPJ.SN IS
  'SUPPLIER ID';

LABEL ON AUTHID.SPJ
 (SN IS 'SUPPLIER ID',
  PN IS 'PART ID',
  JN IS 'JOB ID');
```

4.3 VIEWS

The name *view* well describes its object's function: to provide particular views of base tables. Views are virtual tables, made up of columns and rows from base tables and other views, but their data are not stored separately. Instead the developer defines a view in terms of an SQL SELECT statement. DB2 holds the statement in catalog tables SYSIBM.SYSVTREE and SYSIBM.SYSVLTREE and resolves it into base table references when an SQL statement using the view is bound. The process cannot be seen by users, who perceive and deal with views as if they were base tables. The additional layer of data independence that views provide offers several benefits. Views can:

- Minimize modifications needed in application programs when base tables are restructured. The programs can access views that mirror the original base tables and in some cases update through a view the base tables underlying it.

- Provide access and update security. Rather than allowing users access to complete base tables, developers can grant the use of views that show only columns and rows approved for the users.

- Allow developers to give casual users and programmers easy and efficient access to data from several base tables. The developer creates a view that makes good use of indexes, for example. Users employ that view rather than formulating their own, perhaps inefficient, statements. The developer can also create views that derive aggregate data—averages and the like—or that select data from multiple tables. Users and programmers can simply refer to those views rather than having to write the sometimes complex statements needed to perform the same tasks.

This statement refers to the base tables shown in Fig. 4.5:

```
CREATE VIEW LONDON_SP AS
  SELECT S.SN, CITY, PN, QTY
  FROM S, SPJ
  WHERE CITY = 'LONDON'
  AND S.SN = SPJ.SN;
```

In the statement, the view's name, LONDON_SP, is followed by the keyword AS, indicating that the view is to be created as the SELECT statement that follows. The statement creates this view:

LONDON_SP VIEW

SN	CITY	PN	QTY
S1	LONDON	P1	200
S1	LONDON	P1	700
S4	LONDON	P6	300
S4	LONDON	P6	300

A SELECT statement that references the view,

```
SELECT S.SN, CITY, PN, QTY
FROM   LONDON_SP;
```

will be transformed at bind time into:

```
SELECT S.SN, CITY, PN, QTY
FROM   S, SPJ
WHERE  CITY = 'LONDON'
AND    S.SN = SPJ.SN;
```

The developer may use almost any SELECT statement in a view definition. DB2, however, does not allow creation of views with statements including UNION ALL, UNION, or ORDER BY operations perhaps because the second and third operators could entail costly sorts, and it will not create a view from a statement including a FOR UPDATE OF clause, a clause used in embedded SQL that indicates the selected data will be updated.

Supplier (S) Table

SN	SNAME	STATUS	CITY
S1	SMITH	20	LONDON
S2	JONES	10	PARIS
S3	BLAKE	30	PARIS
S4	CLARK	20	LONDON
S5	ADAMS	30	ATHENS

Job (J) Table

JN	JNAME	CITY
J1	SORTER	PARIS
J2	PUNCH	ROME
J3	READER	ATHENS
J4	CONSOLE	ATHENS
J5	COLLATOR	LONDON
J6	TERMINAL	OSLO
J7	TAPE	LONDON

Part (P) Table

PN	PNAME	COLOR	WEIGHT	CITY
P1	NUT	RED	12	LONDON
P2	BOLT	GREEN	17	PARIS
P3	SCREW	BLUE	17	ROME
P4	SCREW	RED	14	LONDON
P5	CAM	BLUE	12	PARIS
P6	CDG	RED	19	LONDON

Supplier/Part/Job (SPJ) Table

SN	PN	JN	QTY
S1	P1	J1	200
S1	P1	J4	700
S2	P3	J1	400
S2	P3	J2	200
S2	P3	J3	200
S2	P3	J4	500
S2	P3	J5	600
S2	P3	J6	400
S2	P3	J7	800
S2	P5	J2	100
S3	P3	J1	200
S3	P4	J2	500
S4	P6	J3	300
S4	P6	J7	300
S5	P2	J2	200
S5	P2	J4	100
S5	P5	J5	500
S5	P5	J7	100
S5	P6	J2	200
S5	P1	J4	100
S5	P3	J4	200
S5	P4	J4	800
S5	P5	J4	400
S5	P6	J4	500

Fig. 4.5 Suppliers, Part, Job, and Suppliers/Part/Job (SPJ) tables

It gives special handling to views with GROUP BY and HAVING clauses, which also require sorts. Whenever a SELECT statement accesses a view containing one of those clauses, DB2 will perform the necessary sorts and place the sorted rows in a temporary table that satisfies the request. This operation is generally transparent to the view's user. It may lengthen response times if a large number of rows must be sorted. Also views using GROUP BY cannot be updated because of inconsistencies that can be introduced when the temporary tables are changed.

DB2 also will not update certain other views. For example, it makes no sense to update views that include aggregates such as AVG, SUM, and COUNT because DB2 has no way of knowing what values to assign to the base tables. For example, if the average QTY was increased by 100, should DB2 increase each value by 100? Trying to update views that contain MIN, MAX, and DISTINCT values would entail similar ambiguities and logical inconsistencies between the views and base tables. DB2 issues an error code when a program or user tries to update a view containing any of those aggregates and functions. In addition, a view definition of a calculated value or constant cannot be updated although a row can be inserted into such a view.

Nor will DB2 update views created with joins. In other words, DB2 will not update a view when it finds more than one table listed in the CREATE VIEW statement's FROM clause. But developers may use subselects to create updatable views from multiple tables. In some cases, DB2 will update a view drawn from multiple tables with a subselect when it will not update the equivalent view created with a join. In recasting a join statement as a subselect, the developer should take care that the statements are in fact equivalent and that the reformulated statement will perform well. While all subselects can be defined as joins, not all joins have equivalent subselects.

CHECK Option

Besides providing a way to limit user access to authorized columns and rows, views can provide data validation and enforce security policies by checking the validity of updates against the condition defined in the CREATE VIEW statement's WHERE clause. The developer invokes this facility by including the clause WITH CHECK OPTION in the CREATE statement. Consider this example, which refers to the table in Fig. 4.5:

```
CREATE VIEW LONDON_S AS
   SELECT SN, SNAME, STATUS, CITY
   FROM  S
   WHERE  CITY = 'LONDON'
   WITH CHECK OPTION;
```

A user of this view attempting to select, update, or delete a value not covered by its definition will receive an error code. DB2 will not, for example, accept the statements:

```
INSERT INTO LONDON_S VALUES
   ('S20','THOMAS',50,'ATHENS');

UPDATE LONDON_S
   SET CITY = 'ATHENS'
   WHERE CITY = 'LONDON';
```

The primary purpose for the WITH CHECK OPTION is to prevent someone from inserting or updating a row that cannot subsequently be selected. For example, persons with privileges on the LONDON_S view without the check option can successfully execute the above statements even though they will not be able to select the supplier in Athens.

Another use of the WITH CHECK OPTION is to provide automatic validation of data. All predicates specified in the view definition will be checked when an INSERT and UPDATE statement is issued on the view. For example:

```
CREATE VIEW S_CHECK AS
   SELECT SN, SNAME, STATUS, CITY
   FROM   S
   WHERE  CITY IN ('LONDON', 'PARIS', 'ATHENS')
   AND    STATUS BETWEEN 10 AND 30
   WITH CHECK OPTION;
```

In this case, a user can neither accidentally change Smith's status to 5, which is below the allowable range nor insert a new supplier that does not have a status between 10 and 30. The view also requires that all new suppliers be in the specified cities and that no existing supplier can be changed to a city not listed in the IN clause. An index on columns specified in predicates, however, will not be used to locate a row to be updated. Views created on views including a check option are also checked according to the specified criteria.

No special privilege is needed to create a view as long as the new creator can select from the table that the view references.

Levels of Views

Developers can create views on other views and on combinations of views to any number of levels as long as the view references no more than 15 base tables directly or indirectly. As shown in Fig. 4.6, for example, VIEW I can be created over some columns and rows in TABLE A, VIEW II can be created on TABLE A and TABLE B, VIEW III can be created on VIEW I and VIEW II, and so on. While this offers a great deal of flexibility, it can

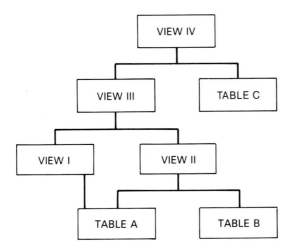

Fig. 4.6 Levels of views

also create a great deal of confusion if levels are piled too high. The higher-level views depend on those at the lower levels. If a lower-level view or table is dropped, higher-level views depending on it will also be dropped automatically and without warning. In Fig. 4.6, for example, if VIEW I is dropped, VIEW III and VIEW IV are dropped. If TABLE A is dropped, all of the views are dropped.

Table Restructuring

Perhaps the most important advantage provided by views comes into play when base tables are restructured. Fig. 4.7 shows an original base table for managing data about a parts inventory. It also shows two tables that restructure the information from the base table, adding an attribute and creating a separate warehouse relation. Applications that used information from the original base table might have been written to use a view of that table, which could have been created with the statement CREATE VIEW P AS SELECT * FROM P_T. In that case, when the base tables are restructured as shown in Fig. 4.7b if the developer creates a new VIEW P identical to the original, the programs accessing it need not be modified. The statement for duplicating the original view from the new tables would be:

```
CREATE VIEW P AS
    SELECT PN, PNAME, COLOR, WEIGHT, CITY
    FROM   PART_T, WAREHOUSE_T
    WHERE  PART_T.PN = WAREHOUSE_T.PN;
```

a Original Table and View
P_T

PN	PNAME	COLOR	WEIGHT	CITY
P1	NUT	RED	12	LONDON
P2	BOLT	GREEN	17	PARIS
P3	SCREW	BLUE	17	ROME
P4	SCREW	RED	14	LONDON
P5	CAM	BLUE	12	PARIS
P6	COG	RED	19	LONDON

CREATE VIEW P AS SELECT * FROM P_T;

b Restructured Table and New View
P_T

PN	PNAME	COLOR	WEIGHT	C FEET
P1	NUT	RED	12	54
P2	BOLT	GREEN	17	72
P3	SCREW	BLUE	17	76
P4	SCREW	RED	14	88
P5	CAM	BLUE	12	56
P6	COG	RED	19	94

Warehouse_T

PN	CITY
P1	LONDON
P2	PARIS
P3	ROME
P4	LONDON
P5	PARIS
P6	LONDON

```
CREATE VIEW P AS
   SELECT PN, PNAME, COLOR, WEIGHT, CITY
   FROM P_T, WAREHOUSE_T
   WHERE P_T.PN = WAREHOUSE_TPN;
```

The base tables underlying the two views shown here are different. The views themselves are the same. If plans used the original view, they would not have to be rewritten when the tables are changed. The plans would simply use the new view, which carries the old view's name.

Fig. 4.7 Using a view when restructuring tables

Notice, however, that the FROM clause includes two tables. DB2 will not update the view, so applications performing updates on the original view will not work with this one. The developer might avoid this limitation if the view can be defined in terms of a subselect rather than a join and will perform satisfactorily. (See Fig. 4.7a):

```
CREATE VIEW P AS
   SELECT PN, PNAME, COLOR, WEIGHT, CITY
   FROM P_T;
```

(See Fig. 4.7):

```
CREATE VIEW P AS
   SELECT PN, PNAME, COLOR, WEIGHT, CITY
   FROM   PART_T, WAREHOUSE_T
   WHERE  PART_T.PN = WAREHOUSE_T.PN;
```

The base tables underlying the two views shown here are different. The views themselves are the same. If SQL statements used the original view, they would not have to be rewritten when the tables are changed. The SQL statements would simply use the new view, which carries the old view's name.

After the base tables are restructured and the view is re-created, the next execution of an application program that accesses the view automatically rebinds the SQL to incorporate the changes. In most cases, views cost only a few milliseconds of CPU time when DB2 binds the SQL, a one-time cost for static SQL. For interactive QMF or LanguageAccess users, that CPU cost is paid each time a view is used. It is a negligible price, however, particularly considering the many benefits views provide.

Views Not Theoretically Updatable

Not all views are updatable in theory. C.J. Date provides an example of a view that is not theoretically updatable that utilizes the tables in Fig. 4.5.

Consider the view created by this statement:

```
CREATE VIEW CITY_PAIRS (S_CITY, P_CITY) AS
   SELECT S.CITY, P.CITY
   FROM   P, S, SPJ
   WHERE  P.PN = SPJ.PN
   AND SPJ.SN = S.SN;
```

This view will contain city pairings, each showing a city where a part supplier is located, taken from Table S, and a city where the user organization stores the part, taken from Table P. Part P1, for example, is kept in London. It is supplied by Supplier S1, also located in London. The row in the CITY_PAIRS table would be London-London. Part P1 is also supplied by

Supplier S5 in Athens, creating an Athens-London pair. Here is the complete view:

CITY_PAIRS VIEW

S_CITY	P_CITY
LONDON	LONDON
PARIS	ROME
PARIS	PARIS
PARIS	LONDON
LONDON	PARIS
ATHENS	PARIS
ATHENS	LONDON
ATHENS	ROME

An organization may find such a view very useful. It will run into difficulties, however, if it tries to update the view and the DBMS allows it. Consider this UPDATE statement:

```
UPDATE CITY_PAIRS
   SET   S_CITY = 'DALLAS',
         P_CITY = 'NEW YORK'
   WHERE S_CITY = 'PARIS'
   AND   P_CITY = 'LONDON';
```

Which city should be updated in the S table? Which in the P table? The obvious ambiguity makes the attempted update meaningless. A similar problem occurs with this DELETE statement:

```
DELETE FROM CITY_PAIRS
   WHERE S_CITY = 'LONDON'
   AND   P_CITY = 'ROME';
```

Are all London suppliers and Rome parts to be deleted from the base tables S and P? And consider this INSERT:

```
INSERT INTO CITY_PAIRS
   VALUES ('DALLAS','NEW YORK');
```

Are NULLS to be inserted in all columns except CITY in the base tables?

Whether a view involving a join is updatable is not always obvious. Indeed the question of theoretically updatable views is a fertile one for researchers. Some views of joins that DB2 will not currently update, however, are theoretically updatable, particularly those joined on the primary and foreign keys. IBM's researchers are likely to provide the ability to update those views in future DB2 releases. For an indepth discussion of view updatability, see E.F. Codd, *The Relational Model for Database Management Version 2*.

4.4 DROPPING OBJECTS

We have devoted two chapters to creating objects. A discussion of deleting them will require only a brief section. A statement for dropping an object uses the keyword DROP followed by the type of object being dropped and its name—for example:

```
DROP TABLE AUTHID.SPJ;
```

Dropping an object automatically causes dependent objects to be dropped. For example, if a tablespace is dropped, all tables, indexes, and views related to that tablespace will be dropped, revoking all privileges that have been granted and invalidating all application plans and packages that reference the objects. Often it is necessary to recreate objects that have been dropped. The easiest method is to save the SPUFI files that contain the create statements and resubmit them for execution. If the files are not available, the CREATE statements can be developed based on selects from catalog tables before dropping objects. There are a number of products on the market that will read the catalog tables and generate the create statements.

4.5 CATALOG TABLES AND DIRECTORY

DB2 automatically records in the catalog tables information on objects as they are being created. It inserts rows into the tables describing the objects. When the objects are dropped, the rows are deleted. Fig. 4.8 summarizes the catalog tables that are updated when an object is created, and Chapter 14 has a diagram showing the relationship between the tables. Information can be obtained from the catalog tables as from any data tables by issuing select statements.

Menu-driven access to the catalog tables is available by choosing the CATALOG VISIBILITY option from the DB2I panel. The sample panel in Fig. 4.9 shows a request for information on a table as indicated by the "L" on line 1. The name of the table, "posystem.spj", is keyed on line 2. The AUTHID of "fleur" (line 3) is being used to make the request and must have privileges to look at the information. The installation default allows any composite AUTHID to see information on objects owned by one of the IDs.

Information about the database is in the catalog table SYSDATABASE. The DBD (database descriptor) itself is in the DBD01 tablespace in the DSNDB01 database. The DSNDB01 database is the directory. It is not possible

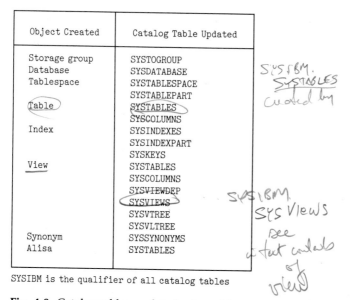

Object Created	Catalog Table Updated
Storage group	SYSTOGROUP
Database	SYSDATABASE
Tablespace	SYSTABLESPACE
	SYSTABLEPART
Table	SYSTABLES
	SYSCOLUMNS
Index	SYSINDEXES
	SYSINDEXPART
	SYSKEYS
View	SYSTABLES
	SYSCOLUMNS
	SYSVIEWDEP
	SYSVIEWS
	SYSVTREE
	SYSVLTREE
Synonym	SYSSYNONYMS
Alisa	SYSTABLES

SYSIBM is the qualifier of all catalog tables

SYSIBM. SYSTABLES created by

SYSIBM. SYS Views see text contents of view

Fig. 4.8 Catalog tables updated when objects are created

to select from the directory although information can be obtained about the DBD by issuing a −DISPLAY DATABASE command. The directory also has information on the status of utilities that have been submitted in the tablespace SYSUTIL and the command −DISPLAY UTILITY can be issued to determine the status. The tablespace SYSLGRNG has information on the RBA (relative byte address) used to determine the range of log records required for recovery, and the report utility can be used to get this

```
= = = =>
Enter object TYPE and NAME          RETRIEVE LIMIT = = = > 0100
1 OBJECT TYPE = = = > L             (See Object list below)
  A ALIAS                           I REVOKE IMPACT
  B COLUMNS                         J STOGROUP
  C DATABASE                        K SYNONYM
  D INDEX                           L TABLE
  E PACKAGE                         M TABLESPACE
  F PLAN                            N VIEW
  G PRIVILEGES                      O VOLUME
  H RELATIONSHIP
2 OBJECT NAME = = = > posystem.spj  (Leave blank for all)
3 CURRENT SOLID = > fleur           (Leave blank for USER)
Press: ENTER to process END to exit HELP for more information
```

Fig. 4.9 Catalog visibility

information. The tablespace SCT02 contains the application plans, and SPT01 contains the application packages. There are no tools for seeing the plans and packages in the directory although it will be seen in Chapter 10 that there are several catalog tables that have information on plans and packages.

4.6 SUMMARY

DB2 offers developers considerable flexibility in designing tables and using views. The choices they make in exercising that latitude—including such seemingly minor points as the order of columns in rows—can have a significant impact on performance. Attention to these points should become a matter of habit for all developers.

EXERCISES

4.1. Write a CREATE statement for an employee table, named EMP_T, in DAY-OURDB.EMPTSP with the following column names and descriptions:

Column name	Data type and length
EMPNO	Alpha 6, nulls are not allowed
FIRSTNME	Alpha from 1 to 12
MIDINIT	Alpha 1
LASTNAME	Alpha from 1 to 15
WORKDEPT	Alpha 3, allow for nulls
PHONENO	Alpha 4
HIREDATE	Date data type
JOB	Alpha 8
EDLEVEL	Numeric values 32K
SEX	Alpha 1
BIRTHDATE	Date data type
SALARY	Packed decimal 9 with 2 decimal places
BONUS	Packed decimal 9 with 2 decimal places
COMM	Packed decimal 9 with 2 decimal places

4.2. Where should FIRSTNME and LASTNAME be placed in the CREATE TABLE statement, and why?

4.3. Assuming FIRSTNME and LASTNAME have been placed most efficiently in the CREATE statement for Table EMP_T, write a CREATE statement for a view named EMP based on that table, which moves those columns to the beginning of the table.

4.4. A table with 10 columns and 100,000 rows requires 1 million more bytes than expected. What is the likely problem?

4.5. The SQL statement SELECT AVG(SALARY) FROM EMP_T yields inaccurate results. Why?

5

Referential Integrity

5.1 INTRODUCTION

Referential integrity refers to a particular kind of consistency that data in a relational database must exhibit in order for the database to remain usable. Consider the Job and SPJ tables shown in Fig. 4.5. If J2 rows were deleted from the Job table, the SPJ table as it now stands would not make sense. The rows in SPJ referring to J2 would be meaningless since there is no longer such a job. The potential for this kind of anomaly exists whenever any changes are made to foreign key columns and whenever primary key columns are updated or deleted. The relational model includes a rule for avoiding these inconsistencies: Every foreign key value, other than null, must have a corresponding primary key value to which it refers. In the example, the deletion of J2 in the J table violates referential integrity because the JN column is a primary key in the Job table and a foreign key in the SPJ table.

Companies also want to avoid certain conditions in a database that would violate their business policies. For example, the company using the Supplier and Part tables may have a business rule stating that parts may be kept only in cities that also have suppliers. Under that rule, every value in the Part table's CITY column must have a corresponding value in the Supplier table's CITY column. Organizations have many such business rules that apply to their everyday operations—employees must be assigned to departments, credit can be extended only to authorized customers, and so on. Not only should the data in databases adhere to these rules, but the database management system should also enforce that adherence.

To avoid referential integrity and business rule violations, database developers must specify rules for how the data can be changed. Ideally the developer would be able to describe the rules to the DBMS, which then enforces them. Without support for rule enforcement from the DBMS, programmers must incorporate that enforcement in the programs that handle the changes. It is preferable to have the database management system enforce the rules thus saving programmers the work of having to code for them in every application that accesses the database. It also insures that the rules are enforced consistently, avoiding the possibility of one or more application programs failing to enforce them.

Several types of rules can be used to enforce referential integrity. DB2 provides enforcement for most of these types in Version 2. The type of rule that is most appropriate for any given database, however, usually depends on the user organization's business requirements—on how the company wishes to control the data. Sometimes an organization may want to use a type of enforcement rule not currently supported by DB2. There will also be a few situations in which an application's rule enforcement can provide better performance than DB2's enforcement. Therefore to provide a general understanding of referential integrity, we will look at all rule types first. Then we will discuss DB2's referential integrity facilities, how to use them, and their performance implications. Finally for those who occasionally need to use application-enforced integrity, we will discuss how to code for the various rules and how to track their use.

If the reader is not familiar with basic SQL data manipulation, Chapter 7 can be read before reading this chapter.

5.2 THE RULES

In the example in which deletion of J2 from the Job table violates referential integrity, the tables' developer might have defined a rule stating that no job could be deleted from the Job table if the SPJ table indicates it is an active job—that is, if the SPJ table still includes that job. This type of rule is called a restrict rule. Users and programs are restricted from making changes that would violate the referential integrity. The system, or host-language program, warns them of the restriction and perhaps suggests alternate courses of action. The user might dispose of parts assigned to Job 2 and delete J2 rows in the SPJ table. Then the deletion of J2 from the Job table would be allowed.

Another way the developer might avoid the problem would be to establish a rule that any time a job is deleted from the Job table any row in the SPJ table including that job would also be deleted. This kind of rule is called a cascade rule because the change that would violate the rule causes a cascade of changes to other parts of the database in order to avoid the violation.

The third rule type neutralizes integrity problems by substituting nulls for values in a foreign key that correspond to the values changed in the related primary key. When J2 is deleted from the Job table, for example, the neutralize rule would require the substitution of nulls for all J2 values in the SPJ table. In this case, the SPJ table would still account for the allocated, but unassigned, parts and database users could find those parts by selecting for nulls in the table's JN column.

Developers may employ any one of these rule types for any type of change depending on the nature of the data and how the organization uses them. Would the organization's inventory procedures account for the parts allocated to a canceled job, for example, if a cascade rule automatically deleted rows with information about those parts? Would the organization prefer to have an employee dispose of the parts and change the table? These rules and design decisions come into play for any type of database change—deletes, inserts, and updates. We will look at additional examples as we discuss the rules' implementations.

5.3 DB2's REFERENTIAL INTEGRITY SUPPORT

DB2 allows developers to designate primary and foreign key columns in the CREATE and ALTER TABLE statements. Then it automatically restricts any changes to the foreign key column that would violate referential integrity—it issues an error message whenever a user or program attempts to update a value in the foreign key to a value not found in the referenced primary key column or to insert a foreign key value not found in the referenced primary key. In addition, DB2 enforces rules governing deletions and updates of primary key values. The developer may specify with the creation of the foreign key that DB2 employ a restrict, cascade, or neutralizing rule when deletions are to be made from the primary key column. And DB2 does not allow updates to a primary key column if the old primary key value exists in the referenced foreign key column.

DB2 verifies that data manipulation adheres to all applicable referential integrity rules as the processing occurs. This is called inflight verification. As processing changes a row's values, DB2 checks for referential integrity violations and takes the specified action if it discovers any. If a restrict rule is in effect, for example, processing stops when a violation occurs. This

Box 5.1   Referential integrity summary

- Each foreign key value must have a matching primary key value.
- An insert into a primary key table cannot violate referential integrity and no checking is required.
- Deletion of a foreign key value cannot violate referential integrity and no checking is required.

The following rules apply to DB2's referential integrity enforcement:

- Changes in primary key values are allowed only for those values that do not have matching foreign key values.
- The insertion of any given foreign key value or an update to that value is allowed only if the matching value exists in the primary key.
- Deletion of a primary key value when a corresponding foreign key value exists
  - will be barred if the foreign key constraint has been specified as RE-STRICT;
  - will cause deletion of the corresponding foreign key values if the constraint has been specified as CASCADE;
  - will set the corresponding foreign key values to null if the constraint has been specified as SET NULL.

---

inflight checking provides improved performance compared with checking in advance—although DB2 does some of that, too—or with allowing processing to continue to a commit work point and then rolling back the processing if a violation had occurred.

Referential integrity processing does require resources, however, which the installation must take into account. For example, if DB2 were enforcing a restrict rule on the JN foreign key, when a user attempted to delete J2, DB2 would have to first search for J2 in the SPJ table, taking the necessary concurrency control locks, performing the I/O operations, and so on. This processing can be very intensive if the number of changes of key values is high.

In most cases, DB2 integrity enforcement will be more efficient than that done by an application. When DB2 enforces the rules, its checking will always use an available index on a primary or foreign key column, whereas for an application's checking, depending on how the checking is coded, the optimizer may not employ an index. In addition, DB2's checking utilizes the Data Manager rather than passing the rows to the Relational Data System, which will not be the case for application-enforced checking. And

DB2's checking does not require passing of values to the application. Avoiding the application's involvement minimizes the path length, the number of instructions that must be executed for checking. Also several utilities aid in maintaining referential integrity. Finally with DB2 enforcement, the catalog tables store information on all integrity rules, eliminating the need to produce and manage written documentation of them.

On the other hand, there are a few situations in which application-enforced integrity might make sense. For example, DB2's rules may not match an organization's policy for using the data in question. In some cases, the organization might rather have a primary key update cascade to the foreign key rather than having DB2 bar the change with its implicit restrict rule. Such a cascade is permitted by the relational model.

And for some batch updates or insertions, performance considerations also suggest use of integrity checking by the application program. For example, consider a situation in which there is a foreign key on the SPJ table's supplier number column to the Supplier table. Suppose the organization were performing a 10,000-row batch insertion to the SPJ table, with each new row indicating the receipt of a part from supplier S1. Before allowing insertion of each new row, DB2 would have to check to see that S1 existed in the Supplier table. A user would know, however, that the check can be made only once for the entire batch.

DB2 does not allow exceptions to integrity rules once they have been defined. In the above example, for instance, the organization may want to have DB2 enforce the rule on the supplier number foreign key at all times except during batch insertions. The LOAD utility, described in Chapter 16, provides a means for shutting off constraint checking during batch insertions. For batch updates, the only way to shut off that enforcement would be to use an ALTER statement to drop the key from the SPJ table. After the batch update, the key could be added again that also requires execution of a utility, CHECK DATA, which we discuss briefly below and more fully in Chapter 16. Still, in most cases users will find it most practical to define referential integrity constraints in the tables and allow DB2 to enforce them. This avoids the need to repeatedly code for rules in applications and to risk incorrect or inconsistent coding. It also allows users to update tables directly through QMF, SPUFI, or other interfaces that include no provisions for code to enforce integrity rules.

Creating Primary Keys

The first step in setting up a new table's referential integrity is to specify the primary key in the CREATE TABLE statement (Fig. 5.1). The syntax is straightforward. After the key words PRIMARY KEY, the column or

```
CREATE TABLE S
  (SN     CHAR(6)  NOT NULL,
   SNAME  CHAR(20) NOT NULL WITH DEFAULT,
   STATUS SMALLINT NOT NULL WITH DEFAULT,
   CITY   CHAR(150) NOT NULL WITH DEFAULT,
   PRIMARY KEY (SN))
IN DAGKWDB.STSP;

CREATE UNIQUE INDEX SNX
  ON S (SN);

CREATE TABLE SPJ
  (SN     CHAR(6)  NOT NULL,
   PN     CHAR(6)  NOT NULL,
   JN     CHAR(6)  NOT NULL,
   QTY    INTEGER  NOT NULL WITH DEFAULT,
   PRIMARY KEY (SN, PN, JN),
   FOREIGN KEY SNFK (SN) REFERENCES S
     ON DELETE RESTRICT,
   FOREIGN KEY PNFK (PN) REFERENCES P
     ON DELETE CASCADE,  --NOT REALISTIC
   FOREIGN KEY JNFK (JN) REFERENCES J
     ON DELETE SET NULL, --NOT REALISTIC
IN DAGKWDB.SPJTSP;

CREATE UNIQUE INDEX SPJX
  ON SPJ (SN, PN, JN);

CREATE INDEX SPJPNX
  ON SPJ (PN);

CREATE INDEX SPJJNX
  ON SPJ (JN);
```

Fig. 5.1 Creating a table with a primary and foreign key

columns that comprise the key are listed in parentheses. DB2 allows only one primary key per table, as the relational model dictates.

The developer must also create a unique index on the key column or columns. This assures that DB2 will enforce the requirement that every primary key value be unique—a requirement called entity integrity in relational terms. If there is no unique index on the specified primary key, DB2 considers the table definition incomplete. DB2 will not allow SQL data manipulation access to an incomplete table but will allow developers to alter the table or create indexes on it.

DB2 allows primary key columns to be declared NOT NULL or NOT NULL WITH DEFAULT. NOT NULL WITH DEFAULT will allow a zero or blank as a primary key value, however, probably not the intended unique identifier. Since NOT NULL WITH DEFAULT makes little sense for a column with a unique index in any case, only one zero or blank will be allowed. A possible exception is the use of timestamp as a primary key that would allow for the automatic recording of the timestamp when the row is inserted.

In IBM parlance, a table with a foreign key is called a dependent table and a table whose primary key is associated with a foreign key is called a parent table. Relational purists resist this terminology because it suggests that the relationship between tables related by keys is hierarchical, which, of course, it is not. We will use the terms primary key and foreign key table in most cases. DB2 allows primary key tables to exist without associated foreign key tables. Such tables are called independent tables. And, of course, tables can have both primary and foreign keys.

Creating Foreign Keys

The foreign key clause in the CREATE or ALTER TABLE statement first creates a name for the referential constraint. In the first example in Fig. 5.1, this name is SNFK. This eight-character name is used in error messages to identify a violated constraint. It is important to specify a constraint name. If it is not given, DB2 will generate a name that will be difficult to track and use when a violation of referential integrity is detected. The same foreign key column can appear in multiple tables, referencing the same primary key table each time, but the referential constraint name must be unique to each table.

The developer specifies in parentheses following the referential constraint's name the column or columns that serve as the foreign key. A foreign key column must be of the same data type and length as the primary key column. A foreign key to a composite primary key must also be a composite made up of the same number of columns with each column having the same data type and length as the corresponding column in the primary key. The sequences of values in indexes on associated foreign and primary key columns may be reversed, however; that is, one may be ascending, the other descending.

Foreign keys need not have indexes, but it is almost always best if they do. If a foreign key does have an index, the optimizer will always use it for referential integrity checking. This is an important performance consideration as will be discussed in Chapter 6 in the section on indexing for performance. The foreign key clause next identifies the single table that the key references. It need not identify that table's primary key column, which is implicit. This feature does not comply exactly with the rules of the relational model, which allow a single referential constraint to reference more than one primary key table. In his book, *The Relational Model for Database Management Version 2* (Reading, Mass.: Addison-Wesley, 1990), Codd describes sibling tables, tables with the same primary key columns but with differing table names. Each sibling table is used for a differing

Box 5.2   Referential integrity information in the catalog tables

- SYSFOREIGNKEYS contains the foreign key constraint name (REL-NAME) and columns that constitute the foreign key.
- SYSRELS contains the foreign key constraint name (RELNAME), name of the parent table, and the primary key delete rule.
- SYSCOLUMNS.KEYSEQ, FOREIGNKEY indicates if the column is part of a primary key or foreign key.
- SYSINDEXES.UNIQUERULE must be P for primary key. SYST-ABLES.CHECKFLAG, CHECKRID, STATUS indicates if the table is in check pending and whether a primary key has been defined. It also has number of dependents of a parent table and number of parents of dependent table.
- SYSTABLESPACE.STATUS indicates if the tablespace is in check pending.
- SYSTABLEPART.CHECKFLAG, CHECKRID indicates if a partition is in check pending.
- SYSCOPY.ICTYPE indicates whether there is a quiese point.

category of information. For example, one Supplier table might be used for domestic suppliers and its sibling used for foreign suppliers with a dependent table containing information common to both. DB2 does not allow a foreign key to reference two parent tables.

The foreign key clause goes on to identify the type of rule to be enforced when rows are deleted from the primary key table. After the keywords ON DELETE, the developer states whether DB2 should RESTRICT the deletion, CASCADE it to the foreign key table, or set the corresponding values in the foreign key to null, SET NULL. In Fig. 5.1, for example, because the developer has specified CASCADE on the PNFK referential constraint, which references the P table, if P10 were deleted from the P table, each occurrence of it, along with the rest of its row, would also be deleted from the SPJ table.

Foreign Keys and Nulls

Foreign and primary key columns need not have the same null attribute. Developers should pay special attention, however, to the null attributes of columns used as foreign keys, particularly composite foreign keys. Inconsistent use of nulls in composite foreign keys could lead to violations of referential integrity.

Whether a foreign key column should allow nulls or not depends on the nature of the data. If in the foreign key table a row's information would make no sense without the associated information in the primary key table, the foreign key column should be declared as NOT NULL. For example, imagine a table, Customer Order, holding information on product orders and including a foreign key to a Customer table that describes customers who have placed the orders. If there can be no order without a customer, there must always be a relationship between the description of an order in the Customer Order table and the description of its customer in the Customer table. Consequently, there must be a foreign key value to the Customer table for every row in Customer Order, and nulls must not be allowed. Some call this an absolute dependency between the two tables.

On the other hand, there need not always be a relationship between rows in primary and foreign key tables. Consider an Employee table describing employees and including a foreign key to a Department table describing the departments to which they are assigned. If the company allows employees to be unassigned, the Employee table's foreign key to the Department table should allow for nulls. Some call such a relationship between primary and foreign key tables a conditional dependency. In this case, whether or not there is a relationship between a row in the Employee table and a department description in the Department table depends on whether or not the employee is assigned to a department. If the company had a rule requiring that every employee be assigned to a department, the relationship between the two tables would be absolute. In the case of composite keys, DB2 considers the entire key null if any one of its columns is null. If an insert into the foreign key columns includes a null, DB2 will allow the insert if it finds a null in any foreign key column. This may result in foreign key values without matching primary key values, a violation of referential integrity. Consider foreign keys on the SN, PN, and JN columns in the SPJ table. If a null appears anywhere in the SN, PN, or JN columns of SPJ, DB2 would allow an insert. This insert would be allowed even though there are no matching primary key values in the P and J tables of P99 and J99.

```
INSERT INTO SPJ
VALUES (unknown, 'P99', 'J99', 200)
```

One way to avoid this problem is to declare all columns in a composite key as NOT NULL. Another way is to declare all of them NOT NULL WITH DEFAULT. The row would not be inserted if P99 and J99 are not primary key values.

Adding Keys

A primary key may be added to an existing table by identifying the key column in an ALTER TABLE statement—for example, ALTER TABLE P PRIMARY KEY (PN). Of course, there must first be a unique index on the primary key column.

Adding a foreign key to an existing table is a bit more complicated. It may be done with an ALTER TABLE statement. For example:

```
ALTER TABLE SPJ
FOREIGN KEY PNFK (PN)
REFERENCES P
ON DELETE RESTRICT;
```

Adding a foreign key, however, places temporary restrictions on the table's use. This is because values that would violate referential integrity may already exist in the foreign key column. After DB2 adds the foreign key, therefore, it does not allow access to the table until the foreign key values have been checked against the corresponding primary key. The table's status is called check pending. The CHECK DATA utility, described in Chapter 16, performs this function. When the utility finds a foreign key value that violates referential integrity, it can delete the value's row and write it in an exception table. (The LIKE function is useful for creating exception tables.) After the utility has removed violations or found none, DB2 lifts the check pending status and allows access to the table.

An ALTER statement can also be used to drop a primary or foreign key and associated referential constraints. When a foreign key is dropped to allow for application-enforced checking of batch updates, the CHECK DATA utility should be executed against the table containing the key after the key is redefined.

5.4 DATA MANIPULATION CONSTRAINTS

When integrity constraints are in effect, a few specific types of data manipulations hold the potential for integrity violations or for unpredictable or anomalous results. DB2 detects some of these situations when it attempts to bind SQL statements that could result in problems. Instead of completing such a bind, DB2 issues an error message. In other cases, DB2 prevents the problems by barring the definition of constraints that could lead to them. When the CREATE or ALTER TABLE statement that poses the problems attempts to execute, DB2 issues an error message.

Let us look at these problematic data manipulations and constraint conditions. Most of the potential problems are due to subtle conditions

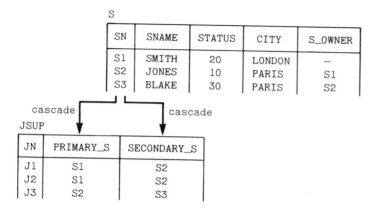

Fig. 5.2 Invalid subselect delete

that are best understood through illustrations. Study of the accompanying examples should clarify the potential problems.

Updating a Primary Key

If DB2 allowed an SQL statement to update more than one primary key value at a time, such processing could produce duplicate values, thus violating entity integrity. Assume, for example, a primary key on an EXAMPLE table's PK column, which includes numeric values ranging in order from 1 to 5. The statement:

```
UPDATE EXAMPLE SET PK = PK + 1
```

would cause each value to be increased by 1. If processing began at the highest value, 5, and worked down in sequence, there would be no problem. There would never be duplicate values. If processing began with any other value—raising 1 to 2, for example—entity integrity would be immediately violated. Since DB2 cannot know the order of processing in advance, it takes no chances and flags such a problematic UPDATE statement as an error at bind time. Similarly, DB2 disallows updates of primary keys with cursors, which hold the same potential problems.

Invalid Delete with Subselect

When a cascade rule is in effect, DB2 will not allow deletions based on a subselect that references the table from which the deletions are being made. This example illustrates the problem: Consider the two tables in Fig. 5.2.

Box 5.3   Potential referential integrity violations

Potential violations detected at bind or run time:

- attempt to delete rows referenced in a subselect
- attempt with a subselect to insert multiple rows in a self-referencing table
- attempt with a WHERE CURRENT OF clause to delete rows in a self-referencing table

Potential violations detected when attempting to define the constraint:

- definition of self-referencing constraint with other than CASCADE constraint
- definition of a delete-connected cycle
- definition of delete-connected tables through multiple paths with differing constraints or with the SET NULL constraint

---

One is the familiar Supplier table, with SN as a primary key. The other is the JSUP table, which shows which suppliers supply which jobs. Each job has both a primary and secondary supplier. The PRIMARY_S and SECONDARY_S columns are foreign keys to the Supplier table, with both the referential integrity rules specified as delete cascade.

The following subselect might be used to delete from the Supplier table all suppliers who are not used as secondary suppliers on any job.

```
DELETE FROM S WHERE SN NOT IN
(SELECT SECONDARY_S
 FROM   JSUP
 WHERE  JSUP.SECONDARY_S = S.SN)
```

The results of this statement, however, will be different depending on the order in which the rows are processed. If SN = S1 is evaluated in the subselect first, the NOT IN clause evaluates as true because S1 is not a secondary supplier. Therefore, S1 is deleted from the Supplier table. Since it is a primary key value, and the cascade rule is in effect, the S1 rows in JSUP are also deleted. When SN = S2 is evaluated in the subselect, the NOT IN clause also returns true, since the previous cascade delete had eliminated the two jobs in which S2 had been secondary supplier. S2, therefore, is also deleted and its deletion cascades to eliminate the J3 row. Now, when SN = S3 is evaluated in the subselect, the NOT IN clause returns true and S3 is deleted.

Suppose, however, that S3 were the first value from the Supplier table to be evaluated in the subselect. In that case, the NOT IN clause would cascade

SN	SNAME	STATUS	CITY	S_OWNER
S1	SMITH	20	LONDON	—
S2	JONES	10	PARIS	S1
S3	BLAKE	30	PARIS	S2
S4	CLARK	20	LONDON	S3
S5	ADAMS	30	ATHENS	S4

S_O

Fig. 5.3 Self-referencing constraints

return false because, at this point in the processing, the J3 row still exists, with S3 as its secondary supplier, and the S3 row will not be deleted. To avoid this kind of anomaly, at bind time, when DB2 encounters a DELETE statement containing this type of subselect combined with a cascade delete rule, instead of binding the statement it issues an error message.

Self-Referencing Constraints

A single table can include both a primary key and a related foreign key. The limitations to changes in the primary key that the foreign key defines are called self-referencing constraints, which enforce hierarchical organizational arrangements. In the supplier example, for instance, if each supplier were owned by another, higher-level supplier, those ownerships might be recorded in a new column in the Supplier table. Fig. 5.3 shows such a modified Supplier table, S_O table, with the S_OWNER column containing the ownership indications. For example, S2 is owned by S1, S3 by S2, and so on. If a foreign key is created on S_OWNER, its rule can enforce the dependent, hierarchical relationships among the suppliers.

By definition, the foreign key in a self-referencing table must specify the DELETE CASCADE rule. The restrict rule would be of little practical value because its enforcement would be limited to barring deletion of any primary key value that had a dependent foreign key value. This would assure that an existing "ownership" relationship could not be removed from the table, but at the cost of greatly limiting changes to the table. In the example, for instance, only S5 could be deleted because it is the only supplier that does not own another.

The DELETE SET NULL rule is not suitable for a self-referencing constraint because it holds the potential for unpredictable results. For example, this statement would call for deletion of any supplier that does not report to another—in other words, any supplier whose S_OWNER value is null:

```
DELETE FROM S_O WHERE S_OWNER IS NULL
```

If DELETE SET NULL were in effect, when the SN = S1 row was deleted, S1 in S_OWNER would be set to null. If the rows were processed in order, when the SN = S2 row was deleted, S2 in the S_OWNER column would be set to null. Eventually, all the rows in this table would be deleted—if the rows were processed in order. If the rows were not processed in order or if the values in the S_OWNER column were not in sequence, fewer rows would be deleted.

With the proper DELETE CASCADE rule in effect, when any primary key value is deleted, all rows with key values below it in the hierarchy of ownerships are also deleted. If S3 were deleted from the S_O table, for example, the deletions would cascade to the SN = S4 row, then to the SN = S5 row. This would be the desired result assuming that a decision had been made to stop doing business with S3 and its subsidiaries.

A self-referencing constraint must be created with an ALTER TABLE statement. This is because the primary key table and primary key must exist before the related foreign key can be defined. If either the DELETE SET NULL or DELETE RESTRICT rule is specified as the self-referencing constraint, DB2 issues an error message when execution of the ALTER TABLE statement defining the invalid constraint is attempted.

Self-referencing tables hold the potential for two other errors. For one, when values are inserted into the self-referencing table, there must be an existing primary key value for every inserted foreign key value. In the example, an attempt to insert a row with an S_OWNER value of S10 would fail because there is no S10 in the primary key. This problem frequently surfaces when a subselect is used to insert values from one table into another, self-referencing table. If DB2 detects such a violation during processing, it issues a negative SQLCODE. The rule is that more than one row cannot be inserted into a self-referencing table with a subselect.

Finally a cursor cannot be used to delete rows from a self-referencing table. The order in which the rows are processed would affect the results.

Cycles

A cycle is a situation in which tables are related to each other through both primary and foreign key relationships. In the simplest case, one table is a primary key table to the other; the second table is a primary key table to the first. For example, consider the tables in Fig. 5.4. One is a modified Job table, or J_S table, that includes a column, SUPER, showing each job's supervisor. Supervisors are employees of course. The JN column is the primary key. The other table is an employee table, which includes a

J_S

JN	JNAME	CITY	SUPER
J1	SORTER	PARIS	E700
J2	PUNCH	ROME	E200
J3	READER	ATHENS	E500
J4	CONSOLE	ATHENS	E300
J5	COLLATOR	LONDON	E800
J6	TERMINAL	OSLO	E100
J7	TAPE	LONDON	E400

restrict

cascade

E

EMPLOYEE	. . .	ASSIGNED_JOB
E100		J6
E200		J2
E300		J4
E400		J7
E500		J3
E600		–
E700		J1
E800		J5

Fig. 5.4 A cycle

column, ASSIGNED_JOB, showing the employee's job assignments. The EMPLOYEE column is the primary key. The SUPER column in the J_S table is defined as a foreign key to the employee table. ASSIGNED_JOB in the employee table is a foreign key to the J_S table. This is a two-table cycle.

Some cycles consist of more than two tables—foreign keys may connect several tables before the loop closes. There are restrictions on the type of delete rules that may be used with either two-table or greater than two-table cycles. The CASCADE DELETE rule may not be used in a two-table cycle. In a cycle with more than two tables, at least one of the foreign keys participating in the cycle must employ the RESTRICT or SET NULL rule. DB2 will issue an error message when a CREATE statement with constraint definitions violating these restrictions attempts to execute.

To understand the kind of problem that might occur in cycles consider what would happen in the example if the foreign key on the SUPER column were defined with the CASCADE rule and that on the ASSIGNED_JOB column were defined with a RESTRICT rule. In that case, every time the row for an employee who is a supervisor is deleted from the Employee table, rows in the J_S table showing that employee as supervisor would also be deleted. Notice what happens when there is an attempt to delete 'E400' from the Employee table. The deletion cascades to the J7 row in J_S table. That deletion, however, is barred by the restrict rule constraining deletions of job numbers that appear in the ASSIGNED_JOB column.

In some cases, even with a valid cycle, some deletions may be impossible. In the example, even if both foreign keys were defined with the restrict rule—a cycle that DB2 would allow—there would be no way to delete most of the rows in both tables. For example, the 'E400' row could not be deleted from the Employee table because of the foreign key restriction on the SUPER column. Neither could the row with 'E400' be deleted from the J_S table because of the ASSIGNED_JOB foreign key's restriction against deleting J7. This kind of difficulty can be avoided in a cycle by defining at least one of the foreign keys with the DELETE SET NULL rule and allowing nulls in the foreign key column.

Delete-Connected Tables

Tables related with a foreign key are called delete-connected tables because a deletion in the primary key table can affect or be affected by the contents of the foreign key table. If the delete rule connecting the two tables is cascade, then tables that are delete connected with the foreign key table are also delete-connected on its primary key table. In other words, a table can be delete connected with its grandparent. In Fig. 5.5a, for example, the J and PJ tables are delete connected by a foreign key on the JN column. Because the JN column's foreign key rule is cascade, the SPJ table, which is delete connected with the PJ table, is also delete connected with the J table.

Problems can arise when two tables are delete connected through more than one path. In Fig. 5.5a, for example, the foreign key relating the J and SPJ tables directly would make those tables delete connected through two paths—the direct connection and the path through the PJ table. Because of the possibility of differing results depending on the order of processing such delete-connected tables, DB2 restricts their definition. The foreign keys that establish a table's multiple delete connections—in the example, PN and JN in the SPJ table—must all be defined to have the same delete rule, and the rule may not be the SET NULL rule. Both must be defined either by the restrict rule or by the cascade rule. DB2 will issue an error message whenever a CREATE or ALTER TABLE statement attempts to define keys that violate these restrictions.

Let us look at one of the problems that might occur if DB2 allowed such multiple path delete connections. In Fig. 5.5b, the foreign key on PN

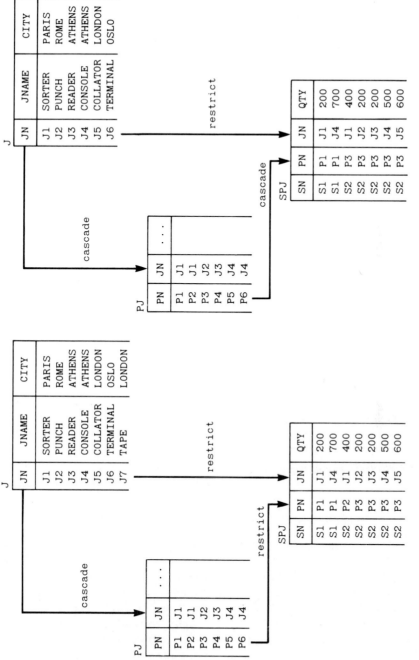

Fig. 5.5 Delete-connected tables

in the SPJ table to the PJ table is defined by the cascade rule. The foreign key on JN in the SPJ table to the J table is defined by the restrict rule. If a statement attempted to delete 'J1' from the J table, if DB2 first processed the cascade rules to the PJ and SPJ tables, because of the cascade J1 would be deleted from all three tables. If DB2 first checked the constraint between the SPJ and J table, it would find J1 as a foreign key value in the J table and restrict all deletions.

ALTER Statements That Invalidate Plans

As we have discussed, DB2 detects the possibility for some of these problematic situations when it binds SQL statements that might raise problems. For example, it will not bind a plan for a statement calling for a cursor update of a primary key column. Suppose, however, that the plan for the cursor update already exists when the primary key is created with an ALTER TABLE statement. In that case, when the ALTER TABLE statement executes, DB2 invalidates the plan and attempts to rebind it on the next attempted execution. That rebind will fail, of course, and the plan will not be usable.

To avoid such unhappy surprises, when developers add a primary key or a foreign key with the CASCADE or SET NULL rule—foreign keys with the RESTRICT rule do not cause any problems—they should try to rebind plans that access the tables. This will uncover any plans that will not rebind successfully, alerting the developer to problems that must be investigated. Alternatively, a developer can look in the catalog tables to determine which plans have been invalidated by the addition of a key. Chapter 14, on application monitoring, describes how to find in the catalog information about the plans and packages that use any given table.

5.5 APPLICATION ENFORCED INTEGRITY

While techniques for coding referential integrity checking in an application are not complicated, the coding itself can be quite complex. We will use simple examples to illustrate the techniques. But real-world situations are likely to be more complicated and not merely because they are likely to entail more complicated logic. An application enforcing integrity must do more than include SQL statements to check constraints and carry out other integrity processing. It must also take steps to prevent changes to the data during the checks, changes that could invalidate the results of the checks.

A description of those steps here would detract from our discussion of referential integrity concepts. An IBM manual, *DB2 Referential Integrity Usage Guide*, describes the data locking strategies required for application enforcement of referential integrity. The following techniques will not provide for referential integrity unless used in conjunction with those locking strategies.

Insert Rules

Inserts of rows containing new primary key values do not require checks of associated foreign keys because the additions pose no threat to referential integrity. Values added to foreign key columns through inserts, on the other hand, must have corresponding primary key values. A row including a job J10 inserted in the SPJ table, for example, would make no sense if there were no J10 in the J table. A program inserting rows in the SPJ table should first check that a row's JN value exists in the J table before allowing the insert.

This check can be coded easily. The following SELECT statement determines whether J10 exists in the J table:

```
SELECT JN
FROM   J
WHERE  JN = 'J10'
```

DB2 communicates the status of a search to programs through SQL-CODEs (discussed in Chapter 9). If DB2 finds any rows in a search, it returns an SQLCODE of zero. After including the above statement in the program, therefore, the programmer can include a test for SQLCODE = 0 and have the program perform the insertion only if the test is positive. Using pseudo-code for clarity, the program might read:

```
SELECT JN
FROM   J
WHERE  JN = 'J10'
IF SQLCODE = 0
   INSERT INTO SPJ (SN, PN, JN, QTY)
   VALUES ('S1','P4','J10',200)
```

Since the insert program is not likely to include the information on J10 required in the J table, a cascade rule probably would not be appropriate. Nor does it appear reasonable to create a job J10 with null values in the J table. The restrict rule seems the best choice in this case, requiring the program to display or print a message indicating that the insert was not allowed.

Update Rules

Updates of primary key values may require changes in foreign key values to maintain referential integrity. Suppose a manager wished to change job

J2 to J10 to indicate a change in its priority. If the change were made in the J table, the existence of any J2 in the SPJ table would violate referential integrity. A cascade update would change all J2s in the SPJ table to J10. Coding for this operation is straightforward:

```
UPDATE J   SET JN='J10' WHERE JN='S2'
UPDATE SPJ SET JN='J10' WHERE JN='S2'
```

A neutralizing rule would change J10 values in the SPJ table to nulls.

A restricted update would allow the change to the J table only if there were no J2s in the SPJ table. This subselect using the NOT EXISTS operator can implement this restricted update rule:

```
UPDATE J   SET JN='J10'
WHERE JN='J2'
AND NOT EXISTS
    (SELECT JN
     FROM SPJ
     WHERE JN='S2')
```

Since the update in this case merely changes the job priority, however, a cascade rule to reflect that change throughout the database might be appropriate.

Updates of foreign keys hold implications similar to those of inserts involving foreign keys. A WHERE . . . NOT EXISTS clause can also be used to implement a restricted rule for foreign key updates. (The EXISTS and NOT EXISTS operators hold a chance of error when they are used to enforce referential integrity because of the possibility of changes to the data between evaluation of the subselect and accompanying update, which will be discussed in Chapter 8.)

Cross-Checking Key Values

A developer can use relatively simple SELECT statements to check whether a database in its current state adheres to referential integrity when only a few tables are involved. The following statement performs a cross-check between two tables with related primary and foreign keys to identify any foreign key values that do not appear in the primary key. The statement refers to the job number example in which JN is the primary key in the J table and a foreign key in the SPJ table. The statement:

```
SELECT SN, PN, JN, QTY
FROM   SPJ
WHERE  NOT EXISTS
    (SELECT JN
     FROM J
     WHERE J.JN = SPJ.JN)
```

returns any row in SPJ containing a job number that does not appear in the J table.

The CHECK DATA utility provides options for cross checking multiple tables. The utility can be used, however, only with DB2 enforced referential integrity. The required foreign keys can be added with an alter statement and dropped after the utility has been executed if it is necessary to enforce the constraints with application code.

5.6 TRACKING INTEGRITY RULES

Referential integrity becomes more complex when many interrelated tables are involved. Programmers will find it difficult to determine or remember integrity rules each time they write a program that changes data in a table. A form like the one in Fig. 5.6 offers a convenient way for developers to record integrity rules for reference by programmers. Each form records rules for how to handle inserts, updates, and deletes of the primary and foreign keys in a single table.

The example form in Fig. 5.6 refers to the S table presented in Fig. 5.7. To illustrate how the form helps manage foreign keys, we have added to the S table an EMPNO column, which is a foreign key to Fig. 5.7's Employee_Responsible table. The Employee_Responsible table includes information about the employee who is responsible for contact with each supplier.

The name of the table for which the rules are recorded is entered at the top of the form. The box in Fig. 5.6 titled "Primary Key" records the rules for dealing with changes to the table's primary key column, or columns for a composite key. Each box titled "Foreign Key" deals with one of the table's foreign key columns. If the table has more than two foreign keys, an additional form would be used.

The primary key column or columns are listed at the left of the Primary Key box. Each column under the heading "Foreign Key Table" deals with a table that contains a foreign key to the primary key. In this case, SN is the primary key column in the S table. The only Foreign Key Table for that column is the SPJ table, which has SN as a foreign key.

The matrix beneath the Foreign Key column indicates the rule to be applied when the primary key has a value updated or removed with a deletion. Cells with a dash indicate that no action is required. Notice that for inserts to the Primary Key column, reference to the Foreign Key column is never required. In the example, if a value in SN in the S table, the primary key, is to be updated, a restricted rule (RR) applies regarding SN in the SPJ table. That is, the update should be allowed only if the value being changed

TABLE NAME: Supplier Table

PRIMARY KEY

COLUMN(S)	FOREIGN KEY TABLE(S) TABLE/ COLUMN(S)			TABLE/ COLUMN(S)			TABLE/ COLUMN(S)			TABLE/ COLUMN(S)			TABLE/ COLUMN(S)		
SN	SPJ														
	SN														
	I	U	D	I	U	D	I	U	D	I	U	D	I	U	D
Insert	—	—	—	—	—	—	—	—	—	—	—	—	—	—	—
Update	—	RR	—	—		—	—		—	—		—	—		—
Delete	—	—	RR	—	—		—	—		—	—		—	—	

Indicate processing for any foreign keys in the table:

FOREIGN KEY

IN ABOVE TABLE COLUMN(S): Empl_No	PRIMARY KEY TABLE TABLE: Employee-Responsible Table COLUMN(S): Empl_No		
	I	U	D
Insert	RR	—	—
Update	—	RR	—
Delete	—	—	—

FOREIGN KEY

IN ABOVE TABLE COLUMN(S):	PRIMARY KEY TABLE TABLE: COLUMN(S):		
	I	U	D
Insert		—	—
Update	—		—
Delete	—	—	—

Fig. 5.6 Referential integrity processing matrix

S Table

SN	SNAME	STATUS	CITY	EMPL_ NO.
S1	SMITH	20	LONDON	0741
S2	JONES	10	PARIS	2561
S3	BLAKE	30	PARIS	2561
S4	CLARK	20	LONDON	0741
S5	ADAMS	30	ATHENS	5222

SPJ Table

SN	PN	JN	QTY
S1	P1	J1	200
S1	P1	J4	700
S2	P3	J1	400
S2	P3	J2	200
S2	P3	J3	200
S4	P6	J3	300
S4	P6	J7	300
S5	P2	J2	200

Employee_Responsible Table

EMPL_NO	NAME	TEL_NO
0741	SMITH	4251
1624	ROGERS	4277
2561	PETERS	4242
3442	JONES	4203
5222	PEPLINSKI	4264

Fig. 5.7 Tables for matrix example in Fig. 5.6

in the S table does not exist in the SPJ table. The same rule applies to deletions.

These rules make sense because information in the SPJ table about the jobs serviced by the original supplier would no longer be associated with that supplier if SN were changed in SPJ. When a cascade rule is called for— that is, when changes to the Primary Key column should cause corresponding changes in the foreign key column—the entry would be "CR" for "cascade rule." That entry might also include an estimate of the number of rows in the foreign key likely to be affected, a useful piece of information for estimating the change's impact on performance.

A Foreign Key column from the table in question is listed at left in the Foreign Key box and the table and primary key to which it refers are identified under the box's Primary Key Table heading. In this case, the EMPNO is the foreign key referring to EMPNO in the Employee_Responsible table. The matrix below the Foreign Key column records the rules for handling changes to the column. If a foreign key value is deleted, no action is required in the primary key. In this case, adding an EMPNO to the S_Table would violate referential integrity if there is no employee with that number. The programmer therefore should apply a restrict rule to additions to the foreign key EMPNO.

5.7 SUMMARY

Referential integrity requires that every foreign key value, other than null, have a corresponding primary key value. If changes to the data were allowed to violate that rule, the tables would soon become meaningless and impossible to use. Several rules governing data changes will protect against referential integrity violations. Developers define the rules to DB2 when tables are created and can subsequently change the rules with the alter statement. DB2 then enforces the rule whenever changes that will affect the key are attempted. Developers must know how to implement all integrity rules and how to use DB2's referential integrity facilities. They must also be aware of limitations on certain data manipulations imposed by DB2's implementation of integrity rules that insure predictable and repeatable results.

EXERCISES

5.1. The statement, ALTER TABLE SPJ PRIMARY KEY (SN, PN, JN), will not execute successfully. What are three possible causes of the problem?

5.2. The following statement will not execute successfully:

```
UPDATE SPJ
   SET   PN = 'P4'
   WHERE JN = 'J2'
```

What is a possible cause of the problem?

5.3. A table, DEPENDENTS, storing information on employees' dependents, has the EMPLOYEE_NO column as a foreign key to the EMPLOYEE table. What delete constraint would be appropriate for handling cases when employees leave the company?

5.4. A table, SUPERVISORS, containing information on which employees are assigned to supervise which jobs, has a foreign key to the employee table. What delete constraint would be appropriate for handling cases when employees assigned as supervisors leave the company?

5.5. An update of the PN column, a primary key in the PARTS table, will not execute. What might be the problem?

6

Indexing for Performance

6.1 INTRODUCTION

An index on a table works much like a book index. Rather than scanning an entire tablespace to find a particular piece of information, the system finds the subject's listing in the index and follows a pointer directly to its location. Just as well-constructed book indexes can save readers time, well-designed indexes in DB2 can save I/O and processor time. DB2 offers developers a number of index options and, via the optimizer, makes the best use of the indexes developers provide. The choices developers make in designing indexes determine how good that best use will be.

DB2 creates indexes by column (or several columns in the case of composite indexes). Developers can create as many indexes as they like, but because DB2 must use resources to maintain indexes—no matter whether they prove useful—developers should choose columns to index and the types of indexes to use with care. These decisions require an understanding of how data are to be used. Although developers need not concern themselves with the details of how DB2 employs specific indexes, an understanding of its indexing scheme will also help them make the best index design choices.

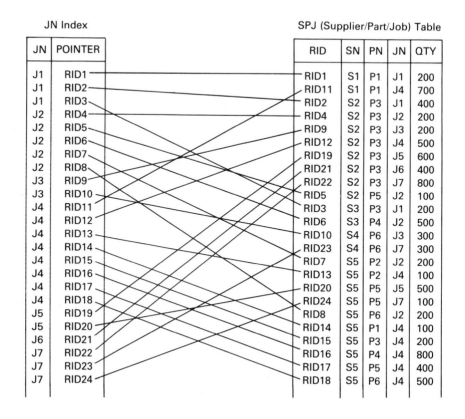

JN Index   SPJ (Supplier/Part/Job) Table

JN	POINTER
J1	RID1
J1	RID2
J1	RID3
J2	RID4
J2	RID5
J2	RID6
J2	RID7
J2	RID8
J3	RID9
J3	RID10
J4	RID11
J4	RID12
J4	RID13
J4	RID14
J4	RID15
J4	RID16
J4	RID17
J4	RID18
J5	RID19
J5	RID20
J6	RID21
J7	RID22
J7	RID23
J7	RID24

RID	SN	PN	JN	QTY
RID1	S1	P1	J1	200
RID11	S1	P1	J4	700
RID2	S2	P3	J1	400
RID4	S2	P3	J2	200
RID9	S2	P3	J3	200
RID12	S2	P3	J4	500
RID19	S2	P3	J5	600
RID21	S2	P3	J6	400
RID22	S2	P3	J7	800
RID5	S2	P5	J2	100
RID3	S3	P3	J1	200
RID6	S3	P4	J2	500
RID10	S4	P6	J3	300
RID23	S4	P6	J7	300
RID7	S5	P2	J2	200
RID13	S5	P2	J4	100
RID20	S5	P5	J5	500
RID24	S5	P5	J7	100
RID8	S5	P6	J2	200
RID14	S5	P1	J4	100
RID15	S5	P3	J4	200
RID16	S5	P4	J4	800
RID17	S5	P5	J4	400
RID18	S5	P6	J4	500

This index includes pointers from each indexed value to the location of every row that includes it. A search for rows with job number 3, for example, would find J3 in the JN index and follow the pointers to the appropriate pages (RID stands for row or record identification).

Fig. 6.1 A simple index

6.2 THE B-TREE

The most rudimentary database index is the simple index (Fig. 6.1), which has one entry for, and a pointer to, every row in the indexed table. The system scans the index sequentially to find the desired entry, an inefficient process. An index on a 6-byte column of a million-row table would fill 2500 pages, for example, which would require a lengthy search for each access. Instead of a simple index, DB2 uses the B-tree (Fig. 6.2), which provides

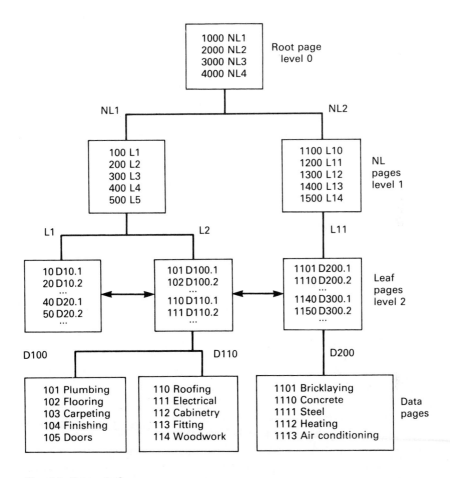

Fig. 6.2 B-tree index

pointers from one level of index pages to another with each level holding increasingly narrower ranges of values. The lowest level holds an entry for each unique value in the indexed column or columns and a pointer to each row. By following a path down through the appropriate ranges, DB2 can find a specific row in a very large database with only a few I/O operations.

Matching Index Scans

A search for information about Flooring Job 102 in a job table could follow a B-tree index on job numbers like that shown in Fig. 6.2. The search begins at the B-tree's top page, called the *root page*. The root page entries represent upper range limits. In the example, the ranges run from 0 to 1000, 1001 to 2000, 2001 to 3000, and 3001 to 4000. The pointers for each range point in this case to nonleaf (NL) pages 1, 2, 3, and 4 respectively. These are called NL pages to distinguish them from the lowest level of pages, called *leaf pages*, which, like a simple index, contain a pointer to every row in the table. Unlike a simple index, the B-tree's leaf pages do not list every entry in the indexed column. Instead they list each unique value followed by pointers to the rows containing each occurrence of the value.

DB2 checks the search value, 102, against the root page's range values; finds it falls within the first range; follows that range's pointer to NL 1; and checks the search value against the ranges there. This time DB2 finds that the value falls in the second range, between 101 and 200, and follows its pointer to leaf page 2. By scanning that page, DB2 finds the search value itself and follows the pointer to the data page containing the value's row, data page 100. This search, called a *matching index scan*, requires in this case only four I/O operations. If the index were frequently used, the root page and some NL pages would likely remain in the bufferpool so only two or fewer I/O would be required.

Nonmatching Scans

DB2 can use the B-tree index in several other ways. Because pointers chain the leaf pages in sequence (indicated by the arrows between leaf page 1 and leaf page 2 in Fig. 6.2), when a sequential retrieval is requested, DB2 may scan across this level rather than starting at the root page and following the tree down to each value. DB2 may begin such a scan, called a *nonmatching index scan*, at the first leaf page and continue until it finds the value or range of values it needs. Or it may perform a matching scan to locate the starting point for the nonmatching scan. For example, DB2 might satisfy a request for data on jobs with identification numbers between 100 and 1000 by performing a matching scan to locate 100 in the leaf pages and then scanning across the leaf pages and retrieving the appropriate rows until reaching 1000. A request for information about jobs with IDs of less than 500 would begin a nonmatching scan at the beginning of the chained leaf pages, stopping at 500. A request for jobs with IDs greater than 500 would perform a matching scan to locate 500 and scan to the end of the leaf pages.

In some cases, DB2 will find the information it needs in the index using a matching or nonmatching scan and not have to read data pages. These searches are called matching or nonmatching scans without data reference. Composite indexes are good candidates for index scans without data reference. A request may want to select SN, PN, and JN. If there was a composite index on those columns in the SPJ table, DB2 could fulfill the request without having to reference the data pages.

Index Lookaside

Index lookaside can be used after absolute positioning (accessing the root and NL pages and locating the required value in the leaf page.) The current leaf page is checked for the next required value. If it is not found, the leaf page to the right is checked. If the value is not found, the immediately higher NL page is checked. If the required value is still not found, matching index scan is used. A matching index scan is sometimes referred to as absolute positioning.

Index lookaside avoids absolute positioning for each value, the buffer manager does not release a page until it moves to the next page, and prefetch can be used on the leaf pages. These factors result in a significant reduction in the number of getpages, physical I/O, lock requests, and CPU time using index lookaside. This technique is particularly useful for the inner table of nested-loop and hybrid joins, correlated subselects, repeated execution of any SQL statement that processes multiple rows, and a singleton select in a programming loop. (Joins and correlated subselects will be discussed in Chapters 7 and 11.) Index lookaside is not an option of the optimizer. It is a technique coded into DB2 processing. Therefore the only indication of its use is a reduction in resource consumption as seen in the accounting trace records or by turning on the performance trace.

6.3   USE OF MULTIPLE INDEXES

DB2 can use multiple indexes on a table to satisfy multiple predicates joined by AND or OR. The qualifying RIDs (row identifiers) are obtained from the indexes for each of the predicates, sorted, and duplicates eliminated—a union process for OR; intersect for AND. From the resulting list, DB2 retrieves the data from the data pages in sequence as they appear on the DASD using list prefetch—up to 32 pages are read with a single I/O-like sequential prefetch.

Consider the following two SELECT statements assuming a separate index on SN and PN.

```
SELECT SN, PN, JN, QTY SELECT SN, PN, JN, QTY
FROM   SPJ  FROM SPJ
WHERE  SN = 'S5' WHERE SN = 'S5'
AND    PN = 'P5' OR PN = 'P5'
```

Figure 6.3 shows the RIDs obtained from the index for S5 and P5 and the RIDs in sequence as a result of a sort. For an AND condition, the RIDs

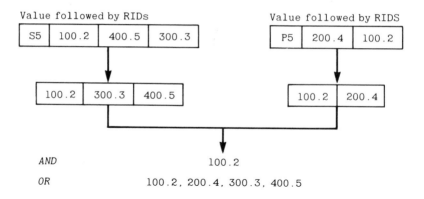

Fig. 6.3 Use of multiple indexes

that appear in both temporary lists are identified. RID of 100.2 is the only row that satisfies both predicates combined by the AND condition so only one I/O is needed to a data page.

Similar processing takes place for an OR condition except that the RIDs that appear in both temporary lists are identified and duplicates eliminated. RIDs of 100.2, 200.4, 300.3, and 400.5 qualify in the example. Notice that the resulting RIDs are in sequence as they appear on DASD allowing for the use of list prefetch. The RIDs are sorted in a RID pool before retrieving pages in sequence using list prefetch. The RID pool will be discussed in Chapter 12.

6.4 BALANCING THE B-TREE

The number of I/O operations necessary for a matching index scan depends on the number of levels in the index. This depends in turn on the table's size, the indexed column's length, and on whether the index includes only unique values or allows redundancy. Appendix B describes how to determine the number of index pages and levels needed given that information. Here we will consider index space requirements from the viewpoint of the index's function.

From that perspective, the key point is that the leaf page level must hold enough index entries and associated pointers to point to every row in the table. For indexes on columns in which each value is unique—called, appropriately, *unique indexes*—the leaf pages must hold one entry and one pointer for every row. The pointer is a 4-byte RID indicating the row's location in the data pages. The first three bytes reference the data page, and the last byte indicates the page directory slot that contains the offset within the page where the row is located. For nonunique columns, the index does not repeat redundant values. Instead it contains an entry for each distinct value along with the RIDs for up to 255 rows that contain the value. If there are more than 255 rows with the value, it is repeated along with the additional RIDs up to 255 and so on. We will limit this discussion on space requirements to unique indexes.

A single index page contains about 3563 bytes of usable space. If the unique index column is 10 bytes in length, an index page will hold about 255 values and their associated pointers (number of entries = 3563 bytes/ (10 bytes length + 4 bytes RID)). If the table contains 255 or fewer rows, the entire index can fit on one page. In this case, the root page is also the leaf page, resulting in a one-level index.

When rows are added to this table—and their index column values to the index—eventually the total will exceed 255; then the index will need more than one page. To provide it, DB2 splits the root page into two pages, each containing half the index values and their pointers. It then creates a new root page with an entry for each of the two ranges' upper values and associated pointers to the appropriate leaf pages. As rows continue to be added, eventually one of the leaf pages will be filled. At that point, DB2 splits the page, dividing its values. It must then account for the new ranges in the root page, replacing the original range entry and pointer with two range values and pointers to the new pages. This is referred to as insert processing. A more efficient method for creating an index is build processing, which will be discussed in Chapter 16.

This splitting process keeps the B-tree in balance, which means that a matching scan for every value in the table requires the same number of reads. If DB2 did not perform this balancing when the leaf page filled and instead merely added another NL page for the additional entries, scans for values down the path containing that range would often have to read both the original and added pages; requiring additional I/O operations. Since the pages would most likely be needed down the most frequently used paths, the extra I/O operations needed in such an unbalanced tree could be especially costly.

Since in the example the root page can hold 255 values and their pointers, DB2 can continue splitting leaf pages within the two-level index until they total that number. At that point, the index can contain about 65,025 values: 255 leaf pages each with 255 values (255 * 255 = 65,025). If more rows are added, DB2 must split the root page again and begin another level—this time a NL level. This three-level index can contain over 16 million unique values. The root page can point to 255 NL pages. Each of the NL pages can point to 255 leaf pages, each of which can point to 255 rows (255 NL pages * 255 leaf pages per NL page * 255 rows per leaf page = 16,581,375 rows).

As rows continue to be added, DB2 will continue to add levels to the index. (Once all values in a leaf or NL page are deleted, the page is removed from the B-tree.) A B-tree of more than three levels can degrade performance for several reasons: A matching scan requires an I/O operation for each level, and the page splitting needed to keep a large index balanced requires I/O and CPU time and causes the index pages to be scattered across DASD. The system catalog table SYSIBM.SYSINDEXES includes the number of levels in each index and the leaf distribution—the percentage of pages separating what should be contiguous leaf pages. A leaf distribution of 20, for example, means that 20 percent of the pages are no longer contiguous—perhaps 60 pages are interspersed between what should be 300 contiguous pages. If a table exhibits poor response times and SYSIBM.SYSINDEXES indicates a frequently used index on it has more than three levels or widely distributed pages, the developer should consider reducing that number. If the excessive number of levels has been caused by page splitting, reorganizing the index—that is, rebuilding it to make physical storage more efficient—will reduce the number of levels and leaf distribution.

Another way to reduce the number of levels, beyond storing the index as efficiently as possible, is to shorten the indexed column or columns—perhaps splitting off part of a long composite index into a separate index to allow more entries to fit on each page. (Columns more than 30 to 50 bytes long make poor candidates for indexes in any case because they fill pages rapidly, requiring frequent page splitting.)

Another way to reduce the number of levels in a clustering index is to partition the table's tablespace. A partitioned tablespace requires one clustering index, which is partitioned into the same number of parts as is the tablespace. In a few cases, including in regard to the clustering index, DB2 manages each partition as if it were a separate tablespace.

Indeed a partition is a separate VSAM dataset. Each index partition therefore indexes only a fraction of the table rows. If a three-level index cannot hold enough entries for the complete table, it may hold enough entries for half the table or some smaller fraction. Indexes to a partitioned tablespace other than the clustering index, however, must cover the entire table. At present, it is best not to use partitioning if more than one index is required on the table in most cases. The cost of maintaining the additional indexes with the utilities is frequently excessive.

6.5 SELECTING COLUMNS TO INDEX

DB2 lets designers create indexes on as many of a table's columns as they wish. Since they may also create composite indexes, they may in fact create

---

Box 6.1   Characteristics of columns that benefit from an index

---

- Primary key and foreign key columns
- Columns that must have unique values
- Columns that have aggregates computed frequently
- Columns used to test for the existence of a value
- Columns that are searched or joined over less than 5 to 10 percent of the rows when considering a nonclustering index
- Columns that are searched or joined over less than 30 to 50 percent of the rows when considering a clustering index
- Columns frequently used together in a WHERE clause can benefit from a composite index to avoid maintaining multiple indexes
- Columns frequently used in an ORDER BY, GROUP BY, and DISTINCT clause

---

more indexes than there are columns. Indexes need processing resources, however. Each time a row is inserted or deleted, for example, a corresponding operation must be performed on each of its table's indexes. Whenever an indexed value is changed, the RID for its entry in the leaf pages must be deleted from its original location and inserted in its new place. Notice in Fig. 6.2, for example, that if the plumbing ID were changed from 101 to 11, the index entry would have to be deleted from page L2 and instered in L1.

Whenever DB2 loads or recovers a table, it must build or rebuild each index to it. Whenever it reorganizes a tablespace, it must also rebuild the indexes. The index itself may need to be reorganized (rebuilt) more frequently than the tablespace as a result of index page splitting. Finally indexes require disk space. Using indexes efficiently is a matter of selecting those whose performance benefits outweigh these costs. The benefits depend on the way the data are to be used and on table size.

Columns to Index

Indexes provide the most benefits when they are used for columns that are frequently searched or joined over a small percentage of their rows, say 5 to 10 percent. Since primary and foreign keys are often used in those ways, they are good candidates for indexes. Indexing columns for which aggregates (counts, sums, and averages) are frequently computed can provide performance gains because DB2 can compute those values directly from the index without having to read data pages. The same principle applies for columns for which minimum, maximum, or distinct values are frequently sought.

If a column must have unique values—a primary key, for example, or a column listing bin identifiers—the designer should create a unique index for it. The optimizer favors unique indexes when equal predicates are specified on the column with the unique index.

6.6   THE VALUE OF CLUSTERING

The clustering index holds the most potential for performance gains. With a clustering index, DB2 takes responsibility for maintaining rows in sequence on the clustering index columns as long as there is free space. The table rows must be sorted according to values in the indexed column (or columns) before the data are loaded or a costly reorganization will be needed. DB2 maintains clustering by placing inserted rows in the indexed column's sequence on available free space in the data pages. DB2 can then process the table in that order efficiently. If it must follow an index sequence that does not correspond to the row sequence—a nonclustering index—it may have to reread data pages to identify all the qualifying rows unless list prefetch is used. As we will see, this difference holds significant performance implications particularly when sets of values or ranges are accessed and when data is processed in sequence.

Clustered Indexes and Retrievals

An example illustrates the value of a clustered index in retrievals. Consider a Part table with 10,000 rows on 200 data pages. Suppose for simplicity that an equal number of parts are located in 20 cities across the country. The cardinality of the city column is 20—that is, 20 distinct values appear in the column. A tablespace scan to select all parts located in Dallas requires 200 I/O operations—one for each page that DB2 must read. Let us see whether an index will improve on that performance.

Since parts are dispersed equally among the 20 cities, each city appears in 5 percent of the rows. This percentage—one divided by the number of distinct values—is the filter factor (FF). Multiplying the FF times the total number of rows yields the number of times the value appears in the column—in this case, 500. Suppose there was a nonclustering index on the city column. The leaf pages would contain an entry for each city followed by the RIDs for the 500 rows in which the city appears (Fig. 6.4). If DB2 had to follow each pointer to retrieve each row, it could require 500 I/O, reading each of 200 data pages 2.5 times on average. (In addition, the B-tree

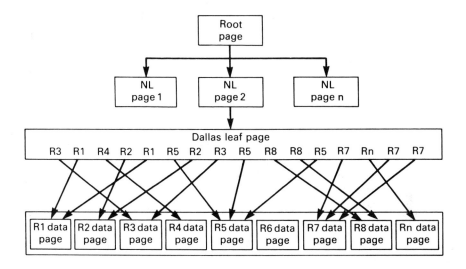

Fig. 6.4 I/O required using a nonclustered index

would have to be traversed 500 times, and if it is a 3-level index, that is
1500 I/O to the index pages in addition to the 500 I/O to the data pages).

In many cases, however, DB2 will use list prefetch for a single index.
Under this approach, it sorts the RIDs, eliminates duplicates, and issues
one I/O for each of up to 32 pages as in the multiple index processing. And
because duplicate RIDs are eliminated, no page need be read more than
once. In the example, only 7 I/O (ceiling 200/32) to the data pages are
needed, the same as a tablespace scan with sequential prefetch. The tablespace scan has an advantage in some cases since no index pages need to be
processed and no sort of the RIDs is required.

A clustering index has advantages for an index with a low cardinality,
20 in this case. All of the Dallas rows will be stored together in the data
pages as indicated in Fig. 6.5. To find information on Dallas parts, DB2
would perform a matching scan to locate the first Dallas entry in the leaf
pages. Then it would keep reading the leaf pages in order, dipping down to
the data pages, until it reached the last Dallas entry. After locating the first
entry, it can use sequential prefetch on the leaf and data page holding Dallas
parts. Since Dallas rows represent about 5 percent of the total, they will
require about 5 percent of the 200 data pages or 10 pages. Prefetch can
reduce the number to 2 I/O. With the clustering index, therefore, DB2 will
find all Dallas parts with only 10 I/O operations plus the few I/O needed
to search the index for the first Dallas entry and scan the leaf pages. The
formula for calculating the number of I/O, excluding index accesses,

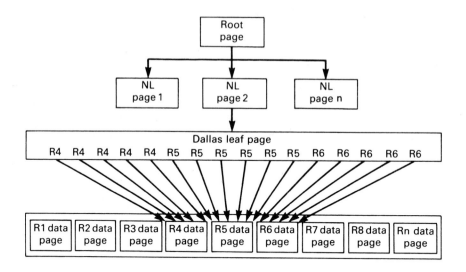

Fig. 6.5 I/O required using a clustered index

needed to locate all rows containing a value when the column containing the value has a clustering index is I/O = (FF * NPAGES).

Using an Index to Avoid a Sort

Clustering is valuable when DB2 must process a column's values in sequence. The three SQL operations, ORDER BY, GROUP BY, and DISTINCT described in Chapter 7 all require such processing. If a column is specified in an ORDER BY, GROUP BY, or DISTINCT operation and there is not a suitable index on the column, DB2 must sort it to put it in sequence before returning even one row to a user. If there is an index with a reasonably high cluster ratio—percent of rows in sequence—it can be used to retrieve the rows in sequence and return the rows immediately one-by-one. The leaf pages are scanned, dipping down to the data pages to pull the rows in sequence. DB2 cannot simply return rows from the data pages in order even if the cluster ratio is 100 percent since at execution time rows may have been inserted out of sequence. (The values on the leaf pages are always maintained in sequence on the indexed values through page splitting.)

Clustering and Joins

A clustered index provides performance gains by allowing for merge joins without a sort on the inner and outer table. DB2 performs joins in three

---

Box 6.2 Characteristics of columns that benefit from a clustering index

---

- Column with a low index cardinality or skewed distribution (if an index is required)
- Column frequently searched or joined over a range of values using predicates such as BETWEEN, >, <, or string search (LIKE)
- Column frequently processed in sequence using the operators ORDER BY, GROUP BY, and DISTINCT
- Primary key column is a good candidate for frequent cursor repositioning, sorting, or range or string searches
- Foreign key column is a good candidate for frequent one to many joins (the many foreign values would be clustered together)

---

ways. In one, the *nested-loop join*, it retrieves a value from the column to be joined in one table, scans the second table's column looking for matches, and creates a joined row for each match it finds. Then it repeats the process, retrieving another value from the first table, called the *outer table*, doing a matching index scan on the second, or inner, table for matches, and so forth. It continues this nested-loop process until all the matches are found. Each time DB2 retrieves a new value from the outer table, it uses index lookaside or does a matching index scan on the inner table.

If on the other hand the column values were stored in sequence, DB2 can find all the matches with just a single pass through the two tables, a process referred to as a *merge join*. If either or both of the two tables had been stored according to a clustering index on the column to be joined, the columns would be in sequence, and the optimizer would probably use the index in a merge join without any additional sort needed for the column.

The hybrid join, which combines elements of the nested-loop and merge joins, also benefits from a clustering index on the outer table since it must be processed in sequence as will be seen in Chapter 11.

Columns That Benefit from Clustering

Box 6.2 summarizes the characteristics of columns that benefit from a clustering index. No one column will have all of the characteristics. Some columns will have some characteristics that indicate that the column should have the clustering index, but other columns will also have some of the characteristics. It is an important but difficult decision and many tradeoffs need to be considered.

The primary key column is often chosen to have the clustering index for cursor repositioning to be discussed in Chapter 9. It is not necessary, however, when using the OPTIMIZE FOR ''n'' ROWS clause also discussed in the chapter. There remains the advantage of having the clustering index on the primary key for batch processing as discussed in Chapter 9. The foreign key is a good candidate for clustering, particularly if there are many foreign key rows for a given primary key value. Joins will be enhanced by having the many foreign key values clustered together on the data pages.

The choice of the column to have the clustering index depends on the type of processing. If mostly equal predicates are specified on a column with a unique index, clustering has no advantage over a nonclustering index that is often the case for the primary key. Also if mostly index only processing is done, clustering has no advantage since the values are always in sequence in the index pages for clustering and nonclustering indexes.

It has been seen that there are significant advantages to having a clustering index. It is important for the designer to designate the clustering index. If no index is created with the parameter CLUSTER, then the first index created or more precisely the index with the lowest OBID (object identifier) will be used to determine where to insert the row. The reorganization utility, however, will not place the rows in sequence on this index, and one of the parameters of the utility cannot be used as will be seen in Chapter 16.

Only one index can be defined explicitly as the clustering index. The cluster ratio is maintained for all indexes, however. Surprisingly, developers have found that several of their indexes will have a reasonably high cluster ratio of around 40 to 60 percent and are used by the optimizer efficiently.

6.7   GENERATING PRIMARY KEYS

Designers frequently place the clustering index on the primary key column. This can result in performance problems if the primary key is a generated value—a sequence number. In some instances, a table will not include a natural primary key column—no combination of the table's meaningful columns other than the entire row will include all unique values. It is still necessary, however, to identify uniquely each row in such a table with a primary key for referential and entity integrity, joins, and reestablishing position after a cursor is closed. In that case, the designer must provide for a column that includes only unique values. There are a number of ways to do this.

One way is to have an application assign numbers to rows in sequence as they are added to the table. There are drawbacks to this solution. The application could keep track of the last number used by storing it in a work table each time a row is inserted. This can result in lock contention, however, since each insert would require a select of the last sequence number and an update of the last sequence number used. Another technique is to use the maximum aggregate to determine the last sequence number stored in the table.

```
SELECT MAX(SEQNO)
FROM   S
```

If SEQNO has a descending index, the first leaf page will contain the last sequence number and can be obtained by DB2 with a one-fetch index scan. The maximum aggregate avoids having to maintain a work table and reduces potential lock contention somewhat. But still the last sequence number must be read, and if the new row is frequently inserted on the page containing the last row inserted in rapid succession, lock contention can result. This would be a likely occurrence if there was a clustering index on the sequence number.

Performance is degraded significantly when maintaining an index on a sequence number. There is potential for lock contention not only on the data pages but also on the index pages for clustering and nonclustering indexes. The new sequence number must be inserted on the last leaf page, which will become full quickly and be split leaving behind a half full page unlikely to receive any additional values. The NL pages will grow with the growth of the leaf pages since they must accommodate references to a large number of half-full leaf pages. And after more inserts, a new root page will need to be added increasing the number of levels in the B-tree. (Recall from Section 3.8 that a page split requires a lock on the next higher page and that could mean effectively locking 40,000 rows.) It will be necessary to reorganize the index frequently, which may be acceptable if the transaction rate is sufficiently low so as not to result in lock contention on the index and data pages.

Another method of generating primary key values is to use a pseudo-random number generator algorithm to assign a number to each new row. The microsecond portion of the TIMESTAMP data type works effectively as a random number generator, supplying up to 999,999 usually unique values. MAX(SEQNO), a random number generator, or microsecond portion of TIMESTAMP may occasionally produce a duplicate number—the TIMESTAMP when more than one processor executes transactions simultaneously or when processing is done across time zones. DB2 will return an SQLCODE of -803 when there is an attempt to add a duplicate to a unique index. The application using either of these devices should test for that code and regenerate a row's primary key value when it is encountered. The complete TIMESTAMP will usually provide unique values but requires 10 bytes, which can add significantly to storage and processing requirements if it is not required for other purposes.

Another problem with generated primary key values is that DB2 cannot be used to enforce referential integrity on the true primary and foreign key. For example, there can be an order in a dependent table without customer information in the parent table.

A generated primary key column will usually have values that are meaningless to users, exacting a performance cost while providing them little benefit. DB2 will have to maintain an index on the column, which will be searched or used in joins only rarely if at all. One compromise solution is to create a composite index, placing the generated column after one or more columns that are frequently searched and joined. Such an index will be slightly less efficient for the meaningful columns than if they had their own. For one thing, fewer meaningful values will fit on each index page. But the arrangement avoids maintaining one virtually useless index on the meaningless primary key. Whenever possible, it is best to use a meaningful primary key.

6.8 INDEX CARDINALITY AND COMPOSITE INDEX DESIGN

In deciding whether to perform a tablespace or index scan, the optimizer analyzes the amount of redundancy in the indexed column (or columns in the case of composite indexes). If the optimizer determines a high level of redundancy, it will probably assume that a tablespace scan will be more efficient than using the index. The RUNSTATS utility analyzes redundancy by counting or estimating the number of distinct values a column or columns contain, called *index cardinality* in DB2's parlance, and estimating the number of rows and pages to be processed.

The optimizer estimates how many rows any given SQL statement is likely to return in relation to the total number of rows or pages. Again assuming an even distribution of values, if the statement is searching for rows based on an equality—WHERE CITY = 'DALLAS', for example— the CITY column's cardinality gives a good estimate of the number of rows likely to be returned. Each distinct value has an equal chance of occurring. If there are 20 distinct values, each has 1 in 20, or .05, chance of occurring. That probability, the FF, is one divided by the column's cardinality. The number of rows likely to include any given value is calculated by multiplying the FF times the number of rows in the table. Generally, the higher the cardinality and the lower the FF for an SQL statement, the more likely the optimizer is to use an index in satisfying it.

If the criteria for searching a single table includes an AND condition—WHERE CITY = 'DALLAS' AND WEIGHT = 100, for example—the probability of any given combination of values occurring is calculated by multiplying the FFs for each predicate. If there are 50 possible weights, that predicate's FF is .02. Combining the FFs for the city and weight predicates in a composite index results in an FF of .0001 (.05 * .02). The optimizer, however, will not always know a column's cardinality. When a statement requires a search of columns included in a composite index, the optimizer may calculate an estimate of the number of rows to be returned from only partial cardinality information. The cardinality information available for any given search on composite index columns depends on the order in which the columns were declared in the index and on the make up of the search criteria. This point will become clear as we look at the cardinality information DB2 keeps and how that information applies to specific searches.

The catalog tables include three cardinality measures:

- FIRSTKEYCARD is the number of distinct values in a single indexed column or in the leading column of a composite index. It is recorded in the catalog table, SYSIBM.SYSINDEXES. The optimizer uses FIRSTKEYCARD to determine redundancy for single-column indexes and for composite indexes if the first column, but not all the columns, is specified.

- COLCARD is the number of distinct values in the first column of a single column or composite index. It is recorded in SYSIBM.SYSCOLUMNS.

- FULLKEYCARD is the number of distinct values in a composite index. It is also recorded in SYSIBM.SYSINDEXES.

If the column is indexed, COLCARD and FIRSTKEYCARD will be the same. If the column is not indexed, the user can request that RUNSTATS estimate the column's cardinality, and it will be placed in COLCARD. Also it is advisable to have RUNSTATS collect the COLCARD for the nonleading columns in a composite index. Having RUNSTATS calculate a cardinality estimate can increase the utility's cost somewhat but generally is a good investment. The optimizer uses COLCARD to determine redundancy for composite indexes in certain cases depending on how an SQL statement's predicate is formulated and to determine join strategies.

If all the columns in a composite index are specified in a statement's predicate as equality criteria, the optimizer uses FULLKEYCARD to determine the FF. If all the columns of a composite index are not specified as equality criteria in the predicate—that is, if the nonleading columns are specified with some other scalar operator or not used at all—the optimizer can use the missing column's COLCARD value to calculate the FF.

Notice that these three values, FIRSTKEYCARD, FULLKEYCARD, and COLCARD, provide information about all the columns in a composite index. Suppose, for example, that there is a composite index on the PN, SN, and JN columns in the SPJ table with the columns having been declared in just that order. In this case, the FIRSTKEYCARD value is the SN column's cardinality. The FULLKEYCARD value is the composite index's cardinality—the number of distinct combinations of the SN, PN, and JN values. In addition, there may be COLCARD values for any of the individual columns as discussed in Chapter 16.

If all the columns in a composite index are specified in a statement's predicate as equality criteria, FULLKEYCARD provides an excellent cardinality value. The search is looking for one particular combination of the composite columns' values. And if the leading column alone is specified as an equality, FIRSTKEYCARD's cardinality value is accurate. If all of the columns are not specified as equality criteria, however—if some are specified with some other scalar operator or not at all—the optimizer must apply special rules.

If the leading column of a composite index is not specified as part of the search criteria, the optimizer will not choose the index for a matching index scan. This is because, without having the leading portion of a composite value to use in the search, DB2 has nothing to match against the B-tree's root page and NL page range values. Consider the composite key on SN, PN, and JN. In this example, SN is CHAR (2), PN is CHAR (5), and JN CHAR (4). Now suppose the table containing these columns has 10,000 rows, ranging from "S1P0001J001" to "S9P9999J999".

(Columns with differing data types can be used in a composite index. If character data types are included, alphanumeric values determine sequence—"blank" then "A" to "Z" then "0" to "9". Trailing blanks complete any character values that do not fill a column. For example, "CDX" comes before "5B_".)

The range values for the example index's root page might be "S2P0001-J001", "S3P0001J001", "S4P0001J001", and so on. This predicate would define a search for the quantity of part number P1280 being used on job J004: WHERE PN = 'P1280' and JN = 'J004'. Because SN is not specified, a matching scan for that value—"??P1280J004"—is not possible because there is no way of knowing what range it falls within. A nonmatching scan of the leaf pages for the value, however, might be more efficient than a tablespace scan, and DB2 might well choose a nonmatching scan in this case. Generally though, it is not efficient to maintain a composite index when the leading column is not usually specified as part of the criteria for searches of the table.

Now consider a search for parts supplied by supplier S4—WHERE SN

= 'S4'. DB2 may perform a matching scan at least through the root page and NL pages where the range value 'S4P0001J0001' points to 'S4' values in the leaf pages. DB2 can then scan the leaf pages to complete the search.

If the predicate includes the first two columns of the three-column composite index, DB2 may be able to complete the search down the B-tree with a matching scan. To find the jobs on which supplier 'S4' supplies part 'P1280', for example, DB2 might follow range values looking for 'S4P1280??' (where ?? represents any value).

In deciding whether to use a composite index for searches when only part of the index is known, the optimizer must perform special cardinality checks. If COLCARD has been updated for the nonleading columns, the optimizer can use that value in its calculations, and sometimes it will use a default value for COLCARD. For example, if the first two columns of a three-column composite have been specified, the optimizer multiplies the FF for the first column times that for the second column to determine the combined FF. FIRSTKEYCARD provides the FF for the first column. If the second column's COLCARD has been updated, it provides that column's FF. If it has not been updated, the optimizer uses a default FF of .04, equivalent to a COLCARD value of 25.

When the middle column or columns of a composite index are the subject of the search, the calculation is a bit more complex. For example, this statement would request the parts supplied by supplier S4 on job J007:

```
SELECT PN
WHERE  SN = 'S4'
AND    JN = 'J007';
```

If COLCARD is available for PN, it is used to calculate the FF for the statement. If not, the optimizer has FIRSTKEYCARD and FULLKEYCARD values to go on. Neither alone gives a good indication of the cardinality of the S4?????J007 combination. Suppose there are 10 supplier numbers. SN, and therefore FIRSTKEYCARD, has a cardinality of 10 and a FF of .10. Multiplying that FF times the number of rows, 10,000, indicates that S4 has 1,000 parts it may supply. But is it likely that S4 supplies all possible parts to any one job or that J7 uses all parts? Using the FULLKEYCARD's FF is equally misleading. That would indicate about how many times each part is likely to be supplied by any given supplier to any given job. In this case if FULLKEYCARD is 5000, yielding an FF of .0002, we can assume supplier S4 supplies each part to job J007 twice (.0002 * 10,000 = 2). But it is unlikely that any supplier supplies only one kind of part to any given job.

When the middle columns of a composite key are not specified in a predicate and COLCARD has not been updated, the optimizer uses interpolation of the FIRSTKEYCARD and FULLKEYCARD values to determine cardinality. IBM has not indicated the formula the optimizer uses in this calculation, but it would be something like this:

```
FFMID = FIRST + ((FULL — FIRST)/(NCI — 1)) * (NCW  1)
```

Where,

```
FFMID = FF if the middle column or columns is missing
FIRST = FIRSTKEYCARD's FF
FULL  = FULLKEYCARD's FF
NCI   = number of columns in the index
NCW   = number of columns in the WHERE clause
```

Using this formula for the example produces an FF of .0501, which means about 500 rows will be returned for the statement (0.0501 * 10,000 = 501). If the rows were evenly distributed, following a nonclustering index DB2 would have to read about 200 data pages plus the cost of reading index pages, sorting the RIDs, and removing duplicates. If the table occupies 200 data pages, it would probably be less costly to perform a tablespace scan than it would be to use a nonclustering index. If the SN-PN-JN index were clustering, only about 10 pages would have to be processed (0.0501 * 200), making use of a clustered index a good choice for the optimizer. (The example does not consider list and sequential prefetch, which can result in all three estimates being divided by 32.)

A matching index scan can be done on each value IN a list of values with a composite or single column index. Consider the following statement:

```
SELECT SN, PN, JN, QTY
FROM   SPJ
WHERE  SN = 'S5'
AND    PN IN ('P1', 'P4', 'P5')
AND    JN > 'J2'
```

Three matching index scans can be performed. First for the values S5, P1, J2; second for S5, P4, J2; and third for S5, P6, J2. A scan of the leaf pages past J2 can be done to satisfy the > predicate on JN after each of the three matching index scans.

Column Order and Performance

The order in which columns are specified in a composite index can have an impact on performance depending on how the data are used. Suppose that there is a composite index made up of the WEIGHT and CITY columns of a Part table, which has 1 million rows. (The table's structure is based on that shown in Fig. 4.4, but for illustration we are changing its description in this example.) If the table is usually used to locate parts of a certain weight in each city, the search may be done in one of two ways: by locating values for the city in question and finding the given weights or by locating values for the weights in question and finding the given city. For example, this statement will determine the part numbers and names of parts in Miami that weigh more than 562 pounds:

```
SELECT PN, PNAME
FROM   P
WHERE  CITY = 'MIAMI'
AND    WEIGHT > 562
```

If this were the typical request made of the P table and if we knew the table contained many fewer rows with 'MIAMI' than with weights greater than 562, putting the CITY column first in the composite index would provide a performance benefit. Suppose there were about 100,000 rows containing 'MIAMI' and about 300,000 with weights greater than 500. If CITY came first in the composite index, range values might include CHICAGO000, CHICAGO500, DALLAS_000, DALLAS_500, MIAMI__000, and MIAMI__500. To satisfy the statement, DB2 could follow the B-tree to the first leaf page for the range MIAMI__500, then scan the leaf pages in sequence for all index values containing weights greater than 562—reading about half the MIAMI values, about 50,000 in all.

If on the other hand weight came first in the composite, a sequence of values would run 500CHICAGO, 500DALLAS_, 500MIAMI_, 570NEW-YORK, 571DALLAS_, 571MIAMI_, and so on. To satisfy the search, DB2 would follow the B-tree to the leaf page that begins the range of values greater than 562MIAMI_. It would then scan all leaf pages with greater values in sequence to find those that include 'MIAMI', reading perhaps all 300,000 index values with weights greater than 562.

The general rule for ordering columns in such a composite index is to place in the first position the column likely to have the fewest rows satisfying the usual search of the indexed table.

Composite Index versus Multiple Indexes

In selecting columns to index, developers should also consider the tradeoff between composite and multiple indexes. If applications frequently access several columns within the same table—that is, when they are often used together in an SQL WHERE clause with AND—and if the developer includes them in a composite index, DB2 will locate them efficiently with a matching index scan. A composite index avoids having to maintain several individual indexes. Composite index cannot be used, however, to satisfy

	SN	PN	JN	QTY
Missed ------------ >	S1	P1	J1	200
Missed ------------ >	S1	P1	J4	700
Missed ------------ >	S2	P3	J1	400
	S2	P3	J2	200
	S2	P3	J3	200
	S2	P3	J4	500
	S2	P3	J5	600
	S2	P3	J6	400
	S2	P3	J7	800
	S2	P5	J2	100
Missed ------------ >	S3	P3	J1	200
	S3	P4	J2	500
Index ------------- >	S4	P6	J3	300
Index ------------ >	S4	P6	J7	300
	S5	P2	J2	200
	S5	P2	J4	100
	S5	P5	J5	500
	S5	P5	J7	100
	S5	P6	J2	200
	S5	P1	J4	100
	S5	P3	J4	200
	S5	P4	J4	800
	S5	P5	J4	400
	S5	P6	J4	500

Fig. 6.6 Missing values with a composite index and OR predicates

ORed predicates since rows could be missed. The following select can be satisfied with multiple index processing if there is a separate index on each of the three columns referenced but a composite index cannot be used in a matching index scan.

```
SELECT SN, PN, JN, QTY
FROM   SPJ
WHERE  SN = 'S4'
OR     PN = 'P1'
OR     JN = 'J1'
```

The S4 rows can be identified with the composite index, but the P1 and J1 rows would be missed if a matching index scan is done to locate S4 followed by a scan forward on the leaf or data pages as shown in Fig. 6.6. Multiple index processing will identify all the qualifying rows. Multiple indexes also have the advantage that the leading column does not have to be specified in the predicate.

DB2
efficiently

EXPLAIN

TABLESPACE

NORMAL FORMS

① Repeating groups

② Columns depends on

maybe
③ Non key column

④ 2 or more independent

update/delete
anomalies
⑤ Symmetric constraint

JOIN between two tables

1:N ☐ ☒

M:N ☐ ☒☐

VCHAR ²⁰⁰⁰ᵇʸᵗᵉˢ LONG upto 2 gigabytes
CHAR ²⁵⁵

index are created
to enforce these

Integrity constraints rules

primary key, foreign key, unique, NOT NULL

check

create table
emp
name NUM (10)
CONSTRAINT
(primary key (empID)

foreign key (empID)
reference employee (empid)

UNIQUE (...)

Oracle Data Dictionary

very useful for developer
DBA

role
privileges,
objects seen by user
performance of DB based on AUDIT file

VIEWS
user_own
all_
dba

Intersection Tables and Foreign Keys

Composite keys are often useful in intersection tables—tables made up of a number of foreign key columns that participate in a composite primary key. The SPJ table with foreign keys to the S, P, and J tables and a composite primary key made up of those columns is a prime example. It is usually efficient to index foreign key columns because they frequently take part in joins. An index on the foreign key can also be used in referential integrity checking and enforcement when changes are made in the corresponding primary key columns. For these reasons, it seems at first that it would be a good idea to maintain an index on all foreign keys in an intersection table. But this may not be the case.

Remember there will already be a composite index on the composite key columns. A unique index on those columns is needed for them to serve as the primary key. DB2 can use that index when it enforces referential integrity rules for the first column in the foreign key and for joins on that column. The leading foreign key index columns, however, should be identical to the primary key index. Otherwise delete cascade (discussed in Chapter 5) cannot use the index.

We have eliminated the need for one index in the intersection table. Do we still need the others? In most cases, the answer depends mostly on the expected update activity on the associated primary key tables. The indexes on the individual foreign key columns will be of limited value for updates, inserts, and deletions from the intersection table. In most of these cases, the composite index will be helpful. But if there will be heavy update activity on a primary key table, DB2 will frequently have to search the foreign key column to enforce integrity, and a separate index on PN and JN will be very useful. For example, an update or delete of a PN in the P table would require a tablespace scan of the SPJ table without an index on PN in SPJ. In addition, a join on PN would require a tablespace scan of SPJ.

Look-up Tables

Look-up tables are simple tables that associate related values—such as state names with their mailing abbreviations (California with CA, for example). Such look-up tables are prime candidates for composite indexes, which can satisfy requests without reference to the data pages. Most look-up tables are small. The composite index, in fact, may fit on one root page that has a good chance of remaining in the bufferpool for long periods. Indeed, a unique index on state code is required since it is the primary key and duplicate state codes should not exist in the table. Adding the state name provides for index only access. It is not important whether the index on state code is clustered or nonclustered since an equal predicate will be used on a unique index.

Index Only Access

A number of different types of SELECT statements can be satisfied using index leaf pages without processing data pages. Index only access is more likely with composite indexes. Assume that all columns referenced in the following examples are indexed and that there is a composite index on SN, PN, JN in the SPJ table.

The aggregates MIN and MAX can be satisfied by a one-fetch index scan. The MIN function requires an ascending index, and MAX requires a descending index for a one-fetch index scan to be used.

```
SELECT MAX (QTY)
FROM   SPJ
```

The aggregates AVG, COUNT, and SUM can be computed with a non-matching index scan and without access to the data pages.

```
SELECT AVG(QTY) FROM SPJ
```

If a predicate is specified, a matching index scan can be used to narrow the search before applying the aggregate.

```
SELECT COUNT(*)
FROM   S
WHERE  SN 'S4'
```

If no predicate was specified—that is, the request is to count all the rows in a table—COUNT(*) will result in any available index being used to determine the number of rows. DISTINCT, although not an aggregate per se, can be satisfied with index only access.

```
SELECT DISTINCT SN FROM S
```

If there is a composite index on CITY and SN in that order, the search could be narrowed to Munich and then SNs retrieved in sequence.

```
SELECT SN
FROM   S
WHERE  CITY = 'MUNICH'
ORDER  BY SN
```

Indexes on the primary key and foreign key in the S and SPJ tables provide for index only processing to narrow the search to S2 and join on SN.

```
SELECT S.SN, PN, JN
FROM    S, SPJ
WHERE   S.SN = SPJ.SN
AND     S.SN = 'S2'
```

Index only processing can be used to satisfy EXISTS and NOT EXISTS tests, again assuming indexes on the primary and foreign keys.

```
SELECT SNAME
FROM    S
WHERE   EXISTS
   (SELECT SN, PN, JN
    FROM    SPJ
    WHERE   SN = S.SN
    AND     PN = 'P5'
    AND     JN = 'J7')
```

Multiple index processing can result in index only processing with separate indexes on SN and STATUS.

```
SELECT SN, STATUS
FROM    S
WHERE   SN      BETWEEN 'S3' AND 'S5'
AND     STATUS BETWEEN 30 AND 50
```

Leaf versus Data Page Scans

Processing all leaf pages can be more efficient than processing all data pages since leaf pages usually have more values per page. Thus fewer I/O are required. An example will demonstrate the point. Assume a composite index of 10 bytes, 100-byte row length and 1,000,000 rows on the table. A tablespace scan would read 28,572 data pages (28,572 = ceiling (1,000,000/ floor (3870/(100-byte row + 8 bytes))). A SELECT that can be satisfied from the index pages would require a nonmatching index scan of only 3938 pages (3938 = ceiling (1,000,000 / floor (3563/(10-byte column + 4-byte RID))). Both leaf and data pages can be processed using prefetch so the estimated number of I/O can be divided by 32 with a 4M-byte bufferpool.

Consideration should be given to including in the index those columns frequently retrieved. Doubling the size of the index in the example would still result in a considerable saving over a tablespace scan. In addition when using index only processing, a nonclustered index is as efficient as a clustered index since all the values are in sequence in the leaf pages and data pages are not being processed.

6.9   WHEN NOT TO INDEX

A common guideline is to avoid indexes on a table in a tablespace containing seven pages or less. The thought is that DB2 would spend less time scanning the entire tablespace for the information it needs than it would maintaining and using an index. There are several cases when an index even on very small tables may be necessary or advisable from a performance point of view. Each table should have a primary key that requires a unique index to guarantee unique values. The optimizer may use an index on such a small table in joins, referential integrity checking, and for index only processing. EXPLAIN has shown the use of an index on a one page tablespace with 9 rows.

Since updates represent most of the index cost, whether the costs will be excessive depends largely on the frequency of updates. If the table is usually only read, an index costs little because updates are rare. If a table experiences periodic bulk updates—effecting more than about 10 percent of its rows—dropping its indexes beforehand and recreating them afterward is likely to save on processing. Chapters 9 and 16 discusses this technique in depth. Periodic execution of the utilities to maintain the tablespaces will require more resources the more indexes there are on the tables when loading, reorganizing, and recovering the tablespaces.

Another reason to use indexes judiciously is that the more indexes there are, the greater is the likelihood of lock contention. Locks against an index page lock more rows than locks against a data page. When a row is inserted into a table with four indexes, at least four index pages will be locked. If the index pages contain 400 row references each, 1600 rows may be affectively locked in addition to the rows on the data page being updated.

Columns to Avoid Indexing

Columns updated frequently make poor candidates for indexes because of the performance cost of maintaining them. Columns with a low cardinality, skewed distribution, or many unknown values also make poor candidates for indexing. These three conditions result in a long synonym chain of RIDs—the value is followed by many RIDs. One reason is that indexes with a long synonym chain require a great amount of processing to update as will be seen. Another is that they are of little or no value for retrieval. Consider the example of a column in a Part table that indicates which of 20 cities in which each part is located when 80 percent of the parts are located in one headquarters city of Dallas. This is an example of a low cardinality of 20 and a skewed distribution of values with 80 percent of values being Dallas. Since the overwhelming majority of rows on every data page will include that city, an index will do nothing to help DB2 locate those rows. It might as well read every data page. Actually a nonclustering index will add excess I/O operations.

Columns with a low cardinality—for example, a column indicating gen-

der in an employee table—demonstrate the inefficiency of indexes with redundant values. About half the values will be male, half female, and the
two will probably be uniformly distributed throughout the table. It makes
little sense to use an index to help locate entries for males or females. DB2
will have to read all the data pages to satisfy such a search. Reading index
pages too can only slow that search. Although it may not be as obvious,
the principle holds for columns with higher cardinalities. The general rule
is to avoid creating an index on any column for which on average distinct
values appear more than once on each data page. This formula calculates
that average figure:

```
AVG  = Average number of appearances for each unique value  on each data page
CARD = Cardinality of the index
FF   = Filter factor = 1/CARD
NR   = Number of rows
NP   = Number of pages
AVG  = (FF * NR)/NP
```

The following calculation is for the Part table, City column example
when 10,000 parts are distributed equally among 20 cities and the entire
table occupies 200 data pages:

```
FF  = 1/20 = .05
AVG = (.05 * 10,000)/200 = 2.5
```

A SELECT can be used to determine the average number of occurrences of a value on a data page for indexes that have been created by PAT:

```
SELECT I.CREATOR, I.TBNAME, I.NAME,
       I.FIRSTKEYCARD, I.FULLKEYCARD,
       C.NAME, C.COLCARD,
       T.CARD, T.NPAGES,
       T.CARD/T.NPAGES/I.FIRSTKEYCARD,
       T.CARD/T.NPAGES/I.FULLKEYCARD
FROM   SYSIBM.SYSINDEXES I,
       SYSIBM.SYSTABLES  T,
       SYSIBM.SYSCOLUMNS C,
       SYSIBM.SYSKEYS    K
WHERE  I.FIRSTKEYCARD > 0
AND    I.FULLKEYCARD  > 0
AND    T.CARD         > 0
AND    T.NPAGES       > 0
AND    I.CREATOR   = 'PAT'
AND    K.IXCREATOR = 'PAT'
AND    C.TBCREATOR = 'PAT'
AND    T.CREATOR   = 'PAT'
AND    T.NAME    = C.TBNAME
AND    T.NAME    = I.TBNAME
AND    K.IXNAME  = I.NAME
AND    C.NAME    = K.COLNAME
```

The calculation of T.CARD/T.NPAGES/I.FIRSTKEYCARD will give the average number of occurrences of a value on a page for a single column and T.CARD/T.NPAGES/I.FULLKEYCARD will give the value for a composite index. It may be worthwhile to evaluate existing indexes to determine how useful they will be in narrowing the search for required values.

Generally it is best to determine before creating an index if the index will be useful. This can be done by counting the number of distinct occurrences of the columns being considered for an index.

```
SELECT COUNT (DISTINCT SN, PN)
FROM   SPJ
```

If there are very few distinct values—less than 20 or less than 5 percent of the total number of rows—try to avoid creating the index. It will be of little value in narrowing the search and will be costly to maintain.

A Skewed Distribution of Values

Let us look more closely at columns that do not have a uniform distribution of values. Suppose company headquarters are in Dallas and 80 percent of the parts are housed there. A column with a skewed distribution of values—some values occur much more frequently than do others—has similar problems as one with a low cardinality, at least for the frequently occurring values. A SELECT like the following one will provide information on the distribution of values in columns that are being considered for indexes.

```
SELECT STATUS, COUNT (*)
FROM   S
GROUP  BY STATUS
ORDER  BY 2
```

Fig. 6.7 shows the number of occurrences for values of status. A status of 900 occurs 50 times, and a status of 10 occurs 250,000 times. Assuming a 1-million row table, an index on status would be useful in locating suppliers with a status of 500 or more. An index would be of little value, indeed it would result in additional I/O to the index pages, to locate suppliers with a status of less than 500. A tablespace scan particularly with prefetch is best to locate frequently occurring values.

There are times when it may be necessary to create an index on a column with a skewed distribution of values in order to locate the infrequently occurring values. Techniques for dealing with a skewed distribution will be discussed in Chapter 11.

Status	Number of occurrences	
900	50	⟵────────── Good use of index
800	150	
700	300	
600	480	
500	875	
⋮	⋮	
50	55000	⟵────────── Poor use of index
40	75000	
30	150000	
20	175000	
10	250000	

Fig. 6.7 Distribution of values

The Cost of Maintaining a Low Cardinality Index

A study conducted by one of the authors (Gabrielle Wiorkowski) with indexes on a million-row table indicates the performance cost of updating indexes with a low cardinality or skewed distribution of values. In the study's first phase, 5000 rows were inserted in the table when it had only one index on a unique column, and the total I/Os for the operation were counted. Then a second index, with a low cardinality, was added. The data were inserted again and I/Os were counted. The process was repeated until five indexes had been added. Fig. 6.8 shows the results.

The table in the study organized information about a manufacturing process. The first index column held a time stamp for each sequential procedure. Consequently each value was unique. The additional columns contained information on various aspects of the procedure, the details of which are unimportant to this discussion. The important point is that each had a different cardinality. The number in parentheses after each column's name indicates the number of times on average each distinct value in the column was repeated. The cardinalities are listed beside CARD. In the OP column, for example, each distinct entry repeated about 5000 times in the million rows and the cardinality is 200. This does not seem to be a tremendous amount of redundancy, but as the study found, it had a significant impact on performance. The other indexes had a higher cardinality. Insertion of 5000 rows required 470 I/O operations when the table had the one unique index. When the OP index was added, 1102 I/Os were needed. As the additional indexes were created in turn, each required relatively few additional I/Os. The second index added 632 I/Os for the insertions, and the next three together increased I/Os by only 273.

In the experiment's second phase, another index was substituted for the

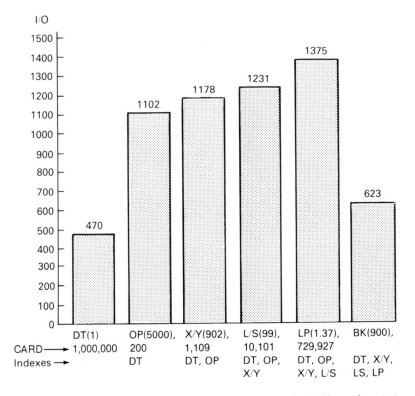

This graph shows the number of I/O operations needed for 5000-row inserts to a 1 million-row table with various combinations of indexes. The average number of times each distinct value repeats in an index is given in parentheses after the index name.

Fig. 6.8 Effect of index redundancy on add I/O count

one with the low cardinality. Because the third index (X/Y), with each distinct value repeated only 902 times and added only 76 I/Os, it was assumed that the cardinality had relatively little impact on performance. Therefore an index with about the same cardinality was chosen to replace OP, with the expectation being that the new index would exhibit a neutral effect on the number of I/Os needed for the insertion. Given that assumption, any reduction in I/Os with the new collection of indexes could be attributed to OP's removal. Indeed when the 5000 rows were now inserted, only 623 I/O operations were needed.

When the low cardinality index was added to and subtracted from the table, its impact was apparent. The conclusion was that even one index with distinct values repeating as frequently as 5000 times each over 1-million rows requires an inordinate amount of I/Os for updates while as many as five indexes with a higher cardinalities—distinct values repeating 900 times over 1-million rows—cost relatively little.

Insert and Delete Processing

A description of the index processing required for inserts and deletes illustrates the high cost of maintaining an index on a column with the same value occurring many times resulting in a long synonym chain. Assume indexes on STATUS and CITY in the S table, and that both indexes have a long synonym chain. The following insertion is made:

```
INSERT INTO S (SN, SNAME, STATUS, CITY)
VALUES ('S1', 'POOLE', 20, 'SYDNEY')
```

Suppose there are more than 10,000 occurrences of STATUS of 20. The value is listed on a leaf page followed by a maximum of 255 RIDs for it. When a new row is inserted, the new RID is placed after the indexed value and all other RIDs are shifted to the right. This results in RIDs being stored out of sequence. For example:

```
(Status of) 20 RID1 RID3 RID5 RID2
```

If the new row is RID7, it will be inserted before RID1. If there is no free space on the page, it is split, which results in an exclusive lock being taken on the NL page during which time no one can use that area of the index.

Similar processing is done to insert the new RID in the CITY index with the similar opportunity for splitting and index page locking.

Deletions require even more processing. Consider the following deletion:

```
DELETE FROM S
WHERE  STATUS = 20
AND    CITY   = 'SYDNEY'
```

First the index on STATUS might be used to locate the row referenced by RID1 so it can be tested for the SYDNEY value. If the row is not for SYDNEY, it is not deleted. The next RID in the STATUS index, RID3, is also tested. If a STATUS 20 row does include SYDNEY, its RID is deleted, and all the others are shifted left. The RID must now also be deleted from the index on CITY after doing a matching index scan for Sydney. If there are a large number of RIDs for SYDNEY, the scan for the RID to be deleted can be quite time consuming and costly. If the cardinality on the CITY column were 20, and there were 1 million rows in the table, there would be about 50,000 RIDs for SYDNEY. It may be necessary to scan up to 50,000

Box 6.3   When not to index

Avoid indexing columns:

- That have a low cardinality
- That have skewed distribution of values
- That have many unknown values
- That are frequently updated
- That are longer than 40 bytes
- That cause lock contention problems

RIDs to find the one to be deleted or perhaps the required RID is tenth in the synonym chain in which case it would be necessary to shift the RIDs left after the deletion. One RID is deleted at a time for a global delete of a set of rows.

An update operation on indexed values is even costlier. It actually requires the deletion of the value in the index followed by the insertion of the new value.

Ideally developers should simply not index columns with a low cardinality, a skewed distribution of values, or many unknown values. All three of these conditions result in a long synonym chain of RIDs as described above. If it is necessary to have such an index, adding another column and creating a composite index can increase cardinality. For example, assume SN has a high cardinality. It might be made the trailing column of in a composite index with STATUS. This is not an elegant solution, but it is effective. A delete of one row was reduced from 40 seconds to 20 milliseconds using this technique.

Research is being done by IBM on simply marking the value as being deleted rather than shifting the RIDs. It remains to be seen if prototyping and testing will result in improved performance. There is also the tradeoff of an increase in the need to reorganize indexes to reclaim space from deleted values.

6.10   MAINTAINING CLUSTERING

Before performing a search for data, the optimizer checks the system catalog to determine which indexes are available and their cardinality. After a table's data are loaded with the load utility, executing the RUNSTATS utility collects statistics describing the table, including the cluster ratio of all indexed columns. As rows are inserted, however, DB2 maintains their sequence according to the designated clustering index only and then for only as long as the free space in the data pages allows. In a table for managing inventory in a warehouse, for example, the developer may declare the column for part number as the clustering index and the column indicating the bin in which each part is stored as a nonclustering index. If initially the parts are assigned by part number to numerically ordered bins, both columns may be in sorted sequence, and DB2 will consider both as clustered. As parts are added and removed, however, this storage scheme will break down as room must be found for parts in bins outside the numerical order. As that happens, the bins column will soon have a lower cluster ratio. Similarly as free space in the data pages is used up and DB2 must place new rows on pages outside their clustering sequence, the column or columns of the clustering index themselves become unclustered, and performance degrades as the benefits of clustering are lost.

When Data Are Considered Clustered

DB2 marks an index's CLUSTERING column in SYSIBM.SYSINDEXES with a "Y" when the developer has specified that the index is to be clustered. The RUNSTATS utility then determines the index's degree of clustering, entering in the index's CLUSTERRATIO column in SYSIBM.SYSINDEXES the percentage of rows in sequence and marking the CLUSTERED column with a "Y" if that percentage is greater than 95. The CLUSTERRATIO value is the important one for the optimizer. In most cases, it uses that value in deciding whether to use the index in an access path. If it contains zero, the optimizer assumes that RUNSTATS has not been executed and looks at the CLUSTERED value. If CLUSTERED = 'Y' the index is treated as a clustering index by the optimizer in many cases.

The optimizer does not use a particular CLUSTERRATIO as an absolute cutoff point for whether it considers an index clustered. Instead it uses the CLUSTERRATIO in formulas that estimate the number of I/O likely to be required if the index is used. IBM has not made those formulas public. One reasonable approach, however, would be to use CLUSTERRATIO to estimate a number of I/O somewhere between what would be required if the index was totally clustered and what would be needed if it was not clustered at all. For example, if each distinct index value occurs 200 times, retrieving rows with a given value stored on random data pages would require about that many I/O. If, on the other hand, those rows would fill only 10 data pages when they were clustered, total clustering would mean they could be retrieved with only 10 I/O. Suppose the CLUSTERRATIO was 80 percent. That percentage of the rows would fill 8 pages (.80 * 10), requiring 8 I/O. The remaining 20 percent of the rows, 40 (.20 * 200), would be stored randomly and would require an I/O each. In this case, the formula estimates that using the clustering index would require 48 I/O.

Performance Degrades as Clustering Declines

DB2 can maintain clustering as long as there is space to insert rows in sequence. If there is no space on the appropriate page, it places it on another page out of sequence (see Section 3.4). As this occurs, the index gradually loses clustering and its benefits. Suppose the CLUSTERRATIO in the above example falls to 50 percent. At that point, using the index would require about 105 I/O to retrieve any given value's rows ((.50 * 10) + (.50 * 200)). Because the optimizer makes its calculation at bind time, unless RUNSTATS is executed and the plan is rebound it cannot be aware of the lost clustering and will continue to use the index even if there might be another more efficient path. Of course, a tablespace reorganization will restore clustering, making the original path efficient again.

The CLUSTERRATIO can be monitored and the tablespace reorganized when the percentage falls below 80. This statement will identify indexes declared as clustered that have fewer than 80 percent of their rows in sequence:

```
SELECT NAME, CREATOR, TBNAME, CLUSTERRATIO,
       CLUSTERING, CLUSTERED
FROM   SYSIBM.SYSINDEXES
WHERE  DBNAME       = 'SPJDB'
AND    CLUSTERING   = 'Y'
AND    CLUSTERRATIO < 0.80
```

A point to remember, however, is that the reorganization utility will not recluster a table if it is in a simple tablespace that includes other tables. For a simple tablespace with only one table or a segmented tablespace, the reorganization utility will unload the table's data and reload them according to the clustering index sequence using the leaf pages to locate the rows in sequence (If SORTDATA is specified, a tablespace scan is used, and the data are sorted in sequence). If no clustering index is declared, the reorganization utility unloads the data using a tablespace scan for all three types of tablespaces and returns the data unclustered. The developer should execute the RUNSTATS utility after reorganization so that the optimizer can determine if an index is clustered and take advantage of it if it is. The optimizer does not automatically develop new access paths for static plans and packages that might use the index. Someone must rebind the plan or package to give the optimizer the opportunity to use the current statistics. Chapter 16 discusses the scheduling of reorganization, RUNSTATs, and rebinds.

6.11 INDEX MONITORING

While developers should choose which columns to index with which index type based on how they expect the data to be used, their expectations will not always be accurate. When the database is in use, however, they can monitor the ways in which indexes are being employed. Two facilities provide information on index usage: the SQL EXPLAIN statement and the catalog table.

SYSPLANDEP and SYSPACKDEP contains the names of tables and indexes used by all static plans and packages, those used with application programs. By selecting an index name from the catalog tables, the developer can find all the programs for which DB2 uses the index. If no programs or only a few do use the index, the developer might want to drop it; apparently little benefit is being derived for the cost of maintaining it. This weeding of little used indexes requires care, however. If the one program that uses a particular index runs frequently or if, when it does run, the index plays a crucial role, dropping it would be a mistake. An index might also be used by the optimizer to satisfy QMF requests or other interactive SQL requests from other software employed by occasional users, and this usage would not be indicated by SYSPLANDEP and SYSPACKDEP. The catalog authorization tables identify occasional users who may be using the table with the index in question.

The EXPLAIN command can be invoked when using SQL interactively from QMF or SPUFI or when SQL is embedded in a host language. The EXPLAIN command inserts rows in a table explaining the access path chosen by the optimizer when it binds a plan. This table indicates the indexes used for each SQL statement in the plan. The facility allows developers to determine the indexes that DB2 uses for each request. They might then explore the effects of restating requests to make better use of available indexes or consider adding an index when it seems there should be one but the EXPLAIN table shows that none is being used. Chapter 13 discusses the EXPLAIN command in more detail.

6.12 SUMMARY

Perhaps the most critical design factors for DB2 performance are decisions about which columns to use as indexes and what types of indexes to use. These decisions depend on an understanding of how indexes relate to data usage and of how DB2 implements indexes. This chapter has provided information on both aspects of the decision-making process.

Tables provide a multitude of indexing options, and usage of any table is difficult to predict. Although indexing is more science than art, developers cannot rely on rules of thumb. They should monitor DB2's index usage and the performance of applications that do—or might—take advantage of indexes. Practice and experimentation as well as awareness of design principles are necessary for optimum index usage.

EXERCISES

The following exercises refer to tables that are designed as the Supplier, Part, and Job tables. The data values and descriptions of the exercises were chosen to present various indexing problems and do not match the data in those tables.

6.1. The supplier table (S) has 10,000 rows occupying 200 data pages. The status column contains 20 distinct values. The following SQL statement is representative of those requiring optimal performance. How should the table be indexed?

```
SELECT SN, SNAME, STATUS, CITY
FROM   S
WHERE  STATUS = 10
```

6.2. The city column, a 12-byte CHAR column in the same S table, includes 10 distinct cities. There are also 20 distinct statuses. What index would be useful for this request?

```
SELECT SN, SNAME, STATUS, CITY
FROM   S
WHERE  STATUS = 10
AND    CITY   = 'DALLAS'
```

6.3. There is an index on PN in the P table and a composite index on SN, PN, and JN in the SPJ table. How might the optimizer use these indexes to find the part numbers (PN) and names (PNAME) used in job J4 as requested by this statement?

```
SELECT PN, PNAME
FROM   SPJ, P
WHERE  JN      = 'J4'
AND    SPJ.PN = P.PN
```

6.4. There is a composite index on SN and SNAME in the S table and SN, PN, and JN in the SPJ table. Could the optimizer avoid reading data pages to select the names of suppliers of part P5 as requested by the following SELECT statement?

```
SELECT SNAME
FROM   S SX
WHERE  EXISTS
   (SELECT SN, PN, JN
    FROM   SPJ
    WHERE  SPJ.SN = SX.SN
    AND    PN = 'P5'
    AND    JN = 'J7')
```

6.5. There is an index on SN and CITY in the S table. What updates are required on the table and indexes for the following procedures?

```
A) INSERT INTO S
   VALUES('S1','JOHNSON',40,'DALLAS')

B) UPDATE S
   SET CITY = 'DALLAS'
   WHERE SN = 'S1'

C) DELETE FROM S
   WHERE SN = 'S1'
```

6.6. Performance is poor when the S and SPJ tables are joined on SN, which is indexed in both tables. What might be the problem and a possible solution?

6.7. Table A's tablespace, tablespace x, has been reorganized. The optimizer, however, has marked Table A's designated clustering index as unclustered in SYSINDEXES. What are possible problems and solutions?

6.8. Under what conditions might three separate indexes on SN, PN, JN have advantages over a composite index on the three columns?

6.9. Are there any advantages to using a clustering or nonclustering index when most predicates will be equal conditions on the indexed column and the index is unique?

6.10. Can list prefetch be used in conjunction with index only processing? Why?

7

Using SQL for Data Manipulation

7.1 INTRODUCTION

The label *structured query language* is a misnomer in that the language it refers to provides much more than query capabilities. It also provides data definition and data control facilities and, as this chapter describes, rich data-manipulation capabilities. The name is misleading in another sense. Although the language serves well for interactive queries and updates, it can also be embedded within host-language programs for database access. With only a few minor additions to the syntax, embedded SQL works exactly the same as interactive SQL.

The primary data-manipulation activities provided by SQL are SELECT, UPDATE, INSERT, and DELETE. The SELECT capabilities provide a powerful, flexible collection of methods for finding desired data within a database. UPDATE, INSERT, and DELETE allow for the changing, addition, and removal of rows, respectively. We will examine all of these capabilities in detail by looking at examples of statements that employ them. The examples refer to the tables presented in Fig. 7.1. By working through the example statements manually—referring to the tables and identifying selected rows, for example—one can easily grasp each statement's meaning.

Supplier (S) Table

SN	SNAME	STATUS	CITY
S1	SMITH	20	LONDON
S2	JONES	10	PARIS
S3	BLAKE	30	PARIS
S4	CLARK	20	LONDON
S5	ADAMS	30	ATHENS

Job (J) Table

JN	JNAME	CITY
J1	SORTER	PARIS
J2	PUNCH	ROME
J3	READER	ATHENS
J4	CONSOLE	ATHENS
J5	COLLATOR	LONDON
J6	TERMINAL	OSLO
J7	TAPE	LONDON

Part (P) Table

PN	PNAME	COLOR	WEIGHT	CITY
P1	NUT	RED	12	LONDON
P2	BOLT	GREEN	17	PARIS
P3	SCREW	BLUE	17	ROME
P4	SCREW	RED	14	LONDON
P5	CAM	BLUE	12	PARIS
P6	COG	RED	19	LONDON

Supplier/Part/Job (SPJ) Table

SN	PN	JN	QTY
S1	P1	J1	200
S1	P1	J4	700
S2	P3	J1	400
S2	P3	J2	200
S2	P3	J3	200
S2	P3	J4	500
S2	P3	J5	600
S2	P3	J6	400
S2	P3	J7	800
S2	P5	J2	100
S3	P3	J1	200
S3	P4	J2	500
S4	P6	J3	300
S4	P6	J7	300
S5	P2	J2	200
S5	P2	J4	100
S5	P5	J5	500
S5	P5	J7	100
S5	P6	J2	200
S5	P1	J4	100
S5	P3	J4	200
S5	P4	J4	800
S5	P5	J4	400
S5	P6	J4	500

Fig. 7.1 Suppliers, Job, Part, and Suppliers/Part/Job Tables

7.2   SELECT STATEMENTS

All SELECT statements take this basic form:

```
SELECT SNAME, CITY
FROM   S
WHERE  SN = 'S4'
```

In general, the SELECT clause indicates the column or columns that are to provide the information; the FROM clause indicates the table or tables that contain those columns; the WHERE clause, or predicate, contains the criteria by which the information is to be selected. A SELECT list may contain up to 750 columns and a FROM clause up to 15 tables.

The WHERE clause identifies rows to be selected. It contains one or more conditions that must be met before a row will be included in the returned set. A condition may be that a row's value must relate to some other value in a particular way. SQL allows the standard comparators: the "equal to" (=), "not equal to" (¬=), "greater than" (>), "greater than or equal to" (> =), "less than" (<), and "less than or equal to" (< =) operators. The comparators are referred to as simple operators and apply to alphanumeric as well as numeric values. Generally alphabetical order determines the relative weight of alphanumeric or alphabetic values.

In the statement above, for example, the WHERE clause stipulates a search for information related to a supplier with a supplier number (SN) equal to S4. The WHERE clause can stipulate multiple search criteria through the use of the AND and OR Boolean operators. In addition, another kind of SELECT statement, called a subselect, may serve as a search criterion. (Section 7.6 describes this facility.)

SELECT *

An asterisk (*) after SELECT indicates that all columns in the selected rows are to be returned. The asterisk avoids the need to specify all the column names or even to know what they are.

SELECT * should not be used in host-language programs, however. Such use would detract from data independence in this way: When an SQL statement selects data for use by a program, the program must have a host variable to receive a value from each column selected. If a column were added to the table, the embedded SELECT * would automatically pass its value to the program. If there is no host variable, DB2 has no place to store the returned value for access by the program. Similarly, if a column were deleted, SELECT * would not return the correct values to the program. If the columns to be selected had been listed, however, the added columns would not have affected the program and the deleted column would effect only the programs referencing the column. In addition, SELECT * detracts from good performance as will be discussed in chapter 11.

This example illustrates the use of SELECT * and the operation of a simple WHERE clause. The problem is to determine from the example tables the jobs that use part number P6 supplied by supplier S5 and the number of parts (QTY) assigned to each of those jobs. The Supplier/Part/Job (SPJ) table in Fig. 7.1 contains all of that information. This statement selects it:

```
SELECT *
FROM    SPJ
WHERE   SN = 'S5'
AND     PN = 'P6'
```

The SELECT * clause indicates that all column values from the appropriate rows are to be returned. The FROM clause indicates the rows are to be found in the SPJ table. And the WHERE clause stipulates that only rows in which SN equals S5 and PN equals P6 are to be returned. Single quotation marks in the statement identify character string values. Before reading the report returned by this SELECT statement, presented below, try locating in the SPJ table the rows that satisfy the WHERE criteria. Here is the report with the needed information:

SN	PN	JN	QTY
S5	P6	J2	200
S5	P6	J4	500

Notice that SELECT * returns the columns in the order in which they were defined in the CREATE TABLE statement, and the column names are returned as headings.

Selecting Nulls

SQL statements that test for the presence of nulls hold the potential for a programming difficulty. It may seem natural for programmers to test for nulls in the same way they test for any other value. A typical SQL statement to locate employees with $25,000 salaries would be:

```
SELECT EMPLOYEE_NO
FROM    EMPLOYEE_TABLE
WHERE   SALARY = 25000
```

The equals sign would not be correct syntax, however, for a statement that seeks null salaries. As DB2 sees it, a null does not equal—or compare in any way with—anything. SQL therefore provides a special predicate using

the verb IS to test for nulls. In this case, the proper statement would be:
WHERE SALARY IS NULL.

SELECT Using OR or IN

A user or programmer can limit a search to rows containing any one of a
number of values by using a series of OR operators in the WHERE clause
or by using the IN operator. Consider a request for information about suppliers S1, S3, and S4. We would like to know the parts supplied by each,
how many of each part is supplied, and the jobs in which they are used. All
of that information is contained in the SPJ table. Using the OR operator,
this statement will return the necessary rows:

```
SELECT SN, PN, JN, QTY
FROM   SPJ
WHERE  SN = 'S1'
OR     SN = 'S3'
OR     SN = 'S4'
```

The SELECT will return all columns from the SPJ table for rows having a
supplier number of S1, S3, or S4. The equivalent statement using the IN
operator is:

```
SELECT SN, PN, JN, QTY
FROM   SPJ
WHERE  SN IN ('S1', 'S3', 'S4')
```

The statement might be read as "Return all column values from the SPJ
table for rows with supplier numbers included in the set of numbers consisting of S1, S3, and S4." The responses to the statements will be the same:

```
SN PN JN QTY
S1 P1 J1 200
S1 P1 J4 700
S3 P3 J1 200
S3 P4 J2 500
S4 P6 J3 300
S4 P6 J7 300
```

Range SELECTS

SQL also allows users to retrieve rows associated with ranges of search values—for example, all rows from the Part (P) table containing weight values
greater than or equal to 12 and less than or equal to 14. The language provides two equivalent ways of formulating these requests. One way uses the
symbolic relationship operators. Those operators would be used to report

on parts with weights included within the range just stated in the following way:

```
SELECT PN, WEIGHT
FROM   P
WHERE  WEIGHT > = 12
AND    WEIGHT < = 14
```

The alternative uses the BETWEEN operator:

```
SELECT PN, WEIGHT
FROM   P
WHERE  WEIGHT BETWEEN 12 AND 14
```

Besides being easier to type and perhaps a bit easier to grasp, this second statement holds performance benefits—explained in Chapter 11—over the one using the symbolic operators. One must remember, however, that the BETWEEN operator includes within its range the numbers used in the statement. A way to remember is to understand that the range defined by the BETWEEN operator is equivalent to that created by the *less than or equal to* and *greater than or equal to* operators. (NOT BETWEEN does not include the end points.)

The report returned by either statement is:

```
PN WEIGHT
P1   12
P4   14
P5   12
```

String Searches

The LIKE operator specifies searches for values that contain any character or string of characters. The operator allows the user to specify the location of the target character or string within a longer string by using underscores and the percent (%) sign. Each underscore represents a character position of any value. The % sign is a wild card standing for any number of alphanumeric values. Examples will illuminate the points.

The following statement requests a search for the name of any supplier in the Supplier (S) table whose name includes a K:

```
SELECT SN, SNAME
FROM   S
WHERE  SNAME LIKE '%K%'
```

The % signs indicate that any combination of characters can precede or follow the K or only the value of K exists in the SNAME. A scan of the S

Table's SNAME column reveals that two values fit the criteria: BLAKE and CLARK.

If a string search is being done within a host-language program, the host-language variable used to provide the value to be found must match the length of the column being searched. If that variable is short, it must be padded with underscores or the % sign. In the example above if the column being searched is CHAR(5), the host variable must contain %K%%%. The additional % signs, not needed with interactive SQL, pad the variable to the required five character length. Such padding is not necessary for a host variable declared as variable in length such as when using COBOL 49 level fields. Chapter 9 discusses host-language variables more fully.

A request for suppliers with a K in the fourth position of their names demonstrates the use of the underscore with the LIKE operator:

```
SELECT SN, SNAME
FROM   S
WHERE  SNAME LIKE '_ _ _K%'
```

The one value satisfying this request is BLAKE.

7.3 NEGATING A PREDICATE

The NOT operator in the WHERE clause allows the SELECT to search for rows that do not meet the stated criteria. The word NOT preceding another operator causes this negation. The symbol ¬= placed before a comparison operator negates it. For example, these statements will return suppliers not located in London or Athens:

```
SELECT SN, SNAME, CITY
FROM   S
WHERE  CITY NOT IN ('LONDON', 'ATHENS')
```

or

```
SELECT SN, SNAME, CITY
FROM   S
WHERE  CITY ¬= 'LONDON'
AND    CITY ¬= 'ATHENS'
```

7.4 AGGREGATES AND OTHER BUILT-IN FUNCTIONS

SQL offers a number of built-in mathematical functions called aggregates for use in the SELECT clause that allow users to request data on the basis of simple mathematical operations or according to several numeric properties. It will, for example, return the sum or average of the values that meet the search criteria, and it will identify the minimum or maximum value found. In addition, SQL allows users to request computations—addition, subtraction, multiplication, division, and combinations of those operations—on the selected data. The operators are AVG, SUM, MIN, MAX, COUNT, and DISTINCT and the familiar mathematical symbols +, −, *, and /. The built-in functions, except for COUNT, ignore nulls in their calculations. Examples best explain the functions' use.

MIN, MAX, and AVG

The SPJ table (Fig. 7.1) contains the quantity of each part each supplier supplies for each job. To find the minimum, maximum, and average number of parts supplied by supplier S2, the SELECT statement must identify the quantities in rows where supplier number is S2 and apply the MIN, MAX, and AVG operators to those amounts:

```
SELECT MIN(QTY), AVG(QTY), MAX(QTY)
FROM   SPJ
WHERE  SN = 'S2'
```

Eight rows satisfy the WHERE clause. In those rows, the minimum QTY value is 100, and the maximum is 800. The average QTY for those rows is 400. The statement returns:

```
MIN(QTY)  AVG(QTY)  MAX(QTY)
   100       400       800
```

Headings above the resulting values may or may not be returned depending on the interactive tool that is being used. They are returned in the order listed in the SELECT clause.

Math in the SELECT Clause

Suppose we want to know the difference between the maximum quantity and the average for parts supplied by S2. A simple adjustment of the SELECT clause, inclusion of a minus sign, provides the answer:

```
SELECT MAX(QTY) − AVG(QTY)
FROM   SPJ
WHERE  SN = 'S2'
```

```
Returns:       400
```

The SELECT clause can handle more complex equations. When functions are used in combination in SELECT equations, SQL follows the standard order of operations. It first computes expressions within parentheses, beginning with the innermost set if parentheses are nested. Then it performs multiplication and division before addition and subtraction. For example, to calculate the difference between maximum quantity and average quantity that we have just found as a percentage of the average, we must divide the difference by the average and multiply by 100. Here is that computation in the SELECT clause:

```
SELECT (MAX(QTY) - AVG(QTY))/AVG(QTY)*100
```

The parentheses enclosing the subtraction are necessary to ensure the operation is performed first, as the computation demands. The answer in this case is 100. Suppose the parentheses were forgotten. The clause would be:

```
SELECT MAX(QTY) - AVG(QTY)/AVG(QTY)*100
```

SQL would perform the division and multiplication first (400/400*100 = 100) and then the subtraction (800 − 100 = 700), not the intended computation.

DISTINCT and COUNT

The DISTINCT operator filters out all redundant column values in the rows satisfying the WHERE clause or, if no WHERE clause is used, of the entire table. For example, the following statement would be used to find the distinct supplier and part numbers that appear in the SPJ table. Notice that DISTINCT applies to all the columns in the SELECT clause even though commas separate the columns.

```
SELECT DISTINCT SN, PN
FROM   SPJ

Returns:

SN PN
S1 P1
S2 P3
S2 P5
S3 P3
S3 P4
S4 P6
S5 P1
S5 P2
S5 P3
S5 P4
S5 P5
S5 P6
```

DISTINCT can work with other built-in functions, removing the repeated values before performing the specified function. For that use, DISTINCT is specified within parentheses, along with the name of the column being acted upon, as shown in the next example demonstrating the COUNT operator.

When followed by an asterisk in parentheses, the COUNT operator counts all rows that satisfy the WHERE condition. If there is no WHERE clause, it counts all rows in the table—for example:

```
SELECT COUNT(*)
FROM   SPJ

Returns:

COUNT(*)
   24

SELECT COUNT(*)
FROM   SPJ
WHERE  PN = 'P3'

Returns:

COUNT(*)
    9
```

When followed by the DISTINCT operator and a column name in parentheses, COUNT returns the number of distinct values in the column—for example:

```
SELECT COUNT (DISTINCT PN)
FROM   SPJ

Returns:

COUNT (DISTINCT PN)
        6
```

Data-Type Conversions

DB2 offers several functions that can be used in the SELECT or WHERE clause for converting the data types of values from columns, host-language variables, and calculations. For example, the keyword DECIMAL can be used to convert any numeric data type into a packed decimal. If the numeric value to be converted is called BALANCE, the command DECIMAL (BALANCE, 6,2) changes it to a packed decimal with a precision of six and two decimal places. A typical conversion of a calculation would be DECIMAL (AVG (BALANCE, 6,2)), which would compute the average of BALANCE and return it with a precision of six and two decimal places. FLOAT(BALANCE) will convert a numeric BALANCE to a double precision floating point number.

The INTEGER function works in a similar fashion to convert any numeric type to an integer. It is particularly useful for rounding off numerals.

For example, INTEGER (AMOUNT + 0.5) will round up and truncate to an integer any numeric AMOUNT with a fractional part of 0.5 or more and round down to an integer any decimal amount with a fractional part less than 0.5. The result is a 4-byte binary number. When INTEGER is used with a mathematical function such as SUM, the order of the functions in a statement is important. For example, the clause INTEGER (SUM (AMOUNT + 0.5)) will sum the AMOUNT values and round off the result. The command SUM (INTEGER (AMOUNT + 0.5)) will round off the AMOUNT values before summing.

The HEX function converts any data type other than LONG VARCHAR to hexadecimal representation. The results are presented as a VARCHAR type with twice as many bytes as the original value. The HEX function is useful for converting values in the START_RBA column of the catalog table SYSIBM.SYSCOPY. This column presents the relative byte address (RBA) to which the RECOVER utility should recover in a log. The utility requires that the RBA be presented in hexadecimal representation.

The DIGITS function converts numeric values to a character string with leading zeros and without a sign or decimal point. If the value is a SMALLINT type, the result is a 5-byte string; if it is an INTEGER type, the result is a 10-byte string; and if it is a DECIMAL, the result has the same number of digits as the original value.

Finally the VARGRAPHIC function converts a character string of 254 bytes or fewer to a double-byte DBCS representation, which is used for Japanese Kanji ideograms.

String Manipulation Functions

DB2 provides several functions for manipulating character strings. The substring function (SUBSTR) extracts a portion of a character string, with numbers presented with the string value's name indicating which alphanumeric value begins the extract and the number of characters to be included. For example, SUBSTR (SNAME, 1,3) instructs DB2 to begin with the first character in the SNAME value and include three alphanumeric values. If the SNAME value were JACKSON, the function's result would be JAC. If there are not enough characters to fill the receiving host variable or column, the result is padded with trailing blanks.

One interesting use for SUBSTR in conjunction with DIGITS is to break apart intelligent identification numbers (those including codes). For example, the seventh digit of a part identification number of INTEGER type might indicate the city in which it is stored. An SQL statement like this might be used to select according to that digit:

```
SELECT CITY, QTY
FROM   INVENTORY
WHERE  SUBSTR (DIGITS (PARTID), 7,1) = '4'
```

In the WHERE clause, DIGITS converts PARTID to a character string, and SUBSTR extracts the seventh character. If that character is '4,' the search criterion is satisfied.

The concatenation function is in a way the reverse of the substring function. Rather than taking strings apart, as SUBSTR does, concatenation puts them together. The function can be used to combine any combination of character variables and literals. Concatenation is used in the SELECT clause to format results or in a WHERE clause to put data in the desired format for processing and is invoked with a double bar sign. In the statement's results, the character string coming before the double bar is joined with that after the double bar. Literals are enclosed in single quotes.

For example, the following statement finds the names and colors of parts stored in London, and returns them, separated by a comma and a space:

```
SELECT PNAME||', '||COLOR
FROM   P
WHERE  CITY = 'LONDON'
```

It returns:

```
NUT  , RED
SCREW, RED
COG  , RED
```

Notice that these results assume that PNAME has been declared as CHAR(5). For CHAR columns, the concatenation takes place after the trailing blanks that pad a value to the column's length. For VARCHAR columns, concatenation takes place immediately after each value's final character. If PNAME had been declared VARCHAR, the results would be:

```
NUT, RED
SCREW, RED
COG, RED
```

Another string manipulation function, LENGTH, counts the number of bytes, or characters, in a CHAR or VARCHAR value, excluding bytes used as null and VARCHAR indicators. LENGTH includes a count of trailing blanks for CHAR columns. VARCHAR columns have no trailing blanks. The result is an integer.

The VALUE Function

The VALUE function provides flexibility for handling nulls and zeros in computations. Without the use of VALUE, for example, division by null

FORMAT	DATE	DATE EXAMPLE	TIME	TIME EX.
ISO (International Standards Organization)	YYYY-MM-DD	1987-05-23	HH.MM.SS	20.10.30
USA (IBM USA Standard)	MM/DD/YYYY	05/23/1987	HH.MM AM	08:10 PM
EUR (European Standard)	DD.MM.YYYY	23.05.1987	HH.MM.SS	20.10.30
JIS (Japaneses Industrial Standard Christian Era)	YYYY-MM-DD	1987-05-23	HH:MM:SS	20:10:30

Fig. 7.2 Date and time data types

or zero would result in a negative SQLCODE, which indicates an error. If the VALUE function is applied to the division by zero or null, the result is a null. The calculation VALUE (AMOUNT/PERCENT) will return null whenever PERCENT is zero or null.

VALUE can also be used to substitute a numeric value for any nulls used in computations. That function is used by identifying the value to be substituted for nulls after the name of the data item used in the computation. For example, in the calculation NET_SALARY—VALUE (INSURANCE, 0), zero will be subtracted from NET_SALARY whenever INSURANCE is a null. Otherwise if the null was subtracted, the result would also be null. Similarly adding a null or multiplying by null results in null.

7.5   DATE AND TIME CALCULATIONS

DB2 offers a number of functions for working with its three date and time data types—DATE, TIME, and TIMESTAMP—and a number of calculations that may be used with the data types. The flexibility of the DATE and TIME data types begins with the formats of the dates and times they represent, which include international, U.S., European, and Japanese standards (Fig. 7.2). The International Standard Organization's (ISO) formats are the defaults that come with DB2, but the system's installer can change these defaults. The default values will be used unless the SQL statement using DATE or TIME specifies otherwise. The format can also be chosen for an application program at precompile time.

The CHAR function is used in SQL statements to specify a format for a DATE or TIME value other than the default. For example, if the default is the ISO standard but the programmer wants to use the USA standard, the CHAR function used with the column name will make the conversion. The syntax is CHAR(DATE_COL, USA), where DATE_COL is the column name and USA is the desired format. The conversion returns the date as a character string.

The CHAR function can also be used to convert the results of date or time calculations to character strings rather than the decimal representation that would otherwise result. For example, CHAR(DATE_COL − 60 DAYS) would subtract 60 days from the value in the DATE_COL column and return the result as a character string. CHAR includes the delimiters— the dashes or slashes—that are part of the DATE representation.

DB2 offers a number of functions for extracting only part of a DATE, TIME, or TIMESTAMP. For example, MONTH(DATE_COLUMN) returns only the month. If DATE_COLUMN held 12/15/1989, 12 would be returned. The DAY and YEAR functions work similarly for the day or year portion of a DATE value. And the HOUR, MINUTE, and SECOND functions return those portions of TIME values. The MICROSECOND function returns the microsecond portion of a TIMESTAMP column.

DATE and TIME values may participate in several types of calculations. One type involves the addition or subtraction of labeled durations. For example, any number of years, months, or days may be added to or subtracted from a DATE value. The syntax simply identifies the date column, followed by a plus or minus sign, followed by the number of units and the unit's name—YEARS, MONTHS, or DAYS. But the result of the addition or subtraction is not so straightforward.

YEAR and MONTH Calculations

In most cases, the YEARS or MONTHS calculation results in the same date as the original DATE value, plus or minus the number of units indicated, regardless of the number of days in the interval covered by the addition or subtraction. Consider the calculation DATE_COL + 1 MONTHS, for example, when the DATE value is '09/30/1989'. Although the following month, October, has 31 days, DB2 does not add that many days. Instead it returns '10/30/1989', the same date plus one month.

Remember, that is in most cases. Some dates, however, exist in some months or years, but not others. For example, the calculation '08/31/1989' + 1 MONTH could not result in '09/31/1989' since September has only 30 days. In these cases, DB2 returns the last day of the appropriate month; in the example, '9/30/1989.' The same principle applies to a labeled duration calculation that would result in February 29 of a nonleap year.

Use of the DAYS units provides more precise results, with the result date being exactly the number of days added or removed from the original date as the number indicated in the calculation—for example, '09/30/1989' + 31 days = '10/31/1989'.

Last Day of Month Calculations

Often a program may have to know the last day of the current month—so that bills can be sent out on that date, for example. But the last date of a month might be the twenty-eighth, twenty-ninth, thirtieth, or thirty-first. The following clause using a combination of DATE and string functions can determine the current month's last date, no matter the month or year.

Imagine a PARTS_ORDERED table that includes a column, SCHED _DATE, showing the scheduled delivery date for all ordered parts. For accounting purposes, we want to know which parts are scheduled to be delivered after the last day of the current month. This statement will find that information:

```
SELECT PN
FROM    PARTS_ORDERED
WHERE   SCHED_DATE >
        DATE(SUBSTR(CHAR(CURRENT DATE, ISO), 1,8)||'01')
        + 1 MONTH - 1 DAY
```

The clause beginning "DATE" determines the current month's last date. Assuming a current date of February 15, 1989, the following list presents the results of each element in the clause, beginning with the innermost parentheses:

```
1. CHAR(CURRENT DATE, ISO)  = 1989-02-15
2. SUBSTR(..., 1,8)         = 1989-02-
3. (...||'01')              = 1989-02-01
4. (...) + 1 MONTH          = 1989-03-01
5. (...) - 1 DAY            = 1989-02-28
```

In the first step, the CHAR function puts the current date into a character string in the ISO format. The second step uses the substring function to truncate that date to just the year and month. Step three's concatenation sets the date to the first of the month. Step four's addition of a month sets the date at the first day of the next month. The final step subtracts a day, resulting in the final day of the current month. DATE at the beginning converts the date to the DATE data type for DB2's use in the comparison.

TIME Calculations

Addition or subtraction of time units to a TIME value is similar to date calculations but without some of the complications. The labeled units are

HOURS, MINUTES, and SECONDS. The time calculations take into account the 24-hour representation for the ISO, European, and Japanese formats and the 12-hour representation for the USA format. For example, if 12 hours were added to a non-USA format TIME value of '16.30.00', the result would be '04.30.00'. If 12 hours were added to a USA format TIME value of '04:30 PM', the result would be '04:30 AM'.

All of the labeled durations available for TIME and DATE values may also be used in TIMESTAMP calculations. In addition, MICROSECONDS can also be used in TIMESTAMP calculations.

Subtracting DATE and TIME Values

DATE values may be subtracted from one another but not added, and TIME values may be subtracted from one another but not added. In addition, DATE or TIME values may be subtracted, respectively, from special values called CURRENT DATE and CURRENT TIME, which represent exactly what their names say. DB2 also provides CURRENT TIMESTAMP and CURRENT TIMEZONE, the latter of which provides the time duration of the local time zone from GMT (Greenwich Mean Time). (GMT is now known as the universal time coordinate). When subtraction of these values occurs, the results take the special form YYYYMMDD, which is a packed decimal type representing the number of years, months, and days that the subtraction yields. For example, if the CURRENT DATE is '06/20/1989', subtracting a DATE value of '03/30/1987' yields 00020300, for 2 years, 3 months, and no days.

DB2 will perform subtractions on dates with differing formats. For instance, using the PARTS_ORDERED table from the above example and assuming SCHED_DATE is in ISO format, DB2 can handle this statement to determine which parts are due to arrive at least two years after December 31, 1989:

```
SELECT PN
FROM  PARTS_ORDERED
WHERE  YEAR(SCHED_DATE - '12/31/1987') > 2
```

Notice that SCHED_DATE is in the ISO format but '12/31/1989' is in USA date format. Notice also that '12/31/1989' is not even identified as a date. It is merely a character string. DB2 recognizes the string's format as a date and treats it as such.

The DAYS Function

The DAYS function provides a way to calculate the number of days between two DATE values. DAYS determines the number of days between a given date and 12/31/0000. That number by itself will rarely be useful; however, by determining the DAYS values for two dates and subtracting one from the other, DB2 finds the number of days separating the two dates. For example, for a DATE_COL1 value of '02/28/1989' and a DATE_COL2 value of '01/31/1989', the calculation DAYS(DATE_COL1)—DAYS (DATE_COL2) returns 28.

Day of the Week

The DAYS function is useful in determining the day of the week of a given date in a column or host variable of DATEREC, for example.

```
SELECT DAYS(DATEREC) — (DAYS(DATEREC) — 1) / 7 * 7
FROM   PARTS_ORDERED
```

should be single word table.

The values returned will be 1, 2, 3, 4, 5, 6, or 7 representing Monday, Tuesday, Wednesday, Thursday, Friday, Saturday, or Sunday.

A similar calculation can be used to determine the Monday on or before DATEREC:

```
SELECT DATE((DAYS(DATEREC) — 1) / 7 * 7 + 1)
FROM PARTS_ORDERED
```

If the Monday after DATEREC is required, the following calculation will provide the date:

```
SELECT DATE((DAYS(DATEREC) — 1) / 7 * 7 + 1 + 7)
FROM PARTS_ORDERED
```

If Tuesday is required, -2, $+2$ rather than -1, $+1$ should be used in the calculation. If Wednesday is required, -3, $+3$ rather than -1, $+1$ should be used. For Thursday and the remaining days of the week increment by -1 or $+1$ for each of the days.

Converting to the DATE Data Type

If dates are stored as character or numeric types in a format DB2 does not accept, the DATE function and string manipulations in an SQL statement can convert them to the proper type and format. Suppose ORDER_DATE is stored as a CHAR(6) type in the form YYMMDD. This statement will convert ORDER_DATE values to a DATE type in the ISO format:

```
SELECT DATE ('19'
             ||SUBSTR(ORDER_DATE,1,2,)||'-'
             ||SUBSTR(ORDER_DATE,3,2)||'-'
             ||SUBSTR(ORDER_DATE,5,2))
```

```
FROM        PARTS_ORDERED
WHERE       SN = 'S4'
```

Looking at an example date helps one understand how the statement works. Suppose ORDER_DATE were 880131.

The statement in the parentheses begins with '19'. Concatenated with that is the substring of ORDER_DATE, beginning with the first position and including two characters—'88'. That yields '1988'. The next concatenation adds the hyphen, '1988-', and the next adds a two-character substring from ORDER_DATE beginning at position 3—'01'. So far, we have '1988-01'. The next concatenation adds another hyphen, and the final one adds the final two characters from the string—'1988-01-31'. The DATE function then converts that character string to the DATE type.

If ORDER_DATE were stored as a DECIMAL or INTEGER, the conversion statement would be only slightly different, having to account first for the conversion from the numeric to character type before the substring function can be used. The following statement handles the conversion of either DECIMAL or INTEGER types:

```
SELECT DATE('19'
       ||SUBSTR(DIGITS(ORDER_DATE),1,2)||'-'
       ||SUBSTR(DIGITS(ORDER_DATE),3,2)||'-'
       ||SUBSTR(DIGITS(ORDER_DATE),5,2))
   FROM   PARTS_ORDERED
   WHERE  SN = 'S4'
```

7.6 SELECTING BY GROUPS

The GROUP BY clause may be used in SELECT statements for searches designed to return a single value—a sum or minimum, for example. But rather than performing the search and returning the value for an entire column, GROUP BY separates the rows into partitions according to similar values in the named column and then operates on each group. In other words, the GROUP BY operator creates a separate group for each distinct value in the named column. Then it performs the select on each group and returns a single row for each group. Grouped by CITY, for example, the Supplier table has three groups: for LONDON, PARIS, and ATHENS. This statement, then, finds the maximum supplier status in each city:

```
SELECT CITY, MAX(STATUS)
FROM   S
GROUP  BY CITY
```

Returns:

```
CITY MAX(STATUS)
LONDON     20
```

```
PARIS      30
ATHENS     30
```

A HAVING clause works like a WHERE clause to qualify a search, but the HAVING clause criteria apply to the groups created with a GROUP BY clause rather than to individual rows—for example:

```
SELECT CITY, MAX(STATUS)
FROM   S
GROUP  BY CITY
HAVING COUNT(*) > 1
```

Returns:

```
CITY MAX(STATUS)
LONDON     20
PARIS      30
```

SQL applies the HAVING clause criteria to each group. In this case, it counts the values in each group, eliminates any group having fewer than two, and returns the maximum value for those remaining.

GROUP BY will establish groups according to the values in more than one column, creating a separate group for each unique combination of values in the columns specified. A select from the SPJ table might group according to supplier number and part number (GROUP BY SN, PN). In that case, the S1-P1 combination represents a group, consisting of two rows, the S2-P3 combination forms a group with seven rows, and so on. The number of columns that may be used in a GROUP BY clause is limited by the total number of bytes in their columns. Theoretically DB2 allows columns totaling 4000 bytes to make up a GROUP BY clause, which should allow enough columns to satisfy almost any request.

Notice that any column included in the SELECT clause of a statement that contains a GROUP BY clause must either have an associated built-in function or appear in the GROUP BY clause. The function will return a single value based on the information in the indicated column for the grouped rows. But which of the group's values would the select return if no function was specified? For example, suppose that in the above statement, the SELECT clause had included the SNAME column. Which supplier name would SQL return with the LONDON row?

7.7 SORTING THE ANSWER SET

An ORDER BY clause, placed at the end of a select, tells SQL the sequence in which to present the response. The user can specify sequencing by one or more of the selected columns. SQL sequences first according to the first column indicated. Then within each group created by the first sequence, it sequences according to the second column indicated, and so on—for example:

```
SELECT JN, PN, QTY
FROM   SPJ
WHERE  QTY > = 400
ORDER BY JN, PN

Returns:

JN PN QTY
J1 P3 400
J2 P4 500
J4 P1 700
J4 P3 500
J4 P4 800
J4 P5 400
J4 P6 500
J5 P3 600
J5 P5 500
J6 P3 400
J7 P3 800
```

The rows are sequenced by job numbers—J1, J2, J4, J5, J6, J7. Then within groups of rows having duplicate job numbers, the rows are sequenced by part number—J4-P1, J4-P3, J4-P5, and so on. As with the GROUP BY statement, the maximum number of columns that may be used with an ORDER BY depends on the total length of the column values with 4000 bytes being the limit.

The ORDER BY clause need not identify the returned column or columns to be used in the sequence by name. Instead it can identify them by their position in the SELECT clause. An equivalent ORDER BY clause for the above statement would be ORDER BY 1, 2. This facility is useful for substituting for long column names. Its use is required if a mathematical operation stipulated in the SELECT clause returns the values to be sorted or to indicate the columns to be sorted in UNION operations (discussed in Section 7.10).

DB2 sequences null values as being higher than any other value. It will sequence in ascending or descending order. Ascending is the default. A user specifies descending order by placing the word DESC after the column in the ORDER BY clause—for example, ORDER BY PN DESC.

7.8 SUBSELECTS

Subselects are selects that work in conjunction with other selects, providing values that determine part of the search criteria. In simple as opposed to correlated subselects, DB2 usually first performs the subselect, or inner select, presented within parentheses below the primary, or outer, select. The value or values returned for the subselect provide values for the search criteria for the primary select.

In correlated subselects, the subselect's search criteria depend on values from the table identified in the outer select. SQL evaluates the outer select first and passes a value to the subselect, which returns values one at a time to be used in completion of the outer select. Both types of subselects can best be explained through examples.

To understand a simple subselect, consider a search for parts that exceed the average weight of all the parts kept in London. A subselect can determine the average weight and pass that value to a primary select that locates the heavier parts:

```
SELECT PNAME, WEIGHT
FROM    P
WHERE   WEIGHT >
  (SELECT AVG(WEIGHT)
   FROM    P
   WHERE   CITY 'LONDON')
```

Returns:

PNAME	WEIGHT
SCREW	17
BOLT	17
COG	19

Subselect Returning Multiple Values

Subselects can also pass multiple values to the primary select, most frequently done by using the IN operator in the primary select to address a set of values returned by the subselect. To determine the part number and name of parts supplied by supplier S2, for example, a subselect could locate S2's part numbers in the SPJ table and pass that set to a select that finds those parts' names in the P table. The statement for this select is:

```
SELECT PN, PNAME
FROM    P
WHERE   PN IN
  (SELECT PN
   FROM    SPJ
   WHERE   SN = 'S2')
```

Returns:

PN	PNAME
P3	SCREW
P5	CAM

The primary select can also use three other operators—ALL, ANY, and SOME—to address sets of values returned by the subselect. Used in the select's WHERE clause, ALL, ANY, or SOME instructs the select to find rows based on their comparison to the values in the returned set. For ALL, each returned row satisfies the comparison against all values in the set. For ANY and SOME, which are equivalent, each satisfies the comparison against at least one value in the set. For example, the following statement determines all parts that weigh more than each and every part stored in PARIS:

```
SELECT PNAME, WEIGHT, CITY
FROM   P
WHERE  WEIGHT > ALL
  (SELECT WEIGHT
   FROM   P
   WHERE  CITY = 'PARIS')
```

The words ANY and ALL are somewhat ambiguous and do not naturally carry to some users the operators' precise meanings. Moreover, SQL's handling of unknown values with respect to these operators can be misleading. Since searches provided by the ANY, ALL, and SOME operators can be performed with equivalent statements using more straightforward terminology, users may be wise to avoid these operators entirely rather than having to deal with their somewhat confusing distinctions. For example, selecting parts that weigh more than each and every part stored in Paris is the same as selecting parts that weigh more than the heaviest part stored in Paris. The MAX operator can identify those rows.

```
SELECT PNAME, WEIGHT, CITY
FROM   P
WHERE  WEIGHT >
  (SELECT MAX(WEIGHT)
   FROM   P
   WHERE  CITY = 'PARIS')
```

Similarly the MIN operator can perform the function of ANY or SOME. To say that a given value is greater than any or some of the values in a set is the same as saying that it is greater than the least value in the set and that the different formulation will return the same results.

Care must be exercised if there is a possibility that no rows will qualify for the subselect when using ALL and MAX interchangeably since the result can differ. If there are no parts in Paris, all weights will be greater than will the empty set, but no weights will be greater than will a null from MAX. If there are parts in Paris, MAX returns the same results as does ALL. MIN and ANY or SOME return the same results regardless of whether rows qualify in the subselect. No weights will be greater than is the empty set, and no weights will be greater than is a null MIN.

Nulls are also troublesome if they appear in rows in a table processed in a subselect. Assume for a moment that the PN column contains a null in the SPJ table and that there is a P99 in the P table. It is necessary to determine information on parts in P that are not used on jobs in SPJ, and the statement used is:

```
SELECT PN, PNAME, COLOR, WEIGHT, CITY
FROM   P
WHERE  PN NOT IN
  (SELECT PN
   FROM   SPJ)
```

The P99 in the P table will not be identified. The rational is that the unknown value in the SPJ might be P99. Either of the following two formulations of the request will identify the P99 that is not currently being used on any job.

```
SELECT PN, PNAME, COLOR, WEIGHT, CITY
FROM   P
WHERE  PN NOT IN
  (SELECT PN
   FROM   SPJ
   WHERE  SPJ.PN IS NOT NULL)
```

The subselect excludes any nulls with the predicate WHERE SPJ.PN IS NOT NULL.

```
SELECT PN, PNAME, COLOR, WEIGHT, CITY
FROM   P PX
WHERE  PN NOT IN
  (SELECT PN
   FROM   SPJ
   WHERE  SPJ.PN = PX.PN)
```

The subselect is comparing part numbers between the SPJ and P tables. It was said earlier that null compares to no value, therefore any nulls will be ignored. These are just a few of the potential problems when dealing with nulls and the reason that most developers declare most columns NOT NULL WITH DEFAULT. Recall from the previous examples that even then a subselect can return null and aggregates can return null in inner or outer selects if no rows qualify as a result of the WHERE clause.

Nested Subselects

A subselect can pass an intermediate answer set to a subselect that uses it in defining the search criteria that allow it to pass an intermediate answer to another subselect, and so on for as many subselects as a search may need. The only limit is that any single SQL statement may not exceed 32K bytes and cannot reference more than 15 tables. In most cases, SQL executes the innermost subselect first and works its way up. For example, a search to locate the part number and name for parts supplied by supplier Jones would be similar to the search presented above in which we found the part numbers and names for parts supplied by S2. In this case, however, an additional subselect is needed to find Jones's supplier number. The necessary statement is:

```
SELECT PN, PNAME
FROM   P
WHERE  PN IN
  (SELECT PN
   FROM   SPJ
   WHERE  SN =
     (SELECT SN
      FROM   S
      WHERE  SNAME = 'JONES'))
```

Returns:

```
PN PNAME
P3 SCREW
P5 CAM
```

Correlated Subselects

In a correlated subselect, the outer select identifies a table from which SQL draws values for use in the subselect. The outer select passes one row at a time from the identified table to the subselect, which uses the column specified in the subselect to perform the subselect. For example, to determine the names of parts used on job 1, the search can check each part listed in the P table against all the parts listed in the SPJ table. If when the part number (PN) from P matches the PN from SPJ, the job number equals J1, the select returns that part's name. This statement satisfies the search:

```
SELECT PNAME
FROM   P PX
WHERE  'J1' IN
  (SELECT JN
   FROM   SPJ
   WHERE  SPJ.SN = PX.PN)
```

To perform this search, SQL first passes the first part number from the P table to the subselect. The subselect uses the part number, P1, from that row in its search. This search finds P1 used in two jobs—J1 and J4—which make up the set returned to the outer select for evaluation with the IN operator. Since J1 is the first value returned, the outer select returns PNAME from the P1 row in the P table—NUT. SQL continues the process by passing to the subselect each subsequent part number from the P table in turn. Try continuing the search using the remaining values from the P table.

7.9 JOINS

In general joins combine information from two or more tables by comparing all the values that meet the search criteria in the designated column or columns of one table with all the values in corresponding columns of the other table or tables. When the values meet the comparison criteria, the rows containing them are joined and used for the select. (This kind of join is called an *inner join. Outer joins,* discussed in Section 7.11, do not require a match in both columns to be joined.)

A simple example illustrates the join concept. To find all suppliers of part P4, their names, cities, and amounts they supply, a search must draw from tables S and SPJ. The first step could be to find the P4 suppliers, identified by supplier number, in the SPJ table. Those rows, shaded in Fig. 7.3, also provide the quantities supplied. The next step is to find the suppliers' names and cities by matching the SN values associated with P4 in the SPJ table with the SN values in the S table—that is, by comparing the values for equality. When a match is found, the combined row provides the information for the select.

The FROM clause of the SELECT statement for the join must include the tables that participate. The WHERE clause identifies the columns to be compared and the type of comparison. Although most joins involve a match of values—called a *natural join*—any of the comparison operators may be used. The statement needed for this join is:

```
SELECT SNAME, CITY, QTY
FROM   S, SPJ
WHERE  S.SN = SPJ.SN
AND    PN   = 'P4'

Returns:

SNAME CITY
BLAKE PARIS
ADAMS ATHENS
```

Although not a requirement, in most cases, the columns on which the tables are joined have the same name, data type, and length. When they have the same name, it must be qualified by the table name—SPJ.SN, for example.

(S) Table

SN	SNAME	STATUS	CITY
S1	SMITH	20	LONDON
S2	JONES	10	PARIS
S3	BLAKE	30	PARIS
S4	CLARK	20	LONDON
S5	ADAMS	30	ATHENS

(SPJ) Table

SN	PN	JN	QTY
S1	P1	J1	200
S1	P1	J4	700
S2	P3	J1	400
S2	P3	J2	200
S2	P3	J3	200
S2	P3	J4	500
S2	P3	J5	600
S2	P3	J6	400
S2	P3	J7	800
S2	P5	J2	100
S3	P3	J1	200
S3	P4	J2	500
S4	P6	J3	300
S4	P6	J7	300
S5	P2	J2	200
S5	P2	J4	100
S5	P5	J5	500
S5	P5	J7	100
S5	P6	J2	200
S5	P1	J4	100
S5	P3	J4	200
S5	P4	J4	800
S5	P5	J4	400
S5	P6	J4	500

Fig. 7.3 A join

Three-way Joins

A SELECT statement may join up to 15 tables, but joins of many tables
are not common. The additional joins are simply added to the WHERE
clause. Suppose, for example, that we wish to find the name of P4 along
with the other information requested in the above search. Part names are
included in the P table, so including that table in the join is one way to
expand the search. In this case, we join the P and SPJ tables on the PN
column. The necessary statement is:

```
SELECT SNAME, S.CITY, PNAME, QTY
FROM    S, SPJ, P
WHERE   S.SN   = SPJ.SN
AND     SPJ.PN = P.PN
AND     P.PN   = 'P4'

Returns:

SNAME CITY   PNAME QTY
```

```
BLAKE PARIS  SCREW 500
ADAMS ATHENS SCREW 800
```

Notice that the CITY column in the SELECT clause is modified by the S table name to distinguish it from the CITY column in the P table, also part of the joined tables.

Joins Using Comparisons Other Than Equality

Any of SQL's comparison operators may be used as the basis on which tables are joined. The following example search, while perhaps of limited utility except to a port authority, demonstrates such a join. In the example, we want DB2 to compare the ship length in the ship table to the dock length in the dock table to determine which docks are long enough to accommodate a ship pulling into port. The SELECT will return the dock ID that can be communicated to the ship. The necessary statement is:

```
SELECT SHIP_LENGTH, DOCK_ID
FROM   SHIP, DOCKS
WHERE  SHIP_LENGTH < DOCK_LENGTH
```

Joining a Table with Itself

SQL can join a table with itself, treating the table as if it were two identical copies of itself. Since the same table must be referred to twice in the FROM clause, a correlation name must be used to distinguish each reference. A correlation name is created with a character string placed after the table name in the FROM clause, with the table name and correlation name separated only by a space. The correlation name can then be used to qualify columns in other parts of a SELECT statement. Correlation names are required when a table is joined with itself but may be used at any time. They are particularly helpful in saving key strokes when a short correlation name substitutes for a long table name. In the example below, I and II represent the correlation names for the SPJ table.

A request to find the combined quantity of parts P2 and P6 for each supplier that supplies both parts for the same job demonstrates a join of a table with itself. To grasp how this join works, imagine that there are actually two SPJ tables, as shown in Fig. 7.4. The statement is:

```
SELECT I.SN, I.JN, I.PN, I.QTY, II.QTY,
       I.QTY + II.QTY
FROM   SPJ I, SPJ II
WHERE  I.SN  = II.SN
AND    I.PN  = 'P2'
AND    II.PN = 'P6'
```

SPJ I

SN	PN	JN	QTY
S1	P1	J1	200
S1	P1	J4	700
S2	P3	J1	400
S2	P3	J2	200
S2	P3	J3	200
S2	P3	J4	500
S2	P3	J5	600
S2	P3	J6	400
S2	P3	J7	800
S2	P5	J2	100
S3	P3	J1	200
S3	P4	J2	500
S4	P6	J3	300
S4	P6	J7	300
S5	P2	J2	200
S5	P2	J4	100
S5	P5	J5	500
S5	P5	J7	100
S5	P6	J2	200
S5	P1	J4	100
S5	P3	J4	200
S5	P4	J4	800
S5	P5	J4	400
S5	P6	J4	500

SPJ I

SN	PN	JN	QTY
S1	P1	J1	200
S1	P1	J4	700
S2	P3	J1	400
.S2	P3	J2	200
S2	P3	J3	200
S2	P3	J4	500
S2	P3	J5	600
S2	P3	J6	400
S2	P3	J7	800
S2	P5	J2	100
S3	P3	J1	200
S3	P4	J2	500
S4	P6	J3	300
S4	P6	J7	300
S5	P2	J2	200
S5	P2	J4	100
S5	P5	J5	500
S5	P5	J7	100
S5	P6	J2	200
S5	P1	J4	100
S5	P3	J4	200
S5	P4	J4	800
S5	P5	J4	400
S5	P6	J4	500

Fig. 7.4 Joining a table with itself

```
ORDER  BY 7 DESC
```

Returns:

I.SN	I.JN	I.PN	I.QTY	II.PN	II.QTY	I.QTY+II.QTY
S5	J2	P2	200	P6	200	400
S5	J4	P2	100	P6	500	600

To evaluate the statement, consider that each row of SPJ I is compared against each row of SPJ II. I.SN must equal II.SN because the request deals with the activity of individual suppliers. I.JN must equal II.JN because the activity relates to one job. Joining rows that meet those criteria and include parts P2 and P6 will provide the answer. Those rows are shaded in Fig. 7.4. In practice the search would probably be narrowed to P2 and P6 before the join.

7.10   UNION

In set operations, a union includes values that appear in either or both of the original sets, with duplicate values excluded from the results. Columns participating in a union must be of compatible data type—broadly defined, a numeric type can be unioned with another numeric type and a character type can be unioned with another character type.

In general, a union consists of multiple SELECT statements combined with UNION operators. Each SELECT identifies the column or columns on which the union is to be performed. The participating SELECT clauses must specify the same number of columns or literals, and literals can be specified instead of columns. The SELECT statements also identify the columns to be included from each table in the union operation. For example, this statement will determine the suppliers included in either or both the S and SPJ tables:

```
SELECT SN
FROM    S
UNION
SELECT SN
FROM    SPJ

Returns:

SN
S1
S2
S3
S4
S5
```

In many cases, rows, or column values, will be selected from each table in a union for different reasons. In those cases, literals printed out with each returned value allow users to keep track of why it was selected. A SELECT clause's literals, which are enclosed in single quotation marks, print out along with the values returned by the select.

Consider, for example, a search for parts that weigh more than 16 pounds and parts that are supplied by S2. The first set of parts can be found in the P table and the second set in the SPJ table. A union of the two sets will return all the parts requested. Literals used with each SELECT will identify in the report the reason each part was included. Since each SELECT associates a different literal with each returned value, duplicate part numbers selected from the two tables may be included. The necessary statement is:

```
SELECT PN, 'WEIGHT > 16'
FROM    P
WHERE   WEIGHT > 16
UNION
SELECT PN, 'SUPPLIED BY S2'
FROM    SPJ
WHERE   SN = 'S2'
```

```
ORDER BY 2, 1

Returns:
```

```
PN
P3 SUPPLIED BY S2
P5 SUPPLIED BY S2
P2 WEIGHT > 16
P3 WEIGHT > 16
P6 WEIGHT > 16
```

If the output is to be sorted, the ORDER BY clause must appear after the final SELECT and must specify the columns to be sorted by their numeric position in the statement. UNION automatically eliminates duplicate rows returned by the participating SELECT statements. The UNION ALL instructs DB2 to leave duplicates in the union's results.

7.11   OUTER JOINS

In the join examples discussed, rows were joined when values in the participating tables compared in a particular way. In some cases, though, it is desirable to include in a join rows from different tables when there are no matching values in both tables for comparison. This is called an *outer join*. An example will clarify the concept.

Consider a search of the EMP and DEPT tables to locate employees who are not assigned to departments and departments that have no employees assigned. An inner join on DEPTNO in the EMP and DEPT tables will find departments that have employees and employees who are assigned to departments. The relational model has an operator for outer joins and the ANSI and ISO SQL2 standard plans to include outer join operators. At present, it is necessary to use subselects to accomplish an outer join using DB2. This example of an outer join requires three sections:

1.   The select to find departments that have employees and employees assigned to departments, the inner join

2.   Two selects with subselects to test for no matches between departments in the DEPT table and departments in the EMP table

3.   Unions of rows from the three selects. UNION ALL is used since there can be no duplicates.

The required statement is:

```
SELECT D.DEPTNO, DNAME, E.EMPNO, ENAME
FROM   DEPT D, EMP E
WHERE  D.DEPTNO = E.DEPTNO
UNION  ALL
SELECT D.DEPTNO, DNAME, '?', '?'
```

```
FROM    DEPT D
WHERE NOT EXISTS
  (SELECT E.DEPTNO
   FROM   EMP E
   WHERE  D.DEPTNO = E.DEPTNO)
UNION  ALL
SELECT '?', '?', E.EMPNO, ENAME
FROM    EMP E
WHERE  NOT EXISTS
  (SELECT D.DEPTNO
   FROM   DEPT D
   WHERE  D.DEPTNO = E.DEPTNO)
```

In the first subselect, each DEPTNO value from the DEPT table is compared with the DEPTNO values in the EMP table. If there is no match, the WHERE NOT EXISTS condition (see below) is satisfied, and that department's row is included in the results, providing departments with no employees. This can be thought of as the left outer join since the DEPT table is the left table in the FROM list of the inner join. The second subselect performs in the same way to find departments that have no match in the employee table and employees who are not assigned to a department. This would then be the right outer join. The statement returns:

D.DEPT	DNAME	E.EMPNO	ENAME
D5	AI	?	?
D1	INFOSYS	E1	FLEUR
D1	INFOSYS	E4	ERIC
D1	INFOSYS	E6	DENNIS
D2	DBADM	E2	TOM
D2	DBADM	E5	KATHY
D3	DATADM	E2	TOM
D3	DATADM	E5	HEATHER
D4	PROGDEV	E1	FLEUR
D4	PROGDEV	E4	ERIC
D4	PROGDEV	E6	DENNIS
?	?	E3	BILL

7.12 INTERSECTION AND DIFFERENCE

In set operations, *intersection* represents the values common to both original sets. *Difference* represents the values of one set that do not also belong to the second set. Fig. 7.5 illustrates these ideas. SQL can calculate intersection and difference by using the EXISTS and NOT EXISTS operators along with correlated subselects. The EXISTS and NOT EXISTS operators return a true or false value to the outer select depending on the evaluation of the subselect with which they are used. For EXISTS, if there is a value satisfying the subselect, the operator returns true. For NOT EXISTS, if there is no value satisfying the subselect, the operator returns true. The outer select includes a row whenever the subselect returns a true evaluation.

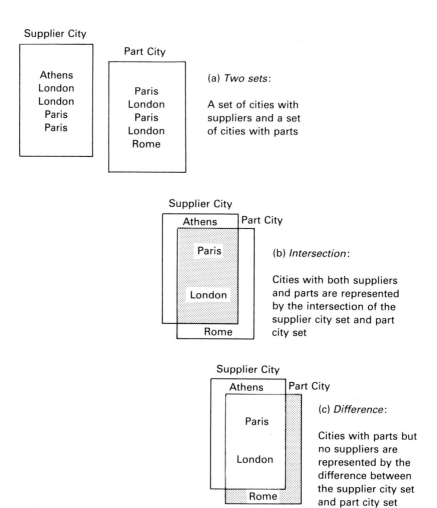

Fig. 7.5 Intersection and difference

A select to determine the cities that have both suppliers and part stocks represents the intersection of the two sets of city values from S and P tables. This statement is used to determine that intersection:

```
SELECT DISTINCT CITY
FROM   S
WHERE  EXISTS
   (SELECT CITY
    FROM   P
    WHERE  P.CITY = S.CITY)
```

```
Returns:

CITY
LONDON
PARIS
```

DB2 performs the search by passing the first city from S to the subselect, which finds a match for LONDON and therefore returns a true evaluation. The outer select therefore includes the row, returning LONDON. Then it continues the process for each subsequent row.

Similarly a search to determine whether there are any cities with parts but no suppliers, found by subtracting the cities in S from those in P, would represent a difference. The statement to determine this difference is:

```
SELECT DISTINCT CITY
FROM   P
WHERE  NOT EXISTS
  (SELECT CITY
   FROM   S
   WHERE  CITY = P.CITY)

Returns:

CITY
ROME
```

If the CITY value from a row in P does not match any CITY value in S, the subselect returns a true value for the NOT EXISTS operator, causing the outer select to return that CITY. In this case, the difference between PART cities and SUPPLIER cities is ROME.

7.13 INSERTING, UPDATING, OR DELETING DATA

SQL allows users to change the values of stored data. The statements required for inserts, updates, and deletes are straightforward.

Inserts

All INSERT statements begin with the words "INSERT INTO" followed by the name of the table to receive the inserts and, in parentheses, the columns to receive the data. The data to be inserted can be specified within parentheses in a VALUES clause, or they can be selected from another table. If all of a table's columns are to receive data, their names need not be specified in the INSERT INTO clause. The following statement, for example, inserts the specified values into all the columns in the S table:

```
INSERT INTO S
  VALUES ('S10', 'JOHNSON', 50, 'DALLAS')
```

If the column names are not specified in the INSERT INTO clause, the values must be listed in the order that the columns were specified in the CREATE TABLE statement. Each inserted value must have a compatible data type and length specified for the column that receives it.

When SQL is embedded in a program, even if all a table's columns are to be included in an insert, it is good practice is to specify them anyway; that way if a new column is added to the table, the insert program will not have to be changed to account for it. (The added column must allow nulls or be specified NOT NULL WITH DEFAULT since the programmed inserts will not provide values for it.) A statement specifying the columns to receive data takes this form:

```
INSERT INTO S (SN, SNAME, CITY)
   VALUES ('S10', 'JOHNSON', 'DALLAS')
```

The inserted values correspond in order to the order of the columns in the INSERT INTO clause. Again, the table columns left out of this statement must be nullable or NOT NULL WITH DEFAULT.

When a SELECT statement is used with an INSERT, the select copies the data it retrieves into the specified table rather than returning it to the user or program. Developers often find the method useful for building a test table from a subset of a production table, as demonstrated by this example:

```
INSERT INTO S_TEST
   SELECT SN, SNAME, STATUS, CITY
   FROM   S
   WHERE  SN < 'S4'
```

Updates

An update, which changes values already stored, includes an UPDATE clause, which indicates the table containing the information to be changed, and a SET clause, which indicates the columns to be changed and their new values. It also uses a WHERE clause to identify specific rows to be changed. Suppose supplier S1 has moved to Dallas and increased its status by 10. Its new name is not known. The necessary update of the S table would require this statement:

```
UPDATE S
   SET CITY   = 'DALLAS',
       STATUS = STATUS + 10,
       SNAME  = NULL
   WHERE SN   = 'S1'
```

Notice that DB2 will update numeric columns based upon mathematical calculations as in the STATUS column. Notice also that an equal sign is used to assign a null to a column, in contrast to the test for a null with a SELECT statement, which requires the special IS operator.

An update can also use a subselect. For example, Supplier Blake has sent an additional 10 each of all parts it supplies to jobs recorded in the SPJ table, but the person wanting to update QTY does not know Blake's supplier number. This UPDATE statement with subselect will handle the change:

```
UPDATE SPJ
SET QTY = QTY + 10
WHERE SN IN
  (SELECT SN
   FROM   S
   WHERE  SNAME = 'BLAKE')
```

Deletes

DELETE statements identify the table from which rows are to be removed and, through a WHERE clause, the specific rows. For example, this statement to delete from the J table jobs performed in Rome:

```
DELETE FROM S
   WHERE CITY = 'ROME'
```

removes the only row that satisfies the WHERE criterion—that for job J2. Subselects can also identify rows to be deleted.

7.14 SUMMARY

SQL provides rich data access and manipulation capabilities. This chapter provides a grounding in those capabilities including information on SQL syntax and on how to employ the SQL operators. Mastering this information is only the first step in learning to use SQL with DB2, however. One must also understand how to use it within programs and understand DB2's implementation of SQL to be able to formulate the most efficient statements. Chapters 9 through 11 discuss how to develop programs for DB2 and efficient use of SQL.

EXERCISES

7.1. What is the danger of using SELECT * in a host-language program? Questions 2 through 4 refer to the tables in Fig. 7.1.

7.2. Write a SELECT statement to determine the names of all jobs using part numbers P1 and P6 and the quantities used. Order the results by job name and quantity; include the part number with each returned row. Determine the results table.

7.3. Use the GROUP BY operator to find how many of part P5 are available, on average, from each supplier that supplies it. The SELECT should provide each supplier number and its average. Determine the results table.

7.4. Write a SELECT statement to determine the job numbers of jobs for which any supplier supplies more P6s than P5s. Include the supplier number in the results. Determine the results.

8

Concurrency Control

8.1 INTRODUCTION

Concurrency control seeks to eliminate the possibility of one user or program changing data while another is in the process of using or changing them, a situation that can lead to errors or inconsistencies in the data. DB2 manages concurrency control with several types of locks that restrict access to data while they are being used. In all but one case, DB2 selects the appropriate lock type based on concurrency control requirements inherent in the transaction. These are called *implicit locks*. In the one exception, programmers may include in applications explicit locks, which the programs issue to lock a table for specific periods.

One example of what can happen when locks are not available demonstrates their utility. Assume the Johnsons have a $1000 checking account balance. Mrs. Johnson withdraws $200 at 10:01:01.001 A.M. At precisely that instant plus a millisecond, before her transaction completes and the new $800 balance is entered, Mr. Johnson withdraws $300. His deduction is taken from the still-intact $1000, and a new balance of $700 is written to the account, overwriting Mrs. Johnson's work. Mrs. Johnson received her $200, but the transaction was lost. Since the final balance should have been $500, the bank also lost. A lock on the account during Mrs. Johnson's transaction would have held Mr. Johnson's transaction at bay. A number

Box 8.1   DB2's locking strategy

DB2 determines its locking strategy for each transaction when it binds the transaction's plan. It bases the strategy on a number of factors:

- The locksizes declared on the tablespaces and indexes in the SQL CRE-ATE statements defining them.
- Type of SQL statements—whether SELECT or UPDATE, for example—within a COMMIT's scope.
- The presence of explicit LOCK TABLE statements.
- The ACQUIRE and RELEASE options chosen by the developer at bind time.
- The isolation level—cursor stability or repeatable read—chosen at bind time.
- The NUMLKTS and NUMLKUS limits.
- The access path chosen.

of other errors are possible when more than one transaction accesses the same data at the same time.

The specific points in a transaction when DB2 acquires or releases locks and the amount of data covered by any particular lock depends on decisions the designer makes during tablespace creation and when issuing a bind command. Locks hold important performance tradeoffs. Overly broad locking results in poor response times as users and programs wait their turns at the data. Overly precise locking provides a high degree of concurrency but requires considerable CPU time and virtual storage for managing the locks. To use locks most efficiently, developers must understand their options for controlling locks and how DB2 will react to their choices.

8.2   TRANSACTIONS, COMMITS, ROLLBACKS

Locks protect data while DB2 performs the logical units of work necessary to complete a database transaction, such as the withdrawal of funds from a savings account or the addition of a part to an inventory. Typically such transactions require a series of updates, insertions, and deletions and internal operations such as fetching and summing data. The total of these steps represents the transaction's logical unit of work. For the savings withdrawal, for example, the transaction must make an entry in the account, adjust and enter the new balance, and adjust and enter the bank's new cash position. To maintain consistency, for a transaction to be successfully completed and recorded, all of its steps must be completed. Otherwise none of the work should be recorded.

Generally DB2 begins acquiring locks on a transaction's affected data when the first SQL statement in a program is executed and holds them until the unit of work is complete or the program terminates. (We will discuss the precise points at which locks are acquired and released.) When the work is complete, DB2 commits it, recording it in an active log dataset for later transfer to storage in the tablespace. Once the change is safely recorded in the log, any locks on the data can be released and the pages can be used by others without requiring additional physical I/O. Programmers can indicate commit points with COMMIT WORK statements within programs, sometimes using them to establish shorter units of work within what initially may have been seen as a logical unit of work and thus creating smaller units of recovery.

The locking arrangement must also make provisions for situations when the transaction does not complete—when the system fails in the midst of the work, for example. In that case, DB2 can follow the information in the log to roll back the status of various system elements to their values at the start of the transaction's processing or at a previous commit point. After the rollback, DB2 releases the locks and issues an error message. Locks themselves can in certain circumstances prevent transactions from completing, a situation called a *deadlock*.

Deadlocks

Certain transactions executing at the same time can lock each other out of data that they need to complete their logical units of work. Since neither can complete its work and commit, neither can release its locks. Nevertheless each waits for the other in a situation called a deadlock or, by some, a deadly embrace.

We will refer to the Johnsons again for a simple example to illustrate deadlocks. Assume that their checking account balance is again $1000 and that they also have a $2000 savings account balance. Assume also that the system is programmed to consider that a transfer from one account to the other is a single transaction, made up of a withdrawal and deposit. Mrs. Johnson attempts to withdraw $200 from the savings account and deposit it in the checking account. At the same time, Mr. Johnson tries to transfer $300 from checking to savings. Mrs. Johnson's transaction begins by locking the savings account so the deduction can be made without threat of a concurrent change. Mr. Johnson's work begins with a lock on the checking

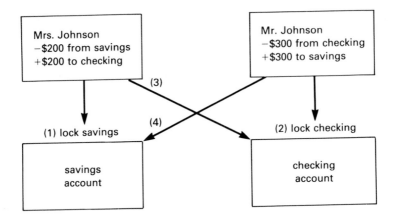

(1) Mrs. Johnson locks the savings account page that contains the row.
(2) Mr. Johnson locks the checking account page that contains the row.
(3) Mrs. Johnson attempts to read the checking account, but it is locked.
(4) Mr. Johnson attempts to read the savings account, but it is locked.

Fig. 8.1 Deadlock

account for the same reason. Mrs. Johnson's transaction tries to continue with an update of the checking account but cannot gain access because of Mr. Johnson's lock. His transaction cannot complete because it encounters his wife's lock on the savings account. Neither transaction can drop its lock until it completes and its work is committed. Neither transaction can complete. Mr. and Mrs. Johnson, or at least their transactions, are in deadly embrace (Fig. 8.1).

DB2 resolves a deadlock by rolling back any action already taken by the transaction in the deadlock that has the fewest log records. This releases that transaction's locks. Usually the transaction rolled back is the one for which a lock was most recently taken. In this example, DB2 will release Mr. Johnson's lock on the checking account, which allows Mrs. Johnson to complete her business. Then Mr. Johnson's transaction can try again.

Inserts and deletes can cause deadlocks because they often require the locking of multiple indexes. The diagram in Fig. 8.2 shows a deadlock arising from an insertion into a checking account table with a concurrent select from that table. The insertion first takes a lock on the appropriate subpage in the table's clustering index (1), followed by a lock on the data page to receive the insertion (2), followed by attempts to lock any other indexes that may have to be updated (4). The select statement, however, may have

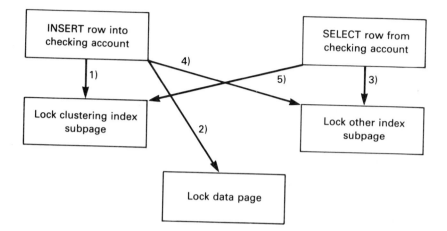

Fig. 8.2 Deadlock due to an insert

taken a lock on one of those other indexes (3), barring the insert's attempt. Meanwhile the select cannot complete because its attempt to use the clustering index (5) is prevented by the insert's lock. The more indexes there are, the more likely it is that lock contention can result.

DB2 checks for deadlocks every 15 seconds unless the system administrator has chosen to change this default value. When it encounters and resolves a deadlock, it issues a message, a negative SQLCODE indicating what action it has taken. The code is −911 if a rollback has been executed and −913 if the program is requested to issue a rollback. (The corresponding SQLSTATE is '40000' and '40502'.) Typically a programmer will have included an error routine in the program that reads the code and reacts accordingly. Depending on the error code and the error routine, the program might automatically reissue Mr. Johnson's transaction or send him a message asking him to reenter the request. CICS provides a transaction restart facility for handling deadlocks that works with DB2 transactions. Under IMS, a deadlock results in automatic requeueing of the transaction, also called a pseudo-abend, resulting in an U777 message.

A DB2 component called the IRLM (IMS resource lock manager) controls all locks. It services them on a first-in, first-out (FIFO) basis. If a lock required by a program is unavailable, it is considered a lock suspension. If the resource is not available within the specified time, a timeout or deadlock will occur. The IRLM returns a −913 to DB2 if it cannot service a lock request within 60 seconds for a transaction or query. If an update has occurred, DB2 returns an SQLCODE of −911 to the program in most cases, and a reason code indicates if it is a deadlock or timeout. (The 60-

second time limit is a default value that the system administrators can change.) The time limit applies to transactions and queries and is multiplied by 3 for binds, by 4 for transaction-driven BMPs, by 6 for IMS fast path, and −STOP DATABASE waits indefinitely with messages written to the console.

8.3 LOCK SIZES AND TYPES

DB2 can lock individual data pages, tables in a segmented tablespace, or entire tablespaces using a variety of lock types that offer a range of concurrency levels. It will also lock index leaf pages or, with subpage locks, fractions of index leaf pages, again using a variety of lock types. A tablespace creator can specify whether DB2 is to use a tablespace, table, or page locksize when applications access the tables. Or the developer can specify a locksize of ANY, indicating that DB2 should choose the locksize whenever the table is accessed. In that case, DB2 usually chooses a locksize of page. The developer also specifies the index locksize when creating the index, although no locks will be taken against indexes when table or tablespace locks are in effect. The developer's decisions on locksizes depend on how the particular table and indexes will be used, with the general tradeoff between response times and CPU and virtual storage usage in effect.

Lock Escalations and Limits

Because page locks require considerable resources, DB2 allows system administrators to limit the number of them that may be taken by any one program or interactive user. Administrators may use two controls, NUMLKTS and NUMLKUS. NUMLKTS causes a page locksize to be promoted to a table or tablespace locksize when any one program or user request has taken a predetermined number of locks on objects in a single tablespace, including data pages, index pages, tables, and the tablespace itself. If a user or program exceeds a predetermined number of locks, specified for NUMLKUS, a −904 (SQLSTATE = '57011') is returned to the program.

The system administrator sets the limits for the entire DB2 system with a default of 10,000 for NUMLKUS. The system administrator uses the NUMLKTS command to limit the number of data-page, index-page, table, and tablespace locks a program or user request can take against objects in a single tablespace having a locksize of ANY. (If the system administrator does not change the initial NUMLKTS limit, the default is 1000.) When a program exceeds the limit, DB2 promotes the lock to a table lock and releases all locks against it except for the tablespace intent lock. If the tablespace is not segmented, the promotion is to a tablespace lock. No SQL-CODE is issued when this occurs to inform the user. This is a good reason to use a locksize of PAGE rather than ANY so that unexpected table or tablespace locks are not taken.

The administrator uses the NUMLKUS command to limit the number of locks a program can hold against all objects in a tablespace created with locksize of PAGE or ANY. If the program exceeds the limit, DB2 issues a negative SQLCODE of −904. The program's error module can then choose to commit or roll back to release the locks. The developer can avoid having a program exceed the NUMLKTS and NUMLKUS limits by having it commit work frequently or by coding a program to issue a LOCK TABLE statement to avoid exceeding a limit. Because of this explicit lock, data- and index-page locks will not be taken against the tablespace, and any previously taken locks will be released.

If system administrators feel that resources are plentiful, they might set NUMLKTS and NUMLKUS at zero, allowing programs to take as many page locks as they need without having the locks promoted to table or tablespace locks or having to process an error condition. This should not be done in the majority of the cases since if the amount of space allocated to the IRLM is exceeded, the IRLM will abend, bringing DB2 down with it. Application programmers can reduce the chances of exceeding the limits by having the program commit work frequently, releasing the locks each time. Use of the cursor stability isolation level for fetching data, discussed in Section 8.4, also reduces the chances that a program will exceed the NUMLKTS and NUMLKUS limits.

DB2 can impose locks against both data and indexes during referential integrity checking. Although the tables may not be explicitly referenced in SQL statements, a count of the locks are included and checked against the NUMLKTS and NUMLKUS limits. This can result in exceeding the limits even though it appears that the limits should not have been exceeded based on an analysis of the explicitly coded SQL statements.

Commit Frequency

The frequency of issuing a commit work can significantly effect performance. IBM tested this effect on DB2 V2.2, 3090/600S with 256M real and 1G expanded storage, using 3380 DASD. The test consisted of updating (not insert/delete) 100,000 rows in a 1,000,000 row table (the 100,000 records used to update the table were in a sequential file).

The results in Fig. 8.3 suggests that a commit after every update should be avoided since over an hour of elapsed time was required. If business requirements permit, a good commit frequency for an online transaction would be about every 5 to 10 updates to minimize CPU time and I/O. A good target for batch processing is to commit every 1000 updates, and a

Commit Frequency	Elapsed mm:ss	CPU mm:ss	I/O mm:ss
1 update	68:31	35:60	27:04
10 updates	16:25	11:26	3:31
100 updates	10:55	9:02	0:55
1000 updates	9:41	8:39	0:08
Lock table	8:50	7:59	0:03

Fig. 8.3 Commit frequency

LOCK TABLE statement reduces resource consumption further. These are reasonable rule-of-thumb figures, but different programs in different environments can require very different CPU and elapsed time to perform the same number of updates. Therefore an installation may want to perform its own tests to determine the best commit frequency for its environment and specific programs.

Share, Update, and Exclusive Locks

DB2 imposes its locks over four lockable units of differing sizes: page, table, tablespace and, for indexes, subpage. (Since DB2 treats pages and subpages alike, we will use *page* to refer to both.) DB2 uses share locks (S), exclusive locks (X), and update locks (U) with both locksizes. *Share locks* allow two or more programs to read simultaneously but not change the locked space, with each taking a share lock. DB2 uses share locks when it responds to SELECT statements. An *exclusive lock* bars all other users from the locked space while an update takes place. Once a program has taken an exclusive lock, no other transaction can read the data or take any kind of lock against it. It is necessary to read a row before it can be updated or deleted, and during this read, a less restrictive *update* lock is taken. The update lock allows others to read the page and acquire a share lock. An update lock must wait for any share locks to be released so that an exclusive lock can be taken before the actual update or delete. The update lock is queued with share locks to get an exclusive lock.

An exclusive lock is always taken before an actual INSERT, UPDATE, and DELETE operation takes place. If DB2 finds a page locked when it attempts to insert a row on it, it places the row on an available unlocked page, an operation that contributes to unclustering but avoids lock delays. If the target index page is locked, however, it waits to get the lock for 60 seconds after which time an error of -911 or -913 is issued, indicating a

Program A has lock				
		X	U	S
Program B	X	–	–	–
can take	U	–	–	Y
lock	S	–	Y	Y

Fig. 8.4 Page lock compatibility

timeout. It must insert the indexed value in sequence as required by the B-tree structure. This is just one of many reasons that, if lock contention occurs, it is often on the index pages.

Promotions and Update Locks

Before changing a value, DB2 must read it. It would seem logical for DB2 to take a share lock (S) against the page for this read and then promote that to an exclusive lock (X) to make the change. It could take an exclusive lock initially, but that would limit concurrency unnecessarily since there would be many cases in which a program would read data in anticipation of changing them but then delay in making the change or not actually make it. The promotion approach, which DB2 implements, lets concurrent users read the data until the last possible moment before the change—if the change is made at all.

This approach also increases the possibility for deadlocks, however. That is because between the time the update transaction takes the S lock and promotes it to an X lock, a second update transaction would be entitled also to take an S lock against the same page. Each share lock would hold, waiting for the other to clear so it could take an exclusive lock and make its change. Neither could clear, of course, because each is preventing the other from taking the X lock it needs to complete.

The U lock avoids these deadlocks in certain cases while still affording a high level of concurrency. A U lock is compatible with S locks but not with other U locks or X locks. Chapter 9 will discuss how to select rows and declare an intent to update or delete the rows. This processing will result in a U lock being taken while looking for a page to change. Before the change is actually made, the lock will be promoted to an X lock after existing S locks are released. (The matrix in Fig. 8.4 shows compatibility among the three page-level locks.)

If and when the program wants to make the change, it waits for preced-

Data Manipulation	Latch Index Root Page	Lock Index Leaf Subpage	Lock Data (Read Row)	Change Lock (Update Row)	Latch Index Root Page	Lock Leaf Subpage
Select	S	S	S	–	–	–
Insert	S	X	X	–	–	–
Update with cursor	S	U	U	X	S	U/X
Update without cursor	S	S	U	X	S	U/X
Delete with cursor	S	S	S	X	S	U/X
Delete without cursor	S	U	U	X	S	U/X

Time ⟶

Fig. 8.5   Page lock types in time sequence

ing S locks to clear and promotes the U to an X lock. (Fig. 8.5 shows the time sequence of locks on pages.) The S locks are likely to clear because none of them represents an update transaction vainly waiting its turn for an X lock. If one of the concurrent transactions were for an update, it would have had a U lock, barring the second update transaction and avoiding a deadlock. Between the time a transaction acquires a U lock and promotes it, other transactions can acquire share locks, enabling them to read the data. The update transaction must wait for all previous S locks to clear before promoting to an X lock for the change if the change is needed. If a change is not made, the U lock is simply dropped at the next commit point.

Update locks are available at the page level and are used when searching for a row to be updated or deleted. They are usually used when a cursor is used to fetch the data and the user has specified an isolation level of cursor stability. The SQL statement DECLARE [name] CURSOR FOR UPDATE OF invokes the use of U locks. (Cursors and the FOR UPDATE OF clause are discussed in Chapter 9.) DB2 will also use U locks while it is searching for data to be updated without a cursor particularly for updates that will effect multiple rows.

8.4   ISOLATION LEVEL

While SQL SELECT statements may return any number of rows, host languages such as COBOL can deal with only one row at a time. If an SQL statement embedded in a host-language program will return multiple rows, the developer must declare in the program a cursor that presents them to

Cursor Stability		Time	Repeatable Read	
Select row	Lock	t1	Select row	Lock first page
		t2	Fetch row	Lock second page
Fetch row on another page	Lock new page	t3	Fetch row	Lock third page
	Unlock previous page	t4		
		t5	Fetch row	Lock fourth page
Fetch row on another page	Lock new page	t6	Fetch row	Lock fifth page
	Unlock previous page	t7		
Commit	Unlock	t8	Commit	Unlock

The Cursor Stability isolation level unlocks each data page after reading it during a transaction. Repeatable Reads holds all page locks a transaction takes until it commits.

Fig. 8.6 Cursor stability versus repeatable read

the host program one at a time, usually within a repeatedly executed block. DB2 can handle locking for these cursor reads in two ways. The choices, called *isolation levels*, are cursor stability (CS) and repeatable read (RR), which is the default. The levels apply to data covered by a PAGE and ANY locksize. Developers and users specify the isolation level at bind time.

Under cursor stability, DB2 takes a lock on the page the cursor is accessing and releases the lock after the cursor moves to another page and a lock is taken (unless FOR UPDATE OF is used). The lock on the last page accessed is released when a commit work is issued or the cursor is closed in most cases. Under repeatable read, it holds all page locks as the cursor moves through the rows and releases them at the next commit point (Fig. 8.6). Cursor stability obviously provides the better concurrency; however, since it allows other users to access the pages a given program has already read in the midst of a process, this isolation level may allow the data to be changed unbeknown to the original program. Consider a program that reads through a table of plumbing parts to be sure all those needed for a particular job are in stock before submitting an order for any of them. If cursor stability were in effect, another program might scoop up the last

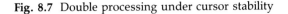

```
SREPORT
PROGRAM   |  SN  |  SNAME  |  STATUS  |  CITY   |
    |
READ 1    |  S1  |  SMITH  |    20    | LONDON  |   UPDATE S
READ 2    |  S2  |  JONES  |    10    | PARIS   |   SET SN='S6'
READ 3   /|  S3  |  BLAKE  |    30    | PARIS   |   WHERE SN='S3'
READ 4  ( |  S4  |  CLARK  |    20    | LONDON  |   Issued by SCHANGE
READ 5    |  S5  |  ADAMS  |    30    | ATHENS  |   SREPORT processes
READ 6  \ |  S6  |  BLAKE  |    30    | PARIS   |   Blake second time
```

SREPORT program uses an index on SN to read rows in supplier number order. Cursor
stability allows SCHANGE program to update S3 to S6 before SREPORT completes,
causing it to process the row twice.

Fig. 8.7 Double processing under cursor stability

number 5 elbow pipe between the time the original program saw it was
available and placed the order including it.

Cursor stability also opens the possibility—though usually only a slight
one—that rows can be mistakenly processed twice or not at all when the
application intended them to be processed once. Consider an application,
SREPORT, that selects suppliers from the Supplier table in Supplier Number order. At the same time, an update program, SCHANGE, is changing
supplier numbers. If SCHANGE increases the Supplier Number of a row
that SREPORT has processed into a range that it is yet to process, SRE-
PORT may well select that row twice. In Fig. 8.7, for example, SREPORT
has processed rows S1, S2, and S3. While it is processing rows S4 and S5,
SCHANGE changes S3 to S6. SREPORT will almost surely process the row
again if the search has been using an index. The update will have added a
pointer from the index for value S6 to the row. Even if the search is using
a tablespace scan that would not return to the page that held the changed
value, it may still encounter the row again if the update had caused it to
be moved. The reverse problem occurs—SREPORT misses a row—when
SCHANGE lowers the row's SN into a range SREPORT has already processed. In addition, locks are not released when a cursor is closed and when
using a singleton SQL statement while RR is in effect.

An isolation level of repeatable read under which SREPORT holds
locks on pages containing processed rows until all processing is complete,
would avoid most of these problems. But whether repeatable read should
be used depends on the application and the facility's processing schedule.
Running batch update and reporting programs in sequence rather than concurrently avoids these double or missed processing problems. Also the seri-

ousness of these problems varies. If the only difficulty that arises from rare processing anomalies is that a plumbing parts inventory might say there are 1020 $0.02 bolts available when there are only 1000, the inconsistency may be tolerable. (The correct number of bolts are in the table. It is a matter of what is read at a given instant.) If on the other hand the application might say a banking customer has $2 million rather than $1 million, there is considerable risk.

Unless the program employing the cursor requires the constancy in the data RR ensures, however, CS is the best choice for isolation level. Besides limiting concurrency by holding numerous locks at the page level, the RR risks the promotion of page locks to a table or tablespace lock if the tablespace has a locksize of ANY or PAGE. If a cursor's SQL statement requires DB2 to create and process an intermediate work file—as it would in processing several types of subselects, for example—RR holds its locks during the processing, which could be a long time. It also risks an error code if the NUMLKUS limit is exceeded. If RR had been specified and at bind time the optimizer does not find a usable index, the optimizer chooses a table or tablespace lock and issues a message, DSNX103I, alerting the developer that the table or tablespace lock will be used to avoid accumulating a lock on every page.

8.5   INTENT LOCKS

When an SQL statement in a transaction first accesses a tablespace covered by a page level lock, DB2 first takes a particular type of lock, called an *intent lock*, at the table level for a segmented tablespace or tablespace level for a nonsegmented tablespace before taking an S, U, or X lock against the page on which the data reside. In a sense, the intent locks act as traffic signals at the table or tablespace level that regulate the use of page-level locks and signal to concurrent transactions whether a particular type of page lock is possible. This function reduces the processing needed to manage the locks while allowing a high degree of compatibility among concurrent locks. For example, if a given transaction needs the data it is about to read to remain unchanged, DB2 could take a share lock against the table or tablespace, which will allow subsequent transactions to read but not to change the data. The transaction must also be sure, however, that no changes are underway before it takes the S lock. That is where the intent lock comes in. For any X lock on a page in the tablespace, which would indicate an imminent change, DB2 will have taken an intent lock on the table or tablespace.

Instead of having to search all page locks to find those applying to a specific page, DB2 can look for the one tablespace intent lock—in this case a share with intent exclusive (SIX) lock. If it finds it, the transaction knows

		Program A has lock					
		X	U	SIX	IX	S	IS
	X	–	–	–	–	–	–
	U	–	–	–	–	Y	Y
Prog.B	SIX	–	–	–	–	–	Y
can	IX	–	–	–	Y	–	Y
get	S	–	Y	–	–	Y	Y
lock	IS	–	Y	Y	Y	Y	Y
	PAGE	–	–	S	S/X	S	S/X

Fig 8.8 Table and tablespace lock compatibility

it must wait for the current changes to be completed before it proceeds with an update.

There are three types of intent locks. Each indicates what read or update activities a transaction employing it is carrying out at the page level, and each allows subsequent transactions encountering it to perform only specific activities. DB2 implements this traffic signal function by assigning a different control level to each type of intent lock. Each type of intent lock exercises this control by either tolerating or barring the concurrent imposition of other intent lock types.

Intent locks are used at the table and tablespace levels for segmented tablespace and at the tablespace level for nonsegmented tablespaces. These three types of intent lock are intent share (IS), intent exclusive (IX), and share with intent exclusive (SIX).

> *Intent share*: The transaction intends to read but not update data pages and therefore take S locks on them; it will tolerate concurrent transactions taking S, IS, SIX, IX, or U locks.

> *Intent exclusive*: The transaction intends to read or change data and therefore take an X lock against the data pages; it will tolerate concurrent transactions taking IX or IS locks.

> *Shared with intent exclusive*: The transaction intends to read or change data; it will tolerate other transactions taking an IS lock on the tablespace, which allows them to read data by taking S-page locks but not change the data.

The matrix in Fig. 8.8 shows the allowable combinations of lock types at the table and tablespace level (including S, U, and X locks) that account for these definitions. The last line in the matrix indicates when page locks can be taken depending on the current tablespace lock. Study of the matrix reveals the type of activity each lock will allow in the data pages beneath it. Note, for example, that if transaction A holds an IX lock, it will allow subsequent transactions to take IX or IS locks, permitting those transactions eventually to take exclusive or share locks, which allow them to change or read a page.

8.6 ACQUIRE AND RELEASE PARAMETERS

Page locks are always taken when they are required during a program's execution, and they are always released when DB2 executes a commit work or rollback statement. (A commit does not release all locks when the CURSOR WITH HOLD clause is used on a CURSOR statement as is discussed in Chapter 9.) To a certain extent, however, developers can control with the bind command parameters the points at which DB2 acquires or releases locks against table and tablespaces, including intent locks. The ACQUIRE parameter choice of USE causes DB2 to impose a table or tablespace lock when it executes an SQL statement that references a table in the tablespace. In response to the alternative ACQUIRE selection, ALLOCATE, DB2 imposes the locks against all tables and tablespaces used by a program when it allocates the program's thread—control blocks that make up the communications path between the program and DB2—just before it executes the first SQL statement in the program. In most cases with page-level locking, a SELECT statement will result in an IS lock at the table level for a segmented tablespace and at the tablespace level for a nonsegmented tablespace, and an UPDATE statement will result in an IX lock. If both the SELECT and UPDATE statements in a program reference the same table, the higher lock of IX will be taken even if the UPDATE statement is not executed because the user wishes to look only at the data and not to update it. The RELEASE parameter choice of COMMIT has DB2 release table and tablespace locks at commit or rollback points; the choice of DEALLOCATE has it hold them until the thread is deallocated and the program terminates. All combinations of ACQUIRE and RELEASE parameter values are permitted except for ACQUIRE(ALLOCATE) with RELEASE(COMMIT) (Fig. 8.9). These choices affect the amount of processing required for managing the locks and whether and when users and programs can access the data.

The ACQUIRE parameter value of USE provides the greater concurrency because the tablespace locks are not imposed until actually needed. When the ACQUIRE selection of ALLOCATE is in effect, DB2 imposes locks well before the program accesses the data, limiting other access to the data before it is absolutely necessary. It may also impose locks when they will not be needed at all, since a given execution of a program may not access all referenced tables and tablespaces while intent locks are nevertheless taken against them. A program for which ALLOCATE is specified must

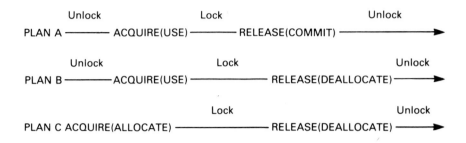

The three possible combinations of ACQUIRE and RELEASE options lock and unlock tablespaces in the above sequences: Plan A is ACQUIRE (USE), RELEASE (COMMIT); Plan B ACQUIRE (USE), RELEASE (DEALLOCATE); and Plan C ACQUIRE (ALLOCATE), RELEASE (DEALLOCATE).

Fig. 8.9 ACQUIRE and RELEASE sequences for tablespace locks

wait for all referenced tables and tablespaces to be available for the required locks before it can execute. This may delay that program's execution, but it does minimize the chance of deadlocks that exists when a number of programs execute concurrently against the same tables and tablespaces. For example, as seen earlier, two programs cannot take IS and X locks at the same time. IS and IX locks are very common for SELECT and UPDATE/INSERT/DELETE statements, however, with page level locking and are compatible.

ACQUIRE(USE) is the default value. It is also the approach DB2 takes when packages are used and for checking referential integrity constraints regardless of the ACQUIRE parameter specified at bind time. DB2 does follow a plan or package's RELEASE parameter for locks it takes for packages and during referential integrity checking.

The RELEASE parameter choice of COMMIT provides for good concurrency because DB2 releases the locks as soon as a commit work is issued rather than holding them, even if they are not needed, until the program ends. Since programmers can include COMMIT WORK statements wherever they like within programs, this parameter choice gives them some control over how long locks are held. When the RELEASE parameter value of COMMIT is in effect, all of a transaction's locks are released at commit time (CURSOR WITH HOLD is an exception to be discussed in Chapter 9). If programmers want to maintain some locks after commits, they must reimpose them perhaps with explicit LOCK TABLE statements. RELEASE-(DEALLOCATE), however, maximizes the benefits of thread reuse and improves performance.

Object Bound	Bind parameter	Value
Plan	ISOLATION	RR
Package	ISOLATION	CS
Plan	ACQUIRE	ALLOCATE
Package	acquire	Always use
Plan	RELEASE	DEALLOCATE
Package	RELEASE	COMMIT

Fig. 8.10 Differing plan and package parameters

Although ACQUIRE(USE) and RELEASE(COMMIT) maximize concurrency, there is a processing cost to consider when DB2 is operating under thread reuse. Thread reuse in CICS and WFI (wait for input) in IMS, allow one or more users to execute a plan multiple times without DB2 having to establish a new thread each time. Thread reuse for a transaction executed more than once or twice a second can result in an increase in transaction rate of 20–50 percent. The higher the transaction rate, the larger the percent increase. ACQUIRE(ALLOCATE) and RELEASE(DEALLOCATE) provide performance advantages when thread reuse is appropriate since a significant percent of the resources required to allocate the thread is in acquiring locks.

Locks with Plans and Packages

Isolation level, acquire, and release parameters specified at bind time can differ between plans and packages, as will be seen in Chapter 10. Locks taken for SQL executed in a plan are held while executing SQL in a package. If a plan is bound with an isolation level of RR and one of its packages is bound with CS, locks taken as a result of RR will be held while SQL in the package is executing. Locks are acquired as SQL in a package are executed even if ACQUIRE (ALLOCATE) was specified for the plan. If a plan is bound with RELEASE (DEALLOCATE), a commit issued in a package will free the locks taken by SQL in the package but not locks taken for SQL executed from the plan. A commit issued in any package or plan (even if bound with RELEASE (DEALLOCATE)) will release the locks taken for SQL bound with RELEASE (COMMIT). Locks can be taken on the same resource by a plan and its packages each bound with different options as shown in Fig. 8.10. For example, a page might be locked first as a result of an SQL statement executed from a package bound with CS, and if later an SQL statement in a plan bound with RR reads the page, the lock will be held as required by repeatable read. Similarly if a plan bound with RELEASE (DEALLOCATE) and a package bound with RELEASE (COMMIT) both access a tablespace that results in an IX, the lock will be held even though the package issues a commit. Lock analysis is simplified if all SQL is in packages with no SQL in the plan.

How to COMMIT

Since transactions may employ more than one database management system, commits and rollbacks are system-wide activities requiring the cooperation of the involved subsystems. DB2 operates within three environments—TSO, IMS, and CICS—each of which handles commits and rollbacks in a different way. Under TSO, the SQL statements COMMIT WORK and ROLLBACK may be used. The syntax of COMMIT is acceptable to some of the DB2 precompilers, but it is best to code COMMIT WORK since it is part of SAA (system application architecture). Under IMS, the CHKP or XRST call causes a commit; ROLL or ROLB causes a rollback. The GU (get unique) call to the IMS I/O PCB (program control block) also causes a commit under IMS. The CICS commands SYNC-POINT, RETURN, and TERMINATE cause a commit, and ROLLBACK causes a rollback. Program termination also commits work under all three environments. DB2 automatically issues a commit when a panel is displayed under CICS or IMS depending on the mode of operation.

When to COMMIT WORK

Generally a COMMIT WORK statement should be included before a program asks for terminal input. If locks are not released until after the input is provided, the individual entering the information has control over how long those locks will be in effect. If that person leaves for a coffee break or answers the telephone before remembering to provide the required input, those locks will be in effect for quite a while, barring others from accessing the data. A commit is issued automatically when displaying a screen using CICS pseudo conversational and IMS.

In some instances, however, particularly when the input is for an update rather than an insertion or deletion, it may be best to keep some locks in force while waiting for the information. For example, when Mrs. Johnson attempts to make a savings account withdrawal, a screen prompting for the amount may well show the balance. There should be a lock on that balance while Mrs. Johnson considers her withdrawal so that Mr. Johnson cannot call it up from another automatic teller machine at the same time.

Box 8.2 Locks used for SQL statements

For the most part, the type of lock DB2 imposes depends on the requirements implicit in the data-manipulation activity it is performing. Here are the types of locks it uses for common SQL statements with a locksize of page, an isolation level of CS, and use of an index to locate the required row:

- A SELECT statement results in an intent share (IS) lock on the table or tablespace and a share (S) lock on the data and index page.
- A SELECT statement with index only access locks no data pages. An IS lock is taken at table or tablespace level.
- S latch is taken on the index root page for most data manipulation statements. (A latch requires one-third the path length of locks.)
- UPDATE and DELETE statements result in U data and index-page locks while searching for data to be updated with or without a cursor.
- INSERT, UPDATE, and DELETE statements result in IX and X locks for update of data and index pages.
- If an index page split occurs, an X lock is taken on the next higher index page.

He may be seeing the current balance, but it will change before he knows it.

A frequently used method for handling this kind of timing problem is to have the program save a copy of the data before they are unlocked. If the user subsequently chooses to update the data, the program can first compare the saved version with a reread of current live data. If there had been no changes, the user's update can be allowed. If the comparison finds differences, the user can be presented with the new values for updating.

A reread of the row can be avoided by issuing an UPDATE statement specifying in the WHERE clause all the values that were displayed to the user. The update will be successful only if the row still exists as it was displayed. For example, part information would be displayed after saving:

```
PN-OLD      = 'P4'
PNAME-OLD   = 'SCREW'
COLOR-OLD   = 'RED'
WEIGHT-OLD  = 14
CITY-OLD    = 'LONDON'
```

The user may change any value and the transaction issues:

```
UPDATE P
   SET PN   = :PN
```

```
              PNAME    = :PNAME
              COLOR    = :COLOR
              WEIGHT   = :WEIGHT
              CITY     = :CITY
      WHERE   PN = :PN-OLD
              PNAME    = :PNAME-OLD
              COLOR    = :COLOR-OLD
              WEIGHT   = :WEIGHT-OLD
              CITY     = :CITY-OLD
```

If no one has made a change to P4 information since the row was displayed, the update will be successful and return an SQLCODE of 0. If DB2 returns SQLCODE = 100, the row no longer exists as it did when displayed or the row was deleted since it was displayed and the user should be informed. If an indexed value has not been changed, DB2 will not update the index. If the user did not change any of the values, the data page is not written to DASD. Thus no additional updates are required by specifying all of the columns in the SET clause.

Techniques used with other DBMS can be used with a variation on the fully qualified update statement. A counter of each update or timestamp column is included in the table and updated each time the row is updated. This column can be used to avoid having to save all columns in the table or all columns displayed to the user. Only the timestamp or counter column needs to be saved and used in the WHERE clause when the update is issued.

Since updates impose exclusive locks, which bar all other access to the locked pages or tablespaces, committing work after heavy update activity is a good idea. With RELEASE(COMMIT) in effect, this releases all table-space locks. It is advisable to group updates together and issue a commit work rather than holding locks while executing host-language code. But programmers will have to have programs reopen any cursors that have not fetched all their rows before a commit.

To accomplish this, they save the last key value and execute an open cursor statement that resumes fetching at the next value. A program may be fetching and displaying information on a set of suppliers from a supplier table for adjustment by the user, for example. Once the adjustment is entered, the program issues a COMMIT WORK to ensure that it is saved. Since the COMMIT WORK closes the cursor, in order to continue display-ing the set of rows at the next row to be processed the program must reopen the cursor at that point in the set unless CURSOR WITH HOLD is speci-fied. (Section 9.3 discusses this procedure in detail.)

8.7 EXPLICIT LOCK STATEMENTS

The LOCK TABLE statement within a program overrides and releases all lock sizes and types that otherwise would be in effect for the accessed tables except for an intent lock held at the table or tablespace level. The explicit table lock allows use of the table locksize for specific programs that update heavily. But the page locksize designated when the tablespace is created applies to all SQL executed. Programmers can use the LOCK TABLE statement to avoid having a program take a large number of page locks. It is a good alternative to repeatable reads when a large percentage of a table's pages are to be updated.

The statement takes the form LOCK TABLE [name] IN SHARE MODE or LOCK TABLE [name] IN EXCLUSIVE MODE. While the statement requires the table's name, in nonsegmented tablespaces, DB2 takes the lock against the tablespace containing the referenced table. The LOCK TABLE locks only the specified table if it is in a segmented tablespace with an intent lock at the tablespace level. The lock does not take effect until the statement executes, even if ACQUIRE(ALLOCATE) had been specified at bind time. If an IX lock is already held, a SIX is acquired. If a SIX, a U, or an X lock is already held, locking table in share mode has no effect. The explicit lock releases according to the RELEASE parameter specified at bind time.

The LOCK TABLE statement, however, will not operate on views or tables located on another DBMS including another DB2 subsystem. If a LOCK TABLE statement attempts to execute against a view, DB2 returns a negative SQLCODE (-156). An error maybe issued at bind time depending upon the precompiler being used to avoid the execution time error condition. A developer wanting to use the LOCK TABLE statement for a view must specify the underlying base table. Installations can use this feature to control use of LOCK TABLE statements. By authorizing developers to use views only, the installation lets DB2 bar their access to base tables, thus enforcing the prohibition against LOCK TABLE statements except in special cases.

8.8   MONITORING LOCKS

There are a number of tools within DB2 that can be used by developers and systems administrators for monitoring locks used by DB2. If lock contention becomes a problem, these tools can be quite useful in determining the locksize and type of locks so that corrective action can be taken. The EXPLAIN command will give the lock type that will be held on tables and tablespaces at execution time. (The use of the EXPLAIN command is discussed in Chapter 13.)

At execution time, a message DSNT501I can accompany -911 or -913 SQLCODE indicating a timeout or deadlock:

```
DSNT501I Type 00000D01, CSECT DSNILMCL, name 00000321.00000105
```

```
----|----1----|----2---|---3----|----4----|----5----
00C9008E 00000301 PROTO .ICLOSE2 .X'0003B6'.X'01'
     Position 01-08 = DB2 error code
     Position 10-17 = Resource type
     Position 19-26 = Database name
     Position 28-35 = Tablespace or index space
     Position 37-45 = Page number (hex)
     Position 47-51 = Index subpage number (hex)
```

Fig. 8.11 Lock contention message

The last group of numbers are the database and tablespace identifiers used by DB2 to locate objects. They are recorded in the catalog tables and DBD. The value of 321 is DBID (database ID) and the value of 105 is OBID (object ID, in this case the tablespace ID). A select with a WHERE clause on OBID and DBID from the catalog tables SYSDATABASE and SYSTABLESPACE can be used to determine the name of object that participated in the lock contention.

Chapter 9 discusses the SQL communication area (SQLCA) data structure used to communicate information between DB2 and a program. The field SQLERRMC contains a message indicating the database, tablespace or index space, page number, and index subpage involved in the lock contention. The message is positional, beginning with the DB2 error code and describing the object involved in the lock contention as indicated in Fig. 8.11.

Programs can write the SQLERRMC message to a table created by the developer called perhaps LOCK_HISTORY along with identifying information like the program name, the SQL statement that resulted in the lock contention, the SQLCODE, the content of SQLERRMC, and the TIMESTAMP. An accumulation of a history of lock contention provides information for resolution of the problem.

Typically the system or database administrator has authority to issue the −DISPLAY DATABASE command. This command gives current locks held and lock waits. Any of three traces can be turned on for general monitoring and accounting. The statistics trace records give the total number of times a condition occurred for all SQL executed in DB2 subsystem. The conditions that are specifically related to locking are suspensions, deadlocks, timeouts, and lock escalations. The accounting trace records give similar information but can be for specific AUTHIDs and plans. These records also give the maximum number of page locks held by a plan that is useful for tuning NUMLKTS and NUMLKUS and for determining if the program needs to issue COMMIT WORK more often to stay within the limits. The performance trace records shows the progression of locks in detail but is very costly to have turned on. It increases the path length threefold, that is three times the usual number of DB2 instructions will be executed while the trace is turned on. Also the results of a performance trace are very lengthy and difficult to read. It is a last resort in problem determination.

8.9 LOCKS ON THE CATALOG TABLES, DBD, AND DIRECTORY

Pages in the catalog tables and the DBD (database descriptor) are locked whenever an object is created or dropped. A lock against catalog table pages or the DBD from a given developer, user, or program may bar others from creating objects or binding SQL. It is advisable to issue a COMMIT WORK after each CREATE, ALTER, or DROP statement to avoid holding locks any longer than necessary. Catalog tables are subject to lock escalation just as are application tables when using a locksize of ANY after accumulating more than 1000 locks. Locks are taken on the DBD for a number of operations including an X lock during object creation, alteration, and deletion; an X lock during index build; an S lock during plan or package bind; and an S lock during execution of utilities (such as LOAD, REORG, or COPY).

Locks are acquired at bind time on the catalog tables, DBD, and directory. An IX lock is taken on most catalog tablespaces, an X lock on the SKCT (skeleton cursor table) and SKPT (skeleton package table) in the directory (also locked for DROP and REVOKE statements), and S lock on the DBD. At execution time, an IS lock is taken on the SYSPLANAUTH and SYSPACKAUTH catalog tables to check execution authority and an S lock on SKCT and SKPT in the directory, and no locks are required on the DBD except for dynamic SQL in which case an S lock is taken.

Strict and generic clustering are used for the catalog tables and their indexes. Strict clustering refers to how rows are stored in the data pages and generic clustering has to do with how indexes are stored. Strict clustering means that a record set—one or more rows that are linked together and that belong to a common root row—will be stored in the same tablespace page. For example, a page in SYSVIEWS will have a row from SYSVTREE, SYSVLTREE, SYSVIEWS, and perhaps several rows from SYSVIEWDEP for views created by a specific AUTHID. The page contains rows from the four tables interleaved on a single page rather than being on four separate pages as would typically be the case for data rows. The page is dedicated to the AUTHID that owns the object so that several developers can be creating views at the same time without the possibility of lock

Box 8.3 Strict and generic clustering

Tables using strict tablespace clustering are summarized. The tablespace using strict clustering is listed followed by the tables whose rows are interleaved within the tablespace.

```
SYSIBM.SYSVIEWS tablespace tables:
  -SYSVIEWS
  -SYSVIEWDEP
  -SYSVTREE
  -SYSVLTREE

SYSIBM.SYSDBASE tablespace tables:
  -SYSTABLESPACE
  -SYSTABLEPART
  -SYSTABLES
  -SYSCOLUMNS
  -SYSFIELDS
  -SYSRELS
  -SYSLINKS
  -SYSFOREIGNKEYS
  -SYSSYNONYMS
  -SYSINDEXES
  -SYSKEYS
  -SYSINDEXPART
  -SYSTABAUTH
  -SYSCOLAUTH

SYSIBM.SYSPLAN tablespace tables:
  -SYSPLAN
  -SYSDBRM
  -SYSSTMT
  -SYSPLANAUTH
  -SYSPLANDEP
  -SYSPLSYSTEM

SYSIBM.SYSPACKAGE tablespace tables:
  -SYSPACKAGE
  -SYSPACKSTMT
  -SYSPACKAUTH
  -SYSPACKDEP
  -SYSPACKLIST
  -SYSPKSYSTEM
```

Tables using generic clustering are summarized. The tablespace using generic clustering is listed followed by the tables and the name of the columns which have generic clustering.

```
SYSIBM.SYSVIEWS tablespace
  -SYSVTREE on CREATOR
  -SYSVIEWDEP on BCREATOR

SYSIBM.SYSDBASE tablespace
  -SYSTABLESPACE on DBNAME
  -SYSTABLES on CREATOR
  -SYSSYNONYMS on CREATOR
```

```
-SYSTABAUTH on GRANTEE
-SYSTABAUTH on GRANTOR
-SYSINDEXES on DBNAME
-SYSINDEXES on CREATOR
-SYSLINKS on PCREATOR

SYSIBM.SYSPLAN tablespace
-SYSPLANAUTH on GRANTEE
-SYSPLANDEP on BCREATOR

SYSIBM.SYSPACKAGE tablespace
-SYSPACKAUTH on GRANTEE
-SYSPACKDEP on BCREATOR
```

contention. In addition, fewer I/O are needed to retrieve information on a view that is referenced in an SQL statement.

The DB2 developers recognized that lock contention is most frequently on index pages. Therefore generic clustering dedicates a subpage of an index to the AUTHID of the owner of the object. Both strict and generic clustering require more DASD space but both reduce the possibility of lock contention when objects are created and plans are bound.

Care should be exercised to avoid defeating the purpose of strict and generic clustering. Some centralized organizations have one person or one department create all of the objects. If one AUTHID is used to create all the objects, strict and generic clustering are rendered meaningless. Even if one AUTHID is used to create only the database and developers create their test objects in the database, there is limited clustering. SYSDBASE tablespace contains 14 catalog tables describing most of the objects in the database. It is suggested that, if there is a centralized organization, different functional AUTHID be used for creating each database. A second way that clustering is lost is when a secondary AUTHID is used by a number of developers to create objects and bind SQL. Again it is not possible to dedicate a data page or index subpage to specific developers since several are using the same AUTHID.

8.10 SUMMARY

It is difficult to point to typical transactions as guides for concurrency control decisions. Two extreme cases, however, summarize the tradeoffs available between resource usage and concurrency levels.

To allow many concurrent programs to change data at the cost of CPU time and virtual storage usage, take these steps:

- Use small lockable units—page for data and subpage of 4 for indexes.
- Have DB2 hold locks for as short a time as possible by employing AC-

QUIRE(USE) and RELEASE(COMMIT) and by setting isolation level at cursor stability. If most SQL statements in the program are executed when the transaction is executed, ACQUIRE(ALLOCATE) and RELEASE(DEALLOCATE) will improve performance. This is particularly important to maximize the benefits of thread reuse.

- In programs, issue frequent commits, hold off updates to as near a commit point as possible, and commit work before waiting for terminal input.

To accommodate mostly read-only programs and batch programs that can afford to limit other program access while using minimum resources:

- Use large lockable units—table for data in a segmented tablespace and subpage of 1 for indexes.
- Use ACQUIRE(ALLOCATE) and RELEASE(DEALLOCATE).

These are the extremes. Each application has a unique mix of transactions with differing performance characteristics and needs that determine the developer's concurrency control choices.

EXERCISES

Exercises 1 through 7 assume a tablespace locksize of "page"; isolation level of CS; ACQUIRE(USE)/RELEASE(COMMIT); index subpage of 4.

8.1. An inventory-receiving transaction updates rows in sequence by purchase order number, which has a clustering index. The receiving personnel, who often execute transactions concurrently, frequently leave their terminals to accept incoming merchandise. They frequently encounter a lock condition. Why? What is a solution?

8.2. Assume the same situation as in Exercise 1 except that rows are inserted rather than updated in sequence. Would the same amount of locking be expected?

8.3. A program abends after updating 5001 rows. What is the problem? Identify possible solutions.

8.4. A customer wants to change reservations at a hotel from January 1 to January 2 and February 1 to February 2 only if rooms are available on both new dates. The reservation transaction finds vacancies on those dates and cancels the January 1 reservation but then finds no room available on January 2. What happened? How can the problem be avoided?

8.5. An application system made up primarily of read-only programs is using more CPU time and virtual storage than expected. What is the problem? Identify a possible solution.

8.6. Deadlocks frequently occur on high-transaction-rate update programs. What is the problem? Provide possible solutions.

8.7. A program with several open cursors issues a commit work before displaying a panel and awaiting input. The program reopens the cursors and finds that rows already processed are being fetched. Why? What is the solution?

8.8. Assume a tablespace locksize of table; isolation level of RR; ACQUIRE (AL-LOCATE)/RELEASE(DEALLOCATE); index subpage of 16. A transaction allows users to read or change rows in a database. The great majority of users choose read only but frequently find themselves locked out. Why? What is a possible solution?

8.9. Assume the same conditions as in Exercise 8 but with a tablespace locksize of PAGE. The bind process issues a message (DSNX103I) warning that the application plan uses a tablespace lock. Why? How can the tablespace lock be avoided?

9

Program Development

9.1 INTRODUCTION

Programs written in a number of host languages—COBOL II, COBOL, PL/1, C/370, FORTRAN, Assembler, APL2, and BASIC—can contain SQL statements that access DB2 data. That is, SQL statements embedded in any of those languages can update a DB2 database or return selected values from the database to a program. Program development for DB2 entails development of the host-language source code, including embedded SQL, and of the host-language data structures needed to receive returned values.

9.2 STATIC SQL

SQL works within host-language programs in two ways—statically and dynamically. With static SQL, the programmer knows the statement to be used and therefore can code for it in the program. This allows the statements' plan to be bound prior to execution and to remain static during execution. (All of the host languages that support SQL can use static SQL except for BASIC and APL2, which, because they are interpretative languages, bind SQL statements each time they are executed.) With dynamic

```
EXEC SQL SELECT SN, SNAME, STATUS, CITY
         INTO   :SN,:SNAME,:STATUS,:CITY
         FROM   S
         WHERE  SN = :SN-IN
END-EXEC.

IF SQLCODE = 0
   MOVE 'YES' TO SN-PRESENT.

IF SN-PRESENT = 'NO'
   EXEC SQL INSERT INTO S( SN, SNAME, STATUS, CITY)
                  VALUES(:SN,:SNAME,:STATUS,:CITY)
   END-EXEC.

IF SN-PRESENT = 'YES'
   EXEC SQL UPDATE S SET  STATUS = :STATUS
         WHERE  SN = :SN-IN
   END-EXEC.

GO TO ACCEPT-NEXT-S.

EXEC SQL DELETE FROM S
         WHERE SN = :SN-IN
END-EXEC.
```

Fig. 9.1 Embedded SQL in a COBOL fragment

SQL, on the other hand, the program formulates statements based upon choices made and entered by the user as the program executes. In this case, the programmer includes code that allows the program to construct the statement, submit it to the bind process, execute it, and deal with its results. (We will discuss static SQL in this section and dynamic SQL in Section 9.9.)

Embedded SQL uses the same syntax that SQL uses interactively with only a few minor additions. One difference is that programmers must use delimiters at the SQL statements' beginnings and ends to set them apart from the host language. The beginning delimiter is always EXEC SQL, which immediately precedes the statement. In COBOL, END-EXEC. signifies the statement conclusion; in PL/1, a semicolon performs that function. FORTRAN recognizes the end of a line as the statement end. Fig. 9.1 is a fragment of a COBOL program showing the four data-manipulation statements. It contains minimal COBOL code to show the SQL and does not show complete COBOL logic. For example, logically it is impossible to reach the DELETE statement.

Host-Language Variables

When a SELECT statement returns values to a program rather than to a user's terminal, the program must have host-language variables to receive them, and the SELECT statement must include information indicating those variables. Host variables in embedded SQL are identified by a colon preceding the variable names. If a host-variable name is split for readability, in COBOL a hyphen must join the two parts (:SN-IN, for example); in PL/1 an underscore joins the two (:SN_IN). DB2 column names may be split with an underscore. These seemingly trivial points are the source of frustration at precompile time. It is easy to remember the distinction but difficult to key the hyphen or underscore depending on whether it is a host-variable or column name. Somewhat like knowing that one drives on the opposite side of the street in London but it does not make the driving any easier.

An INTO clause in an embedded SELECT statement identifies the host variables that are to receive the selected values. Here is a typical SELECT statement embedded in COBOL:

```
EXEC SQL SELECT SN, S_NAME, S_ADDRESS
         INTO  :SN, :S-NAME, :S-ADDRESS
         FROM  S_DETAIL
         WHERE  SN = :SN-IN
END-EXEC.
```

Values from the columns SN, S_NAME, and S_ADDRESS are received by the host variables :SN, :S-NAME, and :S-ADDRESS, respectively.

A single, multilevel host variable in COBOL cited once in an SQL SELECT . . . INTO statement can receive values from multiple columns. Consider the following definition of a COBOL group-level variable S-DETAIL:

```
01  S-DETAIL.
    05  SN        PIC X(2).
    05  S-NAME    PIC X(30).
    05  S-ADDRESS PIC X(60).
```

S-DETAIL can receive values from three columns. The values are assigned to the lower-level variables in the order in which the columns are listed in the SELECT statement. In this example:

```
EXEC SQL SELECT SN, S_NAME, S_ADDRESS
         INTO  :S-DETAIL
         FROM  S_DETAIL
         WHERE  SN = :SN-IN
END-EXEC.
```

SN, S_NAME, and S_ADDRESS are received by the variables SN, S-NAME, and S-ADDRESS, respectively.

As the above examples demonstrate, there can be equivalent SELECT . . . INTO statements using several individual host variables or a single multilevel variable. It is usually better, however, to avoid using multilevel variables. For one thing, if lower-level variables are added or deleted from the multilevel variable, the SQL statement referencing it will no longer work—the columns cited will no longer match the lower-level variables. For another, in order for column values to match the lower-level variables, the statement may have to select more columns than are actually needed for the program, a waste of processing resources.

VARCHAR Variables

The COBOL language deals with variable-length character data through the use of 49-level variables. It is necessary to use a 49-level variable to pass or receive variable-length character values to or from a VARCHAR column. The program must calculate the length of a character value for INSERT and UPDATE statements. This calculation can be done by assigning the value to an array, counting the number of trailing blanks, and subtracting the value from the total length of the string. Another technique is to use the COBOL statement: UNSTRING SNAME-TEXT DELIMITED BY 'bb' COUNT IN SNAME-LENGTH. Then the program assigns that length to the first 49-level of the value's variable. For example, if the SNAME column were VARCHAR, its associated COBOL variable would be:

```
01  SNAME.
    49  SNAME-LENGTH PIC S9(4) COMP.
    49  SNAME-TEXT   PIC X(30).
```

The text portion of the variable is declared as the column's maximum length. If an 01 or 02 text variable were used for a VARCHAR column for values shorter than the maximum, trailing blanks would be stored in the column. In effect, it would not be a variable-length column even though it had been declared as one.

Qualifying a Variable by Table

When the same column name appears in more than one table in the FROM clause, a host-language variable for each column's values must indicate to which table it refers. In a COBOL program, outside of SQL statements, the usual syntax for qualifying a variable applies. Inside SQL statements, however, DB2 requires a different format. For example, if the S_NAME column is included in both the Supplier table and S_DETAIL table, each reference to an S-NAME host-language variable would have to identify the appropriate table. Outside of SQL statements, the COBOL references might be S-NAME OF S-DETAIL or S-NAME IN S-DETAIL. Inside SQL statements, however, the qualification format joins the table and column name with a period. For example, S-DETAIL.S-NAME indicates that the variable refers to the S_NAME COBOL 05 level in the S_DETAIL 01 level. Used in an SQL statement, that format would look like this:

```
EXEC SQL SELECT S_NAME
         INTO  :S-DETAIL.S-NAME
         FROM  S_DETAIL
         WHERE SN = :SN-IN
END-EXEC.
```

Programming for NULLS

If a host program is to receive a value from a column that allows nulls, the program requires variables for both the value and its associated null indicator. A null indicator variable is declared in the program as any other variable. For simplicity programmers usually name the null indicator variable with a variation on the name of its associated variable. For example, a variable to receive values from the SNAME column, which allows nulls, might be called :SNAME. The associated null indicator variable might be called :SNAME-INDNULL.

The null indicator variable must be included in the SELECT . . . INTO statement, as shown in this example:

```
EXEC SQL SELECT SNAME
         INTO  :SNAME:SNAME-INDNULL
         FROM  S
         WHERE SN = :SN-IN
END-EXEC.
```

Notice that no comma or space separates the variable and associated null indicator variable in the statement.

DB2 assigns a null indicator value of 0 if the selected SNAME has a value and a negative value if SNAME is null. As we will discuss, a program can test for these null indicator values and react according to the values it encounters.

Inserting a null also requires special handling. Outside of the SQL INSERT statement, the program must move a negative number to the null indicator for the column receiving the null value. That action would be required, for example, when the STATUS value is null in the following INSERT:

```
MOVE -1 TO STATUS-INDNULL.

EXEC SQL INSERT INTO S
    (SN, SNAME, STATUS, CITY ) VALUE
    (:SN, :SNAME, :STATUS:STATUS-INDNULL, :CITY)
```

Data Conversions

Although host-variable names need not match the names of the columns that provide their values, the data types should be compatible, and the lengths should match. This will not be a problem if DB2 generates the data structures since it creates host-language structures that match the columns' definitions in the catalog tables. Mismatch errors generally occur in working storage variables defined by COBOL programmers. Mismatches can also occur when a SELECT clause's calculation produces a value too large for its variable or when a user keys in a value with the wrong type or length.

DB2 will not allow some mismatches. It issues a negative SQLCODE if a statement attempts to move a number into a numeric data type with insufficient precision to handle it—a value over 32,767 into a small integer, for example. But DB2 will automatically *correct* for some mismatches, allowing processing to continue. For example, it will remove the fractional part of a column's decimal or float value when moving it into an integer or small integer host variable. It will also truncate the trailing characters of a character column's value when moving it to a host variable that is not long enough to hold it. And if a SELECT clause's calculation results in a value too large for its host variable or in an impossible value, a number divided by zero, DB2 simply leaves the variable set at its previous value and issues a negative SQLCODE.

These *corrections* can lead to incorrect or unanticipated results if the programmer is not aware of them. DB2 uses SQLCODEs and null indicator values, however, to describe the data corrections it has made. For example, if a statement moves a value from a nullable integer column into a small integer host variable, it sets the null indicator at −2 and issues an SQL-CODE of +304. If a statement moves a character value into a host variable too short to accommodate it, DB2 also issues a +304 SQLCODE, but this time sets the null indicator to the column's length. Suppose in the above example that SNAME had been declared as CHAR(5), but :SNAME had been declared as a four-byte character type. If the SNAME value selected were BLAKE, :SNAME would take on the value BLAK, :SNAME-IND-NULL would take on 5, and the SQLCODE would be +304.

The following statement illustrates how DB2 handles data mismatches caused by calculations in the SELECT clause:

```
EXEC SQL SELECT SNAME, STATUS/GRADE, SUM(STATUS)
         INTO   :SNAME:SNAME-INDNULL
                :STATUS:STATUS-INDNULL
                :TOTAL-STATUS:TOTAL-STATUS-INDNULL
         FROM   S
         WHERE  SN = :SN-IN
END-EXEC.
```

Whenever GRADE equals zero, DB2 will set :STATUS-INDNULL to -2 and issue a $+802$ SQLCODE. It leaves :STATUS at its previous value. Whenever the sum of STATUS exceeds the maximum value that the TO-TAL-STATUS' data type can accommodate, DB2 reacts in the same way, issuing a $+802$ SQLCODE, setting the null indicator at -2, and leaving the variable at its previous value. If a null indicator is not used in these situations, a -304 or -802 SQLCODE is issued with the same messages as for the analogous positive codes.

To determine if any of these data conversion situations have occurred, the programmer can test for the null indicator's value in host-language code following the SQL statement. The following section describes how to test for SQLCODEs. It is always best to avoid the problem by taking care to have column and host-variable data types match. Not only does that avoid anomalous results but it also saves on the processing DB2 must otherwise perform to *correct* mismatches.

9.3 CURSORS AND REPOSITIONING

A difference between interactive and embedded SQL is that SELECTs in the former may return any number of rows while in the latter the host languages can deal with only one at a time. A programming device called a cursor allows the SELECT to find a set of rows but return them one at a time. Imagine the set of rows being returned to a display screen. A screen cursor could point to the row to be processed, then move to the next row for processing, and so on. A cursor in embedded SQL works in the same way but without the screen.

The developer establishes a cursor with a declarative SELECT statement. (Since it is a declarative rather than executable statement, it can be placed in the data or procedure division of a COBOL program but must physically precede the OPEN.) The declaration takes the form DECLARE SCURSOR CURSOR FOR, in which the cursor's name follows the word DECLARE. Here is a complete example declaration (examples refer to the Supplier/Part/Job tables in Fig. 9.1):

```
EXEC SQL DECLARE SCURSOR CURSOR FOR
         SELECT  SN, SNAME, STATUS, CITY
         FROM    S
         WHERE   STATUS > :OLD-STATUS
         AND     SN     > :OLD-SN
END-EXEC.
```

The program calls on the cursor for processing through two statements: one for opening the cursor and the other for fetching its rows. The OPEN statement readies the SELECT for execution. DB2 attempts to retrieve one qualifying row at a time to pass to the program—unless all rows are required by a sort, for example. The OPEN statement simply uses the key word OPEN followed by the cursor's name: EXEC SQL OPEN SCURSOR END-EXEC. The FETCH statement identifies the cursor to be used and employs an INTO clause to indicate the host variables that are to receive the values from each row:

```
EXEC SQL FETCH SCURSOR INTO :SN, :SNAME, :STATUS, :CITY
END-EXEC.
```

As with the SELECT . . . INTO statement used when a single row is returned, the variables used in a FETCH . . . INTO statement must be of compatible data type with the columns that supply their values.

Typically a FETCH statement is coded within a program loop, which returns after processing a row to receive the next row. DB2 does not process all rows requested by a cursor's statement when the cursor is opened or at the first fetch unless the statement requires a sort or an intermediate work file for a subselect in which case all rows must be processed. Use of an index, which allows rows to be retrieved in order, avoids sorts. In addition, if list prefetch is used, all RIDs (row identifiers) must be retrieved and sorted in most cases before the first row can be returned to the program. Execution of a fetch causes the cursor to advance to the next row. Since the program will usually have to process all selected rows, a test for the existence of rows usually controls the loop. DB2 communicates with programs about processing status through SQLCODEs (Section 9.7). The SQLCODE 100 indicates that the fetch found no rows or no more rows. The program can test for SQLCODE 100 and move out of the loop when it is encountered. The SQLCODE of 0 means one or more rows were found. Alternatively the SQLSTATE can be tested to maintain compatibility among DBMSs that conform to the ANSI and SAA (system application architecture) standard. The SQLSTATE of '02000' means no rows qualify or no more rows qualify, and '00000' means one or more rows qualify. A number of cursors can be opened at one time on a single table or on multiple tables.

Closing and Reopening Cursors

A CLOSE statement—EXEC SQL CLOSE SCURSOR END-EXEC.—closes the cursor. Any COMMIT WORK also closes all cursors in most cases. After a cursor has been closed, it may be reopened without having to be declared again. When it is reopened, its SELECT statement will be evaluated again. If the values that set the SELECT's criteria have not changed, the SELECT will return the same set of rows. This becomes a problem if a program closes a cursor in the midst of processing the set and then reopens the cursor to resume processing. If the program does not change the value that determines the search criteria to reflect the fact that some rows have been processed, the reopened cursor will return the original set. The program will then begin processing rows that have already been processed rather than resuming at the next row in order when the cursor was closed.

A way to avoid this problem is to track the cursor's position as it works through the set of rows and to use the last row processed to reset the search criteria. This technique works only if the search returns unique values in an order that the program can follow. This will always be the case if the search criteria include a primary key column, which by definition includes only unique values, and the results are ordered by that column, which will be the case if DB2 uses an index on that column to retrieve the rows. In most cases, to allow for this cursor tracking technique, a programmer may want to include a primary key in the predicate of a cursor declaration and order the results by that column even when the search does not require it.

The SCURSOR declared above might be used in an application to credit bonuses to suppliers with greater than a certain status, for example. That status may be determined by the application's user, entered in response to a prompt and read into variable :OLD-STATUS. That variable is all that is needed to set the original search criteria to identify the suppliers to be credited. The programmer may want to be able to commit work in the midst of this processing, however, and resume processing at the proper row when the cursor is reopened. Because supplier number (SN) is a primary key, if the SELECT returned the rows in supplier number order, the program could track the cursor's movement precisely through the set. The program sets the original :OLD-SN value at "blank." If the user enters 10 for :OLD-STATUS, SCURSOR'S SELECT statement returns:

SN	SNAME	STATUS	CITY
S1	SMITH	20	LONDON
S3	BLAKE	30	PARIS
S4	CLARK	20	LONDON
S5	ADAMS	30	ATHENS

The cursor initially points to the first row. Then as the rows process according to the FETCH . . . INTO statement, the program saves the current SN in :OLD-SN. If the cursor closes after the program completes its second loop through the statement, :OLD-SN will equal S3. When the cursor reopens, its SELECT statement using that value returns:

SN	SNAME	STATUS	CITY
S4	CLARK	20	LONDON
S5	ADAMS	30	ATHENS

and processing can complete in order.

If the rows are not returned in supplier number order, which is likely in a tablespace scan, this technique would skip rows for processing. Consider the effect, for example, if the cursor's SELECT statement returns rows in this order:

SN	SNAME	STATUS	CITY
S1	SMITH	20	LONDON
S3	BLAKE	30	PARIS
S2	JONES	10	PARIS
S4	CLARK	20	LONDON
S5	ADAMS	30	ATHENS

After the second fetch loop :OLD-SN equals S3. When the cursor is closed and reopened after this fetch, the cursor's SELECT statement will not return the S2 row.

A tablespace scan may or may not retrieve rows in SN order if they are stored in that sequence. (If an index on SN is used to satisfy the select, the rows will be retrieved in supplier number order.) The ORDER BY operator will ensure that the rows are returned in the desired sequence when a tablespace scan is used or another technique is used to locate the rows like the use of multiple indexes or list prefetch on a single index. If the number of returned rows is large, however, performing the sort to satisfy the ORDER BY every time the cursor is opened is likely to be prohibitively expensive. Frequently only 15 rows or the number that will fit on a screen to be displayed to a user is all that is required for online transactions. The OPTIMIZE FOR "n" ROWS ("n" = 15 in this example) clause informs the optimizer that only a small number of rows is required, and it is likely that it will choose to use an index to locate the rows in sequence and avoid a sort. (Chapter 11 discusses how DB2 can use indexes to avoid a sort.)

```
SELECT SN, SNAME, STATUS, CITY
FROM   S
WHERE  SN > :OLD-SN
```

```
ORDER BY SN
OPTIMIZE FOR 15 ROWS
```

Batch programs frequently require the processing of a sizable number of rows for which a matching index scan on a single index would not give as good performance as would other possible access paths. One way to decrease the cost of a sort is to limit the number of rows that the cursor returns each time it is reopened. That can be done by including in the cursor's predicate a criteria limiting the rows returned to those between the last value processed in the sequence and some value about 100–1000 rows beyond that last value. Continuing the example will clarify the point.

In the SCURSOR example, the clause controlling the cursor's reopening has been WHERE SN > :OLD-SN. If 100,000 rows include values greater than :OLD-SN, however, performing that sort each time the cursor reopens will be prohibitive. If the clause were changed to WHERE SN BETWEEN :OLD-SN AND :ENDPOINT and if :ENDPOINT were set at a value that would return only around 100 rows, the sort would not be costly.

Setting an :ENDPOINT requires fairly straightforward logic in the host program's code. But determining the value for :ENDPOINT requires an understanding of the data, and in some cases, determining the value for future processing as the values in the table change can be a challenge. If the column controlling the cursor contains data in numeric order, :ENDPOINT might be set at :OLDSN + 100. If the column contains character data in alphabetic order, the host program might combine the first one or two characters of the last value processed with a string of ZZZs or high values to set the end point. After all of the controlling column's values beginning with one character had been processed, the program would have to increment to the next character, requiring a nontrivial algorithm in most host languages, but not too difficult to do with assembler language.

An alternative would be to have a table storing regularly spaced values that program logic could retrieve as end points. The value selected from the ENDPOINTS table can be compared with the last primary key processed. If the last primary key value exceeds the last ENDPOINT value, the program selects the next highest ENDPOINT value to use in reopening the cursor. The spacing of ENDPOINT values in the table could be changed periodically as the distribution of values changes in the primary key. A clustering index on the columns storing the end point values will avoid sorts and would likely be used with index-only processing.

Cursor Repositioning with a Composite Primary Key

When a cursor is controlled by a composite primary key, reopening in sequence can be complex. Consider a composite primary key on the SN, PN,

SPJ

SN	PN	JN	QTY
S1	P1	J1	200
S1	P1	J4	700
S2	P3	J1	400
S2	P3	J2	200
S2	P3	J3	200
S2	P3	J4	500
S2	P3	J5	600
S2	P3	J6	400
S2	P3	J7	800
S2	P5	J2	100
S3	P3	J1	200
S3	P4	J2	500
S4	P6	J3	300
S4	P6	J7	300
S5	P2	J2	200
S5	P2	J4	100
S5	P5	J5	500
S5	P5	J7	100
S5	P6	J2	200
S5	P1	J4	100
S5	P3	J4	200
S5	P4	J4	800
S5	P5	J4	400
S5	P6	J4	500

Fig. 9.2 Reopening cursors on composite keys

and JN columns of the SPJ table (Figure 9.2). The arrow indicates the last row processed before the cursor accessing the table was closed. The basic approach to finding the next row using a composite primary key is the same as that described above for when a single-column primary key is available. The last key values processed are saved in host-language variables, in this case, :OLD-SN, :OLD-PN, and :OLD-JN. Then this series of selection criteria in the cursor's SELECT statement will reopen it at the next row:

```
WHERE (SN = :OLD-SN AND
       PN = :OLD-PN AND
       JN > :OLD-JN) OR
      (SN = :OLD-SN AND
       PN > :OLD-PN) OR
      (SN > :OLD-SN)
       ORDER BY SN, PN, JN
```

In this case, OLD-SN = 'S2', OLD-PN = 'P3', and OLD-JN = 'J3'. The first portion of the criteria returns the next row, which holds the values 'S2', 'P3', and 'J4'. Notice that no matter what values the host variables hold, the results will always include the next row, and the ORDER BY clause assures it will be the next one processed. As explained in Chapter 11, however, DB2 will not use a matching index scan when it is satisfying an SQL statement that uses the 'OR' operator in this way on a composite index. Therefore processing the test may be expensive.

A second alternative similar to the previous example uses negative logic. It does have the advantage that it allows for a matching index scan on the first column.

```
WHERE (SN =    :OLD-SN AND
       PN =    :OLD-PN AND
       JN <= :OLD-JN) AND NOT
      (SN =    :OLD-SN AND
       PN <    :OLD-PN) AND NOT
      (SN >= :OLD-SN)
      ORDER BY SN, PN, JN
OPTIMIZE FOR 15 ROWS
```

A third alternative that is somewhat easier to code also suffers from the disadvantage of not being able to use an index in all cases. This approach uses concatenation to produce a single value from the values participating in a composite key that can be compared with a single value from the host-language variables containing the last values processed. This statement would handle that test for the SPJ table example:

```
WHERE SN >= :OLD-SN AND
      SN || PN || JN >
      :OLD-SN || :OLD-PN || :OLD-JN
ORDER BY SN, PN, JN
OPTIMIZE FOR 15 ROWS
```

The first WHERE clause may be satisfied with an index on SN provided cardinality is high enough that the optimizer chooses to use the index. It would be more likely to choose the index given the alternative formulation, WHERE SN BETWEEN :OLD-SN AND :HIGH-VALUES. The concatenation, however, causes the predicate to be stage 2. Performance is enhanced with the use of stage 1 predicates as will be seen in Chapter 11.

If the table being accessed is small or processing resources are plentiful, either of the above three approaches will work fine. A fourth approach allows for the series of comparisons needed to check the combinations of values in a composite primary key while at the same time giving DB2 the opportunity to use any available indexes in the searches. With this approach, the host program saves the last set of key values processed by the cursor and the next to the last set. The program then compares those sets of values to determine the criteria to be used in reopening the cursor.

Returning to the example will clarify this approach. Programming the logic for the comparisons requires considerable code. To save space and aid in understanding, we will use pseudo-code in the explanation. The SELECT results would also need to be ordered.

In the SPJ table example, the program saves the SN, PN, and JN values from the last row processed in the :OLD-SN, :OLD-PN, and :OLD-JN variables. It also saves the corresponding values from the previous row in :OLD-SN-2, :OLD-PN-2, and :OLD-JN-2. Finding the next row to process in all cases requires three sets of comparisons and three SELECT statements:

```
1 IF OLD-SN = OLD-SN-2 AND
     OLD-PN = OLD-SN-2 AND
     OLD-JN > OLD-JN-2
     THEN DO 2
     ELSE DO 3
2 SELECT SN, PN, JN, QTY
     FROM   SPJ
     WHERE  SN = :OLD-SN
     AND    JN = :OLD-JN
     AND    PN > :OLD-PN
     ORDER BY SN, PN, JN
     IF NO ROWS RETURNED (SQLCODE = 100)
     THEN DO 4
3 IF OLD-SN = OLD-SN-2 AND
     OLD-PN > OLD-PN-2
     THEN DO 4
     ELSE DO 5
4 SELECT SN, PN, JN, QTY
     FROM   SPJ
     WHERE  SN = :OLD-SN
     AND    PN > :OLD-PN
     ORDER BY SN, PN
     IF NO ROWS RETURNED
     THEN DO 6
5 IF OLD-SN > OLD-SN-2
     THEN DO 2
6 SELECT SN, PN, JN, QTY
     FROM   SPJ
     WHERE  SN > :OLD-SN
     ORDER BY SN
```

Although this method for establishing the row at which to reopen the cursor may require three separate searches, DB2 can use indexes in these searches. Therefore they are likely to require less processing and less time than the single search described earlier without indexes being used. The easiest alternative is to wait until all the rows with the same value in the first column are processed in which case the repositioning would be only on the first column and the first single column index technique can be used. This may be a viable alternative if the values in the first column do not repeat a large number of times.

Scrolling Backward

Users occasionally will want to take second looks at rows returned by a cursor. One way of providing a scrolling capability that presents the rows multiple times is similar to the technique for reopening cursors described above. The program saves the primary key for the row beginning each display panel and uses it to refetch the panel's rows with a new cursor at the user's request. A drawback to this technique is that other processing may change the data between the time when the original rows were displayed and the new cursor is opened. If rows are inserted or deleted, the second series of fetches will return more rows than will fit on the screen or there will be too few qualifying rows. This problem can be avoided by saving the rows returned by a cursor in a temporary table or some other temporary storage available to the program. Under TSO, this might be an ISPF internal table. Under CICS, it could be BMS paging or temporary storage. Under IMS/DC, it could be via the MFS facility or the SPA facility might be used. When the user requests another look at these rows, the program refetches them from the temporary storage. A disadvantage of saving the data is that a good deal of processing is required and the user will frequently not ask to see the data a second time. Also, the program must assure that updates are based on the actual data, not on these temporary copies.

Another approach is to save the primary key for the last row displayed and to use it to select rows with lower primary key values, ordering them by the primary key value in descending order. This approach can be quite effective with the OPTIMIZE FOR "n" ROWS. For example, all the rows with SN < = 'S16' can be retrieved and displayed to the user in reverse order with:

```
SELECT SN, SNAME, STATUS, CITY
FROM   S
WHERE  SN < = 'S16'
ORDER BY SN DESC
OPTIMIZE FOR 15 ROWS
```

A technique for allowing an update of data after a commit saves unnecessary reads when only one row has been displayed. Under this approach, the row's values are saved and used in equality predicates in the UPDATE statement. For example, if a part number and color have been displayed from the P table and the displayed values saved in :PN-OLD and :COLOR-OLD, the UPDATE statement would look like this:

```
UPDATE P
SET    PN    = :PN
       COLOR = :COLOR
```

```
WHERE  PN   = :OLD-PN AND
COLOR       = :OLD-COLOR
```

DB2 will allow the update only if the current values are the same as the previously displayed values. The program should test for an SQLCODE of 100, meaning that no rows were found for the update and the user should be notified. This technique is discussed in more detail in Chapter 8.

Cursor with Hold

The CURSOR WITH HOLD clause in a cursor declaration statement avoids closing the cursor and repositioning to the last row processed when the cursor is reopened. Its use, however, is limited to CICS conversational and batch processing using TSO, CAF, DL/1 batch, and IMS BMP. CURSOR WITH HOLD is not available under CICS pseudo-conversational or IMS interactive processing because DB2 does repositioning similar to what was discussed above, and the value is maintained with the thread. When a screen is displayed online using CICS pseudo-conversational and IMS, a commit is issued, all cursors are closed, the thread is deallocated, and the last position value is lost. Indeed, it is not desirable to hold position while a user is looking at the data or answering a telephone call since it would require holding a lock on the data. CURSOR WITH HOLD can be useful for batch processing. It appears in the cursor declaration statement like:

```
EXEC SQL DECLARE SCURSOR CURSOR WITH HOLD FOR
        SELECT SN, SNAME, STATUS, CITY
        FROM   S
        WHERE  STATUS > :NEW-STATUS
END-EXEC.
```

A FETCH must be the first statement after the COMMIT WORK is issued. Locks are not released on tables, tablespaces, and pages where the cursor is positioned, including pages being processed for the enforcement of referential integrity. Pages with X and U locks are demoted to S locks since all updates have been committed. RELEASE (COMMIT) specified at bind time has no effect. Recall from Chapter 8 that locks can be released as a result of a −911 or −913 SQLCODE from a deadlock or timeout. The cursor position is released when the locks are released. Therefore it may be necessary to code for cursor repositioning even in batch processing if there is a possibility of a deadlock or timeout. LOCK TABLE statements can be issued at the beginning of the program to avoid deadlocks and timeouts.

Embedded UPDATEs and DELETEs

Embedded SQL provides two methods for updating and deleting rows. An embedded UPDATE or DELETE statement can act on all of the rows meeting its WHERE clause criteria in response to a single execution of the statement. Multiple rows therefore may be updated or deleted in a program with the same statement an interactive user would employ for that action. For example, if all parts above a given weight in a particular city were to be reassigned to another city, an application for managing the change might prompt the user to enter the cutoff weight, the city where the parts are to be found, and the city to which they are to be reassigned. If those values were read into variables :WEIGHT-LIMIT, :OLD-CITY, and :NEW-CITY, this embedded statement would update all qualifying parts:

```
EXEC SQL UPDATE P SET CITY = :NEW-CITY,
         WHERE WEIGHT > :WEIGHT-LIMIT
         AND   CITY   = :OLD-CITY
END-EXEC.
```

In some cases, however, the updates or deletions may be done in conjunction with other processing that would require a cursor. If the rows returned with a cursor are to be updated or deleted, the cursor definition must indicate that fact. A FOR UPDATE OF clause alerts DB2 that the update is coming. This warning prevents DB2 from using an index on a column to be updated (unless list prefetch is used). If it were to use an index on a column being updated, some updates would not be applied after the initial update since the index itself would be changed by the update. For example, if an index on the STATUS column were used to retrieve rows, those rows would be returned in STATUS order. An update of STATUS from 10 to 50 would cause the cursor position to skip to a STATUS of 50, missing 20, 30, and 40. If equal predicates are used on the updated column and on all preceding columns, an index can be used to locate the row to be updated.

If the program to reassign parts over a certain weight from one city to another employed a cursor, its declaration would look something like this:

```
EXEC SQL DECLARE PCURSOR CURSOR FOR
    SELECT PN, WEIGHT
    FROM   P
    WHERE  WEIGHT > :WEIGHT-LIMIT
    FOR UPDATE OF CITY
END-EXEC.
```

Notice that the column being updated need not appear in the SELECT clause, although it usually does.

When a cursor is used for updates, the UPDATE statement must use a WHERE CURRENT OF CURSOR clause to indicate the row to be processed—for example:

```
EXEC SQL UPDATE P SET CITY = :NEW-CITY
    WHERE CURRENT OF PCURSOR
END-EXEC.
```

The WHERE CURRENT OF clause causes the row at which the cursor points to be updated. The update does not advance the cursor, however. A FETCH . . . INTO statement is necessary for that.

Certain SELECT statements return values that are not updatable. For example, what values in a column should be changed to "update" the column's average? Since DB2 has no way of answering that question, it bars use of the FOR UPDATE OF clause in cursor declarations that include the AVG function. For similar reasons it will not update rows returned by cursor declarations including the SUM, COUNT, MIN, MAX, and DISTINCT functions or the GROUP BY operator that uses them. The FOR UPDATE OF clause does not work with an ORDER BY. No primary key columns can be specified in the FOR UPDATE OF clause. Finally, unions, joins, and most subselects create temporary work files, as do a number of the other operations, that cannot be updated since the underlying base tables may be changed independently, creating inconsistencies in the data. The FOR UPDATE OF clause may not be used with cursors defined with any of these operations. Also recall from Chapter 4 that a view cannot be updated if it contains most of these conditions, and predicates WITH CHECK OPTION cannot use an index.

Updating with a cursor, with its need for a cursor declaration, FETCH . . . INTO statement, and UPDATE . . . WHERE . . . CURRENT statement, requires considerably more coding than the simple embedded update statement. A primary purpose of the FOR UPDATE OF clause is to hold locks and avoid the update of rows that have been read. But displaying a screen using CICS pseudo-conversational and IMS results in a commit work, which releases all locks. Since the cursor update also precludes the use of indexes on columns specified in the FOR UPDATE OF clause in some cases, it also carries a performance deficit. For these reasons and because in most cases an update without a cursor can carry out the same updates as an update with a cursor, it makes sense to avoid cursor updates except for some batch processing.

Testing for Existence

DB2 issues an error code (-811) if an embedded SELECT returns more than one row and a cursor has not been declared. In some cases, however, programmers may want a program to determine only whether a value exists—once or many times. It is not necessary to declare a cursor to perform such a test. One way to avoid it is to include the existence test in the SQL statement using the EXISTS operator. Another is to use a SELECT without declaring a cursor and test for the −811 SQLCODE, which indicates more than one row would be returned, or for the zero SQLCODE, which indicates exactly one row has been returned. Finally the programmer might use the COUNT operator in the SELECT statement to determine the number of values that satisfy the request. COUNT (DISTINCT) SN WHERE SN = 'S4' allows processing to stop when the first occurrence of S4 is encountered. This last technique has performance advantages if there is an index on the column.

9.4 ORGANIZATION CHART PROCESSING

Organization chart structures are not uncommon in application system design. Most companies have an organization chart similar to the one in Fig. 9.3. Information is frequently stored according to the reporting structure of employees and cost center allocation of budgets and expenses. This type of structure occurs in manufacturing, commonly called bill-of-material processing, where it is necessary to know the components needed to build a product and the subcomponents of each component. For example, a bill-

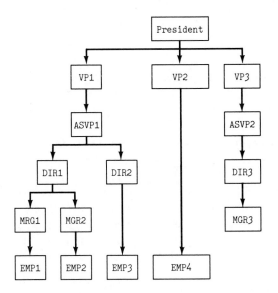

Fig. 9.3 Organization chart

Parent	Dependent	PL	DL
President	VP1	1	2
President	VP2	1	2
President	VP3	1	2
VP1	ASVP1	2	3
VP2	EMP4	2	6
VP3	ASVP2	2	3
ASVP1	DIR2	3	4
ASVP1	DIR1	3	4
ASVP2	DIR3	3	4
DIR1	MGR1	4	5
DIR1	MGR2	4	5
DIR2	EMP3	4	6
DIR3	MGR3	4	5
MGR1	EMP1	5	6
MGR2	EMP2	5	6

Fig. 9.4 Organization chart table

of-material for an airplane would have at the top level the end-product
airplane analogous to the president's level shown in the organization chart.
At the next level down would be the wings of the airplane rather than the
vice presidents, the next level might be the engines rather than the assistant
vice presidents, the next level might be the fan of the engine rather than the
director, and so forth until all components necessary to build the airplane
are accounted for.

An organizational chart or bill-of-materials can be "flattened" into a
table as shown in Fig. 9.4. The top level, the president, appears as the parent, and each position that reports to the president is listed as a dependent
(in the example vice presidents VP1, VP2, and VP3). Each vice president
is also listed in the parent column, with the associated reporting employees
listed as dependents. Each dependent appears as a parent if that dependent
has a reporting employee. EMP1, EMP2, EMP3, and EMP4 do not appear
in the parent column since they have no one reporting to them. The PL
column is a numeric indicator of the level of reporting for the parent, and
the DL column indicates the level of reporting for the dependent. The PL
and DL columns are optional but can be useful for reporting purposes.

The SQL code to perform an explosion to determine all employees who
report directly or indirectly to VP1 is shown along with comments as to the
result of each statement:

```
SELECT DEPENDENT      -- ASVP1 will be returned
FROM   ORG_CHART
```

```
WHERE  PARENT = &VP1

SELECT DEPENDENT       -- DIR1, DIR2 will be returned
FROM   ORG_CHART       -- one at a time when fetched
WHERE  PARENT = &ASVP1

SELECT DEPENDENT       -- MGR1, MGR2, EMP3 will be returned
FROM   ORG_CHART       -- one at a time when fetched
WHERE  PARENT =&DIR1   -- using DIR1 and DIR2

SELECT DEPENDENT       -- EMP1, EMP2 will be returned
FROM   ORG_CHART       -- one at a time when fetched
WHERE  PARENT =&MGR1   -- using MGR1, MGR2, and EMP3
```

The positions are indicated with QMF parameters for ease of understanding. Each parameter would be replaced by a host variable in a program. The first SELECT determines that ASVP1 reports directly to VP1. The second select is used to determine those employees who report directly to ASVP1, DIR1, and DIR2. The third select will determine that MRG1, MGR2, and EMP3 report directly to DIR1. The last select will determine that EMP1 and EMP2 report to MRG1. Using this approach, a select is needed for each level in the organization chart. In addition, a cursor will be necessary for each of the SELECTs along with the logic necessary to save the intermediate values used to determine the next level of reporting and the logic coded in the host language to determine which statement to execute until all reporting levels have been located.

The amount of host language code that needs to be developed can be reduced significantly by having DB2 save the intermediate results using subselects:

```
SELECT PARENT,DEPENDENT,PL,DL
FROM   ORG_CHART
WHERE  PARENT = &VP1 OR PARENT IN
(SELECT DEPENDENT FROM ORG_CHART WHERE PARENT = &VP1 OR PARENT IN
(SELECT DEPENDENT FROM ORG_CHART WHERE PARENT = &VP1 OR PARENT IN
(SELECT DEPENDENT FROM ORG_CHART WHERE PARENT = &VP1 OR PARENT IN
(SELECT DEPENDENT FROM ORG_CHART WHERE PARENT = &VP1 OR PARENT IN
(SELECT DEPENDENT FROM ORG_CHART WHERE PARENT = &VP1 OR PARENT IN
(SELECT DEPENDENT FROM ORG_CHART WHERE PARENT = &VP1 OR PARENT IN
(SELECT DEPENDENT FROM ORG_CHART WHERE PARENT = &VP1 OR PARENT IN
(SELECT DEPENDENT FROM ORG_CHART WHERE PARENT = &VP1 OR PARENT IN
(SELECT DEPENDENT FROM ORG_CHART WHERE PARENT = &VP1 OR PARENT IN
(SELECT DEPENDENT FROM ORG_CHART WHERE PARENT = &VP1 OR PARENT IN -- EMP1, EMP2
returned in work area
(SELECT DEPENDENT FROM ORG_CHART WHERE PARENT = &VP1 OR PARENT IN -- MGR1, MGR2,
EMP3 returned in work area
(SELECT DEPENDENT FROM ORG_CHART WHERE PARENT = &VP1 OR PARENT IN -- DIR2, DIR1
returned in work area
(SELECT DEPENDENT FROM ORG_CHART WHERE PARENT = &VP1 OR PARENT IN -- ASVP1 re-
turned in work area
```

```
(SELECT DEPENDENT FROM ORG_CHART WHERE PARENT = &VP1)))))))))))))))
ORDER BY 3,1,4,2
```

There is a limit of 15 levels using the subselect technique due to the limit of 15 tables being referenced in an SQL statement. This limit applies even if it is the same table name referenced 15 times as is the case for the table ORG_CHART. Also it will be seen in Chapter 11 that an IN subselect results in a tablespace scan that will significantly detract from performance with the 14 subselects in the statement.

Either of the techniques described above for explosions can be used for implosions. For example, an implosion would be used to determine who employee EMP1 reports to directly or indirectly. Each occurrence of the DEPENDENT column would be replaced by the PARENT column and each occurrence of the PARENT column would be replaced by the DEPEN-DENT column.

Good index design will enhance performance for both techniques. A composite index on the parent and dependent columns in that order will provide for index-only processing to accomplish an explosion. If implosions are frequently required, the composite index would be on the dependent and parent columns in that order.

Simple SQL with Increased Table Costs

The SQL can be simplified significantly by storing the explosion in the table. Fig. 9.5 shows a table design where the parent is repeated for each direct and indirect reporting level in the dependent column. The president is not included in the table since only a SELECT * is needed to determine all those that report directly and indirectly to the president. All employees who report directly or indirectly to VP1 can be determined very simply:

```
SELECT DEPENDENT
FROM   EXP_ORG_CHART
WHERE  PARENT = &VP1
```

The expanded organization chart may be acceptable for a small number of rows (say 10,000) and where business professionals need direct ad hoc access. The expanded version would be unacceptable for a large organizational or bill-of-material structure because of the amount of DASD space that would be required and the complexity of updating the data.

9.5 BATCH UPDATE PROCESSING

The task of applying hundreds of thousands of updates to a multimillion row table represents a challenging, though not uncommon, programming

Parent	Dependent	PL	DL
VP1	ASVP1	1	2
VP1	DIR1	1	3
VP1	MGR1	1	4
VP1	EMP1	1	5
VP1	MGR2	1	4
VP1	EMP2	1	5
VP1	DIR2	1	3
VP1	EMP3	1	5
ASVP1	DIR1	2	3
ASVP1	MGR1	2	4
ASVP1	EMP1	2	5
ASVP1	MGR2	2	4
ASVP1	EMP2	2	5
ASVP1	DIR2	2	3
ASVP1	EMP3	2	5
Etc.			

Fig. 9.5 Expanded organization chart table

problem. Seductively easy, and apparently reasonable, approaches can be extremely expensive. We will use a real-world case, altered to use the SPJ example tables, to explore some mass update techniques and their implications.

The production table, SPJ_PROD, has six million rows. Periodically it receives about 500,000 updates from the identically structured SPJ_UP-DATE table. If there is a match on the two tables' primary key columns, the SN, PN, and JN composite, QTY in the SPJ_PROD table's row is updated with the QTY value from the SPJ_UPDATE row. If there is no match, the SPJ_UPDATE row is inserted into SPJ_PROD.

One approach would be to use a cursor statement without a predicate to select the entire SPJ_UPDATE table. Using a programming loop, each primary key value fetched from that cursor is then used in a SELECT statement to search for a match in the SPJ_PROD table. If a match is found, a separate statement updates the row. If there is no match—which is indicated when the select from SPJ_PROD returns an SQLCODE of 100—another statement inserts the row into the SPJ_PROD table. This approach seems reasonable, but when it was tried, processing lasted more than 24 hours before information system personnel gave up and canceled the job.

That approach could be improved upon slightly by using a cursor and a FOR UPDATE OF clause with the SELECT statement searching the SPJ-_PROD table. That would avoid having to find each row being updated twice—once to look for the match and once for the update. But in light of the more than 24-hour processing for the initial approach, saving one search, even if it cut the work in half, would not be savings enough.

Another alternative eliminates the initial SELECT from the SPJ _PROD and the use of the UPDATE with cursor. Instead this approach goes directly to an UPDATE statement on SPJ_PROD without a cursor. In this UPDATE statement, the search criteria specifies equalities on the primary key columns and the values from SPJ_UPDATE are presented by a cursor and programming loop:

```
EXEC SQL UPDATE SPJ_PROD SET QTY = :SPJ_UPDATE.QTY
        WHERE SPJ_PROD.SN = :SPJ-UPDATE.SN
        AND SPJ_PROD.PN = :SPJ-UPDATE.PN
        AND SPJ_PROD.JN = :SPJ-UPDATE.JN
        END-EXEC.
```

If the statement returns an SQLCODE of 100, indicating no row with that primary key was found, the program inserts the row in SPJ_PROD. DB2 can use an index on the primary key in SPJ_PROD to look for the update matches. But even so searches of the 6-million row table, with perhaps as many as 500,000 searches of a 3-level index, plus I/O to the data pages could require considerable processing. This alternative would be appropriate if a small percent of rows would be updated.

Still another possible solution takes an entirely different approach. The idea here is to use two cursor SELECT statements, one selecting from the table providing the update values, the other from the production table. The host-language program compares the selected values and uses the matching values in an UPDATE statement. Because the rows can be returned by the two SELECTs in order, each table need be read only once.

In the example, the cursors' two SELECT statements would be:

```
SELECT SN, PN, JN, QTY
FROM   SPJ_PROD
ORDER  BY SN, PN, JN
```

and

```
SELECT SN, PN, JN, QTY
FROM   SPJ_UPDATE
ORDER  BY SN, PN, JN
```

The returned values are fetched into host-language variables. Each set of values from the production table is compared against corresponding values from the update table. The first set of values from the production table is compared with the first row from the update table. If there is no match, the program checks the second set of values from the production table, then the third, and so on, merging the rows and issuing an update or insert as needed. This process continues until a match is found or until tests in the program logic indicate that the value of the SN-PN-JN combination from the production table is greater than the corresponding value from the update table, which indicates there is no match. (The logic for this test is similar to that described above for reopening a cursor with a composite primary key.)

If a match is found, the appropriate row is updated. If not, the insertion is made. In either case, the program would loop to fetch the second set of values from the update table, begin comparing them against the values from the production table, and so on.

The key to this approach is to design the tables and the SELECT statements in a way that makes it likely that DB2 will use clustering indexes in satisfying both of them. This will allow DB2 to present the rows in order without having to perform costly sorts. And if DB2 does use a clustering index, it is also likely to use sequential prefetch for I/O in which case it brings up to 32 pages at a time into the buffer, rather than 1 page at a time. The two tables must, of course, have indexes with a high cluster ratio on the primary keys. The ORDER BY clause in each SELECT will insure that the rows are returned in order and increase the likelihood that the optimizer will choose to use the indexes to avoid a sort.

The installation faced with this particular problem actually opted for yet another solution because it was not possible to have a clustering index on the primary key in the SPJ_PROD table. Under this approach, an SQL statement deletes rows from the SPJ_PROD table that have primary key values matching those in SPJ_UPDATE. Then all rows from the SPJ_UPDATE table are inserted into SPJ_PROD. These statements provide for those operations:

```
DELETE FROM SPJ_PROD
       WHERE  SN || PN || JN IN
       (SELECT SN || PN || JN
        FROM   SPJ_UPDATE)
```

and

```
INSERT INTO SPJ_PROD
       SELECT SN, PN, JN, QTY
       FROM   SPJ_UPDATE
```

Obviously the coding for this approach is straightforward. But a few other steps are required to make the process efficient. For one thing, if there is an index on SPJ_UPDATE's primary key, DB2 can perform the delete subselect by accessing the index only. For another thing, dropping the indexes on SPJ_PROD before the deletions and insertions avoids the need to delete and insert index values. After the insertions, a way to rebuild several indexes on SPJ_PROD is to unload the table, drop the indexes, sort the dataset in clustering sequence, recreate the indexes, and reload it. One drawback to this approach is that it is not possible to commit work periodically. If there is a failure, the processing must be started again at the beginning. But by using this approach, the installation was able to process the mass update in 3 hours, as opposed to the more than 24 hours required using the initial method.

An alternative that avoids unloading and reloading the data is to drop all of the indexes before the batch processing to avoid updating the indexes. This would be a good alternative if there are few inserts or if the inserted rows are to go at the end of the tablespace. If the inserted rows should be inserted in sequence on the clustering index throughout the tablespace, however, a reorganization of the data would be required after recreating the indexes and a reorganization requires the unloading and reloading of the data. Still there are cases where dropping the indexes, particularly if there are several indexes, and rebuilding them with the procedure discussed in Chapter 16 with a single scan of the tablespace is a viable alternative.

These batch techniques are counterintuitive to DB2 professionals who are accustomed to maximizing performance by encouraging the optimizer to use an index to locate a few rows to be displayed to the user. But batch processing usually requires processing a large percent of the rows in a table. Large in this cases can be more than 10 to 20 percent of the rows. Indeed a number of cases have shown that when updating more than 10 to 20 percent of the rows, a tablespace scan with sequential prefetch is best.

9.6 BENEFITS OF SEQUENTIAL PREFETCH

A tablespace scan is best at times due primarily to the efficiencies of sequential prefetch. Prefetch means that up to 32 pages can be read with a single I/O instruction. The average I/O time for each page read is 1.5 ms (milliseconds) compared to reading each page individually, which requires about 16 ms on a 3390 DASD device.

Sequential prefetch can be used for a tablespace scan and a nonmatching index scan when processing eight or more data or leaf pages. It can be used on the data and index pages after finding a starting position with a matching index scan if the cluster ratio is greater than 80 percent. Prefetch can be used for an update and delete when a cursor is not used. DB2 uses prefetch for its work tablespaces, and the utilities use prefetch of up to 64 pages with a single I/O.

Sequential detection

The benefits of sequential prefetch are so significant that it may be initiated during execution even if not requested by the optimizer. Sequential detection is used to initiate sequential prefetch at execution time if a number of data or index pages are being accessed in sequence. The thresholds for when prefetch can be activated and deactivated can change from one release to another. Currently if five pages of the last eight pages contain required values, prefetch is activated. If five pages of the last eight pages do not contain required values, prefetch is deactivated. Dynamic prefetch can be repeatedly activated and deactivated for any cursor or noncursor SQL statement. It can be of significant benefit in processing the inner table in joins and tests for existence.

EXPLAIN provides information on the access path chosen by the optimizer and is discussed in Chapter 13. EXPLAIN will not show the use of prefetch as a result of sequential detection since it occurs at execution time. The developer can encourage the use of prefetch at bind time, which will be shown when using EXPLAIN as will be seen in Chapter 13. The simplest technique for encouraging the use of prefetch is to not use a predicate. Obviously if a predicate is not coded, a tablespace scan is required, and the optimizer will almost certainly specify the use of sequential prefetch. Techniques for disallowing the use of an index to satisfy a predicate are discussed in Chapter 11. The use of ORDER BY on a column with a high cluster ratio index will encourage the use of prefetch on the data and leaf pages as will the use of range predicates like BETWEEN, less than, and greater than. It is best to avoid repeated execution of a singleton select, rather use a cursor when retrieving more than one row in a program. Issue global update and delete statements without first selecting the rows. As was seen in the batch case study, it is best to process the rows in sequence, which means that the updates to be applied to a table should be sorted in the sequence of retrieval of the table.

9.7   RESTARTABLE BATCH PROGRAMS

Restarting a long running batch update program presents challenges. Let us look at three techniques. A simple approach is to issue no commits during processing. All updates will be rolled back automatically if a failure occurs. This may be acceptable for a 15-minute run, but even then it is more costly than might be thought at first. It can take an hour to apply updates twice, including the rollback. It would require about 15 minutes to apply updates initially, 30 minutes to rollback, and 15 minutes to apply updates a second time. And during most of this time some, perhaps many, of the pages would have exclusive locks excluding all other access. Consequently to avoid the possibility of lengthy rollbacks and holding locks, the batch program should issue commits frequently, perhaps every 1000 rows as suggested in Chapter 8.

When commit works are issued, however, the program must also be able to determine where to resume processing after a failure. The technique for coding this is similar to that for reopening a cursor described above. The primary key value of the last row processed before the commit is saved and used to reestablish position for the resumption of processing. It is not enough for that key value to be saved in the program because it will be lost in the failure when the program abends. However, if that key value is saved in another table, a control table, with the update of that table committed along with the processing on the primary data tables, the value will always be available to the program when it restarts. This control table would contain the last primary key value, control information, intermediate results, and perhaps the commit frequency for future modification if commits need to be more or less frequent.

The restarted program must read the control table to reestablish position and continue processing. Recall that ORDER BY is required to avoid missing rows and an index can be used to avoid a sort. If an index is not available to avoid sorting a large number of rows, end points should be used to minimize the number of rows sorted after each commit. If the input to the update program is on a GSAM file and IMS extended restart is available, it can be used on the input file but cannot be used on the DB2 table to reestablish position when the program is restarted.

A technique often used to avoid developing complex restart logic in a program and to allow for periodic commits is to take an image copy of the tablespaces to be updated before submitting the batch job. If the job fails, the tablespaces are recovered to the image copies. A problem with this technique when using referential integrity is that dependent tablespaces will have check pending set on. This can be avoided by quiescing all the related tables to a RBA (relative byte address) point and recovering to the RBA as will be discussed in Chapter 16. But using both techniques requires that all indexes on all tables must be rebuilt. An alternative is to use DSN1COPY, a service aid also discussed in Chapter 16, to copy all the tablespaces to be updated along with all indexes to sequential files. Then if a failure occurs, DSN1COPY is used to copy the sequential files back to the tablespaces and indexes and rerun the batch job. The use of any of the copy techniques requires that the batch program issue a LOCK TABLE statement to insure that no other program issues an update on the tables since all updates made after the copies will be lost.

9.8   THE SQL COMMUNICATIONS AREA

The SQL communications area (SQLCA) is a data structure that must be included in any host-language program using SQL. The SQLCA provides a

```
01  SQLCA.
    05  SQLCAID    PIC X(8).
    05  SQLCABC    PIC S9(9) COMP.
    05  SQLCODE    PIC S9(9) COMP.
    05  SQLERRM.
        49 SQLERRML PIC S9(4) COMP.
        49 SQLERRMC PIC X(70).
    05  SQLERRP    PIC X(8).
    05  SQLERRD    OCCURS 6 TIMES
                   PIC S9(9) COMP.
    05  SQLWARN.
        10 SQLWARN0 PIC X.
        10 SQLWARN1 PIC X.
        10 SQLWARN2 PIC X.
        10 SQLWARN3 PIC X.
        10 SQLWARN4 PIC X.
        10 SQLWARN5 PIC X.
        10 SQLWARN6 PIC X.
        10 SQLWARN7 PIC X.
        10 SQLWARN8 PIC X.
        10 SQLWARN9 PIC X.
        10 SQLWARNA PIC X.
    05  SQLSTATE   PIC X(5).
```

Fig. 9.6 COBOL'S SQLCA structure

way for DB2 to pass feedback about its operations to the program. As a program runs after each SQL statement executes, DB2 returns, via the SQLCA, codes indicating that the execution was successful or identifying errors or special conditions. The program can then test for these codes and react according to their content—perhaps branching to an error-handling paragraph or subroutine that prints a message and ends the program. This testing may be done with host-language coding following each SQL statement, or it may be done with a WHENEVER statement, which indicates the test and action to be taken for any SQL statement that follows the WHENEVER statement in the program listing.

The SQLCA contains variables for a number of codes and messages. Programmers can hand code the necessary structure, copy it from a source library or have DB2 generate it. An INCLUDE statement allows a host program to include any source code from a library, similar to a COPY statement in COBOL or Assembler and a %INCLUDE statement in PL/1. In COBOL, the code for automatic generation of the SQLCA is EXEC SQL INCLUDE SQLCA END-EXEC. The statement goes in the program's working storage section and generates the code for the SQLCA structure shown in Fig. 9.6.

```
SQLCAID    = 'SQLCA'
SQLCABC    = 136 (length of SQLCA)
SQLCODE    = 0 — Successful execution
           = 100 — No row(s) were found or no more rows were found
           = +N — An informative message
           = -N — An error condition
SQLERRML   = Number of bytes in SQLERRMC, 0 if no message returned
SQLERRMC   = 70-character error message
SQLERRP    = Diagnostic information such as the name of a DB2 module
SQLERRD(1) = Relational Data System (RDS) error code
SQLERRD(2) = Data manager (DM) error code
SQLERRD(3) = The 3rd integer is the number of rows INSERTED/UPDATED/DELETED.
Does not include a count of FK rows deleted with cascade or set null update rule nor
deletes with the mass delete algorithm.
SQLERRD(4) = Embedded dynamic SQL timeron
SQLERRD(5) = Column position of error for embedded dynamic SQL statement
SQLERRD(6) = Buffer manager error code
SQLWARN0   = Blank if the following have no warnings
'W' if one of the following holds a 'W'
SQLWARN1 = 'W' if a column's value was truncated when moved to a host variable
SQLWARN2 = 'W' if one or more nulls were excluded from a function
SQLWARN3 = 'W' if number of host variables does not match column list
SQLWARN4 = 'W' if a dynamic UPDATE/DELETE does not have a WHERE
SQLWARN5 = 'W' if statement applies only to SQL/DS
SQLWARN6 = 'W' if DATE or TIMESTAMP adjusted for different days in month/year
SQLWARN7 = 'W' if nonzero digits were truncated from fractional part of a decimal
number used as the operand of a multiplication or division operation
SQLWARN8 = 'W' if a character that could not be translated was replaced with a
substitute character
SQLWARN9 = 'W' if an arithmetic exception has been ignored during the processing
of COUNT DISTINCT
SQLWARNA = 'W' if at least one character field of the SQLCA has an invalid value
or blank
SQLSTATE = alternative to SQLCODE, value of '00000' to '65535'
```

Fig. 9.7 SQLCA description

SQLCA Return Codes

An examination of the SQLCA structure indicates the kind of information it makes available to a host program. Fig. 9.6 presents a brief description of the SQLCA contents as they correspond to the structure presented in Fig. 9.7. The first two variables, SQLCAID and SQLCABC, identify the communications area and give its length in bytes. The SQLCODE provides the most crucial information. If an SQL statement executes successfully, DB2 returns a zero in SQLCODE. If an error results when the statement is executed, DB2 returns a negative three-digit number to the program in SQLCODE. For example, if the NUMLKUS limit were exceeded, SQL-CODE returns -904. If the statement executes but encounters a special condition that the program might act on, SQLCODE identifies the condition through a positive three-digit number. If no rows or no more rows satisfy a statement, for example, SQLCODE is set to 100. A test for SQL-CODE = 100, then, might tell a program when to exit a loop, for example. (*IBM Database 2 Reference Summary Manual SX26-3771* contains a brief description of the error codes; *IBM Database 2 SQL Messages and Codes Manual SC26-4379* contains complete descriptions of the codes.)

SQLERRMC Contents

The SQLERRMC contains a brief description of the error or special condition identified by the SQLCODE. A program's error-handling paragraph or subroutine might print out SQLERRMC's message during program testing. However, it is not suitable for display to business professionals. Or the program might call on more complete messages of up to 960 characters using sample programs available with DB2—DSNTIAR, written in PL/1, or DSNTIAM, written in Assembler.

If an update statement violates a referential integrity constraint, it is often necessary to know the name of the constraint that was violated. Recall from Chapter 5 that a constraint name was given when defining the foreign key. This name can be found in SQLERRMC when a negative SQLCODE is received, usually beginning with a −53. For example, if a −530 was received indicating that an insert or update would have resulted in an orphan dependent row, the SQLERRMC can be moved to a host-language structure like:

```
IF SQLCODE = -530
   MOVE SQLERRM TO CONSTRAINTS.
```

CONSTRAINTS would be defined in working storage like:

```
01  CONSTRAINTS.
    03  PARM-LENGTH    PIC S9(4) COMP.
    03  REF-CONSTRAINT PIC X(08).
    03  FILLER         PIC X(62).
```

The host-variable REF-CONSTRAINT will contain the constraint name given when the foreign key was defined.

Additional Fields in SQLCA

SQLERRD is an array of six integers representing special codes, each describing some aspect of SQL's handling of a statement. The code of most interest to programmers is the third integer, SQLERRD(3), which indicates the number of rows inserted, updated, or deleted by the statement. It does not include a count of those rows deleted or set null through referential integrity processing or of rows deleted with the mass delete algorithm.

The warnings, SQLWARN0 through SQLWARNA, set a flag (the character W) indicating the existence of a particular condition that will not terminate a program but will affect its results. Conditions pointed out by these warnings include the fact that a column's value was truncated when it was moved to a host variable or that one or more nulls were excluded when a function was calculated. These warnings are most valuable for debugging.

WHENEVER Statements

Programmers need not include code after each SQL statement to examine the SQLCODE values. WHENEVER statements, SQL statements that can be embedded one or more times in the host language's procedural code, provide for branching to a paragraph depending on the content of SQL-CODE. Each WHENEVER statement applies to all of the SQL statements that follow it in the program listing, regardless of the order in which the statements are actually executed. This is because the WHENEVER statements themselves are never executed. Instead DB2's COBOL precompiler is a one-pass precompiler that processes the program from beginning to end and places the code necessary to carry out the WHENEVER statements' functions after each SQL statement in the program. Each WHENEVER statement then applies to the SQL statements following it until the next WHENEVER statement takes control.

Three WHENEVER statements test for three different conditions, all three can be used concurrently within a program. WHENEVER SQLER-ROR checks for negative SQLCODES, which would indicate the statement caused an error. WHENEVER SQLWARNING looks for warnings indicated by an SQLWARN0 of W. WHENEVER NOT FOUND looks for an SQLCODE of 100, indicating that the statement found no rows or no more rows to satisfy the SQL statement. These WHENEVER statements are similar to IF-THEN statements. If the SQLCODE value satisfies the condition, the program performs the stipulated response.

Each WHENEVER statement can respond to the test in one of two ways: by continuing processing regardless of the return code or by branching to an indicated point in the program. Continuation requires simply the word CONTINUE in the statement—WHENEVER SQLWARNING CON-TINUE, for example. CONTINUE is used primarily to aid in maintenance, to express explicitly in the code that the program is not acting upon the indicated test. Thus a programmer need not scan a lengthy program listing just to find that the test was not in effect.

Branching requires the words GO TO and an identification of the point to which control shifts—in a COBOL program, for example, WHENEVER SQLERROR GO TO ERROR-HANDLING, where ERROR-HANDLING represents a paragraph for dealing with the condition. Organizations can deal with error conditions in a variety of ways. The programmer may deal with the problem with code immediately following the statement that caused the error. Many organizations find it more efficient to place all of the error handling within a separate section of the program. This can avoid some redundancy in coding and ease maintenance. Some organizations prefer to have all error handling for all programs in a separate module called by each program. WHENEVER NOT FOUND may be useful for branching to an end-of-job routine. Because programs usually process a number of SQL statements, however, programmers will often want to use a test for SQLCODE 100 and negative SQLCODEs immediately after each statement, and have the program proceed accordingly, rather than using the WHENEVER commands to branch to a routine. Such branching is not consistent with structured programming techniques. It is usually best not to mix WHENEVER and application code tests since in most cases the inserted tests will be done before the coded tests.

9.9 DYNAMIC SQL

Embedded, dynamic SQL is a powerful but costly feature, too costly for use in high transaction rate applications. Dynamically generated SQL statements must be prepared—that is, optimized and bound—just as static SQL would be. Commands within the host-language program therefore must account for that preparation. In addition, if the dynamic statement is a SELECT, the program must be able to determine the data structures needed to receive the selected values and be able to generate those structures, just as the programmer includes the necessary data structures in a host-language program for static SQL by hand coding them or having DCLGEN generate them. (DCLGEN is discussed Chapter 10.) With dynamic SQL, however, a program must dynamically allocate memory to receive the values for them. Consequently dynamic SELECTs can be used most easily with PL/1 and Assembler, the two DB2 host languages capable of allocating memory dynamically.

COBOL and FORTRAN programs can execute dynamic SELECTs. In most cases, however, the programmer must know and include in the program the data type and length of column values to be returned, limiting the usefulness of dynamic SQL. These languages can deal with fixed list SELECTs where the data type and length of columns to be returned are known. Varying list SELECTs present challenges, and subroutines are often used to allocate the required storage as described in the manual *DB2 Note-*

book (GG24-3182). COBOL II has pointer and set constructs that aid in managing varying list SELECT statements. Most of the other SQL statements such as INSERT, UPDATE, and DELETE, which return only SQLCA feedback, not data, work quite easily dynamically within COBOL because there is no uncertainty about the data type and length of returned columns. SQL data definition and data control statements also work easily within COBOL and other host languages.

Dynamic Statements Other Than SELECT

The host program must first include a variable to receive the SQL statement, which should be a varying-length character variable for COBOL and Assembler or a varying or fixed-length string variable in PL/1. The variable should be long enough to accommodate the longest statement a user is likely to require. We will call that variable SQLSTATEMENT. It is declared as any other host variable would be. The programmer may set the variable equal to an SQL statement in this way:

```
MOVE 'UPDATE SPJ SET QTY = QTY + 10
    WHERE SN = 'S3'
    AND   PN = 'P3'' TO SQLSTATEMENT
```

If the dynamic SQL statement, as here, uses constants instead of host-language variables, DB2 will bind and execute it at once in response to a single command, the EXECUTE IMMEDIATE command. The command would look like this:

```
EXEC SQL EXECUTE IMMEDIATE :SQLSTATEMENT END-EXEC.
```

If a dynamic statement is to be reexecuted, however, the EXECUTE IMMEDIATE command is an inefficient way of doing it because it requires that the statement be rebound for each execution. The more efficient approach, and the one needed if the statement uses host-language variables, binds the statement once in response to a PREPARE statement and executes it any number of times in response to EXECUTE statements. (In either case, the optimizer returns its relative cost estimate for a dynamic bind from a host-language program as SQLERRD(4) in the SQLCA.)

For a dynamic SQL statement to be executed repeatedly, a host-language variable is needed to reference the machine language form of the statement after it is bound. We will call the variable SQLBOUND. The embedded SQL statement that orders preparation of the code structure uses the keyword PREPARE, followed by the name of the variable to reference it, followed by the keyword FROM, followed by the name of the source code variable that provides the statement. (Remember that the host-language variable, when used in an embedded SQL statement, is preceded by a colon.) The PREPARE statement for the example would be:

```
EXEC SQL PREPARE SQLBOUND FROM :SQLSOURCE END-EXEC.
```

Because the bind process locks the DBD of all databases containing tables being referenced by the SQL statement, programmers should code for a rollback to release the locks after an unsuccessful PREPARE. A negative SQLCODE indicates an unsuccessful prepare. The program should test for the code and branch to a rollback when the code is encountered.

The statement is now ready for execution, which is invoked by an embedded EXECUTE command. The command simply uses the keyword EXECUTE followed by the name of the prepared plan:

```
EXEC SQL EXECUTE SQLBOUND END-EXEC.
```

Arguments and Parameters

The bind process that results from a PREPARE statement is the same as that done when static SQL is bound except that the resulting plan is not stored in the DB2 directory. Dynamic statements must therefore be bound each time the program runs. The plan is kept in the VS working storage portion of memory, however, allowing a prepared statement to execute more than once without having to be rebound.

A dynamic SQL statement cannot include a host variable. It can, however, use question marks to indicate variables to which values are assigned and passed to the EXECUTE statement—for example:

```
SQLSTATEMENT = 'UPDATE SPJ SET QTY = QTY + 10
               WHERE  SN = ?
               AND    PN = ?'
```

A USING clause in the EXECUTE statement indicates the variables that are to take the places of the question marks. After the statement has been prepared as above, its EXECUTE statement would look like this:

```
EXEC SQL EXECUTE SQLBOUND USING :SN, :PN END-EXEC.
```

The USING clause assigns its variables to the parameters in the order listed. That is, the first variable is passed as an argument to the statement's first parameter, the second variable to the second parameter, and so on. The dynamic statement can execute any number of times with differing values for SN and PN without rebinding.

Dynamic Selects

There are two types of dynamic SELECT statements: *fixed list* and *variable list*. The first is used when the number, types, and lengths of variables needed to receive returned values are known when the host-language program is written. In that case, a COBOL programmer can declare INTO variables in the data division. If the information about the variables will be developed only as the program executes, a variable-list SELECT is needed. In this case, the program must be able to allocate storage for those variables dynamically. This is possible only with PL/1 and Assembler, with COBOL programs calling Assembler, or with Cobol II's pointer and set constructs.

For the variable-list SELECT, DB2 provides the program the information it needs to allocate storage through the SQL descriptor area (SQLDA), a data structure similar to the SQLCA in that both communicate between DB2 and host-language programs. The SQLDA receives a description of the value to be returned from the SELECT statement in the program. DB2 interrogates the catalog tables for the information describing the columns returned by the SELECT and passes that information back to the program. A number of commands are needed to carry out those functions.

The variables for the dynamic SELECT statement's source and code structure are declared just as they would be for non-SELECT statements. The PREPARE statement that invokes the bind process is the same. (The statement to be prepared is restricted, however, in that even if a single value might be returned, the select must use a cursor rather than a SELECT . . . INTO clause. Consequently the PREPARE command will not work with a dynamic SELECT statement that includes INTO.)

An INCLUDE statement, INCLUDE SQLDA, which is similar to IN-CLUDE SQLCA, is required to bring the SQLDA into the program. Then another command, the DESCRIBE statement, is needed to bring the descriptions of the variables the SELECT will return into the SQLDA. The DESCRIBE command takes this form:

```
EXEC SQL DESCRIBE SQLBOUND INTO SQLDA;
```

The syntax is straightforward. The variable containing the statement's code structure—in this case, SQLBOUND—follows the keyword DESCRIBE. The keywords INTO SQLDA are self-descriptive.

The dynamic SELECT statement also requires a cursor. Instead of including the actual SELECT statement in the cursor declaration as would be done with static SQL, the declaration here refers to the variable referencing the statement's machine code—for example:

```
EXEC SQL DECLARE SCURSOR FOR SQLBOUND;
```

It also requires OPEN and FETCH commands. The OPEN statement is the same as in static SQL, but the FETCH statement is slightly different. Instead of using an INTO clause to fetch values into specified host-language variables, FETCH here employs a USING DESCRIPTOR clause, which indicates the values are to be returned to variables identified in the SQLDA—for example:

```
EXEC SQL OPEN SCURSOR;
    DO WHILE . . .
        EXEC SQL FETCH SCURSOR USING DESCRIPTOR SQLDA;
    END;
EXEC SQL CLOSE SCURSOR;
```

Dynamic SQL is a sophisticated feature of DB2 and can be valuable when required. When performance is an issue, however, dynamic SQL should not be used. It requires that DB2 bind a plan each time it executes a statement dynamically (EXECUTE IMMEDIATE) or each time the program is executed (PREPARE and EXECUTE). This can be significant overhead and is not likely to be acceptable if a high transaction rate is required.

9.10 SAMPLE HOST-LANGUAGE PROGRAMS

DB2 provides a number of sample programs that include code that developers will find useful for building their own programs. Most developers keep a skeleton program in their source library to use in developing new programs. DB2's library of sample programs can provide starting points for these skeletons and are in the dataset outprefix.DSNSAMP. The load module for these programs is in outprefix.DSNLOAD where outprefix consists of numerals indicating the current release and version number of DB2, DSN230 for version 2, release 3, for example.

Member DSN8BC3 contains a sample COBOL program, DSN8BP3, a PL/1 program, and DSN8BF3 a sample FORTRAN program. The sample PL/1 program DSNTEP2 is particularly useful. It reads in SQL statements as input and executes them dynamically. It can provide the code needed to execute SQL statements dynamically in a batch job stream or CLIST. The program listings in the sample library have extensive comments explaining the processing done by the programs.

9.11 SUMMARY

DB2 provides for a number of ways to use SQL with a number of programming languages. The syntax for embedded SQL is virtually the same as the standard interactive SQL with the exception of CURSOR manipulation. Cursor repositioning can be a challenge particularly with a composite primary key, and several techniques for cursor management were discussed.

EXERCISES

9.1. What happens with respect to cursors when a screen is displayed using CICS pseudo conversation and IMS? Also what happens to locks held as a result of the FOR UPDATE OF clause?

9.2. What happens with respect to cursors when a screen is displayed using CICS conversation, TSO, and CAF? Are there any potential problems?

9.3. A program for reviewing the number of parts assigned to a given job periodically repeats rows the user has already seen. What is the problem? Provide a possible solution.

9.4. How does DB2 inform an application that an embedded SELECT statement has returned no rows?

9.5. Why is a tablespace scan often best for a batch processing program?

10

Program Preparation and Execution

10.1 INTRODUCTION

DB2 implements SQL as a compiled, rather than an interpreted, language. That is, DB2 compiles all SQL statements in a program into a machine-executable form that can be used any number of times. This provides a performance advantage over an interpretive system that must translate each source statement every time a program runs.

Under older, fully compiled systems, if a database design is changed, programs using the changed portions must be modified and recompiled to create a new run-time version. DB2 avoids this difficulty by separating the host language's procedural code from the SQL code used for data access. It then uses a separate compilation process for each type of code. For the SQL code, compilation is performed with other functions in a process called *bind*. The optimizer, as part of the bind process, finds the most efficient access path to the data required by the SQL statement. The machine-code calls that bind generates to implement this path are called *application plans or packages*. (The distinction between a plan and package will be made in Section 10.6.) The bind process stores information about the application plan and packages in the catalog tables. When a compiled program is to be rerun, DB2 looks in the catalog to determine if the plan or package has been marked invalid because any of the underlying objects it used has been changed or dropped. If so, the plan or package will have already been marked invalid in the catalog, and DB2 automatically creates a new application plan or package by rebinding the SQL statements stored in the catalog table SYSSTMT or SYSPACKSTMT during the original precompile. This avoids the need to revise or process the host-language program in any way.

10.2   THE STEPS IN PROGRAM PREPARATION

The steps required in program preparation and execution are diagramed in Fig. 10.1. The precompiler extracts SQL statements from the host-language code, substituting call statements. When the program runs, these call statements pass control through a language interface module to DB2's database services address space (DSAS), which does the processing called for by SQL statements. The precompiler leaves copies of the SQL statements as comments in the modified host-program source code to maintain understandability. The modified source code is readied for execution through compilation and link editing that allows the programmer to include in the application program compiled code from other libraries.

The precompiler places a copy of the SQL statements in a database request module (DBRM) library member. Each individual program, module, or subroutine that is precompiled separately has one DBRM covering all of its SQL statements. Bind operates on the DBRM to create an application plan or package. It first parses the SQL statement, a process akin to parsing a sentence grammatically. The parsing confirms that all the necessary elements of a statement are present and syntactically correct. Bind also checks that the individual binding the plan is authorized to perform the operations requested by the SQL statements. During bind, the optimizer interrogates the catalog tables describing the database, chooses the access path, and generates the machine code calls needed to execute the statements. DB2 stores information about the plan or package in the catalog tables and also stores the plan or package itself in the directory. The compiled and link-edited program and application plan work together when the program runs. Application plans and packages are broken into sections containing code structures to execute the SQL. Only those sections required as the program runs are brought into the environmental descriptor manager (EDM) memory pool for execution. The plan is located in a directory table using an index on plan name and section. A package is located in a separate directory table using an index on package name, consistency token, and section. The header and directory portion of the plan and packages are brought into the EDM pool and remain there during execution. The sec-

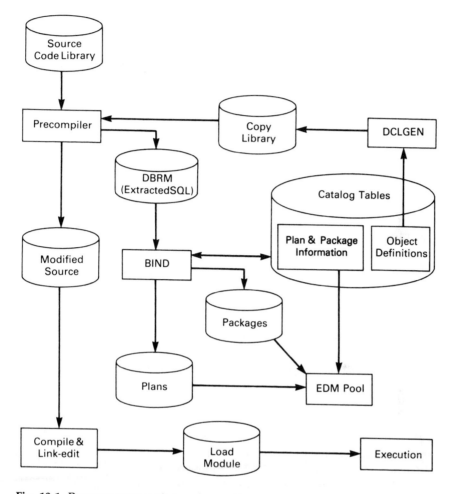

Fig. 10.1 Program preparation and execution

tions are brought into the EDM pool as required by the execution of SQL statements. The plan or package header is used to access the plan or package sections in the EDM pool.

Fig. 10.1 also shows how DB2 can generate data structures for programs written in COBOL or PL/1. A programmer could, of course, code the data structures manually, but for COBOL or PL/1, a facility called *declarations generator* (abbreviated DCLGEN, pronounced "deckle jen") can generate the structures automatically. DCLGEN is available under DB2I or DSN, the two facilities used most frequently in program prepara-

```
┌─────────────────────────────────────────────────────────────────────┐
│                       DB2I PRIMARY OPTION MENU                        │
│  ===>                                                                 │
│                                                                       │
│  Select one of the following DB2 functions and press ENTER.          │
│    1 SPUFI                    (Process SQL statements)                │
│    2 DCLGEN                   (Generate SQL and source language declarations)│
│    3 PROGRAM PREPARATION      (Prepare a DB2 application program to run)│
│    4 PRECOMPILE               (Invoke DB2 precompiler)                │
│    5 BIND/REBIND/FREE         (BIND, REBIND, or FREE appl. plans or packages)│
│    6 RUN                      (RUN a SQL program)                     │
│    7 DB2 COMMANDS             (Issue DB2 commands)                    │
│    8 UTILITIES                (Invoke DB2 utilities)                  │
│    9 CATALOG VISIBILITY       (Invoke catalog dialogs)               │
│    D DB2I DEFAULTS            (Set global parameters)                │
│    X EXIT                     (Leave DB2)                             │
│                                                                       │
│    PRESS: END to exit         HELP for more information               │
└─────────────────────────────────────────────────────────────────────┘
```

Fig. 10.2 DB2I primary option menu (Courtesy of International Business Machines Corporation)

tion. DCLGEN reads from the catalog the descriptions of the tables and views to be used in the program and generates the necessary data structures for them in host-language code.

10.3   DB2 INTERACTIVE

DB2 offers a number of commands for use in readying a program for execution that programmers can use to perform the functions required to convert code from source to executable modules. A convenient alternative is to work through DB2I (DB2 Interactive), which provides a menu interface to the necessary command processor.

DB2I provides options for all the DB2 functions that developers are likely to need. The functions are listed in Fig. 10.2. Choices made at this menu lead to additional panels for invoking the desired functions. Appendix C discusses option 1, SPUFI, and Chapter 16 will cover option 8, utilities. Option 7, DB2 commands, provides for executing commands for such operations as displaying the status of utilities, terminating utilities, and starting or stopping databases or stopping DB2. Option D, DB2I defaults, presents the default panel shown in Fig. 10.3. Default choices entered on this panel apply to all functions performed using DB2I. Default option 1, DB2 NAME, must contain the name given the DB2 subsystem when it was installed. Many installations select their own name for the subsystem, fre-

```
                        DB2I DEFAULTS
 ===>

Change defaults as desired:
   1 DB2 NAME .............         ===> DSN    (Subsystem identifier)
   2 DB2 CONNECTION RETRIES        ===> 0      (How many retries for DB2 con.)
   3 APPLICATION LANGUAGE          ===>        (COBOL, COB2, C, FORT,ASMH,PLI)
                                    COB2
   4 LINES/PAGE OF LISTING         ===> 60     (A number from 5 to 999)
   5 MESSAGE LEVEL ..........      ===> I      (Info., Warning, Error, Severe)
   6 COBOL STRING DELIMITER        ===> '      (DEFAULT, ' or '')
   7 SQL STRING DELIMITER          ===> '      (DEFAULT, ' or '')
   8 DECIMAL POINT ..........      ===> .      (. or ,)
   9 STOP IF RETURN CODE > =       ===> 8      (Lowest terminating returncode)
  10 NUMBER OF ROWS ..........     ===> 20     (For ISPF Tables)

  11 DB2I JOB STATEMENT:    (Optional if your site has a SUBMIT exit)
     ===> //JOB . . . USER = AUTHID
     ===> //*
     ===> //*

  PRESS: ENTER to save and exit     END to exit            HELP for more info.
```

Fig. 10.3 DB2I defaults panel (Courtesy of International Business Machines Corporation)

quently DB2T for test and DB2P for production, rather than staying with the name provided by IBM, DSN. The choice must be entered on the default panel. The default panel's option 9, DB2I JOB STATEMENT, is particularly important since DB2I generates JCL code for several of the DB2I functions. The job statement entered as option 9 will be used for all job streams generated by DB2I. Programmers use the primary menu options 2 through 6 in readying programs for execution. A description of each option will explain the program development steps required by DB2 to satisfy the processes shown in Fig. 10.1.

10.4 GENERATING DATA STRUCTURES

DCLGEN generates COBOL or PL/1 data structures that correspond to the DB2 tables and views to be accessed by the program. DCLGEN also generates DECLARE TABLE statements for those tables and views. DECLARE TABLE statements are SQL statements optionally embedded in the host-language source program. They are similar in syntax to the CREATE statements for the tables they describe. (Fig. 10.4 shows a DECLARE TABLE statement and its corresponding COBOL structure.) The purpose of

```
DECLARE TABLE statement:

EXEC SQL
 DECLARE AUTHID.S TABLE
(SN     CHAR(5)  NOT NULL,
 SNAME  CHAR(20) NOT NULL WITH DEFAULT,
 STATUS SMALLINT NOT NULL WITH DEFAULT,
 CITY   CHAR(15) NOT NULL WITH DEFAULT)
END-EXEC.

Corresponding COBOL data structure:

01 DCL-S.
   10 SN     PIC X(5).
   10 SNAME  PIC X(20).
   10 STATUS PIC S9(4) USAGE COMP.
   10 CITY   PIC X(15).
```

Fig. 10.4 DCLGEN include code

having DECLARE TABLE statements in the source code is to allow the precompiler to check the syntax of the SQL statements referring to the tables and views. If the statement is not present, the precompiler will issue a warning with a return code of 4 for any table or view references that do not have a DECLARE TABLE statement. The precompiler functions independently of DB2 and might even run on a computer on which DB2 is not installed. Having the table and view declarations in the source code allows the precompiler to uncover syntactical errors that otherwise would not be found until DB2 binds the plan. This avoids having to read the catalog tables twice, once during precompile and a second time during bind.

In response to the entries made in the DCLGEN panel (Fig. 10.5), DCLGEN reads the specified table or view definition in the DB2 catalog and generates both the data structure in the specified host language and the DECLARE TABLE statement. Panel option 1 receives the table's or view's name and option 2 the name of the dataset to receive the structures. Option 3 can be used to specify the location of the table or view in a distributed environment. Typically an organization sets up a DCLGEN library for application development projects and application systems in production. The dataset name is made up of that library's name followed by the particular member's name indicated in parentheses. This member name will be used on the INCLUDE statement to bring the member into the host-language program.

If the installation's security system protects the dataset, the programmer enters an individual password in option 4. The programmer indicates in option 5 whether the structure and declaration are new or replacements for existing ones; the choices are ADD or REPLACE. A YES or NO in option 6 indicates whether column labels specified with the LABEL ON

```
                              DCLGEN
 ===>  _

 Enter table name for which declarations are required:
 1 SOURCE TABLE NAME         ===>  S
 2 AT LOCATION..........     ===>       (Optional)

 Enter destination data set:            (Can be sequential or partitioned)
 3 DATA SET NAME........     ===>  'PROJ.AUTHID.COBOL(STABLE)'
 4 DATA SET PASSWORD         ===>       (If password protected)

 Enter options as desired:
 5 ACTION...............     ===>  ADD  (Add new or replace old declaration)
 6 COLUMN LABEL..........    ===>  NO   (Enter yes for column label)
 7 STRUCTURE NAME........    ===>  ST                        (Optional)
 8 FIELD NAME PREFIX         ===>  ST                        (Optional)
```

Fig. 10.5 DCLGEN panel (Courtesy of International Business Machines Corporation)

statement discussed in Chapter 4 should be included as comments in the generated code. Options 7 and 8 allow the programmer to specify prefixes for the table's and its columns' names. Prefixes on the column names can be important because different tables may have identical column names. The FIELD NAME PREFIX, however, is not a true prefix. Rather the value entered on line 8 will have a three-digit sequence number appended for each column in the table. If the structure name is keyed as the table or view name, it overrides the DCL prefix and a warning message of DS-NE903I is issued since it could result in an error in future releases. In addition, the null indicators discussed in Chapter 9 are not generated by the precompiler.

Programmers can also hand code structures or declarations. Indeed those generated by DCLGEN can be modified with an editor. It is advisable to use DCLGEN rather than coding the data structures directly in the program. The use of DCLGEN will insure that each column will have a host variable that matches in data type and length. This is very important to avoid data exceptions and to insure good performance. It will be seen in Chapter 11 that the data type and length of a column and host-variable comparison must match exactly in order for an index to be used to locate the data. In addition, having matching names for columns and host variables eases the development and maintenance of programs. The structures and declarations generated into the dataset are brought into the host-language program with an INCLUDE statement that includes the dataset's

```
                        DB2 PROGRAM PREPARATION
===>

Enter the following:
  1 INPUT DATA SET NAME .....   ===>   'PROJ.AUTHID.COBOL(SUPDATE)'
  2 DATA SET NAME QUALIFIER     ===>   TEMP   (For building dataset names)
  3 PREPARATION ENVIRONMENT     ===>   EDITJCL
                                       (FOREGROUND,BACKGR.,EDITJCL)
  4 RUN TIME ENVIRONMENT ....   ===>   TSO    (TSO, CICS, IMS)
  5 OTHER OPTIONS               ===>

Select functions:              Display panel?      Perform function?
  6 CHANGE DEFAULTS             ===> N (Y/N)        ..............
  7 PL/I MACRO PHRASE .......   ===> N (Y/N)        ===> N (Y/N)
  8 PRECOMPILE.............     ===> Y (Y/N)        ===> Y (Y/N)
  9 CICS COMMAND TRANSLATION    ..............      ===> N (Y/N)
 10 BIND PLAN ..............    ===> Y (Y/N)        ===> Y (Y/N)
 11 BIND PACKAGE ...........    ===> Y (Y/N)        ===> Y (Y/N)
 12 COMPILE OR ASSEMBLE .....   ===> Y (Y/N)        ===> Y (Y/N)
 13 PRELINK.................    ===> N (Y/N)        ===> N (Y/N)
 14 LINK...................     ===> N (Y/N)        ===> Y (Y/N)
 15 RUN....................     ===> N (Y/N)        ===> Y (Y/N)

PRESS: ENTER to process        END to exit         HELP for more info.
```

Fig. 10.6 Program preparation panel (Courtesy of International Business Machines Corporation)

member name. To bring the example structure and declaration generated from Fig. 10.5 into a COBOL program, the following statement must be included in the working storage section:

```
EXEC SQL INCLUDE STABLE END-EXEC.
```

10.5 PROGRAM PREPARATION

Preparing a program for execution entails precompiling, binding, compiling, and linking it. The program preparation panel (Fig. 10.6) takes programmers through those processes as well as the processes necessary to prepare the program for specific operating environments. Notice, however, that programmers can reach precompile and bind individually directly from the primary panel.

The first six entries of the program preparation panel are largely self-explanatory. The INPUT DATA SET NAME generally follows an installation's naming convention that identifies the project name and type of program. DB2 creates a number of temporary datasets in preparing a program—modified source code, print listings, and so on. It uses TEMP as a default in entry 2 as a basis for naming these datasets, adding the user ID and a descriptive term (USERID.TEMP.PCLIST for a precompiler print list, for example). Users can change this default, but then they have to delete the datasets when they are no longer needed. DB2, however, will keep track of and reuse datasets with TEMP in their name, cutting down on housekeeping considerably.

These temporary datasets are important to developers. The precompiler writes errors it detects in USERID.TEMP.PCLIST, for example. Line numbers given for errors refer to the PCLIST listing, not the original source code. (The line numbers will also appear in the PLAN_TABLE, describing the access path chosen by the optimizer for an SQL statement as will be discussed in Chapter 13.) The developer should correct the errors in the original source code in the input dataset from line 1. The precompiled source code is written to USERID.TEMP.COBOL. The modified source code from that file is compiled, and the compiler writes errors it finds in the USERID.TEMP.LIST.

A choice of EDITJCL for option 3 gives the programmer a chance to see and revise the JCL generated to perform the functions selected in options 7 through 15. That JCL is presented via the ISPF EDIT mode. Developers frequently make a copy of the generated JCL, modify it for their specific requirements, and subsequently submit it to avoid having to go through the panels for each program preparation.

Option 6 allows the programmer to check the default panel to see that the proper job statement for the JCL is specified. Options 7 through 15 will lead the programmer through the preparation processes in order. As one step is completed, DB2I automatically moves to the next. When CICS is used, the order of options 8 and 9—precompile before CICS command translation—is important to avoid having the CICS translator issue warnings when it encounters the SQL statements. (Precompile changes the SQL statements from the source program into comments and adds low-level call statements.) Notice that the programmer can choose through the "Display Panel?" option to see and perhaps modify the panel for each process before it performs its function or to have the function performed without seeing the panel. Option 15 allows the programmer to run the program from the program preparation panel using the TSO attach.

Precompile

The precompile panel (Fig. 10.7) can be reached from the program preparation panel or the DB2I primary menu. When the program preparation panel

```
                              PRECOMPILE
   ===>

   Enter precompiler data sets:
   1 INPUT DATA SET ........   ===>   'PROJ.AUTHID.COBOL(SUPDATE)'
   2 INCLUDE LIBRARY .......   ===>   'PROJ.AUTHID.COBOL'

   3 DSNAME QUALIFIER ......   ===>   TEMP     (For building data set names)
   4 DBRM DATA SET .........   ===>   'PROJ.AUTHID.DBRM'

   Enter processing options as desired:
   5 WHERE TO PRECOMPILE      ===>   EDITJCL (FOREGROUND,BACKGROUND,EDITJCL)
   6 VERSION..............     ===>   V1
                                      (Blank, VERSION, or AUTO)
   7 OTHER OPTIONS ........    ===>

   PRESS: ENTER to process         END to exit        HELP for more information
```

Fig. 10.7 Precompile panel (Courtesy of International Business Machines Corporation)

is used, it automatically passes the INPUT dataset name to option 1, the DSNAME qualifier to option 3, and where to precompile it to option 5 in the precompile panel. The user indicates in option 2, INCLUDE LIBRARY, any source library that contributes code via INCLUDE statements to the program being prepared, in particular the library that contains the code structures generated by DCLGEN. The user names in option 4 the DBRM DATA SET, which receives a copy of the extracted SQL code from the precompiler. The library name usually follows an installation's naming conventions. The member name will be the same as the source member name in option 1—SUPDATE in Fig. 10.7. Option 6 provides for specifying a 64-byte name to be used as the version ID with packages. If the entry is left blank, an empty string is the default version ID. If AUTO is used, the version ID will be the same as the consistency token. The version ID is used with packages as will be discussed in section 10.7.

There are additional options that can be entered for entry 7 that can be specified to the precompiler as described in the IBM manual, *Application Programming and SQL Guide (SC26-4377)*. For example, SQL (ALL) requests that the precompiler check that all SQL statements confirm to the SAA (system application architecture) standard. This insures that the SQL will execute against any IBM or non-IBM DBMS that conforms to the standard. SQL (DB2) will cause the precompiler to verify only that the coded SQL statements are correct for execution with DB2.

10.6 THE BENEFIT OF PACKAGES

Some background information is needed to understand the benefit of packages. The transaction managers of CICS and IMS require that the plan be defined for a transaction. Frequently a transaction consists of a number of programs, modules, or subroutines each of which is precompiled separately producing separate DBRM members each of which must be bound. The precompiler produces modified host-language code for each program, module, or subroutine that constitutes a transaction to be processed by a compiler and link editor to produce separate load modules. The precompiler writes a consistency token (pseudo-timestamp) in the DBRM library member and the modified source program that is carried forward to the plan or package and program load module. This consistency token is used by DB2 to insure that the correct plan or package is executed when a load module is executed. If a matching plan or package for the load module cannot be found a −818 SQLCODE is issued. (A −818 will also be issued after a bind when CICS is being used if the CICS NEWCOPY command is not executed.)

If an application plan is used, all DBRM members for a transaction must be bound into a plan and specified to the transaction manager. This makes the development and maintenance of each program, module, and subroutine that constitutes the transaction difficult to manage. When a program requires revision, a new program is added, or an existing program is eliminated, all DBRMs used in the transaction must be identified and bound into a plan. While the bind takes place, the transaction cannot be used. If there is a failure as a result of the change, there are no facilities to fall back to the previous working version. Frequently there are common modules or subroutines that are used by several programs, and it is resource intensive to bind the same subroutine's DBRM into each of many plans that use it. There are performance benefits to having frequently executed programs in a single transaction since that facilitates thread reuse. Packages also avoid the redundancy that results from IMS requiring that the transaction code, plan name, and program name be the same. In addition, it requires considerable I/O and CPU time to bind a large number of DBRM members together each time a change is made to only one program, module, or subroutine and the likelihood of catalog contention is increased. The proper use of packages can avoid these problems and the resources required to bind many DBRM modules into a plan.

Packages, like plans, contain optimized code structures for SQL statements but for only a single program, module, or subroutine contained in a member of the DBRM library. A plan is required when using packages, but it can contain only pointers to packages as indicated in Fig. 10.8 or a mix-

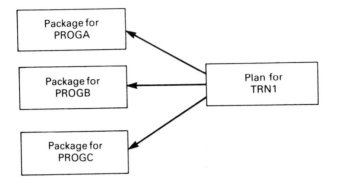

Fig. 10.8 A plan can contain pointers to packages

ture of code structures and pointers to packages. Packages are optional, all DBRM members required by a transaction can be bound into a single plan. If packages are used and a program is changed or added, however, only the DBRM for that program needs to be bound. The plan does not have to be bound since it contains only pointers to packages referenced in the plan.

10.7 BINDING SQL INTO PACKAGES AND PLANS

There are a number of parameters that can be specified when SQL from a DBRM member is bound into a package or plan that effects performance.

Box 10.1 Cost and complexities avoided with the use of packages

---

If a transaction consists of multiple programs, modules, or subroutines, packages avoid complexities and reduce the cost of binds. They:

- Avoid having to identify all programs that constitute the transaction
- Avoid having to identify all programs that use a module or subroutine that is changed
- Avoid having to bind a large number of DBRM members into a plan
- Avoid the costs of a large bind
- Avoid the entire transaction being unavailable during bind and automatic rebind of a plan
- Minimize fall-back complexities if changes resulted in an error
- Minimize catalog contention

```
                            BIND/REBIND/FREE
COMMAND ===> 1

Select one of the following and press ENTER:
1 BIND PLAN          (Add or replace an application plan)
2 REBIND PLAN        (Rebind existing application plan or plans)
3 FREE PLAN          (Erase application plan or plans)
4 BIND PACKAGE       (Add or replace a package)
5 REBIND PACKAGE     (Rebind existing package or packages)
6 FREE PACKAGE       (Erase a package or packages)

PRESS: ENTER to process        END to exit        HELP for more information
```

Fig. 10.9 Bind/rebind/free panel (Courtesy of International Business Machines Corporation)

Most of the parameters apply to both packages and plans; exceptions will be noted. It is necessary to understand the naming convention used with packages before looking at the bind parameters. Packages can have a four part name like:

```
Location.Collection.Package_ID.Version
```

Location is required only if a remote unit of work is being used as will be discussed in Chapter 17. Collection is a user-defined name that is the anchor for packages and that has no physical existence in its own right. Package_ID is the DBRM member name. There must be a one-to-one correspondence between a package and a DBRM member. Different versions must be in different DBRM libraries. The version is recorded in the modified source and DBRM member but is not used to synchronize the package and load module at execution time. The consistency token assigned internally by DB2 at precompile time is used for synchronization.

The BIND PACKAGE command can be generated through the use of DB2I panels. Selection of option 5 from the primary option menu (Fig. 10.2) will result in the display of the BIND/REBIND/FREE panel in Fig. 10.9. Selection of option 4 from this panel and subsequently completing the panel in Fig. 10.10 will result in the generation of JCL and a BIND command. Developers usually tailor the generated commands for their specific requirements and installation standards. Therefore an explanation of each BIND parameter and guidelines for usage of parameter values is based on an example BIND PACKAGE command.

```
BIND PACKAGE   (UNITEST)          -
      LIBRARY  (PROJECT.AUTHID.DBRM) -
      MEMBER   (SUPDATE)           -
```

```
                              BIND PACKAGE
COMMAND ===>

Specify output location and collection names:
   1 LOCATION NAME .............  ===>       (Defaults to local)
   2 COLLECTION-ID.............   ===>       (Required)

Specify package source (DBRM or COPY):
   3 DBRM:      COPY:            ===>    DBRM   (Specify DBRM or COPY)
   4 MEMBER   or COLLECTION-ID   ===>    SUPDATE
   5 PASSWORD or PACKAGE-ID .....  ===>
   6 LIBRARY  or VERSION ........  ===>    'PROJ.AUTHID.DBRM'
                                              (Blank, or COPY version-id)


Enter options as desired:
   7 CHANGE CURRENT DEFAULTS     ===>    NO     (NO or YES)
   8 ENABLE/DISABLE CONNECTIONS? ===>    NO     (NO or YES)
   9 OWNER OF PACKAGE (AUTHID) .. ===>    POWNER (Blank for primary ID)
  10 QUALIFIER.................  ===>    POSTST (Blank for owner)
  11 ACTION ON PACKAGE ......... ===>    REPLACE (ADD or REPLACE)
  12 RETAIN EXECUTION AUTHORITY . ===>    YES    (YES retain user list)
  13 REPLACE VERSION ........... ===>          (SAME, or REPLACE version-id)

  PRESS: ENTER to process         END to exit       HELP for more information
```

Fig. 10.10 Bind package panel (Courtesy of International Business Machines Corporation)

```
OWNER      (POWNER)              -
QUALIFIER  (POTST)              -
SQLERROR   (NOPACKAGE)          -
VALIDATE   (BIND)               -
ISOLATION  (CS)                 -
RELEASE    (DEALLOCATE)         -
EXPLAIN    (YES)                -
FLAG       (I)                  -
ENABLE     (*)                  -
ACTION     (REPLACE)
```

The collection name in parenthesis following the key word PACKAGE, UNITEST in the example, specifies that the package is to become part of the UNITEST collection. The SQL for the bind is to come from the SUP-DATE member in the DBRM library PROJECT.AUTHID.DBRM.

The owner of the package is POWNER. The owner of a plan can bind, rebind, free, or execute the plan. If no value is entered, the default is the use of the primary AUTHID of the binder. Ownership can be shared by making the owning AUTHID a secondary AUTHID to which several AU-THIDs are connected. (Secondary AUTHIDs will be discussed in Chapter

15.) AUTHID should be associated with a function, not an individual, to avoid complexities when the individual transfers to another project or leaves the company. The owner's AUTHID will be recorded in the CREATOR, and the primary AUTHID will be recorded in the BOUNDBY column in the SYSPLAN or SYSPACKAGE catalog tables depending on whether a plan or package is being bound. If privileges are revoked from the owner, the plan or package is marked invalid and must be rebound by an AUTHID with the required privileges when using validate of bind. Ownership of a plan can be changed with a bind or rebind. The old owner retains bind and execute privileges with a grant option on the rebound plan. The OWNER parameter value will be used as the leading qualifier of all unqualified table references in the package or plan unless the QUALIFIER parameter gives another value.

The QUALIFIER parameter value will be used as the qualifier of all referenced tables and views that do not have an explicit qualifier coded. For example, if the FROM clause of an SQL statement contains FROM SPJ, the POTST.SPJ table will be processed with QUALIFIER (POTST) on the bind command. Unlike the owner value, privileges need not be granted to a qualifier value. If the qualifier is not specified, the owner parameter value is used to qualify all unqualified tables and views. It is advisable to use a qualifier rather than an owner value to qualify tables and views to avoid mixing naming conventions with security issues.

The SQLERROR parameter provides for binding SQL statements that reference objects that do not exist at the bind site or for which the binder does not currently hold authority on the referenced objects. The example BIND command uses the default of NOPACKAGE, which means that a package will not be created if either of the conditions are not met. The CONTINUE value will result in a package being created, but statements that caused the error are not executable. SQLERROR (CONTINUE) is required if the DBRM contains SQL for DB2 and non-DB2 DBMS. An attempt to execute unresolved statements results in a negative SQLCODE at execution time. The SQLERROR parameter applies to packages only (not plans).

The VALIDATE parameter is used to specify the method DB2 will use to validate the package or plan. This validation checks the syntax of the SQL statements against the catalog definitions of the tables, views, and columns to which they refer. And it checks the binder's authority to perform the operations the statements call for. Validation can be performed during bind or when the program runs, indicated by the choices of BIND or RUN with the VALIDATE parameter.

Validation during bind is the more efficient procedure because it must be done only once, whereas validation done when the program runs requires repeated partial, or incremental, binds, which detract significantly from transaction rates. In addition under RUN-time validation, the individual executing the plan must have the authority to access all objects processed by the plan, probably broader authority than an organization would want to grant most users. Therefore the default of RUN-time validation should be changed to BIND in most cases as indicated on the example BIND command. RUN-time validation, however, is required for embedded dynamic SQL.

The significance of the bind time parameters—ISOLATION, ACQUIRE, and RELEASE—that effect concurrency were discussed in Chapter 8. Recall that an isolation level of CS (cursor stability) is frequently used rather than the default of RR (repeatable read) to maximize update concurrency. The ACQUIRE parameter does not apply to packages since ACQUIRE (USE) is always used for packages. The RELEASE parameter can be specified with the value of COMMIT or DEALLOCATE for packages and plans.

The EXPLAIN parameter with a value of YES allows programmers to request information on the optimizer's access path selection, a feature that will be discussed in Chapter 13. The default of NO should be overridden with a YES so that the programmer can verify that the access path selected by the optimizer for a package or plan is likely to provide the required performance.

The FLAG parameter value indicates the level of messages to be displayed during the bind. The default of (I) will result in displaying all informational, warning, error, and completion messages; (W) will display only warning, error, and completion messages; (E) will display only error and completion messages and; (C) will display only completion messages.

The ENABLE and DISABLE parameters provide for restricting execution to only specific environments. Either one of these parameters can be specified but not both. Execution of a package or plan can be enabled or disabled for use with CICS, IMSBMP, IMSMPP, IMS, Batch, DB2CALL, DL1BATCH, and SERVER and can further be restricted by connections such as CICS (application ID), IMSBMP (IMS ID), and IMSMPP (IMS ID). The bind parameter ENABLE (CICS) CICS (TST4) will allow only CICS connection name TST4 to execute the package or plan. The DISABLE parameter can be used to allow all connection types except the one specified. For example, all connection types except CICS PRD1 will be allowed with the parameter DISABLE (CICS) CICS (PRD1). The ENABLE/DISABLE parameters are useful for designating a test or production connection. This can avoid a test plan being accidentally executed in a production connection. The number of connection types named should be minimized. A long list detracts from performance since the list must be searched at execution time. ENABLE (*) enables all environments and is the default.

The ACTION parameter indicates whether the package or plan is new or a replacement. ACTION (ADD) will result in an error if the object already exists. It is a good choice in a production environment to avoid accidentally replacing a package or plan. The default value of REPLACE will add the object or replace it if it already exists. BIND with REPLACE is required whenever the host-language program has been changed and precompiled even if the SQL statements and the referenced tables have not been changed. Although the package or plan will be the same if the SQL and tables have not changed, DB2 requires that the consistency token in the load module and package or plan match, necessitating creation of a replacement package or plan when the revised program is precompiled. If the consistency tokens do not match, a −818 SQLCODE is received at execution time.

Coping a Package and Replacing a Version

The SQL statements for a local package can be bound into a package at a remote site or the SQL for a local package can be bound into a different collection within the local site with the BIND PACKAGE command. The SQL statements for a package that has been tested can be copied and bound in the production environment. The source and destination collection cannot be the same when a package is copied within a local site. The following command will take the SQL from the catalog table SYSIBM.SYSPACKS-TMT for the PROGA package (version V1) in the SYSTEST collection, bind the SQL, and place the new package in the UNITEST collection.

```
BIND PACKAGE  (UNITEST)         -
        COPY      (SYSTEST.PROGA) -
        COPYVER   (V1)            -
        OWNER     (POTSTOWN)      -
        QUALIFIER (POUNITST)      -
        ENABLE    (CICS) CICS (REG4)
```

Most of original bind parameters will apply to the new package except for the OWNER, QUALIFIER, ENABLE/DISABLE parameters.

A package can be bound over an existing package with the REPLVER parameter. This can be useful from migrating application systems from a test to a production environment. The following BIND command will replace the PROGA package in the UNITEST collection with a bind of SQL from SYSPACKSTMT to create the package in the SYSTEST collection. It will replace version ID of 'V1' as a result of the REPLVER (V1) and AC-

TION (REPLACE) parameters. It is conceptually like coping the SYS-TEST.PROGA.V1 to UNITEST.PROGA.V1 with a bind of SQL statements for UNITEST.PROGA.V1.

```
BIND PACKAGE  (UNITEST)         -
      COPY    (SYSTEST.PROGA)   -
      OWNER   (POTSTOWN)        -
      QUALIFIER (POUNITST)      -
      ENABLE  (CICS) CICS (REG4) -
      ACTION  (REPLACE)         -
      REPLVER (V1)
```

If UNITEST.PROGA.V1 already exists, the REPLVER (replace version) parameter can be used to replace it. REPLVER (V1) causes the existing V1 package to be replaced in the collection UNITEST. If the UNITEST.PROGA.V1 package does not already exist, the bind will fail. Optionally the original version ID in the SYSTEST collection will remain the same in UNITEST by using REPLVER (SAME). The default of RE-PLVER (SAME) will result in the version ID from SYSPACKSTMT being used for the copy. The REPLVER parameter cannot be used to replace an existing version ID without replacing the package. The COPY and RE-PLVER parameters apply only to packages not plans.

Bind of Packages to a Plan

Packages must be bound to a plan. One or more packages can be named in the PKLIST (package list) parameter on the BIND PLAN command. This bind inserts control information into a plan that points to the package. The STRN plan will point to the SUPDATE package in the UNITEST collection named in the PKLIST as a result of:

```
BIND PLAN  (STRN) MEMBER (MENUPROG) -
     PKLIST (UNITEST.SUPDATE)
```

The DBRM member MENUPROG need not contain any SQL statements. Only security checking is done if there is no SQL in the DBRM. The MEMBER parameter is not required if the PKLIST parameter is specified. A PKLIST can have multiple versions of a package. Specific versions, however, cannot be specified. The consistency token is used to locate the correct package at execution time.

A collection can be established so that all packages bound in the SYS-TEST collection will be part of the TRN1 plan like:

```
BIND PLAN  (TRN1) -
     PKLIST (SYSTEST.*)
```

The plan need not be bound again since an "*" follows the collection name. New packages can be added to the SYSTEST collection for programs that are added to a transaction. Old programs can be modified without a bind of the plan, only the DBRM for the modified program needs to be bound into a package.

A good approach, although not required, is to establish a plan collection with the PKLIST parameter before binding packages. A collection can be created for an application development project or for groups within a large development project. A plan can have multiple collections. For example, a plan with four collections can be established with:

```
BIND PLAN   (STRN) -
      PKLIST (COL1.*, COL2.*, COL3.*, COL4.*)
      . . .
```

Administration of a large development project can be eased with the use of multiple collections. A large number of collections in a production environment, however, can detract from performance. Consider the execution the STRN transaction that requires the SUPDATE package where the package was bound in the COL4 collection. The search for a package COL4.SUPDATE.constoken (where "constoken" is consistency token) would begin in COL1; if it is not found, COL2 would be searched; if it is still not found, COL3 would be searched; if it is again not found, COL4 would be search; if it is still not found, an error message will be received. A lengthy search for a package that can be in any of a long list of collections will delay the start of execution. The search can be shortened by placing frequently executed packages in the first collection or one of the first few collections.

If a package from the same DBRM appears in a multiple collection plan—like COL1.PUPDATE.constoken and COL4.PUPDATE.constoken — the first package found during the search will be used. This may not be the required package. SET CURRENT PACKAGESET can be used in the host-language program to designate the collection to be used. For example, COL4 can be moved to a host variable :CURRENT-COL and the statement SET CURRENT PACKAGESET = :CURRENT-COL issued before the first SQL statement in a package that has been bound to a multiple collection plan is executed. This avoids searching through many collections and has performance advantages. It is best, however, to avoid having multiple packages from the same DBRM in a multiple collection plan in most cases.

Binding SQL into Plans

Most bind parameters apply to both application packages and plans as shown in the Fig. 10.11 intersection diagram. The only parameters that do

```
┌────────────────────────────────────────────────────┐
│  Packages only                                       │
│  SQLERROR                                            │
│  COPY, COPYVER                                       │
│  REPLVER on ACTION                                   │
│              ┌─────────────────────────────────────────────────┐
│              │  Packages & plans                               │
│              │  COLLECTION                                      │
│              │  LIBRARY                                         │
│              │  MEMBER                                          │
│              │  OWNER                                           │
│              │  QUALIFIER                                       │
│              │  VALIDATE                                        │
│              │  FLAG                                            │
│              │  ISOLATION                                       │
│              │  RELEASE                                         │
│              │  EXPLAIN                                         │
│              │  ENABLE                                          │
│              │  DISABLE            Plans only                  │
│              │  ACTION                                          │
│              │                     PKLIST                       │
│              │                     ACQUIRE                      │
└──────────────│─────────────────────NODEFER                     │
               │                     CURRENTSERVER                │
               │                     RETAIN on ACTION             │
               │                     CACHESIZE                    │
               └─────────────────────────────────────────────────┘
```

Fig. 10.11 Parameters that apply to packages and plans

not apply to plans are SQLERROR, COPY, COPYVER, and REPLVER on ACTION. If parameters are not explicitly specified when a package is bound, default values will be used in most cases—not the values specified when the plan is bound. There are a few parameters that apply only to plans—PKLIST, ACQUIRE, RETAIN on ACTION, CACHESIZE, NODEFER, and CURRENTSERVER.

A plan can be bound without packages with a BIND PLAN command similar to the BIND PACKAGE command. The command can be generated using the BIND PLAN panel (Fig. 10.12). Programmers can reach the bind panel from the PROGRAM PREPARATION panel or the BIND/RE-BIND/FREE panel. When the preparation panel is used, it passes the DBRM's library name to the bind panel's option 3. The programmer enters the dataset member's name in option 1. If more than one DBRM is to be bound into a single plan, the programmer can answer yes at option 4, and DB2I will prompt for the additional names. A better choice in many cases

```
                                    BIND PLAN
COMMAND ===>

Enter DBRM data set name(s):
 1 MEMBER    ===> SUPDATE
 2 PASSWORD ===>
 3 LIBRARY  ===> 'PROJ.AUTHID.DBRM'
 4 ADDITIONAL DBRMs? ===> NO                    (YES to list more DBRMs)

Enter options as desired:
 6 PLAN NAME.................    ===>     SUPDATE (Required to create plan)
 5 CHANGE CURRENT DEFAULTS?      ===>     NO   (NO or YES)
 7 ENABLE/DISABLE CONNECTIONS?   ===>     NO   (NO or YES)
 8 INCLUDE PACKAGE LIST? ......  ===>     NO   (NO or YES)
 9 OWNER OF PLAN (AUTHID) .....  ===>     POTSTOWN (Blank for primary ID)
10 QUALIFIER.................    ===>     POUNTST (For tables,views,
                                         aliases)
11 CACHESIZE.................    ===>     1024 (Blank, or value 256-4896)
12 ACTION ON PLAN ............   ===>     REPLACE (REPLACE or ADD)
13 RETAIN EXECUTION AUTHORITY    ===>     YES  (YES to retain user list)
14 CURRENT SERVER............    ===>          (Location name)

PRESS: ENTER to process        END to exit      HELP for more information
```

Fig. 10.12 Bind plan panel (Courtesy of International Business Machines Corporation)

is to choose option 8 by keying YES, and the programmer will be prompted for a list of packages that have already been bound.

Completion of the panel will produce the following BIND PLAN command that will bind the SQL in DBRM member SUPDATE into a plan without using a package. The comment in parentheses and lower case letters after the hyphen indicates the default value, if the parameter is required, or a description.

```
BIND PLAN    (SUPDATE)               - (Required)
     LIBRARY   (PROJECT.AUTHID.DBRM) - (Required)
     MEMBER    (SUPDATE)             - (DBRM member)
     OWNER     (POTSTOWN)            - (Primary ID)
     QUALIFIER (POUNTST)             - (Owner value)
     VALIDATE  (BIND)               - (RUN)
     ISOLATION (CS)                 - (RR)
     ACQUIRE   (ALLOCATE)           - (USE)
     RELEASE   (DEALLOCATE)         - (COMMIT)
     EXPLAIN   (YES)                - (NO)
     FLAG      (I)                  - (Default)
     ENABLE    (*)                  - (All enabled)
     ACTION    (REPLACE) RETAIN     - (No retain)
```

```
CACHESIZE (1024)                    - (Default)
NODEFER   (PREPARE)                  (Default)
```

The ACTION parameter was discussed with respect to packages. There is an additional value that can be specified when binding a plan. The RETAIN value indicates whether execution authority granted previously should remain in effect after the bind. Unfortunately the default is a retain of no and requires that any execute privileges be regranted after a bind. This is more than a security issue; it affects the performance of the plan. Exclusive locks are taken on SYSPLANAUTH and its indexes to delete rows during which time other programs cannot be bound or executed (unless they are granted to the public). It is best to override the default and use a retain of yes. The syntax of this parameter is unlike most. Notice in the above example that RETAIN is not in parenthesis following ACTION as would be similar to the syntax of other parameters. Rather if the keyword RETAIN is present, privileges will not be revoked. If the keyword is not present, privileges will be revoked. In addition, it is one of the few parameters that is specific to BIND and cannot be changed with REBIND.

The CACHESIZE indicates the size of the authorization cache that can be a value from 256 to 4096 bytes or zero. (The cache size specified will be rounded up to the nearest multiple of 256 bytes.) The authorization cache will contain the most recent AUTHIDs that have executed the plan. It is used with the plan in the EDM pool to minimize I/O to the catalog tables SYSPLANAUTH and SYSPACKAUTH to check for the appropriate authority at execution time. The base portion is 32 bytes and each cached AUTHID requires 8 bytes. The default authorization cache size of 1024 bytes will hold the last 124 AUTHIDs that executed the plan. A cache size of zero is a good choice for plans that are not frequently executed by the same AUTHID since it saves space in the EDM pool.

The NODEFER and DEFER parameters are used to determine when a dynamic SQL statement should be prepared in a distributed environment. (Using DB2 in a distributed environment is discussed in Chapter 17.) The default NODEFER (PREPARE) indicates that the prepare of SQL statements are to take place in real time. DEFER (PREPARE) indicates that the prepare will be deferred until the first INSERT, UPDATE, DELETE, EXECUTE, OPEN, or DESCRIBE is issued. Deferring the prepare is a good choice in a distributed environment since it avoids transmitting each prepare, describe, and DML separately.

The CURRENTSERVER parameter is useful to avoid modifying an existing program and plan to be executed at a remote site using a remote unit of work. The plan can be bound with Munich as the current server as:

```
BIND PLAN        (STRN)     -
     PKLIST      (UNITEST.*) -
```

```
OWNER       (POTSTOWN)  -
QUALIFIER   (POUNTST)   -
CURRENTSERVER (MUNICH)  . . .
```

A connection will be made to Munich before the plan is run. The location, Munich, will be recorded in the catalog table SYSPLAN and is used to set the server's special register to Munich at execution time. The plan must be bound locally, even if it contains no SQL to be executed locally. The use of static SQL requires that a package be bound in Munich like:

```
BIND PACKAGE  (MUNICH.UNITEST)      -
     LIBRARY  (PROJECT.AUTHID.DBRM) -
     MEMBER   (SUPDATE)             -
     OWNER    (POTSTOWN)            -
     QUALIFIER (POTST) . . .
```

No further action is required for bind to take place in Munich other than having the location of Munich defined in the SYSLOCATIONS table in the communications database as will be discussed in Chapter 17.

Fall-Back Procedures Using Packages

One of the primary benefits of packages is the ease of developing fall-back procedures. A modified program may not work as required, making it necessary to go back to the previously working program. Assume that the load libraries SYSPROD.LOAD and FALLBACK.LOAD contain the V1 load module and are concatenated in the order specified. The PROGA source code is in SYSPROD.COBOL(PROGA) and FALLBACK.COBOL (PROGA). SYSPROD.DBRM(PROGA) and FALLBACK.DBRM (PROGA) have the SQL statements from precompiles. The plan is bound with SYSPROD and FALLBACK collections like:

```
BIND PLAN  (TRN1) -
     PKLIST (SYSPROD.*, FALLBACK.*)
```

SYSPROD.COBOL(PROGA) is modified, precompiled, compiled, and link edited into SYSPROD.LOAD(PROGA) with V2 specified as the version ID at precompile time. BIND PACKAGE is used to produce a V2 package from the SYSPROD.DBRM library created by the precompiler (optionally COPY and REPLVER parameters can be used). Recall that the precompiler writes a consistency token in the DBRM member that it creates and BIND carries it forward in the package. The precompiler also writes the consistency token to the modified source code that is carried forward to the load module in the compile and linkedit process. Therefore the package and load module will have the same consistency token. When the program is executed, the consistency token in the load module is used to locate the corresponding package.

When PROGA is executed, SYSPROD.PROGA package V2 will be used. If the program does not work as required, fallback can be accomplished by deleting the load module SYSPROD.LOAD(PROGA). When the transaction is next executed, FALLBACK.LOAD(PROGA) and the corresponding package with a matching consistency token will be used since the load libraries are concatenated. Time is now available to correct the source code in SYSPROD.COBOL(PROGA) and go through program preparation specifying V3 at precompile time. When the program is working properly, the components can be placed in the FALLBACK libraries and outdated versions deleted when they are no longer needed. An alternative to using separate source, load, DBRM libraries, and collections can be avoided. Fallback to V1, however, would require PROGA modification, precompile, compile, linkedit, bind package, and run. The use of a single set of libraries does increase the likelihood that earlier code will be lost. Indeed some companies prefer more than the two staging libraries as noted in the first technique using concatenated load libraries. The use of packages provide for a number of alternatives for managing fallback. In any case, the plan can be executed during the bind of a package (not the package being bound).

Managing Sets of Tables with Packages

It may be necessary to manage a set of tables for each corporate division or branch office or for some other functional grouping of the data. All of the tables have the same structure—that is, the same columns with the same data types and lengths—but each division needs to maintain its data in a separate set of tables. (The use of views that identify groups of data in one large table is not always an acceptable alternative.) Information systems professionals, however, do not want to incur the cost of maintaining separate sets of programs. If a change needs to be made to one program, it will have to be made to all the identical programs for each of perhaps 20 or more divisions. One set of programs using a number of sets of tables can be managed through the use of packages.

The BIND PACKAGE and BIND PLAN commands provide for specifying the qualifier to be used for each table and view referenced in an SQL statement. Each set of tables would be created with a qualifier indicating the division that uses the tables, for example DIV1 or DIV2 through DIV20. A single set of programs would be developed and prepared as usual, resulting in a single set of DBRM members. The difference lies in the package bind. Each DBRM member would be bound into 20 collections and all of the collections would be bound into a single plan. An example of binding two division collections followed by a bind of the plan is:

```
BIND PACKAGE   (DIV1COL) MEMBER (PROGA) -
       QUALIFIER (DIV1)   OWNER  (FLEUR) -
       ISOLATION (CS)

BIND PACKAGE   (DIV2COL) MEMBER (PROGA) -
       QUALIFIER (DIV2)   OWNER  (ERIC)  -
       ISOLATION (RR)

BIND PLAN   (ALLDIV) -
       PKLIST (DIV1COL.PROGA, DIV2COL.PROGA)
```

The host-language program would have to determine which of the packages to be used based on who is executing the transaction and plan since all of the packages have the same consistency token as that taken from the set of DBRMs. The program can determine at execution time who is executing the program using the LTERM, USERID, or some other means and move the appropriate collection name into :CUR-DIV followed by the execution of:

```
SET CURRENT PACKAGESET = :CUR-DIV.
```

This will result in accessing the set of tables for the specified division. If the set is not issued, the first package in the list with the same consistency token is used.

A set of tables can be used as an alternative to partitioning a single table. For example, historical data can be managed in separate tables, each with a qualifier indicating the year—CURRENT.SALES, LAST-YEAR.SALES, PREVYEAR.SALES, and for any additional prior years. The use of separate tables provides a number of advantages over the use of a partitioned tablespace as was discussed in Chapter 3.

- Only one tablespace is locked when utilities are executed.
- Utilities can be executed in parallel.
- No need to maintain very large nonpartitioning indexes.
- No need to have a partitioning index that is seldom used for searches or joins.
- No need to drop tablespace to change partitioning index upper range.

The disadvantage of using a set of tables rather than one partitioned tablespace is that developers must use program logic to determine the value to use in the SET CURRENT PACKAGESET statement. A translation table probably would be required to determine which table has which range of

SYSIBM.SYSPLANDEP and SYSPACKDEP: One row for each index, table, view, alias, synonym, and tablespace used by the plan or package.

SYSIBM.SYSSTMT and SYSPACKSTMT: One or more rows with the text of each SQL statement.

SYSIBM.SYSPLAN and SYSPACKAGE: One row for creator, boundby, bind time and date,
plan size, valid, operative, validate, isolation, and so forth.

SYSIBM.SYSPLANAUTH and SYSPACKAUTH: One row for each owner with plan or package
authority.

SYSIBM.SYSPLSYSTEM and SYSPKSYSTEM: One row for each type of system enabled or
disabled.

SYSIBM.PACKLIST: One row for each collection_ID.package in the package list.

SYSIBM.SYSDBRM: One row for each DBRM creator, host language, PDS containing DBRM,
and so forth for plans and packages.

Fig. 10.13 Catalog tables updated with bind

values for tables like ZIPCODE discussed in Chapter 3. In addition, if ad
hoc users process the data, they would need to know which table to access.

Information on Plans in the Catalog

DB2 records information in the catalog tables as summarized in Fig. 10.13
when a plan or package is bound. This information is particularly useful
for impact analysis. If a column is added or deleted from a table or if the
data type of a column is changed, it will be necessary to determine programs
that will be affected. This can be done by selecting from SYSPLANDEP
and SYSPACKDEP to identify all plans and packages that reference the
table. A plan or package that references a table may not reference the column that has been changed. A finer level of identification can be made by
selecting from SYSSTMT and SYSPACKSTMT, which contains the text of
SQL statements. A LIKE predicate can be used to find all references to a
column that has been changed. This search may take some time since it will
require a tablespace scan of all static SQL statements in all applications
systems using DB2. It will take considerably less time, however, than it will
take having several programmers locating and searching through a large
number of program listings. Chapter 14 has a number of SELECT statements from the catalog table to get information on plans and packages.

10.8   REBINDING PLANS AND PACKAGES

The REBIND command is quite distinct from the BIND command. The
REBIND command provides for allowing the optimizer to choose another
access path and to change most of the bind parameters. REBIND gets the

SQL to be bound from the catalog tables (SYSSTMT or SYSPACKSTMT).
BIND gets its SQL from the DBRM library and must be used after a host-language program has been precompiled.

In most cases, DB2 automatically rebinds a plan or package if changes
have invalidated it—if an index, a table, or a view has been dropped or a
privilege revoked. But other times developers—or often the database administrator—may want to rebind plans and packages themselves such as
when an added index may improve performance, when a table's statistics
have changed significantly so that the optimizer might choose a different
access path, when a new release of DB2 has been installed with enhancements that may improve performance, or when the plan or package has
been marked as invalid. If a user-initiated or an automatic rebind fails, DB2
marks the plan or package as inoperative to avoid many repeated rebinds.
It is necessary to perform a bind replace once a plan or package has become
inoperative.

A SELECT from the catalog tables will identify the plans and packages
that have been invalidated (VALID = 'N'), and an automatic rebind will
be attempted. An automatic rebind uses the last owner AUTHID (SYS-
PACKAGE or SYSPLAN.CREATOR) of the person who performed the
bind. VALID = 'A' means that a table or tablespace used by the plan or
package has been altered. A rebind is not required.

```
SELECT NAME, CREATOR, BOUNDBY, VALID
FROM   SYSIBM.SYSPLAN
WHERE  VALID IN ('N', 'A') ;

SELECT COLLID, NAME, VERSION, CREATOR, BOUNDBY, VALID
FROM   SYSIBM.SYSPACKAGE
WHERE  VALID IN ('N', 'A')
```

Plans and packages that are inoperative and require a bind replace can be
identified with:

```
SELECT NAME, CREATOR, VALID,
   OPERATIVE, BINDDATE
FROM   SYSIBM.SYSPLAN
WHERE  OPERATIVE = 'N';

SELECT COLLID, NAME, VERSION, CREATOR,
   BOUNDBY, VALID, OPERATIVE, BINDDATE
FROM   SYSIBM.SYSPACKAGE
WHERE  OPERATIVE = 'N'
```

The syntax of the REBIND command is similar to the BIND command
except that several plans can be rebound as listed in parenthesis after the
REBIND PLAN clause:

```
REBIND PLAN (TRN1, TRN2, TRN3)      -
       ISOLATION (CS)               -
       VALIDATE  (BIND)             -
       ACQUIRE   (ALLOCATE)         -
   \   RELEASE   (DEALLOCATE)       -
       EXPLAIN   (YES)              -
       FLAG      (I)                -
       OWNER     (POWNER)           -
       QUALIFIER (POTEST)           -
       NODEFER   (PREPARE)          -
       CACHESIZE (1024)             -
       ENABLE    (CICS) CICS(REG4)
```

Most parameters can be changed when executing a REBIND command. If parameters are not specified, the last values specified when a bind was performed will remain in effect. The command REBIND PLAN (*) rebinds all plans the user is authorized to bind and does not modify any existing parameters. A global operator like ''(*)'' should be used with care. In this case, all plans granted to the public will be rebound, which is probably not the desired action. Another parameter to use cautiously is REBIND PLAN (STRN) NOPKLIST. This command will cause all collections and packages to be dropped from the STRN plan.

Packages are rebound like plans. The package parameters that cannot be changed with a rebind are: SQLERROR, COPY, COPYVER, and ACTION REPLVER. A specific package (PROGA) and version (V1) of a package in the SYSPROD collection can be rebound with:

```
REBIND PACKAGE (SYSPROD.PROGA.V1)
```

Optionally all packages in a collection can be rebound:

```
REBIND PACKAGE (SYSPROD.*)
```

Like plans, all packages that the user is authorized to bind will be rebound with:

```
REBIND PACKAGE (*)
```

Each package rebind is committed before processing the next package. A package being bound cannot be executed. A plan that references the package, however, can be executed as well as other packages referenced in the plan. Exclusive locks are taken on the SKCT or SKPT table and indexes in the directory where the plan or package is placed when bound. These exclusive locks can interfere with the bind and execution of other packages and plans. The use of packages decreases the likelihood of lock contention since packages are typically small and require less time to bind, resulting in locks being held for a short period of time.

10.9 FREEING PLANS AND PACKAGES

The FREE command can be used to delete plans and packages no longer needed. A package or plan cannot be deleted while it is executing. The TRN1 plan can be freed with:

```
FREE PLAN (TRN1)
```

A specific version of a package can be freed by specifying the fully qualified name. The leading qualifier of location would be included in a distributed environment.

```
FREE PACKAGE (SYSTEST.PROGA.V1)
```

The use of version ID simplifies package identification.
All versions of a package can be freed as:

```
FREE PACKAGE (SYSTEST.PROGA.*)
```

or all packages in the collection SYSTEST can be freed:

```
FREE PACKAGE (SYSTEST.*)
```

or all plans that the developer has authority on can be freed:

```
FREE PLAN(*)
```

Again great caution should be exercised when using an asterisk, particularly when deleting plans. If someone with the highest authorization, SYSADM, invoked FREE PLAN (*), all plans for all application systems and all plans used by DB2 itself such as the DCLGEN, SPUFI, and QMF would be deleted. This accident has been known to happen when well-meaning developers clean up unused plans, costing considerable extra work to restore the unintentionally deleted plans.

Dynamic Plan Allocation

Dynamic plan allocation is an older technique that was occasionally used in previous releases of DB2 to avoid having to bind a large number of DBRM members into a plan. Package bind has significant advantages over this technique but is discussed here briefly for those readers who might be interested. CICS associates a program with a transaction and provides for transferring control of the transaction from one program to another with LINK and XCTL commands. The RCT (resource control table) is used for communication between DB2 and CICS. The following RCT entry associates the plan SPJPLAN with the transaction ID SPJ1:

```
DSNCRCT TYPE = ENTRY, TXID = SPJ1, PLAN = SPJPLAN
```

If the transaction is to be made up of multiple programs, all of the DBRMs resulting from the precompile of the host-language programs must be bound together into the plan SPJPLAN. This can result in a significant administrative burden and the use of CPU and I/O. An extreme but real example has one transaction with 700 programs and 700 DBRMs that must be bound together into a plan each time any one of the programs is changed. Surprisingly the computer resource usage for the bind is rather low considering the number of DBRMs, requiring about 2–3 CPU minutes and 25–30 minutes of elapsed time.

The administrative burden can be decreased by determining from SYS-DBRM the DBRMs that must be bound when a program is precompiled. The following select will result in a list of all DBRM members (NAME) that constitute the SPJPLAN.

```
SELECT PDSNAME, NAME, PLCREATOR,
       PRECOMPTIME, PRECOMPDATE
FROM   SYSIBM.SYSDBRM
WHERE  PLNAME = 'SPJPLAN'
```

An alternative to using one large plan is to select several plans dynamically under one transaction ID. This technique is accomplished with an RCT entry like:

```
DSNCRCT TYPE=ENTRY, TXID=SPJ2, PLNEXIT=YES,
        PLNGME=DSNUCEXT, TWAIT=POOL, . . .
```

PLNEXIT = YES indicates that a plan exit is to be used and PLNP-GME = DSNUCEXT indicates the name of the sample assembler exit provided with DB2 in the sample library (outprefix.DSNSAMP(DS-NC@EXT)). The exit is like any CICS command-level program using COBOL, PL/1, or assembler, and multiple exit programs are supported.

An application program selects the appropriate DBRM member after a SYNCPOINT with LINK or XCTL. DBRMNAME represents a host variable containing the name of the DBRM member, or a literal can be used.

```
EXEC CICS SYNCPOINT
EXEC CICS LINK (or XCTL) PROGRAM(DBRMNAME)
```

The tradeoff for dynamic plan allocation is that thread reuse cannot be used since a thread is created at each SYNCPOINT. There is also the cost of SYNCPOINT with LINK or XCTL itself, which is estimated at 10,000 instructions. The result is a potential transaction rate reduction of 20–50 percent depending on the transaction rate. The benefits of thread reuse are summarized in Box 10.2.

```
                    PROGRAM PREPARATION: COMPILE, LINK, AND RUN
    ===> _

    Enter compiler or assembler options:
     1 INCLUDE LIBRARY              ===>    'PROJ.AUTHID.COBOL'
     2 INCLUDE LIBRARY              ===>    'PROJ.AUTHID.COBLIB'
     3 OPTIONS ................     ===>    NUM, OPTIMIZE, ADV

    Enter linkage editor options:
     4 INCLUDE LIBRARY              ===>    'outprefix.RUNLIB.LOAD' Installa-
                                            tion specific
     5 INCLUDE LIBRARY              ===>
     6 INCLUDE LIBRARY              ===>
     7 LOAD LIBRARY ...........     ===>    'PROJ.AUTHID.LOAD'
     8 PRELINK OPTIONS             ===>
     9 LINK OPTIONS ...........     ===>    AMODE=31,RMODE=ANY - To run above
                                            16 MB line

    Enter run options:
    10 PARAMETERS .............     ===>    VALUE1, VALUE2, VALUE3/
    11 SYSIN DATA SET             ===>    TERM
    12 SYSPRINT DS ............     ===>    TERM

    PRESS: ENTER to proceed        END to exit        HELP for more information
```

Fig. 10.14 Compile, link, and run panel (Courtesy of International Business Machines Corporation)

10.10 COMPILE, LINK, AND RUN

In the compile, link, and run panel (Fig. 10.14), the programmer identifies the libraries contributing code to the program. The program's modified source code from the precompiler will be in USERID.TEMP.COBOL. The installation may also have a source code library of modules and subroutines that may be used by the program. Since these modules are included in the program after precompilation, they cannot include embedded SQL.

The programmer must include an entry in the linkage editor option naming a library that contains a number of modules required by DB2. These include language interface modules for TSO, IMS, CAF, and CICS (modules DSNELI, DFSLI000, DSNALI, and DSNCLI, respectively). The DB2 system installer names the library containing these modules. Although there is no standard, installers usually choose a name similar to "SYS1. DB2.LINKLIB". The default name is "outprefix.RUNLIB.LOAD,".

The final steps in program preparation are to name the load library to receive the compiled and linked program and to set the run options. Option

8 provides for specifying prelink parameters when using C/370. Option 9 provides for running the program above the 16MB line by specifying AMODE = 31, RMODE = ANY. Option 10 provides for specifying parameters to be passed to the program at execution time. Options 11 and 12 provide for specifying input and printer devices. In the example, they are both allocated to the terminal.

10.11 THE DSN PROCESSOR AND EXECUTING PROGRAMS

The DSN command processor is the TSO attach. It is used to perform program preparation functions that require action on the part of DB2 and to execute programs under TSO. The program preparation panels generate DSN statements to execute commands including DCLGEN, BIND, RE-BIND, FREE, and RUN application programs. These commands, preceded by a DSN statement, are included at the end of the generated JCL step. Most TSO commands can also be used from within the DSN command processor. The DSN command processor can be used interactively under TSO, from a CLIST or JCL. Typically the commands are generated by the program preparation panels of DB2I along with the JCL, saved, customized, and submitted as needed.

An example of executing the SUPDATE program in the PROJ.AU-THID.LOAD library and SUPDATE plan using the DSN processor is:

```
DSN SYSTEM (DSN)
    RUN PROGRAM(SUPDATE) PLAN(SUPDATE) -
        LIBRARY('PROJ.AUTHID.LOAD')
END
```

The default name of the DB2 system is DSN. This name is frequently changed to DB2T or DB2P when DB2 is installed on a computer. It is necessary to determine the name assigned at installation time and to use it in place of the DSN in parenthesis in the DSN statement. If the name given is DB2T, the statement will read: DSN SYSTEM (DB2T). The dash at the end of the second line is necessary when the command is executed from JCL or a CLIST to indicate that the statement continues on the next line, which maintains the command's continuous string.

TSO's terminal monitor program (TMP) is used to execute DSN commands in a batch job stream. Fig. 10.15 shows a typical JCL stream for executing a DSN command, in this case the RUN command shown above. The first line sets up the stream's job statement. The EXEC statement invokes the TMP, which is named IKJEFT01. The first three DD statements set up files for the TMP; the next two set up files for the program being

```
//SUPDATE JOB . . . USER = AUTHID
//*
//STEP1     EXEC PGM = IKJEFT01,DYNAMNBR = 30
//STEPLIB   DD DSN = DSN230.DSNLOAD,DISP = SHR
//SYSPRINT DD SYSOUT = A
//SYSTSPRT DD SYSOUT = A
//SYSUDUMP DD SYSOUT = A
//SYSOUT    DD SYSOUT = A
//REPORT    DD SYSOUT = A
//CARDIN    DD DSN = CARDIN.FILE
//*
//SYSTSIN  DD *
DSN SYSTEM(DSN)
RUN PROGRAM(SUPDATE) PLAN(SUPDATE) -
    LIBRARY('PROJ.AUTHID.LOAD')
END
/*
```

Fig. 10.15 Executing a program through JCL

run. "//CARDIN DD DSN = CARDIN.FILE" identifies an input file for the SUPDATE program to read. "//REPORT DD SYSOUT = A" specifies where SUPDATE is to write its report. The statement "//SYSTSIN DD *" indicates the file TMP is to read as if they were entered interactively.

Alternative entry points to the TMP are IKJEFT1A and IKJEFT1B. They have advantages over executing IKJEFT01. The alternative entry points allow condition codes to be passed to the next step in the job stream so that a determination can be made as to whether the next step should be executed, depending on the success of the last step.

Call Attach Facility (CAF)

The CAF (call attach facility) provides for direct control over creation of threads from within an application program. It is used by some developers for batch processing rather than the TMP. It does not have significant performance advantage over TMP-initiated batch processing once the program starts execution. It does have the advantage that condition codes, parameter values, and disposition handling are done as with any standard MVS batch job.

Developers specify the disposition of a dataset after a program has abended by coding the DISP parameter on a DD statement. If the disposition parameter is coded as DISP = (NEW,CATLG,DELETE), the dataset would be deleted if the program abended in standard MVS batch. If IKJEFT01 is used to execute a batch program, however, the dataset will be cataloged— the middle parameter is used. If IKJEFT1A is used, the dataset will be cataloged if there is an application abend—a COBOL call to ILBOABN0,

Assume DISP=(NEW,CATLG,DELETE) on DD statement

Program abend	MVS	IKJEFT1B	IKJEFT1A	IKJEFT01
System abend	DELETE	DELETE	DELETE	CATLG
Application abend	DELETE	DELETE	CATLG	CATLG

Fig. 10.16 Dataset disposition depending upon the environment

a PL/I call to PLIDUMP with the S option, or an assembler ABEND macro is executed. The use of the IKJEFT1B entry point results in the same disposition of the dataset as does standard MVS (Fig. 10.16) If there is a system abend as a result of, say, a data exception (0C7), the dataset will be deleted as indicated in the third parameter. The dump content and abend code passed to the next step in the job varies depending on the entry point used as summarized in Fig. 10.17. Again IKJEFT1B more closely resembles standard MVS batch. In addition, parameters cannot be passed on a JOB or STEP statement to a program using TMP. It is necessary to pass them through the use of a CLIST or on the DSN RUN command. For these reasons, CAF is some times used to execute batch programs. A sample CAF assembler program is in outprefix.DSNSAMP(DSN8CA). CAF is also used occasionally to control when threads are allocated and deallocated. For example, it can be used to avoid holding a thread for the duration of the program execution as the TSO attach does. Conversely it can be used to hold a thread and avoid plan switching from TSO CLISTs. None of the attaches (TSO, IMS, and CICS) need to exist in the MVS address space since CAF is itself an attach facility. CAF can be used from MVS batch, IMS batch (but there is no coordinated commit), and TSO background and foreground.

Program abend	MVS	IKJEFT1B	IKJEFT1A	IKJEFT01
System abend	Appl.	Appl.	Appl.	TSO
Abend code	As is	04C	04C	Not pass
Application abend	Appl.	Appl.	TSO	TSO
Abend code	As is	As is	Not pass	Not pass

Fig. 10.17 Dump content and abend code depending upon the environment

```
//SUPDATE JOB . . . USER=AUTHID
//*
//TERM      EXEC PGM=IKJEFT01,DYNAMNBR=30
//*
//SYSIN    DD *
SELECT * FROM S;
SELECT * FROM P;
/*
//SYSTSIN  DD *
DSN SYSTEM(DSN)
RUN            PROGRAM(DYNSQL) PLAN(DYNSQL) -
               LIBRARY('PROJ.AUTHID.LOAD')
END
/*
//SYSPRINT DD SYSOUT=A
//SYSTSPRT DD SYSOUT=A
//
```

Fig. 10.18 Executing SQL through JCL

Executing SQL through JCL

SPUFI and QMF are frequently used to execute SQL data definition, manipulation, and control statements. There are times, however, when executing a large number of statements would tie up a terminal for too long. Often
statements need to be executed in the evening or scheduled for execution at
specific times. The sample program outprefix.DSNSAMP(DSNTEP2) is a
good tool for this type of processing. It is a PL/1 program provided in
source form and must go through the program preparation process. Fig.
10.18 is an example of the JCL to execute DYNSQL, a prepared copy of
DSNTEP2. The program will accept as input any SQL statement, execute
it dynamically, and write the results to a printer or a file. The example
has the SQL instream but the //SYSIN DD * statement can be changed to
reference a file containing SQL such as a file that has been used to execute
SQL using SPUFI.

    If the organization does not have the PL/1 compiler and run-time li-
braries for program preparation, an assembler version of the program is in
the sample library as outprefix.DSNSAMP(DSNTIAD). The disadvantage
of this version of the dynamic SQL program is that SELECT statements
cannot be executed.

Thread Creation, Use, and Termination Activities

Recall from Chapter 1 that a thread is allocation when the first SQL statement is executed in a program. The thread is a TCB (task control block)
that contains information for communications between DB2 and the appli-

Box 10.2 Thread creation, use, and termination

Activity	Minimize Resources Required
Create thread	
Sign on	
*Write account record	One record for all trans. with thread reuse
*Authorization check	Use authorization cache or grant to public
Load SKCT header	Minimize number of DBRMs bound to a plan
Create CT header	Minimize number of DBRMs bound to a plan
Incremental bind all	Use bind time validation
Acquire all TSP locks	Use acquire allocate if most SQL executed
Load all DBDs	Use acquire allocate if most SQL executed
Open all data sets	Use close of no for tablespaces & indexes
Each SOL executed	
*Load SK section	Size EDM pool to hold frequently used SK
*Create SK copy	Release deallocate avoids space reuse
*Incremental bind	Use bind time validation
*Acquire TSP locks	Use acquire allocate if most SQL executed
*Load DBDs	Use acquire allocate if most SQL executed
*Open data sets	Use acquire allocate if most SQL executed
Process SQL	Use efficient SQL & programming techniques
Commit processing	
Write log records	Commit every 5-10 updates, 1,000 for batch
Release page locks	Above & use lock table for batch
*Release TSP locks	Use release deallocate
*Free SK copy sections	Release deallocate avoids space reuse
Terminate thread (Not done if thread reused)	
*Write account record	One record for all trans. with thread reuse
*Release TSP locks	Not released if thread reuse
*Free SK copy pages	Not freed if thread reuse
*Free working storage	Not freed if thread reuse
*Close data sets	Use close of no for tablespaces & indexes

cation program. A number of activities are performed when a thread is created as are summarized in Box 10.2. An accounting record is written if the accounting trace is turned on. The catalog tables are checked to determine if the AUTHID attempting to execute the transaction is authorized. If an authorization block is used or privileges on the plan are granted to the public, the cost of authorization checking is minimized, particularly for subsequent executions of the transaction. The SKCT (skeleton cursor table) header and directory is loaded into the EDM pool if it is not already present and the CT (cursor table) copy is created for the current executor. If a package is used, the SKPT (skeleton package table) is loaded into the EDM pool if it is not already present, and the PT (package table) copy is created for the current executor. An incremental bind is done unless at bind time the default of run time validation is overridden and bind time validation is requested. All table and tablespace locks are acquired assuming that acquire allocate was requested. This is advisable, as was discussed in Chapter 8, if most SQL statements in the transaction are to be executed. Acquire allocate does result in a larger plan directory where information is kept on the objects manipulated by the plan. The additional space in the EDM pool is probably worth the cost since it results in enhanced performance at execution time.

All DBDs referenced indirectly by naming a table in a FROM clause in a database are brought into the EDM pool, assuming that they are not already present and that acquire allocate was requested. All underlying datasets that house tablespaces and index space are opened if not already open. They will already be opened in most cases if close of no was specified when the objects were created. Beside each activity in Box 10.2 points are summarized that have been discussed throughout the book that will minimize the cost of thread allocation in most cases. The notation "SK" is used to represent SKCT sections for plans or SKPT sections for packages. The activities preceded with an "*" can be avoided on subsequent execution of a plan when thread reuse can be used.

Most of the activities for executing an SQL statement are avoided with thread reuse except, of course, the actual SQL processing itself. The cost of commit processing is reduced as well with thread reuse since table or tablespace intent locks need not be released and CT sections are not freed. Notice that many of the items marked with an asterisk, indicating that the work need not be repeated with thread reuse, are influenced by the acquire and release parameters specified at bind time. Indeed thread reuse saves few resources without specifying ACQUIRE (ALLOCATE) and RELEASE (DEALLOCATE) at bind time. The thread will be terminated only if the transaction assigned to the thread is not executed within 30–45 seconds. Clearly there are significant advantages to thread reuse for frequently executed transactions.

10.12 SUMMARY

This chapter has described how to prepare and execute programs containing SQL, including how to use DB2's facilities for program preparation, DB2I and the DSN processor. Most developers use the DB2I panels to generate the program development JCL a few times, then evolve toward working with the JCL customized to meet their specific requirements and to avoid having to work through the panels repeatedly.

EXERCISES

10.1. What is the function of DECLARE TABLE statements in a program? How can they be coded?

10.2. Revisions are made to a program after going through the complete program preparation process. The revised program is precompiled, compiled, and linkedited, and a rebind is done to produce a new application plan. The program will not execute. What is a possible problem?

10.3. A new program was developed, prepared, and the package bound. The program will not execute. What is a possible problem?

10.4. Write a DSN command to run program SNCHANGE from library SUP-PLY.DJK.LOAD. The application plan carries the program name. The facility has named its DB2 system DB2.

10.5. An application plan just moved from development to production runs exceptionally slowly. Discounting any design deficiencies, what might be the problem?

11

Programming for Performance

11.1 INTRODUCTION

Users who take advantage of SQL's flexibility can formulate a given database request in a number of different ways. DB2 may access the data needed to satisfy any given request in any of several ways. Theoretically the DB2 optimizer should be able to choose the most efficient access path, no matter which equivalent SQL statement is used. DB2's optimizer has not yet reached this ideal. In most cases, the optimizer makes the best choice no matter how the request is stated. But in a few situations, the users' and programmers' decisions in formulating statements can make a difference in performance. This situation will be eliminated over time as IBM software developers improve the optimizer. Nevertheless programmers can improve the performance of their own programs by following a few guidelines for statement formulations. It is necessary to understand how SQL statements are processed in order to apply the guidelines to specific situations, thus there is an emphasis on imparting that understanding in this chapter.

11.2   EFFICIENT JOINS

In a join, DB2 joins rows that qualify for a search from one table with rows that qualify from another table by comparing values from corresponding columns in the join tables. It is important to narrow the search to only the rows required from each table by specifying as many predicates as possible. This minimizes the number of rows to be joined. The number of rows joined usually effects performance more than does the number of tables joined. As the number of rows to be joined goes up multiplicatively, the join costs go up exponentially. In the great majority of cases, it is best to have DB2 perform the join than it is to write application program code to join rows returned from separate SELECT statements. This is because DB2 performs the processing at a lower level within DB2 with fewer instructions executed, and thus a reduced path length is achieved.

DB2 will use indexes in joins only when the columns being joined are of the same data type and length. In most cases, the columns' data types and lengths will match. When they do not, the designer probably made a mistake when creating the tables. If a particular join runs unexpectedly slowly, this error may be the cause. DB2 will not be using an index that the developer knows is there. Developers can use functions for converting data types and lengths to gain compatibility between columns to be joined. Use of these functions, however, negates the possibility of indexes being used to satisfy a statement.

DB2 can implement joins in three ways using a merge join, a nested-loop join, or a hybrid join.

The Merge Join Method

The merge join method requires that the tables to be joined be in sequence. The rows can be retrieved in sequence with a high cluster ratio index or are sorted by DB2. If a sort is required, all predicates are applied before the sort so that a minimal number of rows are sorted. A row is read from one table, designated as the outer table, and the inner table is read to find all matches. A second row is read from the outer table and the inner table is read from its last position to find all matches. The comparisons continue similar to standard match merge processing. Fig. 11.1 is a diagram of the merge join method for accomplishing the join:

```
SELECT C1, C2, C20
FROM   TA, TB
WHERE  C1 = C10
AND    TA.C1 BETWEEN 1 AND 5
```

Notice in Fig. 11.1 that the value of 3 and 4 appears twice in column C1 and must be compared twice to the value in column C10. Similarly the value

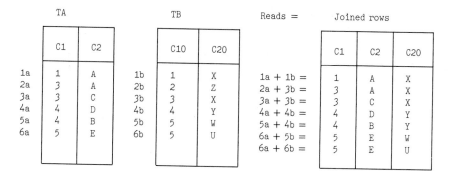

Fig. 11.1 Merge join

of 5 in C10 appears twice and must be compared twice to the matching values in C1. This seemingly trivial point can be quite significant if the value appeared hundreds or thousands of times. Joins are frequently one to many joins—that is one primary key value is joined with many matching foreign key values. It will be seen that the hybrid join has advantages when a value appears in a column many times particularly when the column has a low cardinality.

A merge join will be preferred by the optimizer if the columns being joined have a high cluster ratio index indicating that a large percent of the rows are in the required sequence on the data pages, the tables are very large (particularly many-to-many joins), there is a small bufferpool, or there is no usable index. If the indexes do not have a high cluster ratio, DB2 will sort the qualifying rows before performing the merge. If few columns are selected, the resultant rows to be sorted are shorter resulting in reduced sort costs and increasing the likelihood of a merge join. The requirement for a large sort discourages the use of the merge join method.

If a sort is required on the outer table, the optimizer can derive predicates that were not coded on the SQL statement in order to minimize the number of rows to be processed. Consider determining the parts and their suppliers that were ordered on 1990-09-05:

```
SELECT O.SN, O.PN, DATE_ORDERED, QTY
FROM   ORDERS O, SPJ
WHERE  DATE_ORDERED = '1990-09-05'
AND    SPJ.SN = O.SN
AND    SPJ.PN = O.PN
AND    SPJ.SN BETWEEN 'S2' AND 'S3' -- Derived predicate
AND    SPJ.PN BETWEEN 'P3' AND 'P4' -- Derived predicate
```

While processing the ORDERS table, the outer table in Fig. 11.2, DB2 can determine that only S2, S3, P3, and P4 are required from the SPJ table.

ORDERS

SN	PN	DATE	. . .
S1	P1	1991-01-31	
S2	P3	1990-09-05	
S3	P3	1990-09-05	
S3	P4	1990-09-05	
S4	P1	1991-02-14	
S5	P5	1991-05-10	
S5	P6	1991-06-15	
. . .			
. . .			
. . .			

SPJ

SN	PN	JN	QTY
S1	P1	J1	200
S1	P1	J4	700
S2	P3	J1	400
S2	P2	J2	200
S2	P5	J3	200
S2	P4	J4	500
S2	P3	J5	600
S2	P6	J6	400
S2	P3	J7	800
S2	P6	J2	100
S3	P2	J1	200
S3	P4	J2	500
S4	P6	J3	300
S4	P6	J7	300
S5	P2	J2	200
S5	P2	J4	100
S5	P5	J5	500
S5	P5	J7	100
S5	P6	J2	200
S5	P1	J4	100
S5	P3	J4	200
S5	P4	J4	800
S5	P5	J4	400
S5	P6	J4	500

Fig. 11.2 Derived predicates with a merge join

Two additional BETWEEN predicates are added and evaluated at execution time to narrow the number of rows to be joined in the inner table (the SPJ table).

If the columns to be joined do not have matching nullability in addition to data type and length, a join involving composite indexes will have less than optimal performance if a sort is required. The sort will be on only the first column in the composite index and the nonleading columns will be evaluated at stage 2, which increases the path length. (Section 11.10 discusses the distinction between stage 1 and stage 2 predicates.) As was discussed in Chapter 5, there are times when a foreign key needs to allow for nulls because of a business requirement and the primary key should be declared as NOT NULL. If this is the case and a sort is required, a merge join will not give its best performance.

The Nested-Loop Join Method

The nested-loop join method does not require that the rows to be joined be in any sequence, and preprocessing of the data is seldom required. Thus it

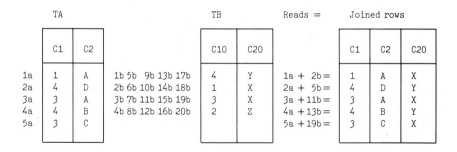

Fig. 11.3 Nested-loop join

is a good technique for joining a small number of rows in particular for cursor repositioning as discussed in Chapter 9. In this approach, DB2 reads the first value from the outer table and then scans the entire inner table looking for matches if there is no index on the inner table join column. Then it reads the second value from the outer table, scans all of the inner table rows, and so on. This process is shown in Fig. 11.3. The repeated scan of the entire inner table can use considerable I/O operations and CPU time and is rarely used.

If there is no index on the inner join column, it is very unlikely that the optimizer will choose the nested-loop join method. If there is an index on the inner table, it is very likely that a matching index scan of the inner table will be done for each qualifying row in the outer table. It is likely that the smaller table will be made the outer table to reduce the number of matching index scans on the inner table. Costs are reduced further by using the index lookaside technique discussed in Chapter 6. Once the required value is found on the leaf page, there is a good chance that the next required value will be on the same leaf page or the next leaf page to the right. A table with a high cluster ratio index is likely to be made the inner table so that the index lookaside and dynamic prefetch described will be efficient. Index lookaside gives significant reductions in the number of getpages, physical I/O, lock requests, and CPU time using index lookaside as discussed in Chapter 6.

Multiple Index Processing on the Inner Table

Multiple index processing can be used on the inner table using all three join methods. An example will show how multiple index processing can be accomplished:

```
SELECT S.SN, SNAME, PN, JN, QTY
FROM   SPJ, S
```

```
WHERE  SPJ.SN = S.SN
AND    QTY    = 100
AND    SNAME  = 'ADAMS'
```

A row with a quantity of 100 can be located in the SPJ table (outer table of a nested-loop join) where it is determined that S2 supplies the part. An index on SN in the S table (inner table of a nested-loop join) can be used to locate the RID (row or record identifier) for S2. An index on SNAME can be used to locate the qualifying RID for ADAMS. If the identified RIDs match, the page is processed. If they do not, the next supplier is obtained from the outer table followed by a matching index scan or index lookaside to locate the RID for S5 and compare it to the ADAMS RID that would match in this example. The processing continues with the third and fourth quantity of 100 in SPJ to complete the join.

The use of a nested-loop join with multiple index usage can have dramatic performance benefits. A join of rows from a 935,000-row table similar to the S table and a 34,000-row table similar to SPJ required 2 hours and 40 minutes of CPU time. When an additional index was added so that multiple index processing could be done, the CPU time dropped to 1 minute. The number of physical I/O dropped significantly as well from 542,936 prefetch I/O to 5630 with processing similar to the join of the S and SPJ tables described.

The Hybrid Join

The hybrid join, as its name indicates, is a mix between a merge and nested-loop join. It is like the merge join in that it requires that the outer table be in sequence; either the rows are retrieved in sequence using an index with a high cluster ratio or the qualifying values are retrieved and sorted. Like a nested-loop join, a matching index scan is used to locate each qualifying value in the inner table index. A difference is that a matching index scan of the inner table is done for only the unique values in the outer table. A further difference is that the hybrid join does not go immediately to the data page. Rather partial rows consisting of the qualifying RIDs from the inner table along with the search value and data values from the outer table are built and written to a temporary work area. For example, the first partial row in Fig. 11.4 is RID 100.1 from table TB with the value of 1 and A from table TA. All partial rows are sorted, duplicates are eliminated, and list prefetch is used to process the data pages of the inner table in sequence as they appear on DASD using skip sequential processing. (Skip sequential processing means that only the pages containing qualifying rows are read even if they are not contiguous.) A sort of the RIDs is not required if the

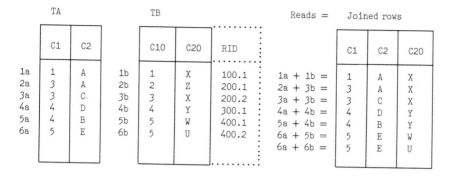

Fig. 11.4 Hybrid join

index has a high cluster ratio (for example, 95 percent) and the RIDs are well ordered.

The hybrid join fits nicely between a merge join that is well suited to joining a large number of rows and a nested-loop join that is well suited to joining a small number of rows. In addition, it has a significant advantage when processing duplicate values in the inner and outer tables. A matching index scan on the inner table is done only for each unique value in the outer table. Even though the value of 3 appears twice in TA (Fig. 11.4), a matching index scan will be done only once using the inner table index. Duplicate processing is also more efficient on the inner table where 5 appears twice. If the two values of 5 appear on the same data page, they will have the same RID but only one I/O will be done to the page since duplicate RIDs are eliminated with the list prefetch processing. The duplicate processing will result in significant savings when joining a primary and many matching foreign key values and when joining columns with a low cardinality on either index and a low cluster ratio on the inner table.

All three join methods can use multiple index processing and list prefetch to qualify rows for the inner table, and all return the rows to the program as they are joined without having to complete the join of all rows. The merge and hybrid join method, however, may require a sort of the qualifying rows before the join can begin. It is only the nested-loop join that never requires preprocessing of the data before beginning the join and returning rows to the program, thus its advantage for quickly returning a few rows to a program even though a large number of rows might qualify but will not be fetched.

A Three-Way Join Using Two Methods

The three join methods can be used in any combination. It is not necessary to complete a two-way join before processing a third table. Rather a row from each of up to 15 tables can be joined and returned to the program one at a time. A three-way join will illustrate the processing that can be done using the SPJ table, which is an intersection table that shows the relationship between the S and P tables. This type of join is frequently required. In this case, it is necessary to determine the supplier name for S3 and the part name of parts supplied by S3.

```
SELECT S.SN, SNAME, P.PN, PNAME
FROM   S, SPJ, P
WHERE  S.SN   = 'S3'
AND    S.SN   = SPJ.SN
AND    SPJ.PN = P.PN
```

The optimizer can choose to do a matching index scan without data reference on an index containing SPJ.SN as the leading column of a composite index to locate all S3s. The S3s can be used as the outer table of a nested-loop join. Notice that a predicate AND SPJ.SN = 'S3' was not specified in the statement. Rather, based on the statistics in the catalog tables, the optimizer chose to add the predicate and apply it first. A composite index on SN, PN, and JN in the SPJ table is used to determine that P3 and P4 are supplied by S3 with index only processing. Once the part numbers are identified, they can be used one at a time in a matching index scan on the P table, which is the inner table of the nested-loop join. Index lookaside and dynamic prefetch can be used in conjunction with the matching index scan on the P table. It brings in the S table as the inner table of a merge join using a unique index to locate the supplier as required by the coded predicate S.SN = 'S3'. A sort is not required for the merge join. The optimizer recognizes that there is a unique index on the S.SN primary key and does not request a sort of one row. This join strategy will perform well even if there are many part numbers qualifying in the SPJ table since index lookaside and dynamic prefetch can be used in conjunction with the matching index scan on the P table.

Redundant Predicates with a Join

In most cases material specific to a prior release of DB2 is eliminated from the book. The use of redundant predicates is mentioned in this edition, however, since it was a widely recommended guideline for joins although it is no longer needed in most cases. This statement is sufficient for the optimizer to determine the best join method and which table should be the outer and inner tables:

```
SELECT JN, PN, PNAME
FROM   P, SPJ
```

```
WHERE   P.PN     = SPJ.PN
AND     SPJ.PN > = 'P5'
```

In prior releases, it was recommended that the search be narrowed on both the P and SPJ table by adding the predicate AND P.PN > = 'P5'. The optimizer adds the predicate automatically and estimates whether it is best to narrow the search on P.PN first rather than SPJ.PN. Any predicate added for access path selection will not be evaluated at execution time if it is not used as part of the access path. The outer table of the join is likely to be the table where the predicate is applied. It is advisable to let the optimizer add a predicate rather than to code it in the statement since a coded predicate will always be evaluated at execution time. This does not mean that SQL in existing programs should be reviewed and the redundant predicate removed. The small amount of CPU time saved would not justify the cost of modifying the SQL in most cases. There are two types of predicate where it is still advisable to code the predicate on both tables to be joined— IN a list of values and LIKE predicates. The optimizer will not automatically add these two types of predicate on the second table to be joined.

Joining a Table with Itself

When DB2 joins a table with itself through a comparison of columns, it will use an index only if the SELECT statement uses correlation names to provide two names for the table. For example, a join of Table TA with itself may be accomplished with this statement:

```
SELECT C1, C2, C3
FROM   TA
WHERE  C1 = C2
```

DB2 will not use an index on either column to accomplish the join. It can take advantage of available indexes if the statement uses correlation names (X and Y in the example):

```
SELECT C1, C2, C3
FROM   TA X, TA Y
WHERE  X.C1 = Y.C2
```

11.3   JOINS VERSUS SUBSELECTS

Any subselect can be rewritten as a join. (The opposite is not true.) Usually the join is the more efficient of the two methods for several reasons. A join's WHERE clause can reduce the number of rows to be processed. The inner select of a subselect frequently qualifies a number of rows that are written to a temporary work area before the processing of the outer select can begin. In contrast, a join can process one row from each of the tables to be joined and return them immediately to the program without processing perhaps a large number of rows from the inner select in an intermediate work area. Finally DB2 cannot use an index in many cases to satisfy a sub-select where it would be able to use the index in carrying out the equivalent join. Examples will clarify these points.

Subselect Compared with a Join

Several types of subselects can return many rows—those beginning with the operator IN, =ALL, =ANY, and =SOME with or without a negation. Indexes can be used to minimize the number of rows processed in the sub-select. For example, the predicate WHERE QTY = 200 will be applied with an index or a tablespace scan to reduce the number of rows qualifying in the following inner select (in parentheses):

```
SELECT PN, PNAME, WEIGHT, CITY
FROM   P
WHERE  PN IN
  (SELECT PN
   FROM   SPJ
   WHERE  QTY = 200)
```

There is no predicate to narrow the search in the outer table of the subsel-ect—the P table. The question is to identify those parts that are being used in a quantity of 200 on jobs. Therefore a tablespace scan is required on the P table, comparing each PN with those identified in the inner select. The number of comparisons is reduced by sorting the inner select result and eliminating duplicates. In the first evaluation, DB2 would compare PN from the first row in the P table, P1, against the PNs in the sorted and reduced work area. In the second evaluation, it would again perform a scan of the SPJ PN work area until a match was found on the second PN value from Table P, and so on. In none of the evaluations would it use an index on PN in the P Table.

In contrast, the alternative join can use indexes on both tables to locate matching values for the statement:

```
SELECT P.PN, PNAME, COLOR, WEIGHT, CITY
FROM   P, SPJ
WHERE  P.PN = SPJ.PN
AND    QTY = 200
```

The join's results would not match those of the subselect exactly, however, because the subselect would not return duplicate rows while the join would. The subselect would return:

PN	PNAME	COLOR	WEIGHT	CITY
P1	NUT	RED	12	LONDON
P2	BOLT	GREEN	17	PARIS
P3	SCREW	BLUE	17	ROME
P6	COG	RED	19	LONDON

and the join would return:

PN	PNAME	COLOR	WEIGHT	CITY
P1	NUT	RED	12	LONDON
P2	BOLT	GREEN	17	PARIS
P3	SCREW	BLUE	17	ROME
P3	SCREW	BLUE	17	ROME
P3	SCREW	BLUE	17	ROME
P3	SCREW	BLUE	17	ROME
P6	COG	RED	19	LONDON

Duplicates can be eliminated from the join results using the DISTINCT operator:

```
SELECT DISTINCT PN,PNAME,COLOR,WEIGHT,CITY
FROM   P, SPJ
WHERE  P.PN = SPJ.PN
AND    QTY  = 200
```

The DISTINCT operator here does require a sort to eliminate the duplicate rows from the join result. And it may be a more costly sort than the one needed to satisfy the subselect in the subselect formulation. That is because the rows returned by the join are longer than those returned by the subselect. In this particular example, the subselect may provide better performance since a sort of shorter rows is required. If the join would not return duplicates, however, negating the need for DISTINCT, the join would perform best.

Indeed the optimizer can transform a noncorrelated or correlated subselect using the IN, =ALL, =ANY, or =SOME operator into an equivalent join and take advantage of any indexes the join would. So that the optimizer can be certain that the subselect and join are equivalent—that they will return identical results in all cases—there are limitations on when it will make these transformations. The key is that the column in the inner select must have a unique index to insure that no duplicates will be returned as a result of the transformation. In addition, the subselect must access only one table; potential join columns must have the same data type and length; the subselect cannot contain a GROUP BY or HAVING clause or use a column function such as DATE and TIME; and the operator on the inner select cannot be negated (such as NOT IN). A nested-loop join is used when the transformation occurs in most cases although a hybrid or merge join are possibilities. If the unique index is dropped, the plan or package will be marked invalid. The next time the plan or package is executed, it will be rebound without the transformation to a join.

If there is a unique index on the SN column in the S tables, the subselect

```
SELECT SN, PN, JN, QTY
FROM   SPJ
WHERE  SN IN
  (SELECT SN
   FROM   S
   WHERE  CITY = 'LONDON')
```

can be transformed into a join.

```
SELECT S.SN, PN, JN, QTY
FROM   SPJ, S
WHERE  CITY = 'LONDON'
AND    SPJ.SN = S.SN
```

Transformation can occur with composite indexes as well. If there is a composite index on CITY and SN in that order, the transformation can occur provided the leading column in the composite index is specified with an equal predicate as is the case in the above example.

Correlated Subselects

Correlated subselects that were introduced in Chapter 7 can be particularly resource intensive since the inner select results cannot be written to a work area and the outer table cannot be evaluated against the work area. (Fig. 7.1 contains the SPJ database tables that will be used for comparing various formulations of requests.)

Consider a search for the names of suppliers of part P5 that are used on jobs as indicated in the SPJ table. The process analysis will be the same if the literal 'P5' is replaced with a host variable.

```
SELECT SNAME
FROM   S SX
WHERE  'P5' IN
  (SELECT PN
   FROM   SPJ
   WHERE SPJ.SN = SX.SN)
```

The subselect cannot automatically be transformed into a join since there is not a unique index on SPJ.PN. It will be necessary to search the SPJ.SN column in the inner select for each unique S.SN in the outer select. The outer SELECT returns the supplier name any time the returned set includes P5. For example, it is necessary to take the first supplier from the S table, say S1, and find all matches in the SPJ table as indicated by the predicate SPJ.SN = SX.SN and identify the parts supplied by S1—in this case P1 and P2, which is written to a temporary work area. Then return to the outer select and determine if P5 is in the work area. Nothing qualifies. The next supplier, S2, is gotten from the S table and located in the SPJ table to identify the two parts, P3 and P5, supplied by S2. Again the processing returns to the outer select to determine if P5 is in the work area, which it is in this case. Notice that each supplier in the outer select must be located in the inner SPJ table and written to a work area with a return to the outer select to determine if the supplier supplies P5. A number of rows in the SPJ table must be read once for each unique SN in the S table. Clearly this processing is resource intensive.

An alternative formulation that returns the same results is to use a join:

```
SELECT SNAME
FROM   S, SPJ
WHERE  S.SN = SPJ.SN
AND    PN   = 'P5'
```

The four P5 rows will be identified in the SPJ table and joined with the S table on SN. The procedure requires at most reads of only four rows in the S table. Developers should be cautious when coding correlated subselects and use joins where possible.

Another type of resource-intensive correlated subselect is demonstrated with an example to locate each supplier, part, and quantity that have a quantity less than the average for all parts.

```
SELECT SN, PN, QTY
FROM   SPJ X
WHERE  QTY <
  (SELECT AVG(QTY)
   FROM   SPJ
   WHERE  PN = X.PN)
```

The AVG aggregate must logically be computed for each value passed from the outer select. The first average QTY is computed for rows containing the first PN (PN=P1, average QTY=333); then all rows with QTY values of less than that average are selected. Next the average QTY is computed for rows containing the second PN (P2, 150), and all rows with QTY less than that are selected, and so on until QTY averages have been calculated for all PNs. The inner select can be evaluated once for each unique PN in the outer table with a matching index scan while performing a table-space scan of the outer table.

Since the subselect returns a single value for each unique PN, DB2 will place it, along with the outer select value that produced it (P1, 333), in a 4K in-memory table. Then, when a subsequent outer select value is to be evaluated, DB2 checks in the in-memory table to see whether the evaluation has already been done. This saving of each unique PN and its average avoids repeated searches of the inner table, provided the values will fit in the 4K in-memory table. If all of the values will not fit in the in-memory table, the space is reused after relocating the required values. An in-memory table can be used for subselects preceded by simple operators ($>$, $<$, $=$, and so forth) and the EXISTS subselect (with or without negation). There cannot be more than 16 columns or 256 bytes in correlated columns. In addition, if there is a unique index on the correlated columns in the outer select, an in-memory table will not be used since there can be no duplicates.

A good way to identify correlated subselects is to ask whether the inner select can be evaluated independently of the outer select. If the answer is no, it is a correlated subselect and caution should be exercised regarding the use of such subselects. If the answer is yes, the inner and outer selects can be optimized independently decreasing complexity and improving performance in many cases.

Testing for Existence

EXISTS and NOT EXISTS subselects are frequently correlated subselects like this one that determines information on parts used on job J2 and the supplier located in Paris.

```
SELECT SN, PN, JN, QTY
FROM   SPJ SPJX
WHERE  JN = 'J2'
AND    EXISTS
  (SELECT S.SN
   FROM   S
   WHERE  S.SN = SPJX.SN
   AND    CITY = 'PARIS')
```

It is likely that a tablespace scan will be performed on the outer table, SPJ, to locate a J2 and the first supplier of parts for that job, S2. An in-memory table for SPJ.SN will be searched for S2. If it is not present, S2 is saved in the in-memory table along with a true or false indicating whether the supplier is located in Paris. S2 can be located in the S table with a matching index scan. The data page can be read to determine if S2 is in

Paris. An index on S.CITY cannot be used. Subsequent S2s from the SPJ table will be found in the in-memory table in many cases, which avoids a search of S.SN for each S2 in SPJ.SN. If S2 is not found because the in-memory space has been reused, the S2 value is saved again. The processing would be repeated for each unique outer table value (SPJ.SN) that supplies parts for J2.

Parts that are used on J2 with the supplier of the parts located in Paris can be determined with a join:

```
SELECT SN, PN, JN, QTY
FROM   S, SPJ
WHERE  S.SN = SPJ.SN
AND    CITY = 'PARIS'
AND    JN   = 'J2'
```

A comparison of the EXISTS processing with a nested-loop join will reveal some similarities and some differences depending on the availability of indexes and on whether the optimizer choses to use the indexes. Assuming that the S table is chosen as the outer table of a nested-loop join, a supplier in Paris can be located, S2. Inner table processing can consist of a matching index scan on a SPJ.SN,PN,JN composite index to locate S2. If J2 is in the leaf page, the required columns on the SELECT clause are retrieved from the data page. If J2 is not in the leaf page, the next supplier in Paris is located, S3, followed by inner table processing to determine if the S3 supplies parts for J2. The outer table processing followed by inner table processing is repeated until there are no more suppliers in Paris. The join has advantages if there is a usable index on S.CITY to narrow the search to suppliers in Paris and an index on SPJ.SN,PN,JN to narrow the search to suppliers that supply parts used by J2. The earlier EXISTS subselect has advantages if there is no usable index on SPJ since only unique SPJ.SNs need to be processed using the in-memory table in most cases.

These mini case studies are intended to impart an understanding of the processing required for different formulations of the same request. An understanding of the processing is necessary when an SQL statement does not provide the required performance so that it can be reformulated into a statement that will perform well.

Comparison of an IN and EXISTS Subselect

An analysis will be done to determine the processing required for an IN subselect compared to an EXISTS subselect. An IN subselect can be used to determine information on parts currently used on jobs.

```
SELECT PN, PNAME, WEIGHT, CITY
FROM   P
```

```
WHERE  PN IN
  (SELECT PN
   FROM  SPJ)
```

First note that the statement cannot be converted to a join since there is not a unique index on SPJ.PN. There is an index on SPJ.SN,PN,JN, however, which probably has fewer pages than there are data pages in the table. There is a good chance that the optimizer will choose to perform a non-matching index scan on SPJ.PN index with sequential prefetch followed by a sort and elimination of duplicates from the subselect result. There is no predicate to narrow the search on the outer P table resulting in a tablespace, comparing each P.PN with the reduced and sequenced SPJ.PN work area.

Information on parts currently used on jobs can also be determined with an EXISTS subselect:

```
SELECT PN, PNAME, WEIGHT, CITY
FROM   P PX
WHERE  EXISTS
  (SELECT PN
   FROM  SPJ
   WHERE SPJ.PN = PX.PN)
```

A tablespace scan is needed on the outer P table as would be the case for IN subselect processing since there is no predicate to narrow the search on the table. For each PN in the P table, a matching index scan is used to locate the part number in the SPJ table. Index lookaside and dynamic prefetch can be used on the inner table. Notice that the processing is similar to a nested-loop join, there is no initial inner-table processing resulting in minimal delay in returning the first row. If there is a usable index on SPJ.PN, EXISTS would perform better than would the IN formulation since processing all SPJ.PN in a work area can be avoided. It is not necessary for the user to wait while all SPJ.PN are processed before the first row can be seen and resources are saved if all qualifying rows are not fetched.

If there is no usable index on SPJ.PN, the IN subselect has advantages. This would be the case in the example. PN is not the leading column of the composite index. The number of SPJ.PNs is reduced and sequenced for examination during a tablespace scan of P. A comparison of NOT IN and NOT EXISTS would be similar to the comparison of IN and EXISTS.

Subselects Returning a Single Value

A subselect returning a single value requires less concern with respect to performance. Use of an index is not barred when comparing an outer select value to an inner select that returns only one value, those that have a simple operator like = or < or > preceding the inner select. If the subselect returns more than one value, an SQLCODE of −811 will be received. The following SELECT statement will determine information on suppliers that are located in the same city as P3.

```
SELECT SN, SNAME, STATUS, CITY
FROM   S
WHERE  S.CITY =
  (SELECT P.CITY
   FROM   P
   WHERE  PN = 'P3')
```

The inner SELECT can be evaluated using an index on P.PN to locate the city where P3 is housed, Rome. An index on S.CITY in the outer SE-LECT table can be used to locate information about the supplier who is located in Rome provided that the S.CITY and P.CITY columns have matching nullability and data types. The execution time evaluation will be as if the statement were coded as:

```
SELECT SN, SNAME, STATUS, CITY
FROM   S
WHERE  S.CITY = 'ROME'
```

A subselect using ANY, SOME, or ALL with a range predicate does not at first appear to qualify only one value in the inner select. Consider determining parts that are too heavy to be shipped on just any available truck due to the weight capacity of the various trucks.

```
SELECT PN, PNAME, WEIGHT, CITY
FROM   P
WHERE  WEIGHT > ANY
  (SELECT TRUCK_LIMIT
   FROM   TRUCK_CAPACITIES)
```

The inner SELECT can be reduced to a single value from leaf pages while performing a nonmatching index scan. In the outer SELECT, DB2 can evaluate that single TRUCK_LIMIT value, say 9000, against part weights with a matching index scan. The execution time evaluation will be as if the statement were coded as:

```
SELECT PN, PNAME, WEIGHT, CITY
FROM   P
WHERE  WEIGHT > 9000
```

This subselect will return the same results and seems more intuitive but is evaluated differently:

```
SELECT PN, PNAME, WEIGHT, CITY
FROM   P
WHERE  WEIGHT >
  (SELECT MIN(TRUCK_LIMIT)
   FROM TRUCK_CAPACITIES)
```

A one-fetch index scan can be used to determine the minimum weight of 9000 assuming an ascending index on the TRUCK_LIMIT column. Again the execution time evaluation will be as if the statement were coded as:

```
SELECT PN, PNAME, WEIGHT, CITY
FROM    P
WHERE  WEIGHT > 9000
```

A matching index scan on WEIGHT cannot be done, however, since an aggregate like MIN can return a null if no values qualify in the inner select—that is, if the truck has to be in Dallas and there are no trucks in Dallas. If there is a small number of TRUCK_LIMIT leaf pages or only a few data pages in the table compared to the number of data pages in the P table or if there is no ascending index on TRUCK_LIMIT, the >ANY subselect formulation would perform best. If the relative size of the tables were reversed and there was an ascending index on a large inner table, however, the use of the MIN aggregate would be best. A 1-fetch index scan on the large table to determine the minimum value and a tablespace scan on a small outer table would give the best performance. It is sometimes necessary to know the size of tables, in addition to understanding how the SQL statements will be processed, in order to identify the reason that a statement will not perform satisfactorily and to be able to formulate a statement that will perform as required.

The processing comparison would be similar for a >ALL subselect and MAX aggregates on columns with a descending index. Recall from Chapter 7 that ALL and MAX will not return the same results if no rows qualify in the inner select. All values will be greater than that of the empty set but no values will be greater than a null from MAX.

Notice that, in the subselects that have been analyzed thus far, both those returning multiple values and those returning a single value, the inner select was evaluated first and written to a temporary work area. Indeed the optimizer usually chooses the best access path for the inner and outer select independently. An exception is a correlated subselect, but even then an in-memory table is used to store intermediate results in some cases.

11.4 INCOMPLETE STATEMENTS

Statements mistakenly left incomplete can waste tremendous amounts of resources. There are several common, costly errors.

Cartesian Products

Perhaps the most wasteful misuse of SQL is a join statement for which the user has forgotten to include a predicate. The result is called a *Cartesian product*, after Descartes, the seventeenth-century mathematician and philosopher who originally defined the product of two vectors in coordinate geometry. In relational terms, a Cartesian product includes a row in the result table for every combination of rows in the participating tables. In other words, the number of rows in a Cartesian product equals the number of rows in one table multiplied by the number of rows in the second table. If S has 1000 rows and SPJ has 10,000 rows, the statement

```
SELECT S.SN, PN, JN
FROM   S, SPJ
```

returns a Cartesian product with 10 million rows. It is unlikely that any application would have use for such a result. A more likely explanation is that the programmer or user forgot to key in the WHERE clause.

A partial Cartesian product can be less obvious. Consider the following select on the catalog tables that estimates the average number of values that appear on a page. Which join condition is missing thus requiring a partial Cartesian product to be performed?

```
SELECT REL.CREATOR, REL.TBNAME, REL.RELNAME
FROM    SYSIBM.SYSRELS REL
WHERE   REL.CREATOR = 'POSYSTEM' AND
   REL.CREATOR || REL.TBNAME || REL.RELNAME
NOT IN
  (SELECT R.CREATOR || R.TBNAME || R.RELNAME
   FROM SYSIBM.SYSFOREIGNKEYS F,
         SYSIBM.SYSRELS        R,
         SYSIBM.SYSINDEXES     I,
         SYSIBM.SYSKEYS        K
   WHERE  F.CREATOR   = R.CREATOR
   AND    F.TBNAME    = R.TBNAME
   AND    F.RELNAME   = R.RELNAME
   AND    R.CREATOR   = I.TBCREATOR
   AND    R.TBNAME    = I.TBNAME
   AND    R.COLCOUNT < = I.COLCOUNT
   AND    I.CREATOR   = K.IXCREATOR
   AND    K.COLNAME   = F.COLNAME
   AND    K.COLSEQ    = F.COLSEQ
   GROUP  BY I.NAME, R.CREATOR, R.TBNAME,
                     R.RELNAME, R.COLCOUNT
   HAVING COUNT(*)  = R.COLCOUNT)
ORDER BY REL.CREATOR, REL.TBNAME, REL.RELNAME
```

The missing join condition is I.NAME = K.IXNAME. An even more subtle oversight involves a composite index. If the first column in a composite index on K.IXCREATOR and K.IXNAME is forgotten, a matching index scan could not be used thereby significantly detracting from the performance of the join.

Indiscriminate Joins

Some programmers unused to SQL's set processing capabilities sometimes fail to limit a join to only the required rows. Accustomed to one-record-at-a-time processing, they feel comfortable joining two entire tables and using the host-language program to test for the desired values. For example, when looking for suppliers of part P5 and the jobs on which it is used, they may join the entire S and SPJ tables with this statement:

```
SELECT S.SN, PN, JN
FROM   S, SPJ
WHERE  S.SN = SPJ.SN
```

Then they use a cursor to fetch the returned rows and test for those containing P5. This join is much more expensive than a join of only the P5 rows from one table with the other, which would be accomplished with this statement:

```
SELECT S.SN, PN, JN
FROM   S, SPJ
WHERE  S.SN = SPJ.SN
AND    PN = 'P5'
```

It is very important to join only the required rows. The number of rows to be joined impacts performance more than the number of tables to be joined in most cases. If the number of rows on each side of a join goes up multiplicatively, join costs go up exponentially. For example, a join of 1000 to 5000 rows times 10 would be a join of 10,000 to 50,000 rows, but the costs would increase a hundred-fold. Another key to efficient joins is to insure that the join columns have matching data types and lengths. If they do not, an index cannot be used.

11.5 LIST PREFETCH WITH MULTIPLE AND SINGLE INDEXES

DB2 can use multiple indexes to narrow a search before issuing I/O to the data pages. Consider the following AND condition.

```
SELECT SN, PN, JN, QTY
FROM   SPJ
WHERE  SN = 'S5'
AND    PN = 'P5'
```

Separate indexes on SN and PN can be used to narrow the search before processing the data pages. The RIDs for S5 are retrieved from the SN index

	SN	PN	JN	QTY
	S1	P1	J1	200
	S1	P1	J4	700
	S2	P3	J1	400
	S2	P3	J2	200
	S2	P3	J3	200
	S2	P3	J4	500
	S2	P3	J5	600
	S2	P3	J6	400
	S2	P3	J7	800
PN index ————————>	S2	P5	J2	100
	S3	P3	J1	200
	S3	P4	J2	500
	S4	P6	J3	300
	S4	P6	J7	300
SN index ————————>	S5	P2	J2	200
SN index ————————>	S5	P2	J4	100
SN & PN index ————————>	S5	P5	J5	500
SN & PN index ————————>	S5	P5	J7	100
SN index ————————>	S5	P6	J2	200
SN index ————————>	S5	P1	J4	100
SN index ————————>	S5	P3	J4	200
SN index ————————>	S5	P4	J4	800
SN & PN index ————————>	S5	P5	J4	400
SN index ————————>	S5	P6	J4	500

Fig. 11.5 Indexes used to identify rows with an AND condition

and the RIDs for P5 are retrieved from the PN index. Fig. 11.5 shows the values for which the RIDs would be identified and the indexes that would be used to identify the RIDs. The identified RIDs are sorted and any duplicates removed. This process is called ANDing the predicates or taking an intersection of the RIDs.

List prefetch is used to retrieve the data pages identified by the RIDs. Recall that list prefetch processes 32 pages with a single I/O. It also uses skip sequential processing. That is if pages 5, 10, 15, 20, and 25 are required, the pages in between are not processed. Since the RIDs are sorted, the pages are retrieved in the sequence as they appear on DASD thus reducing I/O seek time. DB2 processes the data pages only once regardless of how many rows qualify on a page and whether a clustering or nonclustering index is used.

Use of List Prefetch and Sequencing of Data

ORDER BY discourages the use of list prefetch, particularly if there is a good cluster ratio (such as greater than 80 percent) on the column to be sorted and a large percent of the rows are expected to qualify. This is because a sort of the RIDs would almost certainly result in the rows on the data pages being out of sequence and a second sort would be required of the qualifying rows. Even if the cluster ratio is 100 percent at bind time, it cannot be assumed that all rows will be in sequence on the sequenced pages at execution time. There is a good chance that some inserted rows would not be placed in sequence on the clustering index due to a lack of free space after RUNSTATS has been executed and before a SELECT statement is executed. Multiple index processing probably would not be used for the following statement because of the ORDER BY clause.

```
SELECT PN, PNAME, COLOR, WEIGHT, CITY
FROM   P
WHERE  PN BETWEEN 'P2' AND 'P5'
AND    WEIGHT > 700
ORDER  BY PN
```

Multiple index processing can be used with range predicates as well as with equal predicates although in this example it probably would not be used because of the ORDER BY clause. Also the use of list prefetch with a single index on WEIGHT is unlikely for the same reason.

Interdependent Predicates

If two predicates qualify mostly the same rows and a large number of rows qualify, it is best *not* to use an index for one of the predicates to avoid sorting a large number of RIDs unnecessarily. For example, a report is needed on all employees who are > 18 years of age *and* have been with the company > 1 year. (Assume most employees are over 18 and have more than 1 year of seniority.)

```
SELECT EMPNO, EMP_NAME
FROM   EMP
WHERE  AGE > 18
AND    SENIORITY > 1
```

It is best not to have indexes on columns that qualify mostly the same rows since one index would narrow the search sufficiently and two indexes need not be maintained. Both indexes, however, may be required because of frequent searches on age or seniority with infrequent searches on both columns. A technique to avoid the use of one of the indexes used by some developers is to code the least restrictive predicate so that an index cannot be used. Adding a zero to a numeric value or making the length of the host variable longer than the column length is sometimes used. A better alternative that reduces CPU usage is to take advantage of the fact that

ORed predicates on a column cannot use single index processing since rows can be missed. The predicate OR 0 = 1 can be added to a predicate to disallow index usage within parenthesis like: (AGE >18 OR 0 = 1).

These techniques, however, detract from data independence since the distribution of data can change or the optimizer may use a different technique in the future. The use of the clause OPTIMIZE FOR "n" ROWS where "n" is small (such as 15) makes it very unlikely that list prefetch will be used. The SELECT clause has a number of benefits and will be discussed in section 11.6.

Threshold for ANDing of Predicates

There is no architectural limit to the number of predicates that can be ANDed. There are times, however, when ANDing of additional indexes offers no benefits and will incur additional costs. A threshold is used to avoid incurring additional costs when little or no benefits can be achieved. ANDing of predicates will stop when < 32 RIDs qualify from multiple indexes. The search has already been narrowed to a small number of pages and a single I/O to retrieve the 32 pages can be issued using list prefetch. Additional predicates will be applied directly to the row. For example, if < 32 RIDs qualify using the SN and PN indexes, the JN RIDs will not be ANDed with the following SELECT. The JN predicate will be applied directly on the row.

```
SELECT SN, PN, JN, QTY
FROM   SPJ
WHERE  SN = 'S5'
AND    PN = 'P5'
AND    JN = 'J4'
```

Use of Multiple Indexes With OR

Separate indexes on SN and PN can be used to narrow the search before access to the data pages for OR conditions.

```
SELECT SN, PN, JN, QTY
FROM   SPJ
WHERE  SN = 'S2'
OR     PN = 'P4'
```

The process used for an OR condition is similar conceptually to that used for AND conditions, and list prefetch can be used. The RIDs for S2 are retrieved from SN index, and those for P4 are retrieved from PN index. The RIDs are sorted and any duplicates removed. This is referred to as

	SN	PN	JN	QTY
	S1	P1	J1	200
	S1	P1	J4	700
SN index ──────>	S2	P3	J1	400
SN index ──────>	S2	P3	J2	200
SN index ──────>	S2	P3	J3	200
SN index ──────>	S2	P3	J4	500
SN index ──────>	S2	P3	J5	600
SN index ──────>	S2	P3	J6	400
SN index ──────>	S2	P3	J7	800
SN index ──────>	S2	P5	J2	100
	S3	P3	J1	200
PN index ──────>	S3	P4	J2	500
	S4	P6	J3	300
	S4	P6	J7	300
	S5	P2	J2	200
	S5	P2	J4	100
	S5	P5	J5	500
	S5	P5	J7	100
	S5	P6	J2	200
	S5	P1	J4	100
	S5	P3	J4	200
PN index ──────>	S5	P4	J4	800
	S5	P5	J4	400
	S5	P6	J4	500

Fig. 11.6 Indexes used to identify rows with an OR condition

ORing of the predicates or taking a union of the RIDs. Fig. 11.6 shows the values that would be identified with the noted indexes. ORed predicates on the same column with range predicates usually do not result in the use of an index:

```
SELECT SN, SNAME
FROM   S
WHERE  SN < = 'S2'
OR     SN > = 'S4'
```

It would be necessary for DB2 to use a matching index scan to locate S4 and scan forward in the leaf pages to find the supplier name followed by a matching index scan on S2 and a scan backward in the leaf pages. In both cases, it would be necessary to dip down to the data pages to find the supplier name. It is this type of processing that is avoided by doing a tablespace scan with sequential prefetch.

If there is confidence that a small percent of rows will qualify, BE-TWEEN can be used to encourage the use of indexes:

```
SELECT SN, SNAME
FROM   S
WHERE  SN BETWEEN '  ' AND 'S2'
OR     SN BETWEEN 'S4' AND 'ZZ'
```

A matching index scan can be used to identify supplier number $=>$ two
blanks (low values can be used rather than the two blanks) and a scan forward of the leaf pages until S2 is found can be used to identify the qualifying RIDs. A second matching index scan can be used to find S4 and all
those greater than S4 (high values can be used rather than ZZ). The RIDs
are sorted, duplicates eliminated, and list prefetch used. Notice from this
example that multiple index processing can be performed on a single index.

Threshold for ORing of Predicates

There is a threshold for when ORing of predicates will stop. If $>$ 25 percent
of RIDs qualify using, say, the SN and/or PN and/or JN indexes, ORing
of RIDs will stop, and a tablespace scan will be used. This threshold is used
to minimize the sorting of RIDs and to provide for the use of sequential
prefetch. If there is reason to believe that a large percent of rows will be
requested (for example, $>$ 25 percent of RIDs qualify), use the OPTIMIZE
FOR "n" ROWS to inform the optimizer as was suggested for avoiding
index ANDing. It is best to do a tablespace scan immediately rather than
to accumulate 25 percent of the RIDs and then do a tablespace scan.
Thresholds for ORing and ANDing of predicates are also applied at bind
time by the optimizer. These are discussed in Chapter 12.

List Prefetch with a Single Index

Multiple indexes are useful for narrowing the search using several indexes
so that fewer data pages need to be processed. List prefetch can also be
used with single index processing if two or more pages are to be processed.
List prefetch has a number of benefits for multiple and single index processing. No pages need to be reread, pages are read sequentially as they appear
on DASD, seek time is minimized, and skip-sequential processing is used.

   A page may need to be reread without list prefetch because it has multiple qualifying rows. This occurs when a column has a low cardinality or
skewed distribution of values. An example of a low cardinality index on a
city column is used in Chapter 6. The cardinality is 20, meaning that a
search for any one value, say Dallas, qualifies about 5 percent of the rows
and that each page has on average two and a half rows located in Dallas.
Clearly it is desirable to avoid having to read each page two and a half
times, and the elimination of duplicate RIDs with list prefetch does this. A

similar situation occurs with a skewed distribution of values, say 80 percent of the parts, are in the headquarters city and the remaining 20 percent are in branch warehouses. That means there is a good chance that each data page has even more than two and a half parts when a search is done on the headquarters city.

A range search can benefit from list prefetch. If all the parts between P2 and P20 are required, there is a good chance that several qualifying parts will be on a single page. If the index on PN has a high cluster ratio, the benefits of list prefetch are not as great since the cost of sorting the RIDs and eliminating duplicates is not necessary. A high cluster ratio means that most of the values are clustered or grouped together on contiguous pages already and sequential prefetch can be used rather than list prefetch. Therefore list prefetch is more likely to be used if there is a low cluster ratio of say < 80 percent. These factors are considered by the optimizer for both single and multiple index processing using list prefetch. The size of the RID pool where the RIDs are processed is also considered by the optimizer at bind time when determining if list prefetch is a good access path and is discussed in Chapter 12.

Considerations for Use of Multiple Indexes

AND and OR predicates in combination can use ANDing and ORing of RID lists. There is no architectural limit on the number of indexes that are ANDed and ORed although one can run out of work space. RIDs from the first two indexes are combined into, say, temporary list A. RIDs from the third index are combined with temporary list A into temporary list B. RIDs from the fourth index are combined with temporary list B into temporary list C, and so forth with a current maximum set at 200 indexes.

11.6   OPTIMIZE FOR "n" ROWS

In many cases, a SELECT statement may qualify a large number of rows, but only a few are fetched, perhaps only enough to fill a screen to be displayed to a user. Based on the specified predicates, the optimizer chooses a good access path to process a large number of rows, perhaps using multiple indexes, a merge join, a hybrid join, list prefetch, or sequential prefetch. These techniques can be less than optimal for processing only, say, the first 15 rows that qualify. The use of a single index is better than using several indexes and sorting the qualifying RIDs before the first row is returned to the program. A nested-loop join is better than a merge join that requires a sort of the data and a hybrid join that requires a sort of partial rows. The clause OPTIMIZE FOR "n" ROWS should be used to inform the optimizer that only a few rows will be fetched even though many may qualify. The clause cannot be used for the inner table of a subselect and it cannot be used in a CREATE VIEW statement.

DB2 will return all rows that qualify as they are fetched even if they exceed the number of rows specified in the clause. Beware of estimating 15 rows and fetching 10,000 since a good access path for 15 rows is probably not a good access path for 10,000. OPTIMIZE FOR "n" ROWS, where the number of rows is small, will encourage the use of matching index scans and discourage the use of sequential prefetch, list prefetch for single and multiple index usage, and join methods that require sorts. The clause has limited impact on subselect processing where the inner select qualifies many rows since they must all be sorted, have duplicates eliminated, and then placed in a temporary work area. It also has no impact on operations that require sorts like GROUP BY, DISTINCT, and UNION. It is more likely to use an index, even one with a low cluster ratio, however, to avoid a sort for ORDER BY when only a few rows are required.

The optimizer uses the number of rows specified in some of the formulas for estimating the cost of various access paths as will be discussed in Chapter 12. That chapter also discusses the hazards of trying to fool the optimizer. OPTIMIZE FOR "n" ROWS significantly influences the access path chosen by the optimizer and thus the performance of a SELECT statement.

11.7 FUNCTIONS REQUIRING ORDERED ROWS

The ORDER BY, GROUP BY, DISTINCT, and UNION operators may require that rows be sorted, and occasionally the outer table of nested-loop join will use a sort. (ORDER BY and GROUP BY require ordered rows for reasons that are obvious. For DISTINCT and UNION, ordered rows provide the most efficient means to eliminate duplicate values. UNION ALL, which does not eliminate duplicates, does not require a sort.) If the column to which any of the operators requiring ordered values—except UNION— are applied has an index with a high cluster ratio, the optimizer can choose to use the index to locate the rows in sequence to avoid a sort. This is done by scanning the leaf pages and dipping down to the data pages to locate the rows in sequence using sequential prefetch on both the leaf and data pages—but only if the cluster ratio is 80 percent or more and it is estimated that 8 or more pages will qualify. It is not possible simply to scan the data pages even if the cluster ratio is 100 percent since rows could have been inserted out of sequence due to the lack of free space on the target page before the SELECT statement is executed. Recall from Chapter 6 that the values in the leaf pages are maintained in sequence by splitting a page if there is insufficient free space on the page when a value is inserted.

The format of an SQL statement can determine whether DB2 can use an index to avoid a sort. In some cases, DB2 will use an index to avoid a sort for one of a pair of equivalent statements but not the other. For example, a search for distinct values using the DISTINCT operator, which would require a sort, could be satisfied by an equivalent statement using the GROUP BY operator, which might be satisfied by sequential returns through an index, thus avoiding a sort. For example, even if there is a non-unique index on CITY, DB2 would sort the rows to remove duplicates in processing this statement:

```
SELECT DISTINCT CITY
FROM   SPJ
```

It could use the index, however, in processing this equivalent statement:

```
SELECT CITY
FROM   SPJ
GROUP  BY CITY
```

A unique index can be used to avoid a sort for the DISTINCT operator. It is doubtful that a person would intentionally code such a request since all values are distinct by definition with a unique index on the column.

Avoiding a Sort for UNION

An index cannot be used to avoid a sort for UNION. All rows above and below the UNION operator must be retrieved, sorted, and have duplicates eliminated. Consider determining all employees and departments in the company including employees who currently are not assigned to a department and departments that currently do not have employees assigned to them.

```
SELECT D.DEPTNO, DNAME, E.EMPNO, ENAME
FROM   DEPT D, EMP E
WHERE  D.DEPTNO = E.DEPTNO
UNION
SELECT D.DEPTNO, DNAME, '?', '?'
FROM   DEPT D
WHERE  NOT EXISTS
 (SELECT E.DEPTNO
   FROM   EMP E
   WHERE  D.DEPTNO = E.DEPTNO)
UNION
SELECT '?', '?', E.EMPNO, ENAME
FROM   EMP E
WHERE  NOT EXISTS
```

```
(SELECT D.DEPTNO
 FROM   DEPT D
 WHERE  D.DEPTNO = E.DEPTNO)
```

UNION ALL does not require a sort since duplicates are not eliminated and in some cases can be used in place of UNION. UNION ALL is a good alternative to UNION when logically there can be no duplicates as in the above example. If duplicates are acceptable to the program and a large number of rows are expected to qualify, resulting in a large sort, UNION ALL is a good choice to improve performance.

Using Composite Indexes to Avoid Sorts

Frequently DB2 can avoid sorting rows for the GROUP BY, ORDER BY, and DISTINCT operators when the statements using those operators reference columns that are part of composite indexes. Whether or not DB2 can avoid a sort, however, depends on how the columns are used in the statement in relation to their order in the composite index. For example, assume a composite index on SN, PN, and JN, in that order, in the SPJ table. DB2 can use that index to avoid a sort to fulfill the ORDER BY clause in the statement:

```
SELECT SN, PN, JN, QTY
FROM   SPJ
WHERE  SN = 'S4'
ORDER  BY PN, JN
```

It can use a matching scan to find 'S4' rows because the SN column is the leading column. (See Chapter 6 for a full discussion of the use of composite indexes for matching and nonmatching scans.) Because the leaf pages store the index values in SN, PN, JN order, once DB2 has located the 'S4' rows, returning them in order will automatically satisfy the ORDER BY PN, JN request. A sort can be avoided if the trailing columns of a composite index are not specified in the ORDER BY clause. If the statement had requested the reverse order, however—ORDER BY JN, PN, a sort would be required.

When DB2 uses a composite index to satisfy a GROUP BY, it can also avoid a sort of the grouped rows when it is retrieving distinct values from the groups. In some cases, the GROUP BY must be done on the leading column of the composite. Assume a composite index on PN and WEIGHT, in that order, in the P table. DB2 can use the index to group the rows by part number as in:

```
SELECT PN, AVG(DISTINCT WEIGHT)
FROM   P
GROUP  BY PN
```

DB2 need not sort the rows to group the values or to find the distinct weights. If a sort is required, perhaps because of a low cluster ratio, an aggregate like AVG will be computed during the final phase of the sort to avoid passing the data again.

If the statement includes searches of all the columns in the index that were not used in the GROUP BY and DISTINCT operations, the sorts can be avoided no matter which of the indexed columns is used in the GROUP BY or for the DISTINCT operation provided the missing column is specified with an equal predicate. For example, if the composite index is on PN, CITY, and WEIGHT, in that order, in the P table, DB2 can use it to avoid sorts on both the GROUP BY and DISTINCT operations in the statement:

```
SELECT PN, AVG(DISTINCT WEIGHT)
FROM   P
WHERE  CITY = 'SYDNEY'
GROUP  BY PN
```

When DB2 groups rows, it can sometimes avoid a sort to order the results. The columns used in the GROUP BY clause need not be part of the composite index, nor must they be expressed in the clause in any particular order. Again assume the composite on SN, PN, and JN. Because the sample database does not offer a meaningful example, the following example illustrates the concept but probably would not be used in the real world:

```
SELECT SN, PN, JN, QTY
FROM   SPJ
GROUP  BY SN, PN, QTY
ORDER  BY PN
```

Because QTY is not part of the composite index, DB2 would have to sort the rows to perform the GROUP BY operation. The ORDER BY operation, however, would not require an additional sort—even though the GROUP BY clause did not list PN first. The GROUP BY is reordered to PN, SN, QTY, and sorted, avoiding the additional sort. Generally for DB2 to be able to avoid a sort in this kind of situation, the columns used in the ORDER BY clause must be the same as or a subset of those used in the GROUP BY clause.

Sort Times

If a sort cannot be avoided, how long will it take? One 500,000 row sort, with sorted rows of 40 bytes being retrieved, has been timed at 8 minutes and required 6 CPU minutes; a similar sort of 8 million rows took 116 minutes and used 102 CPU minutes on a computer without a sort hardware assist. Reduction in sort times of 38 percent in CPU time and 24 percent in response time was experienced when sorting and fetching 5 million rows on a computer with a sort hardware assist. The savings were more dramatic when only 100 rows were fetched with a savings of 62 percent in CPU and 37 percent in response time.

The length of the rows to be sorted also affects the speed with which the sort can be accomplished. If an SQL statement requiring a sort takes too long, the programmer might consider reducing the number of rows requested by adding additional predicates where possible and reducing the size of the returned rows by eliminating from the SELECT columns that are not essential. If the sort time is still unacceptable, the system administrator should be consulted on the number and size of work tablespaces available to DB2.

The sort begins in DBAS (database services address space) working storage area (250 KB for a user). If more space is needed, the sort spills into the bufferpool, assuming 25 percent of the bufferspace is stealable (no more than 10 percent of the sum of the bufferpools will be taken). If more space is needed, logical work files are allocated on work tablespaces. The default number and size of work tablespaces when DB2 is installed are not sufficient for large sorts. Two rather small work tablespaces are created in the work database DSNDB07 during the installation process unless the system administrator adds more work tablespaces. A good indication of whether there is insufficient work space is to determine if the work tablespaces have gone into secondary extents. (This can be determined by selecting from the catalog tables as described in Chapter 14.) Additional work tablespaces can be created in DSNDB07 like any application tablespace and dropped when they are no longer needed. A difference is that it is necessary to stop and start the database so that the DBD (database descriptor) will be refreshed in the EDM (environmental descriptor manager) pool since the DBD has the volume serial numbers of the disks containing the work tablespaces. The general guidelines for efficient sorts apply: use cylinder or track allocation, and spread the tablespaces across multiple DASD devices and channels.

11.8   PREDICATES THAT DO NOT USE INDEXES

In most cases, DB2 will not use indexes for SQL that include a negation. Use of an index would be inappropriate for a search based on predicates with clauses such as WHERE NOT STATUS = 20 or WHERE STATUS ¬ = 20, for example. In most cases, the ¬= condition does not narrow the search to a small percent of a table's rows but rather means that a majority of the rows will be returned. The same point is true of NOT BETWEEN,

NOT LIKE, and NOT IN conditions. A tablespace scan is the most efficient search method when a majority of rows will be selected.

The ¬> and ¬< conditions are different stories, however. The optimizer can reverse these negative formulations and use an index on the positive formulation. For example, the optimizer can evaluate the clause WHERE NOT STATUS > 20 as WHERE STATUS < = 20 and use an index on STATUS in the search.

The optimizer will not use an index on a search based on the NOT BETWEEN, NOT LIKE, and NOT IN operators, such as for the statement:

```
SELECT SN, PN, JN, QTY
FROM   SPJ
WHERE  QTY NOT BETWEEN 100 AND 800
```

An alternative that can use an index with multiple index processing is (NOT BETWEEN does not include end points):

```
ENDP   = 100-1
BEGINP = 800-1
HIGHP  = 32,767
SELECT SN, PN, JN, QTY
FROM   SPJ
WHERE  QTY BETWEEN 0 AND ENDP
OR     QTY BETWEEN BEGINP AND HIGHP
```

Predicates with Arithmetic Expressions

DB2 will not use indexes in searches based on predicates that use arithmetic expressions. For example, in this statement:

```
SELECT SN, PN, QTY
FROM   SPJ
WHERE  QTY > :QTY / 2
```

DB2 will not use a matching index scan on QTY because of the arithmetic calculation. It is more efficient, therefore, to have the program perform the calculation outside of the SELECT statement. For example, DB2 can use an index to satisfy this statement:

```
QTY    = QTY / 2
SELECT SN, PN, QTY
FROM   SPJ
WHERE  QTY > :QTY
```

Predicates with Scalar Functions

DB2 will not use an index for searches on predicates that include scalar functions, such as those for string, date, and time functions and data type conversions. In the following statement, for example, the use of the MONTH function extracts the month portion of the DATE-RECEIVED column:

```
SELECT PN, DATE_RECEIVED
FROM   SHIPMENTS_RECEIVED
WHERE  MONTH(DATE_RECEIVED) = 4
```

DB2 will not use an index on the DATE_RECEIVED column for the search. This does not mean that DB2 cannot use indexes on columns declared as DATE, TIME, or TIMESTAMP types. It can as long as a DATE or TIME function is not used in the predicate to limit the value being searched.

Literals and Variables

The lengths and precision of literals and host variables used in predicates can determine whether DB2 will use an index in performing a search. Specifically if the corresponding literal or variable is more precise or longer than the value in the indexed column, DB2 will not use an index scan. DB2 will not use an index scan on QTY, for example, if the column was declared integer but the SELECT statement's predicate uses a decimal value for QTY (WHERE QTY > 100.5). If SN has been declared as a 2-byte character column, DB2 will not use an index on it if the predicate uses a longer literal or host value (WHERE SN = 'S2 '). Recall from Chapter 10 that DCLGEN generates data structures to be included in a host-language program and that they will always match the corresponding columns. Care should be exercised when additional host variables are defined in working storage to insure that they match the columns when comparisons are made in predicates.

Composite Indexes

The ways in which DB2 can use a composite index depend on the order in which the component columns have been defined. (Higher to lower order corresponds to left to right order in the definition of the composite index.) The B-tree index structure (described in Chapter 6) limits the use of lower-order columns for matching index scans. One reason is that the high-order column, the first specified as part of the index, must be included in the predicate for the index to be used in a matching scan at all because the search values must be compared to the upper-range values in the root page and nonleaf pages. Another is that if the predicate uses a comparison operator other than equality with a column from a composite index, DB2 cannot use a matching scan on other columns from the composite that are of lower order. It can, however, perform nonmatching scans on those lower-order columns. Examples make this point clearer. Assume a composite index on SN, PN, and JN with the index's columns specified in that order. In response to this statement:

```
SELECT SN, PN, JN, QTY
FROM   SPJ
WHERE  SN > 'S4'
AND    PN = 'P4'
AND    JN = 'J4'
```

DB2 can use a matching index scan on SN to find S4 followed by a nonmatching index scan to find values greater than S4. Because a range operator was used with SN, only nonmatching scans can be used on PN and JN. In response to this statement,

```
SELECT SN, PN, JN, QTY
FROM   SPJ
WHERE  SN = 'S4'
AND    PN < 'P4'
AND    JN = 'J4'
```

DB2 could use a matching scan on SN and PN but only a nonmatching scan on JN. If the highest-order column is not specified at all in the predicate, DB2 may still use a nonmatching scan on the columns if only the indexed columns are requested in the SELECT clause since there are almost always fewer leaf pages than there are data pages.

The LIKE Operator

Again because of the B-tree index structure, DB2 will not use a matching index scan to search for a character string if the leading character is not specified in the LIKE clause. If the leading character or characters are specified, it may use a matching scan to locate values with those beginnings in the index and a nonmatching scan to complete the search for strings with those beginnings and any other characters specified in the clause. If the clause reads WHERE PNAME LIKE 'CH%,' for example, DB2 may perform a matching scan on an index on PNAME. If the clause reads WHERE PNAME LIKE 'CH%J%,' it may use a matching scan to locate strings beginning with CH and a nonmatching scan for strings that also include a J. It may also use a nonmatching index scan to satisfy a string search beginning with "%" or "_".

When the LIKE operator is used with a host-language variable, DB2 in Version 2.3 and above will use an index as described for literals. The content of the host variable is evaluated at execution time and a decision is made about whether a matching or nonmatching index scan can be used. (An explanation of the access path chosen by the optimizer will show the use of a matching index scan.) The DB2 developers exercise caution when they are deciding if an access path should be modified at execution time to avoid adversely effecting performance. The evaluation of a host variable when using a LIKE operator does not require access to the catalog tables and does not require a bind. Therefore performance is not adversely effected and performance can be improved significantly if a matching index scan can be used. Chapter 12 summarizes other factors that are considered at execution time.

Application developers may find that a SELECT statement returns the required results when they are testing interactively with literals, but when the statement is embedded in a host-language program, the part names beginning with CH are no longer found. If the host variable is declared as character data of length 5 for example, DB2 is searching for a string of "CH%bb" (lower case b represents a blank space). A fixed length host variable must be padded with "%" or "_" to its full length like "CH%%%" or "CH%_ _" in order to find any parts beginning with CH. If PNAME is declared as variable length—49 levels in COBOL or VAR in PL/1—the padding is not required provided the length of the search string (3 in this example) is moved into the first 49 level length field.

11.9 THE BETWEEN OPERATOR

SQL provides two ways to request a search for values that fall within a range: by using the symbolic operators $> =$ and $< =$ or by using the BETWEEN operator. These predicates are functionally equivalent but may perform differently, for example:

```
WHERE PN > = 'P2' AND PN < = 'P5'
```

will return the same results as:

```
WHERE PN BETWEEN 'P2' AND 'P5'
```

DB2 may use an index on PN for the search in either case, but it is more likely to use an index for the BETWEEN operator. This is because the optimizer uses default filter factors (FFs) when determining the access path for range predicates and the default is lower for BETWEEN than for other range predicates. Default FFs need to be used for range predicates since the search values are not known until execution time when they are provided by the user and can vary from one user execution of the program to another. Range predicates do not influence the access path at execution time because the formula to determine their use includes statistics from the catalog tables and a bind would be required. SQL with range predicates would need to be executed much like dynamic SQL in order to consider the values provided by the user at execution time. These factors will be considered in more detail in Chapter 12.

The IN operator can also be used to specify a range of values as search criteria. For example, the WHERE clause—WHERE PN IN ('P2,' 'P3,' 'P4,' 'P5')—is equivalent to WHERE PN BETWEEN 'P2' AND 'P5.' But the values used in an IN clause may not—in fact, usually will not—correspond to a range. If the optimizer knows that a search is to cover a range, it will likely choose a matching, followed by a nonmatching, index scan if an appropriate index is available. Since the optimizer cannot assume an IN search covers a range but knows a BETWEEN search does, it is more likely to use a matching, followed by a nonmatching, scan for the BETWEEN operator, even when the clauses are equivalent. It would likely use a matching index scan for each value in the IN list. Even when some of the values of a range may not be wanted in a search, it may be worthwhile to use the BETWEEN operator and have an application program eliminate the unwanted values rather than use an 'IN' predicate that does not include them. Or even better, an additional predicate can eliminate the unwanted rows. For example:

```
WHERE PN BETWEEN 'P2' AND 'P5'
AND PN ¬ = 'P3'
```

In general, BETWEEN is a good operator to use when it is appropriate. It is likely to use an index and use it efficiently.

11.10 STAGE 1 AND STAGE 2 PREDICATES

Box 11.1 summarizes predicates that can use an index, and Box 11.2 summarizes predicates that cannot use an index. The distinction between whether an index can or cannot be used to narrow a search has to do with whether the predicate is stage 1 or stage 2. Stage 1 predicates are applied by the DM (data manager), and stage 2 predicates are applied by the RDS (relational data system). These two components of DB2 work together to perform a database search. DM processes pages in the bufferpool and passes them to RDS, which completes any processing or analysis they require to complete the search. Passing rows from DM to RDS requires CPU cycles. The more rows that DM must pass to RDS to complete a search, therefore, the higher the processing cost will be. DM can perform certain types of searches to identify rows that might satisfy an SQL statement but not others.

Box 11.1   Summary of predicates that can use an index

DB2 may use indexes to satisfy searches called for by:

- WHERE clauses using the comparators =, <, < =, >, > =, ¬>, and ¬< —for example, WHERE SN = 10.
- Predicates using AND to limit the search criteria.
- Predicates using OR to expand the search criteria if the two clauses refer to the same column and both search on an equality.
- Predicates using IN a list of values.
- Predicates using the BETWEEN operator.
- Predicates seeking null values—WHERE SN IS NULL, for example.
- Predicates seeking LIKE character values. If the search value begins with a blank or wild card—WHERE LOCATION LIKE '%BURG' or LIKE '_BURG' for example—DB2 can use a nonmatching index scan. If the search value begins with an alphanumeric value, it can use a matching index scan.
- A WHERE clause limiting a search on the first column or columns of a composite index in which case a matching scan can be used; if the columns used in the predicate do not include the first column of the composite, a nonmatching scan can be used.
- Predicates that search on a value determined by a 'NOT' operator negation of a < or > comparator after transformation to a positive expression—for example, SN > = 50.
- EXISTS and NOT EXISTS subselects can use a matching index scan, assuming a predicate in the inner select.
- A matching index scan can be used on the column preceding the operators >ALL, >ANY, and >SOME subselects (any range operator can be used in place of ">").
- Predicates requiring ORDER BY or GROUP BY operations on clustered columns.
- The aggregates AVG, SUM, and COUNT can use a nonmatching index scan and compute the aggregate without reference to the data pages.
- MIN and MAX use a one-fetch index scan with an ascending and descending index respectively.

Box 11.2 Summary of predicates that cannot use an index

DB2 cannot use indexes to satisfy searches called for by:

- A correlated subselect that cannot be grouped.
- A subselect comparison based on the equal 'IN,' 'ALL,' 'ANY,' or 'SOME' operators, though an index can be used to satisfy the subselect itself.
- An UPDATE statement that updates a column specified in the WHERE condition with something other than an equal predicate.
- A join of a table to itself when a correlation name is not used.
- Predicates that determine search criteria using negation WHERE NOT SN = 10, for example.
- A comparison of a column value with a value that has a different data type or length, DECIMAL(8,2) and DECIMAL(8,3), for example.
- A comparison of a column variable with a longer host-language variable.
- A comparison using an arithmetic expression—WHERE QTY = :QTY/2, for example.
- A predicate using date/time, string, and data type conversion functions.

An important performance goal therefore is to formulate statements so that the DM can perform as much of the search as possible, minimizing the number of rows that must be passed to RDS. In addition, DM does all the index and tablespace scans. RDS does joins and subselects that return multiple rows and searches requiring sorts, data type conversions, and arithmetical operations. If a predicate requires an RDS operation, DB2 will not use an index scan even if one would otherwise be available for use. The distinction between stage 1 and stage 2 predicates will be discussed in detail in Chapter 12.

11.11 MANAGING A SKEWED DISTRIBUTION OF DATA

Developers should avoid indexing columns having a skewed distribution of data as discussed in Chapter 6. Nevertheless, there are times when it would be more efficient to retrieve infrequently occurring values in such a column with an index rather than a tablespace scan. Assume that 80 percent of accounts have a status of 99 and the remaining 20 percent have other status values and that this will always be a representative distribution of values. The application design is such that an account is assigned a status of, say, 1 when an account application is first submitted, of 2 during credit checking, of 3 when credit is approved, of 4 when the first purchase is made, of 5 when payment is due, of 6 when payment is past due, of 7 when payment is received, and finally of 99 when the account is closed. A history of accounts is retained for two years, resulting in accounts with a status of 99 occurring very frequently in the table, but those accounts will seldom be accessed by status in online transactions. Good response time is required, however, when the user requests information on accounts that are past due or that have one of the other statuses that occur infrequently.

One way to encourage DB2 to use the index appropriately is to have the host-language program test the status requested by the user and if the request is not for status of 99, the program can use a SELECT with a predicate on status. Otherwise the program can execute a SELECT without a predicate. Pseudo-code would look like:

```
IF STATUS ¬= 99 -- host-language test

   SELECT ACCOUNT_ID, ACCOUNT_NAME
   FROM   ACCOUNTS
   WHERE  STATUS = :STATUS
      GO TO CONTINUE-PROCESSING.

IF STATUS = 99 -- host-language test

   SELECT ACCOUNT_ID, ACCOUNT_NAME
   FROM   ACCOUNTS
```

The problem with this technique is that it severely detracts from data independence for most application systems. The distribution of values may change in the future, making an index search for what was initially thought to be a frequently occurring value desirable.

In any case, such a problematic solution may not be necessary. RUNSTATS will identify the top 10 occurring values and calculate their percent of occurrence in the table based on the indexed values for nonunique and composite unique indexes. In the case of a composite index, the first column is used for the calculations. The top 10 occurring values will be stored in the column EXITPARM, and the percent of occurrence, in EXITPARML in the catalog table SYSFIELDS. The optimizer assumes that the remaining percentage of rows have a uniform distribution—that is, they all occur an equal number of times. The optimizer can use distribution statistics for all predicates using literals and for dynamic SQL to determine if use of the index will narrow the search sufficiently to be of value or if a tablespace scan with sequential prefetch should be used.

When a host variable is specified in a predicate, the optimizer does not use the information on the distribution of values because it does not know what value will be requested each time a user executes the transaction. Consequently embedded dynamic SQL for which the indexes are used appropriately may be more efficient than static SQL for which they are not. An IBM test, for example, found that retrieval of 77 percent of 510,000 rows required 100 seconds elapsed time and 19 seconds of CPU when the optimizer assumed uniform distribution of all values and used an index inappropriately. When the optimizer considered the distribution of values, the test required only 14 seconds elapsed time and 7 seconds of CPU time. The cost of embedded dynamic SQL is not likely to offset such savings. That cost, however, will be incurred each time the SQL is executed regardless of the frequency of the value sought. In addition, a bind requires that about 30 to 40 pages be read in the catalog tables with the potential for an I/O bottleneck when a high transaction rate is required.

An alternative is to have the application program select from SYSFIELDS where RUNSTATS stored the top 10 occurring values in the column EXITPARM and the percent of occurrence in the column EXITPARML to determine if the value specified by the user and its percent of occurrence is present. Based on this information, the program can issue a select with or without a predicate. The pseudo-code is:

```
SELECT EXITPARML
FROM   SYSIBM.SYSFIELDS
WHERE  TBCREATOR = 'POSYSTEM'
AND    TBNAME    = 'S'
AND    NAME      = 'STATUS'
AND    EXITPARM  = '5'

IF  SQLCODE = 0   -- 1 of top 10 occurring values
AND EXITPARML >10 -- Value occurs in >10% of rows
    SELECT SN, SNAME, STATUS, CITY
    FROM   S
      GO TO CONTINUE-PROCESSING.
IF SQLCODE = 100 -- Not 1 of top 10 values
   SELECT SN, SNAME, STATUS, CITY
   FROM   S
   WHERE  STATUS = '5'
```

Literals are used in the pseudo-code for ease of understanding the example. All literals would be replaced with host variables in a program. This technique requires considerably fewer I/O to the catalog at execution time than would a dynamic bind. In addition, no execution time bind is required. Even this I/O to the catalog table SYSFIELDS can be eliminated by saving the values and percentages in an application table after each RUNSTATS and select from the table at execution time.

11.12 ORDER OF PREDICATE EVALUATION

Under the relational model, the order in which the search criteria are listed in an SQL statement should make no difference to the user. Database management system developers, however, occasionally compromise that principle in the interest of overall performance.

To avoid potential performance deficits, DB2's designers decided to impose priorities on the order in which DB2 performs various evaluations of a row to determine whether it qualifies for a search's results. These priorities are based on both the type of criteria to be checked and the order in which they are expressed. Although setting this priority order improves performance overall, it also means that the order in which predicates are listed can make a difference in performance.

In most cases, this difference will be slight. This is because predicate order plays no part in the optimizer's choice of access path, which depends on its assessment of the availability of indexes, their FFs, table sizes, and a number of other factors. Choice of access path is by far the key determinant of any statement's performance. And because predicate order does not affect access path, it does not affect the number of I/O operations needed for the search. The only processing that predicate order can influence is that needed to complete testing of rows already retrieved through an index or tablespace scan. Except for statements including a complex series of AND and OR predicates, differences in this processing due to predicate order will be insignificant, typically a few micro- or nanoseconds.

In general, in setting a priority order for predicate checking, DB2's developers sought to have it perform first the operations likely to disqualify the most rows when the values being evaluated exhibit uniform distribution. The fewer rows that pass the earlier tests, the less processing that will be required for later tests. Obviously, with uniform distribution, in almost all cases, fewer values in a column will satisfy an equality—match a single value—than will fall within a range—match any one of multiple values. Consequently, if a request calls for both a range and equality search, it usually makes sense to perform the equality test first. If a request entails two equality searches, with a uniform distribution, it should not matter which is performed first. They are likely to eliminate about the same number of rows.

DB2 orders operations within two categories, one for stage 1 predicates (those that will be tested by DM), the other for stage 2 predicates tested by RDS. It evaluates stage 1 predicates before stage 2 predicates. Within each of those categories, DB2 evaluates indexable predicates, those for which it might use an index if one were available, before nonindexable predicates. For example, in the clause, WHERE SN = 'S4' AND NOT SN = 'S2', both predicates are stage 1, but only the first is indexable. Notice that the choice of indexable before nonindexable predicate is the same whether or not there is actually an index on SN.

Within the stage 1 and indexability categories, DB2 orders operations according to predicate type in the following order:

First, it evaluates equality predicates. Besides the obvious equalities (WHERE SN = 'S4', for example), these include the awkward but (to DB2) acceptable use of the IN operator specifying only one value (WHERE SN IN ('S4')), and tests for nulls.

Second, it evaluates predicates that search for ranges—including BE-TWEEN, >, <, and so on.

Next, it considers the IN operator with multiple values.

Finally DB2 evaluates stage 2 subselects and then within these corre-lated subselects.

Within each of these groups, DB2 evaluates predicates in the order in which they are listed in the statement. Parentheses also affect the order of evalua-tions. DB2 evaluates predicates expressed within parentheses before those presented outside them.

What does this order of evaluations mean for performance? Simply, processing will be minimized if the more restrictive "if" tests are performed before the less restrictive tests. Consider the following statement, for ex-ample:

```
SELECT SN, SNAME, STATUS, CITY
FROM   S
WHERE  CITY = 'SAN JOSE'
AND    SNAME = 'SMITH'
```

Assume there are no indexes on table S so DB2 performs the search with a tablespace scan. Because the two predicates are in the same priority group for order of evaluations, DB2 checks them in the order listed. When it evaluates each row, it first checks the CITY value. If CITY does not equal 'SAN JOSE', DB2 need not check the SNAME value. But suppose SMITH appears only a few times in a 500,000 row table, while 'SAN JOSE' appears in 100,000 rows. All of those 100,000 rows pass the first test (CITY = 'SAN JOSE'). But while DB2 goes on to perform the second test for all 'SAN JOSE' rows, only a few of them will pass this second test. If devel-opers knew the table included only a relatively few 'SMITH' rows, they might have coded the SNAME = 'SMITH' predicate first. In that case only a few rows would pass the first test, so the second test would be required only a few times. The formulation would avoid almost 100,000 'if' tests.

(But the CPU time necessary to perform a comparison is in terms of a few micro- or nanoseconds.) If there is a predicate in a lower priority group, like a range predicate, it would be evaluated last regardless of the whether it is coded before, or in the middle of, the equal predicates.

11.13   EFFICIENT UPDATING

Because updates modify the data and associated indexes during the update process, use of indexes to find the rows to be changed presents several problems. DB2 will not use certain indexes for certain types of updates and in some cases will fail to take advantage of usable indexes if the UPDATE statement is improperly worded. We will look at each of these situations.

Indexes and Columns to Be Updated

DB2 will not use an index to locate a column being updated unless the statement includes an equal predicate. Because the update changes the column value and the index value, such an operation could cause a variety of inconsistencies. Consider, for example, this statement:

```
UPDATE SPJ
SET    QTY = :QTY * 1.1
WHERE  QTY > 50
```

Updating a QTY value in this way places it within the predicate's search criteria, causing DB2 to return it for updating, which leaves it still within the search criteria, causing DB2 to return it again for updating, and so on. Such an infinite loop is only one of the anomalies that could occur if DB2 did use an index on a column being updated. When there is a choice therefore, one should avoid specifying in the UPDATE statement's predicate the column being updated particularly if it is a range predicate. Similarly avoid doing an arithmetic calculation in the SET clause since it forbids the use of an index, as was discussed earlier.

Anomalies will not occur if the column specified in the SET and WHERE clauses uses an equal predicate. Therefore DB2 can use an index on SN provided it is not declared as a primary key in satisfying this statement:

```
UPDATE S
SET    SN = 'S9'
WHERE  SN = 'S8'
```

An index cannot be used to locate a row to be updated if the column to be updated and preceding key columns use a range predicate (unless list prefetch is used), the WITH CHECK OPTION is used on view to be updated, or an arithmetic expression is used on a column in the where or set clause.

Further *all* columns in a composite index must be specified with equal predicates to use an index in an update. The following update cannot use an index since PN is not specified in the where clause.

```
UPDATE SPJ
SET    PN = 'P1'
WHERE  SN = 'S1'
AND    JN = 'J1'
```

If PN was specified in the predicate with an equal predicate, a composite index on SN, PN, and JN can be used to locate the row for update.

These restrictions on the use of indexes with an UPDATE statement do not apply to DELETE. Indexes can be used to locate rows to be deleted just as indexes can be used to locate rows to be retrieved with a SELECT statement. Recall from Chapter 6 that the clustering index is always used to determine where to insert a row.

The FOR UPDATE OF Clause

The same principles apply to the use of an index on any column referenced in the FOR UPDATE OF clause of an embedded SQL SELECT statement in performing the statement's search, regardless of whether the referenced columns are actually updated. It is good practice, therefore, to reference in the clause only those columns that are unlikely to have an index. Updating an entire set of rows with an UPDATE statement is more efficient than using the SELECT . . . FOR UPDATE OF and cursor operation to update a row at a time.

UPDATE or DELETE without a Predicate

An UPDATE or DELETE without a predicate will change all the rows in a table. In most cases, such an update would not be intended. Failure to indicate with a predicate the rows to be updated or deleted can be an expensive mistake that is difficult to undo.

Joins and Updates

DB2 will not update a join condition. That is, the update statement's predicate identifying the rows to be modified cannot call for a join. One alternative is to use in the UPDATE statement a predicate similar to that used in an IN subselect to request an operation equivalent to the desired join—for example:

```
UPDATE SPJ SET QTY = 0
WHERE  SN IN
  (SELECT SN
   FROM   S
   WHERE  STATUS = 10)
```

DB2 will update rows returned by such a statement. It will not, however, use an index on SN in the SPJ table to speed its search. It can use an index on STATUS in the S table. The same concepts discussed in section 11.3 on a SELECT . . . IN subselects apply to an UPDATE with an IN subselect.

Another alternative for such updates that makes better use of indexes is to separate the update into component parts—in this case, two selects and an update. This approach requires the use of cursors to handle the intermediate sets. In the example, this alternative would be carried out as described by this pseudo-code, simplified for understandability:

```
DECLARE SCURSOR CURSOR FOR
   SELECT SN FROM S WHERE STATUS = 10
OPEN  SCURSOR
FETCH SCURSOR INTO :SN
DECLARE SPJCURSOR CURSOR FOR
   SELECT QTY FROM SPJ WHERE SN = :SN
   FOR UPDATE OF QTY
OPEN  SPJCURSOR
FETCH SPJCURSOR INTO :TEMP
   UPDATE SPJ SET QTY = 0
   WHERE  CURRENT OF SPJCURSOR
CLOSE SPJCURSOR
** CONTINUE FETCHING SCURSOR **
```

The code's first component selects from the S table supplier numbers (SN) with a STATUS of 10. The cursor on those supplier numbers presents them one at a time to the second SELECT, which returns from the SPJ table the QTY values from rows with matching supplier numbers. In this case, DB2 will use an index on SN in the SPJ table to find those matches.

11.14   STEPS TO CONSIDER IN CODING EFFICIENT SQL

The first step and the goal is to simply code SQL to achieve the required result and to let the optimizer determine the required processing to achieve the result. This will give good performance in the majority of the cases and has a number of advantages. It results in a high level of data independence and minimizes the need to change application programs when the structure of the data changes, new columns are added or deleted, a column is in-

Box 11.3   Guidelines for updates

- Narrow the search for rows to be updated with an equal predicate or on columns that are not to be updated.
- Use UPDATE statement over SELECT . . . FOR UPDATE OF . . .
- If SELECT . . . FOR UPDATE OF . . . is used, reference for updating only those columns not likely to have an index.
- Use a combination of SELECT and UPDATE statements over an equivalent update using a subselect that returns multiple rows.

creased in length, a new index is added, new access strategies are introduced into DB2, and enhancements to the optimizer are made. It reduces the amount and complexity of host-language code that must be developed, tested, and maintained. It also enhances performance by reducing the path length. The more work that can be done by DB2, the fewer instructions that must be executed to return only the required data to the program and the fewer host-language statements that must be executed.

If the first step does not produce acceptable performance, the second step is to reformulate the SQL so that a better access path will be chosen by the optimizer. A number of hints, tips, guidelines, and alternatives have been included in this chapter and throughout the book that should aid in a reformation. If the required performance is still not achieved, the third step and last resort is to break the SQL into parts and introduce procedural code. This technique was used in Section 11.11 to avoid an update with a subselect. It was also used in Chapter 9 for organizational chart processing and as an alternative for cursor repositioning. It does lose the advantages of the first step, however, and should be avoided in a distributed environment since it results in more data being transmitted.

Process Analysis of SQL

A large application system may consist of hundreds of programs the processing of which is not known in detail when the tables and indexes are designed. The text of all static SQL statements is available from SYSSTMT and SYSPACKSTMT and can be analyzed to determine if the tables and indexes are designed for the type of processing that is being done. Capturing dynamic SQL is a bit more of a challenge since it is not stored in the DBRM library discussed in Chapter 10 nor in the catalog tables. All dynamic and static SQL can be captured using IFI (Instrumentation facility interface) as the statements are executed. The SQL text is in record type

63 and outprefix.DSNSAMP(DSNWMSGS) contains information on the record format.

Once the SQL is captured, it can be analyzed to determine if the table and index design is appropriate for the type of processing that is being done. The EXPLAIN command that will be discussed in Chapter 13 can be used to determine the access paths being used. The database design can then be refined based on the analysis. This process analysis is also useful to verify that the SQL generated by CASE tools and fourth generation languages is formulated for good performance.

Use of Efficient Views

Occasional users are not likely to know the steps and guidelines for formulating the most efficient statements. Indeed they need not. Provided developers can anticipate queries, they can create views based on these guidelines that the users can access. The views would use indexes and SQL efficiently, including use of efficient joins. This is an especially valuable technique for ensuring good performance in application systems that process large tables and experience high transaction rates.

11.15 INDEXES ARE NOT ALWAYS BEST

This chapter has concentrated on how to take advantage of indexes. Indexes do not always provide the best access path, however, particularly when a large percentage of rows are being processed in a table and DB2 might use sequential or list prefetch, as was described in an example of batch updating in Chapter 9. Another example is a test performed on an IBM 3090-400 with an 80 MB bufferpool. The table had 250,000 rows of 200 bytes each and a single unique clustered index. A matching index scan retrieving most of the rows in sequence on the clustered index required 10 minutes of CPU time and 25 minutes of elapsed time. The same processing but with rows retrieved in random order took 10 minutes of CPU time and 27 minutes of elapsed time. When the predicate on the index was dropped and an ORDER BY clause added to encourage the use of prefetch, the processing required only 2 minutes, 45 seconds of CPU time and 4 minutes, 15 seconds of elapsed time. Processing a large proportion of a table's rows is frequently more efficient with a tablespace scan than with a matching index scan.

DB2 can use prefetch when 8 or more data or index pages are expected to contain qualifying rows as a result of a select, a cursorless update or delete, a nonmatching index scan using clustered and nonclustered indexes, and after finding the starting position with a matching index scan followed by a nonmatching index scan. If the cluster ratio is > 80 percent, prefetch can be used on the data pages in addition to the leaf pages. DB2 uses prefetch when processing work tablespaces and the utilities use prefetch.

The performance of prefetch for a nonmatching index scan will decrease if there is a high leaf distribution although it is not considered in the decision to use prefetch. If a large number of pages are empty due to deleted rows or free pages or if pages contain rows *not* for the table being processed, the performance of prefetch will degrade. In addition, segmented tablespaces where segments have become dispersed and fragmented when using prefetch will detract from efficient use of prefetch. The sequential detection discussed in Chapter 9 is less likely to initiate dynamic prefetch at execution time, and even if initiated, it will be less efficient with a high leaf distribution.

Several techniques can be used to encourage sequential prefetch. The simplest technique is to use no predicates. Other alternatives are to use a predicate that cannot use an index, use range predicates (for example, BETWEEN, >, <, and so on), or use ORDER BY on a column with a high cluster ratio index. EXPLAIN will indicate whether the optimizer has decided that prefetch should be used. The buffer manager makes the final decision about whether to use prefetch at execution time depending on the percent of usable pages in the bufferpool.

11.16 CAPPING THE COSTS

Application developers have a number of ways to limit the cost of executing any SQL statement. There are time-limit facilities belonging to the various attaches that can be used to control resource usage by programs that include static SQL. There is a governor feature specific to statements executed through QMF. The resource limit facility (RLF) in DB2 provides a flexible way to put a cap on the cost of any dynamic data manipulation statement executed from any program from any location.

There are several options for controlling programs using static SQL. The time limit on TSO sessions set by the TSO administrator applies to programs using DB2. Developers can also specify time limits for jobs or steps on JCL statements. CICS and IMS controls on resource usage also apply to DB2 programs running with those attaches. The QMF governer provides for applying program logic in an assembler program and for limiting the number of rows selected, usage to specific tables, and the use of QMF commands. The RLF limits, however, apply to all dynamic SQL regardless of its source, unlike the QMF governer. The QMF governor can be used in addition to RLF.

RLF limits can apply to an individual and to each dynamic SQL statement in a plan or its packages. The RLF limits are not expressed directly

AUTHID	PLANNAME	ASUTIME	LUNAME
FLEUR	QMF310	40000	blank
FLEUR	blank	20000	SAN JOSE
blank	QMF310	10000	CAPETOWN
blank	SREPORT	7000	PUBLIC
blank	blank	2000	blank
ERIC	blank	null	SYDNEY
BILL	blank	0	DALLAS

Fig. 11.7 DSNRLSTxx table

in CPU seconds but rather in a measure called ASU units. The ASU figure is derived by dividing CPU time by a constant specific to the processor being used. The MVS system programmer can provide this constant from the MVS SRM (system resource manager). A rough idea of the correspondence of CPU and ASU figures based on a 3090–200E is that 30,000 ASU is about 38 CPU seconds. When the EXECUTE IMMEDIATE approach to binding a plan is used, the limit applies to each execution of a statement. In other words, a user is limited in the CPU time he or she may use for any given statement. But the user can execute any statement any number of times regardless of the total time required as long as no single execution exceeds the limit. Both QMF and SPUFI use EXECUTE IMMEDIATE binding. When the PREPARE/EXECUTE approach is used to bind an SQL statement, the limit applies to the total time needed for all executions when the program runs.

The system administrator sets up the limits with RLF tables like the one shown in Fig. 11.7. More than one RLF table may be used to control a system, but only one is active at any one time. For example, one table may set the limits from 9 A.M. to 5 P.M.; another may enforce different limits from 5 P.M. to midnight; and a third still different limits from midnight to 9 A.M. Each table must be named as DSNARLxx or DSNRLSTxx if it is used in a distributed environment. The last two characters are used by the operator to designate the table to be used when starting the resource limit facility with the command: −START RLIMIT = xx.

The example DSNRLSTxx table in Fig. 11.7 illustrates how an administrator can set up the limits. The table includes columns for those assigned individual limits (primary AUTHID), for the plan including its packages to which limits apply (PLANNAME), for the time limit itself (ASUTIME), and optionally for the location of the origin of the SQL data manipulation statement (LUNAME). When a row in the table includes an individual's

AUTHID and ASUTIME only, the limit applies to any statement in any plan or package executed under that AUTHID other than exceptions for that individual that are specified in the table. Similarly when a row lists a PLANNAME and ASUTIME only, the limit applies to any statement executed under that plan or its packages other than specified individual exceptions. If an AUTHID is listed with a *blank* ASUTIME value, the user may use unlimited time for any statement, while a user given "0" ASUTIME may not execute any dynamic statements. And if a row includes *blank* values for both AUTHID and PLANNAME, the ASUTIME time applies to all users and plans not specified in the table. If this row does not exist, the installation default limit is used for all AUTHID and PLANNAME not listed in the table.

In the example, the table limits Fleur to 20,000 ASU units for any dynamic statement she executes coming from San Jose, except for those under QMF, for which her limit is 40,000 ASU units per statement originating locally. Anyone executing statements under QMF310 coming from Cape Town is limited to 10,000 units, except Fleur, with her 40,000 units; Eric, who has unlimited time for statements under any plan coming from Sydney; and Bill, who is not allowed to execute any dynamic statements at all from Dallas. Anyone attempting to execute statements under plan SREPORT is limited to 7000 ASU units coming from any location, other than those same exceptions. The general limitation, other than the exceptions discussed, is 2000 units from any location.

What happens if a statement exceeds an ASU limitation? DB2 issues an SQLCODE of −905 and an SQLSTATE of '57014'. If the statement is using a cursor, the host-language program may test for that code and branch to a routine that closes the cursor and perhaps prepares another cursor with different search criteria likely to require less CPU time. Any work done by a noncursor dynamic statement that exceeds a limit will be rolled back automatically. Since a roll back requires more processing than the original work that is rolled back, setting limits that users frequently exceed on update may turn out to be more expensive than setting higher limits closer to their actual needs. Even if only SELECT statements are used, the limit should be adequate to satisfy most requests. Otherwise the user will receive a −905 after using the specified CPU time and no results. They may repeatedly reformulate the statement in an attempt to stay within the time limit, using the specified CPU time and receive no results for each attempt. This can waste more CPU time than if they had been given a higher limit originally.

Controlling Binds with RLF

Additional columns can be included in the RLF table to control binds of plans and packages. The column RLFFUNC indicates what function the row applies to: '1' means that bind operations are not allowed; '2' means that the row will govern binds by collection and package names; ' ' (blank) means that the row will govern by plan name. The column RLFBIND indicates whether binds are allowed: 'N' means that binds are not allowed for packages or plans; and 'Y' means that binds are allowed for packages or plans (requires RLFFUNC = '1'). The column RLFCOLLN contains the name of a collection that the row applies to if RLFFUNC = '2'. The column RLFPKG contains the name of a package that the row applies to if RLFUNC = '2'. If the column value for RLFPK is blank, the row applies to all packages in a named collection or all plans if RLFFUNC = ' '. If any one of the four columns is used, all are required as well as the LUNAME.

11.17 PERFORMANCE RESULTS

Just how fast will DB2 perform? The answer is highly dependent on the application system and the environment, but IBM benchmark tests give indications. IBM says a benchmark of DB2 Version 2.2, on an IBM 3090 Model 200E with 128 MB main memory and 256 MB expanded memory, handled transactions with an average of 16 SQL statements embedded in COBOL II programs at a rate of 55.5 transactions per second. This was at 89.1 percent CPU utilization, using IMS/DC non-WFI as the transaction manager. The same test using CICS with pool threads gave 54.6 transactions per second at 92.6 percent CPU utilization. Thread reuse results in a 20 percent increase in transaction rate in most cases. The transaction composition was 80 percent selects and 20 percent updates. The data was on eight 3380D, and six replicates were used. The bufferpool had 32 MB and CTHREAD (create thread) was set at 150. Execute privileges were granted to the public. MVS/ESA, DFP 3.1, IMS/VS 2.2 or CICS/MVS 2.1 was used.

Version 2.2 running on a more powerful configuration—a 3090–600E under MVS/ESA with 256 MB of main memory and 265 MB of expanded memory—was benchmarked by IBM at 186 transactions per second and with WFI at 285 transactions per second. A transaction using four SQL calls to debit bank accounts ran at 300 transactions per second. This benchmark is thoroughly documented in the manual *DB2 V2R2 Performance Report (GG24-3461)*. A credit card authorization transaction using two to four SQL calls attained 438 transactions per second at TRW.

11.18 SUMMARY

The ability to use SQL efficiently depends not only on an awareness of efficient requests—particularly those that allow DB2 to make good use of indexes—but also on an understanding of how DB2 implements the language. This chapter has pointed out the requests that will and will not allow DB2 to use indexes. It also described how to formulate requests so that DB2 will be most likely to determine the most efficient access paths. Chapter 12, which describes the optimizer, provides further insights into how an application's design and development can affect performance.

EXERCISES

11.1. A join is taking an excessive amount of time. What are some factors that should be considered to reduce the processing time?

11.2. Consider the following statement:

```
SELECT SN, PN, JN, QTY
FROM   SPJ
WHERE  SN = 'S3'
AND    PN = 'P4'
```

Can a composite index on SN, PN, JN be used to satisfy the select? Can a separate index on SN and PN be used to satisfy the select? Would a composite index or separate indexes yield the best performance? If the predicate is WHERE PN = 'P4', would the composite or individual indexes be best?

11.3. Assume 250,000 rows in table TA and the index cardinalities and cluster ratios noted. Which indexes might the optimizer use? The "?" represents a host variable, "Card" means index cardinality; and CR means cluster ratio of the index.

```
SELECT C1, C2, C3, C4, C5
FROM   TA
WHERE  C2 BETWEEN ? AND ? -- Card=50,000, CR=100%
AND    C3 BETWEEN ? AND ? -- Card=30,000, CR= 11%
```

11.4. Using the same assumption as in exercise 11.3 but the cardinalities noted, which indexes might the optimizer use?

```
SELECT C1, C2, C3, C4, C5
FROM   TA
WHERE  C2 BETWEEN ? AND ? -- Card=150,000, CR=57%
AND    C3 BETWEEN ? AND ? -- Card= 30,000, CR=11%
```

11.5. Using the same assumptions as in exercise 11.3 but equal predicates rather than range predicates, which indexes might the optimizer use?

```
SELECT C1, C2, C3, C4, C5
FROM   TA
WHERE  C2 = ? -- Card=150,000, CR=57%
AND    C3 = ? -- Card= 30,000, CR=11%
```

11.6. A statement with an OR condition is taking an excessive amount of time. What might the problem be, and what action can be taken to reduce the processing required?

11.7. Statements with ORDER BY, GROUP BY, DISTINCT, and UNION are requiring an excessive amount of time. What factors should be considered to improve performance?

11.8. Statements with a 'NOT' condition are taking an excessive amount of time (WHERE NOT C1 = 100 and a statement with WHERE C1 ¬= 100).

11.9. Over 20 percent of the rows in a 1 million-row table need to be updated. Should the SQL be coded to encourage the use of indexes?

11.10. The programmer has entered UPDATE P SET PN = 'P5'. What is the error? How will DB2 respond?

11.11. Assume an index on QTY in the P table. This statement processes slowly:

```
SELECT PN
FROM   P
WHERE  QTY > :QTY + 100
```

How might it be recast to improve performance?

11.12. Assume an index on PN, a CHAR(2) column in the SPJ table. This statement executes slowly:

```
SELECT SN, PN
FROM   SPJ
WHERE  PN > 'P5'
```

Correct the error that is slowing performance.

11.13. Indexes are not being used in many statements where it is expected that an index would be used. What might the problem be?

11.14. Programs that have had good performance are now executing slowly. What are some factors that should be considered?

12

The Optimizer

12.1 INTRODUCTION

The optimizer's primary function is to determine efficient database search strategies for satisfying SQL statements. It is DB2's central component, in effect, its intelligence. The optimizer can be thought of as an expert system that incorporates the knowledge of the database administrator and system programmers and the expertise of many researchers into the science of database access. Catalog tables store knowledge about a database—the sizes of tables, the availability of indexes, and more. The optimizer processes an SQL statement in terms of that information to determine the possible access paths to the needed data. It then applies the experts' rules for determining relative costs of the various search options. This calculation yields an estimate of the least costly access path, which DB2 implements when it executes the statement.

An SQL statement to select information about suppliers in the S table (Fig. 12.1) that supply job 7 with fewer than 200 of any part would read like this:

```
SELECT SN, SNAME, STATUS, CITY, JN, QTY
FROM   S, SPJ
WHERE  S.SN = SPJ.SN
AND    JN   = 'J7'
AND    QTY  < 200
```

S (Supplier Table)

SN	SNAME	STATUS	CITY
S1	SMITH	20	LONDON
S2	JONES	10	PARIS
S3	BLAKE	30	PARIS
S4	CLARK	20	LONDON
S5	ADAMS	30	ATHENS

J (Job Table)

JN	JNAME	CITY
J1	SORTER	PARIS
J2	PUNCH	ROME
J3	READER	ATHENS
J4	CONSOLE	ATHENS
J5	COLLATOR	LONDON
J6	TERMINAL	OSLO
J7	TAPE	LONDON

P (Part Table)

PN	PNAME	COLOR	WEIGHT	CITY
P1	NUT	RED	12	LONDON
P2	BOLT	GREEN	17	PARIS
P3	SCREW	BLUE	17	ROME
P4	SCREW	RED	14	LONDON
P5	CAM	BLUE	12	PARIS
P6	COG	RED	19	LONDON

SPJ (Supplier/Part/Job Table)

SN	PN	JN	QTY
S1	P1	J1	200
S1	P1	J4	700
S2	P3	J1	400
S2	P3	J2	200
S2	P3	J3	200
S2	P3	J4	500
S2	P3	J5	600
S2	P3	J6	400
S2	P3	J7	800
S2	P5	J2	100
S3	P3	J1	200
S3	P4	J2	500
S4	P6	J3	300
S4	P6	J7	300
S5	P2	J2	200
S5	P2	J4	100
S5	P5	J5	500
S5	P5	J7	100
S5	P6	J2	200
S5	P1	J4	100
S5	P3	J4	200
S5	P4	J4	800
S5	P5	J4	400
S5	P6	J4	500

Fig. 12.1 Supplier, Job, Part, and Supplier/Part/Job tables

Box 12.1   Basic access paths available to the optimizer

- Index access using a matching index scan, nonmatching index scan, multiple index usage, IN (list) processing, and one-fetch index scan.
- Use of an index to avoid a sort.
- Asynchronus list prefetch after processing RIDs using single or multiple index processing.
- Tablespace or table scan using asynchronous prefetch.
- Nested loop, merge, or hybrid join and in various combinations for >2-way joins.
- Function evaluation at data retrieval time during final phase of a sort.

Several search strategies will fulfill that request. A DBMS might form the Cartesian product of the S and SPJ tables, creating a new virtual table with a row for every combination of rows from S and SPJ. Then it would search for rows including both J7 and quantities of fewer than 200. If the S table had as few as 1000 rows and SPJ had 10,000, a Cartesian product would have 10 million rows, making this type of search costly indeed—consequently the optimizer will never use this type of search when a large number of rows would result. A viable approach would be to perform a tablespace scan on SPJ, searching for rows with J7 and quantities fewer than 200, and to join those rows with the Supplier table on supplier number. If there were an index on job number, using it would provide a second, more efficient option. To choose the more efficient of the two viable searches, the optimizer would have to know the sizes of the tables and whether there was a useful index.

The catalog tables hold that kind of information. The optimizer would have to know what information to look for and how to evaluate it for any given statement. That knowledge is embodied in the optimizer's rules, many of which are formulas.

The optimizer's ability to find the most efficient path to the data needed to satisfy a request frees the user or programmer from having to know the database structure. In marked contrast, users and programmers accessing databases within hierarchical or network database management systems must be familiar with the relationships between records.

Fig. 12.2 shows a small portion of a network database. Pointers, instances of special data types within records, which are indicated by arrows in the figure, connect related records. To request information from the Em-

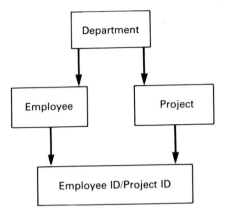

Fig. 12.2 Network database

ployee ID/Project ID records, the user must know that there are pointers to them from Employee and Project records. And the user must include that information in the request. This is called navigating through the database. When changes are made to the database's design, users and programmers must learn about them and will probably have to modify programs to navigate through the new routes.

DB2's optimizer, on the other hand, can detect changes to the database's physical design in catalog table descriptions and itself find a new access path for any SQL statement that requests information from the changed database. Indeed, the optimizer should do better than a programmer in efficiently accessing a database because it can store and apply more information about the database than most people are able to remember—and it can keep up to date with changes much more quickly and accurately than the most studious programmers.

Data Independence

The separation of the request for data from the need to specify its structure is called *data independence*. It has great practical value. Freed from concerns about access paths, programmers and users can work more quickly and effectively. Database administrators can change a database design without causing programmers to have to rewrite applications that access the database. And since design changes can be made easily, the database administrator can improve performance for applications by restructuring tables, adding or deleting indexes, and so on during the tuning process. DB2 developers are able to introduce new access techniques without requiring existing programs or queries to be changed.

Because the optimizer provides for data independence in a relational database management system and independence is of such great value, relational products are likely to compete to a large extent on the basis of their optimizers' capabilities. Ideally an optimizer chooses the best access path no matter how a user chooses to formulate a request. DB2's optimizer has not been perfected to the point where this is true in every case, but no other product's optimizer has reached that goal either. (A way to determine whether a database management system has a good optimizer is to find out whether it collects statistics for the optimizer's use. Then a simple test of the optimizer would be to order the predicates of a data request in several ways and observe response times for each formulation. If the optimizer is effective, in most cases, response times should not vary.) Researchers in a number of companies and universities are working on improving optimizers, and gains have and will continue to come steadily.

IBM guards information about how DB2's optimizer works quite closely. It is known, however, that DB2 grew out of earlier research, the System R project, about which much has been published. It is known that many of the principles on which System R operated have been retained in DB2. Information on the System R project, IBM's statements about DB2's optimizer, and information gleaned from the EXPLAIN command, which provides an explanation of the optimizer's access path choices (Chapter 13), provide the basis for this chapter.

Four Phases of Statement Processing

The optimizer contributes to statement processing in four steps:

1. Parsing checks that the statement is formulated correctly and breaks it down into the components upon which the optimizer bases its search strategy.

2. Optimization identifies the access path possibilities, estimates the cost of each, and selects for execution the one with the lowest cost. It also checks that the individual seeking to use the statement is authorized to perform its operations on the data that will be accessed.

3. Code generation produces machine code calls needed to execute the access path.

4. Execution includes additional authorization checks and communication between the plan or package and the components that perform the search.

All SQL data manipulation statements are processed the same with the exception of the INSERT statement. There is no optimization for an INSERT per se. An INSERT always uses the clustering index or if none is declared

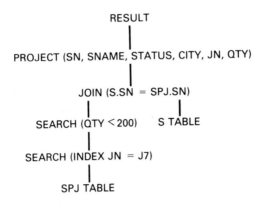

Fig. 12.3 Parse tree

the index with the lowest object ID to determine where a row is to be inserted. The SELECT, UPDATE, and DELETE statements go through a compile process (interpretative techniques are not used). We will look more closely at each of the four phases of the compilation process.

12.2 PARSING

Parsing analyzes an SQL statement much as a grammarian would analyze a natural-language sentence. The parsing process checks that the statement is syntactically and semantically correct and identifies the basic components that give the statement its meaning. The syntax check ensures that the statement exhibits the proper grammatical form for SQL. As a sentence must have a noun, verb, and period at the end, for example, an SQL statement must include certain keywords, commas between column names, and so on. The optimizer enforces these grammatical rules in the syntax check. In the semantic check, it sees that the statement's content is correct by verifying in the catalog tables that the referenced tables and columns exist.

The parsing process constructs a parse tree to identify the statement components that may be acted upon. An SQL statement parse tree is analogous to a parse tree a student might construct for a sentence. The tree branches down from the desired "RESULT" to the steps that must be performed to achieve it (Fig. 12.3). In effect, a separate search must be performed for each nested subselect and each part of a union operation. In most cases, when a statement includes subselects or unions, the optimizer constructs a separate section, called a *query block*, for each one.

12.3 OPTIMIZATION

During optimization, the optimizer decomposes, or breaks down, statements into elements it can operate on. It replaces any views used in a statement with their base table references, for example. It adds the view's tables and predicates to the parse tree and creates additional query blocks if the view includes subselects. It also decomposes predicates, recasting some to gain efficiencies. A WHERE clause might be coded as:

```
WHERE SPJ.PN = P.PN
AND   P.PN = 'P3'
```

If P3 is required from the P table, then P3 must also be required from the SPJ table based on the join predicate, SPJ.PN = P.PN. The optimizer will add the predicate AND SPJ.PN = 'P3' so that it can determine if narrowing the search on SPJ before the join will result in a more efficient access path. If the additional predicate does not provide a good access path, it will not be included in the plan or package to avoid incurring the CPU time at execution to evaluate an additional condition. If the developer had coded the additional predicate, it would be evaluated at execution time.

Some transformations done by the optimizer to improve performance can be quite sophisticated. Consider a composite index on SN, PN, and JN with the statement:

```
SELECT SN, PN, JN, QTY
FROM   SPJ
WHERE  SN = 'S5'
AND    (PN BETWEEN 'P1' AND 'P3'
OR     PN BETWEEN 'P6' AND 'P7')
```

The first thought would be that only a matching index scan can be done for SN = 'S5' with perhaps a scan of the leaf pages to narrow the search to the part numbers required, but in fact, the optimizer can transform the statement into:

```
SELECT SN, PN, JN, QTY
FROM   SPJ
WHERE  (SN = 'S5' AND PN BETWEEN 'P1' AND 'P3')
OR     (SN = 'S5' AND PN BETWEEN 'P6' AND 'P7')
```

This formulation provides for two matching index scans on two of the columns in the composite index with multiple index processing for the OR condition. Box 12.2 summarizes cases where the optimizer can automatically transform coded SQL to improve performance. The transformations will occur only if the same results will be achieved and under the conditions discussed in previous chapters.

After the optimizer reformulates the coded SQL, it then creates a tree

Box 12.2 Summary of cases where the optimizer can transform coded SQL to achieve a better access path

- NOT condition can be transformed to a positive expression.
- IN, =ALL, =ANY, =SOME subselect can be transformed in to a join.
- Equal and range predicates specified on one join table are added for the other join table such as:

```
WHERE TA.C1  = TB.C10
AND    TA.C1  > 10
AND    TB.C10 > 10 -- Added automatically by optimizer
```

- All join combinations are evaluated even though only some are coded (sometimes referred to as transitive closure) such as:

```
WHERE TA.C1   = TB.C10
AND    TB.C10  = TC.C100
AND    TC.C100 = TA.C1 -- Added automatically by optimizer
```

- Simple ORed predicates are converted to IN (list) when evaluating the use of a single index:

```
WHERE TA.C1 = 10
OR     TA.C1 = 30
```

Transformed to:

```
WHERE TA.C1 IN (10, 30)
```

- Columns can be reordered to avoid a sort.
- Predicates can be derived on the inner table of merge join to narrow the search if a sort is required on the outer table.
- Subselects are not processed as they appear:
  Subselects preceded with the operator IN, =ALL, =ANY, =SOME can be transformed to a join.
- Correlated subselect with simple operators (with or without not), EXISTS, and NOT EXISTS can use an in-memory table to minimize repeated scans of the inner table.
- Subselect preceded by a simple operator is evaluated as a simple predicate.
- Subselect preceded with a range predicate on ANY, SOME, ALL can be reduced to a single value and evaluated as a simple predicate.

of alternate access paths using these more efficient formulations. With the tree complete, the optimizer has the statement's information in the form it needs to develop an access path to satisfy the statement's request.

Before assessing the available access paths, the optimizer completes semantic and syntax checks for which it must obtain information from the catalog tables. These include verifying that the data types in the statement are compatible with the operations the statement will perform. The statement cannot ask that character strings be added, for example. It also checks that the individual performing the bind is authorized to perform the operations called for in the statement.

At the heart of the optimizer's work is its analysis of the catalog table's statistics describing the target tables and the index availability. The optimizer gains efficiencies from these analyses in a number of ways. For one simple example, a predicate will not be satisfied if either of the criteria combined with an AND operator is not satisfied. For the clause WHERE C1 = 10 AND C2 = 'ABC', it is more efficient to search the column that will narrow the search the most first since it may not be necessary to perform the second search at all. If 10 is not found in C1, there is no need to look for 'ABC' in C2. The optimizer will check for any indexes on C1 and C2 and compare their filter factors to determine which approach is likely to narrow the search the most or whether multiple indexes should be used.

An objective of the optimizer is to determine which predicate should be evaluated first at execution time. If a predicate disqualifies a row, additional predicates need not be evaluated. A boolean term predicate (simple or compound) is one where if the predicate is evaluated false, the entire WHERE clause is false. An example will illustrate the point:

```
SELECT C1, C2, C3, C4, C5
FROM    TA
WHERE   C1 = 10
AND    (C2 = 20
OR      C3 = 30)
```

The column C1 must have a value of 10 to qualify a row. If 10 is not in C1, the row does not qualify, and there is no need to test additional conditions and use additional CPU time. If single index processing is chosen, an index on C1 will be used first. It will be considered a boolean term predicate and a best matching predicate.

A predicate's filter factor (FF) estimates the percentage of a table's rows that will satisfy the query. The higher the FF, indicating that a higher percentage of rows will be returned, the less likely the optimizer will be to use an index. Much of the table will have to be read in any case. The smaller the FF, indicating that a relatively few rows must be found, the greater the

```
SYSIBM.SYSTABLES
CARD                     Number of rows in the table (cardinality)
NPAGES                   Number of pages that contain rows of the table
PCTPAGES                 Percentage of tablespace pages that contain rows of tables
EDPROC                   blank = EDITPROC not used

SYSIBM.SYSINDEXES
CLUSTERRATIO             Percent of rows in clustering sequence
CLUSTERED               Y if 95 percent of rows are in clustered sequence
FIRSTKEYCARD            Number of distinct values in indexed column
FULLKEYCARD            Number of distinct values in composite index
NLEAF                    Number of active leaf pages in the index
NLEVELS                 Number of levels in the index tree

SYSIBM.SYSCOLUMNS
COLCARD                  Number of distinct values in column
HIGH2KEY                Second highest value in the column (first 8 bytes)
LOW2KEY                 Second lowest value of the column (first 8 bytes)
FOREIGNKEY             B if bit data, S if SBCS data, M if mixed mode

SYSIBM.SYSTABLESPACE
NACTIVE                 Number of pages up to the high preformatted page

SYSIBM.SYSFIELDS
EXITPARM                Indexed value for 1 of 10 most frequently occurring value
                        (first column of a composite index)
EXITPARML              Percentage of rows * 100 that contain the value in EXITPARM
Most columns contain -1 until RUNSTATS is executed
```

Fig. 12.4 Statistics used by the optimizer

likelihood that the optimizer will consider an index efficient. The concept of the FF is similar to the usual notion of probability.

The statistics describe a number of facts about each table being accessed: the number of rows, the number of pages that contain rows, the number of distinct values in each indexed column, the second highest and second lowest values in each indexed column, information on the distribution of data, the cluster ratio of each index and more. (Fig. 12.4 lists catalog statistics that the optimizer uses.) When executed, the RUNSTATS utility obtains these statistics by performing a tablespace scan and analyzing the indexes. Most catalog statistics used by the optimizer can be updated with SQL, a somewhat risky activity we will discuss in Section 12.8. The optimizer uses the statistics in a number of formulas that estimate the costs of various search options. If RUNSTATS has not been executed, the optimizer uses default values in the calculations (see Fig. 12.5). It is impossible to overestimate the importance of executing RUNSTATS after data are loaded and before SQL statements are bound. One company found statements requiring more than 20 minutes in CPU time before RUNSTATS had been

- If RUNSTATS has not been executed,
    - Default statistics are used by the optimizer

SYSIBM.SYSTABLES

CARD	10,000
NPAGES	501 = CEILING (1 + CARD/20)
EDPROC	blank = EDITPROC not used

SYSIBM.SYSINDEXES

CLUSTERRATIO	0 (95% if CLUSTERED = Y)
CLUSTERED	Y (if CLUSTER used when index was created)
FIRSTKEYCARD	25
FULLKEYCARD	25
NLEAF	33.33 = CARD/300
NLEVELS	2

SYSIBM.SYSCOLUMNS

| COLCARD | 25 |
| FOREIGNKEY | S for SBCS data |

SYSIBM.SYSTABLESPACE

| NACTIVE | 501 = CEILING (1 + CARD/20) |

- Uniform distribution of data assumed

Fig. 12.5 Default statistics used if RUNSTATS not executed

executed on the tablespaces took only seconds after RUNSTATS was executed.

The Timeron

The cost of a search is a function of the number of I/O operations required to move pages from disk to main storage and the amount of processing that must be done to search those pages and manipulate the located rows. DB2 uses a number of formulas to determine the access path it will use. The following formula calculates a search cost estimate, called a *timeron*, for users' considerations:

$$Cost = (W1 * I/O) + (W2 * \text{processor cost})$$

W1 and W2 are weighting factors designed to give more or less importance to the I/O or processing costs. Those weighting factors are secret to IBM. Indeed there is speculation among outside observers that W1 is not used at all or that its value is 1, while W2 is 0.5, giving CPU costs only half the weight of those for I/O for most medium-sized processors. The processor weighting factor depends on the CPU model being used as determined from the MVS relative performance power SRM (system resource manager). The size of the bufferpool is also considered in determining the access path.

- FF is an estimate of the percent of rows that will qualify according to coded predicates

Predicate	FF/Formula
WHERE C1 = :HV WHERE C1 IS NULL WHERE C1 IN (:HV, :HV, . . .) WHERE C1 > = Value WHERE C1 > Value WHERE C1 < = Value WHERE C1 < Value WHERE C1 BETWEEN V1 AND V2	1 / COLCARD 1 / COLCARD Number of values in list / COLCARD (HIGH2KEY-Value) / (HIGH2KEY-LOW2KEY) (Value-LOW2KEY) / (HIGH2KEY-LOW2KEY) (High V-Low V) / (HIGH2KEY-LOW2KEY)

:HV = host variable or literal value
Value = V = literal value

Fig. 12.6 Basic FF formula

The CPU model and bufferpool size can differ on a production computer compared to a computer used for testing. If they do differ, the access path can be different in production and test environments.

The timeron is a unitless number that indicates only the search's relative cost. It can be found in the SQLCA (SQL communications area) in field SQERRD(4) as discussed in Chapter 9. QMF users see the timeron divided by 1000 for the chosen path prior to executing a search. The value of the QMF relative cost estimate will be discussed in Chapter 13.

Estimating I/O Costs

The optimizer estimates the number of I/O operations required for many of the possible access paths by using statistics describing the table to be searched in a formula specific to the type of search required. An important element in estimating the number of I/O is the FF, an estimate of the percentage of rows that will qualify as results. To determine the number of I/O needed, the FF is multiplied by the number of rows or pages in the table and adjusted using the cluster ratio of the index in many cases. Fig. 12.6 lists some of the FF formulas currently used by DB2. If the predicate calls for a search based on an equality and there is an index on the column being searched—WHERE PN = 'P4', for example—the FF equals 1 divided by the cardinality of the column, stored as FIRSTKEYCARD in the catalog table SYSIBM.SYSINDEXES. The term COLCARD is used when describing the optimizer and its formula. In fact, COLCARD, FIRST-KEYCARD, or FULLKEYCARD is used in the formula depending on the

COLCARD	BETWEEN, LIKE	>,>=,<,<=
>=100,000,000	3/100,000	1/10,000
>= 10,000,000	1/ 10,000	1/ 3,000
>= 1,000,000	3/ 10,000	1/ 1,000
>= 100,000	1/ 1,000	1/ 300
>= 10,000	3/ 1,000	1/ 100
>= 1,000	1/ 100	1/ 30
>= 100	3/ 100	1/ 10
< 100	1/ 10	1/ 3
-1	1/ 10	1/ 3

Fig. 12.7 Default FFs for range predicates and LIKE

type of index and the specific predicate. Figure 12.4 gives definitions for the cardinalities and HIGH2KEY and LOW2KEY. When the optimizer finds that RUNSTATS has not been executed or the COLCARD is less than 4, it uses a default FF of 1/25 for equal predicates. For range searches— those using the BETWEEN operator, for example—the current default FFs are summarized in Fig. 12.7. DB2 adjusts the FF formula as the COLCARD increases using a step function so that the FF decreases incrementally for larger table sizes. Since in general the lower the FF, the greater the likelihood the optimizer will choose an index, decreasing the default value as the cardinality and table size increases improves the chances of the optimizer choosing to use an index over a tablespace scan for larger tables.

After the FFs have been determined using formulas like those in Fig. 12.6 or the defaults for predicates in Fig. 12.7, they are multiplied by the number of rows or pages in the table in most cases. Additional factors are included in formulas to estimate the number of I/O that will be required. An example using the cluster ratio will demonstrate how this can be done. If the cluster ratio is zero (or less than 5 percent), a good estimate of the number of I/O is the FF multiplied by the number of rows in the table. Assuming an FF of 1/20 for an equal predicate on an indexed column with a cardinality of 20 and a table with 10,000 rows, the estimated number of I/O is 500. Recall from Chapter 6 where these figures are used to estimate the number of I/O required to find all the parts in Dallas that list prefetch would probably be used with such a low cardinality. List prefetch would reduce the number of I/O to the 200 pages occupied by the table. If the cluster ratio is 100 percent, it is a simple matter to multiply the FF by the number of pages in the table (.05 * 200) giving an estimate of 10 I/O. If the cluster ratio is 80 percent, however, it means that 80 percent of the rows are in sequence on the data pages and 20 percent are not. This can be factored into the formula by multiplying 80 percent by the 10 I/O that would be required if the cluster ratio were 100 percent and adding 20 percent multiplied by the 200 I/O that would be required if there was no clustering. This gives a more accurate estimate of 48 I/O (.80 * 10 + .20 * 200).

The optimizer factors in the use of multiple indexes for AND and OR conditions plus the cost of sorting the RIDs (row identifiers) and performing an intersection or union of the RIDs followed by list prefetch in its formula to determine a good access path. The optimizer will consider using list prefetch with a single index to avoid reading a page multiple times because of a low index cardinality or a skewed distribution of values in a column with a low cluster ratio index. If there is a skewed distribution and one of the top 10 occurring values is requested, the percent occurrence in SYSFIELDS (Fig. 12.4) can be used as the FF. Recall from Chapter 11 that the distribution statistics are used only for dynamic SQL and predicates with a literal to avoid run-time optimization.

If the OPTIMIZE FOR "n" ROWS clause is used, the FF formula and the formula to estimate the number of rows are not needed. The value specified for "n" is used as the estimated number of rows to be retrieved in some cases. Calculating the number of pages that will contain that number of rows is straightforward (floor (page size / row length) * "n"). It is still necessary, however, to factor in the cluster ratio, possible use of multiple indexes, whether list prefetch with a single index should be used, and so forth.

The calculated FFs are combined according to the boolean factors in the WHERE clause. Consider a WHERE clause with two predicates and the FFs noted after each predicate:

```
WHERE C1 = 10 -- FF = .05
AND   C2 = 90 -- FF = .20
```

It is estimated that 5 percent of the rows will have a value of 10 in C1 and 20 percent of the rows will have a value of 90 in C2. The WHERE clause requires that a row have both a value of 10 and 90 in columns C1 and C2. It is less likely that a row will meet both conditions than that it will meet either one of the conditions taken individually. This is taken into account by multiplying the two FFs for each of the predicates. Fig. 12.8 shows the formula as FF(P1) * FF(P2) for a WHERE clause with two predicates (P1 and P2).

Tablespace Scans

In estimating I/O costs, DB2 takes into consideration whether sequential or list prefetch can be used. Asynchronous prefetch allows multiple pages

WHERE Clause	Formula
WHERE P1 AND P2 WHERE P1 OR P2 WHERE NOT P1 WHERE C1 IN Subselect	FF(P1) * FF(P2) FF(P1) + FF(P2) − FF(P1) * FF(P2) 1 − FF(P1) Expected cardinality of subselect result divided by product of cardinalities of all relations in the subselect from list

P1 = Predicate expression
P2 = Predicate expression

Fig. 12.8 Formulas to combine FFs according to boolean factors

to be input to the bufferpool in a single operation. All I/O operations are controlled by execute channel programs (EXCPs). Usually only one page is transferred per EXCP. With sequential or list prefetch, up to 32 pages can be transferred for a single EXCP in response to an SQL statement that results in a tablespace scan or a nonmatching index scan. If the CLUSTER-RATIO is greater than 80 percent, prefetch may be used on the data pages as well as the leaf pages. For utility operations, up to 64 pages can be input for a single I/O. Bringing pages into the bufferpool in groups rather than individually saves considerable I/O time—a random page read takes about 16 ms, a prefetch about 1.5 ms using 3390 DASD. In addition, significantly less CPU time is required to initiate 1 I/O rather than 32 I/O. For prefetch to use these maximums—32 or 64 pages per I/O—the bufferpool must be 4 megabytes or larger. When the bufferpool is smaller, fewer pages will be prefetched.

The optimizer estimates the number of pages to be scanned based on the catalog values, NPAGES for segmented tablespace, and NACTIVE for nonsegmented tablespaces. If PCTPAGES (percent of tablespace pages that contain rows of the table) is low, the optimizer might choose to scan the leaf pages of an index with a high cluster ratio dipping down to the data pages for a nonsegmented tablespace. For segmented tablespaces, the space map pages will be used to pull off just those data pages that contain rows of the table being scanned. This avoids scanning pages without rows for the table—such as pages with deleted rows, free pages, or pages with rows from other tables in the case of nonsegmented tablespaces.

Processing Costs

The processing cost is a function of the number of calls between the data manager (DM), which processes pages from the bufferpool and performs

Box 12.3   Summary of stage 1 predicates

- Stage 1 predicates are of the form: WHERE C1 OP V1. The operator OP may be simple operator (such as $=$, $>$, $<$, and so on), IN a list of values, BETWEEN, LIKE, or testing for null.
- Data type and length of C1 and V1 must match.
- Predicates may be joined by boolean operators (AND, OR). OR is converted to IN a list of values where possible.
- Comparison of date/time data types are stage 1.
- Negated predicates are stage 1 but an index will not be used.
- The aggregates AVG, SUM, and COUNT are computed at stage 1 with some processing at stage 2 depending on the access path chosen.
- MIN and MAX can be satisfied at stage 1.
- The column preceding a noncorrelated subselect that returns a single value using $>$ALL, $>$ANY, and $>$SOME can be evaluated at stage 1.

most searches, and the relational data system (RDS), which handles more complex processes. The DM does all index processing and tablespace scans and applies all stage 1 predicates. A stage 1 predicate is by definition a predicate evaluated primarily by the DM. The qualifying columns and rows are then passed to the RDS, which applies all stage 2 predicates. A stage 2 predicate is by definition a predicate evaluated primarily by the RDS. Passing rows, column by column, from the DM to the RDS requires CPU cycles, about 0.005 ms per column. The more columns and rows that the DM must pass to the RDS to complete a search, therefore, the higher the processing cost will be. An important performance goal therefore is to formulate statements so that the DM can narrow as much of the search as possible, minimizing the number of rows that must be passed to the RDS and the path length—the number of instructions that must be executed.

If an SQL predicate requires RDS processing, DB2 will not use a matching index scan even if one would otherwise be available. Many stage 2 predicates applied by RDS require some mathematical calculation, data type conversion, or processing that only the RDS can perform. The RDS also does processing for joins, subselects that return multiple rows, and sorts after the DM has narrowed the search using stage 1 predicates.

The summary of stage 1 predicates in Box 12.3 is very similar to the summary of predicates that can use an index in Box 11.2. This is because the DM does all index processing. Notice that the summary of stage 2 predicates in Box 12.4 is very similar to the summary of predicates that cannot

Box 12.4   Summary of stage 2 predicates

- A predicate comparing different data types: WHERE C1 > 1.1 if C1 is an integer, for example.
- A predicate with an arithmetic condition: WHERE C1 + C2 > C3.
- A predicate with a scalar function including date/time functions and string functions.
- A subselect predicate using IN, =ALL, =ANY, =SOME. Some processing is done at stage 1.
- A subselect predicate using EXISTS or NOT EXISTS. An index cannot be used on an inner-table predicate. An index can be used on the inner-table "join" predicate.
- A correlated subselect. If inner select returns a single value and the select has already been evaluated for a given correlation value, the inner select will not have to be reevaluated if the outer select value is in the in-memory table.
- A predicate that joins a table with itself if correlation names for the table are not used.

use an index in Box 11.3. Some predicates, however, are evaluated partly at stage 1 and partly at stage 2 as noted in the summary.

Stage 1 and 2 Evaluation of a WHERE Clause

A WHERE clause can be evaluated partly at stage 1 and partly at stage 2. Consider a tablespace scan for a statement like:

```
SELECT C1, C2, C3, C4, C5, C6, C7, C8, C9, C10
FROM   TA
WHERE  C1 = 7689
AND    C2 > C2 + C3
```

Table TA has 10,000 rows. Each distinct value in C1 represents about 20 percent of the total. Assume the C2 value will exceed the C2 plus C3 values about 30 percent of the time. The C1 predicate is stage 1, which will result in the DM scanning 10,000 rows and passing 2000 rows to RDS. RDS will scan the 2000 rows and apply the stage 2 predicate on C2 after performing the addition of C2 and C3. The qualifying 600 rows will be returned to the user.

If the first predicate had been stage 2—had it been written WHERE C1 = 7689.0, for example—the DM would have had to pass all 10,000 rows to the RDS. The additional 8000 rows with 10 columns would increase the CPU time by about 400 ms (milliseconds)—8000 * 10 * 0.005 ms. Use of stage 1 predicates whenever possible improves performance because the DM filters out rows that otherwise would have to be passed to the RDS at the cost of CPU processing time.

Some predicates are evaluated at stage 1 or 2 depending on the processing required. An example will demonstrate this point.

```
SELECT SN, SUM(QTY)
FROM   SPJ
GROUP  BY SN
```

If an index can be used to avoid the sort for the GROUP BY, all predicates are stage 1, a single column function is used (not SUM(QTY + 10)), and the function is on the inner table of a join (if there is a join), the summation will be done by the DM. If these criteria are not met or a sort is required to satisfy the GROUP BY, the aggregate is computed during the final phases of the sort by the RDS. This example applies to the SUM, AVG, and COUNT aggregates.

Sequenced Answer Sets

Besides the calls between DM and RDS, any sorts the RDS must perform to satisfy a statement also contribute to the processing cost and are included in the estimate.

For operators that require rows to be returned in sequence—either the final answer set or an intermediate answer set—the optimizer estimates the cost of sorting the returned rows as opposed to using an available index to return them in order. The operators ORDER BY, GROUP BY, UNION, and DISTINCT require sequenced answer sets. A merge and hybrid join also requires that rows be in sequence either by pulling the rows off in sequence using the leaf pages of an index or by performing a sort. The optimizer includes an estimate of the costs for any required sorts in the CPU time estimate.

Also included when estimating the CPU time required is whether EDIT-PROC is being used to compress or encrypt the data and whether character conversion is required.

Referential Integrity Constraint Checking

In determining access paths, the optimizer does not consider any processing that may be necessary for referential integrity constraint checking. No code is added to a plan or package for referential integrity checking. The DM gets information about the constraints from the DBD (database descriptor) and performs all referential integrity processing using index only processing (assuming indexes have been created). This means that DB2 enforced referential integrity will usually outperform application enforced integrity. In other words, the path length is shorter for DB2 enforced integrity. It is not necessary for the processor to pass values to the RDS and the user address space for checking by the application program.

Choosing the Access Path

Before building a tree for each alternative access path, the optimizer eliminates obviously expensive paths, such as most of those that require formation of Cartesian products. The optimizer then estimates the costs of various access paths. The number of possible paths can be large.

Consider a statement requiring a join of three tables, each with four access paths that might satisfy the request (a path using any of three indexes or a tablespace scan). The four access paths could be used in 64 different ways (4 * 4 * 4). The joins might be performed in any one of six orders—Table A with Table B and the results with Table C, Table A with Table C and the results with Table B, and so on (3 * 2 * 1). Then three types of joins—nested loop, merge, or hybrid join—must be considered for each of the two join pairs (3 * 2). In this case, there are 3456 possible paths—(4 * 4 * 4) * (3 * 2 * 1) * (3 ** 2). Efficient optimization depends on the ability to recognize and eliminate early those access paths certain to be poor performers. The DB2 optimizer would discard a good many of these 3456 possibilities and analyze closely only some of them.

If a particularly good access path is discovered, the optimizer will discontinue the evaluation of alternative paths. For example, predicates on columns with a unique index (SN, PN, and JN) are the best access paths for:

```
SELECT SN, PN, JN, QTY
FROM    SPJ
WHERE   SN = 'S4'
AND     PN = 'P6'
AND     JN = 'J3'
AND     QTY = 300
```

An index on QTY will not be considered. A single matching index scan can be done on the unique index. It is considered the best matching index scan. The UNIQUERULE column in SYSINDEXES is checked for a value of "U" or "P" to determine if the index is unique. If the table cardinality is equal to the index cardinality, it was a unique index at the time that RUNSTATS was executed. The optimizer cannot assume that the index will be unique, however, when the SQL is executed and does not consider it a best matching index scan. Chapter 14 has a SELECT statement that will identify potentially unique indexes. The developer should verify that the columns will always contain unique values and create a unique index to insure the best performance.

12.4 CODE GENERATION

After calculating the estimated costs of the access path possibilities, the optimizer selects the low-cost estimate and builds from the access path tree the application plan or package for the search in Access Specification Language (ASL). It then generates from the ASL the machine-language calls needed to execute the plan or package. The generation process uses code structures—prewritten code for possible processes—and adds structures particular to the statement. Commonly used structures are stored in the RDS and called from the plan or package.

12.5 EXECUTION

When a dynamic SQL statement is entered through SPUFI, QMF, or a user-written application, DB2 builds and executes an application plan immediately in working storage, where it is bound. It is not saved. If an SQL statement is embedded in a host-language program, the optimizer stores information about the application plan or package in the catalog tables and the plan and package itself in the directory for retrieval at execution time.

When static SQL is used, at execution time, DB2 checks an authorization table (SYSIBM.SYSPLANAUTH or SYSIBM.SYSPACKAUTH) to ensure that the individual attempting to execute the plan or package is cleared to do so. DB2 also checks the catalog tables to be sure the application plan or package is still valid—that is, that all necessary objects are still available. If the privilege to manipulate the objects in the plan or package has been revoked from the plan or package's owner or if a dependent object has been dropped, DB2 attempts an automatic rebind.

Application plans and packages consist of machine code, most of it calls to code in RDS, to satisfy all of a host-language program's SQL statements. DB2 usually brings only part of the application plan or package from the directory via BP0 into the environmental descriptor manager (EDM) memory pool at any one time. The EDM communicates the instructions for carrying out a search to the RDS, which works with the DM in fulfilling the request (Fig. 12.9). When a thread is established between the application program and DB2, DB2 brings in the header portion of the application plan and the package containing control information. Only

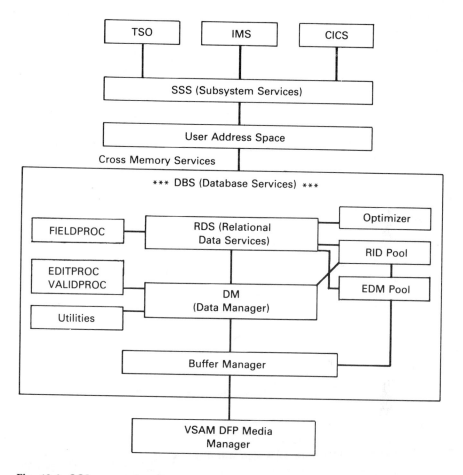

Fig. 12.9 SQL processing flow

when the program calls for a particular statement to be executed does DB2 move the plan or package section for it into the EDM pool. DB2 first looks for a needed section in the EDM pool. If it is not there, the EDM manager checks for it in the bufferpool before it is read from the directory. Since a program will not always execute all of its SQL statements, this arrangement saves I/O, processor time, and memory.

Fig. 12.9 shows the relationship between RDS and DM in the database services address space (DBAS), where most database operations are performed. Threads are established between the DBAS and each interactive user or host-language program through systems services address space (SSAS). The RDS and DM also interface with any EDITPROC, FIELD-

PROC, or VALIDPROC routines related to tables being accessed. Physical I/O is initiated by the buffer manager, which interfaces to the VSAM DFP (data facility product) media manager that actually issues the physical I/O. DM applies stage 1 predicates to the data and index pages brought in the bufferpool.

DB2's utilities for loading data, backing them up, and so on have been designed to work directly with the DM, avoiding the need to work through RDS. This saves processing time compared with user-written code as will be seen in Chapter 16.

12.6 THRESHOLDS APPLIED AT BIND AND EXECUTION TIME

Thresholds are applied at bind time to determine if a particular access path will result in good performance, depending on the resources made available to DB2. If the resources are already used at execution time, further thresholds are applied to avoid using an access path that requires resources already in use.

List Prefetch Thresholds Applied at Bind Time

The RID pool is used to sort the RIDs and eliminate duplicates before using list prefetch for multiple and single index processing as is discussed in Chapter 11. The size of the RID pool influences the optimizer as to whether list prefetch will be chosen as an access path and whether it will be implemented at execution time. The default size of the RID pool is 2172K. The amount of space in the RID pool allocated initially for a RID sort is calculated as 40 K multiplied by CTHREAD (create thread maximum is 30 by default with a maximum of 2000). Additional space is taken in 4K blocks (16K) for the RID sort. If, during processing of the RIDs, there is insufficient space, the RID sort expands in the RID pool depending on the sum of BP0, BP1, BP2, and BP32 with a maximum size of 200M to avoid an individual RID sort taking excessive space.

The optimizer will not choose list prefetch at bind time if it estimates that sufficient resources may not be available at execution time. If more than 125,000 RIDs are estimated to qualify using list prefetch with a single index or multiple indexes, list prefetch will not be chosen as an access path assuming a default BP0 size of 4M. The threshold applied at bind time is based on several factors and can be considerably more than 125,000 RIDs, depending primarily on the size of the bufferpools. The maximum number of RIDs that can be processed can be estimated as:

125,000 = 1,000,000 / (4-byte RID + 4 bytes control data)

The value of 1 million is 50 percent of 2M, which is 50 percent of default BP0 of 4M. If a larger RID pool is required, an unused bufferpool (for example, BP1) can be defined as, say, 2M, which will allow the RID sort to go into an additional 1M of the RID pool and, in this example, allow for processing twice as many RIDs. Basically the estimated number of RIDs times 8 cannot exceed 50 percent of the RID pool, which can be up to 50 percent of sum of bufferpools. (The initial size of 40K * CTHREAD, maximum of 200M, and sum of all bufferpools are not included to simplify the example.)

Increasing the amount of space in the RID pool for a user sort will encourage the optimizer to use list prefetch as might be desired for a batch job processing a large number of rows. Recall the case in Chapter 11 where the CPU time was reduced from 2 hours and 40 minutes to 1 minute through the use of multiple index processing with list prefetch. It is dangerous, however, to increase the amount of space allowed for a RID sort artificially by defining an unused bufferpool. It can encourage the optimizer to choose list prefetch for an online transaction that executes during a time of high RID pool usage and causes other transactions to degrade in performance due to the unavailability of space.

Thresholds at Execution Time

The systems administrator needs to monitor the use of the RID pool closely. If there is insufficient space in the pool at execution time, even though the optimizer requested list prefetch, it will not be used or its use will be discontinued after processing the indexes and perhaps after starting the sort of the RIDs. The accounting statistics found in SMF 101 record type provides counts on the number of times list prefetch was executed successfully, the number of times it was requested by the optimizer but no storage was available at execution time, and the number of times list prefetch was started but was canceled due to limits being exceeded.

Recall from Chapter 11 that if more than 25 percent of the RIDs qualify using ORed predicates, list prefetch will be changed to sequential prefetch at execution time. If less than 32 RIDs qualify using some but not all ANDed predicates, the additional indexes chosen by the optimizer will not be used since the search has already been narrowed to a point where one I/O can be issued to bring the 32 pages into the bufferpool.

The optimizer indicates whether sequential prefetch *should* be used. The decision about whether it *is* used is made by the buffer manager at execution time. It will use prefetch if more than 10 percent of the bufferpool pages are marked stealable—another good argument for using a large bufferpool.

Although not an execution time threshold per se, recall from Chapter 9 that sequential detection is used to initiate dynamic prefetch at execution time even though prefetch was not requested by the optimizer. Indeed sequential prefetch can be dynamically turned on and off, depending on the number of pages found to be in sequence at execution. If five pages contained qualifying rows within the last 8 pages, dynamic prefetch is activated. If five pages do not contain qualifying rows within the last 8 pages, dynamic prefetch is deactivated. (These types of thresholds are frequently adjusted by DB2 developers from one release to another.) Also the value used in a string search with a LIKE predicate is evaluated at execution time to determine if a matching or nonmatching index scan should be used.

12.7 STATISTICAL INTERDEPENDENCE OF COLUMNS

The optimizer's FF equations for statements selecting rows based on the values in a composite index assume that the distribution of values in the different columns are statistically independent—that the distribution of values in one column is unrelated to the distribution of values in another. Very often this is not the case. For example, if some suppliers specialize in certain types of parts, the distribution of SN values and PN values in the SPJ table can be very different from what would be expected if both columns exhibited uniform distribution of values and the distributions were independent of each other. (IBM manuals call interdependent columns correlated columns.)

Recall that the distribution of values is considered for predicates using a literal and dynamic SQL in terms of the percent of occurrence of the top 10 occurring values. The distribution statistics are not used for host variables and are collected for only the first column of the composite index, which may not be representative of the entire composite index. The following example assumes that the first column is not representative and that host variables are used in the predicates, resulting in the optimizer assuming a uniform distribution of values.

This statement using the COUNT operator yields the frequency with which each combination of a composite index on SN and PN value is distributed:

```
SELECT SN, PN, COUNT(*)
FROM   SPJ
GROUP  BY SN, PN
ORDER  BY 3 DESC
```

	P1	P2	P3	P4	P5	P6	Total
S1	2000	0	0	0	0	0	2000
S2	0	0	7000	0	1000	0	8000
S3	0	0	1000	1000	0	0	2000
S4	0	0	0	0	0	2000	2000
S5	1000	2000	1000	1000	3000	2000	10000
Total	3000	2000	9000	2000	4000	4000	24000

a

	P1	P2	P3	P4	P5	P6	Total
S1	.083	0	0	0	0	0	.083
S2	0	0	.292	0	.042	0	.333
S3	0	0	.042	.042	0	0	.083
S4	0	0	0	0	0	.083	.083
S5	.042	.083	.042	.042	.125	.083	.417
Total	.125	.083	.375	.083	.167	.167	1.000

b

Fig. 12.10 Joint distribution of values

If the assumption of uniform and independent distributions were true, the results would show each SN/PN combination occurring about the same number of times. But suppose DB2 returns these results:

```
SN PN COUNT
S2 P3 7000
S5 P5 3000
S5 P6 2000
S5 P2 2000
S4 P6 2000
S1 P1 2000
S5 P4 1000
S5 P3 1000
S5 P1 1000
S3 P4 1000
S3 P3 1000
S2 P5 1000
```

Rearranging this data into a matrix like that in Fig. 12.10a gives a clearer indication of the distribution of the various pairs of values. It shows that PN values are unevenly distributed, with the most frequently occurring value being P3. The SN values are also skewed, with S2 being the most frequent. Now, by dividing each occurrence of a combination by 24,000, which is the total number of rows, we obtain the percentage of rows that will be returned for a statement whose search criteria specifies the combination, for example:

```
SELECT SN, PN, QTY
FROM   SPJ
WHERE  SN = 'S2'
AND    PN = 'P3'
```

The matrix in Figure 12.9b shows those percentages. The optimizer would use a formula like the following to estimate the FF for any combination of values. (The factors for adjusting for the cluster ratio are not included to simplify the example.)

```
FF = FF(P1) * FF(P2)
```

The FF for the SN column would be 1 divided by SN's cardinality, or 1/5. The FF for the PN column would be 1 divided by PN's cardinality, or 1/6. Therefore, the statement's FF would be 1/5 * 1/6, or .033. Notice the differences between this estimate of the percentage of returned rows for any combination and the actual percentages shown in Fig. 12.10b. In cases where the difference is great, such as that for the S2, P3 combination, the optimizer's access path choice based on the estimate may be inefficient. The .033 FF would likely cause DB2 to use a composite index on SN and PN in all searches based on a combination of those values. But the developer may not want the index to be used for the more frequently occurring combinations such as S2-P3.

This example of interdependent columns in a composite index with a skewed distribution of values is a combination of the problems of dealing with interdependent predicates and a skewed distribution of values as was discussed in Chapter 11. Most of the techniques for dealing with the two problems do not apply in this example since the problems exist together. We might want the optimizer to use indexes on SN and PN for all the AND queries other than the S2 or P3 combination, which would probably be more efficiently located with a tablespace scan.

The following pseudo-code illustrates how to force a tablespace scan for searches of SN and PN values of S2 or P3 and let the optimizer select the access path for the others:

```
IF :SN = 'S2' AND :PN = 'P3'
   SELECT SN, PN, QTY
   FROM   SPJ
   WHERE (SN = :SN or 0 = 1)
   AND   (PN = :PN or 0 = 1)
ELSE
   SELECT SN, PN, QTY
   FROM   SPJ
   WHERE  SN = :SN
   AND    PN = :PN
```

For the first SELECT, program logic following the SELECT would have to discard the relatively few rows that do not include S2 and P3. Again, data independence has been lost. The technique discussed in Chapter 11 of selecting the distribution statistics from the catalog tables or a copy of the statistics would be useful provided that the leading column of the composite index is representative of the distribution.

12.8 FOOLING THE OPTIMIZER

There are times when application developers believe that they know more about the characteristics of the data than is available to the optimizer. They would like to influence or force a specified access path, thinking that it would result in improved performance over the access path chosen by the optimizer. This is possible by updating the statistics used by the optimizer. The primary benefit of updating the statistics, however, is to allow for simulating large production tables in a test environment using small test tables and for capacity planning. All statistics can be updated with the exception of the 10 most frequently occurring values and their percent of occurrence. The rows describing the distribution statistics can be deleted using the MODIFY utility. For example, the rows describing the CITY column distribution in the S table will be deleted from SYSFIELDS by:

```
MODIFY STATISTICS TABLE (AUTHID.S)
              COLUMN (CITY)
              DELETE NONUNIFORM
```

Correcting for Outliers

When a column includes a few extremely high and low values, the optimizer may inaccurately estimate the proportion of rows included in a range—and make the improper choice about whether to use an index to find values in that range. For example, the optimizer uses a formula like the following to determine the FF for a statement requiring a *greater than* search of a column's upper range:

```
FF = (HIGH2KEY - V1) / (HIGH2KEY - LOW2KEY)
```

The value V1 setting the range's high point (for example, WEIGHT 900). HIGH2KEY is the second highest value in the column; LOW2KEY, the second lowest. DB2's developers used the column's second highest and second lowest values in the formula rather than highest and lowest values to eliminate extreme values that are not representative of the distribution of values and nulls. Sometimes that correction is not enough to give a true picture of the column.

Consider a WEIGHT column in the Part table in which almost all parts have a weight of between 100 and 1000 pounds. RUNSTATS has found, however, a HIGH2KEY of 8000 and a LOW2KEY of 10.

Assume there are frequent searches of the Part table for parts weighing more than 900 pounds. The optimizer would calculate the FF for that search as follows:

```
FF = (8000 - 900) / (8000 - 10) = .89
```

This indicates that 89 percent of the rows would satisfy the search and the optimizer would probably not choose to use an index to find them. However, we know that the extreme values found by RUNSTATS for HIGH2-KEY AND LOW2KEY provide a distorted view of the column. By updating those values to 1000 and 100 respectively, we can change the optimizer's calculation for the range search:

```
FF = (1000 - 900) / (1000 - 10) = .10
```

With this FF, indicating only 11 percent of the rows will be returned, the optimizer would very likely choose to use a clustering index or perhaps a nonclustering index using list prefetch to avoid processing pages more than once. One major problem with this technique is that it would be effective only for predicates using literals and dynamic SQL and would not be needed if distribution statistics are collected. Recall that default FFs are used for range predicates when host variables are used.

Forcing an Access Path

It is necessary to have a great deal of information in order to force an access path. An indepth understanding of how the optimizer chooses an access path is required, not a trivial task as has been seen in this chapter. What values should be used to cause the desired access path? How will the data be processed by a large number of programs in the application system and by casual users for ad hoc processing? If catalog statistics are updated directly with an UPDATE statement, RUNSTATS cannot be executed since it replaces the updated values or the values will have to be updated after each execution of RUNSTATS.

Consider the following statement and statistics. Which index should the optimizer choose to use?

```
SELECT SN, PN, QTY
FROM   SPJ
WHERE  JN  = 'J1'
AND    QTY < 20000
```

Relevant statistics:

SPJ has 10,000 rows on 100 pages

JN has an index with 50 unique values

QTY has a clustering index with 6000 unique values

QTY has a LOW2KEY of 10,000 and a HIGH2KEY of 40,000

Most developers will think that using the index on JN would provide the best access path since an equal predicate is specified, and they will be tempted to force the use of the index by setting the index cardinality approximately equal to the cardinality of the table:

```
UPDATE SYSIBM.SYSINDEXES
SET FIRSTKEYCARD = 10000
WHERE NAME    = 'JNINDEX'
AND   TBNAME  = 'S'
AND   CREATOR = 'POSYSTEM'
```

But before using the update, let us take a closer look at the statistics, FF calculations, and estimate I/O to the data pages:

1.   The JN FF estimates that 2 percent (1/50 = 0.02) of the rows would qualify, requiring 100 I/O plus a sort of the RIDs for list prefetch or 200 (0.02 * 10,000 rows) if list prefetch is not used.

2.   100 I/O would be required for a tablespace scan since there are 100 pages (The estimates are not divided by 32 since sequential or list prefetch can be used in all three cases).

3.   The QTY FF would estimate that 34 percent (ceiling (20,000 − 10,000) / (40,000 − 10,000) = 0.333) of the pages with rows in sequence on QTY with a clustered index would require 34 I/O (0.34 * 100 pages) and no sort is required.

The calculations indicate that the QTY index would require significantly fewer I/O than would using the JN index. The point is that what appears initially to be a good access path may not be, or even if it did result in a better access path for a specific statement, it may cause a poor access path for other SQL statements in the many application programs.

The Peril of Tampering with Statistics

Developers tempted to fool the optimizer should consider a number of important issues. First is the danger of suboptimization. By inducing the optimizer to choose a better path for one statement, one may be forcing it to choose a poor path for other statements. One way of avoiding that problem is to modify the statistics, bind the application plan or package with the desired path, and reset the statistics to their original values. Such an approach is hazardous since any automatic rebind will use the current statistics. (A better approach is to use the OPTIMIZE FOR 1 ROW clause, which will make it very likely that an index will be used in many cases. Even this approach, however, has many of the hazards discussed below.)

Another danger is that the situation that prompted the modification in catalog statistics may change over time. Changes to the data's characteristics from updates and insertions can turn what was once a good access path into a poor performer. And changes in the way an organization uses a table can also make a good access path decision look bad. The developer's optimization choices that seemed proper when a table was used solely for batch programs may not appear so when the organization gives users access to the table for online transactions and ad hoc queries. In addition, application developers may add or drop indexes and the DB2 developers are likely to add new access strategies and continue to enhance the optimizer, which could not be taken advantage of when "fooling" the optimizer.

The choice to modify the statistics can produce an administrative nightmare. The organization would have to set up controls for the execution of RUNSTATS to avoid undoing the alterations. Careful documentation would be required to explain why values were chosen. Bound plans would have to be reviewed periodically to determine that the rationale for the statistics used when they were bound continues to hold. Finally all decisions to fool the optimizer would have to be reexamined with each new release of DB2 containing changes in the optimizer's algorithms and default values.

The optimizer is almost always the best judge of access paths and, although it may sometimes be tempting to "fool" the optimizer by changing the statistics, doing so will rarely be worth the cost.

12.9 SIMULATING PRODUCTION DATA IN A TEST ENVIRONMENT

Frequently small tables are used in a test environment even though the tables will be large in a production environment. This is done to avoid using an excessive amount of DASD space while testing programs. An alternative to loading full production data during testing is to update the statistics to be like what is expected in the production data. The challenge is determining the statistics that should be used for the updates. One approach is to estimate the statistics based on a knowledge of the data. Interviews of the business professionals for whom the application system is being developed will provide some information. They will have a good idea of the number of rows in the tables, and the number of pages can be calculated without much difficulty. But the cardinality of the columns, particularly of those that are indexed, is very important but not so easily estimated. In addition, the distribution of values in terms of the second highest and lowest values, the top 10 occurring values, and their percent occurrence is difficult to estimate.

An alternative that will provide more representative test data is to take a sample of the data that will be used in the production environment. It is very likely that the data already exists on DASD or tape as used by previous application systems, and it will be necessary to extract it when the system is migrated to production. Writing the extract programs early provides for taking a sample of the data to be used during testing of the new DB2 programs. A 10 percent sample is a good target.

The optimizer would in most cases choose the same access path for a 100,000 row table as it would for a similar 1-million row table if the indexed columns in each have about the same distribution of values. The index cluster ratios should contain typical values. A cluster ratio of 100 percent will probably not exist most of the time when tables are being updated and reorganized periodically. The test table should be loaded with data that closely matches the COLCARD, FIRSTKEYCARD, and FULLKEYCARD of the data in the production table. If index cardinality cannot be reproduced exactly (if the large production table has an index with a large number of distinct values), the cardinality of the test table indexes should be proportionate to the table size. For example, if a 1-million row production table has 10,000 distinct values, a 100,000 row test table might have 1000 distinct values, maintaining the 10 to 1 ratio. The developers should try to have the test table's distribution of values match that of the production table's; that is, if each SN value occurs ten times for every PN value in the production table, the test data should show the same relationship. If a skewed distribution of values will exist in a column in the production data, then the skewed distribution should be proportionate in the test data. Finally each column's distribution of values as reflected by the top 10 occurring values and the second highest and second lowest values in the test table should correspond to the production table.

One way to develop a test table with the same statistical characteristics as the production table is to select rows from the production table at random. Numbers between zero and one from a random number generator can be multiplied times the number of rows in the table to extract rows to be included in the test table's sample. For example, in a 1-million row table, if the random number generates .835722, the production table's 835,722nd row should be included in the test table (.835722 * 1,000,000). A simple pseudo-random number formula to generate numbers between zero and one is to take the remainder of a value divided by a prime number. If it is difficult, time consuming, or resource intensive to process the data using the random number, you might simply use every tenth row from the production table.

The access paths chosen by the optimizer for the test tables will be very similar in a 10 percent sample of large tables. The EXPLAIN command can be used to determine the access path that will give a good indication of the performance of the SQL when using the large production tables. The elapsed time used by a test program particularly when using a tablespace scan will not be the same. The cost of a tablespace and nonmatching index scan go up linearly, however, as the size of the table increases. If a scan of 100,000 rows requires one minute, a scan of 1 million rows will require about ten minutes.

Testing is much simpler if the production tables already exist. Then the catalog statistics for the production data can be used to update the catalog for the test tables. This means that large tables for testing or maintenance do not have to be maintained for an application system to be phased into use. Even though the test table may be very small, the optimizer will choose the same access path for it as for the larger production table if their statistics match.

It is very important to have representative test data or statistics in the catalog table. If test data is not representative of production data, test performance will not be representative of production performance.

12.10   CAPACITY PLANNING

Capacity planning requires an estimate of the CPU time and the I/O operations required. Before these estimates can be made, it is necessary to have a great deal of information on how the data will be processed and the actual SQL that will be used. Formulas for estimating the CPU time are given in Fig. 12.11, and those for estimating the I/O time are in Fig. 12.12. Elapsed time is frequently the maximum between the CPU and I/O times. The factors used in the formulas are based on tests done by IBM on a 3090-180S using V2.2. More detailed information is available from the manual, *Capacity Planning for DB2 Applications (GG24-3512).*

It can be seen from the formulas that extensive information is required on the type of processing that will be performed, the indexes, the table sizes, and the number of rows expected to qualify. Even with this detailed information, the estimates depend on many factors including the computer model and DASD used, the workload anticipated, and the bufferpool size and use.

Software companies offer packages to calculate the I/O and CPU cost based on formulas similar to those in Fig. 12.11 and 12.12. These software

- Factors based on 3090-180S timings with 1 engine using V2.2
  - Assume simple predicates since predicate evaluation time is ignored
- Matching clustering and nonclustering index with data access
  - I/O drive time will be more for low cluster ratio index since more pages will need to be read

    - CPU ms = (0.1818 + (0.005 * NC)) * NRQ + (NDMS * 0.0182) + I/O drive time

- Matching clustering and nonclustering index without data access
  - Applies to scan of all leaf pages with NIQ = all entries

    - CPU ms = (0.1818 + (0.005 * NIC)) * NIQ + (NDMS * 0.0121) + I/O drive time

- Index ANDing

    - Total CPU ms   = Ix-only access + RID sort + AND/OR comp + Data access
    - Ix-only Scans = SUM(0.3030 + (0.1212*NP) + (0.0054*NRIDS) + I/O Drive)
    - RID Sort   = 0.0121 * NRIDT
    - AND/OR comp   = 0.0038 * number of AND/OR comparisons
    - Data access   = 0.1515*NDP + (0.1878 + 0.0051 * NC) * NRQ + I/O Drive

- Tablespace Scan
  - The time to return the qualifying rows is 0.1272 ms per row qualified.

    - CPU ms = (0.1515 + (0.005 * NC)) * NRQ + (NR*0.0121) + I/O drive time

- ORDER BY sort (plus cost of obtaining result set)
  - Formula assumes no merges required for sort

    - CPU ms   = Sort cost + FETCH overhead
    - SORT cost = 3.94 + (0.1078 + (0.0036 * NC)) * NRQ
    - FETCH cost = (0.0545 + (0.0021 * NC)) * NRQ

Fig. 12.11 Formulas for estimating CPU time

packages avoid the time required to do the calculations or to develop a program to perform the calculations. But in any case, a great deal of information about the application system processing is required, and the estimates are only as good as the estimates of the processing anticipated.

Rule-of-Thumb Estimates

Fig. 12.13 gives a rough estimate of CPU time in ms by statement type. These rule-of-thumb estimates are based on the same tests and carry the

- ### Unique index matching index scan without data access
  - I/O ms = (((KL+6) * NDMS) / ((1-0.nn) * 4K) * 2ms

- ### Nonunique index matching index without data access
  - I/O ms = ((4 * NDMS) / ((1-0.nn) * 4K) * 2 ms

- ### Matching clustering index with data access
  - Above index estimate plus data I/O = NDP * 2 ms

- ### Matching nonclustering index with data access
  - If < =2 pages, assume no list prefetch
  - I/O ms = 20 ms * (1 + (1 or 2))

- ### If >2 pages, assume list prefetch
  - I/O ms = (2*20 ms) +MIN(NRQ,NPT) * 2 or 10 ms if low cluster ratio index

- ### Index ANDing
  - Total cost = Data cost + SUM (index costs)
  - Data cost = MIN (NRQ,NPT) * 2 msec or 10 ms
  - Index cost = NLP * 2 ms
  - MLP   = ((KL + 6) * NDMS) / ((1-0.nn) * 4K)

- ### Tablespace scan
  - I/O ms = NPT * 2 ms

- ### Legend
  - CPU ms = CPU time in milliseconds
  - I/O ms = I/O time in milliseconds
  - nn   = Percent free space allocated
  - KL   = Key length
  - NIC   = Number of index columns retrieved
  - NIQ   = Number of index entries qualifed
  - NC   = Number of columns selected
  - NDMS   = Number of rows or index entries scanned
  - NDP   = Number of data pages accessed
  - NLP   = Number of leaf pages
  - NP   = Number of pages accessed in each index
  - NPT   = Number of pages in the table
  - NRIDS = Qualifying RIDs form each index scan
  - NRIDT = Sum of (qualifying RIDs from each index scan)
  - NR   = Number of rows in the tablespace
  - NRQ   = Number of rows qualifying (from index ANDing)

Fig. 12.12 Formulas for estimating I/O time

Operation	Indexes	Cost
Select	1	1.1
Index only	1	0.9
Open cursor (+ repositioning)	–	0.15
Fetch (average/row)	1	0.22
Close cursor	–	0.15
Commit with read only	–	1.0
Commit with update (+ I/O to log)	–	1.8
Insert	0	1.0
	1	1.6
	2	2.3
Delete, no cursor	1	2.1
	2	2.8
Update, no cursor	1	2.4
(2 columns updated)	2	3.3
Sort with fetch	–	0.5
Sort	–	0.3
Sort with hardware assist	–	0.1
Create/terminate thread	–	4.0

Fig. 12.13 Rule-of-thumb estimates

same warnings as do the formulas for estimating CPU and I/O time. Examples will demonstrate how to interpret the figures. A select of one row using an index required 1.1 ms of CPU time, and when the select could be satisfied without access to a data page, the time was reduced to 0.9 ms. Notice that the cost of an insert goes up significantly as the number of indexes increases. An insert with no index requires 1.0 ms; with one index, the time goes up by about 50 percent to 1.6 ms; and with two indexes, the time goes up to 2.3 ms. The cost of a delete without a cursor is similar to that for an insert, which indicates that the index had a high index cardinality. A rough estimate of the cost of sorts is 0.3 ms per result row sorted. A computer with a sort hardware assist reduces the time by one-third to 0.1 ms.

In addition to estimating the cost for each SQL statement, it is necessary to consider the cost of establishing a thread, which is 4.0 ms in the test case with execution authority granted to the public.

12.11 SUMMARY

The original architecture of the optimizer as was developed in System R is sound and is being enhanced with each version and release of DB2. It has been seen that many factors are considered in the formula and a number of rules are applied. The cluster ratio is considered for all indexes. Sequential prefetch is considered for tablespace and nonmatching index scans and list prefetch is considered with single and multiple index usage. The distribution of data is used in determining the access path for dynamic SQL and predicates with literals. The optimizer can reformulate SQL statements in a number of cases for improved performance. Thresholds are applied at bind and execution time to provide good performance across many SQL statements that will be executing with different workloads. It is advisable to reserve modifying statistics used by the optimizer for test data and capacity planning. The next chapter will provide information on how to determine the access path chosen by the optimizer using EXPLAIN.

EXERCISES

12.1. What is the purpose of statement parsing?

12.2. What elements go into determining the cost of satisfying an SQL request? How does the optimizer estimate them?

12.3. Why is it important to execute RUNSTATS after data have been loaded?

12.4. How does the optimizer estimate access costs if the catalog tables do not contain statistics on a table being accessed?

12.5. For static SQL, when is the code for a statement loaded from the directory into the EDM pool?

13

The EXPLAIN Command

13.1 INTRODUCTION

Developers and administrators can obtain information about the optimizer's choices for access paths in three ways: (1) They may get an indication of an SQL statement's relative cost from the timeron value; (2) they may query the catalog tables that store information about application plans and packages; and (3) they may use the EXPLAIN statement to instruct the optimizer to describe its chosen access path for a given statement. All of these methods provide information that helps developers design more efficient databases and formulate more efficient SQL statements.

The developer can use the three methods together to analyze and modify database design and SQL statements. An unusually high timeron displayed by QMF might spur a developer to look more closely at the formulation of the SQL statement. The catalog tables provide overview information about all of the statements in a program. The catalog tables SYSPLANDEP and SYSPACKDEP, for example, list all the indexes used by a program's application plan and packages. It does not relate the index usage to particular statements, however. The EXPLAIN command does provide detailed, specific access path information about particular statements. A developer might query SYSPLANDEP and SYSPACKDEP to determine which indexes are and are not being used by plans and packages in an application system. If an index is not used or is seldom used, it might be dropped.

Chapter 14 discusses how to use the catalog tables for monitoring and tuning. This chapter describes how to use the EXPLAIN command.

13.2 REQUESTING THE EXPLANATION

The developer can request, through an option in the DB2I bind panel or with a DSN processor bind or rebind command, that DB2 explain the optimizer's access path choices for all embedded statements in a program. The explanations are presented in a table named PLAN_TABLE. On the bind panel, the developer enters YES for the EXPLAIN option. With DSN, the developer enters EXPLAIN (YES) on the bind command. The request for explanations may also be made when an application plan or package is rebound. If the explanations were already requested at the initial bind or rebind time, however, DB2 will provide them each time the plan or package is rebound without the developer's having to ask for them again.

Developers may want to track decisions made by the optimizer each time DB2 automatically rebinds an application plan and package in production by retaining the EXPLAIN option when moving the application program to production. Tracking will make the automatic rebinds a bit more costly, but the cost may be worthwhile if the explanations indicate changes in the optimizer's access path choices that might affect performance.

A developer can also request an explanation for an interactive statement under SPUFI or QMF by including an EXPLAIN command immediately before the statement. The same command can also be used with individual dynamic SQL statements embedded in host-language programs. The command may take several forms. The basic formulation is EXPLAIN PLAN FOR. The developer will want to have DB2 append an identifying number to the explanation with the formulation EXPLAIN PLAN SET QUERYNO = N FOR, using the numeral N as the identifier. The QUERYNO identification helps a developer keep track of access paths for different statements within a program and for different SQL formulations of the same request. A third formulation of the EXPLAIN command, EXPLAIN ALL FOR, produces the same results as the basic statement and seems meant for use with a future enhancement to the command. Such future explanations may include filter factors (FFs), estimates of the number of rows to be returned or updated, and other information about referenced columns and table structures.

If the request for explanations is made via the bind command, the precompiler automatically assigns a sequence number to each line of the program. The sequence number beside the SQL statement in the precompiler output (USERID.TEMP.PCLIST as discussed in Chapter 10) will be seen as the QUERYNO in the PLAN_TABLE. A technique for associating the

rows in the plan table with the SQL statement explained is to select from
SYSSTMT:

```
SELECT NAME, PLNAME, PLCREATOR,
    SEQNO, STMNO, SECTNO, TEXT
FROM   SYSIBM.SYSSTMT
WHERE  NAME = 'PL1'
```

The text for SQL statements in a package can be obtained like:

```
SELECT NAME, PKNAME, PKCREATOR,
    SEQNO, STMNO, SECTNO, TEXT
FROM   SYSIBM.SYSPACKSTMT
WHERE  NAME    = 'PK1'
AND    COLLID  = 'UNITEST'
AND    VERSION = 'V1'
```

NAME in the predicate is the name of the DBRM member being explained. STMTNO will match the QUERYNO in the plan table. TEXT will
contain an image of the SQL statement for which the explanation applies.
The reports on SYSSTMT and SYSPACKSTMT along with the plan table
report will aid in analyzing the explanation of a number of SQL statements
in a program.

13.3 PREPARATION FOR EXPLAIN

DB2 responds to an EXPLAIN request by placing information about the
optimizer's choices in a plan table created by the individual who makes the
request. That is, there must be a table, called PLAN_TABLE, created under the AUTHID used by the individual requesting the explanation. A
PLAN_TABLE can be shared among a project team by using a secondary
AUTHID. This makes it more difficult to manage and interpret the results,
however. The plan table includes a column for each piece of information
DB2 provides about a plan and package as well as a column for the QUE-
RYNO and a VARCHAR column that the developer can use for remarks.
This column can be used to record the actual SQL statement to which an
explanation refers. After the EXPLAIN request, optionally an UPDATE
statement sets the character values of the SQL statement being studied as
the REMARKS column's value. For example, the following statement requests an explanation of a simple query:

```
EXPLAIN PLAN SET QUERYNO = 1 FOR
SELECT SN, SNAME
FROM   S
WHERE  CITY = 'DALLAS'
```

This UPDATE statement will include the query itself in the REMARKS column of the explanation:

```
UPDATE PLAN_TABLE SET REMARKS =
'SELECT SN, SNAME
 FROM   S
 WHERE  CITY    = DALLAS'
 WHERE  QUERYNO  = 1
 AND    QBLOCKNO = 1
 AND    PLANNO   = 1
```

The UPDATE statement's predicates limit the REMARKS entry to one row in the explanation with a maximum length of 254 bytes.

The plan table will have a row for each step needed to fulfill the statement's request. There will be one or more rows for each query block in a statement, with each subselect or part of a UNION requiring a query block. For each query block, there will be a row for each table accessed and for any additional sort that must be performed to complete a request. Fig. 13.1 shows the CREATE statement for the plan table that must be executed before EXPLAIN can be used.

The developer wanting to use the EXPLAIN facility must create a table with the exact columns shown, either by keying it in or copying it from the sample library provided with DB2 (outprefix.DSNSAMP(DSNTESC)). Another technique for creating the table is ask a friend for SELECT privileges on their PLAN_TABLE and use the LIKE parameter to create the table in your tablespace and database:

```
CREATE TABLE PLAN_TABLE LIKE FRIEND.PLAN_TABLE
  IN DAGKWDB.DAGKWTSP;
```

Additional columns can be added with the ALTER statement. Since DB2 will not automatically enter information in any additional columns when it fills the plan table, those columns should be declared as allowing nulls or NOT NULL WITH DEFAULT. This will avoid an error when DB2 attempts to insert a row in the plan table.

Fig. 13.2 lists brief explanations of the information provided in each column. Several of the columns are particularly useful in monitoring table and index usage and tuning the design:

- The QBLOCKNO indicates a separate statement section, frequently a subselect or union, requiring a query block. Rows containing the same QBLOCKNO apply to the same subselect. Nested subselects are numbered in order, beginning with 1 as the top level and descending, but are not executed in QBLOCKNO sequence in most cases.

- The PLANNO value indicates which step within a query block the row

```
CREATE TABLE PLAN_TABLE
(QUERYNO           INTEGER      NOT NULL,
 QBLOCKNO          SMALLINT     NOT NULL,
 APPLNAME          CHAR(8)      NOT NULL,
 PROGNAME          CHAR(8)      NOT NULL,
 PLANNO            SMALLINT     NOT NULL,
 METHOD            SMALLINT     NOT NULL,
 CREATOR           CHAR(8)      NOT NULL,
 TNAME             CHAR(18)     NOT NULL,
 TABNO             SMALLINT     NOT NULL,
 ACCESSTYPE        CHAR(2)      NOT NULL,
 MATCHCOLS         SMALLINT     NOT NULL,
 ACCESSCREATOR     CHAR(8)      NOT NULL,
 ACCESSNAME        CHAR(18)     NOT NULL,
 INDEXONLY         CHAR(1)      NOT NULL,
 SORTN_UNIQ        CHAR(1)      NOT NULL,
 SORTN_JOIN        CHAR(1)      NOT NULL,
 SORTN_ORDERBY     CHAR(1)      NOT NULL,
 SORTN_GROUPBY     CHAR(1)      NOT NULL,
 SORTC_UNIQ        CHAR(1)      NOT NULL,
 SORTC_JOIN        CHAR(1)      NOT NULL,
 SORTC_ORDERBY     CHAR(1)      NOT NULL,
 SORTC_GROUPBY     CHAR(1)      NOT NULL,
 TSLOCKMODE        CHAR(3)      NOT NULL,
 TIMESTAMP         CHAR(16)     NOT NULL,
 REMARKS           VARCHAR(254) NOT NULL,
 PREFETCH          CHAR(1)      NOT. NULL,
 COLUMN_FN_EVAL    CHAR(1)      NOT NULL,
 MIXOPSEQ          SMALLINT     NOT NULL,
 VERSION           VARCHAR(64)  NOT NULL,
 COLLID            CHAR(18)     NOT NULL)
   IN DAGKWDB.DAGKWTSP;
```

Fig. 13.1 CREATE PLAN_TABLE

describes. The developer refers to PLANNO to determine the order of steps, which also indicates the order in which the tables are accessed in many but not in all cases.

- The METHOD codes indicate the access strategy: 0 indicates that the table specified in the row is the first accessed; 1 indicates the step uses a nested-loop join; 2, a merge join; and 4, a hybrid join; and 3 indicates an additional sort is required to satisfy the request, frequently to satisfy an ORDER BY clause.

- The PREFETCH value indicates whether sequential prefetch or list prefetch is to be used.

- The ACCESSTYPE values indicate whether a tablespace scan or index will be used to access the data. An index can be used singularly or in combination with other indexes, or a one-fetch index scan can be used.

Report	Column	Explanation
QN	QUERYNO	Set QUERYNO = N on EXPLAIN or assigned by DB2
QBN	QBLOCKNO	A number indicating a subselect or union block
–	APPLNAME	Name of application plan or blank for dynamic SQL
–	PROGNAME	Name of DBRM or blank for dynamic SQL
PN	PLANNO	Number of step where QBLOCKNO is processed
		Each new table accessed has a new step
MET	METHOD	0, first table accessed
		1, nested loop join (inner table)
		2, merge join (inner table)
		3, additional sorts needed
		4, hybrid join
–	CREATOR	Creator of the table accessed in the plan step
TNAME	TNAME	Name of the table accessed in the plan step
–	TABNO	Distinguishes different references to a table
PRE	PREFETCH	S, sequential prefetch
		L, list prefetch
		, (blank), no prefetch or unknown
AT	ACCESSTYPE	I, index scan
		I1, one-fetch index scan
		R, tablespace scan
		N, IN list of values, index access
		M, multi index scans, followed by MX, MI, or MU
		MX, one of many index scans
		MI, intersection of multiple indexes
		MU, union of multiple indexes
		, (blank) insert or update/delete where curretof
MC	MATCHCOLS	Number of matched columns
–	ACCESSCREATOR	Creator of the index
IXNAME	ACCESSNAME	Name of index if AT = I, I1, N, MX
IXO	INDEXONLY	Y, If no data access
MX	MIXOPSEQ	n,3,2,1,0 Step sequence for access type MX/MI/MU
CEV	COLUMN_FN_EVAL	R, evaluation at data retrieval time
		S, evaluation during sort
		, (blank), stage 2, at sort time or unknown
U	SORTN_UNIQ	Y, sort on new table to remove duplicate rows
J	SORTN_JOIN	Y, sort on new table for method 2 (merge join)
O	SORTN_ORDERBY	Y, sort on new table for ORDER BY
G	SORTN_GROUPBY	Y, sort on new table for GROUP BY
U	SORTC_UNIQ	Y, sort on composite to remove duplicate rows
J	SORTC_JOIN	Y, sort on composite for method 2 (merge join)
O	SORTC_ORDERBY	Y, sort on composite for ORDER BY
G	SORTC_GROUPBY	Y, sort on composite for GROUP BY
TSL	TSLOCKMODE	Tablespace lock used
–	TIMESTAMP	YYYYMMDDHHMMSSTH when EXPLAIN was processed
–	REMARKS	Can be used by developers
–	VESION	Package version identifier
–	COLLID	Package collection identifier

Fig. 13.2 PLAN_TABLE Explanation

- The ACCESSNAME value identifies any index used by the row's plan step.

- The MIXOPSEQ column is used for multiple index processing. This column will contain a sequence number indicating the step for access types MX, MI, and MU. These indicate, respectively, whether the row is for one of many index scans, the intersection of multiple indexes, or the union of multiple indexes. The sequence number of zero is the last step of the multiple index processing.

- The COLUMN_FN_EVAL value indicates whether the function evaluation is done during data retrieval (R) or during a sort (S), and a blank indicates the processing is to be decided at run time. This indicator is frequently used with the functions of MIN, MAX, AVG, SUM, and COUNT.

- The SORTN and SORTC columns explain the reasons for the sort or sorts performed for the step. The SORTN columns refer to rows retrieved directly from a base table; the SORTC columns refer to rows in an intermediate answer set created as part of the statement's processing. Each column represents a particular reason for a sort: UNIQUE if it is to remove duplicates for a union or a distinct specification, JOIN if it is to allow for a merge join, ORDERBY to order the results, and GROUPBY to perform a GROUP BY process. A "Y" in a column indicates the reason a sort is required by the step described in that row.

- The TSLOCKMODE column provides codes indicating the type of table or tablespace lock the step requires: X for exclusive, SIX for share intent exclusive, IX for intent exclusive, S for share, IS for intent share, and U for update.

13.4 ANALYZING THE PLAN TABLE

The information in the plan table can point a developer toward a number of performance improvements. If the plan table indicates that the statement requires sorts, for example, the developer might explore the effects of a new index that might make the sorts unnecessary. If the plan table shows that an index designed for use in processing particular statements has not been used, the developer might consider dropping the index to save the cost of maintaining it or investigating why the optimizer has not chosen to use the index. The TSLOCKMODE column will indicate when a plan is using unexpected and inappropriate table or tablespace locking, pointing the developer toward an investigation of the cause. And a developer can accumulate a history of explanations in the plan table to explore the implications

Box 13.1 Plan table analyses and resulting actions

Developers can use the plan table to determine:

- Type of index scan used.
- Use of multiple indexes.
- Plans that do not use an index.
- Use of sequential or list prefetch.
- Plans that require a sort.
- The table or tablespace lock type.

As a result of a plan table analysis, the developer may want to:

- Create indexes.
- Drop indexes not being used.
- Restructure tables.
- Reformulate SQL statements.
- Change isolation levels.
- Reorganize indexes or tables, execute RUNSTATS, and rebind plans and packages.

of changes to a statement's formulation, to the table or index design, and to the optimizer with a new release. DB2 may choose to use an index in response to one of several equivalent statements but not the others, for example, and a series of explanations will uncover the difference.

Another valuable approach is to accumulate explanations for all plans and packages in an application system to allow developers to determine the overall impact of dropping or creating indexes or restructuring the table designs. Some companies find it worthwhile to use EXPLAIN to evaluate applications systems and tools offered by third-party vendors. This allows a company to determine the access paths that the programs will use and thus their probable performance without investing in a full benchmark test.

Remote unit of work packages can be explained. The rows will be inserted into the plan table at the remote site.

Interactive versus Embedded SQL

When using interactive SQL to analyze statements that will be embedded in a host language, the developer should keep in mind that the optimizer's choices may differ for the two types of execution. For range searches and searches of a column with a skewed distribution, for example, the optimizer may choose a different access path for a statement using host variables in the search criteria than for one in which the criteria are set by literals. This is because the optimizer has no way of knowing at bind time what the variable's value will be since it has not been provided by the user and will vary from one user execution to another. Consequently if the developer uses known values in the interactive statement, the optimizer may choose to use an index that it would not use for the comparable embedded statement or the opposite.

One way to compensate for the differences is to use a parameter marker, a question mark indicating an unknown value, in place of values in the interactive statement. Consider interactive execution of the following examples:

```
SELECT SN, PN, JN, QTY
FROM   SPJ
WHERE  QTY > ?
```

and

```
SELECT SN, PN, JN, QTY
FROM   SPJ
WHERE  QTY > 10
```

Of the two examples, the optimizer's access path selection for the first should more closely approximate what its choice would be for the comparable embedded statement that uses a host variable to set the QTY criteria value.

Selecting from the Plan Table

The developer selects information from the plan table as from any other table. Many developers find it convenient to order the returned rows by QUERYNO, QBLOCKNO, PLANNO, and MIXOPSEQ. If the plan and packages are explained repeatedly during testing or if explain is left on in production to tract rebinds, adding the TIMESTAMP column on the ORDER BY clause will group the rows for a single execution of explain. The SELECT statement can use the QUERYNO column to limit the returned rows to specific statements explained. If no QUERYNO values are specified in the predicate, all the rows in the plan table will be returned.

While developers will sometimes find it useful to select only one or two columns from the plan table—to check the names of tables accessed or indexes used—usually they will want to see most of the plan explanation in order to relate its various elements. Because the table is relatively large, the developer may want to use QMF to reformat the report so that it fits easily on a screen. An alternative when using SPUFI is to create a view with narrow column names and eliminate columns that are not essential:

```
CREATE VIEW PLAN_VIEW
  (QN,QBN,PN,MET,TNAME,PRE,AT,MC,IXNAME,
   IXO,MX,CEV,U,J,O,G,UC,JC,OC,GC,TSL,REMARKS) AS
SELECT QUERYNO,QBLOCKNO,PLANNO,METHOD,TNAME, PREFETCH,
  ACCESSTYPE,MATCHCOLS,ACCESSNAME,INDEXONLY,
  MIXOPSEQ,COLUMN_FN_EVAL,SORTN_UNIQ, SORTN_JOIN,
  SORTN_ORDERBY,SORTN_GROUPBY,SORTC_UNIQ,
  SORTC_JOIN,SORTC_ORDERBY, SORTC_GROUPBY,
  TSLOCKMODE,REMARKS
FROM PLAN_TABLE;
```

The following example shows a reformatted report. Fig. 13.2 shows the correspondence between the column names used in the report and PLAN_TABLE.

Here is a simple query including an explain request followed by a SELECT statement for retrieving the resulting explanation:

```
EXPLAIN PLAN SET QUERYNO = 1 FOR
SELECT SN, SNAME
FROM   S
WHERE  CITY = 'DALLAS'

SELECT *
FROM   PLAN_VIEW
ORDER BY QN, QBN, PN, MX
```

The formatted report might look like this:

QN	QBN	PN	MET	TNAME	PRE	AT	MC	IXNAME	IXO	MX	CEV	U	J	O	G	U	J	O	G	TSL
1	1	1	0	S	L	I	1	CITYX	N	0		N	N	N	N	N	N	N	N	IS

The AT column value, which represents the ACCESSTYPE value from PLAN_TABLE, indicates that the optimizer has chosen an index scan. The IXNAME column, which stands for the ACCESSNAME column in PLAN_TABLE, gives the name of the index, CITYX. The MC value, for MATCHCOLS, of greater than zero shows that the scan is a matching index scan. An MC value of zero would indicate a nonmatching scan; a value of more than one indicates the number of columns in a composite index being used in the matching scan. The IXO, for INDEXONLY, value of N, for no, means that the scan does not retrieve values from only the index but must also access the data pages. A Y, for yes, would indicate the request is being satisfied without the need to access data pages.

13.5 SAMPLE EXPLANATIONS

The following sample plan table reports illustrate particular types of explanations.

Use of Multiple Indexes and List Prefetch

This select statement can use multiple indexes. DB2 will use list prefetch after performing an intersection of the RIDs from the city and status indexes, sorting the RIDs, and eliminating duplicates.

```
EXPLAIN PLAN SET QUERYNO = 1 FOR
SELECT SN, SNAME
FROM   S
WHERE  CITY   = 'DALLAS'
AND    STATUS = 10
```

QN	QBN	PN	MET	TNAME	PRE	AT	MC	IXNAME	IXO	MX	CEV	U	J	O	G	U	J	O	G	TSL
1	1	1	0	S	L	M	0		N	0		N	N	N	N	N	N	N	N	IS
1	1	1	0	S		MX	1	CITYX	Y	1		N	N	N	N	N	N	N	N	IS
1	1	1	0	S		MX	1	STATUX	Y	2		N	N	N	N	N	N	N	N	IS
1	1	1	0	S		MI	0		N	3		N	N	N	N	N	N	N	N	IS

PRE = L in the first row shows that list prefetch can be used and AT = M indicates that multiple indexes will be used. AT = MX in the second row indicates that the CITYX index will be used in the multiple index operation (MX = 1). The third row indicates that the STATUX index will be used in the multiple index operation (AT = MX, MX = 2). The CITYX and STATUX indexes are processed serially. The last row indicates that an intersection of the RIDs (row identifiers) will be performed after sorting the RIDs and eliminating duplicates (AT = MI, MX = 3). Notice that RID sort is not explicitly shown in the plan table and will not be shown any time list prefetch is used. The sort is implicit in list prefetch. An exception is when the RIDs are sorted for a hybrid join.

A Sort

The developer seeks an explanation for the following statement, which has encountered long response times:

```
EXPLAIN PLAN SET QUERYNO = 1 FOR
SELECT  SN, PN, JN, QTY
FROM    SPJ
```

```
WHERE    QTY BETWEEN 100 AND 300
ORDER BY QTY;
```

The same PLAN_TABLE SELECT statement and QMF format as were used in the previous example return this report:

QN	QBN	PN	MET	TNAME	PRE	AT	MC	IXNAME	IXO	MX	CEV	U	J	O	G	U	J	O	G	TSL
1	1	1	0	SPJ	S	R	0		N	0		N	N	N	N	N	N	N	N	IS
1	1	2	3				0		N	0		N	N	N	N	N	N	Y	N	IS

The AT code, R, indicates that a tablespace scan is used to find the rows. A Y in O, which represents the SORTN_ORDERBY column from the plan table, indicates that DB2 performs a sort to satisfy the ORDER BY command. If the tablespace and answer set are large, both processes can be very time consuming. The developer decides to create a clustering index on QTY in the SPJ table and runs the statement again, setting the QUERYNO to 1 in the EXPLAIN command, and in the SELECT against the plan table. The report now reads:

QN	QBN	PN	MET	TNAME	PRE	AT	MC	IXNAME	IXO	MX	CEV	U	J	O	G	U	J	O	G	TSL
1	1	1	0	SPJ	L	I	1	QTYX	N	0		N	N	N	N	N	N	N	N	IS
1	1	2	3						N	0		N	N	N	N	N	N	Y	N	IS

The AT value, I, and MC value, 1, indicate that a matching index scan will be used on the new index, QTYX, now indicated in the IXNAME column. EXPLAIN does not explicitly indicate that a scan of the leaf pages follows the matching index scan, but this can be deduced based on the fact that a BETWEEN predicate is used and list prefetch (PRE = L) is being used. Still a sort of the data is required because list prefetch is used, which requires a sort of the RIDs. The sort of the RIDs is not explicitly specified in the plan table but can be deduced based on the knowledge that list prefetch by definition requires a sort of the RIDs. Once the RIDs are sorted, it is highly unlikely that the rows on the pages will be in sequence. This would be true only if the cluster ratio is 100 percent each time the statement is executed. Therefore if the rows must be in a sequence, they must be sorted in most cases.

It is decided that the sort of the RIDs and rows is not acceptable. The index on QTY is dropped and recreated as a clustering index followed by a reorganization of the data to get the rows in sequence, execution of RUN-

STATS so the optimizer knows about the clustering index, and a reexecution of EXPLAIN.

QN	QBN	PN	MET	TNAME	PRE	AT	MC	IXNAME	IXO	MX	CEV	U	J	O	G	U	J	O	G	TSL
1	1	1		SPJ		I	1	QTYX	N	0		N	N	N	N	N	N	N	N	IS

The clustering index is being used to avoid a sort of the data and no sort of the RIDs is required. Clearly this is the better of the three access paths. These three examples demonstrate how performance can be improved in an iterative fashion by varying factors and checking the effect using EX-PLAIN. The index on a quantity column is unlikely in a table, but it does demonstrate the point using the SPJ database.

A Join

The explanation for a statement including a join provides particularly important information, including the type of join and whether sorts are required. This statement, to locate suppliers that both supply parts and have offices in Dallas, as well as the name and quantity of those parts, requires a three-way join:

```
EXPLAIN PLAN SET QUERYNO = 1 FOR
SELECT S.SN, P.PN, QTY, S.CITY
FROM    S, P, SPJ
WHERE   S.CITY = 'DALLAS'
AND     S.SN   = SPJ.SN
AND     P.CITY = S.CITY
```

The explain table will look like this:

QN	QBN	PN	MET	TNAME	PRE	AT	MC	IXNAME	IXO	MX	CEV	U	J	O	G	U	J	O	G	TSL
1	1	1	0	S	L	I	1	SCITYX	N	0		N	N	N	N	N	N	N	N	IS
1	1	2	1	SPJ	L	I	1	SPJX	N	0		N	N	N	N	N	N	N	N	IS
1	1	3	2	P	L	I	1	PCITYX	N	0		N	Y	N	N	N	N	N	N	IS

Step PN 1 shows that the optimizer has chosen to use a matching scan of the SCITYX index on the S table to identify suppliers in Dallas (AT = I, MC = 1, IXNAME = SCITYX). In the next step, it uses a matching scan of the SPJX index (AT = I, MC = 1, IXNAME = SPJX) to find the SPJ table rows for the supplier, say S4, identified from a data page in step

1. The MET value of 1 in the step PN 2 row indicates that DB2 will perform a nested-loop join to find the matches. That the plan accesses the S table first (MET = 0 in the PN 1 row) indicates that DB2 will use the rows returned from PN 1 as the join's outer table.

The explanation's third row shows that the use of an index on the P table (AT = I) to find rows using the PCITYX index after adding a predicate P.CITY = 'DALLAS'. Step 3 also includes a sort of the rows from this scan (J = Y) in order to perform a merge join (MET = 2) of the two sets. The table beside the MET = 2 is the inner table in the merge join.

Implicit Predicates and Transformations

In certain situations, the optimizer will determine that an SQL statement with a different formulation than the one being executed would provide the same results more efficiently, as discussed in Chapter 11. In those cases, it will create a plan or package for the more efficient formulation and indicate the change in the explanation.

For example, this subselect to determine parts that are used on jobs results in the following explanation when there is no unique index on PN in the Part table:

```
EXPLAIN PLAN SET QUERYNO = 1 FOR
SELECT SN, PN, JN, QTY
FROM   SPJ
WHERE  PN IN
   (SELECT PN
    FROM   P)
```

QN	QBN	PN	MET	TNAME	PRE	AT	MC	IXNAME	IXO	MX	CEV	U	J	O	G	U	J	O	G	TSL
1	1	1	0	SPJ	S	R	0		N	0		N	N	N	N	N	N	N	N	IS
1	2	1	0	P	S	I	0	PNX	Y	0		N	N	N	N	N	N	N	N	IS
1	2	2	3				0		N	0		N	N	N	N	Y	N	Y	N	

Notice that QN = 2, QBN = 2, and PN = 2 indicates that two sorts are performed. This is somewhat misleading. Actually one sort of the subselect results is done for two reasons—to eliminate duplicates and to sequence the results for more efficient processing. An attempt is made to find a match for each PN in SPJ in the sorted subselect work area during a tablespace scan of SPJ. When a match is found, the search can stop since the subselect values are in sequence and fewer values need to be searched since duplicates are eliminated in the subselect work area.

If there is a unique index on the primary key in the Part table, the optimizer will automatically transform the subselect to a join and the explanation would look like this:

QN	QBN	PN	MET	TNAME	PRE	AT	MC	IXNAME	IXO	MX	CEV	U	J	O	G	U	J	O	G	TSL
1	1	1	0	SPJ	S	R	0		N			N	N	N	N	N	N	N	N	IS
1	1	2	1	P		I	1	PNX	Y			N	N	N	N	N	N	N	N	IS

A nested-loop join is frequently used with this type of automatic transformation with the original outer select table as the outer table in the join. Recall that if the unique index is dropped, the plan or package will be marked as invalid and an automatic rebind will occur the next time the plan or package is accessed and no transformation is possible. If a NOT IN subselect is used, it cannot be transformed to a join.

Another type of modification done by the optimizer occurs when an equal predicate is specified on one of the tables to be joined but not on the other table. The optimizer will automatically add the additional equal predicate when choosing the access path as was discussed in Chapter 11.

For example, the statement for the following join specifies that the search will be limited according to SN in the SPJ table:

```
EXPLAIN PLAN SET QUERYNO = 1 FOR
SELECT S.SN, SNAME, PN, QTY
FROM    SPJ, S
WHERE   S.SN   = SPJ.SN
AND     SPJ.SN = 'S2'
```

In selecting the join's inner table, however, the optimizer may decide it is more efficient to limit the search by SN in the S table, an equivalent approach. In that case, it would choose an access path as if the statement had been formulated as follows:

```
EXPLAIN PLAN SET QUERYNO = 1 FOR
SELECT S.SN, SNAME, PN, QTY
FROM    SPJ, S
WHERE   S.SN = SPJ.SN
AND     S.SN = 'S2'
```

The plan table might look like this:

QN	QBN	PN	MET	TNAME	PRE	AT	MC	IXNAME	IXO	MX	CEV	U	J	O	G	U	J	O	G	TSL
1	1	1	0	S		I	1	SNX	N	0		N	N	N	N	N	N	N	N	IS
1	1	2	2	SPJ	L	I	1	SPJX	N	0		N	Y	N	N	N	N	N	N	IS

Notice that in step PN 1 the explanation shows that the optimizer has chosen to access the S table first, indicating it is using the "S2" rows from that table as the outer table in the merge join, even though the original statement does not appear to require such a step. Also notice that a sort is not required on the S table even though it is a merge join. The optimizer has recognized that the index is unique on SN and that the equal predicate (AND S.SN = 'S2') added will qualify only one row. There is no need to sort one qualifying row. The same principle applies to range predicates. If only SPJ.SN > 'S2' had been specified as the predicate, the optimizer would automatically add the predicate S.SN > 'S2'.

There is a sort required for the SPJ table as indicated on the second line that it is assumed will not give acceptable performance. It is decided to create a clustering index to avoid the sort and execute EXPLAIN to insure that the sort is avoided:

QN	QBN	PN	MET	TNAME	PRE	AT	MC	IXNAME	IXO	MX	CEV	U	J	O	G	U	J	O	G	TSL
1	1	1	0	SPJ	L	I	1	SPJX	N	0		N	N	N	N	N	N	N	N	IS
1	1	2	2	S		I	1	SNX	N	0		N	N	N	N	N	N	N	N	IS

The creation of the clustering index on SPJ is indeed used to avoid the join sort. In addition, the SPJ has become the outer table for the merge join.

Testing for Existence

Generally, correlated subselects are poor performers. There are situations, however, when correlated subselects, particularly those using EXISTS or NOT EXISTS, perform better than do the alternatives, as the EXPLAIN example below shows.

Consider the following comparisons of tests for referential integrity violations, one using a NOT EXISTS subselect, the other a NOT IN subselect. In the example, Supplier and Parts tables, SN in the SPJ table is a foreign key to the S table. Therefore any SN value in SPJ must have a corresponding value in S. The following statement will test for that condition:

```
EXPLAIN PLAN SET QUERYNO = 1 FOR
SELECT *
FROM   SPJ
WHERE  NOT EXISTS
   (SELECT S.SN
    FROM   S
    WHERE  S.SN = SPJ.SN)
```

The equivalent statement using NOT IN is as follows:

```
EXPLAIN PLAN SET QUERYNO = 2 FOR
SELECT *
FROM    SPJ
WHERE   SN NOT IN
   (SELECT SN
    FROM    S)
```

Again if any rows are returned, the tables violate referential integrity.

QN	QBN	PN	MET	TNAME	PRE	AT	MC	IXNAME	IXO	MX	CEV	U	J	O	G	U	J	O	G	TSL
1	1	1	0	SPJ	S	R	0		N	0		N	N	N	N	N	N	N	N	IS
1	2	1	0	S		I	1	SNX	Y	0		N	N	N	N	N	N	N	N	IS
2	1	1	0	SPJ	S	R	0		N	0		N	N	N	N	N	N	N	N	IS
2	2	1	0	S	S	I	0	SNX	Y	0		N	N	N	N	N	N	N	N	IS
2	2	2	3				0		N	0		N	N	N	N	Y	N	Y	N	IS

Notice that DB2 used a matching index scan on SN for the NOT EX-ISTS formulation. Not noted in the plan table report is the fact that index lookaside and sequential detection can be used to activate dynamic prefetch on the leaf pages. A nonmatching scan is used for the NOT IN formulation plus a sort is required on the SNs returned from the inner select. Even though there are two sorts indicated (U = Y, O = Y), only one is performed but for two reasons: to eliminate duplicates and to place the values in sequence. Recall from Chapter 11 that subselects that return multiple rows will always result in the values being reduced to distinct values in sequence to reduce the processing on the inner table answer set.

Based on this analysis, the NOT EXISTS formulation will perform better than the NOT IN formulation. This is true in most cases. Indeed in a test comparing these two formulations against a sample database, the first was completed in 25 CPU seconds; the second ran for 120 CPU seconds before being canceled.

Converting between EXIST and IN subselects must be done with care since they do not always yield the same results. A subselect returns a true or false value when using EXIST or NOT EXIST. When using an IN or NOT IN subselect, however, the statement can return null if no rows qualify. In addition if there is a null SN in S (a primary key should be not null), the NOT EXISTS statement can return rows. The NOT IN statement will not return rows unless WHERE SN IS NOT NULL is added to the subselect.

This plan-table report also has an example that shows that the application plan or package does not necessarily execute in QBN sequence.

Noncorrelated subselects usually execute from the lower levels up, for example. In this sample, QN 2, QBN 2, and PN 1 and 2 execute before QN 2 and QBN 1. The PN steps within a query block are executed in the order indicated.

Although NOT EXISTS can provide relatively good performance, it should not be used with total abandon. Extending the current example shows how different formulations of statements using NOT EXISTS can result in different performance. The example also illustrates the importance of requesting only the information needed. Suppose the query defined above were expressed with the following three formulations:

```
EXPLAIN PLAN SET QUERYNO = 1 FOR
   SELECT SN
   FROM   SPJ
   WHERE  NOT EXISTS
     (SELECT S.SN
      FROM   S
      WHERE  S.SN = SPJ.SN)

EXPLAIN PLAN SET QUERYNO = 2 FOR
   SELECT SN
   FROM   SPJ
   WHERE  NOT EXISTS
     (SELECT *
      FROM   S
      WHERE  S.SN = SPJ.SN)

EXPLAIN PLAN SET QUERYNO = 3 FOR
   SELECT *
   FROM   SPJ
   WHERE  NOT EXISTS
     (SELECT *
      FROM   S
      WHERE  S.SN = SPJ.SN)
```

The **PLAN_TABLE** might look like this:

QN	QBN	PN	MET	TNAME	PRE	AT	MC	IXNAME	IXO	MX	CEV	U	J	O	G	U	J	O	G	TSL
1	1	1	0	SPJ	S	I	0	SPJX	Y	0		N	N	N	N	N	N	N	N	IS
1	2	1	0	S		I	1	SNX	Y	0		N	N	N	N	N	N	N	N	IS
2	1	1	0	SPJ	S	I	0	SPJX	Y	0		N	N	N	N	N	N	N	N	IS
2	2	1	0	S		I	1	SNX	Y	0		N	N	N	N	N	N	N	N	IS
3	1	1	0	SPJ	S	R	0		N	0		N	N	N	N	N	N	N	N	IS
3	2	1	0	S		I	1	SNX	Y	0		N	N	N	N	N	N	N	N	IS

The optimizer chose two separate access paths for the three statements. In the first case because only the SN values were requested, it was able to take advantage of index-only access on both tables. The second case is the same as the first case even though SELECT * is in the subselect since a true or false is returned as a result of testing the predicates. In the third case, the SELECT * in the outer select required a tablespace scan of the SPJ table.

IN Compared with BETWEEN

The sample explanations reinforce some of the guidelines for performance discussed in Chapter 11. Recall that it was suggested that the BETWEEN predicate frequently performs better than does the IN a list of values predicate even if all the values are not required within the range of BETWEEN (P3 is not required). First assume a low cluster ratio index on PN when EXPLAIN is executed for the IN and BETWEEN statements:

```
EXPLAIN PLAN SET QUERYNO = 1 FOR
SELECT SN, PN, JN, QTY
FROM    SPJ
WHERE   PN IN ('P2', 'P4', 'P5')

EXPLAIN PLAN SET QUERYNO = 2 FOR
SELECT SN, PN, JN, QTY
FROM    SPJ
WHERE   PN BETWEEN 'P2' AND 'P5'
AND     PN ¬= 'P3'
```

QN	QBN	PN	MET	TNAME	PRE	AT	MC	IXNAME	IXO	MX	CEV	U	J	O	G	U	J	O	G	TSL
1	1	1	0	SPJ	S	R	0		N	0		N	N	N	N	N	N	N	N	IS
2	1	1	0	SPJ	L	I	1	PNX	N	0		N	N	N	N	N	N	N	N	IS

The IN list of values predicate resulted in a tablespace scan of the SPJ table using sequential prefetch (QN = 1, PRE = S, and AT = R). BETWEEN gives a better access path to return the same result with a matching index scan and list prefetch (QN = 2, PRE = L, AT = I, and MC = 1).

An index with a high cluster ratio makes it more likely that the index on PN will be used for the IN a list of values predicate.

QN	QBN	PN	MET	TNAME	PRE	AT	MC	IXNAME	IXO	MX	CEV	U	J	O	G	U	J	O	G	TSL
1	1	1	0	SPJ	S	N	1	PNX	N	0		N	N	N	N	N	N	N	N	IS
2	1	1	0	SPJ	L	I	1	PNX	N	0		N	N	N	N	N	N	N	N	IS

With the high cluster ratio index, the access path for IN is using sequential prefetch on the leaf pages after doing a matching index scan (PRE = S, AT = N, and MC = 1), and the access path for BETWEEN remains the same.

A Union with Subselects

The following statement determines the suppliers who have and do not have parts listed in the SPJ table using subselects and a UNION. The QBN number next to each statement section corresponds to the QBN number in the row or rows of the plan table report that explain that section:

```
        EXPLAIN PLAN SET QUERYNO = 1 FOR
QBN = 1.SELECT SN,'PARTS IN SPJ    ',QTY
        FROM   SPJ
        WHERE  SN IN
          (SELECT SN
           FROM   S)
        UNION
QBN = 2 SELECT SN,'PARTS NOT IN SPJ', -1
        FROM   S
        WHERE  SN NOT IN
QBN = 3   (SELECT SN
           FROM   SPJ)
```

The plan-table report will look like this:

QN	QBN	PN	MET	TNAME	PRE	AT	MC	IXNAME	IXO	MX	CEV	U	J	O	G	U	J	O	G	TSL
1	1	1	0	SPJ	S	R	0		N	0		N	N	N	N	N	N	N	N	IS
1	1	2	1	S		I	1	SNX	Y	0		N	N	N	N	N	N	N	N	IS
1	1	3	3				0		N	0		N	N	N	N	Y	N	N	N	
1	2	1	0	S	S	I	0	SNX	Y	0		N	N	N	N	N	N	N	N	IS
1	3	1	0	SPJ	S	I	0	SPJX	Y	0		N	N	N	N	N	N	N	N	IS
1	3	2	3				0		N	0		N	N	N	N	Y	N	Y	N	

The QBN order follows the order in which the query block appears in the statement. Notice that the rule of thumb used thus far would suggest that there should be four query blocks since the key word SELECT appears four times even though in fact there are only three query blocks. Analyze the plan-table report for a moment—to determine the reason for only three query blocks—before reading the explanation.

In the example, DB2 will:

1.   Satisfy QBN 1 after transforming the first subselect into a join. If there is a unique index on the column in the subselect, it will be transformed into

a nested-loop join as indicated in the first two lines of the plan-table report.

2. Satisfy QBN 3 by accessing the SPJ table (TNAME = SPJ) with a nonmatching index scan without accessing the data pages using the index SPJX (AT = I, MC = 0, IXNAME = SNX, IXO = Y).

3. Find for the QBN 2 block the SNs for suppliers in the S table that are not represented as supplying parts in the SPJ table by accessing only the SNX index with a nonmatching scan (IXNAME = SNX, AT = I, MC = 0, IXO = Y). A nonmatching index scan usually requires the scan of fewer pages that does a tablespace scan. A large table will usually have a large number of index pages, however.

4. Finally a sort of all the suppliers, who do and do not supply parts to jobs in the SPJ table along with the literal tag, will be done for the UNION. Notice that the sort for unique values (U = Y) appears on the third line as step 3 for query block number 1. Obviously this sort cannot be done until the suppliers above and below the UNION have been retrieved even though the plan-table report indicates it is done before the subselect below the UNION when reading the query blocks in sequence. One cannot always assume that the functions will be executed in the order shown in the plan-table report.

The sort can be eliminated altogether in this case. If UNION ALL rather than UNION had been used, the sort would not have been needed since duplicates would not have to be removed. Logically there can be no duplicates. A supplier cannot both supply and not supply parts. Also in this case, there can be no duplicates assuming that SN is the primary key with a unique index. Of course, UNION ALL does not always return the same results as UNION since it does not eliminate duplicates.

View Materialization

EXPLAIN can be used to determine when view materialization has taken place since the view name will appear as the table name. In the great majority of cases the base table name will appear in the PLAN_TABLE even though the SQL statement references a view. If developers follow a naming convention in which view names incorporate the table names, explanations will be more easily understood. If view materialization has taken place, the view name will appear in the explanation rather than the table name for the step that results in a temporary file being built for the view result. The following view definition, select on the SPJ table, and plan-table report demonstrates the point.

```
CREATE VIEW PNAVG (PN, AVG_QTY) AS
SELECT PN, AVG(QTY)
FROM    SPJ
GROUP BY PN

EXPLAIN PLAN SET QUERYNO = 1 FOR
SELECT SN, SPJ.PN, QTY
FROM    SPJ, PNAVG
WHERE   SPJ.QTY > PNAVG.AVG_QTY
```

QN	QBN	PN	MET	TNAME	PRE	AT	MC	IXNAME	IXO	MX	CEV	U	J	O	G	U	J	O	G	TSL
1	1	1	0	SPJ	S	R	0		N	0		N	N	N	N	N	N	N	N	IS
1	1	2	1	PNAVG	S	R	0		N	0		N	N	N	N	N	N	N	N	
1	2	1	0	SPJ	S	R	0		N	0		N	N	N	N	N	N	N	N	IS
1	2	2	3				0		N	0	S	N	N	N	N	N	N	N	Y	

The third and fourth lines in the report for query block 2 are actually executed before the first and second lines for query block 1. Again this is based on deduction. The last line shows a sort for the GROUP BY during column evaluation (CEV = S, G = Y). Logically this must have been done before query block 1, which operates on the result of the view materialization in a temporary file with the name of the view (TNAME = PNAVG). The temporary file, PNAVG, is used as the inner table of a nested-loop join.

EXPLAIN can be used for any data manipulation statement. The analysis thus far has concentrated on SELECT statements. The access path selection will be the same for UPDATE and DELETE. There is no access path selection for INSERT statements. The clustering index or the index with the lowest OBID (Object ID) is always used to determine where a row is to be inserted. The use of this index, however, will not be shown in the PLAN_TABLE.

Recall from Chapter 11 that an index cannot be used on a column being updated in the SET clause, regardless of whether the index is unique or nonunique, if a predicate with an operator other than equal is used. QN 1 and 2 lines are for the first UPDATE statement in the following example. The difference is that SNX is a nonunique index for QN 1 and a unique index for QN 2 and for the second update of QN 3.

```
EXPLAIN PLAN SET QUERYNO = 2 FOR -- QN 1 is the same UPDATE
UPDATE S
SET    SN = 'S9'
WHERE  SN = 'S5'

EXPLAIN PLAN SET QUERYNO = 3 FOR
UPDATE S
SET    SN = 'S9'
WHERE  SN > 'S5'
```

QN	QBN	PN	MET	TNAME	PRE	AT	MC	IXNAME	IXO	MX	CEV	U	J	O	G	U	J	O	G	TSL
1	1	1	0	S	L	I	1	SNX	N	0		N	N	N	N	N	N	N	N	IX
2	1	1	0	S		I	1	SNX	N	0		N	N	N	N	N	N	N	N	IX
3	1	1	0	S	S	R	0		N	0		N	N	N	N	N	N	N	N	IX

The access path for QN 1 and QN 2 are the same except that, when SNX is declared as a nonunique index, list prefetch (PRE = L) is used. QN 3 requires a tablespace scan (AT = R) since an operator other than equal is used. Notice that the table or tablespace lock is intent exclusive (TSL = IX) for the updates and that all the previous SELECT statements resulted in an intent to share (TSL = IS). (Recall from Chapter 8 that these types of locks are taken at the table or tablespace level depending on whether the tablespace is segmented or nonsegemented).

A Delete with Multiple Indexes

There are no restrictions on the use of an index with a DELETE statement and the access path selection will be the same as if a SELECT statement had been issued with the same predicates. An explanation of a DELETE statement will demonstrate this and answer another question: Under what conditions will three separate indexes on SN, PN, and JN be used when there is also a single composite index on all three columns?

```
EXPLAIN PLAN SET QUERYNO = 1 FOR
DELETE FROM SPJ
WHERE  SN < 'S1'
AND    PN > 'P1'
AND    JN > 'J1'

EXPLAIN PLAN SET QUERYNO = 2 FOR
DELETE FROM SPJ
WHERE  SN = 'S1'
AND    PN > 'P1'
AND    JN > 'J1'

EXPLAIN PLAN SET QUERYNO = 3 FOR
DELETE FROM SPJ
WHERE  SN = 'S1'
AND    PN = 'P1'
AND    JN = 'J1'

EXPLAIN PLAN SET QUERYNO = 4 FOR
DELETE FROM SPJ
WHERE  PN = 'P1'
AND    JN = 'J1'
```

QN	QBN	PN	MET	TNAME	PRE	AT	MC	IXNAME	IXO	MX	CEV	U	J	O	G	U	J	O	G	TSL
1	1	1	0	SPJ	S	I	1	SPJX	N	0		N	N	N	N	N	N	N	N	IX
2	1	1	0	SPJ	L	I	2	SPJX	N	0		N	N	N	N	N	N	N	N	IX
3	1	1	0	SPJ		I	3	SPJX	N	0		N	N	N	N	N	N	N	N	IX
4	1	1	0	SPJ	L	M	0		N	0		N	N	N	N	N	N	N	N	IX
4	1	1	0	SPJ		MX	1	JNX	Y	1		N	N	N	N	N	N	N	N	IX
4	1	1	0	SPJ		MX	1	PNX	Y	2		N	N	N	N	N	N	N	N	IX
4	1	1	0	SPJ		MI	0		N	3		N	N	N	N	N	N	N	N	IX

QN 1 shows the use of a matching index scan followed by a scan of the leaf pages on the first column of the composite index (AT = I, MC = 1, IXNAME = SPJX). Recall from Chapter 6 that a matching index scan cannot be used on low-order columns unless the high-order columns have equal predicates specified. QN 2 has an equal predicate on the high-order column resulting in the same access path except now the matching index scan is on two of the columns (MC = 2). When all three columns have equal predicates, a match is done on all three columns (MC = 3). In most cases, the composite index is chosen over the individual indexes on each column. QN 4 shows that it is only when the leading column of the composite index is not specified in the predicates that the single-column indexes are used with multiple index processing. A second condition for the optimizer preferring the individual indexes is when an OR operator rather than an AND operator is used. The composite index cannot be used with an OR operator since rows can be missed. This analysis suggests that a composite index is better than individual indexes when the high-order columns are usually specified and the operator AND is used. Individual indexes would be needed only if these conditions are not met in most cases.

Locking Choices

The type of lock DB2 takes against a table or tablespace when it is satisfying a given statement has important performance implications. The TSLOCK-MODE value in the PLAN_TABLE (TSL in the sample reports) indicates DB2's lock choice. (Chapter 8 discusses the factors that influence that choice and the varying degrees of concurrency allowed by each of the table and tablespace lock types.) If the explanation indicates that one of the more restrictive locks will be used, the developer can investigate the various influencing factors to determine whether any might be altered so as to change the lock choices.

An application's isolation level can determine the choice between an Intent Share (IS) and the more restrictive Share (S) lock for a SELECT statement, for example. An isolation level of repeatable read (RR) will cause DB2 to choose an S lock on the table or tablespace for a SELECT that requires a tablespace scan. An isolation level of cursor stability (CS) will result in an IS lock, which allows other transactions to change pages in the tablespace. If an explanation for a SELECT shows the use of an S lock and if the search is a tablespace scan, the developer might investigate the application's isolation level. The catalog tables SYSPLAN and SYSPACK-AGE contains a column that indicates each plan's and package's isolation level. (Chapter 14 describes how to use the catalog tables for that kind of investigation.)

EXPLAIN has no way of knowing which pages will be locked and the type of lock that will be taken since the page locks are not taken until the plan or package is executed. The only way to determine this is to start a performance trace, which will indicate when each data and index page is locked and unlocked and the type of lock taken. Turning on the performance trace causes system monitoring facility (SMF) type 102 data records to be written by the subsystem services address space of DB2 describing the processing being done by DB2. Performance traces may be performed according to specific plans, authorization IDs, and DB2's resource managers. These traces consume considerable resources and typically are used by system administrators during off-peak hours.

13.6 WHEN TO INVESTIGATE PERFORMANCE

It is advisable to test SQL statements interactively using QMF or SPUFI before embedding the statements in a host-language program for several reasons. The first is to insure the SQL is providing the information required. If it is not, then more or less host-language code will be written than is necessary. The second reason is that one can get an early indication of performance by observing response time and the QMF relative cost estimate. The last reason is to execute EXPLAIN early to identify any potential performance problems. It is best to discover that an SQL statement is not performing as required before developing and testing a great deal of host-language code that would have to be changed and retested when it is necessary to change the SQL processing.

Recall from Chapter 12 that the relative cost estimate is the timeron used by the optimizer in determining the access path. The timeron is useful for comparing different formulations of the same *request* but has little value in determining which of two different requests will perform best. In addition, as mentioned earlier, the optimizer will not always choose the same access path for a statement when it is executed from a program as when it is executed interactively. A question mark ("?") can be used in place of a host variable or literal when testing interactively to achieve the same access path for static and dynamic SQL. The timeron for embedded

---

Box 13.2   Factors affecting the QMF relative cost estimate

Factors affecting a search's cost—and therefore QMF's timeron, DB2's estimate of that cost—include whether:

- RUNSTATS has been executed
- Statistics have changed since the previous RUNSTATS execution
- A clustering index has become unclustered
- Rows have overflowed to near or far pages
- The number of levels in the index has increased
- Literals or host variables have been used

---

dynamic SQL statements is recorded in the SQLERRD(4) field in the SQLCA.

Actual CPU and I/O processing

EXPLAIN provides good information on expected performance. If a table-space or nonmatching index scan is being used on a large table, subsecond response will not be achieved. A matching index scan is likely to provide the needed response time. More information is needed at times, however, in terms of the actual CPU and I/O processing required. Some companies routinely provide developers with performance reports indicating the total CPU time, DB2 I/O time, physical I/O, and logical I/O from the buffer-pool. This information is available by plan name and AUTHID in accounting (class 1, 2, and 3) and statistics (class 1) records. In addition, these statistics will give information on whether sufficient resources are available to DB2, the resources are being used to their full capacity for the workload, or DB2 has low priority relative to other work being done on the computer. These factors are indicated by excessive wait time for I/O and CPU in the statistics. If resources are not available when they are needed, performance will be poor regardless of how well the database design and SQL statements are developed and tuned.

Explaining Production Plans and Packages

It is important to know the statistics available to the optimizer when EXPLAIN is executed for two reasons. First it aids in understanding the path chosen by the optimizer. Without knowledge of the statistics, the developer may attempt to achieve a "better" access path when in fact the best access path has been chosen based on the statistics. Second, a record of these statistics should be kept along with the PLAN_TABLE so that when the access

The following statements request statistics used by the optimizer in choosing an access path. The analyst should know these statistics when EXPLAIN is executed in order to access the explanation accurately.

```
Table size:
SELECT NAME,CREATOR,CARD,NPAGES,PCTPAGES,EDPROC
FROM    SYSIBM.SYSTABLES
WHERE   DBNAME = 'DASPJDB'
AND     AND TYPE = 'T'

SELECT NAME, DBNAME, NACTIVE
FROM    SYSIBM.SYSTABLESPACE
WHERE   DBNAME = 'DASPJDB'

Index and clustering information:
SELECT NAME, UNIQUERULE, CLUSTERRATIO
        CLUSTERED, FIRSTKEYCARD, FULLKEYCARD,
        NLEAF, NLEVELS
FROM    SYSIBM.SYSINDEXES
WHERE   DBNAME = 'DASPJDB'

Cardinality and second highest and lowest values:
SELECT NAME, TBNAME, COLCARD, HIGH2KEY, LOW2KEY
        HEX (HIGH2KEY), HEX(LOW2KEY)
FROM    SYSIBM.SYSCOLUMNS
WHERE  (TBNAME  = 'S' OR TBNAME = 'P')
OR      TBNAME  = 'SPJ')
AND     COLCARD = > 0

Distribution information:
SELECT TBNAME, NAME, EXITPARML, EXITPARM
        HEX(EXITPARML), HEX(EXITPARM)
FROM    SYSIBM.SYSFIELDS
WHERE   TBCREATOR = &TBCREATOR
AND     TBNAME    = &TBNAME
AND     WORKAREA  = 0

Table layout:
SELECT NAME, COLTYPE, LENGTH, SCALE,
        NULLS, FOREIGNKEY, COLNO
FROM    SYSIBM.SYSCOLUMNS
WHERE   TBCREATOR = &TBCREATOR
AND     TBNAME    = &TBNAME
ORDER BY COLNO
```

Fig. 13.3 SELECT statements that report on statistics used by the optimizer

path changes in a production environment it is possible to determine the reason and whether the new access path is better or worse. Fig. 13.3 presents the SELECT statements needed to get the information. An alternative to selecting from the catalog tables is to have the utility RUNSTATS report on the statistics used by the optimizer as was discussed in Chapter 16.

There are a number of advantages to retaining a PLAN_TABLE containing an explanation of production plans and packages. It provides for tracking changes in access path due to a change in statistics, restructuring tables, adding or dropping indexes, new DB2 releases, and so on. All plans and packages should be explained when they are bound for production use with representative production data. It is best to leave EXPLAIN on so that if automatic rebinds occur they will be recorded in the plan table. All manual rebinds will be recorded as well. The cost of leaving EXPLAIN on is low—a few rows will be inserted into the PLAN_TABLE when a bind or rebind is performed. The TIMESTAMP column will indicate when the rebinds occurred. The production PLAN_TABLE should be monitored periodically to determine if there have been changes to the access path.

13.7 SUMMARY

The EXPLAIN feature provides a powerful monitoring tool. Using the feature is relatively easy. Using it effectively requires an understanding of the performance principles described throughout this book. By using EXPLAIN to investigate the optimizer's choices and by watching how they change with changes in statements or database design, the user can study many of these principles. Practice with EXPLAIN will help users perfect the performance of their application systems.

EXERCISES

In completing the exercises, refer to the following statement and its accompanying explanation. For each question, indicate the elements of the plan table that provided your answer.

```
EXPLAIN PLAN SET QUERYNO = 1 FOR
SELECT S.SN, SNAME, PN, QTY
FROM   SPJ, S
WHERE  S.SN = SPJ.SN
AND    S.SN = 'S2'
ORDER BY S.SN, SNAME
```

QN	QBN	PN	MET	TNAME	PRE	AT	MC	IXNAME	IXO	MX	CEV	U	J	O	G	U	J	O	G	TSL
1	1	1	0	SPJ	S	I	1	SPJX	N	0		N	N	N	N	N	N	N	N	IS
1	1	2	1	S		I	1	SNX	N	0		N	N	N	N	N	N	N	N	IS
1	1	3	3									N	N	N	N	N	N	Y	N	

13.1. What type of join will the plan use?

13.2. What index is used to access the SPJ table? Is the index scan matching or nonmatching?

13.3. Which table is the outer table for the join?

13.4. What is the purpose of the third plan step?

13.5. What tablespace lock type is used for each table?

14

Application Monitoring

14.1 INTRODUCTION

DB2's catalog tables, besides furnishing the statistics upon which the optimizer bases its access path decisions, also provide a wealth of information to assist database administrators (DBA) and developers with their choices. A DBA can monitor the amount of space available in a tablespace, index, or partition, for example, or the percent of table rows out of clustering sequence. This information indicates when reorganization of the tablespace may be desirable. (Figs. 14.1 and 12.4 describe the tables that provide monitoring information.) Or, a developer considering dropping an index that is not being used by a program can determine from the catalog what other programs use the index. This chapter will explore these and other ways DBAs and developers can use the catalog.

14.2 QUERYING THE CATALOG

DBAs and developers use SQL statements to query the catalog tables as they would any other tables. (They can update the catalog tables only with special authorization because doing so could compromise the statistics' integrity. Fig. 14.2 lists actions that cause DB2 to update the catalog tables.) The catalog includes about 38 tables, many with a dozen or more columns. (Appendix A in the DB2 SQL Reference Manual describes all the catalog tables.) It takes DBAs and developers some practice to learn their way

```
SYSIBM.SYSTABLEPART

CARD      Number of rows in the tablespace or partition.
NEARINDREF Number of rows moved to a nearby page due to
            row length increase.
FARINDREF  Number of rows moved to a faraway page due to
            row length increase.
PERCACTIVE Percentage of space occupied by active rows
            containing actual data from active tables
            (not space from deleted rows).
PERCDROP   Percentage of space occupied by rows from
            dropped tables.


SYSIBM.SYSINDEXPART

CARD      Number of rows referenced by the index or
            index partition.
NEAROFFPOS Number of times the next row was not in
            sequence of index but was in a near page
            (within + or - 32 pages).
FAROFFPOS  Number of times the next row was not in
            sequence of index but was in a faraway page
            (greater than + or - 32 pages).
LEAFDIST   Percentage of leaf pages that are not
            contiguous during a sequential access of the
            index.

Most columns contain -1 until RUNSTATS is executed.
```

Fig. 14.1 Tables used for monitoring and tuning

around the catalog tables. This chapter presents queries designed to extract some of the more useful monitoring information. These queries are only samples, however; individuals must customize them to fit the needs of their particular investigations and the practices of their installations. The catalog contains data on all objects within a DB2 system, for example, but investigators will often want to retrieve information about a particular application.

An alternative to keying and executing the SELECT statements on the catalog tables directly is to use the CATALOG VISIBILITY option from the

```
The following activities update catalog tables:

■   Creation and deletion of objects

■   Granting and revoking authorizations

■   Program preparation (binding and freeing plans and packages)

■   Executing the RUNSTATS, STOSPACE, COPY, or REORG utility
```

Fig. 14.2 Population of catalog tables

DB2I primary panel. A number of options are available as was discussed in Chapter 4. There are times when the flexibility of customized SELECT statements are needed to provide the required information. Also the statements may need to be executed from JCL on a scheduled basis.

In many organizations, one individual creates all the objects for an application development team or production application. In that case, to locate information about only that application in the catalog tables, the investigator can use that individual's AUTHID code in the query to limit the search. (This ID code is called CREATOR or an obvious derivative such as IXCREATOR in the catalog tables.) If an application system uses one database, the query can be limited by the database name. Or if the application system uses several databases, their names can be cited together with the OR operator in a WHERE clause to select information about the application.

The catalog table names are fairly long, and some of the SELECT statements for accessing them will be complex; therefore use of correlation names for the table names may save considerable typing. Because some of the column names from different tables are similar, qualification of each column's name with its table's correlation name, even when not needed for a correct SQL statement, usually enhances a statement's understandability.

The catalog table queries may be entered through SPUFI or QMF. A difference between the two is that SQL statements developed under SPUFI require termination with a ";" delimiter. Those developed under QMF do not. The examples in this chapter were developed using QMF. QMF offers some advantages for monitoring the catalog. It will prompt the user for object names, for example. To use that feature, the investigator places an ampersand at the beginning of a character string in an SQL statement where the prompt is to come. If the SQL statement is stored in a QMF query, investigators can use it repeatedly for monitoring as required.

Before using the catalog tables for monitoring, investigators should be sure their statistics are up to date. Executing the RUNSTATS utility for a tablespace or index updates the statistics describing it. RUNSTATS should be executed after the table or index has been loaded or after significant update activity. These statements identify tablespaces or indexes for which RUNSTATS utility has not collected statistics. For tablespaces:

```
SELECT NAME, CREATOR, NACTIVE
FROM   SYSIBM.SYSTABLESPACE
WHERE  NACTIVE = -1
```

For indexes:

```
SELECT NAME, CREATOR, FIRSTKEYCARD
FROM   SYSIBM.SYSINDEXES
WHERE  CARD = -1
```

Box 14.1   How DBAs use the catalog tables

DBAs may use catalog tables to determine:

- Which application plans and packages use which indexes.
- An index's structure, whether unique or clustered, or the number of levels.
- The need for reorganization as determined from SYSTABLEPART and SYSINDEXPART.
- The status of image copies.
- The amount of physical space used and remaining.
- Who has authorization to create objects.
- Which tablespaces, tables, and indexes are within a database.
- Which plans and packages use objects in a database.
- Who created an object and who owns it.
- Which tables, tablespaces, and indexes constitute a database.

14.3   SAMPLE QUERIES RELATED TO PERFORMANCE

Fig. 14.3 shows the relationship between the catalog tables that describe objects in a database. These catalog tables will be used in the following sample queries to test for conditions that may directly affect performance.

Box 14.2   How programmers and analysts use catalog tables

Programmers and analysts may use catalog tables to determine:

- Which plans and packages use which indexes.
- Which plans and packages use which tables and views.
- Which aliases and synonyms have been created on tables and views.
- Table size, the number of rows, and amount of physical space used.
- Who is authorized to select from or update which tables and views.
- Who is authorized to execute which plans and packages.
- Which plans and packages might be affected by a column change.
- A table's structure, its columns, and the column's data types and lengths.
- Which SQL statements are used in a plan or package.

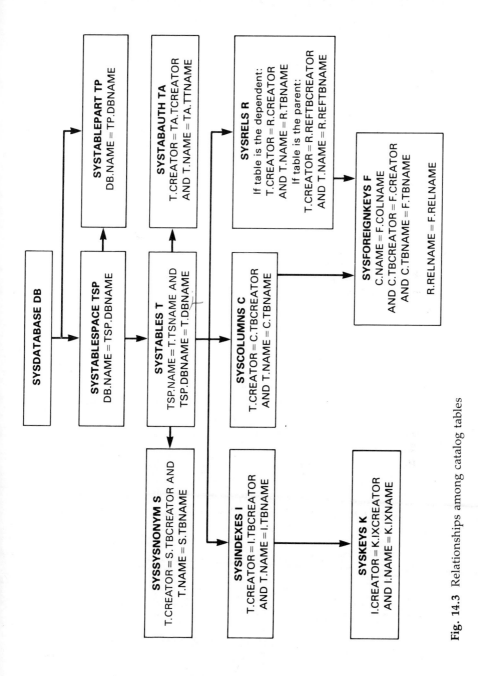

Fig. 14.3 Relationships among catalog tables

441

Tablespaces with Multiple Tables

A DBA can use this statement to identify all tablespaces that contain more than one table, as Chapter 3 explains, usually an inefficient situation if the tablespace is not segmented:

```
SELECT T.NAME, T.NPAGES, T.CREATOR, T.TSNAME
FROM    SYSIBM.SYSTABLES T,
        SYSIBM.SYSTABLESPACE TS
WHERE  T.TSNAME   = TS.NAME
AND    TS.NTABLES > 1
AND    T.NPAGES   > 7
AND    TS.SEGSIZE = 0
```

The statement returns the name of any tablespace with more than one table and the names and creators of the tables in each of these tablespaces. The T.NPAGE > 7 criteria eliminates multiple-table tablespaces in which all tables are smaller than seven pages and TS.SEGSIZE = 0 results in identifying only nonsegmented tablespaces.

The CLOSERULE

A developer indicates with the CLOSERULE whether DB2 is to close the tablespace or index space's underlying VSAM datasets after each user access or keep them open until the database or DB2 is stopped. The choice of opening and closing datasets, which requires I/O operations and CPU time, or keeping them open, which requires additional resources as was discussed in Chapter 3, therefore has performance implications. A CLOSE-RULE choice of YES instructs DB2 to open and close the datasets. NO instructs it to keep accessed datasets open. The following statements will identify the CLOSERULE choices for the tablespaces and index spaces for a given database:

```
SELECT NAME, CREATOR, CLOSERULE
FROM   SYSIBM.SYSTABLESPACE
WHERE  DBNAME = 'DASPJDB'

SELECT NAME, CREATOR, CLOSERULE
FROM   SYSIBM.SYSINDEXES
WHERE  DBNAME = 'DASPJDB'
```

The CLOSERULE column values are YES or NO. Investigators may want to look only for spaces in the database that have one or the other. They may do this by adding the search criterion AND CLOSERULE = 'N' or AND CLOSERULE = 'Y' to these statements. Frequently used tablespaces and index spaces should have a CLOSERULE of 'N' as was discussed in Chapter 3. An alternative is to count the number of tablespaces and indexes with a CLOSERULE of no. DSMAX, which has a default of 1000 should be adjusted to the sum of data sets with a close of no plus the number of datasets with close of yes that are frequently accessed at the same time. The maximum number of open datasets dictated by MVS/SP 3.1.1 and DFP 3.2 is 10,000.

Implicitly Created Tablespaces

If a table is created without designating the tablespace to be used, DB2 will automatically create the tablespace using default parameters. Chapter 3 discussed the fact that some of the defaults are not suitable for many tablespaces. For example, parameters that should be used in most cases are SEG-SIZE 64 (default is a nonsegmented tablespace) and CLOSE of NO. In addition, the default of 12K bytes of primary and secondary quantities may not be adequate. Tablespaces that have been created implicitly by DB2 can be identified by:

```
SELECT DBNAME, NAME
FROM   SYSIBM.SYSTABLESPACE
WHERE  IMPLICIT = 'Y'
```

Tables with No Indexes

Tables larger than seven pages should usually have indexes. The following statement identifies all tables that do not and their creators:

```
SELECT CREATOR, NAME
FROM   SYSIBM.SYSTABLES T
WHERE  TYPE = 'T'
AND    NOT EXISTS
  (SELECT I.TBNAME
   FROM   SYSIBM.SYSINDEXES I
   WHERE  I.TBNAME   = T.NAME
   AND    I.TBCREATOR = T.CREATOR)
```

Not all tables identified in this report may require indexes. For example, most of the processing on an identified table may involve a large percentage of rows, a situation in which an index may not improve efficiency. However, all tables identified by the report should be investigated.

The WHERE TYPE = 'T' search criterion in the statement filters out views and aliases that are also described in the SYSTABLES table but that cannot have indexes.

Tables with No Clustering Index

There are significant benefits to having a clustering index on each table as was discussed in Chapter 6. The tables that have only nonclustering indexes can be identified with:

```
SELECT I.TBCREATOR, I.TBNAME, I.CREATOR,
       I.NAME, I.CLUSTERING
FROM   SYSIBM.SYSINDEXES I
WHERE  NOT EXISTS
       (SELECT X.TBCREATOR, X.TBNAME
        FROM   SYSIBM.SYSINDEXES X
        WHERE  X.CLUSTERING = 'Y'
        AND    X.CREATOR    = I.CREATOR
        AND    X.NAME       = I.NAME)
ORDER BY I.TBCREATOR, I.TBNAME
```

If no clustering index is declared, the first index created (to be precise the index with the lowest OBID[object identifier]) is used to determine where to insert a row but is not used in a reorganization to maintain clustering.

Very Small Tables with Indexes

Indexes on very small tables—those having seven pages or less—usually waste resources. Indeed DB2 will not use an index in many cases on a table that small in its own tablespace. This statement identifies indexes on small tables:

```
SELECT T.NAME, I.NAME, T.NPAGES
FROM   SYSIBM.SYSTABLES T,
       SYSIBM.SYSINDEXES I
WHERE  T.CREATOR = I.TBCREATOR
AND    T.NAME    = I.TBNAME
AND    T.TYPE    = 'T'
AND    T.NPAGES  < 7
```

There are a few good reasons for having an index on a small table, however. If the table were used as the inner table in a nested-loop join, the index would be useful. It would also be useful for referential integrity constraint checking, for enforcing unique values, and for index-only processing of look-up tables.

Tables with Multiple Indexes

Tables that are frequently updated or reloaded with large amounts of data should not have many indexes. This statement identifies tables with three or more indexes:

```
SELECT TBNAME, TBCREATOR
FROM   SYSIBM.SYSINDEXES
GROUP BY TBNAME, TBCREATOR
HAVING COUNT(*) > 2
```

Since SYSIBM.SYSINDEXES has a row for each index, a count of the rows for each table—grouped by table name and creator—indicates those tables with more than two indexes.

Indexes with a Low Cardinality

Indexes with highly redundant values, that is, a low cardinality, are of little or no value in selects and require excessive I/O and CPU time during updates. The following two statements determine the amount of redundancy in an indexed column. The first statement returns—for each index in a database—a COLCARD value, which is the number of distinct values in the column, and a CARD value, which is the total number of rows in the table. If there are significantly more rows than there are distinct values, the column is probably too redundant to make a useful index:

```
SELECT C.TBCREATOR, C.TBNAME, C.NAME, T.CARD,
       C.COLCARD, HIGH2KEY, LOW2KEY
FROM   SYSIBM.SYSCOLUMNS C,
       SYSIBM.SYSTABLES T
WHERE  T.DBNAME     = 'DASPJDB'
AND    C.TBCREATOR = T.CREATOR
AND    C.TBNAME    = T.NAME
AND    C.COLCARD    > 0
ORDER BY TBCREATOR, TBNAME, NAME
```

Chapter 6 describes the formula for determining the average number of times a distinct, indexed value appears on a page and explains the performance implications of that measure of redundancy. The following statement retrieves the information necessary to complete that formula for a given index and performs the calculation. The formula requires the number of rows in the table (T.CARD), the number of pages the table uses (T.NPAGES), and the number of unique values in the indexed column (I.FIRSTKEYCARD) or for composite indexes (I.FULLKEYCARD). Putting that information together requires this four-way join:

```
SELECT I.CREATOR, I.TBNAME, I.NAME,
       I.FIRSTKEYCARD, I.FULLKEYCARD,
       C.NAME, C.COLCARD,
       T.CARD, T.NPAGES,
       T.CARD/T.NPAGES/I.FIRSTKEYCARD,
       T.CARD/T.NPAGES/I.FULLKEYCARD
FROM   SYSIBM.SYSINDEXES I,
       SYSIBM.SYSTABLES  T,
       SYSIBM.SYSCOLUMNS C,
       SYSIBM.SYSKEYS    K
WHERE  I.FIRSTKEYCARD > 0
AND    I.FULLKEYCARD  > 0
AND    T.CARD         > 0
```

```
AND    T.NPAGES        > 0
AND    I.CREATOR   = 'POSYSTEM'
AND    K.IXCREATOR = 'POSYSTEM'
AND    C.TBCREATOR = 'POSYSTEM'
AND    T.CREATOR   = 'POSYSTEM'
AND    T.NAME    = C.TBNAME
AND    T.NAME    = I.TBNAME
AND    K.IXNAME  = I.NAME
AND    C.NAME    = K.COLNAME
```

The fifth line contains the formula for single-column indexes and the sixth line one for composite indexes to estimate the average number of occurrences of a value on a data page. The first four lines of the WHERE clause eliminates rows for which RUNSTATS has not been executed; the middle four lines limit the report to indexes created by the individual with an authorization ID of POSYSTEM. The last four lines govern the join of the four tables contributing to the report.

The cardinality of columns can be investigated before creation of an index takes place. If there are very few distinct values of less than 20 or of less than 5 percent of the total number of rows, it is best not to have an index on the column or columns. The following statement will list the distinct occurrences of the SN and PN columns in the SPJ table.

```
SELECT DISTINCT SN, PN
FROM   SPJ
```

The COUNT operator can also be used to determine distribution of values. For example, the following statement and its results indicate that the combination of SN and PN columns would make a poor index because of skewed distribution.

```
SELECT SN, PN, COUNT(*)
FROM   SPJ
GROUP BY SN, PN
ORDER BY 3 DESC
```

SN	PN	
S2	P3	7000
S5	P5	3000
S5	P6	2000
S5	P2	2000
S4	P6	2000
S1	P1	2000
S5	P4	1000
S5	P3	1000
S5	P1	1000
S3	P4	1000
S3	P3	1000
S2	P5	1000

Identifying Unique Indexes

When an index has been declared by its creator to be unique, DB2 will not allow a duplicate value to be entered in the column. If an indexed column contains all unique values but has not been declared unique, the developer may want to check with the table users to determine if values in the column or columns should always be unique. A unique index is favored by the optimizer when equal predicates are used on the columns with the unique index as was discussed in Chapter 12. This statement identifies all potentially unique indexes in a DB2 system:

```
SELECT I.NAME, I.CREATOR, I.UNIQUERULE
FROM   SYSIBM.SYSINDEXES I,
       SYSIBM.SYSTABLES  T
WHERE  C.COLCARD > 0
AND    I.UNIQUERULE  = 'D'
AND    I.FULLKEYCARD = T.CARD
AND    I.CREATOR     = T.CREATOR
AND    I.TBNAME      = T.NAME
```

When the number of rows in a table (T.CARD) equals the number of unique values in its indexed columns (I.FULLKEYCARD), the index is unique. A UNIQUERULE value of D indicates duplicates are allowed in the index. A UNIQUERULE of U or P means the index has been declared unique and the P indicates that it is a primary key.

Columns Used in an Index

The following statement identifies the columns designated as an index by a given creator and allows analysis of composite indexes:

```
SELECT I.CREATOR, I.NAME,
       K.COLSEQ, K.COLNO, K.ORDERING
FROM   SYSIBM.SYSKEYS K,
       SYSIBM.SYSINDEXES I
WHERE  I.TBCREATOR = &TBCREATOR
AND    I.TBNAME    = &TBNAME
AND    I.CREATOR   = K.IXCREATOR
AND    I.NAME      = K.IXNAME
ORDER BY I.NAME, K.COLSEQ
```

COLNO gives the column's numerical position in the table; COLSEQ gives its numerical position in the index if the index is composite; ORDERING indicates whether the index has been designated to use ascending or descending order.

Plans and Packages with Repeatable Read

At bind time, a developer can indicate through the isolation-level choice how DB2 should manage concurrency control locks acquired on behalf of the application. Under a level of repeatable read, DB2 accumulates locks until the application issues a commit or the thread is deallocated. Under cursor stability, DB2 releases a page lock as soon as a row on another page is accessed as long as the page has not been updated. Repeatable read tends to limit the number of concurrent users. Response times are likely to increase as some applications wait for other applications to complete. The following statement identifies all application plans and packages in a DB2 system with an isolation level of repeatable read and their creators:

```
SELECT NAME, CREATOR, 'PLAN', 'PLAN'
FROM   SYSIBM.SYSPLAN
WHERE  ISOLATION = 'R'
UNION ALL
SELECT NAME, CREATOR, COLLID, VERSION
FROM   SYSIBM.SYSPACKAGE
WHERE  ISOLATION = 'R'
```

Tablespace-Level Locks

Locking at the table or tablespace level can limit concurrency. DB2 imposes a table or tablespace lock whenever a tablespace created with a locksize of table or tablespace is accessed and sometimes when a tablespace with a locksize of ANY is accessed. Page locks will be promoted to table or tablespace locks more often under a locksize of ANY than PAGE. This statement identifies tablespaces created with table, tablespace, and ANY locking:

```
SELECT NAME, DBNAME, CREATOR, LOCKRULE
FROM   SYSIBM.SYSTABLESPACE
WHERE  LOCKRULE IN ('S', 'T', 'A')
```

Index Subpage Size

Indexes created with large index subpages—a full index page or half subpage—may limit concurrency during updating. The SYSIBM.SYSINDEXES table indicates index page or subpage size in terms of bytes: A full page is 4096 bytes; a half page is 2048 bytes; and so on. This statement identifies indexes created with full or half pages:

```
SELECT NAME, CREATOR, PGSIZE
FROM   SYSIBM.SYSINDEXES
WHERE  PGSIZE > = 2048
```

If the table served by an identified index has limited concurrency, decreasing the subpage size to 1/4, 1/8, or 1/16 of a page may solve the problem. A larger subpage, perhaps 1, may be required to reduce page splitting overhead due to heavy insert and update activity concentrated on a few index pages. Index page splitting causes an exclusive lock on the next higher level in the index, barring use of the index down the locked path.

Tables and Their Indexes by Plan or Package

Since the use of an index usually improves performance, it is often useful to know which indexes the optimizer has chosen to use for each table accessed by a plan or package. If more than one SQL statement within the plan or package uses the table that has the index, this report will not indicate which table accesses actually use the index. The report does provide enough summary information to guide further analysis, perhaps through use of the EXPLAIN statement, which was discussed in Chapter 13. The following statement provides a report on the tables and indexes used by a plan:

```
SELECT DNAME, BNAME, BTYPE
FROM    SYSIBM.SYSPLANDEP
WHERE   DNAME = &PLAN
AND     BTYPE IN ('I', 'T')
```

A similar statement will provide information for a package:

```
SELECT DNAME, DCOLLID, HEX(DCONTOKEN), BNAME, BTYPE
FROM    SYSIBM.SYSPACKDEP
WHERE   DNAME = &PACKAGE
AND     BTYPE IN ('I', 'T')
```

DNAME is the plan or package name. DCOLLID and DCONTOKEN are the collection ID and consistency token of the package. BNAME is the name of an object used by the plan or package. BTYPE is the object's type: T for table, I for index, V for view, S for synonym, A for alias, or R for tablespace. This SELECT statement concerns tables and indexes. Figs. 14.4 and 14.5 shows the relationship between the catalog tables that have information about plans and packages.

Plans and Packages That Use a Given Index

Before dropping an index, a developer should determine which application plans and packages would be affected. The following statement identifies plans and packages that use a given index:

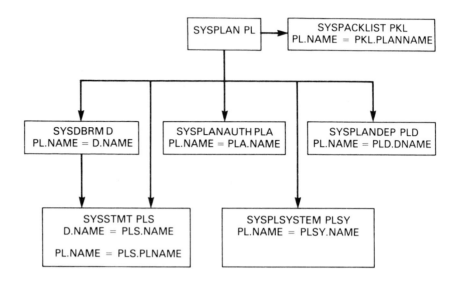

Fig. 14.4 Relationships among plan tables

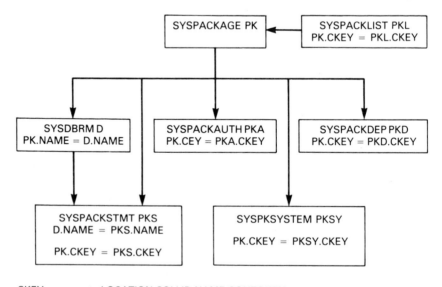

CKEY represents LOCATION.COLLID.NAME.CONTOKEN
- SYSPACKLIST does not include CONTOKEN
- SYSPKSYSTEM does not include LOCATION at present

Fig. 14.5 Relationships among package tables

```
SELECT PLD.DNAME, PL.CREATOR, 'PLAN', 'PLAN'
       PLD.BNAME, PLD.BCREATOR
FROM   SYSIBM.SYSPLANDEP PLD,
       SYSIBM.SYSPLAN    PL
WHERE  PLD.BTYPE    = 'I'
AND    PLD.BCREATOR = &IXCREATOR
AND    PLD.BNAME    = &INDEXNAME
AND    PLD.DNAME    = PL.NAME
UNION ALL
SELECT PKD.DNAME, PK.CREATOR, PK.COLLID, PK.VERSION,
       PKD.BNAME, PKD.BCREATOR
FROM   SYSIBM.SYSPACKDEP PKD,
       SYSIBM.SYSPACKAGE PK
WHERE  PKD.BTYPE    = 'I'
AND    PKD.BCREATOR = &IXCREATOR
AND    PKD.BNAME    = &INDEXNAME
AND    PKD.DNAME    = PK.NAME
```

If only a few plans and packages use the index, the developer can analyze the impact that dropping the index would have on them. The statement, however, does not identify statements commonly entered through SPUFI or by QMF users which might benefit from the index. DB2 does not save access information for dynamic SQL statements. Developers can identify users authorized to access an indexed table. Then they can contact those users to determine how and how often they use the table. After considering how frequently the statements are used, the investigator can estimate the likely effects of dropping the index and decide how to proceed.

Another way of investigating how an index is being used by dynamic SQL statements is to examine saved QMF queries, which are stored in the table Q.OBJECT_DATA. If a statement references an indexed column, the investigator can use EXPLAIN to determine whether the optimizer chooses to use the index in satisfying the query. The Q.OBJECT_DATA does not store dynamic SQL statements that have not been saved. The table can be altered and the AUDIT parameter added to capture frequently used dynamic statements for later investigation.

Plans and Packages That Use a Given Table or View

Developers find it helpful to know which plans and packages use a particular table or view. This information helps them identify unused or unnecessary tables or views that might be dropped and also helps them identify plans and packages that, if they are rebound, may result in an improved access path due to statistics changing dramatically, the addition of an index, or the installation of a new DB2 release. This statement identifies plans and packages that use a particular table or view:

```
SELECT DPL.DNAME, PL.CREATOR, 'PLAN', 'PLAN', DPL.BNAME
FROM   SYSIBM.SYSPLANDEP DPL,
```

```
        SYSIBM.SYSPLAN     PL
WHERE (BTYPE          = 'T' OR BTYPE = 'V')
AND    DPL.BNAME     = &TABLEVIEWNAME
AND    DPL.BCREATOR = &TABLECREATOR
AND    DPL.DNAME     = PL.NAME
UNION ALL
SELECT DPK.DNAME, PK.CREATOR, PK.COLLID, PK.VERSION, DPK.BNAME
FROM    SYSIBM.SYSPACKDEP PKD,
        SYSIBM.SYSPACKAGE PK
WHERE (BTYPE          = 'T' OR BTYPE = 'V')
AND    DPK.BNAME     = &TABLEVIEWNAME
AND    DPK.BCREATOR = &TABLECREATOR
AND    DPK.DNAME     = PK.NAME
```

The reports will not identify dynamic SQL users of the table or view. The authorization tables are useful for finding that information.

Views on a Table

It is advisable to determine all views that have been created on a table before dropping the table since the drop will also drop all views:

```
SELECT V.DCREATOR, V.DNAME, V.BCREATOR,
       V.BNAME, T.REMARKS
FROM   SYSIBM.SYSVIEWDEP V,
       SYSIBM.SYSTABLES T
WHERE  V.DCREATOR = T.CREATOR
AND    V.DNAME     = T.NAME
AND    V.BTYPE     = 'T'
AND    V.BCREATOR = &TABLE_CREATOR
AND    V.BNAME     = &TABLE_NAME
ORDER BY V.DCREATOR, V.DNAME
```

This select will determine all direct dependent views (only one level) for a given view:

```
SELECT V.DCREATOR, V.DNAME, V.BCREATOR,
       V.BNAME, T.REMARKS
FROM   SYSIBM.SYSVIEWDEP V,
       SYSIBM.SYSTABLES T
WHERE  V.DCREATOR = T.CREATOR
AND    V.DNAME     = T.NAME
AND    V.BTYPE     = 'V'
AND    V.BCREATOR = &VIEW_CREATOR
AND    V.BNAME     = &VIEW_NAME
ORDER BY V.DCREATOR, V.DNAME
```

Objects Dependent on a Given Table or View

The previous statements can be expanded with the UNION operator to identify views and indexes dependent on a table as:

```
SELECT CREATOR, '.', NAME, 'INDEX',
       TBNAME, TBCREATOR
FROM   SYSIBM.SYSINDEXES
WHERE  TBCREATOR = &OBJQUAL
AND    TBNAME    = &OBJNAME
  UNION
SELECT V.CREATOR, '.', V.NAME, 'VIEW',
       D.BNAME, D.BCREATOR
FROM   SYSIBM.SYSPLANDEP D,
       SYSIBM.SYSVIEWDEP V
WHERE  D.BNAME    = &OBJNAME
AND    D.BCREATOR = &OBJQUAL
AND    D.DNAME    = V.NAME
  UNION
SELECT P.CREATOR, ' ', D.DNAME, 'PLAN',
       D.BNAME, D.BCREATOR
FROM   SYSIBM.SYSPLANDEP D,
       SYSIBM.SYSPLAN P
WHERE  D.BNAME    = &OBJNAME
AND    D.BCREATOR = &OBJQUAL
AND    D.DNAME    = P.NAME
ORDER BY 4,1,3
```

Similar information can be obtained on packages by replacing SYSPLAN-DEP with SYSPACKDEP and SYSPLAN with SYSPACKAGE.

Synonyms on a Table or View

All synonyms on a table or view will be dropped when the table or view is dropped. They probably should be re-created when the table or view is re-created. If a synonym is dropped, DB2 will invalidate all application plans and packages using it. If the synonym is re-created, DB2 will automatically rebind the application plan or package on its next execution. The following statement associates a synonym (NAME in SYSIBM.SYSYNONYMS) with its table's or view's name (TBNAME):

```
SELECT NAME, CREATOR, TBNAME, TBCREATOR
FROM   SYSIBM.SYSSYNONYMS
WHERE  TBNAME = 'SPJ'
```

Each synonym must be re-created under the AUTHID of the individual who uses the synonym. A person with SYSADM privileges or one sharing a secondary AUTHID with the creator of the synonym can execute SET CURRENT SQLID = 'authid' and create the synonym under that SQLID.

Indexes Not Used

If an index is not used within any plan or package, chances are good that maintaining the index is a waste of resources. This statement identifies such indexes:

```
SELECT NAME, TBNAME, CREATOR
FROM   SYSIBM.SYSINDEXES
WHERE  CREATOR ¬= 'SYSIBM'
AND    NAME NOT IN
  (SELECT BNAME
    FROM   SYSIBM.SYSPLANDEP
    WHERE  BTYPE = 'I')
UNION ALL
SELECT NAME, TBNAME, CREATOR
FROM   SYSIBM.SYSINDEXES
WHERE  CREATOR ¬= 'SYSIBM'
AND    NAME NOT IN
  (SELECT BNAME
    FROM   SYSIBM.SYSPACKDEP
    WHERE  BTYPE = 'I')
```

The reports will not identify dynamic SQL users whose statements might use particular indexes. An earlier section, "Plans and Packages That Use a Given Index," describes how to investigate dynamic statements.

Invalid Plans and Packages

DB2 invalidates an access plan or package when an object that is used is dropped, when referential integrity constraints covered by the SQL have been altered, or when privileges are revoked. DB2 will then automatically try to rebind the plan or package the next time an attempt is made to execute it. If a rebind fails, DB2 marks the plan or package inoperative (OPERATIVE='N') and does not attempt additional rebinds. Developers may want to identify invalidated plans and packages for at least two reasons. First if there are a large number of invalidated plans and packages, developers may wish to rebind them during off-hours, saving considerable I/O to the catalog tables and CPU time during prime time for each plan or package that DB2 would have rebound. Second they can determine whether dropping indexes or other objects has invalidated any plans or packages. An 'A' in the VALID column indicates that a table or tablespace used by the plan or package has been altered. A rebind is not required. This statement identifies invalid plans and packages that reference objects that have been altered:

```
SELECT COLLID, NAME, VERSION, CREATOR, BOUNDBY, VALID
FROM   SYSIBM.SYSPACKAGE
WHERE  VALID IN ('N', 'A')

SELECT NAME, CREATOR, BOUNDBY, VALID
FROM   SYSIBM.SYSPLAN
WHERE  VALID IN ('N', 'A')
```

If an automatic rebind or user initiated rebind has failed, the plan or package is marked inoperative and an explicit bind replace or rebind with an

AUTHID that has authority on the objects being manipulated by the plan or package is required.

```
SELECT COLLID, NAME, VERSION, CREATOR,
   BOUNDBY, VALID, OPERATIVE, BINDDATE
FROM   SYSIBM.SYSPACKAGE
WHERE  OPERATIVE = 'N'

SELECT NAME, CREATOR, VALID,
   OPERATIVE, BINDDATE
FROM   SYSIBM.SYSPLAN
WHERE  OPERATIVE = 'N'
```

Plans and Packages Validated at Run Time

DB2 can validate that all objects needed by a plan or package exist and that all necessary authorizations have been granted using either of two approaches: once, when the SQL is bound, or repetitively, each time it runs. The latter approach, called RUN validation, is required for embedded dynamic SQL but requires more run-time resources than does the former method, called BIND validation. RUN validation can also cause contention on the catalog tables. Plans and packages in production therefore should use BIND validation. This statement identifies those that do not:

```
SELECT NAME, CREATOR, 'PLAN', 'PLAN'
FROM   SYSIBM.SYSPLAN
WHERE  VALIDATE = 'R'
UNION ALL
SELECT NAME, CREATOR, COLLID, VERSION
FROM   SYSIBM.SYSPACKAGE
WHERE  VALIDATE = 'R'
```

VARCHAR Columns

As was discussed in Chapter 4, a column declared as VARCHAR type should result in saving 20 bytes or more of trailing blanks and be the rightmost column in its table. Developers can use this statement to identify VARCHAR columns, and then investigate whether they meet those criteria:

```
SELECT DISTINCT TBCREATOR, TBNAME,
       COLNO, NAME, COLTYPE, LENGTH,
       SCALE, NULLS, COLCARD,
       HIGH2KEY, LOW2KEY
FROM   SYSIBM.SYSCOLUMNS
WHERE  TBCREATOR ¬= 'SYSIBM'
AND    TBCREATOR ¬= 'Q'
AND    TBNAME IN
   (SELECT DISTINCT TBNAME
    FROM   SYSIBM.SYSCOLUMNS
```

```
WHERE  COLTYPE = 'VARCHAR'
OR     COLTYPE = 'LONGVAR')
```

The predicate clauses—WHERE TBCREATOR ¬= 'SYSIBM' AND TBCREATOR ¬= 'Q'—eliminate from the report information describing catalog and QMF tables.

14.4 WHEN TO REORGANIZE

Developers should consider reorganizing a tablespace or index space under a number of conditions:

- When more than 20 percent of a table's rows are out of clustering sequence.
- When a number of rows have overflowed their original pages to near or far pages.
- When space from dropped tables in nonsegmented tablespaces can be reclaimed.
- When there has been heavy update activity.
- When data were loaded with an application program.

The statements in this section help to identify these conditions.

Unclustered Indexes

The Catalog tables indicate the degree of clustering in two ways. In one, CLUSTERRATIO indicates the percent of rows in clustering sequence. If the CLUSTERRATIO is less than 80 percent, reorganization is advisable. In the other, the CLUSTERED column of SYSIBM.SYSINDEXES indicates when more than 5 percent of rows are out of clustering sequence. Although the optimizer uses the CLUSTERED value only if CLUSTERRATIO has not been updated, developers might find it useful in their investigations.

The following statement determines the CLUSTERRATIO for all indexes in the database SPJDB:

```
SELECT NAME, CREATOR, TBNAME,
       CLUSTERRATIO,
       CLUSTERING, CLUSTERED
FROM   SYSIBM.SYSINDEXES
WHERE  DBNAME = 'SPJDB'
```

The predicate AND CLUSTERING = 'Y' can be added to report on only the indexes that were created as clustering indexes.

If the optimizer has chosen to use an index as a clustered index in a plan, as the percent of rows in clustering sequence decreases, performance for the plan degrades. Simply rebinding the plan will not solve the problem because, if the CLUSTERRATIO is unchanged, the optimizer will continue using the index.

The data should be reorganized to regain clustering. If the data has lost clustering, there is a good chance that a good deal of index page splitting has occurred and that the indexes would benefit from reorganization as well.

Plans that use a clustering index with a CLUSTERRATIO less than 80 percent can be identified by:

```
SELECT DNAME, BNAME, TBNAME
FROM   SYSIBM.SYSPLANDEP   P,
       SYSIBM.SYSINDEXES   I,
       SYSIBM.SYSINDEXPART IP
WHERE  P.BNAME    = I.NAME
AND    P.BCREATOR = I.CREATOR
AND    I.NAME     = IP.IXNAME
AND    I.CREATOR  = IP.IXCREATOR
AND    BTYPE      = 'I'
AND    CLUSTERING = 'Y'
AND    CLUSTERRATIO < 80
```

The performance of these plans will improve in most cases after a reorganization of the data. Similar analysis can be done for packages by replacing SYSPLANDEP with SYSPACKDEP. Optionally the SELECT referencing SYSPLANDEP can be unioned with a SELECT referencing SYSPACKDEP.

Index Leaf Distribution

The LEAFDIST column in the SYSIBM.SYSINDEXPART tables gives the percentage of noncontiguous leaf pages to total leaf pages in an index. Non-matching index scans, index lookaside, and sequential detection decrease in efficiency as the LEAFDIST increases. Reorganization of the index should be considered if the LEAFDIST is 20 or more. This statement identifies those indexes:

```
SELECT IXNAME, LEAFDIST
FROM   SYSIBM.SYSINDEXPART
WHERE  LEAFDIST > = 20
```

Number of Index Levels

The more index levels there are, the more I/O operations are required for matching index scans. As was explained in Chapter 6, in most cases an index of greater than three levels occurs as a result of index page splitting to maintain a balanced B-tree. This statement identifies indexes with more than three levels:

```
SELECT NAME, INDEXSPACE, NLEVELS
FROM   SYSIBM.SYSINDEXES
WHERE  NLEVELS > 3
```

Ideally one would test for the number of levels in the index after the index was built, and if that number is exceeded, the index should be reorganized.

Overflow Rows

When a variable-length row expands beyond the amount of space left on its page, DB2 relocates it and leaves a pointer to its new location. Accessing such a row then requires two I/O operations: one to find the pointer and one to find the row. Reorganization should be considered when about 3 to 5 percent of a table's rows have been relocated. This statement provides the percentage of rows that have been relocated:

```
SELECT TSNAME, NEARINDREF, FARINDREF, CARD,
       (NEARINDREF + FARINDREF)*100/CARD
       PCTFREE, FREEPAGE
FROM   SYSIBM.SYSTABLEPART
WHERE  CARD > 0
AND    ((NEARINDREF + FARINDREF)*100/CARD) > 0
```

NEARINDREF gives the number of rows relocated to a near page, and FARINDREF gives the number relocated to a more distant page as was discussed in Chapter 3. Increasing the percent of free space can avoid the movement of rows if the rows expanded in length are scattered throughout the data pages. In any case, consideration should be given to dropping the tablespace and recreating it as a segmented tablespace if rows are moved frequently. Free space for the expanded row can be found much more efficiently by accessing only the space map pages with a segmented tablespace rather than having to scan data pages as is necessary with nonsegmented tablespaces.

14.5   SPACE MANAGEMENT

System administrators, DBAs, and developers often want to know how much disk storage has been allocated for DB2 datasets and how much is actually being used by them. These statements request answers to those questions. If too much or too little space has been allocated, the tablespace can be altered and the appropriate amount of space specified. The new space allocation will be made available when the tablespace or index is reorganized, recovered, or when load replace is executed. The STOSPACE utility, which updates catalog statistics on space usage, should be executed before the following analyses are performed; otherwise the SPACE column will contain zero. In addition if storage groups are not used, the SPACE column will contain zero, and the following statements will be of no value in most cases.

Allocated Space

This statement identifies the DASD volumes and amount of space within them allocated to DB2 storage groups:

```
SELECT NAME, SPACE, SPCDATE, VOLID
FROM   SYSIBM.SYSSTOGROUP,
       SYSIBM.SYSVOLUMES
```

NAME identifies the storage group; SPACE gives the amount of allocated space in kilobyte units; VOLID gives the DASD volume; and SPCDATE gives the date the STOSPACE utility was last run. If developers create their own VSAM datasets USING VCAT rather than using a storage group, the STOSPACE utility does not record in the catalog tables the amount of space allocated. Some information is available using LISTCAT on the ICF catalog, but a number of values will contain zero since DB2 processing of VSAM datasets does not result in all values being updated with USING VCAT.

A technique for getting the space statistics into the catalog tables is to alter the tablespace (changing it to using a storage group), execute the STOSPACE utility to collect the space figures, and (if it is required) alter the tablespace back to USING VCAT.

Pages Allocated versus Pages Used

The following statement identifies the number of pages allocated to and used by a tablespace:

```
SELECT T.TSNAME, TP.PQTY, T.NAME,
       T.NPAGES, T.CARD
FROM   SYSIBM.SYSTABLEPART TP,
       SYSIBM.SYSTABLES T
WHERE  TP.TSNAME = T.TSNAME
AND    CREATOR   = &TABLECREATOR
AND    TYPE      = 'T'
```

NPAGES gives the number of pages in the tablespace on which rows actually appear. It does not include pages that have been formatted but do not have active rows. PQTY is the primary space allocation in 4-kilobyte page units. Comparing NPAGES with PQTY is valid only if there is only one table in the tablespace.

Space Used

The following statement indicates how much space has actually been preformatted and used by a DB2 system as of the last time RUNSTATS and STOSPACE were executed and the percentage of allocated space that amount represents:

```
SELECT NAME, SPACE, NACTIVE,
       NACTIVE*PGSIZE*100/SPACE
FROM   SYSIBM.SYSTABLESPACE
WHERE  SPACE > 0
```

NACTIVE provides the number of preformatted and used pages; PGSIZE gives the page size. Each row in the report represents a tablespace. If the percentage of space used is less than 80 percent and the database administrator expects little growth, he or she might consider reallocating space for the tablespace. A low utilization percentage may, however, indicate that space from dropped tables is not being used and should be reclaimed through reorganization.

Space Unavailable after a Table Has Been Dropped

When a table is dropped, its space in a nonsegmented tablespace is unavailable for use until the tablespace is reorganized. This statement identifies nonsegmented tablespaces that contain unusable space for that reason and the percentage of each such tablespace that is unavailable:

```
SELECT TSNAME, DBNAME, PERCDROP
FROM   SYSIBM.SYSTABLEPART
WHERE  PERCDROP > 0
```

This situation would not be a problem in segmented tablespaces, which can immediately use space from dropped tables.

Determining Space Available

The following statement determines the amount of free space (PERCACTIVE) available in a tablespace or partition:

```
SELECT TSNAME, DBNAME, PERCACTIVE
FROM    SYSIBM.SYSTABLEPART
WHERE   DBNAME = 'DASPJDB'
```

If PERCACTIVE is above the desired amount, free space can be re-gained through reorganization.

Multiple Extents

When DB2 has had to use the secondary storage allocation for a tablespace, the tablespace is said to occupy multiple extents, a situation to be avoided. If data are in secondary extents, they are probably not near those in the primary allocation, unnecessarily increasing disk seek times during data access. This statement identifies tablespaces likely to occupy multiple extents, in this case a storage group with a name beginning 'SPJST'.

```
SELECT TSNAME, PQTY, SQTY, SPACE,
       SPACE*100/(PQTY*4)
FROM   SYSIBM.SYSTABLEPART,
       SYSIBM.SYSTABLESPACE
WHERE  TSNAME     = NAME
AND    PARTITIONS = 0
AND    STORNAME   LIKE 'SPJST%'
```

If the percentage derived by the calculation in line 2 is relatively high—as determined by an installation's experience—the tablespace is likely to occupy multiple extents.

Index Space Used

The following statement calculates the space used for indexes in the database in primary and secondary extents as a percentage of the primary allocation for all indexes in the DASPJDB database.

```
SELECT NAME, PQTY, SQTY, SPACE,
       SPACE*100/(PQTY*4)
FROM   SYSIBM.SYSINDEXES,
       SYSIBM.SYSINDEXPART
WHERE  NAME = IXNAME
AND    PARTITION = 0
AND    DBNAME = 'DASPJDB'
```

If the percentage is high, the index is in multiple extents. It should be altered to increase the primary quantity before the next reorganization.

Placement of Indexes and Tablespaces

Performance on large tables can be improved by placing indexes and table-spaces on separate volumes and channels so that more parallelism in I/O can be achieved. Competition for resources can be reduced by placing indexes and tablespaces on different devices. This would apply to joins where benefits can be gained by placing indexes on separate volumes and channels from the tables that they reference. The statement will identify the VOLIDs of tablespaces and indexes created using storage groups.

```
SELECT I.TBCREATOR, I.TBNAME, I.CREATOR,
       I.NAME, P.PARTITION, P.STORNAME,
       P.VCATNAME, V.VOLID
FROM   SYSIBM.SYSINDEXPART P,
       SYSIBM.SYSINDEXES   I,
       SYSIBM.SYSVOLUMES   V
WHERE  P.IXCREATOR = I.CREATOR
AND    P.IXNAME    = I.NAME
AND    P.STORNAME  = V.SGNAME
AND    P.STORTYPE  IN ('T', 'I')
ORDER BY I.TBCREATOR, I.TBNAME
   I.CREATOR, I.NAME, P.PARTITION
```

Placement of Work Tablespaces

Performance of sorts will be enhanced with good placement of work tablespaces. They should be placed on devices that are not busy and spread across multiple devices. Less than optimum placement can decrease throughput. The work tablespace in the DSNDB07 database like data tablespaces can be altered and placed in different storage groups to achieve the objectives before a reorganization.

```
SELECT DBNAME, TSNAME,
       STORNAME, VCATNAME,
       NEARINDREF, FARINDREF
FROM   SYSIBM.SYSTABLEPART
WHERE  DBNAME = 'DSNDB07'
ORDER BY DSNAME, TSNAME
```

Tablespace Copies

Whenever an image copy of a tablespace is made for recovery purposes, information about the copy is recorded in SYSIBM.SYSCOPY. This information is used by the recovery utility. But it can also help system administrators and DBAs track the status of copies to determine, among other things, if the current copy schedule is satisfactory. This statement produces a report on the status of copies of tablespaces in the DASPJDB database, including information on when the copies were made:

```
SELECT TSNAME, ICTYPE, TIMESTAMP, DSNAME
FROM   SYSIBM.SYSCOPY
WHERE  DBNAME = 'DASPJDB'
```

DSNAME is the name of the dataset containing the copy. ICTYPE indicates the type of copy that has been made or that a copy is required according to the following codes:

F = Full image copy

I = Incremental image copy

P = Partial recovery point

Q = Quiesce

R = LOAD(REPLACE) LOG(YES)

S = LOAD(REPLACE) LOG(NO)

W = Reorg LOG(NO)

X = Reorg LOG(YES)

Y = Load LOG(NO)

Z = Load LOG(YES)

Copies taken when a tablespace was loaded or reorganized with the LOG of NO option (ICTYPE = 'W' or ICTYPE = 'Y') and when a partial recovery was done without a full image copy (ICTYPE = 'P') are of particular interest to developers because a tablespace cannot be updated or recovered until such a copy has been made. This statement identifies such tablespaces:

```
SELECT TSNAME
FROM   SYSIBM.SYSCOPY
WHERE  ICTYPE IN ('Y', 'W', 'P', 'S')
```

Monitoring 32K Bufferpools

Because reading or writing one 32-kilobyte page may require eight times as much I/O transfer time and physical I/O as one 4-kilobyte page, tablespaces should be assigned to the 32-kilobyte bufferpool only if its table's rows exceed 4 kilobytes. This statement identifies tablespaces in BP32:

```
SELECT NAME, DBNAME, CREATOR, BPOOL
FROM   SYSIBM.SYSTABLESPACE
WHERE  BPOOL = '32K'
```

Determining the Size of a Plan and Package

An estimate of the size of a plan can be determined with the calculation:

```
PLSIZE + CACHESIZE + AVGSIZE * MAX(SECTNO)
```

A plan base section (PLSIZE), the average size of the sections (AVGSIZE), and the cache size can be determined from SYSIBM.SYSPLAN for a plan, in this example the SUPDATE plan:

```
SELECT NAME, PLSIZE, AVGSIZE, CACHESIZE
FROM   SYSIBM.SYSPLAN
WHERE  NAME = 'SUPDATE'
```

The number of sections (MAX(SECTNO)) in a plan can be determined from SYSIBM.SYSSTMT:

```
SELECT PLNAME, NAME, MAX(SECTNO)
FROM   SYSIBM.SYSSTMT
WHERE  PLNAME = 'SUPDATE'
GROUP BY PLNAME, NAME
```

Similar analysis can be done for a package, PROGA in the example, by replacing SYSPLAN with SYSPACKAGE and SYSSTMT with SYS-PACKSTMT like:

```
SELECT COLLID, NAME, VERSION, PKSIZE, AVGSIZE
FROM   SYSIBM.SYSPACKAGE
WHERE  COLLID  = 'UNITEST'
AND    NAME    = 'PROGA'
AND    VERSION = 'V1'

SELECT COLLID, NAME, VERSION, MAX(SECTNO)
FROM   SYSIBM.SYSPACKSTMT
WHERE  COLLID  = 'UNITEST'
AND    PKNAME  = 'PROGA'
AND    VERSION = 'V1'
```

The size of the **PROGA** package is about:

```
PKSIZE + AVGSIZE * MAX(SECTNO)
```

The size of plans and packages are useful in determining if the EDM pool is sized properly for the plans and packages to be executed. The use of the EDM pool is discussed in Chapters 1, 3, and 10.

Sizing the EDM Pool

An estimate of the maximum size of the EDM pool can be calculated from the catalog tables based on currently bound plans and packages. If all plans were executed concurrently and all plan sections were loaded, the following statement would give a good estimate.

```
SELECT P.NAME, P.PLSIZE, P.AVGSIZE, S.NAME,
       MAX(S.SECTNO) * P.AVGSIZE,
       (MAX(S.SECTNO) * P.AVGSIZE) + P.PLSIZE
FROM   SYSIBM.SYSPLAN P,
       SYSIBM.SYSSTMT S
WHERE  P.CREATOR = S.PLCREATOR
AND    P.NAME    = S.PLNAME
AND    S.SECTNO  > 0
```

```
GROUP BY P.NAME, S.NAME, P.PLSIZE, P.AVGSIZE
ORDER BY P.NAME, S.NAME
```

Similar analysis can be done for packages by replacing SYSPLAN with SYSPACKAGE and SYSSTMT with SYSPACKSTMT.

It is also necessary to estimate the size of DBD (database descriptors) when sizing the EDM pool. This can be done for all databases that have been created with:

```
-DISPLAY DATABASE(*)
```

This analysis will provide information on the upper limit of EDM pool size requirements for the current work load.

14.6 TRACKING REFERENTIAL INTEGRITY STRUCTURES

The REPORT utility provides comprehensive reports on referential integrity structures. However, it will sometimes be helpful to find information about them by querying the catalog directly. Here are a few statements for locating basic information about referential integrity structures.

The following statement identifies all tables created by POSYSTEM that include a primary key and are part of a referential integrity structure.

```
SELECT CREATOR, TBNAME, RELNAME,
       REFTBCREATOR, REFTBNAME
FROM   SYSIBM.SYSRELS
WHERE  REFTBCREATOR = 'POSYSTEM'
ORDER BY CREATOR, TBNAME, RELNAME
```

REFTBNAME is the name of the primary key table in a relationship; RELNAME, the name of the relational integrity constraint.

This statement identifies tables created by POSYSTEM that include a foreign key.

```
SELECT REFTBCREATOR, REFTBNAME,
       RELNAME, DELETERULE,
       CREATOR, TBNAME
FROM   SYSIBM.SYSRELS
WHERE  CREATOR = 'POSYSTEM'
ORDER BY REFTBCREATOR, REFTBNAME, RELNAME
```

Tables without Primary and Foreign Keys

This statement identifies tables that do not have a primary key.

```
SELECT CREATOR, NAME
FROM   SYSIBM.SYSTABLES
WHERE  TYPE = 'T'
```

```
AND    STATUS = ' '
ORDER BY NAME
```

And this statement identifies tables that do not have any foreign keys.

```
SELECT CREATOR, NAME, DBNAME
FROM   SYSIBM.SYSTABLES
WHERE  TYPE = 'T'
AND    CREATOR || NAME
NOT IN
  (SELECT DISTINCT CREATOR || TBNAME
   FROM SYSIBM.SYSRELS)
ORDER BY NAME
```

Foreign keys do not have to be indexed, but it is usually best if they are. If there is an index on a foreign key, DB2 will always use it to enforce the key's constraints. Without an index, a tablespace scan of each dependent table will be required whenever the primary key is updated or deleted and for joins involving the foreign key. The following statement identifies foreign keys created by POSYSTEM for which there are no indexes.

```
SELECT REL.CREATOR, REL.TBNAME, REL.RELNAME
FROM   SYSIBM.SYSRELS R
WHERE  REL.CREATOR = 'POSYSTEM' AND
       REL.CREATOR || REL.TBNAME || REL.RELNAME
NOT IN
  (SELECT R.CREATOR || R.TBNAME || R.RELNAME
   FROM SYSIBM.SYSFOREIGNKEYS F,
        SYSIBM.SYSRELS      R,
        SYSIBM.SYSINDEXES   I,
        SYSIBM.SYSKEYS      K
  WHERE F.CREATOR    = R.CREATOR
  AND   F.TBNAME     = R.TBNAME
  AND   F.RELNAME    = R.RELNAME
  AND   R.CREATOR    = I.TBCREATOR
  AND   R.TBNAME     = I.TBNAME
  AND   R.COLCOUNT < = I.COLCOUNT
  AND   I.CREATOR    = K.IXCREATOR
  AND   I.NAME       = K.IXNAME
  AND   K.COLNAME    = F.COLNAME
  AND   K.COLSEQ     = F.COLSEQ
  GROUP BY I.NAME, R.CREATOR, R.TBNAME,
           R.RELNAME, R.COLCOUNT
  HAVING COUNT(*) = R.COLCOUNT)
ORDER BY REL.CREATOR, REL.TBNAME, REL.RELNAME
```

14.7 DETERMINING FUNCTION AND OBJECT PRIVILEGES

The following statements will help a system or database administrator determine who is authorized to perform which functions on which data.

Authorization to Update a Column

This statement identifies individuals, plans, and packages that may update a given column—in this case, a column with salary information:

```
SELECT GRANTOR, GRANTEE, TNAME, COLNAME
FROM   SYSIBM.SYSCOLAUTH
WHERE  COLNAME = 'SALARY'
```

GRANTEE includes the IDs of those authorized to update the column and the names of plans or packages that update it. The statement does not identify those authorized to execute those plans and packages. That information can be obtained by using the plan names derived from the previous statement in a statement like this one:

```
SELECT GRANTEE, GRANTOR, NAME
FROM   SYSIBM.SYSPLANAUTH
WHERE  NAME = 'SUPDATE'
```

A similar analysis can be done for packages by replacing SYSPLANAUTH with SYSPACKAUTH.

Those Using a Table or View

When an individual responsible for a table considers dropping it or views based on it, he or she should be sure to consult with those authorized to use it. This consultation gives the authorized users a chance to explain the need for the table or views, or it at least informs users that the table or views will no longer be available. The first SELECT of this UNION statement identifies those authorized to manipulate a table; the second SELECT identifies those authorized to use individual columns:

```
SELECT GRANTOR, GRANTEE, TCREATOR, ' ',
       TTNAME, ALTERAUTH, DELETEAUTH,
       INDEXAUTH, INSERTAUTH,
       SELECTAUTH, UPDATEAUTH
FROM   SYSIBM.SYSTABAUTH
WHERE  TCREATOR    = &CREATOR
AND    TTNAME      = &TAB
AND    GRANTEETYPE = ' '
AND    GRANTOR    ¬= GRANTEE
AND    UPDATECOLS ¬= '*'
  UNION
SELECT GRANTOR, GRANTEE, CREATOR, '*',
       COLNAME,
       ' ', ' ', ' ', ' ', ' ', ' ',
FROM   SYSIBM.SYSCOLAUTH
WHERE  CREATOR     = &CREATOR
AND    TNAME       = &TAB
AND    GRANTEETYPE = ' '
```

```
AND    GRANTOR ¬= GRANTEE
ORDER BY 1,4
```

The search is on GRANTEETYPE of "blank," which indicates an individual rather than a plan or package. The UPDATECOLS ¬= '*' criterion in the first SELECT limits the search to tables or views for which authorization has been granted for all columns. The following statement, simpler than the previous one, also identifies persons authorized to use a table but not plans and packages that access the table:

```
SELECT TTNAME, GRANTEE, DATEGRANTED
FROM   SYSIBM.SYSTABAUTH
WHERE  GRANTEETYPE ¬= 'P'
AND    TTNAME      = 'S'
AND    TCREATOR    = 'POSYSTEM'
AND    GRANTOR     ¬= GRANTEE
```

High-Level Authorizations

The SYSIBM.SYSUSERAUTH table identifies those authorized to carry out the functions of system administrator and database administrator. In general, these functions include the ability to create such high-level objects as databases and storage groups, to display the status of databases, to start and stop DB2, to start and stop databases, and to grant authorities. This statement, for example, identifies those who may create databases:

```
SELECT GRANTEE, CREATEDBAAUTH
FROM   SYSIBM.SYSUSERAUTH
WHERE  CREATEDBAAUTH ¬= ' '
```

The SYSIBM.SYSDBAUTH table identifies the privileges granted on objects in a database. This statement indicates the persons authorized to use objects in the DASPJDB database and the types of authorizations for these individuals:

```
SELECT GRANTEE, CREATETABAUTH, CREATETSAUTH,
       DBADMAUTH, DBCTRLAUTH,
       DBMAINTAUTH, DISPLAYDBAUTH,
       DROPAUTH, IMAGCOPYAUTH, LOADAUTH,
       REORGAUTH, RECOVERDBAUTH,
       REPAIRAUTH, STARTDBAUTH,
       STATSAUTH, STOPAUTH
FROM   SYSIBM.SYSDBAUTH
WHERE  NAME = 'DASPJDB'
```

14.8 DOCUMENTATION

The Catalog tables can provide online much of the information about database systems that installations typically have to maintain in hard-copy documentation. The statements in this section produce some of the more useful reports. The reports might be made part of an application system's hard-copy documentation with its currency being verifiable online as required.

Table Layout

The most basic form of database documentation in nonrelational systems has traditionally been the file layout. This statement produces the analo-gous documentation in a relational system: the table layout. This statement returns a table's column names, their data types, lengths, and positions in the table:

```
SELECT NAME, COLTYPE, LENGTH, SCALE,
       NULLS, FOREIGNKEY, COLNO
FROM   SYSIBM.SYSCOLUMNS
WHERE  TBCREATOR = &TBCREATOR
AND    TBNAME    = &TBNAME
ORDER BY COLNO
```

Objects and Programs in a Database System

This statement determines all the tablespaces, tables, and indexes within a given database, in this case database TIED0100:

```
SELECT TSP.NAME, TSP.CREATOR, T.NAME,
       T.CREATOR, I.NAME, I.CREATOR
FROM   SYSIBM.SYSTABLESPACE TSP,
       SYSIBM.SYSTABLES     T,
       SYSIBM.SYSINDEXES    I
WHERE  TSP.DBNAME = 'TIED0100'
AND    I.DBNAME   = 'TIED0100'
AND    T.DBNAME   = 'TIED0100'
AND    TSP.NAME   = T.TSNAME
AND    T.NAME     = I.TBNAME
```

This statement identifies all the plans and packages that access a given data-base system—in this case, DASPJDB:

```
SELECT PL.NAME, T.DBNAME, 'PLAN', 'PLAN'
FROM   SYSIBM.SYSPLANDEP    PLD,
       SYSIBM.SYSPLAN       PL,
       SYSIBM.SYSTABLESPACE T
WHERE  PLD.BTYPE = 'R'
AND    T.DBNAME  = 'DASPJDB'
AND    T.NAME    = PLD.BNAME
AND    PLD.DNAME = PL.NAME
UNION ALL
SELECT PK.NAME, T.DBNAME, PK.COLLID, PK.VERSION
```

```
FROM    SYSIBM.SYSPACKDEP    PKD,
        SYSIBM.SYSPACKAGE    PK,
        SYSIBM.SYSTABLESPACE T
WHERE PKD.BTYPE = 'R'
AND    T.DBNAME  = 'DASPJDB'
AND    T.NAME    = PKD.BNAME
AND    PKD.DNAME = PK.NAME
```

Change Impact Analysis

One of the primary functions of documentation is to help developers assess the impact of changes to an application system. When a column is changed, for example, programs, plans, and packages that use it may have to be revised. This statement helps developers locate tables that include a column—in this case, column SN—with the plans and packages that access those tables:

```
SELECT C.TBNAME, C.TBCREATOR, PLD.DNAME, 'PLAN', 'PLAN'
FROM    SYSIBM.SYSPLANDEP PLD,
        SYSIBM.SYSCOLUMNS C
WHERE C.NAME    = 'SN''
AND    C.TBNAME  = PLD.BNAME
AND    PLD.BTYPE = 'T'
UNION ALL
SELECT C.TBNAME, C.TBCREATOR, PKD.DNAME, PKD.COLLID
FROM    SYSIBM.SYSPACKDEP PKD,
        SYSIBM.SYSCOLUMNS C
WHERE C.NAME    = 'SN'
AND    C.TBNAME  = PKD.BNAME
AND    PKD.BTYPE = 'T'
```

The statement identifies plans and packages that access any column in the table containing the column in question but perhaps not that column itself.

The following query, which may require a more costly search, will identify plans and packages that have statements that use the column with the indicated spelling:

```
SELECT PLNAME, PLCREATOR, 'PLAN', 'PLAN'
FROM    SYSIBM.SYSSTMT
WHERE  TEXT LIKE '%SN%'
UNION ALL
SELECT NAME, PLCREATOR, COLLID, VERSION
FROM    SYSIBM.SYSPACKSTMT
WHERE  TEXT LIKE '%SN%'
```

The SYSIBM.SYSSTMT and SYSIBM.SYSPACKSTMT table stores each SQL statement within existing plans and packages. The search for each reference to the column may be costly if there are a large number of plans and packages because there is no index on the TEXT column.

14.9 SUMMARY

The catalog tables contain a wealth of information useful to system administrators, DBAs, and developers. Accessing it with standard SQL statements is straightforward once the user becomes familiar with the available information and the table and column names. This chapter has provided a number of statements to get users started.

EXERCISES

14.1. Which catalog tables must be accessed to determine which plans and packages use a particular index?

14.2. If the catalog tables indicate that no plans and packages use an index, why shouldn't the index be dropped immediately?

14.3. What is a good way to determine whether a supposedly clustering index has lost clustering?

14.4. Can space management be done effectively when USING VCAT is used to create tablespaces and indexes rather than using storage groups?

14.5. Which column in which catalog table can indicate that tables in a particular tablespace cannot be updated and that the tablespace cannot be recovered? What are the column values that indicates that situation?

15

Security Control

15.1 INTRODUCTION

DB2 maintains control over its facilities and databases by allowing an action only when the catalog tables show that the user is authorized to take that action. Administrators exercise control by granting privileges in a variety of ways: by authorizing a collection of privileges grouped by job function, by assigning individual privileges, and by granting others the authority to grant privileges. DB2 also confers certain implied privileges; an object's creator, for example, has the implicit right to alter or drop the object. In addition, DB2 cooperates with the security controls of the various attaches and, through exit programs, with external security packages.

Controls cover five types of activities:

1. Database activities, including starting and stopping databases, creating tables and tablespaces, and using a variety of utilities for loading, recovering, reorganizing, and copying data.

2. Table activities, including data manipulation, index creation, and table alteration.

3. Subsystem activities, including creation of databases and storage groups.

4. Plan and package activities, including bind and execution.

5. Use activities, including the use of bufferpools, storage groups, and tablespaces.

These privileges can be assigned in five hierarchical groupings: SYSADM, SYSCTRL, DBADM, DBCTRL, and DBMAINT. A sixth grouping of privileges, SYSOPR, applies specifically to operators. An individual with system administrator privileges (SYSADM) may perform all of these activities; one with database administrator privileges (DBADM) may perform all activities but subsystem ones within assigned databases; an individual with database control authority (DBCTRL) may perform all activities but subsystem ones within assigned databases; and one with database maintenance authority (DBMAINT) may perform about half the database activities within assigned databases. (Fig. 15.1 shows the authorization groupings.)

Some privileges provide for managing the data without being able to select and update it. SYSCTRL has most privileges of SYSADM but cannot access any tables nor execute any plans or packages. DBCTRL, DBMAINT, and SYSOPR, which have much more limited use of DB2 facilities than does SYSADM, cannot access data with SQL. These privileges may be necessary if the organization has top secret data that very few people are allowed to access but others need in order to manage the database objects.

Under the authorization groupings, for example, an individual holding

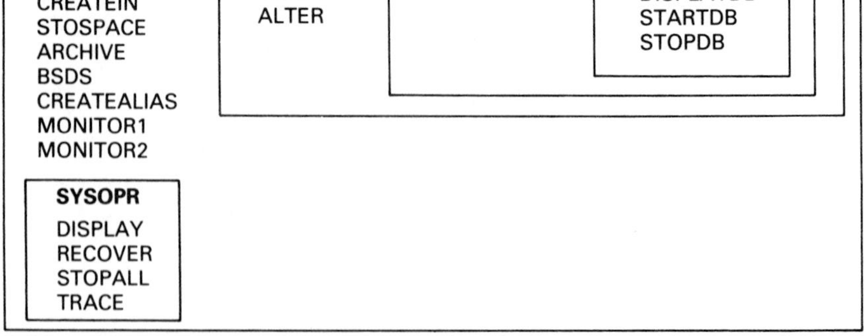

Quiesce utility requires IMAGCOPY privileges
Report utility requires RECOVERDB privileges

Fig. 15.1 Administrative authorities

DBCTRL privileges may create a table (CREATETAB) or a tablespace (CREATETS), display a database's activity (DISPLAYDB), start or stop a database (STARTDB, STOPDB), execute the COPY and QUIESCE (IMAGCOPY), execute the recover and report utility (RECOVERDB), perform reorganizations and repairs (REORG, REPAIR), execute the RUNSTATS utility (STATS), drop a database (DROP), and load tables (LOAD). Someone holding DBADM can perform all the functions of DBCTRL and DBMAINT and may also create, alter, and delete indexes and tables as well as select and update data in the tables.

Administrators may also grant individual privileges to individuals to extend those they hold under a functional grouping. The system administrator may grant bind privileges (BINDADD) to an individual authorized to carry out DBADM activities, for example.

Finally two authorization levels, Install SYSADM and Install SYSOPR, provide the privileges required to install DB2. These include authority to recover and repair the directory and catalog tables. DB2 does not check the catalog tables for these authorities because those tables may not be available when these privileges are needed. The holder of Install SYSADM authority can grant or revoke SYSADM privileges. Once a person has been granted SYSADM privileges they can pass the privilege on to others. Fig. 15.2 describes the catalog tables that DB2 updates when privileges are granted and revoked. Notice the correspondence between the five types of privileges and the tables.

Table privileges

SYSIBM.SYSTABAUTH contains the privileges held by users on tables and views.

SYSIBM.SYSCOLAUTH contains the UPDATE privileges held by users on individual columns of a table or view.

Plan and package privileges

SYSIBM.SYSPLANAUTH contains the privileges held by users over plans and packages.

SYSIBM.SYSPACKAUTH contains the privileges held by users over packages.

Subsystem privileges

SYSIBM.SYSUSERAUTH contains the system privileges held by users.

Database privileges

SYSIBM.SYSDBAUTH contains the privileges held by users over databases.

Use privileges

SYSIBM.SYSRESAUTH contains the privileges held by users over bufferpools, storage groups, and tablespaces.

Fig. 15.2 Catalog tables that record authorizations

15.2   THE SYSTEM ADMINISTRATOR

At most installations, one designated system administrator holds SYSADM privileges, with one or two other individuals also holding them as backups. The system administrator typically assigns the various grouped and individual privileges to database administrators who pass along privileges to developers. Installations may decide to assign privileges according to any of a variety of schemes. In a production environment, the administrators will assign privileges sparingly, with an eye toward maximum data protection. A development group, on the other hand, might emphasize flexibility, giving a large number of developers a wide range of capabilities.

Besides the ability to grant and revoke privileges, system administrators have authority to take any other possible action within the DB2 system. They can revoke privileges granted others, select from or update any table, and alter or drop objects created by others. The system administrators' powers are not absolute, however; they cannot bar a table's creator from selecting from or updating it, nor can they keep an object's creator from dropping the object. And although there are few checks on an administrator's actions, those actions can be monitored through a trace. Since there should be only a few individuals with system administrator's privileges, such a trace should cost relatively little in processing resources. Another alternative is to use SYSCTRL, which allows all operations on objects, except the privilege does not allow for selecting and updating the data and execution of plans and packages.

Security Checked at Execution Time

Much development work revolves around the creation and testing of tables. DB2's security and control scheme therefore allows a table's developer considerable room for action. A table's creator has implicit authority to perform table activities on it: including select; update; alter; drop; create views and indexes; issue the LOCK TABLE, LABEL ON, and COMMENT ON statements; and use the LOAD and RUNSTATS utilities on the table. Several other authorities needed by developers can be granted explicitly—to start or stop a database or display its status or to execute the reorganization, repair, copy, or runstats utilities—as individual privileges or as part of a functional group on a named database.

A table's creator can also share privileges to act on it by passing them along to everyone with access to the DB2 system or to selected individuals. They in turn can pass along to others the authority to pass along some of the privileges.

15.3   GRANT AND REVOKE STATEMENTS

GRANT, REVOKE, and other control statements are in fact a type of SQL. When the statements execute, DB2 updates the catalog tables that contain information about authorizations (Fig. 15.2). These catalog tables are also updated automatically when objects are created to account for implicit privileges held by the creators.

All SQL control statements take a similar form, indicated in the following examples:

```
GRANT PRIVILEGES
   ON OBJECT_NAME
   TO AUTHID (OR PUBLIC)
```

and

```
REVOKE PRIVILEGES
   ON OBJECT_NAME
 FROM AUTHID (OR PUBLIC)
```

The statements are largely self-explanatory. The name of the specific privilege being granted or revoked follows the keyword GRANT or REVOKE. A single statement may grant or revoke multiple privileges. In that case, the privileges' names are separated by commas. GRANTs can be very specific. For example, the privilege to update or delete rows from a table does not carry the privilege to select from it. The keyword ALL after GRANT confers privileges for all table activities.

Those receiving or losing a privilege are identified by their AUTHIDs. (Section 15.10 describes how DB2 manages identifiers. In most cases, they are nonmnemonic character strings. For clarity, the examples in this chapter use names as AUTHIDs.) A single statement can also grant or revoke privileges to more than one individual. In that case, the grantees' AUTHIDs are separated by commas. If the grantor wishes to extend a privilege to all users, the keyword PUBLIC will be used rather than specific IDs or PUBLIC AT ALL LOCATIONS if privileges are to be granted to all locations in a distributed environment.

If grantors wish to pass along the authority to grant a privilege, they complete the GRANT statement with the clause WITH GRANT OPTION. Those receiving the privilege can in turn pass it along in the same way. A privilege may be passed to an unlimited number of users via this option. Usually, however, an organization will institute a policy to limit the number of users receiving any given privilege this way. An administrator can use the catalog authorization tables to monitor the number of times privileges have been passed along. Section 15.9 discusses how DB2 handles revocations of privileges granted via the WITH GRANT OPTION.

15.4 GRANTING AND REVOKING TABLE PRIVILEGES

George has created a table, SPJ, and therefore holds a number of implicit privileges on it, including the authority to alter or drop it or to create a view or index on it. Implicit privileges are limited, however. For example, a table's creator cannot automatically execute utilities other than LOAD and RUNSTATS on the table. Privileges to execute the other utilities must be granted individually or as grouped privileges on a database. (Fig. 15.3 summarizes a table creator's implicit privileges and their limitations.)

One of George' privileges is the authority to pass along privileges on table SPJ to others. He would like anyone with access to DB2 to be able to select from that table. He would use this statement to grant that privilege:

```
GRANT SELECT
    ON GEORGE.SPJ
    TO PUBLIC;
```

He would like Aaron to be able to insert and delete rows and execute the grant:

```
GRANT INSERT, DELETE
    ON GEORGE.SPJ
    TO AARON;
```

Later George wishes to revoke those privileges. He has two statement choices:

```
REVOKE INSERT, DELETE
    ON GEORGE.SPJ
    FROM AARON;
```

or

```
REVOKE ALL
    ON GEORGE.SPJ
    FROM AARON;
```

```
A table's creator has the implicit authority to:

  ▪    Alter or drop the table.
  ▪    Create a view or index on the table.
  ▪    Select, insert, update, and delete rows from the table.
  ▪    Use the LOAD or RUNSTATS utility on the table.
```

Fig. 15.3 Implicit privileges held by a table's creator

In either case, Aaron's authority to pass along the privilege is also automatically revoked. And the statement also revokes all privileges Aaron has granted under authority of the original GRANT statement.

Update authority may be granted for an entire table or only specific columns, with the designated columns indicated in parentheses:

```
GRANT UPDATE (SNAME, CITY)
    ON GEORGE.SPJ
    TO HEATHER, ADAM;
```

The update privileges may not be revoked by column, however, only by the entire table. George could not revoke Heather or Adam's privilege to update only the SNAME column, for example. Instead he must revoke update privileges for the entire table:

```
REVOKE UPDATE
    ON GEORGE.S
   FROM HEATHER, ADAM;
```

To give Fleur all table activity privileges on his SPJ table, George would use this statement:

```
GRANT ALL
    ON GEORGE.SPJ
    TO FLEUR;
```

He can revoke all those privileges with a REVOKE ALL statement.

```
REVOKE ALL
    ON GEORGE.SPJ
  FROM FLEUR;
```

15.5 PLAN AND PACKAGE PRIVILEGES

The authority to bind and execute plans, packages, and collections can be controlled in a variety of ways. Most of the bind privileges provide the authority to bind, rebind, free, and execute plans and packages and assume that the binder has select and update privileges on the tables being manipulated in the program. Most organizations grant BINDADD to application developers that allow them to bind new plans and packages and to hold all bind privileges on their objects. Eric can be granted the privilege like:

```
GRANT BINDADD
    TO ERIC;
```

The BIND privilege assumes that the plan or package has been previously bound. An AUTHID that binds a plan or package with BIND authority will have the same privileges as if the bind had been done with BIN-

DADD authority. SUPDATE has been bound by Eric and he can give all bind privileges to Heather with this statement:

```
GRANT BIND
    ON PLAN SUPDATE
    TO HEATHER;
```

Once Heather has bound the plan, Eric,will not be able to execute the plan assuming that he does not hold SYSADM privileges.

The BINDAGENT privilege provides for managing plans and packages without being able to execute them. The privileges must be granted by the owner or SYSADM. The AUTHID that has been granted BINDAGENT can bind a plan or package on behalf of the owner by specifying the OWNER parameter but cannot execute or free it. The primary AUTHID is placed in the BOUNDBY column.

If packages are being used in conjunction with plans, the CREATE IN privilege is required in addition to BINDADD or BIND. CREATE IN privileges provide for binding packages in a collection. The following GRANT statement will allow Heather to bind SQL into packages in the SYSTEST collection:

```
GRANT CREATE
    IN COLLECTION SYSTEST
    TO HEATHER;
```

The CREATE IN privilege, like the BINDADD and BIND privileges, provides for binding, rebinding, freeing, and execution of packages.

An AUTHID can be given privileges on all occurrence of packages in all collections. Recall from Chapter 10 that a set of tables can be managed with packages and the SET CURRENT PACKAGESET statement. For example, the following grant will allow Eric these privileges.

```
GRANT CREATE
    IN COLLECTION *.PROGA
    TO ERIC;
```

The use of the global operator (*) requires SYSADM authority. Plan owners do not have privileges on each package in their plan. Heather can be given privileges on all packages in a collection by SYSADM like:

```
GRANT CREATE
    IN COLLECTION SYSTEST.*
    TO HEATHER;
```

Similarly Bill can be given the privilege to execute all packages in the SYSTEST collection by SYSADM like:

```
GRANT EXECUTE
    ON PACKAGE SYSTEST.*
    TO BILL;
```

Package Privileges with a Remote Unit of Work

Remote bind of packages requires that the binder hold BINDADD and CREATE IN privileges at the server site. Alternatively, if the package owner has COPY privileges at the local DB2 site, the package can be copied to the server site. The BIND PLAN PKLIST function is performed at the local DB2 site and privileges must be held at the local DB2. The owner of a plan must have EXECUTE privilege on each package or collection. The user of a plan must have EXECUTE privilege on the plan and each remote package or collection. The situation can be simplified by granting bind, copy, and execute privileges in a group like:

```
GRANT ALL
    ON PACKAGE PACKA
    TO ERIC;
```

EXECUTE Privileges

Initially after a plan or package is bound, the only AUTHID that can execute it other than SYSADM is the one who bound it. That AUTHID can use GRANT EXECUTE statements to pass execution privileges on the plan or package to others. Those given execution privileges on a plan or package need not hold individual privileges on the tables the plan or package uses when using static SQL. If embedded dynamic SQL is used, privileges must be granted on the tables manipulated in the plan and packages.

This statement gives Bill the authority to execute plan SUPDATE:

```
GRANT EXECUTE
    ON PLAN SUPDATE
    TO BILL;
```

If packages are used with the plan, privileges need to be granted on all packages in a collection or specific packages. The most common security management technique is to grant execution privileges on all packages in a collection—for the SPJCOLL collection in the example:

```
GRANT EXECUTE
    ON SPJCOLL.*
    TO BILL;
```

An alternative is to grant execution privileges on specific package, for example, the PROGA and PROGB packages:

```
GRANT EXECUTE
   ON SPJCOLL.PROGA, SPJCOLL.PROGB
   TO DAWN;
```

Grants on individual packages can cause complexities. An example will demonstrate the point. Assume that Dawn is granted BINDADD and EXECUTE privileges on PROGA and PROGB packages. She binds a PROGC package and does an explicit bind of a plan naming PROGA, PROGB, and PROGC DBRMs (database request modules) in the package list. If Dawn's privileges on PROGA or PROGB are revoked, the entire plan is marked as invalid. The complexities can be avoided by granting privileges on the SPJCOLL collection.

Security Checked at Execution Time

Each time an AUTHID executes a plan or package, it is necessary to check that privileges have been granted. The first check is against the authorization cache in the EDM (environmental descriptor manager) pool to determine if the AUTHID has previously executed the plan. If the cache is still in the pool, that is, if the space has not been reused, a minimal amount of CPU time is required. If the AUTHID is not found, DB2 checks to see if the AUTHID has SYSADM privileges. If not, explicitly granted privileges are checked, and finally implicit privileges are checked. This can require considerable I/O and CPU time.

The sequence of checking is performed only once as the transaction is executed repeatedly by the same AUTHIDs when using the authorization cache. Recall from Chapter 10 that the CACHESIZE can be specified as from 256 to 4096 bytes when the plan is bound. The base portion of the authorization cache is 32 bytes and each cached AUTHID requires 8 bytes. Once the authorization cache is filled, a current AUTHID will be replaced by the next AUTHID that executes the plan. Optionally the cache size can be zero for those plans that are not executed frequently by the same AUTHID to avoid taking unnecessary space in the EDM pool.

DB2 may be made to defer to CICS or IMS security completely for applications when they are moved to production. In fact, this can improve performance by avoiding some of DB2's privilege checking. To turn an application's security over to IMS or CICS, DB2 execution authority for the application's plans and packages is granted to the public. A bit in the execution plan indicates it is a public plan. When a user attempts to execute the plan, DB2 checks for the bit, finds it, and does no further security checking. CICS or IMS security mechanisms would have to have been previously determined if the person can execute the transaction.

An unauthorized user would find it difficult to circumvent the CICS or

IMS security by attempting to take advantage of the public access to the plan or package under TSO or through the call attach facility. Screen control would continue to be handled by the other attach. And if an external security package protects the datasets holding the plan and packages, the host-language source code, the SQL in the DBRM library, and the load module, security should be good despite the public privilege granted under DB2 in most cases. In addition, the ENABLE/DISABLE parameters can be specified at bind time to designate the execution environment as was discussed in Chapter 10.

15.6 SUBSYSTEM PRIVILEGES

System administrators can authorize and revoke grouped privileges in a number of ways at the subsystem or database level. The CREATEDBA grant gives the grantee the authority to create databases and hold DBADM authority over them. Once the grantee has created the databases, the CREATEDBA grant can be revoked. The individual can no longer create databases but retains DBADM authority over those he or she already created. The CREATEDBC grant allows creation of databases but confers only DBCTRL authority over them. (Fig. 15.4 summarizes subsystem privileges.)

In most cases, privileges granted as part of a group may not be revoked individually. If a programmer holds DBADM authority over a database, for example, a statement to revoke that individual's authority to create tablespaces in the database would have no effect. To achieve that end, the administrator would have to revoke the DBADM authority and grant each of its component privileges—except for CREATETS—individually.

Most of the remaining subsystem privileges that have not been discussed—STOSPACE, ARCHIVE, BSDS, MONITOR1, and MONITOR2 are privileges on operations usually performed by the systems administrator and are seldom granted individually. An exception is the CREATEALIAS privilege, used primarily in a distributed environment. An AUTHID must have the privilege to create an alias, but the person using the alias need have privileges only on the underlying table or view to which the alias refers. Aliases are discussed in Chapter 17.

15.7 DATABASE PRIVILEGES

System administrators may also grant grouped privileges over specific databases. For example, the statement:

```
GRANT DBADM
    ON DATABASE DASPJDB
    TO FLEUR;
```

- SYSADM allows almost all privileges.
- SYSCTRL has almost all SYSADM except the privilege does not allow selecting or updating data and execution of plans and packages.
- CREATEDBA allows the creation of databases and DBADM authority over the databases created.
- CREATEDBC allows the creation of databases and DBCTRL authority over the databases created.
- CREATESG allows the creation of storage groups.
- CREATEALIAS allows for creating aliases on tables and views.
- BINDADD allows the binding of new plans and packages.
- BINDAGENT allows the binding of plans and packages without select/update privileges on the data.
- CREATE IN allows for adding a package to a collection.
- STOSPACE allows for execution of the STOSPACE utility.
- ARCHIVE allows for execution of the ARCHIVE LOG command.
- BSDS allows for execution of −RECOVER BSDS.
- MONITOR1 allows for starting traces except those that contain secure data such as SQL statement text and audit data.
- MONITOR2 allows for starting all traces with all options.
- SYSOPR allows usage of display, recovery, stopall, and trace.

Fig. 15.4 Subsystem privileges

gives Fleur all privileges on all objects in the database.

A number of privileges may also be granted individually at the database level. For example, the statement:

```
GRANT CREATETS, CREATETAB
   ON DATABASE DASPJDB
   TO ADAM, HEATHER;
```

authorizes Adam and Heather to create tablespaces (CREATETS) and tables (CREATETAB) within the database DASPJDB.

The use of utilities can be granted on a database like:

```
GRANT IMAGCOPY, REORG
   ON DATABASE DASPJDB
   TO IVA;
```

will allow Iva to execute the COPY and REORG utilities on any tablespace in DASPJDB.

15.8 RESOURCE USAGE PRIVILEGES

Use privileges can be granted on a bufferpool, storage group, or tablespace. System and database administrators generally grant the use privileges developers need to exercise their create privileges. If developers are to use storage groups to create tablespaces and indexes in a database, for example, they must be granted use of storage groups in which to create them. And if they are to create tablespaces or indexes, they must have use of bufferpools.

The GRANT and REVOKE statements for use privileges are very similar to the usual format except that USE OF is used. For example, all individuals who create physical objects will need the use of a bufferpool, granted with a statement like this:

```
GRANT USE OF BUFFERPOOL BPO
    TO PUBLIC;
```

This statement will give Fleur the use of DASD space to create physical objects in the DASPJSTO storage group:

```
GRANT USE OF STOGROUP DASPJSTO
    TO FLEUR
```

Granting privileges on storage groups provides for controlling the use of DASD space. Fleur will be able to use only the DASD volumes identified in the DASPJSTO storage group. If a finer level of space control is required, a tablespace can be created with a designated amount of space and privileges to use the tablespace granted:

```
GRANT USE OF TABLESPACE DASPJDB.DASPJTSP
    TO FLEUR;
```

Now Fleur will be able to use only the amount of space specified when the tablespace was created.

15.9 REVOKE CASCADES

When a privilege that has passed along a line of developers via the WITH GRANT OPTION is revoked from one of them, grantees further down the line also lose it. Assume that Fleur has granted Eric the privilege to update the SPJ table WITH GRANT OPTION, and Eric has passed the privilege to Heather, for example. If Fleur revokes the privilege from Eric, the revocation automatically cascades to Heather and anyone to whom she has passed the privilege.

An individual may receive the same privilege from more than one grantee and pass it along to others. In that case, the effect of the revoke cascade depends on the timing of the GRANTs and REVOKEs. David may also grant Eric the privilege of updating table SPJ. When Fleur revokes the privilege from Eric, he retains it because of David's grant. Whether Heather retains the privilege depends on the timing of the grants and revocations. If Eric had passed the privilege to her before David had granted it to him, she will lose her privilege when Fleur revokes it from Eric. Fig. 15.5 demonstrates this timing effect.

It is advisable to use the CATALOG VISIBILITY option of DB2I to get a revoke impact analysis before revoking a privilege. This is particularly important if the WITH GRANT OPTION has been used or if a high level privilege like SYSADM or DBADM is revoked. Otherwise more privileges may be lost than was initially thought would be. The impact analysis will provide the information necessary to regrant privileges that were revoked due to a cascade effect. GRANT statements can be generated directly from the catalog tables like the grants being generated on all tables beginning with "PO":

```
SELECT DISTINCT 'GRANT SELECT ON',
   GRANTOR||'.'||TTNAME, 'TO', GRANTEE, ';'
FROM   SYSIBM.SYSTABAUTH
WHERE  SELECTAUTH = 'Y'
AND    TTNAME LIKE 'PO%'
AND    GRANTOR ¬= GRANTEE
```

Revoking privileges can also affect plans and packages. If a plan's binder loses a privilege that the plan requires, DB2 will mark it invalid and attempt a rebind when the plan is next executed. (The same principles apply to packages but only the specific packages affected). Assume that Eric has SELECT and UPDATE privileges on table SPJ when he binds plans that select from and update the table. The plan that selects from SPJ will be

---

```
Assume the WITH GRANT OPTION has been used to pass a privilege from one person to
another:

   MONDAY    Fleur grants privilege to Eric
   TUESDAY   Eric grants privilege to Heather
   WEDNESDAY David grants privilege to Eric
   THURSDAY  Eric grants privilege to Dawn
   FRIDAY    Fleur revokes privilege from Eric

Eric retains privilege under David's grant, and Dawn retains the privilege based
on David's grant. Heather, however, loses the privilege because it was based only
on Eric's grant from Fleur, which has been revoked.
```

Fig. 15.5 Timing of grants and revokes

marked invalid if Eric's SELECT privilege is revoked, and the plan that updates will be marked invalid if his UPDATE privilege is revoked. If any automatic rebind fails, which would happen after Eric's privileges were revoked (assuming they were not regranted), the plan is marked inoperative. This avoids perhaps many unsuccessful rebinds taking excessive resources. Once a plan is marked inoperative in the catalog table, it is necessary to do a bind replace. (The example assumes the use of plans without packages. If package are used, the same principles apply.)

An organization frequently has a large number of professionals developing application systems on DB2, and a privilege may be granted a large number of times. One person stated that execute privilege on a plan had been granted 72 times. This is an extreme case, but it is not unusual for privileges to be granted several times. Redundant grants can increase the size of the authorization tables and detract from performance. They can be identified by selecting from each of the authorization tables summarized in Fig. 15.2 and by using REVOKE statements executed to remove the rows. A select to identify redundant grants on plans looks like:

```
SELECT GRANTEE, NAME, COUNT(*)
FROM   SYSIBM.SYSPLANAUTH
GROUP BY GRANTEE, NAME
HAVING COUNT(*) > 2
ORDER BY 3 DESC
```

If multiple AUTHID granted the privilege, a REVOKE statement is required for each grantee. An alternative for SYSADM that minimizes the number of revokes that must be issued is:

```
REVOKE PRIVILEGES
   ON SUPDATE
  FROM ROBERT -- or PUBLIC
    BY ALL
```

A similar procedure can be used on all of the authorization tables summarized in Fig. 15.2.

15.10   THE AUTHID

DB2 uses two types of authorization identification, primary and secondary AUTHIDs, to control and track system utilization. The security mechanisms of the various attaches—TSO, CICS, and IMS—provide the individual's primary AUTHID (Fig. 15.6). The secondary AUTHIDs, which are provided by an external security package invoked via installation-written exit programs, can be shared by groups of developers.

AUTHIDs are used in the catalog tables to associate users with privi-

Under CICS, the system administrator specifies in the DB2 DSNCRCT table the AUTHID or the source of the ID to be used by DB2 as the primary AUTHID. The RCT (resource control table) might indicate these ID sources:

```
AUTH = USERID   - CICS user ID
AUTH = GROUP    - RACF group ID (used with secondary AUTHIDs)
AUTH = USER     - Operator ID from the SNT (3 characters padded on the right with
                  5 blanks)
AUTH = TERM     - Terminal ID (4 characters padded with 4 blanks)
AUTH = SIGNID   - VTAM application name for the CICS system
AUTH = (string) - < = 8 character string
AUTH = TXID     - Transaction ID (4 characters padded with 4 blanks)
```

Under IMS, the following sources may provide the primary AUTHID:

```
IMS sign-on ID
LTERM ID
PSB name
USER parameter on job statement
RACF entries
```

Under TSO, the user logon ID serves as the primary AUTHID

Fig. 15.6 Sources for primary AUTHID

leges and with their activities, such as creation and use of objects. The AUTHID belonging to the creator of a table, view, index, or alias is made part of the object's name as a qualifier that must be included in data manipulation statement references to the object with two important exceptions.

1.   If the current SQLID of the individual executing the statement interactively matches the qualifier, that individual need not include it in the reference.

2.   If the binder of the plan or package specifies the qualifier or owner parameter with an AUTHID, that AUTHID provides the qualifier for otherwise unqualified tables and views referenced in the plan or package.

Use of the QUALIFIER parameter on the bind statement provides for specifying the qualifier to be used for all unqualified tables and views referenced as was discussed in Chapter 10. It has the advantage that no privileges need to be granted to the qualifier.

The secondary AUTHID allows developers working on the same project to share both the set of privileges associated with the identification and the ownership of objects. A user can be assigned up to 245 secondary AUTHIDs, but usually would need only a few. (The sample programs outprefix.DSNSAMP(DSN3SATH) and outprefix.DSNSAMP(DSN3SSGN) provide sample secondary AUTHID exits: the first for connections to DB2, the second for sign-on through CICS or IMS.) Typically an installation will set up a secondary AUTHID for each application system and assign the ID to all individuals working on the application. The OWNER parameter in the bind command allows the binder to assign a secondary AUTHID as a plan or package owner, allowing those sharing the ID to perform binds.

Together an individual's primary and secondary AUTHIDs provide what IBM calls composite privileges. An individual can use DB2 under either a primary or secondary AUTHID or both. Looked at from the opposite side of the issue, DB2 will use either or both primary and secondary IDs to control or track an operation, depending on what the operation is.

For some operations in which the primary or secondary ID might be used, the command entered interactively or embedded in a host-language program determines which is actually in effect. The ID specified by the command is called the current SQLID. The command takes the form SET CURRENT SQLID = 'VENDOR'. The current SQLID is indicated by a string of eight or fewer characters matching the user's primary AUTHID or one of his or her secondary AUTHIDs or by a host-language variable containing the string. Another method for setting the current SQLID employs the keyword USER. When the command SET CURRENT SQLID = USER is embedded in a program or entered interactively, the user's primary AUTHID is set as the SQLID. The USER keyword, which we will discuss more fully, provides a means for having the same embedded SQL data manipulation language statement provide different levels of access depending on the program's user. The SQLID specified by the SET CURRENT command remains in effect until it is superseded by another command, until the user's DB2 connection is terminated, or until a new CICS or IMS sign-on or resign-on is received.

For most operations, including execution of most SQL statements, DB2 checks the initiating individual's authority under their composite privileges. DB2 allows the operation if the catalog tables indicate the individual has the necessary authority under the primary or a secondary AUTHID. For some operations, however, including the use of a synonym, granting and revoking privileges, and the creation of unqualified objects, it checks the privileges held only by the current SQLID.

Ownership of Objects

An object's owner automatically has all privileges on the object and can grant them to others. DB2 tracks *ownership* of objects by placing the owner's ID in the CREATOR column of the object's associated catalog table— SYSDATABASE for databases, SYSTABLES for tables, and so on. When individuals qualify an object's name with one of their IDs, DB2 records that ID in the object's CREATOR column to indicate ownership. In either case, the primary AUTHID is recorded in the CREATEDBY column so that the creator can be traced.

DB2 allows users with SYSADM, DBADM, and DBCTRL authority to create certain objects that carry AUTHIDs of others. (Those with SYSADM authority can create tables, indexes, aliases, and views for others. Those with DBADM and DBCTRL authority can create tables and indexes for others.) To do this in the object's CREATE statement, the creator uses the other's AUTHID as the qualifier of the object's name. The person whose AUTHID has been used then holds all implicit privileges on the object, without having been granted the privilege to create the object.

DBADM has all privileges over all objects in a database in most cases. An exception has to do with views created by others. An example illustrates the exception and why it exists. Say that Fleur and Eric both have DBADM privileges over separate databases and each person grants Heather SELECT privileges on one of their tables. Heather can create a view encompassing the two tables in the two databases since only SELECT privileges on a table is required to create a view. Neither Fleur nor Eric will be able to select from the view since it involves reference to a table that they do not have privileges on. This is logical, but what is frustrating to those with DBADM authority is that they cannot use a view even if it is created solely on tables within their specific database. The restriction is a result of the way privileges are recorded in the catalog tables. In addition, SYSADM authority is required to create a view for an AUTHID that is not one of DBADM composite IDs.

To allow a development group to share an object's ownership when a developer using dynamic SQL creates an object without a qualifier, DB2 places the developer's current SQLID in the CREATOR column. Of course, the developer should have the current SQLID set to the group's secondary AUTHID. DB2 still keeps a record, however, of the individuals who actually created the unqualified objects by placing their primary AUTHIDs in the CREATEDBY column of the object's catalog table.

When a plan or package creates an object with static SQL, the plan or package's owner, indicated in SYSPLAN.CREATOR or SYSPACKAGE.CREATOR, who may or may not be the individual executing the plan or package, becomes the object's owner. Therefore, the plan or package's owner must have the required privileges to create the object. DB2 places the binder's primary AUTHID, kept in SYSPLAN.BOUNDBY or SYSPACKAGE.BOUNDBY, in the object's CREATEDBY column.

Ownership of Plans and Packages

A plan or package's owner is recorded as the primary AUTHID of the individual who bound it, unless that person indicates in the bind command a secondary AUTHID shared by others. To do that, the binder uses a command like BIND PLAN (SREPORT) OWNER (VENDOR). In this case, all those with VENDOR as a secondary ID share the plan's ownership and the privileges that go with it. If the owner parameter is not specified, the primary AUTHID of the binder is the owner. The same principles apply to packages.

A plan's owner can transfer ownership to any other of that owner's composite IDs during a rebind or bind replace by indicating the new owner in the rebind command—for example, REBIND PLAN (SREPORT) OWNER (PROJECT). The new owner identification, PROJECT, is indicated for SREPORT in SYSPLAN.CREATOR. The former owner, however, automatically retains privileges on the plan after a rebind. A bind replace, without the RETAIN parameter, is needed to remove the former owner's privilege.

15.11 RESTRICTING ACCESS TO PARTS OF TABLES

Often an installation will want to allow some users access to only certain rows or columns of a table, allowing them to look at all information in an employee table except some salaries, for example. Views offer one way to limit access to a table according to data elements. The USER keyword used in conjunction with an authorization table provides another. We will discuss views first then authorization tables.

Views as Security

Views provide a way to limit access to tables according to data element values. The only privilege required to create a view is to have access to the underlying table. A developer might create a view on a salary table that includes only rows containing salaries below a limit, for example. Users granted data manipulation privileges on that view will be able to access only those rows, not the full base table. Views can also limit access to columns. Columns not included in the view's SELECT statement will not be available to the view's users.

Privileges may be granted and revoked on views in a number of ways. A view's creator automatically holds the same privileges on it as on the underlying tables. If the creator loses a privilege on a base table, he or she automatically loses it on the view. All other users granted that privilege on the view also lose it. Assume, for example, that Eric has SELECT and UPDATE privileges on the SPJ table. He also has SELECT and UPDATE privileges on views he creates from the table. If his UPDATE privilege on SPJ is revoked, he retains his views on it but can no longer update them.

If he loses his privilege to SELECT from SPJ, the views are automatically dropped as are any views created against them.

Use of views to limit access can become unwieldy when access is to be granted according to a number of criteria. For example, suppose one wanted to allow one group of users to see information in the Supplier table only for suppliers located in London, another group to see information on suppliers in Paris, and a third to see information on those in Athens. To accomplish this, the developer creates three views, each including rows only with those city values. Then program logic can test for the user's authorization ID and use the appropriate view. Creating all the views and coding this logic can become a burden if there are to be numerous categories of access to a table. In those cases, the authorization table technique may be easier to manage.

Authorization Tables

Under this technique for limiting access to a table, the developer creates an authorization table, usually requiring only two columns: (1) for the authorization IDs of those allowed access and (2) for the values by which access is to be limited. When a user attempts to access the primary table, a statement selects from the authorization table that has the limiting values. The access statement then uses the value or values in its search criteria. An example will clarify the process.

Consider the problem described above of limiting access to the supplier table by city. The developer would create an authorization table, SUP_AUTH, with the authorization IDs of each user in the AUTHID column, and with the associated city or cities each user is authorized to access information about in the AUTH_CITY column. Recall that the USER keyword refers to the primary AUTHID. The following statement will determine the city value that the individual executing the plan or package is entitled to access and pass it to the host-language variable AUTH_CITY:

```
SELECT AUTH_CITY
INTO  :AUTH-CITY
FROM   SUP_AUTH
WHERE  AUTHID = USER
```

That city value can then be used in the search criteria for the statement the user executes to access the supplier table, for example:

```
SELECT SN, SNAME
INTO  :SN, :SNAME
FROM   SUPPLIER
WHERE  CITY = :AUTH-CITY
```

An alternative, when the user should have access to information about more than one city, employs a subselect to do the authorization checking:

```
SELECT SN, SNAME
INTO  :SN, :SNAME
FROM   SUPPLIER
WHERE  CITY IN
       (SELECT AUTH_CITY
        FROM   AUTHORIZATION
        WHERE  AUTHID = USER)
```

This technique can be simplified through the use of a view. For example:

```
CREATE VIEW AUTH_S (SN, SNAME, STATUS, CITY)
  SELECT SN, SNAME, STATUS, CITY
  FROM   S
  WHERE  CITY IN
       (SELECT AUTH_CITY
        FROM   AUTHORIZATION
        WHERE  AUTHID = USER)
```

A SELECT from AUTH_S view will return only the suppliers that the person executing the program is authorized to see.

Recall that an index cannot be used on the column preceding the IN operator with a subselect. In these examples therefore, a tablespace scan would be required on the supplier table for each access. If there is a unique index on AUTH_CITY, an automatic transformation to a join for selects will give improved performance. A composite index provides for index only access to AUTHID and AUTH_CITY.

Still another technique uses the current SQLID in conjunction with RACF, an external security package. A RACF group is defined for each city with each individual who is allowed access to information on that city assigned to the group. A sign-on exit sets the current SQLID to the city group name. An alternative is to prompt the user for the city name for which access is desired and place the name in the host variable :AUTH-CITY; the set will fail with a −553 SQLCODE if the city is not one of the user's composite IDs. If the set executes, a view like that used above controls the user's access, except that the CURRENT SQLID rather than USER determines the access criteria:

```
CREATE VIEW AUTH_S (SN SNAME, STATUS, CITY)
SELECT SN, SNAME, STATUS, CITY
FROM   S
WHERE  CITY = CURRENT SQLID
WITH CHECK OPTION
```

The advantages of this technique are that it avoids the need either for an authorization table or for IN subselects and joins. The disadvantage is that users cannot be given access according to multiple criteria, in this case according to more than one city value.

Access to the Catalog Tables

Some organizations are concerned that allowing developers the authority to select from the test catalog table may violate their security policy since they will be able to see information about objects in all databases. A view can be created that allows a developer to see information about only those objects in the databases that were created with a qualifier that agrees with one of their composite AUTHIDs. A view is required on each of the catalog tables like the one on SYSCOLUMNS that allows for developers to see the table layout of all tables in all databases that were created by one of their composite AUTHIDs.

```
CREATE VIEW AUTHID.SYSTABLES AS
   SELECT NAME, COLTYPE, LENGTH, SCALE,
          NULLS, FOREIGNKEY, COLNO
   FROM   SYSIBM.SYSCOLUMNS
   WHERE  TBCREATOR = USER
   OR     TBCREATOR = CURRENT SQLID
   ORDER BY COLNO;
```

Privileges are then granted on the view to the public:

```
GRANT SELECT
   ON AUTHID.SYSTABLES
   TO PUBLIC;
```

Catalog Visibility Privileges

Catalog visibility is an option on the DB2I menu panel as was discussed in Chapter 4. The installation default allows the developer to see information on objects authorized through any of the developer's primary or secondary AUTHIDs. Additional privileges can be allowed by populating the control catalog table SYSIBM.DSNCNTLCAT. The table is created through the installation procedure with one row for install SYSADM, and the table must exist with one row.

   The table contains a column USERID to record the AUTHID that is allowed to see objects owned by, or privileges granted to or by, an ID in the OWNERID column. For example, the first row in the control catalog table (Fig. 15.7) allows Eric to see information about objects owned by, or privileges granted to or by SPJSYS. The second row allows Fleur to see information about all objects with a blank OWNERID which would be a good choice for a SYSADM AUTHID. The third row allows anyone to see

SYSIBM.DSNCNTLCAT

USERID	OWNERID
ERIC FLEUR PUBLIC PUBLIC	SPJSYS TESTSYS

Fig. 15.7 Control catalog Table

information about objects owned by, or privileges granted to or by TEST-SYS. The last row can exist in the table with no other rows. It allows anyone to see information about all objects in the catalog tables.

15.12   DATA DEFINITION CONTROL

An external interface can optionally be used to control the creation of objects with the data definition control facility. Partial or complete control of creating objects can be turned over to a security department that uses security software to protect data at a company or to a computer-aided systems engineering (CASE) tool. The use of this facility does *not* avoid existing DB2 authorization checks; rather it imposes additional constraints. The creation, alteration, and dropping of all objects can be controlled by naming only the application plans or collections that are allowed to perform these operations. Exceptions can be allowed by naming objects that can be created by registered or unregistered plans or collections. Optionally control can be exercised by naming each object that can be created by registered or unregistered plans or collections. Exceptions can be allowed for additional objects not specified to be created by registered or unregistered plans or collections.

The use of data definition control support must be requested by the system administrator on the DSNTIPZ install panel. Two registration tables will be created through the installation process for registering objects and application plans or collections. The default name of these tables are DSN_REGISTER_OBJT and DSN_REGISTER_APPL. The DSN_REGISTER_OBJT table is used to register some or all objects that can be created. The table is not required if creation of all objects is controlled by naming the only those plans or collections that are allowed to create objects. If exceptions are allowed (some objects can be created with unregistered plans or collections), exception objects must be explicitly registered in the object table. The DSN_REGISTER_APPL table is used to register

DSN_REGISTER_OBJT

QUALIFIER*	NAME*	TYPE*	APPLMATCHREQ	APPLIDENT	APPLIDENTTYPE
	DASPJSTO	S	Y	BACHMANP	P
	DASPJDB	D	Y	BACHMANP	P
DAPOSDB	DAPOSTSP	T	Y	IEWP	P
FLEUR	POSTABLE	C	Y	IEFC	C
SYSADM		D	N		
TESTDB		T	N		

* Primary key

Fig. 15.8 Table for Registering Objects

plans and collections that are allowed to. create objects. The table is not required if all objects that can be created are named in the object registration table. If exceptions are allowed (some registered plans and collections can create unregistered objects), accept must be specified for option UN-REGISTERED DDL DEFAULT on the install panel. The object and application registration tables are checked before accepting DDL statements.

An example will demonstrate how the registration tables can be used. Consider a case where the organization needs to control creation of objects with exceptions through CASE tools. Registered objects must be created, altered, and dropped by specified plans or collections. Unregistered objects can be created, altered, and dropped by unregistered plans or collections. The system administration needs to specify the DSNTIPZ install options:

```
CONTROL ALL APPLICATIONS  ===>  NO
REQUIRE FULL NAME         ===>  NO
UNREGISTERED DDL DEFAULT  ===>  ACCEPT
```

Rows are inserted into the DSN_REGISTER_OBJT table describing objects that can be created. The columns QUALIFIER and NAME in Fig. 15.8 contains the qualifier and name of objects that can be created, TYPE contains a code indicating the type of object (S for storage group; D for database; T for tablespace; C for table, view, index, synonym, or alias), APPLMATCHREQ has a "Y" if the plan or collection must be in the application registration table or "N" if this is not required, APPLIDENT contains the name of the plan or collection, APPLIDENTTYPE contains a "P" if the application is a plan or a "C" if it is a collection.

Rows are inserted into the DSN_REGISTER_APPL table describing plans and collection that are or are not allowed to create objects. The column APPLIDENT in Fig. 15.9 contains the name of plans and collections, APPLIDENTTYPE has a "P" if the application is a plan or "C" if it is a

DSN_REGISTER_APPL

APPLIDENT*	APPLIDENTTYPE*	DEFAULTAPPL*	QUALIFIEROK*
BACHMANP	P	Y	Y
IEWP	P	Y	N
IEFC	C	Y	N
FOCUSC	C	N	N

* Primary key

Fig. 15.9 Table for Registering Applications

collection, DEFAULTAPPL has a "Y" if the application is allowed to create objects or "N" if the application is not allowed to create objects, QUALIFIEROK has a "Y" if only the qualifier specified in DSN_REGISTER_OBJT.QUALIFIER can be used or "N" if any qualifier can be used.

The registration tables in Figs. 15.7 and 15.8 specify that the DASPJ-STO storage group and DASPJDB database must be created using the BACHMANP plan. The BACHMANP plan must be in DSN_REGISTER_APPL table as indicated by "Y" in the APPLMATCHREQ column and the plan is allowed to create objects as indicated by "Y" in the DEFAULT_APPL column. The DAPOSTSP tablespace must be created in the DAPOSDB database by the IEWP plan. The QUALIFIER value of DAPOSDB is the database name for a tablespace. QUALIFIEROK value of "N" means only DAPOSDB is valid. The FLEUR.POSTABLE must be created by the IEFC collection. The TYPE value of "C" means that a table, view, index, synonym, or alias can be created. If the QUALIFIER column was blank and QUALIFIEROK had a "Y", any qualifier could be used. SYSADM and TESTDB can create any database and tablespace using any plan or collection (NAME = blank and APPLMATCHREQ = N). TESTDB is restricted to creating tablespaces in TESTDB database. The three qualifiers FLEUR, SYSADM, and TESTDB will require appropriate grants to AUTHIDs with the same name in addition to the entries in the object registration table.

The last two SYSADM and TESTDB rows do not have an application identifier or type (APPLIDENT and APPLIDENTTYPE columns). Therefore, SYSADM and TESTDB can create any objects. Actually these rows are not required since the installation options chosen allow any unregistered objects to be created by any application plan or package. The rows would be needed if the organization needed to control the creation of all objects with exceptions for SYSADM and TESTDB. The last row in the application registration table disallows the creation of objects by the FOCUSC by specifying "N" for DEFAULTAPPL.

Additional columns can be included in the application registration table for documentation (APPLICATIONDESC), tracking the AUTHID that inserted the row (CREATOR), when the row was inserted (CREATETIMESTAMP), the AUTHID that updated the row (CHANGER), and when the row was updated (CHANGETIMESTAMP). These additional columns are optional.

15.13 SUMMARY

DB2 offers a rich, flexible set of control facilities. Development organizations can deploy them in a variety of combinations to achieve any level of control, from centralized to decentralized. A centralized scenario, which places control over almost any activity in the hands of one or two individuals, may be appropriate in organizations developing highly sensitive systems. Most development groups find a more flexible, decentralized approach more convenient and appropriate. The following examples suggest how an organization can allocate privileges to achieve either a centralized or decentralized arrangement.

Centralized Control

Under this scenario, a system administrator with SYSADM privileges creates all storage groups, databases, and tablespaces. The system administrator grants a database administrator authority to create tables (CREATETAB), to bind new plans and packages (BINDADD and CREATE IN), and to use the tablespaces. The database administrator grants programmers SELECT, INSERT, UPDATE, and DELETE authorities on the tables that the database administrator creates.

After a programmer has written a program and precompiled it, which requires no authorization, that programmer submits it to the database administrator. The database administrator performs the first bind and grants bind and execute privileges for the plan and packages to the programmer, who can then test and modify the program and perform the necessary bind replace operations. When testing is complete, the database administrator revokes the programmer's privileges, loads the production data, performs a bind replace, and grants execute authority to the business professionals who will use the program.

This approach requires considerable management attention, so much that an unwieldy bureaucracy is likely to grow up around it. Programmers will have to fill out request forms to have the database administrator create their tables, bind their new plans and packages, and accept their completed programs. They will have to schedule time for those chores. Even in a small development group, this approach is sure to delay development. In a large group, it may be unworkable.

Decentralized Control

For decentralized control, the system administrator creates a storage group and grants use of it to all members of a development team. He or she also grants all members CREATEDBA, BINDADD, and CREATE IN privileges. The development team is then authorized to perform any activity required to develop and test an application system. The system administrator provides the same privileges to a production administrator, who when the application system is turned over, can obtain the CREATE statements from the developer's SPUFI files or use a product like DBMAUI to generate them. The administrator executes the statements using the production AUTHID and binds all the plans and packages. Developers cannot modify or use the tables and programs in the production system, although they still have the original test objects for future enhancements. While the developers have considerable flexibility during development, this arrangement provides a sharp line between development and production, affording a good deal of protection for the application in the production environment.

EXERCISES

15.1. Eric creates a table, ERIC.EMPLOYEE, with NAME, EMPNO, TITLE, and SALARY columns. He grants UPDATE authority on the table to George. Later Eric decides to revoke George's privilege to update the salary column but not the others. What statement or statements can Eric use to take that action?

15.2. George and Paul have update authority WITH GRANT OPTION on the SPJ table. Paul passes the privilege to Frank, who passes it to Mary. George also passes the privilege to Frank. Frank later passes the privilege to update SPJ to Terry. Paul then decides to revoke Frank's privilege to update SPJ. Who retains that privilege?

15.3. The system administrator grants CREATEDBA authority to George. After George creates database XYZDB, the administrator revokes George's CREATEDBA authority. What authority does George hold on XYZDB before losing CREATEDBA authority? After?

15.4. Frank has been given authority to execute plan SUPDATE, which updates the S table; he has not been authorized, however, to update that table. Can he execute the plan?

15.5. How can Mary and Sally both bind a plan without one losing the privilege?

16

Utilities

16.1 INTRODUCTION

DB2 offers a number of utilities for analyzing and managing the physical storage of data. A user may employ any of several methods to execute each utility, each method differing in ease of use and the degree to which it allows users to customize the utility's executions. Customization may be desirable for a number of reasons. If a load were to require an unusually large sort, for example, the user might wish to modify the load utility's default sort procedure. The easier the execution method, the less flexibility it allows. Ranked from easiest and least flexible to most complex and most flexible, there are four methods of executing the utilities:

1. By completing DB2 Interactive (DB2I) panels and having them generate the execution code.

2. By coding DSNU command processor statements.

3. By customizing JCL supplied with DB2 in the DSNUPROC procedures.

4. By running JCL from DSNUPROC customized through DSNUTILB.

The execution methods are interrelated in that the higher-level methods actually invoke the lower-level methods. A user may enter at any level depending on the extent of customization required. A useful technique is to have

Administrators
STOSPACE: Collects and records physical storage space allocation statistics in
the catalog tables.
REPAIR: Replaces invalid data with valid data.
MODIFY: Deletes records of unwanted image copies and related log records from SYS-
IBM.SYSCOPY and SYSIBM.SYSLGRNG directory.

Developers
LOAD: Loads data into DB2 tables from sequential file or SQL/DS unload tape.
RUNSTATS: Collects and records statistics from tablespaces or indexes in the cata-
log tables.
CHECK INDEX: Checks indexes for consistency with the tables they reference.
CHECK DATA: Checks for violations of referential integrity and optionally deletes
rows, and checks table and index consistency.
REORG: Restores storage efficiencies for a tablespace or indexes.
COPY: Creates a full or incremental image copy of a tablespace or partition.
MERGECOPY: Merges incremental copies with other incremental copies or a full image
copy.
REPORT: Produces a report on all tables and tablespace in a referential integrity
structure and datasets needed for a recovery.
RECOVER: Recovers data to a current state using the log and image copies.
QUIESCE: Establishes a point of consistency for a list of tablespaces to provide
for recovering a referential integrity structure to a point in time.

Fig. 16.1 Utilities used by administrators and developers

DB2I generate the code and to customize it under the EDITJCL function.
The name of the file containing the JCL will be given.

Users employ utility control statements similar in format to SQL to
specify utility options. The user completes a utility control statement with
a file editor and saves it in a partitioned or sequential dataset. The "UTILI-
TIES" option of DB2I incorporates the utility control statement in the execution code.

We will look more closely at the execution methods and statements in
exploring the individual utilities. Three of the utilities are used primarily by
system administrators; the others are used mostly by developers (Fig. 16.1).
This chapter concentrates on the latter.

16.2 THE LOAD UTILITY

The load utility loads data from a sequential file into one or more tables in
a tablespace. A load consists of several phases, each of which performs
distinct load processes. Besides initialization and termination, the phases
are RELOAD, which reads and loads all records and writes any index values
into temporary files; SORT, which sorts the index values; and BUILD,
which builds the indexes. There is also a phase for referential integrity
checking, checking for duplicate values in columns with a unique index,

```
DSNEUPO1                      DB2 UTILITIES
===>
Select from the following:
 1 FUNCTION ==> EDITJCL       (SUBMIT job, EDITJCL, DISPLAY, TERMINATE)
 2 JOB ID   ==> LOADSPJ       (A unique job identifier string)
 3 UTILITY  ==> LOAD          (CHECK, CHECK DATA, COPY, DIAGNOSE, LOAD, MERGE,
                               MODIFY, QUIESCE, RECOVER INDEX, RECOVER TABLE-
                               SPACE, REPORT, REPAIR RUNSTATS, STOSPACE.)

 4 CONTROL CARDS DATA SET     ==> 'PROJ.AUTHID.CNTL(LOADSTMT)'

To RESTART a utility, specify starting point, otherwise enter NO.
 5 RESTART  ==> NO            NO, At CURRENT position, or beginning of PHASE)
 *Data set names panel will be displayed when required by a utility.

PRESS: ENTER to process       END to exit         HELP for more information
```

Fig. 16.2 The utilities panel

and phases for handling and reporting on violations. As Chapter 6 discusses in detail, it is often more efficient to build indexes during loads than to create them afterward.

Users can choose several load options through the DB2I utility panel (Fig. 16.3) or with DSNU. In item 2 of the utility panel, DISCDSN, for example, the user can specify a discard dataset in which the utility saves records it cannot load for later review and correction by the user.

The LOAD DATA statement gives users a number of options for controlling the load process, including the following functions:

- Load some fields from the input file and ignore others.
- Load only data that meet a specified condition—with values equal to or greater than a specified value, for example—so that only desired rows are included.
- Load records from one file into multiple tables in a tablespace based upon input data values.
- Load some fields into columns in one table and other fields into columns in another table in a tablespace.
- Specify a discard dataset to receive records that cannot be loaded.
- Load can replace existing data or add additional data.
- Load a referential integrity structure.
- Load one or all partitions of a tablespace.
- Convert input data from one numeric type to another or from one char-

acter type to another. (The utility will convert between character and numeric types in some special cases to be discussed.)

- Alter the length of input data items.
- Restart the load at a phase or current position.

Loading from the Utilities Panel

These are the users' options for each panel item in Fig. 16.2:

- 1 FUNCTION. Users can choose to submit the job that is set up through the panel directly for execution, view and edit the generated JCL, display the utility's status—whether running or idle—or stop the utility. The commands for invoking these functions are, respectively, SUBMIT, EDITJCL, DISPLAY, and TERMINATE.

  The JCL generated from a load panel is kept in a dataset named DSNULOA.CNTL, prefixed with the user's TSO ID. If users select function EDITJCL, completing the panel places them in the DSNU-LOA.CNTL dataset in the edit mode. After making any changes, the user can submit the job. If users expect to rerun this or a similar job, they can copy the dataset to save the JCL. The original dataset will be written over the next time the user executes a different load. If the JCL has been copied, users can execute it, or a modification of it, later rather than having to regenerate the JCL through the utility panel.

- 2 JOB ID. Users enter a unique identifier for the utility. If users make no entry, a utility ID is generated. The utility ID can be used as the identifier to have the utility status displayed or the utility terminated.

- 3 UTILITY. Users specify the utility to be used—in this case, LOAD.

- 4 CONTROL CARDS DATASET. Users indicate the partitioned or sequential dataset that contains the load control statement. In Fig. 16.2 PROJ.AUTHID.CNTL is the name of a PDS (partitioned dataset), and LOADSTMT in parentheses is the name of the member that contains the load control statement. DB2I will incorporate the contents of PROJ.AUTHID.CNTL(LOADSTMT) in the correct sequence when it builds the JCL in the DSNULOA.CNTL file. Users may want to save DSNULOA.CNTL and modify the LOAD DATA statement for subsequent load jobs. They will find it following the JCL statement "//SYSIN DD *".

- 5 RESTART. Users can choose to restart a load after a failure at the load's current position or at the beginning of the utility phase being executed. The phase in which the input data are read and loaded is called RELOAD. Other phases are initialization (UTILINIT), sorting

```
DSNEUP02
                              DATA SET NAMES
  ==>
Enter data set name for LOAD or REORG TABLESPACE:
  1 RECDSN   ==> 'PROJ.AUTHID.SPJDATA'

Enter data set name for LOAD:
  2 DISCDSN  ==> 'PROJ.AUTHID.DISCARD'

Enter output data sets for local/current site for COPY or MERGECOPY:
  3 COPYDSN  ==>
  4 COPYDSN2 ==>

Enter output data set(s) for recovery site for COPY:
  5 RCPYDSN1 ==>
  6 RCPYDSN2 ==>

PRESS: ENTER to process        END to exit        HELP for more information
```

Fig. 16.3 Dataset names for utilities

of any indexes (SORT), building of any indexes (BUILD), deletion of duplicates in unique indexes (INDEXVAL), enforcement of referential integrity (ENFORCE), discarding of violations (DISCARD), report on errors (REPORT), and termination (UTILTERM). Users can determine the status of a utility job by indicating the JOB ID after the DISPLAY command on the DB2I utilities panel. Alternatively the command −DISPLAY UTILITY LOADSPJ can be entered from the DB2I commands panel.

When RESTART is done from the current position, loading is actually resumed from the last commit point with commit points falling at about every 100 pages for most utilities. The RESTART command parameters are CURRENT, PHASE, and NO. Users will use NO when the utility is first submitted. RESTART(CURRENT) will give the best performance and can be used for most utilities.

If a utility job has not completed successfully and it is not to be restarted, users must terminate it before resubmitting it. Another utility with the same JOB ID cannot be executed until the original is terminated, even if the original job ends abnormally. The JOB ID has been written to SYSUTIL in the directory for restart purposes. Termination is performed from line 1 of the utilities panel with the JOB ID used to identify the job on line 2. Alteratively the −TERM UTILITY (LOADSPJ) command can be entered from the DB2I commands panel. Termination of the utility is required to clear it from a directory table used by DB2 for restart purposes.

These are users' options for each panel item in Fig. 16.3:

- 1 RECDSN. Users specify the dataset containing the data being loaded. In the JCL in DSNULOA.CNTL, they will find the name of the dataset following "DSN" in the statement "//SYSREC DD DSN=".

- 2 DISCDSN. Users may indicate a dataset to receive records that the utility is unable to load. In the example, the LOAD utility will write records that it cannot load to the dataset PROJ.AUTHID.DISCARD.

- 3 COPYDSN. Users specify the name of a dataset to contain an image copy as discussed in section 16.6.

- 4 COPYDSN2. User specify the name of a dataset to contain a second image copy as discussed in section 16.6.

- 5 RCPYDSN1. Users specify the name of a dataset to contain an image copy for off site recovery as discussed in section 16.6.

- 6 RCPYDSN2. Users specify the name of a dataset to contain a second image copy for off site recovery as discussed in section 16.6.

The LOAD DATA Statement

The LOAD DATA statement takes the following basic form:

```
LOAD DATA
    RESUME NO
    SORTDEVT SYSDA
    SORTNUM 4
    LOG NO
    DISCARDS 1000
    INTO TABLE AUTHID.S WHEN (50:51) = 'ST'
    (SN  POSITION (1)    CHAR(2),
     PN  POSITION (3:4)  CHAR(2),
     JN  POSITION (*)    CHAR(2),
     QTY POSITION (*+2) INTEGER EXTERNAL(3))
```

The RESUME command instructs the utility on how to handle data already in the receiving dataset. There are three options:

- RESUME NO: Indicates that the dataset is to be empty. If it is not, the load will not execute. This is the default option.

- RESUME NO REPLACE: Causes the utility to write over existing data.

- RESUME YES: Instructs the utility to add new rows to an existing table.

Under all the RESUME options, the LOAD utility extracts indexed values and places them in a temporary file during a single pass of the input file. The temporary file is sorted so that LOAD can efficiently build the

Box 16.1 Utilities and concurrent processing

Some utilities allow programs or users to access the data even while the utility is executing. In some cases, such as MERGECOPY, they allow both reads and updates. In some cases, they allow concurrent processing during one phase of execution but not another such as REORG, which allows access during the unload phase but not during the reload phase. The following list describes the processing allowed by the various utilities and any restrictions on it:

Utilities that allow processing

- RUNSTATS: Reads and updates when SHRLEVEL is set to change; reads only when SHRLEVEL is set to reference.
- COPY: Reads and updates when SHRLEVEL is set to change; reads only when SHRLEVEL is set to reference.
- REORG: Reads and updates during UNLOAD.
- MERGECOPY: Reads and updates.
- RECOVER-PAGE: Reads and updates of pages not on the same track.
- STOSPACE: Reads and updates.
- CHECK: Reads only.
- MODIFY: Reads and updates except on SYSIBM.SYSCOPY and SYSIBM.SYSLGRNG tables.

Utilities that do not allow concurrent processing

- LOAD.
- REORG (during the RELOAD phase).
- RECOVER tablespaces and indexes.
- REPAIR.

B-tree indexes. The utility does not sort the input records. Therefore it is important to sort the input file on the clustering index columns before the load is executed. One company reported that a load resume of yes required 10 hours to add 3 million rows but after sorting the rows the job required only 38 minutes. This is because the rows were inserted in ascending sequence at the end of the tablespace and the end of the index, which allowed for build mode to be used on the index. Regardless of which RESUME option is used if the sequential file containing the input data is in sequence on the clustering index columns and there is only one index, the utility will not sort the indexed values since the values will be extracted in sequence from the sequential file.

Under the insert mode used under RESUME YES, the utility adds values to each index page in sequence, which has significantly better performance than does an application program that will insert values throughout the index pages in most cases, frequently having to process index pages multiple times. The insert mode used by the LOAD utility when using RESUME YES is more efficient than what can be done with an application program but may still require a reorganization of the indexes to achieve the best performance and minimize the space required for the indexes. One installation improved performance by a factor of 10 by reorganizing indexes built with this insert method. Also RESUME YES will not reuse space from deleted rows because doing so would require a tablespace scan to find the available space. The new rows are placed at the end of the existing data.

Test results indicate the importance of using LOAD RESUME YES whenever possible rather than adding rows with an application program even for adding one to five percent new rows. It required 78 elapsed seconds to insert one percent of 262,000 rows into table with 2 indexes but only 43 elapsed seconds when using load resume. The difference becomes more dramatic as the number of rows added increases even when the increase is a fairly low percentage. It required 377 elapsed seconds for an application program insertion of five percent of the rows but only 91 elapsed seconds when using load resume. The difference may have been even more significant had LOG NO been used.

A major advantage of load resume is that all index values are sorted before they are placed in the B-tree. This means that each index page needs to be updated only once. In contrast, an application program would be inserting the index value basically at random, having to update the same index page multiple times.

The SORTDEVT parameter refers to the type of device holding the temporary files to be used for sorting index values; SORTNUM indicates the number of temporary datasets to be used in the sort. In almost all cases, the choices will be SYSDA, meaning a direct access storage device, and four or more temporary datasets. Particularly for large tables, placing sort work files and output on tape will slow the process. (Box 16.2 describes LOAD options that affect performance for indexes requiring large sorts.) SORTDEVT is required if the table being loaded has indexes. If SORTNUM is omitted, the sort program will use a default number of temporary work datasets.

The LOG NO command instructs the utility not to record data in the recovery log as they are loaded. The log's primary function is to record images of changes made to loaded tables for use in recovery from a failure.

Box 16.2 Loading large tables

DB2's default values for the load utility are suited to tables of up to a few hundred thousand rows with a few indexes. With larger tables and those with many indexes, the user may want to modify the generated JCL for the load if column values must be sorted for indexes. These are the key modifications:

- The amount of main memory allocated for the utility, its region size, should be increased from the default of 1 megabyte to 4–5 megabytes, which allows more rows to be sorted in memory before being written to a temporary work area.

- Blocking factor, which determines the amount of data read in a single I/O operation, should be set at one-half a track or 22K for a 3380 or 28K for a 3390 device for good performance. The size and number of sort-work datasets, which temporarily hold partially sorted data during the process, should be increased. One or two large sort-work datasets have advantages over several smaller work datasets on a single DASD device. If multiple DASD devices and channels are available, several smaller work datasets spread across multiple DASD devices and channels and separated from the input and output datasets will result in a more efficient sort. DB2 uses the same dataset to sort all of a table's indexed columns. It uses the longest indexed column to determine the record size for all indexed columns and adds 12 bytes for each value. Therefore use the length of the longest indexed column plus 12 bytes as the record size for all indexed columns times the number of indexes times the number of rows when figuring the sort-work dataset's size. The work space should be about 2.15 times the size of the data being sorted. Cylinder allocation on DASD will improve sort performance. These guidelines also apply to the REORG and RECOVER utility, which will use a sort to rebuild indexes.

The RECOVER utility reconstructs a table or partition by updating a copy of it with the changes recorded in the log between the time the copy was made and the time of failure. No copy exists when the data are initially loaded, of course. A log of the loaded records therefore would provide the only way to recover a newly loaded tablespace until a copy of it is made. If the user does not specify LOG NO, the utility automatically uses the log.

Recording data in the log during a load can increase the time required for the load significantly, however. A load of a 100,000-row table with a 115-byte row length can require log data amounting to more than 2 million bytes if LOG YES is specified but only about 108,000 bytes with LOG NO. For large loads, in particular, it is usually faster to load without the log and make a copy of the tablespace immediately after for use in recovery. In fact, a tablespace loaded with LOG NO cannot be recovered (the copy pending status is set) until a full image copy has been made. Therefore DB2 will not allow tables in such a tablespace to be updated until a full copy has been made. (Section 16.6 describes how to make this copy.)

A second way to overcome the limitation is by using the FORCE option for the ACCESS parameter when starting the database that holds the table. A third method is to use the REPAIR utility with the NOCOPYPEND option. By using the second or third methods, the user relieves DB2 of the responsibility of being able to recover after a failure. In other words, recovery will be impossible. Consequently, these options should be used with care. It is not necessary to remove the copy-pending status if the table is read only. In this case, if there is a failure, the data can be reloaded.

The INTO TABLE clause in the control statement indicates the table that is to receive the data. If there is a one-to-one correspondence in data type and length between the input file fields and table columns, the LOAD DATA statement may end with this line. If the file fields do not match the table columns, however, the statement must explicitly assign the file's field positions to the table's columns and indicate the data types. This is done with the parameters in parentheses following the INTO TABLE clause.

The user may describe the location of fields on the sequential file with several formulations. With the formulation shown above, the starting position of the input data for each table column is indicated in parentheses following the field name and the keyword POSITION. An asterisk by itself indicates the input begins immediately after the previous field. An asterisk followed by a numeral indicates the input begins a specific number of positions after the previous field. The length of the field, indicated in parentheses after its data type, determines the number of bytes of input data to be loaded into the column.

LOAD permits data type conversions from character to numeric types using the INTEGER EXTERNAL and DECIMAL EXTERNAL options. INTEGER EXTERNAL converts numbers of display or character type to their binary representations. For example, it would convert HEX'F7F8F3' to binary 783. DECIMAL EXTERNAL translates from display to packed decimal representation.

Another formulation for assigning positions (shown below), the field positions of the input data to be loaded in each table column are specified as a range with start and end points separated by colons. The following formulation, for example, indicates that the SNAME column in the S table is to receive input data from positions 5 through 19:

```
SNAME POSITION (5:19) CHAR
```

Notice that the length of the CHAR field need not be indicated, assuming that the field and column lengths match, since LOAD will use the length specified when the table was created.

Loading Decimals

The load utility will handle three decimal representations—packed, zoned, and external. The packed decimal representation requires no special handling other than declaring it as DECIMAL PACKED. Rather it simply follows the CREATE TABLE's specification for the column's length and decimal placement. The utility converts the zoned and external representations in ways that are not so obvious. The representations are best explained through an example.

Consider a table declared as follows:

```
CREATE TABLE COSTS
   (COST    DECIMAL (8,2)
    DISCOUNT DECIMAL (8,2))
```

The sequential input file contains records with 16 positions. The first 8 positions are the COST data in zoned decimal representation; the second 8, the DISCOUNT data in external representation. The file looks like this:

```
Record 1 00000503    503
Record 2 0000050L −  503
Record 3 0000050L − .503
```

Notice that the zoned representation does not include decimal points or leading signs. The load utility follows the CREATE TABLE statement's specification in positioning the decimal point. The sign is encoded in the representation. Here, for example, the L is a -3; the value 0000050L (in hexadecimal) equals -503. The external representation includes both sign and decimal place with each occupying a position.

The LOAD statement for this file would look like this:

```
LOAD DATA
INTO TABLE AUTHID.COSTS
(COST      POSITION (1:8)  DECIMAL ZONED,
 DISCOUNT  POSITION (9:16) DECIMAL EXTERNAL (8,1))
```

The specification of the length and decimal position for the external representation in the LOAD statement (8,1), along with the explicit placement of a decimal in the input data, override the table's definition for the column (8,2). The following results of the statement SELECT * FROM

COSTS after the data are loaded illustrates these points and indicates how the utility converts the various fields:

```
COST DISCOUNT
   5.03   50.30
  -5.03  -50.30
  -5.03  -   .50
```

Notice that for the zoned representation, the utility has placed the decimal point two places to the left of the last place in the input data, as indicated in the table's definition. For the external representation, it has placed the decimal one place to the left of the last place. In the case of Record 3, the explicit decimal point takes precedence, causing the utility to truncate the third digit to the right of the decimal in order to accommodate the column, which allows only two digits to the right.

A variety of conversions are available as detailed in the manual *IBM Database 2 Command and Utility Reference.*

Loading Specific Records

A WHEN clause instructs the utility to load only records meeting a given condition. In the following statement, for example, the statement WHEN (50:51) = 'ST' instructs the utility to load only those records with ST in columns 50 and 51:

```
LOAD DATA
DISCARDS 1000
INTO TABLE AUTHID.P CONTINUEIF (80:80)='C'
  WHEN (50:51) = 'ST'
  (PN     POSITION (1:2)      CHAR,
   PNAME  POSITION (5:24)     CHAR,
   COLOR  POSITION (30:35)    INTEGER,
   WEIGHT POSITION (90:93)    INTEGER
          DEFAULTIF (90:93)    = -1,
   CITY   POSITION (100:114) CHAR
          NULLIF    (100:102) = '***')
```

'IF' Conditionals for Logical Records and Nulls

Several LOAD parameters instruct the utility on how to proceed if it encounters certain conditions. The CONTINUEIF parameter, for example, instructs the utility to view consecutive physical records as one if the last position in the preceding record contains the character C.

NULLIF and DEFAULTIF provide directions for the handling of nulls and place holders. Input files sometimes use an actual character or numeric value—usually one with no contextual meaning—to hold a place in a given field when its value is unknown or not applicable. DB2, on the other hand, provides null values for that purpose. The NULLIF and DEFAULTIF provide for translations from the place holders to nulls or zeros and blanks. In the statement above, the NULLIF command instructs the utility to place a null value in the CITY column if it finds asterisks in positions 100 through 102. Besides allowing nulls, DB2 permits table creators to specify that a column receive zeros whenever a record does not include data for it. That column designation is NOT NULL WITH DEFAULT. The DEFAULTIF command provides a similar capability for the load utility. When the utility encounters a place holder designated by the DEFAULTIF command, it inserts a zero if the column is numeric and a blank if it is character. In the example, the DEFAULTIF command causes the utility to load zeros into the WEIGHT column any time it encounters -1 in positions 90 through 93. If a column is declared NOT NULL when its table is created, the loaded record must provide some value for it—either the load fails or the record is written to the discard dataset if discard processing is requested as is the case in the example.

The WHEN Conditional

When the number of fields to be loaded into a given table varies from month to month, the WHEN conditional can be used to instruct the utility about how many fields there are to be loaded and where they should be placed. Such a conditional LOAD statement indicates both the record position where the utility will find a code instructing it on how to proceed and the action it should take if the code equals a specified value.

Suppose there might be from one to three expense fields to be loaded depending on the record's content. The code numbers 1, 2, or 3 can be placed in a specified position in the input dataset to indicate how many fields are in fact present. Then the WHEN command describes where that code resides and what to do with the field the code indicates exists. The LOAD statement might look like this:

```
LOAD DATA
   INTO TABLE AUTHID.EXPENSES
   WHEN (18) = '01' (EXPENSE1 POSITION (20:29))
   WHEN (18) = '02' (EXPENSE1 POSITION (20:29),
   EXPENSE2 POSITION (30:39))
   WHEN (18) = '03' (EXPENSE1 POSITION (20:29),
                     EXPENSE2 POSITION (30:39),
                     EXPENSE3 POSITION (40:49))
```

The statement can include as many WHEN conditions as are needed.

Loading VARCHAR

When VARCHAR data are loaded, each variable length input field must be preceded by a two-byte binary number indicating its length. If that indicator is not included, the utility will add trailing blanks to fill out the column to the maximum length declared in the CREATE TABLE statement. In effect, the utility will treat the column as CHAR as it exists on the sequential file rather than VARCHAR, the desired data type on the table. A COBOL program that writes the sequential file must calculate the number of characters before the trailing blanks and place it in the first 49 level length field as was discussed in Chapter 9. If there is no length field, the LOAD statement must describe the input as CHAR, even if the column to receive the field is declared as VARCHAR. If there is a length field, the statement must describe the input field as VARCHAR.

Loading DATE and TIME Data

Date and time input data must be input as character types, with the punctuation included for whichever format is being used. For example, under the default ISO format, an input date must include the hyphens, as in 1989-04-21. If the date or time column has been specified as NOT NULL WITH DEFAULT, the load utility will automatically load the system's date or time when the load starts execution for any missing values in the input data.

This may or may not be the desired result. Suppose there are columns in the Parts table indicating the date and time when a part was ordered and the date and time it was received, but the part has not been received. The row is inserted after the order is placed but before it is received. The program writing the sequential file can use a date of 0001-01-01 or 9999-12-31 for future or unknown dates depending on application design requirements.

There is an exception to the requirement that date and time values must be in character format for the load utility. The load utility will accept as input the DB2 internal date and time format written by the reorganization utility. Developers can use the reorganization utility to unload a tablespace into a sequential file and use that file as input to the load utility. This technique requires that the parameter UNLOAD be used when executing the reorganization utility. The control statement for load can specify the name of the date and time column and allow for the default date and time data type. That is, the data type should not be specified as DATE EXTERNAL.

CONTINUEIF

The CONTINUEIF command instructs the utility to treat the input record following a designated indicator as logically belonging to the preceding record. The command specifies the alphanumeric character that is to serve as the indicator and the position where the utility is to check for it. In the example, the utility is to read an input file as a continuous record when it encounters a "C" in position 80. That is, the record following the "C" is treated as a continuation of the record that contained it. This feature often helps in converting data used by an application program that deals with multiple record types to a DB2 table.

Loading Data with an Application Program

The load utility has significant advantages over loading data with an application program. It builds multiple compact indexes with one pass of the data after sorting the indexed values using DFSORT and uses the efficient build rather than insert mode on indexes. Load leaves the specified percent free in the data and index pages, which cannot be done with an application program. Load communicates directly with DM without going through RDS, which reduces the path length. Load can use asynchronous deferred writing after accumulating up to 10 percent of the buffer space in updated pages per dataset. Load does not have to check for broken pages as do insert and delete. Logging can be turned off on a load.

If it is necessary to load the data with an application program, consideration should be given to reorganizing the data afterward to gain free space for future insert and update activity. At a minimum the indexes should be reorganized since most of the index pages will be half full as a result of using insert mode. It is best to create indexes after an application program has inserted the rows so that build mode can be used.

If there are multiple indexes, the procedure outlined in Box 16.3 will save having to pass the tablespace and extract the indexed values for each index created. In any case, the developer will need to manage any duplicate values when using a unique index.

Discarding Records That Cannot Be Loaded

The keyword DISCARD on the load control statement followed by a number informs the load utility to write any records that cannot be loaded to a sequential file and continue the load. If discards are not requested, the first record that cannot be loaded will cause the load to abend. It will be necessary to find and correct the problem and issue − TERMINATE LOADSPJ before resubmitting the load. Load detects one error at a time if no discard dataset has been specified. In that case, each error record will need to be corrected, the load terminated, and resubmitted—a rather long, costly, and frustrating experience.

Box 16.3   Creating indexes efficiently after an application program load

When adding a large number of rows, it is almost always more efficient to use the LOAD utility than to have an application program perform the load. If an application program does handle the load, an inefficient insert mode is used to build indexes. A multistep, somewhat unwieldly procedure employing the DSN1COPY and RECOVER utilities, however, can avoid that mode when an application program must be used to load the data. The procedure requires considerable time and effort. And because DSN1COPY does not update the catalog tables, there is a slight risk that data could be lost—and if lost be difficult to recover—if he or she makes a mistake. But the method saves considerable I/O and CPU time. Here is the procedure, step by step:

- Create a temporary tablespace exactly like the tablespace containing the table to have the indexes. We will call the temporary tablespace TEMP and the current tablespace CUR. Stop the current tablespace to avoid changes to it during the index creation procedure. The STOP statement names the tablespace and the database to which it belongs, in this case DAGKWDB. The statement is: −STOP DATABASE (DAGKWDB) SPACENAM (CUR).

- Use the DSN1COPY Utility to copy the CUR tablespace into a sequential dataset, in this case called SEQ. Use DSN1COPY to copy TEMP to CUR. Start the current tablespace to allow creation of the indexes. The statement is: −START DATABASE (DAGKWDB) SPACENAM (CUR).

- Create the required indexes—AUTHID.SNX and AUTHID.PNX, for example.

- Stop Tablespace CUR again.

- Use DSN1COPY to copy SEQ into CUR. Start Tablespace CUR. Recover the indexes with the statement RECOVER INDEX (AUTHID.SNX, AUTHID.PNX).

The parameter value after DISCARD indicates the number of records to be discarded before LOAD abends. The number should not be too large since discarding records is costly and time consuming. If the error is actually just a keying error on the LOAD statement, all or most records could be written to the discard dataset. Conditions that cause records to be written to the discard dataset and not written to the tablespace are:

- Data conversion errors
- WHEN clause condition not met by the record
- Record belongs to another partition
- Duplicate values in a column with a unique index
- —RESUME NO results in all duplicates being discarded
- —RESUME YES results in added duplicates being discarded
- Records that violate referential integrity constraints

Duplicates in a column with a unique index are discovered while building the index. Recall that the first phase of the LOAD utility, RELOAD, simple reads the data from the sequential file and lays it out on the tablespace. It is not until index processing is done that the duplicates are discovered. References to the rows that contain the duplicate values are removed from all indexes and the rows are marked as deleted in the tablespace. The deleted row space is reusable and the rows will not be retrieved when accessing the data using a tablespace scan or indexes.

Inserting Rows into a Table from Another Table

A handy technique for inserting a small number of rows into a table is an insert with a SELECT. This statement, for example, will insert a subset of the SPJ rows into the identical SPJTEST table:

```
INSERT INTO SPJTEST
   SELECT SN, SNAME, STATUS, CITY
   FROM   SPJ
   WHERE  SN BETWEEN 'S2' AND 'S4'
```

If more than 100,000 rows are to be loaded, however, the LOAD utility is more efficient, particularly if the table receiving the rows has several indexes.

16.3 LOADING REFERENTIAL INTEGRITY STRUCTURES

Because input data might violate referential integrity constraints, the load process for tables that participate in a referential integrity structure requires special handling. With one approach, the load utility will recognize from the catalog tables that constraints exist and automatically enforce them, checking for violations during the load and writing to a discard dataset any rows in violation. Or the user can instruct the utility to not perform constraint checking during the load by specifying ENFORCE NO in the LOAD statement.

Enforcing constraints during a load, which is the default mode, requires more processing and will slow the load down a bit. When the load is complete, however, all of the referential structure's tablespaces and indexes may be used immediately. On the other hand, if the load has been performed without checking, DB2 does not allow the dependent tables to be used until they have been checked, a condition known as check pending. The CHECK DATA utility can be used to lift the check pending status. There are other ways to remove the restrictions, however, including two dangerous methods that circumvent constraint checking. And although loading with ENFORCE NO is the primary reason DB2 sets the check pending status, it will do so for several other reasons to be discussed when the possibility of violations exist. Let us look more closely at constraint enforcement during loads and at the check pending status.

The LOAD Statements

An entire referential integrity structure can be loaded from a single input file into a single tablespace, which for reasons discussed in Chapters 3 and 5 should usually be a segmented tablespace. The process of executing the LOAD and CHECK DATA utilities in order to get a referential integrity structure up and running can be relatively complex. If the various tables participating in the structure occupy the same tablespaces, managing the process is less difficult.

The following LOAD statements call for the loading of the referential integrity structure of the S, P, J, and SPJ tables from a single sequential file into a single tablespace with constraint checking:

```
LOAD DATA ENFORCE CONSTRAINTS
INTO TABLE AUTHID.S WHEN (1:3) = 'S '

LOAD DATA ENFORCE CONSTRAINTS
INTO TABLE AUTHID.P WHEN (1:3) = 'P '

LOAD DATA ENFORCE CONSTRAINTS
INTO TABLE AUTHID.J WHEN (1:3) = 'J '

LOAD DATA ENFORCE CONSTRAINTS
INTO TABLE AUTHID.SPJ WHEN (1:3) = 'SPJ'
```

The SPJ table has a foreign key to each of the other tables, and there is a possibility that those keys have values not included in the primary keys. With ENFORCE CONSTRAINTS in effect, the load utility will not load rows that have no matching primary key value, and will, optionally, write them to a discard dataset. In addition, if there are other rows in the same load that depend on these discarded rows for their adherence to referential integrity, the utility also will not load these dependent rows. Such violations are called secondary errors.

If the LOAD statement specifies ENFORCE NO, check pending will be set on for dependent tables. Check pending can be caused by several other actions that hold the potential for referential integrity violations. For example, both adding a foreign key to a populated table or performing a load replace of a primary key table can result in check pending. Load replace of the parent table will result in check pending being set on for all dependent tables since primary key rows with dependents could have been replaced. Recovery of some, but not all, tablespaces in a referential integrity set can cause referential integrity violations and thus results in check pending status. We will discuss another potential source of referential integrity problems in recoveries, lack of synchronization of the tables to what is called a quiesce point, in the section on recoveries. Basically if there could potentially be a foreign key value without a matching primary key value, check pending will be set on.

Under check pending, DB2 bars all SQL data manipulation against the covered rows and prohibits the copying or reorganization of the tablespace. Even an attempt to update a primary key value is not allowed since it would require processing dependent tables. Attempts to perform any of these actions receive a resource unavailable message. DB2 does allow the execution of LOAD REPLACE, CHECK DATA, REPAIR, RUNSTATS, and RECOVER utilities against the tablespace. DB2 also allows DROP and ALTER statements applying to the objects under check pending status. In fact, dropping a table or constraint that holds a potential violation is one rather severe way to remove check pending.

The check pending status can be removed in several ways. The involved tables can be reloaded under the REPLACE mode with ENFORCE CONSTRAINTS in effect; the tablespace can be recovered to a quiesce point; or the tables or constraints with the potential violations can be dropped. Two other methods tell DB2 to drop the restrictions and ignore the problem, an action that results in a highly compromised database. Under one method, the system administrator uses the REPAIR utility to reset the status. Under the other, the affected database is started with the ACCESS parameter set at FORCE. Neither method is recommended but REPAIR is somewhat better since starting the database with access of force ignores all possible problems.

Using CHECK DATA

The usual way to reset check pending status is to execute the CHECK utility against the tablespace or affected portion. This utility compares the participating primary and foreign keys to assure that the data satisfy the referential constraints. Optionally, it will copy invalid rows to an exception table and delete them. The utility will also issue a report identifying the deleted rows. We will discuss the utility's features more closely in the following description of the CHECK DATA statement used to execute the utility:

```
CHECK DATA TABLESPACE DASPJDB.STSP
            TABLESPACE DASPJDB.PTSP
            TABLESPACE DASPJDB.JTSP
            TABLESPACE DASPJDB.SPJTSP
SCOPE PENDING
FOR EXCEPTION
      IN AUTHID.SPJ USE AUTHID.SPJEX
EXCEPTIONS 100
DELETE YES
SORTDEVT SYSDA
```

The statement calls for the checking of tablespaces holding all the tables with foreign keys against the tablespace holding the primary key table, in this case DASPJDB.SPJTSP. Although foreign key tables can be checked individually, it is best to do all those in a referential structure that needs checking at the same time. This is because DB2 can keep the leaf pages for the primary key column being checked in the bufferpool for comparison with all of the foreign keys' values, rather than having to input the primary key values repeatedly for each foreign key.

Using the SCOPE parameter in the CHECK DATA statement, the user can instruct the utility about how much of the tablespace to check. A selection of SCOPE PENDING tells it to check only those rows covered by the CHECK PENDING status. The choice of SCOPE ALL tells it to check the entire tablespace. First, the user must determine how much of the tablespace the pending status covers.

DB2 records check pending status in the catalog in SYSTABLESPACE.STATUS, SYSTABLEPART.CHECKFLAG, SYSTABLEPART. CHECKRID, SYSTABLES.CHECKFLAG, AND SYSTABLES.CHECKRID. These catalog columns tell whether check pending is in effect, and if so, its scope—the portion of the tablespace covered. Check pending may cover an entire tablespace, a partition, or rows beyond a specific row ID. (A database access table DBAT, which is an internal table kept in main memory, also stores check pending status. The DISPLAY DATABASE command provides the information.) If the CHECKFLAG values are blank, the tablespace or partition is not in check pending status. If those columns contain 'C', the check pending status is in effect.

If CHECKRID contains a row ID, it indicates that a LOAD REPLACE with ENFORCE NO has added rows to an existing table. The identified row and those with higher RID values are covered by the check pending status. The SCOPE PENDING selection would be appropriate for the CHECK DATA statement. If CHECKRID contains zeros, it indicates that the entire tablespace is covered by the check pending status. The SCOPE ALL choice would be appropriate.

The following statements determine tables and tablespaces covered by check pending and the scope of that coverage:

```
SELECT NAME, CHECKFLAG, HEX(CHECKRID), 'TABLE'
FROM   SYSIBM.SYSTABLES
WHERE  CHECKFLAG = 'C'
UNION
SELECT TSNAME, CHECKFLAG, HEX(CHECKRID), 'TABLESPACE'
FROM   SYSIBM.SYSTABLEPART
WHERE  CHECKFLAG = 'C'
ORDER BY 1, 4;
```

The FOR EXCEPTION, EXCEPTIONS, and DELETE parameters in the CHECK DATA statement instruct the utility on how to deal with referential integrity violations it discovers. The utility will generate an error message identifying the table, constraint name and RID of rows in violation. If DELETE YES is specified, it will write the rows to an exception table and delete them. The EXCEPTIONS parameter specifies the number of errors the utility should detect before terminating the job. This parameter should be set at a relatively low number, such as 100. If there are more errors than that, they may be the result of a general error in the data, and running the utility job all the way through would likely be a waste of time and resources.

In order for DB2 to allow use of the EXCEPTIONS and DELETE facilities, an exception table must have been created to receive the deletions. That table is identified in the FOR EXCEPTIONS clause of the CHECK DATA STATEMENT. The exception table should be identical to the foreign key table that may contain the violations with the addition of one column to hold the RID (row or record identifier) of the rows in violation and another, which is optional, to hold a timestamp for when the utility began executing. The timestamp is useful since repeated execution of the utility will insert rows into the same exception table. Other columns may be included for remarks, installation codes, and so on. But, since the utility will not insert any values to those columns, they must be declared as nullable or as NOT NULL WITH DEFAULT. The exception table can be created easily with a CREATE . . . LIKE statement, followed by ALTER statements to add the extra columns. For example:

```
CREATE TABLE SPJEX LIKE SPJ;
ALTER TABLE SPJEX ADD RID CHAR(4);
ALTER TABLE SPJEX ADD TIMESTAMP TIMESTAMP;
```

After errors have been corrected in the exception table, the rows can be inserted into the foreign key table.

The final CHECK DATA statement parameter, SORTDEVT, indicates the device the utility is to use for sorts. A sort of the foreign key prior to processing may be necessary but only if there is no index on the foreign key or if the index contains additional columns.

CHECK INDEXes

The CHECK INDEX utility does not check referential integrity per se. Rather it checks that all rows in an indexed table are in fact indexed and that all row IDs in the index actually point to rows. Discrepancies in indexes are rare, usually caused by a storage device fault. Since DB2 uses indexes in referential integrity checking, however, errors in indexes can cause referential integrity violations to be missed.

The CHECK INDEX statement format can call for specific indexes or for all indexes in a tablespace to be checked. The first approach looks like this:

```
CHECK INDEX NAME (AUTHID.SNX, AUTHID.SPJX)
```

After the keyword NAME, the indexes to be checked are included in parentheses. The second method simply identifies the tablespace:

```
CHECK INDEX TABLESPACE SPJTSP
```

If there is reason to believe that there could be inconsistencies in the indexes, CHECK INDEX should be performed on primary and foreign key indexes before executing CHECK DATA.

A Simplified Approach

The most convenient method for loading a referential integrity structure is to load the primary key table first, then the foreign key tables with EN-FORCE CONSTRAINTS. That way the primary key table can be read while the foreign key tables are being loaded. Duplicates in the primary key can also be discarded, corrected, and inserted into the parent table prior to loading the foreign key rows.

If the primary and foreign key tables are in the same tablespace, the latter must be loaded with RESUME YES—the primary key table already exists in the tablespace and the foreign key table's rows must be added to it. This results in the load utility building the foreign key table's indexes through the inefficient insert mode. Nevertheless the benefits of having the referential integrity structure within the single, segmented tablespace, may outweigh the performance costs of this insert mode. The technique described in Box 16.3 can be used to build indexes on the foreign key after the data are loaded.

It is almost always better to have the load utility enforce referential integrity constraints than to load with ENFORCE NO and have the CHECK DATA utility handle enforcement. For one thing, the check pending status imposed after a load with ENFORCE NO curtails the data's usefulness considerably. Another reason the ENFORCE CONSTRAINTS load is preferred is that it is likely to be less costly. In one test run on an IBM 3090 200E under MVS/ESA, a load of a foreign key table with 1.5 million 100-byte rows and a primary key table with 500,000 rows required 17 minutes elapsed time under ENFORCE CONSTRAINTS. Under ENFORCE NO, the same load required 12 minutes, and the CHECK DATA utility took another 8 minutes—in all 3 minutes longer.

16.4 RUNSTATS

The RUNSTATS utility reads tablespaces and indexes to collect statistics describing the data, such as the number of pages and rows and the number of distinct values in an index. RUNSTATS stores these statistics in the catalog tables (Figs. 16.4 and 16.5). DB2's optimizer uses the catalog statistics in selecting efficient access paths. Developers also use the statistics to monitor and tune tablespaces by determining reorganization needs and managing space.

RUNSTATS should be executed immediately after a table and its indexes have been created and the data loaded. Then, in general, the utility should be run again whenever changes to a table may have changed the statistics in ways that could affect performance. If an index is added, for example, RUNSTATS should be run before plans that use the table referenced by the index are rebound to allow the optimizer to take advantage of the index.

The utility might also be run after heavy updating but only if that updating has an impact on the statistics. If added rows have the same number of unique index values as the table contained when RUNSTATS was last executed, for example, the index cardinality statistics will remain the same. The updates will have little effect on the optimizer's choice of access path for most processing using a unique index. One way to determine how often to execute RUNSTATS is, prior to an execution, to save in a table, perhaps called STAT_HISTORY, copies of the values in the catalog tables being updated. After the execution, the user can compare the two sets of statistics. If there is little difference, particularly in the cardinalities and cluster-

SYSIBM.SYSTABLES

```
CARD         – Number of rows in the table (cardinality)
NPAGES       – Number of pages that contain rows of the table
PCTPAGES     – Percentage of tablespace pages that contains rows of table
EDPROC       – blank = EDITPROC not used
```

SYSIBM.SYSINDEXES

```
CLUSTERRATIO – Percent of rows in clustering sequence
CLUSTERED    – Y if 95% of rows are in clustered order
FIRSTKEYCARD – Number of distinct values of indexed column
FULLKEYCARD  – Number of distinct values of composite index
NLEAF        – Number of active leaf pages in the index
NLEVELS      – Number of levels in the index tree
```

SYSIBM.SYSCOLUMNS

```
COLCARD      – Number of distinct values in column
HIGH2KEY     – Second highest value in the column (first 8 bytes)
LOW2KEY      – Second lowest value of the column (first 8 bytes)
FOREIGNKEY   – B if bit data, S if SBCS data, M if mixed mode
```

SYSIBM.SYSTABLESPACE

```
NACTIVE      – Number of pages up to the high preformatted page
```

SYSIBM.SYSFIELDS

```
EXITPARM     – Indexed value for 1 of 10 most frequently occurring values (first
               column of a composite index)
EXITPARML    – Percentage of rows * 100 that contain the value in EXITPARM
```

Most columns contain −1 until RUNSTATS is executed

Fig. 16.4 Statistics updated by RUNSTATS and used by the optimizer

SYSIBM.SYSTABLEPART

```
CARD         – Number of rows in the table space or partition
NEARINDREF   – Number of rows moved to a nearby page due to row length increase
FARINDREF    – Number of rows moved to a faraway page due to row length increase
PERCACTIVE   – Percentage of space occupied by active rows containing actual data
               from active tables (not space from deleted rows)
PERCDROP     – Percentage of space occupied by rows from dropped tables
```

SYSIBM.SYSINDEXPART

```
CARD         – Number of rows referenced by the index or index partition
NEAROFFPOS   – Number of times the next row was not in sequence of index but was in a
               near page (within + or −32 pages)
FAROFFPOS    – Number of times the next row was not in sequence of index but was in a
               faraway page (greater than + or −32 pages)
LEAFDIST     – Percentage of leaf pages that are not contiguous leaf pages during a
               sequential access of the index
```

Most columns contain −1 until RUNSTATS is executed

Fig. 16.5 Statistics updated by RUNSTATS and used for space management

ing indicators, the execution was not necessary. The STAT_HISTORY table can accumulate a history of statistics that an administrator can analyze to determine an appropriate schedule for executing RUNSTATS. SELECT statements from the catalog tables in Fig. 16.4 can be used to identify the statistics used by the optimizer. If the statistics change dramatically over time with some going up while others go down, RUNSTATS may need to be run more frequently. If all statistics move in the same direction, RUN-STATS may not be needed as frequently.

The analysis of an accumulation of statistics will provide information on how frequently the data and indexes should be reorganized. RUNSTATS provides the option to produce only statistics used to determine reorganization requirements and to manage space or only the statistics used by the optimizer. In addition, the user can choose to report on the statistics without updating the catalog table for analysis purposes.

The optimizer can take advantage of updated statistics in building efficient access paths only if the applications are rebound after the statistics are updated. Executing RUNSTATS on tablespaces used for applications in production programs therefore will have no effect until the application plans are rebound. With interactive SQL, under QMF or SPUFI, or with embedded dynamic SQL, plans are bound each time a statement is executed. Executing RUNSTATS on tablespaces used by these applications should provide immediate benefits, therefore, if the statistics reflect that an index's cardinalities or cluster ratios have changed, for example.

The RUNSTATS Statement

The format of the RUNSTATS statement is straightforward. The RUN-STATS TABLESPACE keyword is followed by the name of the tablespace on which the utility is to be run, which is prefaced by the name of the database in which it resides. It should also specify whether the utility should develop statistics on the tablespace's indexes.

The following statement will update statistics on the table or tables in tablespace DAGKWSPJ in database DAGKWDB and all of its indexes:

```
RUNSTATS TABLESPACE DASPJDB.DASPJTSP
         INDEX (ALL)
         SHRLEVEL REFERENCE
         UPDATE ALL
         REPORT YES
```

ALL in parentheses after INDEX indicates that RUNSTATS should obtain statistics on all indexes on all tables in the named tablespace, including the distribution statistics if a nonuniform distribution of values is detected. The user might request statistics on one or more specific indexes in the tablespace by specifying them in parentheses after the keyword INDEX. If the keyword INDEX is not used, RUNSTATS will not obtain statistics on any indexes.

The SHRLEVEL options are REFERENCE and CHANGE. If the developer specifies REFERENCE, while RUNSTATS executes, users and programs will be able to read but not update the table or tables in the tablespace. If the developer specifies CHANGE, others will be able to update the table or tables during utility execution. SHRLEVEL of change requires 5 to 10 percent more CPU time than SHRLEVEL of reference.

UPDATE ALL indicates that all statistics in the catalog tables are to be updated, which is the default. There are two classes of statistics to chose from by specifying UPDATE OPTIMIZER that will update the statistics in Fig. 16.4 or UPDATE SPACE that will update statistics in Fig 16.5. Updating only the statistics used for space management avoids the possibility of loosing current access paths with rebinds using new statistics. Also UPDATE NONE can be used in conjunction with REPORT YES to avoid a different access path. Statistics are collected and reported but the catalog tables are not updated. REPORT YES provides a report on the statistics and is a good choice regardless of the UPDATE parameter specified. The default is REPORT NO.

A RUNSTATS statement can obtain statistics on indexes only, which is useful when an index has been added, to determine if an index has a low cluster ratio or if a great deal of index page splitting has occurred. This will be less costly than updating statistics on the data since only the leaf pages of the index need to be scanned. This statement, for example, requests statistics on two indexes, ISN and IPN:

```
RUNSTATS INDEX (AUTHID.ISN, AUTHID.IPN)
   SHRLEVEL CHANGE
```

If the developer requests statistics on more than one index, all indexes must be on tables in the same tablespace.

The following statement shows the format for requesting statistics on specific tables and columns in a tablespace:

```
RUNSTATS TABLESPACE DASPJDB.DASPJTSP
   TABLE (S)
   TABLE (SPJ) COLUMNS (PN, JN),
   INDEX (ALL)
   SHRLEVEL REFERENCE
   UPDATE ALL
   REPORT YES
```

RUNSTATS uses a sampling method to estimate COLCARD, HIGH2-KEY, and LOW2KEY statistics on nonindexed and nonleading columns of composite indexes. The TABLE parameter with the table name indicates that these statistics should be collected on all columns. If the COLUMNS parameter is specified with specific columns, only those column statistics will be updated with a limit of 10 nonindexed columns. (The optimizer's use of these statistics is described in Chapter 12.) Updating statistics on nonindexed columns requires additional processing. These statistics, however, provide useful information for the optimizer in choosing a good access path, particularly for the nonleading columns of composite indexes when all columns are not specified with equal predicates in the WHERE clause.

The DB2I panel choices for RUNSTATS are essentially the same as those for LOAD. Datasets need not be designated for receiving records, discards, or copies, of course. The generated JCL will be placed in the DSNURUN.CNTL dataset.

STOSPACE Utility

STOSPACE is like RUNSTATS in that it collects statistics and records them in the catalog tables. Unlike the statistics collected by RUNSTATS, those collected by STOSPACE are not used by the optimizer but by users when determining if space should be increased or decreased with the ALTER statement before a reorganization. SELECT statements to compare the amount of space used and allocated are covered in Chapter 14. These statements will not give accurate results (some will not even execute) unless the SPACE columns have been updated by STOSPACE. The SPACE column in SYSINDEXES, SYSTABLESPACE, and SYSSTOGROUP is updated with the amount of space allocated. The date of STOSPACE execution is recorded in SPCDATE. Space allocation is collected for objects in storage groups but not for objects created as shared read only data and those created using VCAT. A technique that can be used to collect space statistics when using VCAT is to use the ALTER statement to change from using VCAT to using STOGROUP, execute STOSPACE utility, and use alter again to return to the use of VCAT. The control statement to collect space allocation in the storage groups DASPJSTO and DAZIPSTO is:

```
STOSPACE STOGROUP (DASPJSTO, DAZIPSTO)
```

16.5   REORGANIZATION

The REORG utility reorganizes data on physical storage to recluster rows, positioning overflowed rows in their proper sequence, to reclaim space in a tablespace after a table has been dropped, to restore free space, and to provide for newly allocated space specified by an ALTER. These functions will be needed after heavy insert, update, and delete activity and after seg-ments of a segmented tablespace have become fragmented and dispersed. The question of reclaiming space from dropped tables is particularly impor-tant when QMF users frequently create and drop tables within a tablespace although these problems do not exist in a segmented tablespace. Catalog monitoring, perhaps using a STAT_HISTORY table like that described in the section on RUNSTATS, can indicate when reorganization is necessary. Proper scheduling of reorganizations significantly improves performance of all application programs.

The REORG Statement

A REORG statement can apply to a tablespace and its associated index-spaces or to an indexspace alone. When an indexspace only is reorganized, the data pages are not processed—only the leaf pages are scanned. The format is straightforward: the command REORG TABLESPACE, followed by the tablespace name or REORG INDEX, followed by the index name. The utility's phases include an unload, a sort—if SORTDATA is specified or if indexes are involved—and a load. A sort of the data and index values requires the sort device (SORTDEVT) and the number of work files to be used in the sort (SORTNUM). Those choices depend on the same consider-ations as those described for a load in Box 16.2.

The statement might also specify that the load phase is not to use a log. The parameter is LOG NO, just as in the LOAD statement. It carries the same restrictions on updates and recoveries as LOG NO does when it is used with the LOAD utility and should be followed with a full image copy.

The statement to reorganize the DASPJTSP tablespace looks like:

```
REORG TABLESPACE DASPJDB.DASPJTSP
   LOG NO
   SORTDEVT SYSDA
   SORTNUM 6
   SORTDATA
```

The statement to reorganize the ISN index looks like:

```
REORG INDEX AUTHID.ISN
   SORTDEVT SYSDA
   SORTNUM 4
```

A reorganization of indexes may be all that is needed. This is particu-larly true if data is usually inserted in ascending sequence beyond the exist-ing data with an ascending clustering index. Indeed it is important to reor-ganize the indexes frequently in such a situation since they will have undergone a good deal of page splitting. Another case where reorganization of data need not be frequent is when most processing uses a matching index scan to locate only a few rows. Locating a few rows with a matching index scan can be done efficiently regardless of where those few rows are located in the data pages.

The SORTDATA Parameter

The reorganization utility unloads the data by scanning the leaf pages of the clustering index to locate the rows to be unloaded in the sequence of the clustering index unless the parameter SORTDATA is used. Scanning the leaf pages can be a costly process since it is necessary to skip around DASD locating the rows in sequence with a good chance that the same data page will have to be accessed repeatedly. Tests using SORTDATA have shown significant reductions in elapsed times with rather high cluster ratios—a 20 percent reduction with a cluster ratio of 95 percent and a 74 percent reduction with a cluster ratio of 80 percent. The elapsed time is increased by only 4 percent with a cluster ratio of 100 percent. These tests suggest that SORTDATA be used for the majority of reorganizations.

If SORTDATA is not used, REORG unloads the data depending on whether a segmented or nonsegmented tablespace is used, whether there is a clustering index declared on a table, and whether there is more than one table in the tablespace. If it is a segmented tablespace, each table is unloaded individually in sequence, using the clustering index leaf pages, and reloaded in clustering sequence with each table's segments in contiguous space. If there is no clustering index, rows are unloaded in the physical order of segment blocks and each table's segments will be contiguous when reloaded. If it is a nonsegmented tablespace and there is one table in the tablespace, rows are unloaded in sequence using the clustering index leaf pages like a segmented tablespace. If there is more than one table in a nonsegmented tablespace, however, data is not reclustered since the data is unloaded with a tablespace scan.

Expanding or Contracting Space

The REORG utility can be used to expand or contract space under VCAT. (Under STOGROUP, a simple DB2 ALTER statement can expand or contract space.) If VCAT had been used to create the tablespace, the tablespace's VSAM datasets can be deleted and re-created with the required space. A PAUSE clause is required in the REORG statement to allow these steps. A statement with that parameter looks like this:

```
REORG TABLESPACE DASPJDB.SPJ
   UNLOAD PAUSE
```

The user restarts REORG, specifying PHASE as the restart point on line 8 of the utilities panel. Optionally the JCL can be modified by placing RESTART (CURRENT) or RESTART (PHASE) on the EXEC DSNU-PROC statement.

An assembler program, DSNTIAUL, in the sample library, outprefix.DSNSAMP, is a good alternative for unloading data. This program is useful for transporting data from one DB2 database to another, for frequent reloading of test data, and for restructuring tables. The name of a table, along with a WHERE clause, can be specified to indicate the rows to be unloaded. Alternatively a view can be created identifying specific columns and rows and the name of the view specified to DSNTIAUL. The extracted sequential file can then be loaded into another table. DSNTIAUL creates LOAD control statements for the new tables but should be modified to use LOG NO in most cases. A number of developers have reported that it offers performance advantages over REORG unload. The performance of DSNTIAUL can be enhanced further, particularly in terms of CPU time reductions, by increasing the blocking factor in the assembler program (not in the JCL as might be expected). The sample program and JCL to execute it can be found in the sample library outprefix.DSNSAMP with the member names of DSNTIAUL and DSNTEJ2A.

16.6 COPY, MERGECOPY, AND RECOVER

If a tablespace or index is lost—through a storage media failure, perhaps— the copy, mergecopy, and recover utilities allow for its restoration.

The installation uses the COPY utility periodically to copy the tablespace or only the pages containing changes. The former copies are called *full image copies*; the latter are *incremental image copies*. DB2 records before and after images of all insert, update, and delete activity in log datasets. If a failure occurs, the mergecopy utility might be used to merge incremental copies into a new full image copy. To restore the tablespace, the recover utility writes the most recent usable image copy to DASD and applies all updates from the log beginning with the first one after the copy was made. If the incremental copies have not been merged, the same pages frequently will have to be processed for each copy if the pages are updated between incremental copies. DB2 recovers indexes by rebuilding them with a single pass of the tablespace, using a procedure similar to the LOAD and REORG utilities. This eliminates the need to copy the index.

Fig. 16.6 shows the interaction of the elements that go into a recovery. The copy utility records in the catalog table SYSIBM.SYSCOPY the fact that a copy has been made. The recover utility determines from this information what copies are available and required for the recovery. SYS-

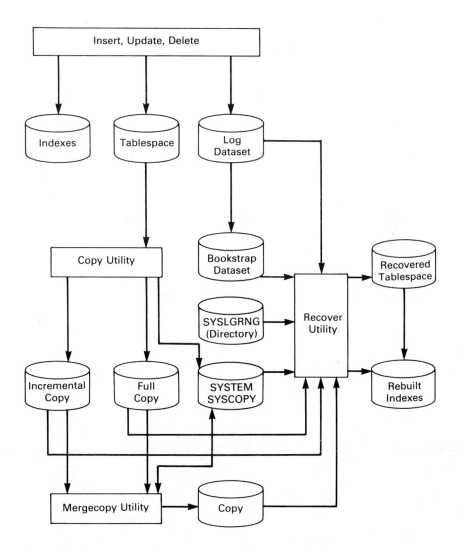

Fig. 16.6 Backup and recovery

LGRNG contains the starting point in the log. The bootstrap dataset (BSDS) contains an inventory of the log datasets. The recover utility uses the BSDS to determine the active and archived log dataset, needed for the recovery. The image copy is written to the tablespace, and the updates that were made after the copy are located in the log and applied to the copy.

The copy and recovery process offers a tradeoff between performance and tablespace availability. Copying requires processor time, but the longer the time between copies, the longer it takes to recover. That is because during recovery, logged updates have to be applied to the copy to bring it up to date. The more changes there have been to the data, the longer it takes to update the copy. If a table is updated frequently, frequent copying is necessary to avoid lengthy recoveries.

The incremental image copy provides a middle-ground solution to this tradeoff problem. Rather than using resources to make more frequent full image copies, incremental copies can be made periodically to record changes. DB2 keeps each incremental copy in a separate dataset. The merge utility can be used to merge all incremental copies to create a new full image copy periodically to decrease the time needed for recovery. Merge is not required, but if it is not done, the recover utility will have to do the merge before the recovery can start. The cost of the merge itself can be quite significant if many updated pages must be merged.

For tables that experience low update activity, taking periodic incremental copies is faster and more efficient than full image copies. But when the utility takes an incremental copy, it must check a bit map, bits are set to one on the tablespace's space map page that indicates which pages have experienced any change since it was last copied. If more than 5 to 10 percent of the pages have been changed, copying the whole tablespace will usually be more efficient than locating each page individually. With a full copy, DB2 can use asynchronous prefetch, processing 64 pages at a time and requiring about 4-5 ms per page. With an incremental copy, it reads only one page at a time with an average of about 25 ms per page. The utility produces a report including the number of pages copied and percentage of changed pages. This is useful information for scheduling copies.

If a tablespace has few updates, the installation may want to make daily incremental copies and a new full image copy each week. The schedule depends on the number of updates to the tablespace, the acceptable time of recovery, and the cost of making the copies. If copies have not been merged, the RECOVER utility will merge all copies before applying the copy to the tablespace.

Accumulating more incremental copies than there are available tape drives can delay the recovery process. If there is an insufficient number of tape drives for the copies to be mounted, WORKDDN (intermediate work dataset) can be used to merge the copies that can be mounted. WORKDDN will subsequently be merged with additional copies on available tape drives. The RECOVER utility will merge the oldest copies, using available tape drives. If all copies cannot be merged with available tape drives, the most recent copies will not be used. Rather RECOVER will go back further in the log and apply updates to the oldest copies that were merged. A good guideline is to take a full image copy or to merge the incremental copies before the number of copies exceeds the number of available tape drives to avoid delays in the recovery process.

The COPY Statement

The COPY statement indicates whether the copy is to be full or incremental, the device type that is to hold the copy dataset, and the share level. A typical statement would look like this:

```
COPY TABLESPACE DASPJDB.DASPJTSP
   SHRLEVEL REFERENCE
   FULL YES
   COPYDDN (L1DDNAME, L2DDNAME)
   RECOVERYDDN (R1DDNAME, R2DDNAME)
```

The FULL NO parameter causes the utility to make an incremental copy and FULL YES a full image copy. Full image copy is the default choice.

SHRLEVEL REFERENCE allows access to the tablespace for reads during the copy process. SHRLEVEL CHANGE allows updates to the tablespace's data during copying. (DB2 permits this share level only if the tablespace has been created with a locksize of page or any.) Copying while updates are being made requires additional resources, and recoveries made with these copies take longer than if the changes do not have to be accommodated. In addition, a partial recovery to an image copy made with SHRLEVEL CHANGE will result in a message indicating that the object has been recovered to an indeterminate point. The data pages may have changed during the copy, and they may not be reflected in the space map page.

As many as four image copies of a tablespace can be created simultaneously with a single pass of the tablespace. Two copies can optionally be made for the local site (in case one copy is lost or damaged) and two copies can optionally be made for a recovery at another site (in case of a disaster). The COPYDDN parameter lists in parentheses the DD names to be used for each of two local copies—(L1DDNAME, L2DDNAME). The RECOVERYDD parameter lists in parentheses the DD names to be used for each of two copies for off-site recovery—(R1DDNAME, R2DDNAME). Fig. 16.7 shows how these DD names are used within a job step to execute the COPY utility.

If both local and recovery site copies have been made in the past and only local or recovery copies are made, a full recovery may not be possible at one of the sites and a warning will be issued:

```
//COPYSPJ EXEC DSNUPROC,SYSTEM=DDT,UID='CSPJ',UTPROC=''
//L1DDNAME DD DSN=LOCALC1,UNIT=SYSDA,VOL=SER=SERID1,
//           SPACE=(TRK,(15,1)),DISP=(NEW,CATLG,CATLG)
//L2DDNAME DD DSN=LOCALC2,UNIT=SYSDA,VOL=SER=SERID1,
//           SPACE=(TRK,(15,1)),DISP=(NEW,CATLG,CATLG)
//R1DDNAME DD DSN=REMOTC1,UNIT=SYSDA,VOL=SER=SERID1,
//           SPACE=(TRK,(15,1)),DISP=(NEW,CATLG,CATLG)
//R2DDNAME DD DSN=REMOTC1,UNIT=SYSDA,VOL=SER=SERID1,
//           SPACE=(TRK,(15,1)),DISP=(NEW,CATLG,CATLG)
//DSNUPROC.SYSIN   DD  *
  COPY TABLESPACE DASPJDB.DASPJTSP
       COPYDDN     (L1DDNAME, L2DDNAME)
       RECOVERYDDN (R1DDNAME, R2DDNAME)
       FULL YES
       SHRLEVEL REFERENCE
/*
```

Fig. 16.7 Job step to execute copy utility

```
DSNU406I FULL IMAGE COPY SHOULD BE TAKEN FOR BOTH LOCAL SITE AND RECOVERY SITE
```

The MERGECOPY statement is similar to the COPY statement, identifying the tablespace in question and the device type to hold the output dataset. Share level need not be indicated since updates or reads of the tablespace are not affected by the merge process. The merge statement must indicate, however, whether the utility is to merge the incremental copies with the previous full image copy or only with themselves. The command NEWCOPY YES indicates the merge is to produce a new full image copy; NEWCOPY NO merges only the incremental copies. All incremental copies and the full copy will be merged with this statement:

```
MERGECOPY TABLESPACE DASPJDB.DASPJTSP
  NEWCOPY YES
  COPYDDN (M1DDNAME, M2DDNAME)
```

When COPY or MERGECOPY is executed from the DB2I utilities panel, one or two datasets must be specified in items 3 and 4, COPYDSN and COPYDSN2, to receive the full image or incremental copy. The JCL generated by the panel for COPY is written to the dataset DSNU-COP.CNTL, prefixed by the user's TSO ID.

RECOVER

Recovery can be performed on both a tablespace and its associated indexes or on indexes alone. If a tablespace is recovered, its indexes must also be recovered unless only the tablespace was damaged and the table and indexes agree. The statement for either is straightforward: the keyword RECOVER followed by the keyword TABLESPACE or INDEX, followed by the object's name:

```
RECOVER TABLESPACE DASPJDB.DASPJTSP
```

or

```
RECOVER INDEX (AUTHID.ISN, AUTHID.IPN)
```

If there is reason to believe that the indexes do not require recovery but that is not certain, CHECK INDEX can be used to make the determination and will require significantly fewer resources than will doing a tablespace scan and rebuilding the indexes. The statement would look like:

```
CHECK INDEX NAME (AUTHID.SNX, AUTHID.SPJX)
```

or

```
CHECK INDEX TABLESPACE SPJTSP
```

Multiple tablespaces can be recovered with a single pass of the log datasets. This is particularly important when recovering a tablespace that has related tables in other tablespaces. Indeed, if all related tablespaces are not recovered together, a check pending state will result. If partial recovery of some, but not all, tables related through referential integrity is required, it is necessary to name all related tablespaces in the RECOVER control statement.

```
RECOVER TABLESPACE DASPJDB.DASPJTSP
        TABLESPACE DASPJDB.DALOCTSP
        TABLESPACE DASPJDB.DAEMPTSP
        TABLESPACE DASPJDB.DADEPTSP

RECOVER INDEX (ALL)
        TABLESPACE DASPJDB.DASPJTSP
        TABLESPACE DASPJDB.DALOCTSP
        TABLESPACE DASPJDB.DAEMPTSP
        TABLESPACE DASPJDB.DADEPTSP
```

If the tablespaces are not related to each other, recovering one tablespace at a time can have performance advantages since sections of the log can be skipped.

If the utilities RECOVER, LOAD, and REORG abend without a successful restart, recovery pending can be set on. Like copy and check pending, no updates can be make to the tables in the tablespace while recovery pending is on, and like check pending, no SELECT statements can be issued. It is best to restart the failed utility to turn off the recovery pending status. In many cases, it is not possible to simply terminate the utility and resubmit it.

16.7   RECOVERING REFERENTIAL STRUCTURES

Recovery of referential structures requires synchronization. If primary and foreign key tables were recovered to different points in time, they would likely end up in violation of referential integrity. If, for example, the recovery of a foreign key table covers more time than the recovery of the primary key table, values that have been added to the foreign key during the extended period may not have been included in the primary key table at the point of its recovery. DB2 manages and enforces synchronization of the recovery of referential structures through the QUIESCE utility.

The QUIESCE utility establishes a point at which a set of tablespaces are in a consistent state. The set, identified to the utility in the execution statement, need not be a referential integrity structure. But since the utility's primary purpose is to allow recovery of referential structures, the included tablespaces usually make up a referential structure.

The underlying situation the QUIESCE utility deals with is the fact that COMMIT WORK statements do not cause DB2 to apply updates to the tablespace immediately. Rather COMMIT WORK statements turn responsibility for recording the updates over to DB2, which may collect them in the log dataset and bufferpool for a period of time before applying them. This makes the processing more efficient. Up to 10 percent of the bufferpool can contain updated pages for a single dataset that can be written to DASD in 32 pages chunks sequentially as the pages appear on DASD using one of the write engines. This deferred write not only makes the writing of updated pages efficient, it also means that anyone who needs to read or update the pages will not have the cost of a physical I/O to DASD if the pages are still in the bufferpool. An alternative that will force updated pages to DASD is to stop the database specifying tablespace names. Updated pages in the bufferpool, however, are not accessible by others without physical I/O to DASD. In addition, all the underlying VSAM dataset for the named tablespaces and indexspaces in the database will be closed.

The execution of QUIESCE causes DB2 to apply all outstanding updates from the bufferpool for the tablespaces included in the execution statement. At the same time, QUIESCE records the point at which the updates were applied in terms of the relative byte address (RBA). The RBA is analogous to a sequence number of the log record, in fact, it is an offset from the beginning of the log with a maximum value of 2^{48}. The RBA allows the RECOVER utility to identify the image copy from SYSCOPY, the active or archival logs from the BSDS and the starting point in the log from SYSLGRNG in the directory for use in the recovery.

The QUIESCE utility records the RBA in the catalog table SYSCOPY along with other information about image copies. The individual executing a recovery can locate RBA or image copy information for use in the RE-COVER statement by querying SYSCOPY or executing the REPORT utility. We will discuss how to do that shortly, but first we will cover how to execute the QUIESCE utility.

All of the tablespaces in the set to be synchronized must be identified in the QUIESCE statement. One of the reports generated by the REPORT utility is designed to identify the tablespaces to include. The REPORT TA-BLESPACESET statement will generate a listing of the tables in a tablespace and the relationships among them. The REPORT statement must identify only one of the tablespaces with a table participating in the referential structure. If that tablespace is related through a referential constraint to a table in a different tablespace, that tablespace and its tables will also be included in the report. For example, the following statement requests a report on tablespace DASPJDB.DASPJTSP and related tablespaces:

```
REPORT TABLESPACESET
       TABLESPACE DASPJDB.DASPJTSP
```

That statement might generate a report like that shown in Fig. 16.8. By studying the relationships listed in the report, one can identify delete-connected tables, cycles, and self-referencing tables.

Notice that the EMP and DEPT tables reference each other and thus participate in a cycle. The DEPT table is both a parent and a dependent, and thus participates in a self-referencing relationship.

The QUIESCE statement then includes all the tablespaces identified in the TABLESPACESET report. Using the report from Fig. 16.8, the QUIESCE statement would look like this:

```
QUIESCE TABLESPACE DASPJDB.DASPJTSP
        TABLESPACE DASPJDB.DALOCTSP
        TABLESPACE DASPJDB.DAEMPTSP
        TABLESPACE DASPJDB.DAEPTSP
```

When QUIESCE is executed, it must take a share lock on each tablespace. If it cannot obtain share locks on all of the included tablespaces within 60 seconds, the default setting, it terminates and issues a resource unavailable message. It must then take an exclusive lock on any tablespaces that have outstanding updates in the bufferpool and log. The utility will also terminate if an included tablespace is in copy pending, check pending, or recover pending status. QUIESCE requires only minimal I/O operations and CPU

```
REPORT TABLESPACESET
        TABLESPACE DASPJDB.DASPJTSP
```

TABLESPACE	TABLE	DEPENDENT TABLE
DASPJDB.DASPJTSP	AUTHID.S	AUTHID.SPJ
		AUTHID.S_BUYER
	AUTHID.P	AUTHID.SPJ
	AUTHID.J	AUTHID.SPJ
		AUTHID.J_ASSIGN
	AUTHID.SPJ	
DASPJDB.DALOCTSP	AUTHID.VALID_CITY	AUTHID.S
		AUTHID.P
		AUTHID.J
	AUTHID.VALID_STATUS	AUTHID.S
DASPJDB.DAEMPTSP	AUTHID.EMP	AUTHID.S_BUYER
		AUTHID.J_ASSIGN
		AUTHID.DEPT
	AUTHID.J_ASSIGN	
	AUTHID.S_BUYER	
DASPJDB.DADEPTSP	AUTHID.DEPT	AUTHID.EMP
		AUTHID.J_ASSIGN
		AUTHID.DEPT

Fig. 16.8 Reporting on referential integrity structures

cycles—only enough to apply usually few updates from the bufferpool and logs and record the RBA.

A good procedure for preparing to recover a related set of tablespaces is to QUIESCE all related tablespaces to insure that all pending states are off and that all updates in the buffer pool are written to the tablespaces and indexes, then to take an image copy, and finally to QUIESCE all related tablespace once again to provide for a partial recovery to a RBA.

The RBA and image copy information needed for recovery can be obtained through the REPORT utility using the REPORT RECOVERY statement or by querying SYSCOPY directly. The REPORT RECOVERY statement identifies the tablespace for which the information is sought. The statement looks like this:

```
REPORT RECOVERY
        TABLESPACE DASPJDB.DASPJTSP
```

Fig. 16.9 shows a partial sample report. The TYPE column shows the image copy type (ICTYPE) for each copy. (The ICTYPE codes are: F, full image copy; I, incremental image copy; Q, quiesce; P, partial recovery point; R, LOAD(REPLACE) LOG(YES); S, LOAD(REPLACE) LOG(NO); W, RE-ORG LOG(NO); X, REORG LOG(YES); Y, LOAD LOG(NO); Z, LOAD

```
REPORT RECOVERY
TABLESPACE DASPJDB.DASPJTSP

  ▪   Information from SYSCOPY (catalog table)


                            DS   FILE               SHR DEV
TIMESTAMP                 TYPE  NUM  SEQ  START RBA  LVL TYPE  REQD DSNAME
1988-06-08-11.10.00.278362 *O*  0000 0000 000008CF501A          Y
1988-06-08-11.10.06.548910 *X*  0000 0000 000008CF98EE          N
1988-06-14-14.16.25.843679 *O*  0000 0000 000008E05F8A          Y
1988-06-14-14.17.18.039184  F   0000 0000 000008E0BD09 R  SYSDA N   C8145GD. . .
1988-06-14-04.16.15.387643 *O*  0000 0000 000008F19D98          Y
1988-06-14-10.09.20.843913 *O*  0000 0000 000008F2CFE9          Y
1988-06-14-10.11.01.560183  F   0000 0000 000008F411F3 R  SYSDA N   C8145GD. . .
1988-06-14-09.11.08.495230 *O*  0000 0000 000008F58320          Y
1988-06-14-09.12.15.334827  F   0000 0000 000008F5C674 R  SYSDA N   C8145GD. . .
1988-06-14-09.13.08.358720 *Q*  0000 0000 000008F72B8C          Y


  ▪   Information from SYSLGRNG (directory table)
DSNU583I - DSNUPPLR - REPORT RECOVERY TABLESPACE DASPJDB.DASPJTSP SYSLGRNG ROWS
 UCDATE     UCTIME     START RBA        STOP RBA
 060888    10200532   0000088F5573    0000088F6994
 060888    10211502   000008C6E2BD    000008C6F9E1
 060888    22190320   000008CDD8D8    000008CDEED0
 060888    22211177   000008CF9C6D    000008CFB2B7
 061488    08373692   000008E0A5E3    000008E0BC84
 061488    19230279   000008F3F918    000008F30F6D
 061488    19253341   000008F5AE3C    000008F5C4EE


DSNU583I - DSNUPPLR - REPORT RECOVERY TABLESPACE DASPJDB.DASPJTSP BSDS VOLUMES
 START TIME       END TIME        START RBA       END RBA     UNIT   VOLSER
19882882420449  19883882620449  0000000000000  000000368FFF  3380   WAV01
19883882420538  19883882620538. 0000000369000  00000038FFFF  3380   WAV01
19883882437183  19883882437183  0000000390000  000000397FFF  3380   WAV01
```

Fig. 16.9 Reporting on information used for recovery

LOG(YES).) The report also lists the start RBA for the quiesce point or image copy and the name of the dataset that holds the copy. The information from SYSLGRNG is used to determine where in the log to start to apply updates to the image copy that is placed in the tablespace. If the image copy RBA is less than the SYSLGRNG RBA, updates will be applied starting from the SYSLGRNG RBA in the log dataset.

A sample query that produces some of the same information from SYS-COPY looks like:

```
SELECT TIMESTAMP, HEX(START_RBA), ICTYPE
FROM   SYSIBM.SYSCOPY
WHERE  DBNAME = 'DASPJDB'
AND    TSNAME = 'DASPJTSP'
ORDER BY TIMESTAMP
```

The HEX operator puts the RBA in hexadecimal representation, which is the form required in the RECOVER statement. The ICTYPE allows identification of the quiesce points and image copies. An ICTYPE of P, W, or Y means the tablespace is in copy pending state.

TORBA or TOCOPY

Recovery can be made to an image copy or to a specific RBA. Recovery to the RBA provides more flexibility, allowing recovery to a specific point in time as identified from the reports discussed. Consider, for example, a tablespace for which an image copy was taken on a Sunday. On Wednesday the installation discovers that Tuesday's updates were in error. Recovery to the image copy taken on Sunday would lose Monday's correct updates. Recovery made to an RBA from late Monday or early Tuesday would save Monday's work.

In a recovery to the image copy, the dataset containing the copy, identified in SYSCOPY, is specified in the RECOVER statement. The copy used in RECOVER TOCOPY should be made with SHRLEVEL REFERENCE or else data pages could be changed in the course of the copy without being reflected in the space map pages. If the recovery to the copy uses a copy made with SHRLEVEL CHANGE, DB2 issues a warning and recovers the object to an indeterminate point. The RECOVER TOCOPY statement looks like:

```
RECOVER TABLESPACE DASPJDB.DASPJTSP
    TOCOPY C8145GD.DASPJTSP.TIC.G0007V00
```

In recovery to RBA, the START_RBA from SYSCOPY is designated in hexadecimal notation. Recovery to RBA will recover updates made up to the point of the RBA, but not include those made at that point. The RECOVER TORBA statement looks like:

```
RECOVER TABLESPACE DASPJDB.DASPJTSP
    TORBA X'000008A50B9C'
```

Multiple tablespaces can be recovered simultaneously by identifying them all in the RECOVER statement. When the multiple tablespaces are part of a referential integrity structure, however, the recovery should be not only to an RBA but to an RBA that is a quiesce point and all of them should be included in the statement. If either requirement is not met, some or all of the dependent tables will be placed under check pending. A RECOVER statement for a referential integrity structure would be:

```
RECOVER TABLESPACE DASPJDB.DASPJTSP
    TABLESPACE DASPJDB.DALOCTSP
```

```
TABLESPACE DASPJDB.DAEMPTSP
TABLESPACE DASPJDB.DADEPTSP
TORBA X'000008A50B9C'
```

All of the indexes in each tablespace must also be recovered. The RE-COVER utility actually rebuilds the indexes, so an image copy or RBA need not be specified. The RECOVER INDEX statement need identify only the tablespaces for which the indexes are to be recovered. Individual indexes may be specified for recovery or the word ALL can be used to indicate all indexes in the tablespace are to be recovered. (If the recovery fails after some indexes have been rebuilt, only the remaining indexes need to be recovered.) For example:

```
RECOVER INDEX (ALL)
        TABLESPACE DASPJDB.DASPJTSP
        TABLESPACE DASPJDB.DALOCTSP
        TABLESPACE DASPJDB.DAEMPTSP
        TABLESPACE DASPJDB.DADEPTSP
```

A full image copy of all tablespaces recovered with TOCOPY or TORBA must be made before updates can be made. The RECOVER utility is restartable in case of failure. If the job is terminated before completion, however, the tablespaces are placed in a recover pending state, which means among other things that no data manipulation statements can execute against the tablespace.

REPAIR Utility

The REPAIR utility can be used to set the three pending states off if it is not possible to determine the reason for the pending states and correct them. All or any one of the pending states can be forced off. The following statement forces off all three pending states—check pending, copy pending, and recovery pending.

```
REPAIR SET TABLESPACE DASPJDB.DASPJTSP
    NOCHECKPEND
    NOCOPYPEND
    NORCVRPEND
```

An alternative method for circumventing the pending states is to start the tablespace with access of force. The disadvantage of this technique is that the user will not know about other problems that may exist.

```
-START DATABASE (DASPJDB) SPACENAM (DASPJTSP) ACCESS (FORCE)
```

Neither approach corrects the problem that resulted in the pending state. The problems are ignored and DB2 will not be able to maintain data integrity.

```
DSNU105I + DSNUGDIS - USERID = RUNSPJ
             UTILD = RUNSPJ
             PROCESSING UTILITY STATEMENT 1
             UTILITY = RUNSTATS
             PHASE = RUNSTATS   COUNT = 90400
             STATUS = ACTIVE
DSN9022I + DSNUGCCC '-DISPLAY UTILITY' NORMAL COMPLETION
```

Fig. 16.10 Status report of the RUNSPJ utility

REPAIR can also be used to dump, delete, and modify rows. This may be necessary in an emergency until there is time to isolate and correct the problem properly. For example, foreign keys without a parent can be deleted very quickly without executing the CHECK DATA utility. The row with a RID of X'0000070C' can be deleted like:

```
REPAIR
  LOCATE TABLESPACE DASPJDB.STSP
  RID (X'0000070C') DELETE
```

The REPAIR utility should not be used routinely but is useful in an emergency condition where there is insufficient time to handle the problem properly.

Determining the Status and Phase of a Utility

The DISPLAY UTILITY command can be used to determine the status and phase of a utility. The syntax of the command is straightforward. Fig. 16.10 is an example of the result of the display. The command −DISPLAY UTILITY(RUNSPJ) will display the status and phase of the utility assigned the name RUNSPJ. The command −DISPLAY UTILITY(*) will cause display of the status and phase of all utilities known to DB2 that were submitted under the AUTHID of the individual who issued the command.

Service Aids

Service aids are somewhat like utilities but with one important difference. They operate outside the control of DB2. Indeed DB2 does not have to be operational for most of them. The problem is that, if there is a failure, DB2 cannot assist in a recovery. DSN1COPY is probably the most often used service aid. Chapter 9 suggested using it for making a copy of the tablespace and indexes before a batch program was executed that might fail and require recovery to the point before the program started. Its use has the ad-

Box 16.4 Service Aids

Service aids that operate outside the control of DB2

- DSN1COPY can be used to copy tablespace and index spaces to/from sequential files, perform DBID/OBID translation, reset log RBA to 0, and print dumps of data and index pages.

- DSN1CHKR can be used to check for broken hashes and links and to verify the integrity of the catalog tables and directory.

- DSN1LOGP can be used to produce a summary or detailed report of the recovery log.

- DSN1PRNT can be used to print contents of tablespaces, indexes, image copies, and sequential datasets created by DSN1COPY.

- DSN1SDMP can be used to force dumps when selected DB2 events occur or after a utility abend and to write DB2 trace records to a user defined MVS dataset.

---

vantage that the indexes do not have to be rebuilt. Box 16.4 summarize the service aids.

16.8 SUMMARY

DB2's utilities are important to performance in two ways. First, they allow for efficient management of the physical storage. Second, used properly, they contribute to optimum performance of databases. The utilities themselves require resources. Therefore careful use of the utilities can save on processing costs.

EXERCISES

16.1. Table A, the only table in its tablespace, cannot be updated when the COPY or RUNSTATS utility is executed on the tablespace. What is a possible cause, and what can be done to allow such updates?

16.2. Data were loaded in sequence of the clustering index, but SYSIBM.SYSINDEXES shows a very low cluster ratio for the clustering index. What might be the problem? Provide a possible solution.

16.3. An index will not fit in the space calculated for it. Assume the calculation was correct. What are possible problems? How might they be solved?

16.4. Performance was good, on a prototype database that contained data on one of a company's four divisions. When the tablespaces were reloaded with data from all divisions, performance fell. What is a possible problem? Identify a solution.

16.5. A tablespace cannot be updated or recovered. What are possible problems and solutions?

16.6. An attempt was made to restart a load with LOG NO and a restart of PHASE. Why does the restart fail? How might the restart be accomplished?

16.7. A recovery takes longer than expected. What might be the problem? Provide a solution.

16.8. What DML statements are allowed when COPY PENDING, CHECK PENDING, or RECOVERY PENDING is set on? In general, what utilities can be executing when the pending states are set on?

17

Distributed Database

17.1 INTRODUCTION

IBM began a staged implementation of distributed database management system capabilities for DB2 beginning with Version 2 Release 2 with a planned evolution to a fully functional distributed database management system. The goal is a database management system in which data can be distributed among multiple computers on a network with each site being able to operate as an independent database management system but with the group cooperating—and appearing to users—as a single system. Eventually the distribution will be able to include nodes running not only DB2 but also IBM's other systems application architecture (SAA) database management systems, SQL/DS, SQL/400, and OS/2 EE database manager (DM). Already these DBMSs can participate in a distributed environment.

Distributed databases hold several advantages. Data are distributed and processing performed across multiple systems, allowing the work to be shared by multiple processors. Availability of data is enhanced because the failure of one site has a limited effect on other sites. And last but not least, providing easy access to remote data will make it easier for users to perform their jobs.

If processing frequently spans multiple sites, however, these benefits can give way to deficits. For example, communications over a satellite typically adds a half second to response times—a quarter second to send a request and a quarter second to receive it. And then there is the processing cost of communications hardware, software, and network services to consider. Generally processing over a communications link requires two or three orders of magnitude as much time as local, channel-to-channel processing.

As to availability, if multiple nodes must be continuously available for processing that spans nodes, failure at one affects the entire system. If each site were available 98 percent of the time, system-wide availability would be only 96 percent for two sites (.98 * .98) and only 92 percent for four sites (.98 * .98 * .98 * .98).

Because of the tradeoffs of costs and benefits in a distributed database system, users should choose applications to be distributed carefully. A warehouse inventory control system is an example of an application that is a good candidate for distributed data. Warehouses generally service local areas, so most of the processing can be done locally, but occasionally a local warehouse might need to search for a product at another site. These occasional searches do not require high communications costs nor does occasional centralized reporting. Both the system-wide searches and central reporting, however, would be much more timely and convenient on a distributed system. Other candidate applications include branch banking, regional insurance offices, and retail sales. Demand for distributed databases in these and other businesses is likely to spur continuous development of distributed capabilities.

17.2 THREE TYPES OF DISTRIBUTED CAPABILITY

IBM has defined at least three types of distributed capabilities, two of which are currently supported and one of which is a future goal. The two supported are what the company calls remote unit of work (UOW) and distributed UOW. A UOW is a transaction made up of a related set of SQL statements. Under remote UOW, DB2 on one computer can send multiple, related SQL statements to another DBMS on a remote computer. (Fig. 17.1 shows two remote UOWs.) The remote site performs the processing for the statements, but the sending site controls whether to commit or roll back the UOW. It is necessary to issue a CONNECT TO statement to change from one remote DBMS to another. The location and AUTHID part of the table name is not required in the following example.

Under distributed UOW, the CONNECT statement is not required; however processing is supported only between multiple DB2s. Again the sending site maintains control over commits or rollbacks of the transaction. When the sending site issues a COMMIT WORK, DB2 at that location takes responsibility for insuring that all updates are applied or rolled back. The UOW sent to another site may or may not be executed. The third type

```
CONNECT TO :LONDON
INSERT INTO S
          (SN, SNAME, STATUS, CITY)
     VALUES ('S10', 'JONES', 50, 'LONDON')
INSERT INTO SPJ
          (SN, PN, JN, QTY)
     VALUES ('S10', 'P40', 'J7', 400)
COMMIT WORK

CONNECT TO :SYDNEY
UPDATE P
   SET CITY = 'PERTH'
  WHERE PN   = 'P60'
DELETE FROM J
  WHERE JNAME = 'ELECTRICAL'
    AND CITY  = 'SYDNEY'
COMMIT WORK
```

Fig. 17.1

of distributed processing is a distributed request that allows a single SQL statement to span sites. We will discuss this capability, not yet supported, in a moment.

Read access across all nodes is provided under all of the attaches. But there are limitations on updates in the distributed environment. All updates that are part of a UOW must be performed at only one site. Under IMS and CICS, updating is restricted to the site originating the transaction. Under TSO, batch TSO, or the CAF (call attach facility), the single update site may be remote, and there is nothing to prevent the originating site from issuing multiple UOWs with the updates for each performed at differing sites. For example, an application program in Dallas might issue updates on tables in London followed by a commit work and then issue updates on tables in Sydney followed by a commit work, and so on. Version 2.3 does not support the coordination of updates. For example, updates in London will be applied even if the updates in Sydney fail.

Remote UOW conforms to DRDA (distributed relational database architecture) but distributed UOW does not since it was developed before DRDA. Remote UOW supports static and dynamic SQL data manipulation, data definition, and data control. Distributed UOW supports only data manipulation that is always bound at the remote site using dynamic SQL. Neither capability allows for execution of utilities on the remote data.

In the first stages, a referential structure will have to reside at a single site. Consider the challenge of allowing a user to delete a primary key row in Dallas with a cascade rule that could cause the deletion of a number of rows in foreign key tables located in London and Sydney. What if the site in London was not available or there was a failure halfway through the cascade delete in Sydney after the deletes in London were complete? Avoiding such problems could detract severely from performance. Not avoiding them opens the way for the introduction of errors.

17.3   DISTRIBUTED REQUEST

The third distributed capability defined by IBM but not supported initially is the distributed request, which comes closer to the generally accepted definition for fully distributed databases. A distributed request would allow a single SQL statement to span sites, perhaps joining or unioning rows from tables in Dallas, London, and Sydney. Such a capability would allow a referential structure to be dispersed across multiple locations and be maintained automatically by DB2, including a cascade delete like that described above.

Allowing transactions to span multiple machines requires, among other things, use of a two-phase commit. Under the two-phase commit, the participating nodes in a transaction first communicate with each other the fact that each has completed its portion of the transaction and is ready to commit. The initiating site will ask each site if it is ready to commit, receive the response, and if all are ready, ask each site to commit. If a positive response is received and all have committed successfully, all is well. The challenge is coordinating a failure. What if a positive response is received from all but one site? Perhaps there was a failure at that site and updates could not be committed. All other sites have committed and locks have been released. The updates cannot be removed; rather it will probably be necessary to save the updates that have not been applied and apply them when the site is available. Another complicating factor is that the site did commit but there was a transmission failure and the positive response was never received. Two-phase commit is a challenge and is resource intensive.

Distributed requests also require global optimization that considers the size of the answer set at each location, the size of each computer, and the communication links that connect the sites to determine what work should be done where. Consider the problem of a join on a 10,000-row table in London with a 500-row table in Sydney with results to be sent to Dallas. Should the join be performed in London, Sydney, or Dallas? The answer depends on the processing resources at each site and the likely number of rows that will qualify, among other things. Answering such questions will require an optimizer with a global view of the distributed system. We may see this sophisticated capability in the middle to late 1990s.

IBM has the research in place to accomplish this distributed processing goal. They began research on distributed database management with R* (pronounced R star) in 1980 after completion of the System R prototype in 1979. R* was concerned with distributed processing across peer DBMS.

Researchers also recognized that distributed processing would also be required across mini-and microprocessors with their respective database management systems. Thus additional research, code named Starburst, began in 1982 and continues today. The DBTI (Database Technology Institute) developed DRDA and is currently furthering its development.

17.4 LOCATION TRANSPARENCY

Location transparency refers to the idea that with a distributed database a user should not have to know the location of requested data. The goal is to have the DBMS determine the location of the data from the catalog tables and the communications database. Some location transparency is provided in DB2 through the addition of a third qualifier to table names: LOCATION.AUTHID.NAME. The location qualifier, as its name suggests, indicates the location of the data and eliminates the need to have unique table names across all DB2 sites. The three-part name can be used anywhere the previous two-part names could be, except with the LOAD utility, which accepts only the two-part name. In addition, a synonym cannot be created on an object using a three-part name.

An alias can be used to avoid having to code the full three level name of a table or view. The statement CREATE ALIAS SPJ FOR DALLAS.VENDOR.SPJ would allow a user to use the reference, SPJ, without being aware of the location of the table or the AUTHID of the table. (City names are used for location to clarify the examples. Location transparency, however, will be enhanced if a functional name rather than a city name is used.) It is necessary to have privileges to create an alias, but once it is created, the person who uses the alias need only have privileges on the underlying table or view. The catalog tables are used to translate an alias to its fully qualified name, allowing DB2 to locate remote data when the SQL statement contains only the alias. SYSTABLES has an "A" in the TYPE column indicating that the row applies to an alias.

A few points to remember about aliases: A synonym created on an alias is actually created on the underlying object. An object need not exist when an alias for it is created, but DB2 will issue a warning if an alias is created on an object that does not exist at the local site. DB2 will not check for the existence of the object at remote sites when using a distributed UOW. If an object underlying an alias does not exist when a plan referencing the alias is bound at the remote site, DB2 issues a warning if the VALIDATE(RUN) parameter is used and an error if VALIDATE(BIND) is used. Because an alias is used, when a table is moved to a new location, plans using the table need only be rebound as long as each UOW can still be executed at only one remote site following the move when using a distributed UOW.

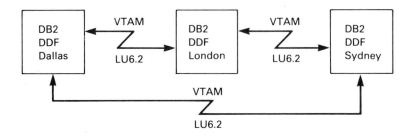

Fig. 17.2 Distributed data facility (DDF)

17.5 LOCAL AUTONOMY

Distributed capabilities include support for the concept known as local autonomy: Each site can operate independently of the distributed system. Applications using local data only are not affected by being part of the distributed system. Failure at one location in a network, for example, will not affect local processing at another location or remote requests to or from the remaining active sites. Moreover through new security arrangements and the ability to set local priorities for the processing of remote requests, local administrators can maintain tight control over their own data and resources. Optionally control can be exercised at a central site with a remote UOW.

The Distributed Data Facility (DDF)

DDF is an optional fourth address space required for the management of distributed data. (See Fig. 17.2.) DDF need not be installed if the DB2 system is not to participate in distributed processing. But each DB2 participating in distributed processing must have an active DDF address space. The DDF address space can be started automatically as part of DB2 startup or started when needed dynamically with a −START DDF command. Distributed processing can also be stopped automatically with a −STOP DDF, which will quiesce all distributed processing. That is, new requests will be rejected but currently active requests will be satisfied.

A request to be satisfied at a remote site is passed to the local DDF after creating an allied thread, which establishes a link using VTAM (virtual telecommunications access method), APPC (advanced program to program communications), and the LU (logical unit) 6.2 protocol. The request is transmitted to the remote DDF that establishes a database access thread (DBAT). After it is executed at the remote site, the results are returned via the remote DDF to the requesting local DDF, which in turn returns the

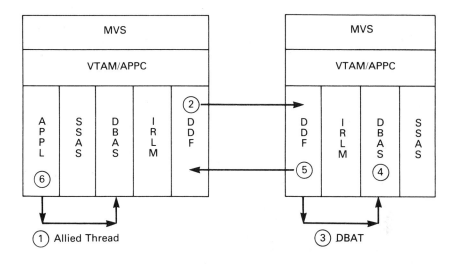

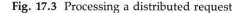

1. Allied thread created when first SQL request is issued
2. Request passed to local DDF which sends it to remote DDF
3. DBAT (Database Access Thread) created by remote DDF
4. SQL prepared and executed by remote DBAS
5. Results returned by remote DDF to local DDF
6. Local DDF passes results to application program
7. Remote DBAT terminated when remote access is done

Fig. 17.3 Processing a distributed request

result to the requesting application program. This processing is diagramed
in Fig. 17.3. The actual execution of the remote SQL is done in the DBAS
(database address space). The IRLM (IMS resource lock manager) handles
locks similar to what would be done for local processing. The remote SSAS
(system services address space) handles logging and the recording of statistics at the remote site.

One way for a local site to control remote access to its resources is by
turning the DDF on or off. For example, DDF might be stopped during
peak processing hours, barring outside access during that time and switched
on during off hours. In addition, each remote site given access to a local
site must be identified in the SYSIBM.SYSLUNAMES table of the local
site's communications database (CDB), a database used to control distributed database communications. Another way to control local access is for
the system administrator to set the dispatching priority of the DDF address
space lower than that for the other DB2 address spaces. This will favor

processing of local requests over remote requests. Once the program starts executing, however, its priority is that of the address space where it is executing.

The Communications Database (CDB)

The CDB is required for any DB2 installation initiating remote processing. The CDB functions somewhat like the catalog and directory to control distributed database communications. The CDB differs from the catalog and directory in one important way. The CDB tables are created and populated by the user like any data tables, not by the system as is done for the catalog and directory. If there are errors or omissions in the table entries, the distributed capabilities will not function.

Generally the CDB tables describe the characteristics of the VTAM links to be used for remote requests, identify the nodes that requests can be received from or sent to, translate locations referenced in table names in SQL statements to the logical unit name of the node containing the data, and handle the security needed for remote requests. Fig. 17.4 shows a diagram of the tables, and Fig. 17.5 lists the CDB tables, briefly describes their functions, and tells when during remote processing they are accessed, an indication of the processing cost they contribute. Let us look at some of the highlights of the tables here.

The table SYSIBM.SYSLUNAMES is at the heart of the CDB. It names the logical units that can participate with the site in distributed requests, containing one row for each DB2 site to which a request can be sent and one row for each site from which a request can be received. DB2 accesses SYSLUNAMES the first time a remote site is referenced. An LUNAME is the name of a DB2 site as known by VTAM; LOCATION is the name of a site as known by users. Some column values in SYSLUNAMES indicate other tables that are to assist in controlling the communication.

For example, a Y in column USERNAMES indicates that the CDB table SYSUSERNAMES is to be used to translate the local AUTHID of the individual requesting remote access to his or her remote ID, called NEWAUTHID. NEWAUTHID will be discussed in the following section. A Y in column MODESELECT indicates that table SYSMODESELECT should be used to determine the request's class of service—in effect, the transmission techniques and route to be used. Typically, there will be a default mode. SYSMODESELECT, however, can provide for an alternate route for specified AUTHID, PLAN, and LUNAME. If USERNAMEs or MODESELECT has Ys but there are no corresponding rows in the SYSUSERNAMES or SYSMODESELECT tables, DB2 issues an error message indicating that the resource is unavailable.

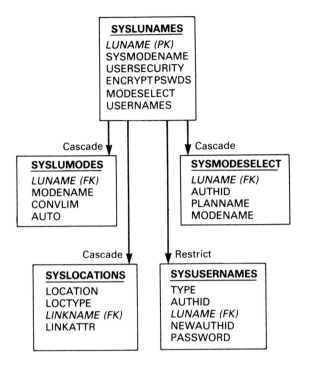

Fig. 17.4 Communications Database

SYSLUNAMES: Defines characteristics of logical units, the remote sites, that
                 the local site may send to or receive from; includes one row for
                 each site; accessed the first time and LUNAME is referenced.

SYSLUMODES: Defines characteristics of VTAM sessions to be used in communi-
                 cations with each remote site; accessed only when DDF is started.

SYSLOCATIONS: Translates location segment of three-part table name to a logical
                 unit name, LUNAME; accessed when SQL statement includes a LOCA-
                 TION.

SYSMODESELECT: Identifies class of communications service, MODENAME, to be used
                 for each session; class may be assigned by AUTHID, PLANNAME, and
                 LUNAME; accessed the first time a program or user is referenced.

SYSUSERNAMES: Translates local AUTHID to remote NEWAUTHID; accessed the first
                 time a connection is made.

Fig. 17.5 Communications database tables

AUTHID	LUNAME	NEWAUTHID
ERIC	DALLAS	DALLAS1
FLEUR	LONDON	blank
HEATHER	null	ALLSITES
DAVID	null	blank
blank	SYDNEY	REMOTEOK
blank	PERTH	blank

Fig. 17.6 SYSUSERNAMES

The CDB table SYSLUMODES is used to set the number of *conversations* to be allowed between sites during an LU 6.2 session. The DDF uses two types of conversations—system conversations for communicating status information and user conversations for communicating SQL requests, results, and commit and rollback messages. A system conversation starts with the first remote request and ends when DB2, DDF, or VTAM is stopped. A user conversation starts when a thread is established and ends when it is terminated, but more than one conversation may be used with a given thread. DB2 accesses SYSLUMODES when DDF is started. The tables can be updated at any time, but changes will not take effect until DDF is restarted.

17.6   SECURITY

To extend security to the concept of local autonomy, DB2 provides for the translation of a requesting AUTHID to an AUTHID to be transmitted to the remote site for authorization checking, which is the NEWAUTHID column in the SYSUSERNAMES table. The NEWAUTHID value must be granted privileges at the remote site to perform the requested operations. When users make requests to the remote site, DB2 uses the entries in SYSUSERNAMES to translate their local IDs to the appropriate remote ID and transmits the NEWAUTHID value with the request. (Translations of IDs with inbound requests may be done as well.) The table includes columns for local AUTHIDs, the LUNAMEs of remote sites, and the NEWAUTHIDs associated with each user's access to each remote site (see Fig. 17.6). The translation is done for the AUTHID executing dynamic SQL and for the binder AUTHID when using static SQL.

Nulls and blanks have special meanings in SYSUSERNAMES. A blank under AUTHID means that any AUTHID being used at the local site will be translated to the ID in NEWAUTHID for the associated remote location—except for those expressly given a NEWAUTHID for that site. In Fig. 17.6, for example, all users not named in the table at the local site have the NEWAUTHID of REMOTEOK when submitting a request to SYDNEY. A null in LUNAME means that the local user has the associated NEWAU-THID at all remote locations. And a blank in NEWAUTHID means that the user's AUTHID is to be used as the NEWAUTHID. If there is a value other than null or blank in AUTHID, it will be translated to the NEWAU-THID value and transmitted to the remote site. For example, ERIC will be translated to DALLAS1 when he executes a dynamic SQL statement or binds a package in Dallas.

Security for distributed database activities actually begins with the authorization to start or stop DDF. RACF or other security software can also verify the connection authorization at the remote DDF. The remote user must have received table privileges from the site where the data resides when using dynamic SQL to process the tables specified in the transmitted SQL statements. The GRANT/REVOKE statements have a parameter to allow a local site to provide access to a table to the PUBLIC AT ALL LOCATIONS.

17.7 PROGRAM DEVELOPMENT IN A DISTRIBUTED ENVIRONMENT

The relational model, including the structural and integrity parts as well as the manipulative part, makes distributed database management possible and practical. The set constructs defined in the relational model as implemented in SQL makes distributed processing economically feasible. A single SQL statement can be transmitted to a remote site where it acts on one or on a large number of rows, returning an SQLCODE indicating that the insert, update, or delete was or was not successful. In the case of a SELECT, the number of rows to be returned to the requesting site can be narrowed to just those required. It is not necessary to transmit all the rows and have the application determine those that are needed. Nor must the rows be requested and transmitted one at a time as would be done with a nonrelational DBMS. DB2 takes the efficiency of set processing a step further with a facility called block fetch.

It could be costly in communications and processing time to send one row at a time between two DB2 systems as a result of a SELECT statement even after narrowing the search to just the requested rows. And it would also be wasteful to transmit all of the requested rows if the application or user decides to process only some of them. To avoid these problems when a cursor is used to select rows from a remote site, block fetch groups, say 100 rows from the cursor, and to transmit them together, rather than transmitting one row at a time. For example, a SELECT may request 1000 rows from a 10,000-row table located remotely. The block fetch would return perhaps a 100-row block to the requesting DB2. An attempt will be made to fill the 32K-byte block with result rows to maximize performance. It releases the share locks on the remote data pages as the rows are processed when using the isolation level of cursor stability (CS) and holds them until a commit work is issued when using repeatable read (RR).

The block of data is built in the local DSAS (database services address space) and transmitted to the remote DSAS from where rows are fetched by the program. Two 32K-byte buffers can be allocated per DBAT. Buffer-pools BP0, BP1, BP2, and BP32 are not used.

DB2 uses the block fetch only when it can be sure that the selected rows are not to be updated. (Updates of the blocked rows would cause synchronization problems at the remote site.) DB2 can tell from the cursor statement whether the retrieved rows are to be updated in many cases. It is best that the developer specify in the cursor statement the FOR FETCH ONLY clause to indicate that no rows are to be updated so that it is clear that block fetch will be used. If the statement specifies FOR UPDATE OF, DB2 will not allow a block fetch. If neither clause is used, DB2 will still use block fetch if the cursor statement itself indicates updates are disallowed, if, for example, it includes an ORDER BY, GROUP BY, column function, join, and so forth. Both dynamic and static SQL will use the block fetch.

DB2 executes all SQL statements that reference remote data as dynamic SQL at the site where the table is stored when using a distributed UOW. The DB2 DBRM (database request module) must be bound at the DB2 local site even if it contains no SQL acting on tables at the local site. Unbound remote SQL will be in the plan and will be bound at the remote site before the plan is executed at the remote site. At bind time at the remote site, the AUTHID of the original binder of the plan is checked for the appropriate privileges. If the plan contains true embedded dynamic SQL, the AUTHID of the *runner*, the person executing the plan or interactive SQL, is checked for the appropriate privileges.

Alias references are resolved at bind time, which provides for the movement of objects without requiring modifications to programs and the SQL that they contain. This plays a major role in location transparency. SYS-PLANDEP stores information about local dependent objects for impact analysis but not remote dependent objects. Alias dependencies are recorded, however, so that the objects can be traced to some extent.

If there is a communication or DB2 failure, a −904 SQLCODE will be received indicating an unavailable resource. A commit work can be issued and will result in a −901 indicating that a rollback has been done at the local and remote sites after which additional SQL can be executed successfully. If a commit work is not issued, a -906 SQLCODE will be received for each subsequent statement accompanied by a message that the statement cannot be executed because the function is disabled due to prior error.

Other factors to be considered in a distributed environment are that a LOCK TABLE statement cannot be issued on a remote table and that deadlocks are treated as a timeout at the local site, not rolled back. Character conversion allows international companies to distribute DB2 data between countries using different character sets. If there is a possibility that tables on SAA (system application architecture) DBMS other than DB2 are to be processed from a program, it is advisable to test the SQLSTATE rather than the SQLCODE. Chapter 1 discussed the fact that SQLSTATE will return the same or similar conditions for all SAA DBMS and provide compatibility with ANSI SQL2 which allows for use of DBMSs from companies other than IBM.

Packages in a Distributed Environment

The use of packages with a remote UOW provides for a remote bind of static SQL followed by repeated executions. (A distributed UOW results in the static SQL being bound each time it is executed.) The DBRM member PROGA is bound at each site with statements such as:

```
BIND PACKAGE (LONDON.PROGA) MEMBER (PROGA) -- London bind
BIND PACKAGE (SYDNEY.PROGA) MEMBER (PROGA) -- Sydney bind
BIND PACKAGE (DALLAS.PROGA) MEMBER (PROGA) -- Dallas bind
```

PROGA will be executed in Dallas and contains SQL statements that will be executed in London, Sydney, and Dallas. The DBRM must be bound into a package at each of the sites where the SQL is to be executed. The location part of the package name must be defined in the table SYSLO-CATIONS. In addition, a plan must be bound containing the three packages at the requesting site, at Dallas in the example:

```
BIND PLAN    (TRN1) -
     PKLIST  (LONDON.PROGA, SYDNEY.PROGA, DALLAS.PROGA)-
     CURRENTSERVER (SYDNEY)
```

PROGA might contain the following SQL statements:

```
SELECT PN, PNAME, WEIGHT, CITY
FROM   P                     -- Table in Sydney
WHERE  PN = 'S4'

COMMIT WORK
CONNECT TO :LONDON
```

```
SELECT PN, PNAME, WEIGHT, CITY
FROM   P                    -- Table in London
WHERE  PN = 'S4'
```

The first SELECT statement will be executed in Sydney since the CUR-
RENTSERVER (SYDNEY) was specified when the plan was bound. The
second SELECT will be executed in London or the content of the host variable :LONDON as specified in the CONNECT TO statement. Notice that
a commit is required before the CONNECT statement can be executed. Of
course, it is best to issue a CONNECT to Sydney in the program rather
than having to know that the current server had been specified as Sydney
when the package was bound. But the example is designed to show the
function of the current server.

It is possible to switch between a remote UOW (RUW) and a distributed UOW (DUW) through the use of CONNECT RESET like:

```
COMMIT WORK
CONNECT RESET

SELECT PN, PNAME, WEIGHT, CITY -- DUW using dynamic SQL
FROM   STOCKHOLM.POS.P         -- Table in Stockholm
WHERE  PN = 'S4'               -- Can use an alias

SELECT PN, PNAME, WEIGHT, CITY
FROM   P                       -- Table in Dallas on
WHERE  PN = 'S4'               -- Requesting DB2
```

The first SELECT is using a fully qualified table name although an alias
could have been created so that only the table name of P could be referenced. The second SELECT is accessing the P table at the requesting site
of Dallas.

Performance in a Distributed Environment

The transmission of large amounts of data should be avoided when using
DB2 distributed capabilities. One test required 25 minutes to transmit
500,000 rows using a 64K-bps (bits per second) communication link. There
is also the CPU time required to buffer messages, package them into
frames, compute check sums, bind sessions, and control data flow, and
transmission that applies when using both communications links and channel-to-channel communications between multiple DB2s on the same computer. A rule of thumb figure that can be used to estimate the CPU time
required by DDF is 1.2 ms (milliseconds) per message. A SELECT of one
row would require three messages: one to send the request, one to receive
the result row, and one to receive the SQLCODE for a total of 3.6 ms. The
time needed is reduced significantly when using block fetch even for a few

rows. The rule of thumb is 2.6 ms total to send a request and receive 32K bytes of data.

Costs are reduced with set processing since fewer messages must be formatted and transmitted. Whenever possible it is best not to select a row and then issue an update or delete on that row. Rather issue global update and delete statements. This approach has performance advantages for remote as well as for local processing as was discussed in Chapter 11. Another point mentioned in that chapter, and one that is even more important in a distributed environment is, to narrow the search to just the rows needed using all applicable predicates.

17.8 DISTRIBUTED ENHANCEMENTS

In addition to the DDF address space and the block fetch feature, a number of components of DB2 provide for a distributed database environment. Most of these features are needed to ensure local autonomy and location transparency.

The resource limit facility (RLF) can limit the amount of CPU usage for interactive or embedded dynamic SQL DML issued locally or received from a remote site through an additional column indicating the site in the limit table. If the RLF is not used, the system administrator can specify that there is no limit (NOLIMIT) or the amount of CPU time that can be used by a remote request, that remote requests will not be accepted (NORUN), or that from 1 to 5 million ASU can be specified, indicating the maximum amount of CPU time that can be used by each SQL statement in DSNZPARM. The facility does not apply to static SQL. RLF can be used, however, to control whether BINDs are allowed as was discussed in Chapter 11. The audit facility will track access or attempted access from remote sites as it does from local sites.

The DISPLAY DATABASE command will give the location name of a lock requester and lock holder, and DISPLAY THREAD command can be specific to a location. DISPLAY LOCATION provides statistics about threads that have a distributed data relationship. A trace can be specific to a location with the LOCATION parameter when the trace is started, stopped, or displayed. The performance trace has been enhanced to trace the resource managers of DDF. Statistics can be collected on message traffic at the transaction, SQL statement, and data sent/received level.

17.9 SUMMARY

A decade of research and prototyping of distributed database management built on top of two decades of research and prototyping of the relational model will be realized in stages over the next few years. This is just in time to logically reunite data that have been dispersed on diverse hardware and software spread over many, if not all, of the seven continents. Distributed database processing makes it possible to return to the original goal of database management, the sharing of corporate data across the organization with the ability to access it regardless of where it is located.

EXERCISES

17.1. The statement, UPDATE SPJ SET SN = 'S2' WHERE JN = 'J3', issued in Sydney against the SPJ table in Dallas, receives a resource unavailable message. What are possible reasons for the message?

17.2. The above statement receives an error message. What is a possible reason?

17.3. Turnaround time for the above remote request increases dramatically, although there have been no major changes in the data or access path. What are possible reasons?

17.4. Describe the purpose of the FOR FETCH ONLY clause.

17.5. Name two important technical innovations that must be implemented to allow for distributed requests.

A

Tablespace Size Estimations

A tablespace's space requirements depend on the design of the table or tables it will hold. The table design described in the CREATE TABLE statement determines the length of each row, which in turn determines the number of rows that will fit on each page and therefore the number of pages needed for the table. The number of pages needed provides the basis for the amount of space specified for the tablespace's VSAM dataset. To determine space requirements the developer needs to know the row length, usable space per page, and number of rows in the table.

To calculate row length, add the length of each column declared in the table. Each character column requires 1 byte per character length declared. For VARCHAR columns, use the average number of characters to be stored in the column plus 2 bytes for the VARCHAR column length indicator. INTEGER columns require 4 bytes and SMALLINT columns 2 bytes. Each column that allows nulls requires an extra byte for the null indicator. The number of bytes required for each data type is listed in Fig. 4.2. In addition, each row has a 2-byte entry in the page directory, indicating among other things the distance in bytes from the beginning of the page to the record's beginning. Each row is also identified with a 6-byte row prefix (RP). The row plus the 6-byte RP is a record. The first byte of the RP is a row type indicating that the record is a normal, overflow, or pointer record. The next 2 bytes contain record length which is the row length plus the 6-byte RP.

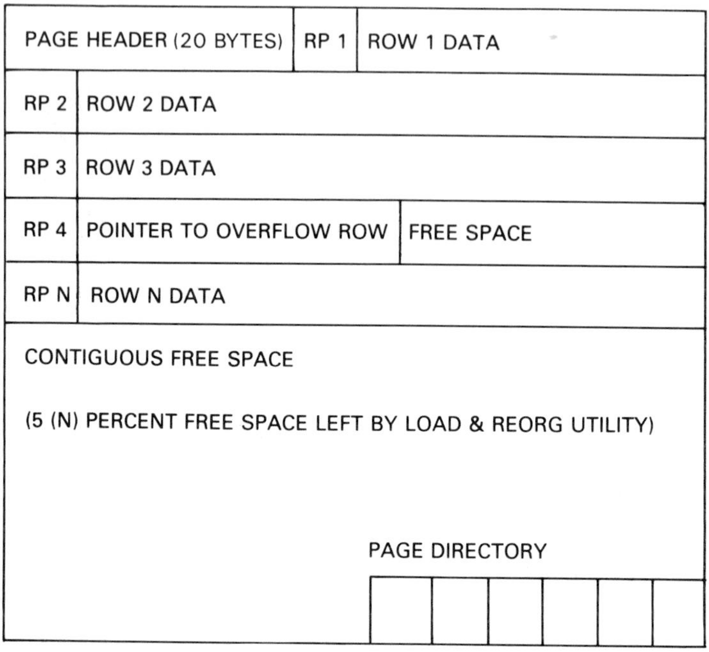

PAGE HEADER (20 BYTES)	RP 1	ROW 1 DATA	
RP 2	ROW 2 DATA		
RP 3	ROW 3 DATA		
RP 4	POINTER TO OVERFLOW ROW	FREE SPACE	
RP N	ROW N DATA		
CONTIGUOUS FREE SPACE (5 (N) PERCENT FREE SPACE LEFT BY LOAD & REORG UTILITY)			
		PAGE DIRECTORY	

Fig. A.1 Page layout

The OBID (object ID) comes next in 2 bytes. The final byte in the RP matches the row's entry in the page directory, which is the map ID entry. The total space needed for each row, then, is its length plus 8 bytes for the data management information: the 2-byte directory entry and 6-byte RP.

A number of calculations can be saved if the table has already been created. The record length can be determined from SYSTABLES with the SELECT statement:

```
SELECT RECLENGTH
FROM   SYSIBM.SYSTABLES
WHERE  CREATOR = 'AUTHID'
AND    NAME = 'SPJ';
```

Each data page contains 4096 bytes. (Fig. A.1 shows a data page layout.) When DB2 searches for a row, it first reads the page header (which takes 20 bytes) to find the correct page and then the directory to find the row's location. The header contains the page number in the page set, the log RBA when the page was last updated, and the free space available on the page. The last two bytes on the page are trailer information. The first of the two bytes is the subscript of the first free entry in the page directory, indicating deleted rows, and the second byte is used to indicate if the page is broken. The header and trailer reduce usable space on the page. Free space left by the load and reorganization utilities as specified when the tablespace is created also reduces space available for rows when the data are loaded or reorganized. The load and reorganization utilities leave the percentage of free space after the header and trailer has been deducted.

To determine the number of rows that will fit on each page, divide the usable space by the amount of space needed by each row. Since DB2 will not split rows between pages, any fractional value should be ignored, a fact indicated by the "floor" operator in the following example. Then to calculate the number of pages needed, divide the number of rows in the table by the number of rows per page. Since DB2 will not dedicate only a fraction of a page to a table, any fractional result should be raised to the next whole number, indicated by "ceiling" in the formula.

The usable page size is calculated as:

```
4096 page size
 -22 page header and trail area
-204 byte for 5 percent free space
 ---
3870 Usable page size
```

The formula for calculating the number of pages required is:

```
Number of pages = ceiling (N of rows / floor (3870 / (row length + 8)))
```

A sample calculation for a row length of 100 bytes with 1 million rows is:

```
28,572 pages = ceiling (1,000,000/ floor (3870 / (100+8)))
```

Space for free pages can be added to the estimate by dividing the estimated number of pages by the FREEPAGE value of say 63 and adding that to the original estimate:

```
29,026 = 28,572 + (28,572 / 63)
```

Finally the estimate can be made more precise by calculating the number of space map pages discussed in Chapter 3 and adding one for the header page.

These calculations can be tedious and time consuming for a large number of tables. The burden can be relieved somewhat by inserting rows into a table created by the developer describing the table name, the number of rows in the table, the row length, and the length of the columns in an index like:

SPACE_CALC Table

TNAME	N_ROWS	ROW_L	INDEX_L
S	1,000,000	139	20
SPJ	2,700,000	32	28
P	3,000,000	70	22
J	1,000,000	116	20

A SELECT statement from the SPACE_CALC table can be used to estimate the number of data pages and leaf pages (index space calculations are described in Appendix B):

```
SELECT TNAME, N_ROWS, ROW_L, INDEX_L,
       (N_ROWS / (3870 / (ROW_L  + 8 ))), -- Data pages
       (N_ROWS / (3563 / (INDEX_L + 4 )))  -- Leaf pages
  FROM  SPACE_CALC
```

The report generated will look like:

TNAME	N_ROWS	ROW_L	INDEX_L	DATA PAGES	LEAF PAGES
S	1,000,000	139	20	38,461	6,801
SPJ	2,700,000	32	28	28,125	24,544
P	3,000,000	70	22	61,224	22,057
J	1,000,000	116	20	32,258	6,801

If the developer wants DB2 to create the tablespace's dataset in a storage group, he or she must convert the number of pages needed to 1K-byte units, the unit value used with the primary quantity (PRIQTY) parameter in the CREATE TABLESPACE statement. This conversion requires multiplication of the number of pages needed times four—since there are 4K bytes per page. Here is the calculation for the example:

```
PRIQTY = (N pages * 4)
       = (29,026 * 4)
       = 116,104
```

If the developer creates the tablespace's VSAM dataset, the estimate should be converted to cylinders or tracks for the best performance. DB2 will do this automatically when using storage groups.

B

Estimating Index Sizes

Estimating the space needed to store an index is similar to estimating a table's space requirements. It differs, though, in a few important details. The first step is to determine the usable space on an index page. As with a data page, an index page contains 4096 bytes. A page header takes 29 bytes. Subpage management also requires overhead space. Each subpage requires 21 bytes plus the index column length for overhead, except for a 1 subpage, which needs 17 bytes. An index page specified with SUBPAGE 4 on a 6-byte column therefore would require 108 bytes of subpage overhead—27 bytes per subpage, 4 subpages. The total subpage overhead is 17 if the subpage size is 1. The percentage of free space allocated by the load or reorganization utility is calculated on the amount of space left after the header and subpage overhead have been subtracted. Here is a sample usable space calculation for an index page:

```
4096 page size
 -29 page header
-108 subpage overhead =
     (index length+21)*4 subpages
-396 10 percent free space for insertions
---
3563
```

The next step, calculating the number of index entries per page, is straightforward. Divide the usable space by the space needed for each entry, which is the indexed column's length plus a 4-byte RID (row or record identifier) and 1 extra byte if the column allows nulls. Entries cannot be split across pages, so fractional values should be ignored. The formula and an example follows.

```
Index entries per page = floor (3563 / (index length + 4))
356 = 3563 / (6 + 4)
```

The final step, calculating the number of pages, requires an understanding of the index's B-tree scheme. In a B-tree, index entries are distributed among several levels of pages: a single root page at the top of the tree, one or more levels of nonleaf (NL) pages that point to leaf pages, and the leaf pages themselves, which hold all the index entries. (Fig. 6.2 diagrams a B-tree index.) Because the NL pages must provide a balanced, or equal-length, path to all the leaf page values and because a limited number of pointers can fit on each NL page, the B-tree may require more than one NL layer. The calculation itself reveals how many levels are needed and how many pages each will have.

For this portion of the calculation, we need the number of entries per page, which we have determined, and the total number of entries, which equals the number of rows in the table for a unique index. We will use a 1-million row table for the example and assume that the index is unique—all its values are different. The leaf page level contains an entry for each row in the table. Determining the number of pages needed for that level is a matter of dividing the total entries—1 million—by the entries per page—356. Fractional values should be raised to the next whole number—in the example, 2809.

```
2809 = 1,000,000 / 356 (leaf pages)
```

The next level, a NL level, must provide one pointer to each leaf page. Determining the number of NL pages needed requires taking the number of leaf pages and dividing by the number of entries per page (2809 / 356) and again raising fractions to the next whole number. In this case, only 8 NL pages are needed to provide a pointer for each leaf page. If there were a much larger number of leaf pages or many fewer entries per page, the B-tree would require another level to provide a balanced path. The calculation is repeated until the result is 1, which represents the root page needed to point to the NL level. The number of pages needed for the entire B-tree is the sum of the pages required at each level. As a formula, the calculation looks like this:

```
N level pages = ceiling (number of rows / index entries on page)

N-1 level pages = ceiling (previous level pages / index entries on page)
```

```
Root level when ceiling (previous level / entries per page) is less than or equal
to 1
```

In the example, the number of pages needed for a 1-million row table with an index length of 6 is:

```
2809 = 1,000,000 / 356 (leaf pages)
   8 =     2,809 / 356 (NL pages)
   1 =         8 / 356 (root page)
---
2818 Total index pages
```

If the index were not unique, it would not require this much space. The table's redundant values need not be repeated in the index for each occurrence. Only the RID for each row containing the repeated value need be listed along with one entry per subpage for the value itself. An equipment inventory table may have an index on a model number column, for example. The index need not repeat the model number for each row in which it appears. Instead it would list the model number once, along with the RIDs for the rows that include it (the model number is repeated every 254 RIDs). The amount of space saved depends on the amount of redundancy in the column being indexed. In the space calculation, we can adjust for redundancy by considering each index value and RID as a separate entry and calculating the average length of each entry. If the indexed column length is 10 bytes, for example, and each value is repeated about five times, the index requires six entries—the value and five RIDs. The value is 10 bytes and each RID is 4 bytes, for an average of 6 bytes per entry. Use this amount in place of the column-length- plus-RID figure in the unique index calculations for the leaf pages.

C

Using SPUFI

Developers usually use SPUFI (SQL processing using file input), a component of the DB2I (DB2 interactive) menu-driven application tool, to create database objects. SPUFI provides facilities for setting up the files needed for the SQL CREATE statements and the output from their execution, for editing the statements and browsing the output, and for other aspects of the object creation process. Users can also develop and run any SQL data definition, data manipulation, or data control statements through SPUFI.

SPUFI is the first choice on DB2I's primary option menu. Before going to SPUFI the first time, however, the user should customize some of the underlying DB2I facilities. This is done through the DB2I defaults panel (Fig. C.1), choice 6 on the DB2I primary menu (Fig. 9.5).

The first change should be on line 1, the name of the installation's DB2 system. The initial name on the panel will likely be DSN, the name IBM gives to the system. It should be changed to the name the system's installer chose—in all probability, DB2T for test or DB2P for production. If the developer will be using COBOL, most of the other defaults should be appropriate with the exception of line 6, which has as the default "DEFAULT" and instead should have a single quote.

While at the default panel this first time, the developer may want to set up a personal JOB statement for programs developed under DB2I. The statement, entry 9 on the DB2I defaults panel (Fig. C.1), is included by

```
                              DB2I DEFAULTS
    ===>

    Change defaults as desired:

     1 DB2 NAME . . . . . .     ===> DSN    (Subsystem identifier)
     2 DB2 CONNECTION RETRIES   ===> 0      (How many retries for DB2 con.)
     3 APPLICATION LANGUAGE     ===> COB2   (COBOL, COB2, C, FORT,ASMH,PLI)
     4 LINES/PAGE OF LISTING    ===> 60     (A number from 5 to 999)
     5 MESSAGE LEVEL . . . .    ===> I      (Info., Warning, Error, Severe)
     6 COBOL STRING DELIMITER   ===> '      (DEFAULT, ' or '')
     7 SQL STRING DELIMITER     ===> '      (DEFAULT, ' or '')
     8 DECIMAL POINT . . . .    ===> .      (. or ,)
     9 STOP IF RETURN CODE > =   ===> 8      (Lowest terminating returncode)
    10 NUMBER OF ROWS . . . .   ===> 20     (For ISPF Tables)

    11 DB2I JOB STATEMENT:    (Optional if your site has a SUBMIT exit)
       ===> //JOB . . . USER = AUTHID
       ===> //*
       ===> //*

    PRᵀ  ᴶ: ᶠᵁTER to save and exit     END to exit          HELP for more info.
```

Fig. C.1 DB2I defaults panel

DB2I in the JCL that it generates for program preparation and execution of utilities. The statement contains installation-specific information about jobs such as accounting and billing data, maximum processing time allowed for a job, and so on. The developer should provide this information. The developer will also have to include on the JOB statement an AUTHID through the clause USER = AUTHID. The AUTHID is passed to DB2 for authorization checking or may be intercepted by the installations security software and another value passed to DB2. Once the statement and panel defaults have been set, they should have to be changed only rarely.

The user can now move to the SPUFI panel (Fig. C.2) through choice 1 on the primary menu. The first visit to the SPUFI panel should be brief, long enough only to move through choice 5 to the current SPUFI defaults panel (Fig. C.3). Most of the SPUFI defaults that come with the system, those defining output datasets and output formats, are appropriate for most installations. Developers may want to give some consideration to the first two default choices: for isolation level and the maximum number of lines that a SELECT executed through SPUFI may return.

Isolation level addresses concurrency control locking strategies. SPUFI comes with an isolation level default of RR (repeatable read), which provides maximum data protection. For reasons described in detail in Chapter

```
                              SPUFI
   ===>

   Enter the input data set name: (Can be sequential or partitioned)

   1 DATA SET NAME. . .   ===> 'PROJ.AUTHID.SPUFI(CREATES)'

   2 VOLUME SERIAL. . .   ===> (Enter if not cataloged)

   3 DATA SET PASSWORD    ===> (Enter if password protected)

   Enter the output data set name : (Must be sequential data set)

   4 DATA SET NAME. . .   ===> 'PROJ.AUTHID.SPUFIOUT'

   Specify processing options:

   5 CHANGE DEFAULTS     ===> YES (Y/N -Display SPUFI defaults panel?)

   6 EDIT INPUT. . . . .  ===> YES (Y/N -Enter SQL statements?)

   7 EXECUTE. . . . . .   ===> YES (Y/N -Execute SQL statements?)

   8 AUTOCOMMIT. . . . .  ===> YES (Y/N -Commit after successful run?)

   9 BROWSE OUTPUT. . .   ===> YES (Y/N -Browse output data set?)

   For remote SQL processing:

   10 CONNECT LOCATION. . ===>

   PRESS: ENTER to process       END to exit      HELP for more information
```

Fig. C.2 SPUFI panel

8, most developers will want to change this default to CS (cursor stability), which provides maximum concurrency. The default for maximum number of rows returned is 250. If a SELECT statement returns fewer rows than expected, it may be because of the value set here.

Once the DB2I and SPUFI defaults have been set, the developer can go to work using the SPUFI panel. (Changing selection 5 to NO will avoid display of the SPUFI defaults each time SPUFI is used.) Line 1 takes the name of the sequential or partitioned dataset that will receive the SQL statements. Any number of SQL data definition, manipulation, or control statements may be entered into this input file. Line 4 takes the name of the dataset that receives the executed SQL statements and their results. It must be a sequential dataset. DB2 will create this file with the dataset characteristics on lines 3 to 6 of Fig. C.3 if it has not been created previously. A record

```
                        CURRENT SPUFI DEFAULTS

  ===>

  Enter the following to control your SPUFI session:

  1 ISOLATION LEVEL      ===> CS (RR=Repeatable Read,CS=Cursor stability)

  2 MAX SELECT LINES     ===> 250 (Maximum number of lines to be
                                   returned from a select)

  Output data set characteristics:

  3 RECORD LENGTH . . .  ===> 4092 (LRECL=Logical record length)

  4 BLOCK SIZE . . . . . .===> 4096 (Size of one block)

  5 RECORD FORMAT . . .  ===> VB (RECFM=F, FB, FBA, V, VB, OR VBA)

  6 DEVICE TYPE . . . . . ===> SYSDA (Must be DASD unit name)

  Output format characteristics:

  7 MAX NUMERIC FIELD    ===> 20 (Maximum width for numeric fields)

  8 MAX CHAR FIELD . .   ===> 80 (Maximum width for character fields)

  9 COLUMN HEADING . .   ===> BOTH (NAMES, LABELS, ANY or BOTH)

  PRESS: ENTER to proceed          END to exit          HELP for more info.
```

Fig. C.3 SPUFI defaults

length of 133 on line 3 will provide for a nicely formatted report without line wrapping.

A YES in line 6 will place the developer in the ISPF editor, which is used for keying in the statements. Each statement must be terminated with a semicolon. And statements creating objects should be followed by COMMIT WORK statements, which commit the catalog table updates needed to create the objects. Objects should be created in hierarchical order—that is, a database must be created before its tablespaces, tablespaces before their tables, and so on. Chapter 3 describes this hierarchy.

Finally SQL statements are executed with a YES in line 7. The work done by SQL data manipulation statements may be committed automatically with a YES in line 8 and the results browsed with a YES in line 9.

The following is a listing of a SPUFI file used to create all of the objects in the SPJ database that have been used in examples throughout the book. The two hyphens '--' are used for comments and to control which statements should not be executed in the file. For example, if all objects in the database need to be recreated the hyphens can be removed on the first two lines so that the database and all of its objects will be dropped before recreating the objects.

```
-- DROP DATABASE DASPJDB;
-- COMMIT WORK;

   CREATE DATABASE DASPJDB
     STOGROUP DASPJSTG
     BUFFERPOOL BPO;
   COMMIT WORK;

-- ************** Create Supplier Objects ****************
-- Drop tablespace or lower level objects rather than the database
-- if revisions are required to only lower level objects.
-- 'Comment out' creates that do not require revision before execution.

-- DROP TABLESPACE STSP;
-- COMMIT WORK;

   CREATE TABLESPACE STSP
     IN DASPJDB
     USING STOGROUP DASPJSTG
       PRIQTY 100000
       SECQTY 4
       ERASE NO
     PCTFREE 10
     FREEPAGE 20
     SEGSIZE 64
     LOCKSIZE PAGE
     BUFFERPOOL BPO
     CLOSE NO;
   COMMIT WORK;

   CREATE TABLE S_T
     (SN     CHAR(6) NOT NULL,
      SNAME  CHAR(20) NOT NULL WITH DEFAULT,
      STATUS SMALLINT NOT NULL WITH DEFAULT,
      CITY   CHAR(15) NOT NULL WITH DEFAULT,
      PRIMARY KEY (SN))
   IN DASPJDB.STSP;
   COMMIT WORK;

   CREATE UNIQUE INDEX SNX
     ON S_T (SN)
     USING STOGROUP DASPJSTG
       PRIQTY 5000
       SECQTY 4
       ERASE NO
     PCTFREE 20
     FREEPAGE 20
     CLUSTER
     SUBPAGES 4
     BUFFERPOOL BPO
     CLOSE NO;
   COMMIT WORK;
```

```
CREATE VIEW S AS SELECT * FROM S_T;
COMMIT WORK;

-- Creating a view involving >1 table can be placed in
-- the section after the primary table.

-- An alternative is to place the CREATE VIEW after each
-- table involved in the view since any dependent table
-- that is dropped would also cause the view to be dropped.
-- Initially the view must be after all dependent tables.

-- CREATE VIEW LONDON_SP AS
--    SELECT S.SN, CITY, PN, QTY
--    FROM   S, SPJ
--    WHERE  CITY = 'LONDON'
--    AND    S.SN = SPJ.SN;

-- COMMIT WORK;

-- A SPUFI file can be used to create all objects in a database

-- An alternative is to have a SPUFI file for each tablespace
-- and its dependent objects

-- ************* Create Part Objects ******************

-- DROP TABLESPACE PTSP;
-- COMMIT WORK;

   CREATE TABLESPACE PTSP
     IN DASPJDB
     USING STOGROUP DASPJSTG
       PRIQTY 5000000
       SECQTY 4
       ERASE NO
     PCTFREE 10
     FREEPAGE 63
     SEGSIZE 64
     LOCKSIZE PAGE
     BUFFERPOOL BP0
     CLOSE NO;
   COMMIT WORK;

-- An alter might be added to a SPUFI file and the
-- original creates commented out.
-- This can be done with the ISPF editor using 'C' on a line containing
-- only '--' and 'OO' beginning the block and ending the block to cause
-- the '--' to precede the line.

-- ALTER TABLESPACE DASPJDB.PTSP
--    PCTFREE 15
--    FREEPAGE 15
--    CLOSE YES;
-- COMMIT WORK;

   CREATE TABLE P_T
     (PN    CHAR(6)  NOT NULL,
      PNAME CHAR(20) NOT NULL WITH DEFAULT,
      COLOR CHAR(6)  NOT NULL WITH DEFAULT,
      WEIGHT SMALLINT NOT NULL WITH DEFAULT,
```

```
       CITY   CHAR(15) NOT NULL WITH DEFAULT,
       DATE_RECORDED DATE NOT NULL WITH DEFAULT,
       PRIMARY KEY (PN))
    IN DASPJDB.PTSP;
    COMMIT WORK;

    CREATE UNIQUE INDEX PNX
       ON P_T (PN)
       USING STOGROUP DASPJSTG
         PRIQTY 10000
         SECQTY    4
         ERASE NO
       PCTFREE 15
       FREEPAGE 10
       SUBPAGES 4
       BUFFERPOOL BP0
       CLOSE NO;
    COMMIT WORK;

    CREATE INDEX PCITYX
       ON P_T (CITY)
       USING STOGROUP DASPJSTG
         PRIQTY 15000
         SECQTY    4
         ERASE NO
       CLUSTER
       PCTFREE 20
       FREEPAGE 15
       SUBPAGES 4
       BUFFERPOOL BP0
       CLOSE NO;
    COMMIT WORK;

    CREATE VIEW P AS SELECT * FROM P_T;
    COMMIT WORK;

-- ***************** Create SPJ Objects ******************

-- DROP TABLESPACE SPJTSP;
-- COMMIT WORK;

    CREATE TABLESPACE SPJTSP
       IN DASPJDB
       USING STOGROUP DASPJSTG
         PRIQTY 5000000
         SECQTY       4
         ERASE NO
       PCTFREE 10
       FREEPAGE 63
       SEGSIZE 64
       LOCKSIZE PAGE
       BUFFERPOOL BP0
       CLOSE NO;
    COMMIT WORK;

    CREATE TABLE SPJ_T
       (SN  CHAR(6) NOT NULL,
        PN  CHAR(6) NOT NULL,
```

```
      JN  CHAR(6) NOT NULL,
      QTY INTEGER NOT NULL WITH DEFAULT,
      PRIMARY KEY (SN, PN, JN),
      FOREIGN KEY SNFK (SN) REFERENCES S_T ON DELETE RESTRICT,
      FOREIGN KEY SNFK (PN) REFERENCES P_T ON DELETE RESTRICT,
      FOREIGN KEY SNFK (JN) REFERENCES J_T ON DELETE RESTRICT)
   IN DASPJDB.SPJTSP;
   COMMIT WORK;

-- An ALTER might later be added to the SPUFI file.

-- ALTER TABLE SPJ_T
--   ADD LOCATION VARCHAR(40) NOT NULL WITH DEFAULT
--   VALIDPROC VALLOC;
-- COMMIT WORK;

   CREATE UNIQUE INDEX SPJX
     ON SPJ_T (SN,PN,JN)
     USING STOGROUP DASPJSTG
       PRIQTY 40000
       SECQTY     4
       ERASE NO
     CLUSTER
     PCTFREE 20
     FREEPAGE 15
     SUBPAGES 4
     BUFFERPOOL BP0
     CLOSE NO;
   COMMIT WORK;

   CREATE VIEW SPJ AS SELECT * FROM SPJ_T;

   CREATE VIEW LONDON_SP AS
     SELECT S.SN, CITY, PN, QTY
     FROM   S, SPJ
     WHERE  CITY = 'LONDON'
     AND    S.SN = SPJ.SN
   COMMIT WORK;

-- Document the contents of the SPJ table
   COMMENT ON TABLE AUTHID.SPJ IS
   'SPJ SHOWS THE RELATIONSHIP BETWEEN
    SN, PN, JN AND HAS THE PN QUANTITY';

   COMMENT ON AUTHID.SPJ
   (SN IS 'SN IS THE SUPPLIER ID',
    PN IS 'PN IS THE PART ID',
    JN IS 'JN IS THE JOB ID')

-- Provide alternative column heading for QMF and SPUFI reporting

   LABEL ON COLUMN AUTHID.SPJ.SN IS
   'SUPPLIER ID';

   LABEL ON AUTHID.SPJ
   (SN IS 'SUPPLIER ID',
    PN IS 'PART ID',
    JN IS 'JOB ID')

   COMMIT WORK;
```

Answers to Exercises

CHAPTER 1

1.1. DB2 attaches to TSO, IMS, and CICS. They cooperate with DB2 to provide data communications, transaction control, and security.

1.2 Yes, but the program must execute under the attach facility for which it was prepared.

1.3. DB2 consults the catalog to determine that the existing application plan or package has been invalidated. A rebind is automatically executed to determine a new access path.

1.4.
```
SELECT NAME, SALARY
   FROM   EMPLOYEE
   WHERE  ASSIGNMENT = 'ACCOUNTING'
   AND    SALARY > 50000;

   NAME  SALARY
   RALPH 36000
```

1.5.
```
SELECT NAME, LOCATION
   FROM   EMPLOYEE
   WHERE  NAME = 'PETERS'
   AND    EMPLOYEE.ASSIGNMENT = PROJECTS.ASSIGNMENT;

   NAME    LOCATION
   PETERS  LOS ANGELES
```

1.6. I/O will usually have a greater impact on response time or the rate at which transactions can be processed although this is changing as MVS/ESA makes additional memory available.

CHAPTER 2

2.1 Normalized Design. (Note: Primary keys are preceded by an asterisk.)

```
Student              Professor              Department

*ID                  *ID                    *ID
 Name                 Name                   Name
 Address              Age                    Location
 Dept. ID (Major)     Date of Employment
 Dept. ID (Minor)     Dept. ID
                      Education

 Grades               Professor Courses
*Student ID          *Professor ID
*Course ID            Course ID
 Grade

 Course               Text
*Course ID           *Course ID
 Course Name          Text Name (Text name could be in Course
                                table if there is a one-to-one
                                relationship between texts and
                                courses.)
```

2.2. The foreign keys are the Dept. ID (Major) and Dept. ID (Minor) in the Student table, Dept. ID in the Professor table, Student ID and Course ID in the Grades table, Professor ID and Course ID in the Professor Courses table, and Course ID in the Text table.

2.3. A join will be required between the primary and foreign keys whenever information is required from more than one table. For example, if information is required on the students, the courses they have taken, and their grades, a three-way join will be required over the Student, Course, and Grades tables.

CHAPTER 3

3.1. `CREATE DATABASE DAYOURDB`
`        STOGROUP SYSDEFLT`
`        BUFFERPOOL BPO;`

3.2. `CREATE TABLESPACE EMPTSP`
`        IN DAYOURDB`
`        USING STOGROUP DASPJSTG`

```
        PRIQTY 20000
        SECQTY     4
        ERASE NO
      PCTFREE 5
      FREEPAGE 63
      LOCKSIZE PAGE
      CLOSE NO
      BUFFERPOOL BP0
      SEGSIZE 64
      DSETPASS SESAME;
```

3.3. ALTER TABLESPACE DASPJDB.EMPTSP
      PCTFREE 10
      BUFFERPOOL BP1;

3.4. Table A and Table B may share a tablespace that has a locksize of TABLESPACE or ANY. Using an ALTER TABLESPACE statement to change the locksize to PAGE may solve the problem. Placing the tables in separate tablespaces is another possible solution. Another possible cause of the problem is that the UPDATE program issues an explicit tablespace lock, which might be removed. Placing the tables in a segmented tablespace is a good alternative.

3.5. Lock contention may be on the index rather than the tablespace. Raising the index's subpage value, which reduces the subpage size, will allow a higher concurrency level. Or the tables may be very small, perhaps only two or three pages, so that one-half to one-third of the table is locked for each update. More free space per page will distribute the rows across more pages. An alternative that will keep fewer rows per page with insert activity is to add additional unused columns to the row to make it longer.

3.6. PN could represent a partitioning index on Table P. Partitioning indexes cannot be updated. The alternative to an update is to Delete PN 10 and Insert PN 100. (Beware of cascade or set null rules if the table has dependent tables.) PN may have a unique index, which already includes PN 100. Finally Table P may be a view of joined base tables, which cannot be updated. PN may be a primary key, and there is a value of 10 in a foreign key column of one of the dependent tables.

3.7. The table includes more values than anticipated. Expand the size of the final partition or create an additional partition.

3.8. Table A may share a tablespace with Table B, a large table. If there is no usable index for Table A, DB2 will access it by scanning the tablespace, which includes Table B. Placing the tables in a segmented tablespace solves the problem.

3.9. The bufferpool needs to be made larger. If the table is very large, consider placing the indexes in a separate bufferpool to increase the likelihood that the index pages will not have to be read repeatedly.

CHAPTER 4

4.1.
```
CREATE TABLE EMP_T
    (EMPNO      CHAR(6)      NOT NULL,
     MIDINIT    CHAR(1)      NOT NULL WITH DEFAULT,
     WORKDEPT   CHAR(3)                             ,
     PHONENO    CHAR(4)      NOT NULL WITH DEFAULT,
     HIREDATE   DATE         NOT NULL WITH DEFAULT,
     JOB        CHAR(8)      NOT NULL WITH DEFAULT,
     EDLEVEL    SMALLINT     NOT NULL WITH DEFAULT,
     SEX        CHAR(1)      NOT NULL WITH DEFAULT,
     BIRTHDATE  DATE         NOT NULL WITH DEFAULT,
     SALARY     DECIMAL(9,2) NOT NULL WITH DEFAULT,
     BONUS      DECIMAL(9,2) NOT NULL WITH DEFAULT,
     COMM       DECIMAL(9,2) NOT NULL WITH DEFAULT,
     FIRSTNME   VARCHAR(12)  NOT NULL WITH DEFAULT,
     LASTNAME   VARCHAR(15)  NOT NULL WITH DEFAULT)
    IN DAYOURDB.EMPTSP;
```

4.2. FIRSTNME and LASTNAME should come last. Placing VARCHAR types last provides the best performance since DB2 need not determine the beginning and end of each column on physical storage after the VARCHAR columns.

4.3.
```
CREATE VIEW EMP AS
    SELECT EMPNO, FIRSTNME, MIDINIT, LASTNAME, WORKDEPT,
    PHONENO, HIREDATE, JOB, EDLEVEL, SEX, BIRTHDATE,
    SALARY, BONUS, COMM
    FROM   EMP_T;
```

4.4. The CREATE TABLE statement failed to specify NOT NULL or NOT NULL WITH DEFAULT for all 10 columns, requiring use of 1 byte as a null indicator for every value in every column. Specifying NOT NULL or NOT NULL WITH DEFAULT for a column eliminates the need for the indicator for all of the column's values.

4.5. The salary column has been specified NOT NULL WITH DEFAULT, and some rows contain zeros for unknown salaries. The solution is to use the statement, SELECT AVG(SALARY) FROM EMP_T WHERE SALARY ¬= 0. Or the table might be changed to allow nulls in the salary column. The SELECT statement would ignore null values in taking the average.

CHAPTER 5

5.1. One of the columns may not be declared NOT NULL or NOT NULL WITH DEFAULT, there may not be a unique index on the columns, or the executor does not have alter privileges on the table.

5.2. DB2 does not allow a global update of a primary key.

5.3. A cascade delete would make sense in this case because there will be no reason to maintain active information on an individual's dependents when that individual is no longer employed. However, there may be a requirement to archive data on the former employee.

5.4. A SET NULL constraint would be appropriate because, although the employee has left the company, the supervisory job remains to be filled.

5.5. A foreign key in another table may include that value. DB2 enforced referential integrity will not allow the update of a primary key value upon which a foreign key value depends.

CHAPTER 6

6.1. An index on status would be counter productive because each value occurs, on average, 2.5 times on each data page. SN or SNAME would be candidates for the clustering index, depending on which will be most frequently joined or searched over a range of values or require frequent sorts.

6.2. A composite index on status and city would be useful. There are 200 possible status-city combinations (20 distinct status codes * 10 distinct city codes). Assuming they are evenly distributed, on average a combination would appear once on every four pages. The index, therefore, would be efficient. It is doubtful that separate indexes on STATUS and CITY would be as good as a composite index. About 500 RIDs would qualify using an index on STATUS and about 1000 RIDs would qualify using an index on CITY. The RIDs would have to be sorted and duplicates eliminated plus the cost of processing the two indexes.

6.3. A nonmatching index scan on the leaf pages of the SN-PN-JN composite index could find PN for all J4 rows. A matching scan on the PN index could lead to PNAME in the P table's data pages.

6.4. All information can be obtained from the index pages. A scan of the SN-PN composite index in SPJ finds the SN next to each occurrence of P5. A match against supplier numbers in the S table's SN-SNAME index locates the supplier names. And as soon as the EXISTS finds a value, the search can stop.

6.5. (A) Values will be inserted into the S table. Values and pointers will be inserted into the SN index and CITY index. (B) In the CITY index, the pointer to the S1 row from its previous city's entry will be removed and added to the Dallas entry. The row will be updated in the data pages. (C) The row will be deleted from the S table. The pointers to it in the CITY and SN indexes will be deleted.

6.6. The supplier number may have a low cardinality with a nonclustering index. An alternative problem might be that the two SN columns were mistakenly declared as different data types or lengths, in which case, DB2 would not use the indexes in a join. Recreate one of the tables to make the two columns consistent.

6.7. There may be more than one table in the tablespace, in which case the REORG *utility will not recluster.* A solution is to place the tables in a segmented tablespace or to place Table A in its own tablespace. Or the problem might be that the RUNSTATS utility was not executed after reorganization. SYSINDEXES, therefore, has not been updated to reflect the reclustering.

6.8. If the leading column of the composite index (SN) is not specified in the WHERE clause, the individual indexes can be used but a composite index cannot be used in a matching index scan. ORed predicates can use the individual indexes but not the composite index in a matching index scan. (Rows can be missed using a composite index with ORed predicates.)

6.9. No. An equal predicate will result in a matching index scan to locate the one row requested regardless of whether the rows are in sequence on the data pages.

6.10. No. List prefetch refers to how data pages are processed. Index only processing means that data pages are not processed. Sequential prefetch can be used on the index pages.

CHAPTER 7

7.1. The program must have a variable to receive a value from each column in the results row. If a column is added to the table accessed by the program, SELECT * will return it, and the program will abend. SELECT * severely detracts from data independence and should be avoided.

7.2.
```
SELECT JNAME, QTY, PN
FROM    SPJ, J
WHERE   SPJ.PN = J.PN
AND     PN IN ('P6', 'P1')
ORDER BY JNAME, QTY
```

JNAME	QTY	PN
CONSOLE	100	P1
CONSOLE	500	P6
CONSOLE	700	P1
PUNCH	200	P6
READER	300	P6
SORTER	200	P1
TAPE	300	P6

7.3.
```
SELECT SN, AVG(QTY)
FROM    SPJ
```

```
GROUP BY SN
HAVING PN = 'P5'
```

SN AVG(QTY)

S2   100
S5   333

7.4.
```
SELECT FIRST.SN, FIRST.JN
FROM   SPJ FIRST, SPJ SECOND
WHERE  FIRST.SN  = SECOND.SN
WHERE  FIRST.JN  = SECOND.JN
AND    FIRST.PN  = 'P6'
AND    SECOND.PN = 'P5'
AND    FIRST.QTY > SECOND.QTY
```

SN JN

S5 J4

CHAPTER 8

8.1. Since the rows are added in sequence, new transactions frequently attempt to access the same data and index page. And when the receiving personnel leave their terminals during a transaction, they leave the locks in force. A solution is to commit work before displaying the input panel and after each update operation. Commits must be issued under TSO, the call attach facility and CICS conversational. Commits are automatic when using IMS and CICS pseudo-conversational.

8.2. There should be less locking on inserts because DB2 will insert a row in a near page if it finds the first-choice page locked; however, frequent reorganization is needed to regain clustering and avoid having the pages scattered across DASD.

8.3. Have the program commit work more frequently or issue an explicit table lock before mass updates. In any case, the program should check for a negative SQLCODE and handle the condition to avoid an abend. But contention on the clustering index can be a significant problem.

8.4. The reservation transaction under CS dropped its lock on the January vacancy while checking for the February vacancy. By the time it returned to update the reservation, another transaction had taken the vacancy. An isolation level of RR would hold all locks until the entire transaction completed. An alternative is to make the February reservation before canceling the January one.

8.5. Since read-only programs can share data, locking at the page level is excessive and unnecessary. Alter the tablespace locksize to tablespace. An alternative would be to have the read-only programs issue explicit tablespace locks.

8.6. Frequent commits should be included in the update transactions. The update transactions should also test for SQLCODE −911 and −913 and retry the transaction that has been rolled back to clear a deadlock.

8.7. The program did not save the last key value processed before the commit closed the cursor. It should save the last key value and reopen the cursor at the next value after the commit.

8.8. ACQUIRE(ALLOCATE) is causing table locks to be taken when the program starts executing even though the user seldom chooses the transaction option that does updating. To improve concurrency, change locksize to page, isolation level to CS, and the release parameter value to commit. Then have the program issue frequent commits.

8.9. With isolation level of RR, the optimizer uses a tablespace lock if no index is available. Reformulate the SQL statement so that it can use an index or create an index for it. Or rebind the plan with cursor stability.

CHAPTER 9

9.1. All cursors are closed and locks are released including those held for the FOR UPDATE OF clause.

9.2. Cursors are not closed and locks are not released unless a COMMIT WORK is issued before the screen is displayed. This can be a problem since no one can select or update the pages locked while the user is deciding on the appropriate response or perhaps answers the telephone or goes on a break or out to lunch.

9.3. The application is using a cursor to present the rows. When a COMMIT WORK executes, the cursor is closed. When it reopens, it selects the original set of rows and resumes processing at the beginning. The program could track the cursor's progress through the set and adjust the cursor statement to accommodate it when the cursor is reopened as is explained in Section 9.3.

9.4. DB2 issues SQLCODE 100 to indicate a SELECT has returned no rows or no more rows.

9.5. Batch programs often process a large percentage of the rows in a table—that is the reason they are batch programs. A tablespace scan is usually best when processing more than about 10 to 20 percent of the rows because of the efficiencies of sequential prefetch.

CHAPTER 10

10.1. DECLARE TABLE statements allow the precompiler to check the syntax of a program's SQL statements. DECLARE TABLE statements can be hand-coded or generated by DCLGEN from DB2I. DCLGEN has significant advantages since it insures that the data types and lengths of host variables will match those of the columns.

10.2. If a program has been precompiled, its application plan must be bound with BIND REPLACE. A rebind will result in an SQLCODE of -818 at execution time.

10.3. A plan must be bound specifying the new package in the PKLIST clause in addition to binding the package. Optionally a collection can be established so that package binds can reference the collection and the plan bind can be avoided. This is a good approach.

10.4. DSN SYSTEM(DB2)
```
     RUN PROGRAM(SNCHANGE) PLAN(SNCHANGE) —
         LIBRARY('SUPPLY.DKJ.LOAD')
END
```

10.5. The plan was bound without accurate statistics in the catalog tables. Perhaps RUNSTATS was not executed after production data were loaded.

CHAPTER 11

11.1. Join performance will be improved with indexes on the join columns (preferably a high cluster ratio index). The data type and length of the columns to be joined must be the same to use an index. The nullability of join columns needs to match for a merge join that requires a sort for the best performance. Narrow the search in the select with the join to avoid joining all rows if all rows do not require a join. Consult with the systems administrator on the size and usage of bufferpool BP0. A large bufferpool can significantly improve join performance.

11.2. A composite index can be used to narrow the search on SN and PN. An intersection of the RIDs from SN and PN indexes can be performed followed by list prefetch. A composite index would be best for the WHERE clause specified in the SELECT statement. If the predicate is WHERE PN = 'P4', separate indexes would be best since the leading column of the composite index is not specified in the predicate.

11.3. The optimizer is likely to use the C1 index since it has a cluster ratio of 100 percent. Multiple index usage is unlikely if there is a high cluster ratio.

11.4. The optimizer is likely to use multiple index processing on C2 and C3 indexes since both indexes have a fairly low cluster ratio.

11.5. The optimizer is likely to use the C2 index only since it is expected that a small percentage of the rows will qualify with an equal predicate and cardinality of 150,000 in a 250,000 row table.

11.6. Perhaps more than 25 percent of the RIDs qualify, and after accumulating the RIDs, DB2 is changing to a more appropriate tablespace scan to process the large percentage of data. The clause "OR $0=1$" can be added to a predicate with index usage within parentheses to avoid the use of an index.

11.7. ORDER BY, GROUP BY, DISTINCT and UNION require a sort if the columns involved do not have a high cluster ratio index or an index that can be used to retrieve the rows in sequence for a small percentage of rows. An index with a high cluster ratio would not benefit UNION. UNION ALL, however, can be used to avoid a sort if no duplicates rows will qualify or if duplicates are acceptable to the program. Consult with the systems administrator to determine if the bufferpool needs to be increased in size for the workload or if it is necessary to create more work tablespaces, to rephrase the statement, to use temporary tables, or to create appropriate indexes.

11.8. 'NOT' and '¬=' predicates cannot use an index. These conditions do not narrow the search significantly.

11.9. The SQL should probably be coded to encourage sequential prefetch to avoid traversing the B-tree 200,000 times. Index lookaside and dynamic prefetch on the leaf pages would make index processing more efficient as was discussed in Chapter 6. Accessing both the index and data pages, however, can be avoided with a tablespace scan. In addition, consideration should also be given to dropping the indexes before a large number of inserts or deletes (or updates of indexed columns) to avoid maintaining the indexes followed by recreating the indexes as was discussed in Chapter 9.

11.10. There is no predicate to identify the rows to be updated. DB2 will set all part numbers (PN) to P5.

11.11. DB2 cannot use an index on a column that is part of an arithmetic operation in the predicate. Perform the arithmetic outside the SELECT:

```
QTY = QTY + 100

SELECT PN
FROM   P
WHERE  QTY > :QTY
```

11.12. DB2 is not using the index on the PN column because the PN value in the statement does not match the PN column's length. The WHERE clause should read: WHERE PN > 'P5' not 'P5 '.

11.13. Perhaps RUNSTATS has not been executed. The optimizer does not have accurate statistics and is taking defaults if RUNSTATS has never been executed.

11.14. Consider monitoring the catalog tables and determine if the tablespaces need to be reorganized. (Chapter 14 has some sample SELECT statements that will prove useful.) A clustering index may have become unclustered by a large percent (such as more than 20 percent) after filling the available free space in the data pages. Again consider increasing the size of the bufferpool. Perhaps the overall use of DB2 has increased, resulting in contention for bufferspace, and perhaps the buffers are going critical (95 percent of pages are marked in use).

CHAPTER 12

12.1. Parsing checks a statement's syntax.

12.2. The cost of a database search includes I/O operations and CPU processing. The optimizer estimates costs by using catalog statistics describing the tables being accessed in formulas specific to the type of search being performed.

12.3. RUNSTATS collects statistics describing the table, tablespace, and indexes that the optimizer uses to determine a good access path.

12.4. In the absence of statistics, the optimizer uses default values to estimate costs.

12.5. A plan section for an SQL statement is loaded into the EDM pool only when it is to be executed.

CHAPTER 13

13.1. A merge join (MET = 2 in PN = 2).

13.2. Index SPJX is used for a matching scan (XNAME = SPJX, AT = N, MC = 1).

13.3. SPJ is the outer table.

13.4. To sort the answer set to satisfy the ORDER BY command (MET = 3, O = Y). This sort can be avoided by removing SNAME.

13.5. Intent to share lock at the tablespace level (TSL = IS).

CHAPTER 14

14.1. SYSIBM.SYSPLANDEP and SYSIBM.SYSPACKDEP.

14.2. The catalog tables do not store information on dynamic SQL application plans. Dynamic SQL users may be using statements that take advantage of the index.

14.3. Check the CLUSTERRATIO column in SYSIBM.SYSINDEXES.

14.4. The catalog tables have a limited amount of information on the amount of space used in tablespaces and indexes since the SPACE column in several catalog tables have zero when USING VCAT. The SPACE column is used in divisions and multiplications.

14.5. If a tablespace has an ICTYPE value of Y, W, or P in the SYSIBM.SYSCOPY tables, tables in it cannot be updated and it cannot be recovered.

CHAPTER 15

15.1. The following statements are needed to revoke only one column of update privileges granted on table ERIC.EMPLOYEE:

```
REVOKE UPDATE
    ON ERIC.EMPLOYEE
  FROM GEORGE;

GRANT UPDATE (NAME, EMPNO, TITLE)
    ON ERIC.EMPLOYEE
    TO GEORGE;
```

15.2. George, Paul, Frank, and Terry retain the privilege.

15.3. George holds DBADM authority over the databases he has created, even after losing CREATEDBA authority.

15.4. Frank may execute SUPDATE without having authority to update the S table.

15.5. If Mary and Sally have a shared secondary AUTHID of SPJSYS and bind the plan with OWNER(SPJSYS), the problem is avoided.

CHAPTER 16

16.1. SHRLEVEL of REFERENCE has been specified on the COPY or RUNSTATS utility, which prohibits the updates. SHRLEVEL of CHANGE will provide concurrency while COPY or RUNSTATS executes.

16.2. RUNSTATS was not executed on the tablespace after the data were loaded. Execute RUNSTATS. Or the index may have become unclustered after the data were loaded. In this case, executing REORG will restore clustering, and execution of RUNSTATS will record that fact in the catalog tables.

16.3. The data may have been loaded with a host-language program rather than with the LOAD utility. Allocate additional space and recover or reorganize the index after the index has been created in insert mode. Alternatively create the index after the rows have been inserted.

16.4. Addition of the new data may have significantly changed the distribution of values, making the optimizer's choice of access path inappropriate. Execute RUNSTATS to update the catalog statistics and rebind the application plans to allow the optimizer to take the changes into account.

16.5. If the LOG NO parameter was specified for the LOAD or REORG utilities or a partial recovery was done, DB2 will not allow updates or recovery of the data until a full-image copy has been taken.

16.6. A load specified with the LOG NO parameter cannot be restarted at a phase. Restart the load using the CURRENT parameter.

16.7. The recovery may be using incremental copies. Execute MERGE-COPY periodically to avoid a merge of the copies during the recovery process.

16.8. COPY PENDING allows SELECT only. CHECK PENDING and RECOVERY PENDING allows no DML. COPY PENDING allows any utility to be executed. CHECK PENDING allows for COPY, REORG, LOAD REPLACE, CHECK, and REPAIR utilities to be executed. RECOVERY PENDING allows RECOVER, LOAD REPLACE, and REPAIR utilities to be executed.

CHAPTER 17

17.1. Dallas's DDF may not be started. SYSUSERNAMES may not indicate the user's authorization to execute the statement. Or SYSMODESELECT may not indicate the communications mode to be used.

17.2. The table underlying the SPJ alias may not have been defined or privileges may not have been granted to the AUTHID attempting to execute the statement.

17.3. The Dallas site may have lowered the dispatching priority of the DDF address space, placing local requests ahead of remote requests. Or the transmission mode may have been changed to a slower communications route.

17.4. The FOR FETCH ONLY clause alerts DB2 that a remote request does not entail an UPDATE. This allows DB2 to use the block fetch to transmit 32-K blocks of rows together.

17.5. The two-phase commit and global optimization.

Index